CONTEMPORARY LEARNING THEORY AND RESEARCH

Roger M. Tarpy

Bucknell University

The McGraw-Hill Companies, Inc.

New York   St. Louis   San Francisco   Auckland   Bogotá   Caracas   Lisbon
London   Madrid   Mexico City   Milan   Montreal   New Delhi
San Juan   Singapore   Sydney   Tokyo   Toronto

TO JEAN
colleague, friend, muse

Contemporary Learning Theory and Research

1 2 3 4 5 6 7 8 9 0   DOC DOC 9 0 9 8 7 6

ISBN 0-07-063117-4

This book was set in Palatino by GTS Graphics, Inc.

The editors were Brian McKean and Jack Maisel; the production supervisor
was Annette Mayeski.
The cover was designed by BC Graphics.
The photo editor was Alexandra Truitt.
Project supervision was done by York Production Services.

Library of Congress Cataloging-in-Publication Data
Tarpy, Roger M.
      Contemporary learning theory and research / Roger M. Tarpy.
          p.   cm.
      Includes bibliographical references and index.
      ISBN 0-07-063117-4 (main text : alk. paper).—ISBN 0-07-063118-2
      (instructor's manual/test bank : alk. paper)
          1. Learning, Psychology of.   I. Title.
      BF318.T36 1997
      153.1'5—de21   B6-36652

http://www.nthcollege.com

CONTENTS

CHAPTER 1
Historical Background to the Study of Learning

CHAPTER 2
Science, Psychology, and the Study of Learning

CHAPTER 3
Basic Procedures in Pavlovian (Classical) Conditioning

CHAPTER 4
Variables That Affect Classical Conditioning

CHAPTER 5
Classical Conditioning Phenomena

CHAPTER 6
Theoretical Perspectives in Classical Conditioning

CHAPTER 7
Conditioning of Biologically Adaptive States

CHAPTER 8
Basic Procedures in Instrumental (Operant) Conditioning

CHAPTER 9
Variables That Affect Instrumental Learning

CHAPTER 10
Instrumental-Conditioning Phenomena

CHAPTER 11
Theoretical Perspectives in Instrumental Conditioning

CHAPTER 12
Adaptive Specializations in Learning

CHAPTER 13
Generalization and Discrimination

CHAPTER 14
Memory

CHAPTER 15
Complex Cognitive Functioning

ABOUT THE AUTHOR

Roger M. Tarpy is a professor of psychology at Bucknell University, where he received the Lindback Award for Distinguished Teaching in 1982. An expert in the field of animal learning, Dr. Tarpy earned his AB at Amherst College, an MA at the College of William and Mary, and a PhD at Princeton University. In addition to many scholarly articles, Dr. Tarpy has published six books. The most recent include *Principles of animal learning and memory* (1982), *The individual in the economy: A survey of economic psychology* (1987, with S. E. G. Lea and P. Webley), and *Psychology* (1993, with K. G. Shaver).

PREFACE

As I put the finishing touches to this manuscript, I am struck by the conflicting emotions it evokes. Most salient is my enormous sense of pride, satisfaction, and relief—pride and satisfaction from completing a project of this scope, and relief at no longer having to cope with deadlines and the like. There is, however, another discernable feeling—one of keen anticipation. This reaction arises from knowing that this volume, like all books, reflects a series of compromises, and that, although compromise is usually a sought-after outcome, it may cause discomfort in some quarters (indeed, a common political adage is that a good compromise occurs only when all parties are dissatisfied!).

What are these compromises? The three most important concern *what* material to include (and thus what to exclude), *where* to put it, and *how* to present it. The "what" issue is, by far, the easiest to deal with. Although an author automatically biases coverage when choosing to discuss certain experiments or particular concepts at the expense of others, such bias is evident in any good book. In fact, a book with no point of view, no selectivity, does very little to advance the general knowledge within the field.

The "where" issue is more vexing. Where in the book does one discuss, say, learned helplessness? In the section on higher mental processes or basic instrumental learning? These decisions are difficult because the interpretation one gives to a concept or topic depends on the context in which that topic is reviewed, yet readers vary as to where in a text they expect to see particular topics covered (and, by inference, in the interpretations they give to the topic).

Finally, the "how" question creates the most challenging and interesting tension of all. On the one hand, authors hope that the level of discourse will make the material understandable and accessible to all, or most, college students. On the other hand, authors are pained to give a shallow or simplified version of an area that they find endlessly fascinating and varied. They wish to avoid simplicity because, as experts in the field, they know that the issues are not at all simple.

I have tried to cope with these compromises in a variety of ways. First, I have attempted to write a book that is sufficiently inclusive, scholarly, and rigorous as to appeal, I hope, to many of my colleagues in the field. At the same time, I have kept the student squarely in mind by placing much of the advanced material, and most of the supporting evidence, which students normally find distracting and counterproductive, in endnotes. Thus, students, who are inexperienced in the field of learning, may read an unencumbered version of the text and derive a good sense of the contemporary principles of learning by confining themselves to the text. More advanced scholars, on the other hand, may delve further into a topic by consulting the additional ideas and references cited in the endnotes.

Second, to make the book as useful as possible to undergraduate readers, I have used several pedagogical devices—interim summaries, which provide a review of the material in each major section of a chapter, and a glossary, which provides a definition of most major terms used in the text. Finally, I have tried to gain clarity and appeal by keeping in mind that the ultimate task of any book is to portray the forest, not simply all of the trees.

Although I formally dedicate this book to my wife, Jean E. Roberts, I acknowledge two general groups of people who deserve my undying gratitude—my colleagues in the field of animal learning, whose brilliant and inspired research has made the writing of this book a pleasure beyond words, and my students, whose curiosity and interest have made me take a project of this kind seriously. For a list of the former individuals, please consult the bibliography at the end of this text.

In addition, I would like to thank a number of people who have helped me directly in carrying out this project. My colleagues in the Department of Psychology at Bucknell University, especially Kay Ocker, Ruth Craven, and Mary Gavitt, and all the members of the Bucknell community, who have, over the years, provided generous support for this project and countless others. One would be hard pressed to find a more congenial atmosphere in which to work. The people at McGraw-Hill have been outstanding in every respect— professional, competent, and insightful—and I can't thank them enough for supporting me in every way possible. All authors should be so blessed. These include Jane Vicunas, Brian McKean, and Katie Redmond. I am also very grateful for the careful and efficient work of the production staff, which includes Mary Jo Gregory, Jack Maisel, Lori Stambaugh, and Alexandra Truitt.

Finally, I would like to express my appreciation to a group of colleagues who, at various stages of development, read some, or all, of the manuscript. Their comments were most valuable, and I beg their indulgence for the errors that still remain. They are Peter Holland, Karen Hollis, Alex Kacelnik, Stephen Lea, Ralph Miller, Dave Riccio, Jean Roberts, Todd Schachtman, Kelly Shaver, Dale Swartzentruber, and Ed Wasserman.

Harpswell, ME   Roger M. Tarpy
July 9, 1996

CHAPTER 1

Historical Background to the Study of Learning

EVOLUTION: WHY LEARNING?

Imagine that you are hurtling through space in a magical starship and that you have godlike powers to create new worlds and species. You come upon an uninhabited planet and decide to ply your magic. Here is the challenge: Precisely what kind of species would you create? What characteristics would you give the creatures so that they could live successfully on this planet?

When asked to engage in this whimsical game of imagination, many students say that the new species should have strong legs, to escape from predators, or the ability to talk, so that individuals may share their feelings and communicate important messages. Others argue that the new animals should have keen senses, so that they can find food, or specialized abilities for recognizing mates. Many of the sentiments express the idea that the species should be decidedly humanlike. This view is thoroughly understandable; after all, humans are enormously successful and much to be admired, and they stand at the center of our egocentric universe.

This argument misses a very important point, however. To be successful—that is, to survive, reproduce, and remain safe—a species does not have to be humanlike. The individuals simply must conform in some important way to the demands posed by their surroundings. If one were to imagine populating a new world, the first task, therefore, would be to survey the world and determine what conditions exist, and only then begin to create an animal that fits those conditions.

Very often, when students play this creation game, someone, sensing that the title of the course ("Learning") may have something to do with the answer, suggests that the new species should be able to learn. The advantages of learning are so obvious that the suggestion seems entirely reasonable. However, to be successful as a species, is it really necessary to be able to learn? Many species, probably the vast majority, on the planet Earth do not learn very much at all.[1] Sponges are perfectly content to sit passively on the ocean floor, filtering out

Spiders spin elegant and complicated webs instinctively, without ever learning to do so.
© *Cesco Ciapanna, The National Audubon Society Collection/Photo Researchers*

plankton. Mayflies are born one morning and, following a frenzy of mating activity, die by sunset. Spiders spin elegant and complicated webs and yet are never instructed to do so. Even so-called complex animals perform inborn behaviors. Sheepdogs, for instance, perform their amazing feats without ever being taught. The point is that although learning appears to be highly advantageous, and at times even essential, it is by no means necessary for survival.

Innate Behavior and Its Benefits

Most species do not engage in any meaningful learning because they do not have to. Their innate abilities are sufficient for coping with the demands of the ecological niche in which they reside. For example, many respond to **innate releasing mechanisms** by performing highly adaptive, **innate behaviors.**[2] Innate releasing mechanisms are specific stimuli that trigger the appropriate unlearned behavior. Consider the sexual behavior of a fruit fly. If a female is isolated early in life so that she never experiences other members of her own species, and then later, she is offered sexual access to several different males, only one of which is of her own species, she will unerringly choose the correct male.[3] The male of her species is a releasing mechanism for triggering mating behavior. The same argument may be applied to many other species and a variety of life-sustaining behaviors, including foraging for food and water and recognition of predators.[4] In short, most species display some kind of innate behavior; these are highly adaptive behaviors that are programmed in the genetic codes of the individual and require no learning whatsoever.

How do we know that a behavior is innate? Is it possible that apparently innate behaviors really are learned without us realizing it? Determining whether a behavior is innate or learned can be quite difficult, but there are some general guidelines. First, behaviors are innate when the individuals who perform them have been isolated from birth and thus have had no prior opportunity to learn them.[5] This is, perhaps, the surest way to know. Second, innate behaviors are highly stereotyped; they are performed in a ritualistic and inflexible fashion. Consider the grooming behavior of the male Mandarin duck, who performs a preening ritual on his wing feathers. Even when some of the feathers have been cut, the drake still continues to preen with its bill at exactly the place that the feathers previously occupied. Third, innate behaviors are subject to modification across generations, through selection. This means that, like prize roses or giant vegetables, behavioral characteristics may be selectively bred. The field of behavior genetics is largely devoted to this issue. Finally, innate behaviors are performed even when the individuals are placed in a different context. Squirrels, for instance, will continue to cache nuts even when housed in a small wire cage that provides no suitable site for storing the nuts.[6]

Costs of Learning

In addition to the suitability of innate behavior, there is a second reason why many species have never evolved the capacity to learn. In evolutionary terms, evolving a capacity to learn involves significant costs. Johnston (1981) discusses five such costs. First, if coping with environmental demands depended on learning, then there surely would be a period of time prior to the learning when the animal would be unable to cope and therefore highly susceptible to attack. On the average, such animals would be at a severe disadvantage and unlikely to survive. Second, if parents had to train their offspring, then fewer offspring could be afforded, because such training would involve added time and energy that would place the parents at a selective disadvantage. It would be easier for the parents, from an evolutionary perspective, not to have children who had to be taught. Third, if reproductive behaviors had to be learned, then the species would be at risk because an individual might never survive long enough to learn to reproduce; the animal might be preyed upon before it had a chance to learn. Fourth, having an ability to learn means that an animal would have to have greater neurological complexity. A species would not evolve a large and complex brain that is capable of learning without also incurring some biological costs. Finally, having the ability to learn implies that an animal would be highly disabled if learning failed to take place. The animal would have no recourse, no alternative mode of action if, for some reason, it did not learn what it was supposed to.

Benefits of Learning

Let us return to the original question—is it really necessary for a species to be able to learn? Given that instinctual behavior often suffices, and that the evolution of the capacity to learn involves enormous costs, it would appear that learning is superfluous, if not burdensome.

This is not always the case, however. Being able to learn may be an extremely valuable asset. To help explain this point, first consider a famous example of modern-day natural selection—namely, the peppered moths in nineteenth-century Great Britain. Most of the moths were light in color, although a small percentage contained dark pigmentation. One reason why the light variety was more prevalent was that the places on which they landed briefly were tree trunks covered with lichen (a light green plant); their light color against the light-colored tree trunks made it difficult for predator birds to detect them. The dark-colored variety easily stood out against the trees and thus were easily preyed upon by birds. By midcentury, however, the soot from the factories that fueled England's Industrial Revolution had badly darkened the trees within range of the urban populations. Now, the dark-variety moth was at a selective advantage; they were hard to detect on the dark, sooty tree trunks, whereas the light variety stood out and were easily preyed upon. The balance between light and dark moths shifted dramatically. The black variety became common, whereas the light variety became rare. Interestingly, in the rural areas of England, far from the sooty factories, no change in the distribution of moths was evident; light-colored moths still predominated.

If we generalize from this example, we may identify the primary advantage for learning. Learning is a valuable asset when the environmental conditions are likely to change suddenly.[7] If the changes in the environment are sufficiently slow, then a species may evolve new innate capacities to cope. If, however, there is variability in the environment, and the variability is relatively sudden and unpredictable from one generation to the next, then learning is important. In other words, the ability to learn is not critical, provided the species lives in a stable environment. Learning becomes valuable, however, if the environment is likely to change, because learning endows the species with the ability to cope.

What kinds of environmental changes affect the evolution of a species? There are many. Volcanic upheavals, viral infections, migration or population dispersion, pressures from other evolving populations of species, and climatic changes that cause alterations in the availability of food resources are but a few.

The fate of the peppered moth in Victorian England is a noted example of natural selection in the modern era. The light colored moth, barely visible in the photo, blended in with the green lichen which covered trees thus concealing the moth from predators. The dark colored variety, however, easily stands out against the light background.
© *M. W. F. Tweedie, The National Audubon Society Collection/ Photo Researchers*

Qualifications

Learning endows an animal with flexibility, and it liberates it from being a rigid, stereotyped individual in the face of a changing environment. There are some important qualifications, however. First, flexibility is really a by-product of the selection of specific traits, rather than the evolution of some kind of general intelligence. As Plotkin (1983) stated, "The generic function of learning is a special form of phenotypic flexibility [which] cannot be isolated as some abstracted quality or attribute. It has to be associated with specific traits—flexibility in . . . preference [for mates], flexibility in choice of diet, flexibility in adoption of a dialect, flexibility in moving about space, and so on. . . . [For example,] there are animals that are flexible in habitat choice but inflexible in vocal output" (p. 122). This means that we may understand the learning process only in terms of the functions of specific learned behaviors. The principles involved in learning, say, to select an appropriate diet may differ substantially from those that govern the learning to avoid predators.[8]

A second and related caution is that learning and instinct interact; they coexist. For many years, scientists have believed that the dichotomy between innate and learned—between nature and nurture—is too simplistic. So-called innate behaviors are executed within an environmental context and thus are affected by the environment. Similarly, so-called learned behaviors operate in terms of innate behavioral templates or behavior potentials. That is, the genetic structure of an individual creates predispositions that are modified by experience (see Chapters 7 and 12).[9]

INTERIM SUMMARY

From the point of view of evolution, successful animals do not need to have the capacity to learn, provided that their behavior copes with the demands of the environment. Their innate behaviors are suitable. Moreover, the evolution of learning involves significant costs (for example, the need for parents to instruct their offspring detracts from the well-being of the parents, thus posing a risk for the parents' survival). Learning, nevertheless, has evolved in many creatures. The likely reason is that it helps organisms to cope with sudden and unpredictable changes in the environment. If new behavioral strategies can be created through the learning process, then those individuals are at a selective advantage, relative to others who do not have the ability to change their behavior.

WHAT IS LEARNING?

Learning is not easy to define formally because there are many different perspectives, each emphasizing a different facet of this complex process. A definition of learning could refer simply to the overt behavior. For instance, the fact that someone successfully drives an automobile suggests that the person has learned to drive. A definition of learning also could refer to an internal state of knowledge. Many dictionaries define learning in this fashion as "knowledge acquired by study."[10] In everyday language, we talk about knowing the Greek alphabet, the names of the bones in the inner ear, or the stars in the constellation Cassiopeia. Because both of these perspectives (overt behavior and internal states) are important viewpoints in contemporary learning theory, each is considered in more detail in the following sections.

Learning as Acquired Behavior

From an evolutionary perspective, the idea of learning as overt behavior is important. Genes build an organism that has many characteristics. Some are morphological traits, such as eye color or limb structure, and some are internal neurological mechanisms that control, or provide a capacity for, behavior. Natural selection operates on both types of traits. Thus, animals are at a selective advantage if they possess certain beneficial morphological characteristics or if they possess certain neurological structures that allow for adaptive behavior.

Stated differently, having morphological traits that are advantageous, or behaving in a manner that is advantageous for survival, puts the individual at a selective advantage. Over the many millions of years of biological evolution, such animals were more likely, on the average, to rear their offspring successfully and thus to perpetuate their genes. The point is that the behavioral manifestation of learning is important for survival and adaptation. *What the animal does* is of the utmost importance because, from the point of view of evolution, it is the animal's behavior, not its knowledge, that constitutes its coping strategy.

Learning as Knowledge

Learning may also be viewed as a transition from the state of ignorance to a state of knowledge. It is easy for humans to appreciate this point because we have been taught facts, values, and general knowledge our entire lives. Other creatures also possess knowledge, however. For example, animals know their territory; they know how to find food or water by using various landmarks; and they know where to expect to meet predators, even though they do not always behave in a manner that reveals such knowledge to a human observer. The challenge posed by animal learning research, then, is to know precisely what knowledge an animal has acquired, and the rules by which knowledge is obtained.

If learning means knowledge acquisition, then what do animals learn about? This is a difficult question to answer, even in the case of human beings, with whom we can communicate easily. We may, however, make an educated guess. First, an animal learns about stimuli in its environment because many stimuli serve as a signal for some important outcome. The sight of a distinctive tree or a certain path, for instance, may cause an animal to expect to find a water source nearby (the animal has learned to associate the tree or path with the water source). A robin searches for worms in a backyard after a summer rain because the water glistening on the blades of grass signals that worms may be near the surface.

Second, an animal learns about its own behavior. It learns that if it performs a given action, then a certain outcome will be forthcoming. A pet dog, for example, knows that it will receive food if it "shakes hands" with its owner.

Usually, both kinds of knowledge occur together. Think of what happens when you purchase a can of soda from a vending machine. You recognize that the machine (the stimulus) contains cans of soda. The stimulus has significance or meaning in that respect. You also recognize that your own behavior is important in securing a soda. Putting coins in the slot leads to the delivery of the can. Simply knowing that soda is associated with, or predicted by, the machine does not, by itself, produce the soda. You must also have a separate bit of knowledge—namely, that performing the correct sequence of actions is necessary as well.

Definition of Learning

Considering that both aspects of learning (the overt behavior and the knowledge state) should be included in a formal definition, **learning** may be defined in the following way: "Learning is an inferred change in the organism's mental state which results from experience and which influences in a relatively permanent fashion the organism's potential for subsequent adaptive behavior."[11]

The first part of this definition emphasizes that learning is always inferred from performance. If there is no behavior to observe, then we may never be sure that learning has taken place. This so-called learning-versus-performance distinction is extremely important because it suggests that there may be laws that control performance that are distinct from those that control the creation of knowledge (see also Chapter 2). Stated differently, it may be possible to discover how an organism acquires knowledge, or at least the specific environmental conditions under which the knowledge is formed, without being able to explain why the organism, in fact, performed the behavior generated by the knowledge.

A second feature of the definition is that learning involves an inferred change in the mental state of the organism. We may not be able to identify the neurological structures that underlie this mental state, but, in theory at least, they must exist. Knowledge must somehow be coded or represented in the neurological structure of the organism. Surely, movement of the muscle fiber, which constitutes the overt performance, cannot appear out of thin air. Performance must be initiated, or determined, by some prior neurological state that had been created or altered during the learning process.

A third feature is that learning stems from experience. This aspect of the definition allows us to distinguish learning from, say, instinct. As noted earlier, instinctual behaviors are present at birth; no instruction is required for the organism to be able to perform those behaviors. Behaviors that cannot be performed without instruction, however, reflect learning.

A fourth consideration is that learning is a relatively permanent change. The knowledge and the behavior potential persist through time. This aspect guards against mistaking a temporary change in behavior due to, say, fatigue, for learning.

A final aspect of the definition refers to learning as being a change in the potential to behave. Again, the distinction between the knowledge state and the overt behavior requires this stipulation. An individual could develop knowledge and yet not perform in such a way as to demonstrate that knowledge. The individual would have the potential to behave even though the behavior is not actually occurring. A good example is the effect of satiation on behavior. Imagine that a laboratory rat learns to traverse a complicated maze, involving right and left turns, to reach a food reward. It may know which turns are correct, but if the rat is not hungry, and thus not motivated to search for food, it may not demonstrate its knowledge of the maze. Learning therefore generates a potential for behavior, although that potential may not be expressed at every moment.

INTERIM SUMMARY

Learning may be viewed from two distinct perspectives. First, learning refers to the development of overt, adaptive behavior (learning to drive a car, for instance). Second, learning refers to acquired knowledge (for example, knowing historical dates). In this text, both perspectives are used. Consequently, learning is defined as an inferred change in the organism's mental state, which results from experience and which influences in a relatively permanent fashion the organism's potential for subsequent adaptive behavior. Each aspect of this definition emphasizes an important quality of learning—for example, that learning represents a potential for behavior, not simply the behavior itself.

SOURCES OF KNOWLEDGE

As just discussed, the psychology of learning attempts to provide a theory of how knowledge is acquired. Many scholars throughout history have addressed this question.

Greek Philosophers

Not surprisingly, the problem of the origins of knowledge was a theme of the Greek philosophers. Their philosophies are still important today because they provide a foundation for current thinking. Next, we briefly discuss two Greek philosophers: Plato and Aristotle.[12]

Plato.

The Greek philosopher Plato (427–347 B.C.) wrote about two dozen compositions, called "dialogues," most of which featured his famous teacher, Socrates, arguing various theoretical positions. One of these contained a theory of human knowledge. Plato believed that knowledge or truth is inherent in every person.[13] To illustrate his reasoning, Plato told of a slave boy who had had no formal education and thus did not possess any acquired knowledge of geometry, and yet through careful questioning, the boy was led to utter a geometric truth—namely, the Pythagorean theorem (the square of the hypotenuse of a right triangle is equal to the sum of the squares of the other two sides). Plato claimed that the boy must have been born with the knowledge; the question-and-answer procedure merely served to draw it out. For Plato, then, knowledge was the inherent possession of truth, an understanding of reality without having learned about it through sensory experience.[14]

Aristotle.

In the year 375 B.C. Plato established his famous school, the Academy, to teach various academic subjects, such as mathematics and rhetoric. Among the 10 to 15 students was Aristotle (384–322 B.C.). Aristotle was originally a staunch defender of Platonic thinking. After Plato's death in 347 B.C., however, Aristotle developed ideas that differed from those of his mentor. Some of these ideas bear upon a theory of knowledge.

Aristotle began his famous treatise "Metaphysics" with the following statement: "All men by nature desire to know. An indication of this is the delight with which we take in our senses." For Aristotle, knowledge is gained through the senses—that is, through experience. Thus, in contrast to Plato's view that the enduring nature of objects was known intuitively, Aristotle believed that the properties of objects could be ascertained only by sensory examination of the objects themselves. Clearly, Aristotle's disagreement with Plato involved *how* knowledge is gained, not about *what* is being learned.

Aristotle's ideas were important to the development of modern psychology for many reasons. First, his emphasis on biological systems provided an intellectual foundation for the areas of motivation and physiological psychology. Second, his laws of association and his theories of memory provided a basis for the modern science of learning and cognition. Most important, however, his recognition that knowledge is gained through the senses provided an important stepping-stone for the founders of modern psychology in the nineteenth century.

Descartes

One of the greatest philosophers of the modern age was René Descartes (1596–1650). Within psychology, Descartes is best known for his psychophysical **dualism,** his theory that mind and body are separate realities. Body is the physical aspect of a human being, one's skin and bones. It is governed by natural, physical laws. Mind, on the other hand, is the rational soul of humankind. Mind is an entity, but it has no physical or material form. Mind is the spiritual and free aspect of our reality, and it is possessed only by humans.

Given these two domains—mind and body—Descartes claimed that there are two kinds of behaviors. The first is reflexive behavior, based on the mechanical laws of physics. Descartes's theory of reflexive behavior is illustrated Figure 1-1. The child's foot touches the fire, and the stimulation is transmitted to the brain, which, in turn, reflexively releases "animal spirits" that travel back down the nerve and cause a withdrawal reaction. This sequence of actions is the **reflex arc,** which represents one of the simplest kinds of information-processing systems. The reflex arc has (a) an incoming impulse or input (nerve to the brain), (b) a point in the spinal cord or brain where the

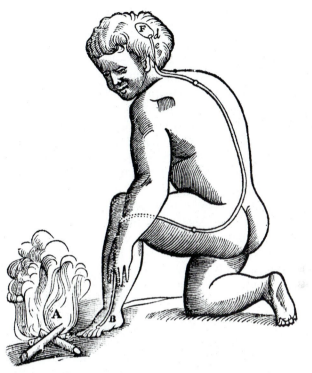

FIGURE 1-1. Diagram of Descartes' theory of the reflex arc, in which the stimulus (heat from the fire) is transmitted to the brain causing a reflexive withdrawal of the hand. *The Bettmann Archive/Corbis*

incoming impulse is processed and transferred to an outgoing impulse, and then (c) the outgoing impulse.

The other kind of behavior, appropriate only to humans, is based upon, and governed by, reason. Here, the mind gains control over actions through its will.[15] Because humans possess a soul, they alone are said to be able to engage in rational action, governed by the rules of the mind, not the laws of physics and chemistry.[16]

Descartes supported this dualism with the following example: If an arm is cut off, the body is surely diminished; it can no longer function as effectively as a whole body. However, a severed limb does not alter or diminish the mind in any way. A person's reasoning process remains unchanged. Thus, the two realms must be separate aspects of human existence.

Empiricism

In the early seventeenth century, several people set the stage for a transition from Descartes's dualism to **empiricism,** the philosophical basis for contemporary psychological theory. One such person was Thomas Hobbes (1588–1679).

Hobbes, a contemporary of Descartes, believed that everything that happened was due to "matter in motion." Hobbes did not separate mind from body, but rather accepted a single reality (the physical reality) and explained mind and soul in terms of this single concept. Thus, mind was not the unextended, formless reality advocated by Descartes, but rather was simply the action of the nervous system. Brain excitations were equivalent to thinking.

This was an important development because if the mind really is equivalent to the brain (if thinking is the same as brain excitations) then stimuli that impinge on, or affect, the brain also affect the contents of the mind. In other words, if knowledge is nothing more than a physical state of the brain, and if experience (the environment) affects the brain state, then knowledge must be created entirely from experience.

The doctrine of empiricism argues that all knowledge, with the possible exceptions of logic and mathematics, is derived from experience. In its pure form, empiricism stipulates that knowledge cannot exist without experience. Although this pure version of empiricism has been challenged, empiricism continues to dominate modern psychology.

Locke.

John Locke (1632–1704), the great British philosopher, is generally regarded as the founder of empiricism as a formal philosophy. Locke was concerned with the origins of knowledge. Unlike Plato, however, Locke argued that there are no innate ideas. Instead, we acquire ideas and knowledge from experience. In fact, Locke believed that the mind at birth is like a blank slate, a "tabula rasa." Experience provides knowledge in the mind, just as writing upon the slate provides knowledge or information not previously contained on the slate.

Locke further claimed that there are two kinds of mental activity or ideas: ideas of sensation and ideas of reflection. Sensations are simple, indivisible ideas that arise from the objects that one experiences in the real world. Experiencing colors or sounds are examples of ideas of sensation. Reflections, on the other hand, are originally based on sensations but no longer dependent on them. Perceiving, thinking, and knowing are examples of ideas of reflection. All ideas, no matter how complex, are derived from a combination of simple sensations and reflections. Thus, if we are to understand human knowledge, we must study how stimuli give rise to sensations, as well as how an individual reflects upon prior sensations.

Hume.

Given the empiricists' conviction that knowledge is derived through the senses, it fell to others to develop formal principles by which knowledge is created. The British philosopher David Hume (1711–1776) gave the clearest expression of these principles.[17] His ambition was to discover the principles of mental life in much the same way that astronomers had discovered principles concerning order in the heavens.

Hume claimed that there are two kinds of mental contents, impressions and ideas. Impressions are the forceful and vivid perceptions that occur when we hear, see, feel, love, hate, desire, or will. Ideas, on the other hand, are thoughts and memories; these are fainter copies of impressions, although they are derived from impressions. Hume further argued that there are three fundamental principles, **laws of association** that describe the way in which these mental contents are created or combined. First is the **law of resemblance,** or similarity. An impression may trigger a particular idea because the two are similar. For example, a picture of a house (impression) may elicit a thought of one's own house (idea), because the impression and the idea are similar.

Second is the **law of contiguity.** The importance of this law cannot be exaggerated, because it has served for 200 years as a guiding principle in psychology, especially in the area of learning. Contiguity means closeness in place or time. This law claims that one idea can trigger the memory of another idea if the impressions on which the ideas are based had been experienced contiguously. Once the first impression occurs, then the idea based on that impression triggers the idea of the second impression. For example, the picture of a house elicits the idea of one's own house (this is the principle of resemblance), but it also triggers additional ideas (for example, the neighbor's house next door or the family car in the driveway) because the impressions that served as the source of the two ideas were contiguous in time (typically, one sees one's own home at about the same time as one sees a neighbor's home or one's car in the driveway). Experiencing the two impressions simultaneously causes their corresponding ideas to become associated. Later, when just one impression is given, the idea of the other is elicited.

Third is the **law of cause and effect.** Hume argued that this rule of association was really secondary to the other two laws, particularly the law of contiguity. According to the law of cause and effect, if two events are contiguous in space and time, with one of the events always preceding the other, the person will come to believe that the first event is the cause of the second event.

Modern Learning Theory

Ebbinghaus.

The laws of association directly influenced the study of learning. There is no better example of this than the work of Hermann Ebbinghaus (1850–1909). According to Ebbinghaus (1885/1964), the study of the development of an association between two mental events could best be accomplished by using stimuli that were devoid of all prior associations (otherwise, one's assessment or measurement of the development of a new association would be confused with, or impeded by, the presence of already-existing associations). In some of his studies, therefore, Ebbinghaus used so-called nonsense syllables (BIJ or LQX), which he believed had no inherent meaning.[18] Ebbinghaus spent many hours associating one stimulus with another, and then reciting them back. In doing so, he put many of the principles of association, developed over a century earlier, to a direct test. For example, he determined whether stimuli that were written close together on the list would be more firmly associated than syllables that were not close together.

Ebbinghaus's research confirmed many of the ideas first proposed by the British Empiricists. For instance, forward associations are stronger than backward ones (if syllable "A" precedes syllable "B," then "A" evokes the memory of "B" more easily than "B" evokes the memory of "A").

Pavlov.

Research on the development of associations was also advanced by the Russian physiologist Ivan Pavlov (1849–1936). As is well-known, Pavlov (1927) demonstrated that dogs associate the clicking sound of a metronome with food, such that, after repeated presentations of the two stimuli, the metronome itself elicits the salivation response that originally had been triggered only by the food (see also Chapters 3–7). Pavlov argued that the two events—the biologically neutral stimulus (metronome) and the biologically powerful stimulus (food)—had become associated. Like Ebbinghaus, Pavlov was really putting the laws of association to a test. Indeed, Pavlov's work launched the study of the associative learning process in modern times.[19] Much of the material presented in this book reflects his legacy.

Thorndike.

The other person identified as an innovator and pioneer in modern learning theory is E. L. Thorndike (1874–1949). Thorndike's (1898) contribution was in the area of instrumental conditioning (see Chapters 8–13). In his original studies conducted with cats, a subject was placed in a cage containing a lever. In the process of trying to get out of the box, the cat—inadvertently at first—hit the lever, at which point, the door sprang open, and the animal was allowed to eat some food placed nearby. Thorndike then repeated the process, discovering that over the course of training, the cat became progressively better at escaping from the box. It learned to press the lever in a speedy and efficient manner, presumably through a process of reward.

INTERIM SUMMARY

Philosophers have, for centuries, speculated about the origins of knowledge. Greek philosophers set the stage by claiming that knowledge either is innate (Plato) or is derived from experience (Aristotle). René Descartes advocated a duality between mind and body, the former being an unextended or formless reality and representing reason and intellect (which was possessed by humans alone). A third historical antecedent to the study of learning processes was the work of the British Empiricists, who claimed that knowledge is derived from experience exclusively (the empiricist position). To describe *how* knowledge was created, the Empiricists formulated the laws of association, which included the laws of similarity, contiguity, and cause and effect. These laws described the means by which ideas become associated, and they were tested by various pioneers in learning research, including Ebbinghause, Pavlov, and Thorndike.

WHY STUDY LEARNING?

A previous section of this chapter emphasized how learning may be important for the survival of a species. Psychologists have additional reasons, however, for wishing to study the learning process.

Curiosity

The most abstract reason, one that some consider noble but perhaps difficult to grasp, is that one may derive great satisfaction from understanding how the world works. Humans are curious creatures; we wish to understand our world, including, most importantly, ourselves. This quest takes many forms. Some people take exotic trips to discover new lands or explore new frontiers. Others are interested in how things work from a biological, chemical, or physical point of view. Nonetheless, what better thing to study than the learning process! It is one of our most precious, complex, and fascinating talents. In a sense, a detailed knowledge of the learning process helps us to understand the very essence of humanity.

Education

Knowledge is not always acquired simply for its own sake. Much knowledge has practical benefits. This is certainly true of learning. Practically speaking, learning theorists have devised a variety of techniques to help students cope with their studies. One example is programmed learning, also termed **programmed instruction.** The most common kind of programmed learning takes the form of specialized textbooks that present concepts or factual information in small units or chunks, often in the form of a question. The student chooses the answer believed to be correct and then consults an answer form to discover whether it is, in fact, accurate.[20] If it is, then the student is reinforced for answering correctly and proceeds to the next question. If it is not, then the student returns to an earlier point in the sequence and begins again. The basic idea is that the material specifies each small incremental step leading to the larger concept or idea. Each step is relatively easy, so the student not only experiences a high rate of success, but also proceeds to new material only after mastering the earlier material.[21]

Programmed instruction is not really any different from conventional instruction. It simply tries to optimize the underlying elements of instruction (for example, the specific behaviors that students make, the clarity with which questions are posed, and the immediacy with which feedback is given). Few would deny that feedback is important in learning; when feedback is given immediately, and abundantly, and when it is contingent only on correct performance, then the learning process proceeds more efficiently.

An interesting variation on this idea is the use of programmed learning at the level of an entire course.[22] The course typically is structured according to small units of material, such as chapters in a textbook or study guide. The student progresses through the course only by mastering each unit successively. Failure to master a unit does not result in a penalty but merely delays the student's progress. Courses designed in this fashion often enjoy considerable success, relative to those using the conventional teaching approach.[23] Again, the important idea is that the small steps that make up the lesson are identified and isolated, and the procedures that help encourage progress, such as providing immediate feedback, are maximized.

Mental Health

From its inception, psychology has been associated with the field of mental health. The study of learning bears directly on this issue. More specifically, learning theorists have studied so-called maladaptive behavior and have devised effective treatment plans for dealing with such behavior.

Explaining Phobias.

One topic addressed quite directly by learning theorists is that of phobias. **Phobias** are maladaptive, irrational fears, for example, the fear of spiders or small, enclosed spaces. They are maladaptive and irrational in the sense that the feared stimulus, in reality, may pose no real danger to the person, and yet the person behaves as if he or she were under considerable threat.

Many psychologists claim that phobias are learned. One of the most famous demonstrations of acquired fear was shown by Watson and Raynor (1920). Their subject, Little Albert, was an 11-month-old infant who initially had no fear of a white laboratory rat; in fact, Albert showed curiosity toward the animal, approaching and touching it. By pairing the white rat with a loud aversive "bang" made by a hammer striking a piece of metal, a fear reaction was learned. Little Albert showed considerable anxiety, crying not only when presented with the white rat, but also when presented with other stimuli, such as a rabbit, a dog, a cotton ball, and a Santa mask. Following this demonstration, many psychologists came to believe that other fears and phobias are acquired in this fashion. Normally innocuous stimuli become associated with some form of trauma and thus become fearsome themselves; that is, the stimuli retain their fear-evoking properties even though they pose no threat.[24]

Such a simplistic theory of phobias has not been strongly supported in recent years.[25] First, Watson and Raynor's famous study has not been replicated.[26] More important, there are many problems associated with this theory.[27] For example, people who have strong phobic reactions often cannot identify any traumatic event that may have caused the reaction to be learned.[28] Similarly, some individuals suffer serious traumas and yet do not develop phobias.[29]

Portrait of John Watson, the founder of Behaviorism.
UPI/Bettmann Newsphotos/Corbis

The argument that learning theory cannot fully explain the origin of phobias does not mean that learning principles are irrelevant to the problem. Many *are* important because they provide a background or context both for the treatment of the phobias and for exploring new ideas or principles related to the development of fear.[30] Thus, learning plays an important role in this area of psychology, even though the explanation of phobias is not a simple extension of conventional learning theory.

Behavior Modification.

No area of practical concern in psychology is more dependent on the study of learning than the area of **behavior modification** (also called **behav-**

ior therapy).[31] Behavior modification refers both to a general theory of treatment and to a set of specific techniques that are designed to help alter the frequency of maladaptive behavior.

Behavior therapy stands in sharp contrast to psychodynamic (Freudian) psychotherapy. The latter places heavy emphasis on underlying causes for psychological problems, such as events from the patient's childhood, and it assumes that most psychological problems stem from the unconscious. Behavior modification, in contrast, assumes that maladaptive behaviors are learned according to conventional laws of learning and thus may be treated with various techniques discovered in the learning laboratory. Behavior therapy rejects the classical trait approach (that maladaptive behaviors arise from an inner trait or personality disorder), claiming instead that the environmental situation plays a critical role in generating maladaptive behaviors. In other words, rather than viewing mental illness and the accompanying maladaptive behaviors as a by-product of some underlying disturbance or disease, behavior therapy focuses on the behavior as a learned reaction and attempts to eliminate it by using principles borrowed from the learning laboratory.[32]

How does behavior therapy treat maladaptive behavior? There are many specific techniques, but generally, it tries to accomplish two things. First, behavior therapy attempts to eliminate or suppress unwanted behavior. One tactic is to identify the reinforcers that sustain the behavior and then to withdraw them so that the behavior declines. Another is to follow an unwanted behavior with a mildly aversive outcome, such as ceasing to pay attention to the patient, or withdrawing a desirable commodity, such as candy. An interesting example of this was shown by Porterfield, Herbert-Jackson, and Risley (1976). The treatment involved young children at a child-care center who frequently engaged in disruptive behaviors, such as hitting or pushing other children, throwing tantrums, and breaking toys. Whenever these behaviors occurred, the misbehaving child was immediately removed from the play area for a short period of time (usually about a minute) and was required to sit at the edge of the room, observing the other children play but not being able to join in. Such a treatment had a beneficial effect. The incidence of disruptive behavior was reduced dramatically.

Second, behavior therapy tries to teach appropriate and adaptive behaviors. For example, a study by Riordan, Iwata, Finney, Wohl, and Stanley (1984) treated children who were so physically handicapped that they required hospitalization. The problem on which the authors focused was the children's eating behavior—specifically, the children's refusal to eat the food that was normally served. Concerned that the children were jeopardizing their health, the authors decided that intervention was warranted. They first determined which food item was most preferred. The preferred food was then used to reinforce eating in general. For instance, a child was given a portion of the normal meal, and if normal eating occurred, then he or she was immediately given the highly preferred food. Dependence on receiving the preferred food was gradually reduced to the point where the children were consuming a healthy and appropriate diet on their own.

INTERIM SUMMARY

Learning research has affected society in many ways. First, it has contributed much knowledge about the behavior of many species, including humans. More important, it has developed theories and methods that offer significant practical benefit in many social settings. Most obvious are its contributions to education, specifically programmed instruction. In addition, learning research has also had an impact on the field of mental health. For example, theorists have furthered our understanding of behavioral disorders such as phobias and have developed specific treatment plans in the form of behavior therapies.

WHY STUDY ANIMALS?

The aforementioned reasons for studying learning (to understand how this important process operates, and to develop practical programs for improving education and mental health) focus on the problem of learning in humans. Why then do psychologists often study nonhuman animals, such as laboratory rats and pigeons? The claim is simple. Using animals in learning research may yield valuable insights about human behavior. In other words, by studying learning in animals, we may also understand, at least to some degree, the underlying principles that govern human behavior. Most learning theorists are not interested merely in the fact that dogs salivate in the manner described by Pavlov, that pigeons peck at lighted plastic buttons to receive grain, or that rats run through complicated mazes to find bits of food in the goal box. Those behaviors are only incidental to the ultimate purpose—namely, discovering general principles that control learning in all creatures.

Such a claim makes sense, however, only if two things are true. First, the use of animals to study learning must offer some advantage over using human subjects. Second, the process of generalizing the principles of learning from animals to humans must be valid and legitimate. That is, rats and humans must be sufficiently similar in the way they learn to warrant studying animals instead of humans. Let us examine both of these claims.

Advantages in the Use of Animal Subjects in Research

There are three strategic reasons why studying animals may be a worthwhile venture. First, animals offer a simplicity not found in humans. They have a need for food, water, and sexual mates, and some may have a need for social interaction, but we assume that these processes are somewhat less complicated than they are in humans. If so, we may be better able to understand how learning works by studying it on a simpler level.

Second, and perhaps most important, learning experiments may be controlled to a greater degree when nonhuman animals are used as subjects than when humans are studied. For instance, subjects may be equated in terms of their genetic makeup or the conditions under which they are raised (thus ensuring that all have experienced the same environment during development). It is impossible to do this in humans.

Finally, we may conduct experiments using animals that we could never possibly do with humans. For example, it would be unethical to deprive humans of items such as food or water in order to motivate them to perform in a learning experiment. Furthermore, humans, unlike rats and pigeons, become bored quickly when confronted with simple tasks. Humans have language and insight, causing them to develop behavioral strategies unlike those possessed by other animals (see Chapter 9). In short, many controlled experiments using rats and pigeons cannot be performed with human subjects, either because humans are too intelligent or because, practically and ethically speaking, it would be inappropriate to do so.

Generalizing from Animals to Humans

What about the second claim? Are we able to generalize the learning principles discovered from studying animals to human beings? Many believe that such generalizations are entirely legitimate. The primary reason is that the behavior of humans and other species has been constrained throughout evolution in similar ways. Every creature, human and nonhuman alike, must move about in the same gravitational field. The supply of various food items is limited to an equal degree for all species that eat those items. The amount of caloric energy required to move a certain mass at a given speed through a particular medium is determined by the laws of physics and biology and is thus the same for all species. In other words, the fact that all animals experience similar limitations on their behavior suggests that evolution has helped to shape learning processes that are common and universal.

Consider the following analogy. Creatures who live in the sea are faced with a common constraint—namely, the drag on, or resistance to, movement caused by the surrounding water. For some animals, such as sponges, this poses very little problem because they cling to stationary objects and allow food to filter through their system. However, the story is quite different for species that are mobile, such as fish. Most fish, as well as, say, dolphins, have evolved a streamlined body that offers relatively little resistance to water as they swim. Fish and dolphins look alike in this respect, but they are decidedly unrelated genetically (dolphins are mammals, not fish). In other words, despite the fact that fish and dolphins are fundamentally different, evolutionary pressures have selected a relatively streamlined shape in both species.

The same claim may be made for learning processes. Conditions in the environment pose similar constraints for those who must learn about, or behave within, those conditions. For example, troops of monkeys that forage on fruits must be able to recognize which fruits are in season, when trees have become relatively barren through excessive feeding, or whether one grove of fruit trees offers greater prospects for nourishment than another. However, other creatures who utilize these food resources are also faced with the same constraints—namely, that there are only so many fruits on a given tree, and that the fruits go out of season. In summary, every animal must deal with the world or the environment as it occurs in nature; to deal with it is to solve the problems that it poses within the limitations or constraints present. The fact that all species that occupy a similar niche must play by the same environmental rules suggests that common learning strategies may have evolved.

We must certainly be cautious here, because generalizing from one species to another may not always be warranted. Learning principles may not hold as universally as we might wish. Humans are not rats or pigeons; they are much more intelligent, and their behavior may be qualitatively different from that of other animals, if for no other reason than that humans have language. Perhaps humans have the same underlying learning processes as other animals but do not always display them in the same way. Instead, perhaps humans share only some of the basic learning processes with other animals. Ultimately, one must discover empirically whether the principles of learning discovered in rats, pigeons, and dogs actually do apply in any direct fashion to human beings.

INTERIM SUMMARY

The ultimate goal of learning research is to understand the learning process in general, particularly that of human beings. Learning research using nonhuman subjects has certain advantages, however. It focuses on learning systems that are simpler than those found in humans, it establishes a relatively high degree of control in its experimental situations, and it studies organisms that, unlike humans, perform without becoming indifferent to the learning task. Whether one can fully understand human learning from studies of nonhuman animals is still debated. However, because many creatures have evolved with respect to a single set of environmental constraints, it is reasonable to believe that considerable overlap in learning styles exists.

ENDNOTES

1. Although Mayr (1974) and others make this point, there is no way to verify the exact proportion of species that can learn. Of the thousands upon thousands of species that are known to exist, so few have been tested.
2. Mayr (1974) Uses the term closed programs to refer to genetic configurations producing behaviors that are not modified by experience.
3. Brown (1965).
4. See Curio (1993) for a review.
5. See Mayr (1974) for a discussion of these distinctions.
6. Proving that humans have instincts is nearly impossible because none of these conditions can be achieved effectively. For instance, humans cannot be isolated from birth, selectively bred, or placed in constraining contexts.
7. See Plotkin (1983); Plotkin & Odling-Smee (1979).

8. See Davey (1989) for a discussion.
9. Mayr (1974) calls these open programs because the behavioral program established in the genetic code can be modified through experience.
10. *The Oxford Encyclopedic English Dictionary* (1991).
11. Tarpy and Mayer (1978), p. 37. This definition is considerably more detailed than many in specifying the nature of the process. For example, Johnston (1981) states; Learning is "any process in which, during normal, species-typical ontogeny, the organization of an animal's behavior is in part determined by some specific prior experience. In the absence of the requisite experience, either some behavioral ability will be altogether lacking, or its organization will be different from that of similar individuals for whom the experience was available" (p. 70). Although such a definition is useful for its emphasis on behavioral organization and species-specific development, the breadth of its basic claim—that learning can be any process that is determined by prior experience—seems excessively broad.
12. For an excellent reference on the history of psychology, see Viney (1993).
13. Plato's *Meno*.
14. This point is important because it argues that knowledge is unrelated to the activation of sense organs. For example, knowing the truth about a noise after the noise has stopped is not the same as hearing the noise in the first place. Knowing, therefore, does not equal sensing.
15. See Watson (1978).
16. This argument suggests a fundamental discontinuity between humans and other species. Such a discontinuity was seriously challenged by Darwin's theory of evolution, however. Modern learning theory has clearly sided with Darwin in claiming that a meaningful continuity *does* exist between humans and other species, and thus that a comparison between species is not only legitimate, but intellectually useful.
17. Many of the principles of association were discussed in Hume's (1739) *Treatise on human nature*. David Hartley (1705–1759) and George Berkeley (1685–1753), contemporaries of Hume's, also made important contributions in the area of empiricism and associationism; see Watson (1978).
18. This argument, however, was thoroughly rejected by later research, which showed that syllables often do have meaning, even though they appear to be entirely nonsensical.
19. Although Watson's original article on Behaviorism (Watson, 1913) focused on stimulus-response reflexes and the formation of habits, his use of Pavlov's research on conditioning occurred in his noted presidential address to the American Psychological Association. There, Watson made the conditioned reflex the centerpiece of his theory of behavior; see R. I. Watson (1978).
20. Material may also be presented by a so-called teaching machine. These devices organize and present material in a systematic manner and provide the student with a means of responding to the questions. Skinner (1950b) is credited with introducing teaching machines, but many others have contributed to this field.
21. Although it sounds like an excellent approach to education, programmed instruction has met with mixed reactions. For one thing, it may not improve retention of the material (although, admittedly, it may require less time than conventional teaching techniques to master the material; see Nash, Muczyk, & Vettori, 1971). Second, a single series of questions in a programmed text does not always conform to the line of thinking or reasoning that a given person actually uses in learning that material, thus making progress quite difficult for many students.

22. Keller (1968).
23. See McMichael and Corey (1969).
24. See Mowrer (1950).
25. See Emmelkamp (1985).
26. Demonstrations of this kind are now considered to be unethical.
27. See Denny (1991); Mineka (1985b).
28. Liddell and Lyons (1978); Murray and Foote (1979).
29. Jacobs and Nadel (1985).
30. See Bandura (1977); Zentall and Galef (1988).
31. Many credit Wolpe (1958) with providing the first thorough and compelling statement of behavior therapy. Since that time, hundreds of accounts of this area have been published. Two good sources are Bellack, Hersen, and Kazdin (1985), who review much of the work from the point of view of various syndromes, and Masters, Burish, Hollon, and Rimm (1987), who focus more directly on the techniques of behavior therapy.
32. Eysenck (1952) wrote an influential paper in which psychotherapy was criticized for not producing improvement in patients at a rate beyond what would be achieved if no treatment whatsoever were given. For an interesting dialogue on this subject, see Breger and McGaugh (1965), and Rachman and Eysenck (1966); see also Rachman (1963).

CHAPTER 2

Science, Psychology, and the Study of Learning

LEARNING RESEARCH AND THE SCIENTIFIC METHOD

Chapter 1 provided a historical background to the study of learning. This chapter focuses on how psychologists study the learning process and on the general kinds of theories they have created. Let us begin by examining the sense in which the psychology of learning depends on, and is informed by, the methods established in the natural sciences.

Goals

Science serves four major goals or objectives. First, it attempts to describe the phenomenon in question accurately, completely, and without bias. A description allows us to establish the facts that are known at present. There is both scientific and practical value in doing this. For example, farmers and scientists alike are interested in knowing which kinds of insects are harmful to crops and which are helpful. The same is true for the study of learning. Psychologists wish to know, for example, the kinds of behaviors that are learned, the conditions under which such learning takes place, and the treatments that enhance or inhibit learning. Without these descriptions, psychology would have no base on which to develop theories about the learning process.

The second **goal of science** (and of scientific psychology) is explanation. Explanations are informed speculations or theories about why a phenomenon occurs. For example, we might explain the fact that some plants are resistant to invasion by insects in terms of the chemicals in the plants' leaves that are toxic or aversive to parasites. Similarly, we might speculate that a person's ability to learn is related to the individual's IQ or level of motivation.

The third and fourth goals of scientific inquiry are related. One is prediction and the other is control. Having an adequate description and explanation of a phenomenon allows one to predict when the phenomenon will occur. Accordingly, if one is able to predict when an event will happen, then one may be able to control it—that is, to manipulate conditions such that the event will or will not occur.[1] These goals are particularly important to learning theorists because many wish to improve learning by altering the conditions under which it takes place. Describing and explaining how a person learns may be sufficient for the theorist, but being able to predict and control the learning process may be the more important goal for the practitioner.

Basic Methods in Scientific Research

The task of describing and explaining learning phenomena says very little about how one goes about achieving these goals. The methods for generating scientific knowledge have been the focus for philosophers and scientists for centuries.[2]

Hypothesis Testing.

The classical view of the scientific method suggests that the first step taken by any scientist is the formation of a hypothesis. A **hypothesis** is a theoretical argument, an "if . . . then" statement, a hunch about the way the world operates with respect to the phenomenon in question. All of us unconsciously test hypotheses in just about everything we do. We behave according to some hunch, belief, or speculation about what is appropriate at that moment; rarely do we act completely out of the blue. For instance, we communicate or interact with another person in a congenial way because we believe (hypothesize) that he or she is our friend. If we felt that the person was our adversary, then we would act in a wholly different manner; our actions would be guided by an entirely different hypothesis. In short, how we behave in our private lives is based on our unconscious theory or hypothesis about what behavior is appropriate. The same is true when we function as a scientist, except that the hypothesis is much more formalized, and we are more conscious of engaging in the speculation.

Once a hypothesis has been formed, then a test of it may be designed. Although the details of how this is done are beyond the scope of this book, nevertheless, some basic ideas are reviewed in the following sections. Any empirical test of a hypothesis requires the specification of both the research design and the independent and dependent variables. The research design is a scheme or overall plan for collecting and analyzing the data. It specifies which variables or treatments are to be used, which behaviors are to be measured, and, overall, the details of the experiment.

Independent Variable.

The **independent variable** is the treatment or condition that, according to the hypothesis, affects the behavior that is being studied. Direct manipulation is the most common way of establishing an independent variable. Specifically, the investigator gives different levels of a treatment to different groups of subjects (or, perhaps, to a single group of subjects but at different time periods). For example, if we hypothesize that the magnitude of a food reward affects learning (say, large rewards produce better learning than small rewards), then we could manipulate the reward size systematically and observe directly whether this is the case. Here, the magnitude of the reward would be the independent variable. To know whether the independent variable influenced the behavior, a comparison between groups would be made. If the groups performed differently, *despite being statistically similar in all other respects*, then the independent variable would be said to have affected the subjects (because the treatment was the only dimension on which the groups differed).

Another way of establishing an independent variable is to measure the subjects on some dimension and then to separate them into groups on the basis of the measurement. For instance, if we hypothesize that body size affects running speed, we might take a group of individuals, rate them on body size, place them in different groups based on body size (small, medium, or large body size), and then observe which groups have the fastest average running speed. Again, because the groups are essentially the same except for the one characteristic measured in the study (body size), we can conclude that body size affects running speed if, indeed, group differences are found.

Dependent Variable.

The **dependent variable** is the one that depends on, or is influenced by, the independent variable; it covaries with, and reflects the effect of, the independent variable. In psychology, the dependent variable is typically a behavioral measure—for example, the rate at which a certain action is performed. A dependent variable must be sensitive enough to change systematically and noticeably with variations in the independent variable. If it does not, then one has no way of knowing whether the independent variable truly affects the behavior.

Following the formulation of the hypothesis and the specification of the experimental design, the next step is to accept or reject the hypothesis, based on the empirical test. To do this, the data are subjected to statistical analysis (if appropriate), and, based on that analysis, the hypothesis is accepted or rejected. One typically hopes to conclude that the independent variable, in some fashion or another, affects the dependent variable as predicted by the hypothesis.

INTERIM SUMMARY

The goals of science include description, explanation, prediction, and control. These same goals are pursued by psychologists who study the learning process. The first step in attempting to reach these goals is to formulate a hypothesis. This "if . . . then" statement specifies the theoretical relationship between a treatment (independent variable) and a behavioral result (dependent variable). When subjects differ only with respect to the independent variable, then differences in their behavior may be attributed to the effect of that variable.

INFERENCE IN SCIENCE

Rarely are scientists interested merely in the presently known facts for their own sake. Rather, they are more interested in explaining the overall nature of the system being studied.[3] The nature of the system cannot be observed directly, however; it must be inferred from the facts.

Inferred States

For psychology, inference involves inducing or concluding something general about a subject, based on its behavior. Imagine the following example. You are sitting at your desk reading an assignment, and suddenly, the door flies open and a friend enters crying. The facts of the situation—the crying behavior—are not really of central importance. The more challenging and critical task is to explain why the behavior occurs, to infer something general about your friend, based on the crying behavior.

What would you say? There are many possibilities. For example, your friend just received upsetting news; stubbed his or her toe on the stairs; a cinder flew into your friend's eye, causing it to tear; your friend is crying tears of joy at having just been told that she or he won the lottery; or your friend is seriously ill from having eaten spoiled food. The possibilities are virtually endless.

One way to choose the most sensible hypothesis is to describe the behavior in great detail, looking for evidence of a cause. For example, we might observe whether the person is grimacing in pain while holding his or her toe, blinking excessively as if to rid the eye of a cinder, clutching a letter with a despairing look on her or his face, or holding his or her stomach while moaning. From these more precise descriptions, we may be able to make a general inference about causality—that is, about the independent variable that produced the behavior. We would be able to do so only because, in the past, we have witnessed certain events and the behavioral reactions that they produce. For example, we may have witnessed toes being stubbed (independent variable) and the person then grimacing in pain (dependent variable); or a person reading a telegram (independent variable) and then sobbing in grief (dependent variable); or dust flying into a person's eye and then the ensuing tears. In short, by carefully observing the behavior, and then relating the details of the observation to previous experience, one may arrive at a fuller explanation of what caused the behavior in the first place.

In the preceding example, the behavior occurred spontaneously, so we had to infer causality from the behavior itself. In the formal study of psychology, however, a behavior is created in the laboratory under controlled conditions. Here, one tries to assess the cause experimentally. Let us illustrate this using another example. Assume that we place a laboratory rat in a maze containing multiple pathways, and we allow it to explore the various turns and alleyways (see Figure 2-1). When it finally reaches the goal box, we deliver a small

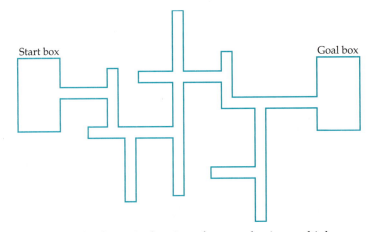

FIGURE 2-1. A schematic drawing of a maze having multiple pathways.

morsel of food. We then repeat this procedure 10 times, counting the number of wrong turns the animal makes on each trial. We notice that the number decreases systematically through training. Initially, the subject took quite a few wrong turns, but by the tenth trial, it was running to the goal box quickly and efficiently.

We have performed two operations. First, we consistently and immediately followed each correct entry into the goal box with the delivery of food. Second, we accurately measured the subject's behavior on each trial. These correspond to the independent and dependent variables discussed previously. The independent variable is the delivery of food reward, and the dependent variable is the behavior of the animal—here, the number of errors per trial.

What allows us to infer a causal relationship between the independent and dependent variables? For one thing, the fact that the decrease in errors follows a consistent pattern over the length of the training suggests that something is affecting the behavior in a systematic manner. More important, though, we may assess the effect of the independent variable by comparing the behavior of this subject (or group of subjects that are treated alike) to the behavior of another animal (or group) that is not given the food reward. If *all* subjects are essentially the same except for the fact that the former got the independent variable (food), whereas the latter did not, then that single difference must be responsible for producing the observed difference in behavior.

Inference in Learning Research

Learning theorists often infer more than the mere fact that the subject learned. They may infer something general about the nature or state of the organism that bears upon its capacity to learn. To illustrate this point, let us expand on the previous example. Assume that we take the rat who had previously been fed in the goal box, and we discontinue its reward. At least for a short period of time, the animal will continue to make the response even though it gets no food at the end. From this behavior, we may infer that the animal possesses some amount of a trait called "persistence." The longer the animal continues to perform, the more persistence it has. Persistence is simply the name we give to the unobserved state that controls the animal's performance when confronted with these conditions (hungry, placed in a familiar alleyway, and given no food in the goal box).

What have we achieved? At the very least, we have identified an abstract, general property of the animal, based on the relationship between our treatment (independent variable) and the resulting behavior (dependent variable). We may even elaborate on the rules by which this trait affects behavior—for example, by varying the kinds of reward in the goal box (food pellets versus water), the magnitudes of reward, the levels of hunger, or the kinds of alleyways.

Drawing inferences about traits such as persistence is precisely the same challenge that other sciences face. Consider an example from chemistry. Chemicals are known for their capacity to evaporate, especially when heated. Imagine that we place a chemical solution in a beaker and accurately measure the volume of the fluid. We then heat the solution to a specified temperature, for a given length of time, and measure the volume a second time. The volume of liquid remaining in the beaker after heating is less than what it was prior to heating. From this, we may infer that the chemical has a certain property, called "volatility," the strength of which is shown by its behavior—namely, the amount of evaporation per unit time. In fact, we may say that this particular chemical is highly volatile if, compared to some other chemical, a great deal of it evaporates when heated.

Volatility then is an abstract property of the chemical; it is not something we can touch or measure directly, but it is a property that we may infer, based on the relationship between the input (the independent variable, the heat) and the outcome (the dependent variable, the volume evaporated). Just as one may infer that a chemical solution has a certain degree of volatility, one may also infer that an animal possesses a certain level of persistence. Both are abstract properties or qualities of the system being studied, and both are measured in terms of the behavior of the system.

INTERIM SUMMARY

The independent and dependent variables are directly observable, but the nature of the overall system (the internal learning process itself) must be inferred from the relationship between the independent and dependent variables. In other words, learning cannot be observed directly, but psychologists may infer its general properties by observing behavior under controlled circumstances. This is analogous to the procedures used in the natural sciences, where the characteristics of, say, a chemical are inferred from the way it behaves under certain controlled conditions.

PROBLEMS IN MAKING INFERENCES

Drawing inferences about the learning process is challenging and difficult. Several issues are relevant to this problem. One is knowing whether the dependent variable is a valid measure of the mechanism or process that is presumably affected by the independent variable.

Test Validity

There is no simple way to confirm that a dependent variable is valid, but it is thought to be so when several different experimental approaches show agreement. Let us illustrate this point with an example from the research on frustration.[4] Rats are trained to run in a double alleyway (see Figure 2-2). Specifically, they are placed in a start box; allowed to run down the first alleyway to goal box 1, where they receive a food reward; and then allowed to run down a second alleyway to a second goal box, where they receive food once again. Once the rats learn to do this proficiently, food reward in the first goal box is omitted. The subjects now run unusually fast in the second alleyway, faster than subjects for whom reward in the first goal box is not omitted.[5]

We explain this outcome by inferring that the subjects experienced frustration in goal box 1. The facts agree with the two general assumptions of frustration theory. First, frustration occurs when the animal expects to receive reward but does not. Second, frustration is a negative motivational state and thus, like hunger or fear, energizes behavior.[6] Given these assumptions, it makes sense to interpret the increase in speed in the second alleyway as being due to the presence of frustration.

Are we sure that we have a valid measure of frustration? Perhaps speed in the second alleyway reflects the action of some other process or mechanism. For example, rather than creating frustration, the omission of reinforcement in the first goal box may reduce the lethargy left over from being fed on the previous trial.[7] Or perhaps omitting the first reward may enhance the attractiveness of the second reward.[8] In other words, how do we interpret the increase in speed in the second alleyway? Is it due to the presence of frustration, does it indicate that the subject has ceased to be sluggish, or does it mean that the subject simply has more interest in obtaining the reward in the second goal box?

If we accept the notion that the internal state called "frustration" caused the increase in running speed, then we must validate our measure of frustration. The best way to do this is to use a variety of tests and to look for

FIGURE 2-2. A schematic drawing of a double alleyway, having two goal boxes. Speed in the second alleyway is often used as a measure of frustration experienced in goal box 1.

agreement among them. For example, we might test whether the omission of the expected reward also energizes other kinds of behavior, such as jumping out of the box or engaging in aggression.[9] Similarly, we might use a different kind of incentive in goal box 1—say, sugar water or access to a sexual mate—and observe whether omission of that reward also causes running speed to increase in the second alleyway.[10] In each case, results similar to those found in the original study should be obtained if, indeed, the assumptions of the frustration hypothesis are true, and we are using a valid measure of frustration. In conclusion, although we may never be entirely sure that we are measuring an animal's internal state accurately (that is precisely why it is an inference and not a direct observation), nevertheless, by using a number of different tests, we may demonstrate agreement in the results and thus become more confident that our overall understanding of the system is accurate.

Learning Versus Performance

Perhaps a more serious problem to the task of drawing inferences is the so-called **learning versus performance distinction.** Recall from Chapter 1 that learning may be viewed as the acquisition of knowledge. Performance, on the other hand, is what the psychologist actually measures; it is the overt behavior of the organism. The psychologist must always rely on performance to study the underlying learning process. The state of knowledge is inferred from the animal's performance.

The problem with using performance to infer learning is that learning and performance may involve, or be governed by, independent processes. As shown in Figure 2-3, the learning processes, which dictate and control the

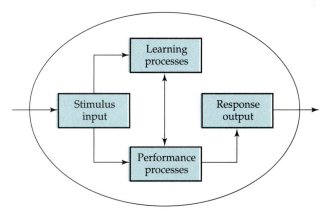

FIGURE 2-3. A schematic diagram illustrating the interaction between two hypothetical sets of processes, one dealing with the acquisition of knowledge (learning processes) and the other dealing with the production of overt behavior (performance processes).

acquisition of knowledge, may be different from the performance processes, which affect, govern, or control the response output centers. Although the diagram represents a very simplified view of behavioral control, it nevertheless implies that the processes or mechanisms involved in learning (acquiring information) may be distinct from those that govern performance. This is the source of the problem.

Various manipulations that affect one of these sets of processes may not affect the other set. A given treatment may affect learning but not performance, or it may change performance without affecting learning. Because the psychologist relies on overt behavior to assess changes in the animal's knowledge state, it is not always possible to know whether a given independent variable actually affects learning exclusively, or performance, or both.

Let us illustrate the problem with the example used previously of a rat learning a complicated maze. This time, however, assume that we do not reward it with food in the goal box. The animal is allowed to explore the choice points and alleyways on each trial, but when it finally arrives in the goal box, no food is given. If we measure the number of errors per trial, we find little systematic change over training; the number of wrong turns remains fairly high throughout.[11] Judging from its error rate, then, the subject does not seem to know which turns lead to a dead end and which lead toward the goal box. Furthermore, its error-filled performance contrasts sharply with that of another animal who is fed in the goal box on each trial and thus learns to run rapidly and efficiently toward the goal, making few errors in the process.

Now imagine that we begin giving food to the first animal in the goal box. This changes the subject's behavior dramatically. It now performs the running task quite proficiently. It leaves the start box and quickly proceeds to the goal box, making virtually no errors along the way. In other words, the animal suddenly (that is, without additional training) performs the correct response even though, based on its initial performance, we had no reason to believe that it knew how to do so. This is an example of learning without performance. The animal learned about the turns in the maze during its initial exploratory phase but did not perform in a fashion that reflected its knowledge (until later, when it began to receive food reward in the goal box).[12]

The opposite case is where performance changes without learning being affected. Using the same example, assume that we give food to rats each time they run to the goal box. Some of the animals receive a large reward in the goal box, whereas others get only a small reward. We are likely to show that performance is affected by reward size. The animals receiving the large reward run faster than the subjects receiving the small amount of food. In terms of their knowledge of the maze, however, measured by the number of errors they commit or the rate of improvement in their running behavior, the groups may be the same. In other words, magnitude of reinforcement may have a pronounced effect on the subject's motivation to perform (as measured by speed), but it may have little or no effect on the subject's knowledge of the maze (as measured by its error rate).[13]

INTERIM SUMMARY

Drawing valid inferences about the learning process is difficult for two reasons. First, there is no simple way to confirm that an inference is valid, except by using a variety of tests and checking to see whether the results are consistent with the hypothesis. A second problem is the learning-versus-performance distinction. Learning is the inner (inferred) process by which organisms acquire knowledge; performance is the overt (observed) behavior. Certain manipulations may affect one but not the other. Thus, inferring that learning has occurred from a change in performance may not be justified.

THEORY IN SCIENCE

Assuming that we have drawn a valid inference, and that we are using a valid measure, what kinds of theories have psychologists developed concerning the learning process? In a sense, that is precisely what this book is about. However, to help prepare for a more detailed discussion of learning theories in Chapter 11, let us examine what scientific theories in general are like.

What Is a Theory?

Several views have been offered concerning what a good scientific theory involves. Here, we present a classical view and a contemporary view.

Classical View.

The classical view, described by historians and philosophers of science, represents an idealistic model.[14] It is based primarily on theories in physics, notable those developed by Isaac Newton. For centuries, Newton's theories have served as a model for the other sciences. Indeed, many in psychology have wanted to emulate them.[15] Psychology, however, may not be the same kind of science as physics, and thus, emulation may be wholly inappropriate.[16]

According to the classical view, a theory is a set of propositions or statements. Some of these are axioms (self-evident truths) about which no one argues, and some are merely assumptions. These propositions and statements are chained together through logic to form theorems. Theorems, in turn, provide testable predictions. If the theorems and facts agree, then we claim that the theory is a good one.

The classical view also makes reference to two kinds of principles that a theory contains.[17] First, there are internal principles. These characterize the basic processes, abstract concepts, and entities of the science. Second, there are bridge principles. These relate how the internal processes and concepts relate to the real world—that is, to observable and measurable aspects of the physical environment.

Portrait of one of history's greatest scientists, Isaac Newton.
Here, Newton is shown conducting his noted experiment
in which he showed that white light is a mixture of colored
light.
© *Omikron, The National Audubon Society Collection/Photo*
Researchers

An example of this formalized system is Boyles's law, which relates the volume of gas to its pressure. According to this law, the pressure of a fixed quantity of gas is inversely proportional to its volume (when maintained at a constant temperature). If one takes a fixed amount of gas and reduces its volume (that is, compresses the gas), the pressure of the gas against the sides of the container increases. Boyles's law may be used to illustrate the difference between internal and bridge principles. The internal principles, the unobservable or theoretical constructs, involve both the idea that molecules exist and move in space, and the laws concerning the relationship between pressure and volume. These ideas are purely abstract, in that we cannot observe them directly. We cannot see molecules moving in space, nor can we see or touch the theoretical relationship between pressure and volume.

We relate these abstract and unmeasurable entities to the real world, however, by means of bridge principles. For example, bridge principles stipulate that pressure is measured by a specialized instrument called a "pressure gauge"; that molecules exert a force against the side of a container, just as other physical entities exert pressure against surfaces; and that the pressure of a physical substance against a given surface increases when there are more units of that substance. Without these bridge principles, the purely internal theoretical principles would yield no testable implications.[18]

Contemporary View.

Not all philosophers of science believe that the classical view applies to sciences other than physics.[19] For one thing, most sciences did not originate from the older tradition of physics, and thus their theories should not be judged by the same criteria of success as theories in physics.

Furthermore, many claim that psychology, in particular, does not conform to the ideal model of science (nor should it attempt to do so) because it is qualitatively different from physics. For instance, in distinguishing psychology from physics, Jaynes (1966) offered an interesting metaphor—"Physics is like climbing a mountain: roped together by a common asceticism of mathematical method, the upward direction ... is always certain, though the paths are not.... Instead of the difficult simplicity of physics, psychology is full of an easy complexity ... it is less like a mountain than a huge entangled forest ... it is directions [that the student] is looking for, not height" (p. 94). In other words, unlike theories in physics, psychological theories are not hierarchical; they are not based on a single foundation such as mathematics or mechanics, but rather offer diverse perspectives for a wide variety of seemingly independent behavioral phenomena.

Criteria of a Good Theory

Regardless of whether scientific theories comply with the classical view, each may be evaluated in terms of how adequately it fits certain criteria. There are five qualities that contribute to a theory's value. First, a theory must be testable. Its internal, abstract concepts must be related to the external world by bridge principles in such a way that the concepts can be verified objectively.[20] Second, a good theory is simple and parsimonious, not encumbered by constructs that are unnecessary for explaining the available data. Third, a good theory has generality; it provides some unified account of a diverse set of findings and phenomena. If, for example, a theory explained only a single fact, then it would have limited appeal. Imagine if Boyles's law explained the behavior of only a single kind of gas! The law would be useless as a general description of the behavior of all gases. A fourth characteristic of a good theory is that it is fruitful. The theory helps to generate new predictions and new ideas; it guides new research. By unifying a set of observations under a single set of principles, many new testable propositions are derived. Finally, although it may seem obvious, a good theory must agree with the facts. Surprisingly, this is not always the case. Theories are occasionally retained despite the observation that they do not comply with the known data, partly because no good alternative theory is available.[21]

Testability, simplicity, generality, fruitfulness, and agreement with data are characteristics of **good theories.** However, it is not always possible to say whether a given theory is a good theory, because it may take many years before the relevant data are collected and evaluated. In fact, our knowledge about truth changes continuously. We often look back on history and marvel at how misinformed we were about the so-called truth.

Consider Descartes's theory about how the nervous system operates (see Chapter 1). Such a theory now seems quaintly naïve, but at the time, there was no compelling reason to believe that it was seriously flawed. The point is that we do not ever know with complete certainty what is true. We may have a justifiable faith that some things are more likely to be true than others. For instance, we are justified in believing that nerves transmit their information both chemically and electrically, rather than hydraulically as Descartes believed. There is, however, nothing that absolutely precludes our theories from changing in the future, as new information becomes available. Given our general knowledge about the way the physical world operates, the available technology, and our inclination to view data with a particular bias, we therefore must evaluate theories in terms of how well they fit the facts, not on how closely they conform to the classical view of theory.

INTERIM SUMMARY

The classical view of a good scientific theory is exemplified in the work of Isaac Newton in physics. These formal systems contain abstract concepts, as well as bridge principles that relate the concepts to the real world and allow the concepts to be observed and measured. Many contemporary philosophers believe that psychology does not conform to this classical model. Regardless, the quality or goodness of a theory may be judged according to certain criteria. These stipulate that a good theory is testable, parsimonious, general, and fruitful (it generates new ideas and research), and it must agree with the known facts.

THEORETICAL APPROACHES TO LEARNING

What kind of theory has psychology generated with regard to the learning process? In this section, we consider three major kinds of theory. Each is covered in detail in Chapter 11, so our purpose here is simply to outline the general nature of these approaches and to provide a brief evaluation of them.

Cognitive Theories

Cognitive theories represent a powerful approach to the study of behavior. They are called "teleological theories" because they make reference to, define, and describe the purpose or goal toward which behavior is directed, rather than the causes of behavior. According to cognitive theories, subjects are behaving in accordance with a goal, even though the form of the response may vary.[22] The goal, in a sense, explains why the subject behaves as it does. For example, when we observe a dog chasing a cat, we say that the dog has a goal—namely, to catch the cat. Although the details of the behavior may be complex (for example, the dog may zigzag, jump against the trunk of a tree, and bark), all of the component behaviors are intended to serve the ultimate goal of catching the cat.[23]

Cognitive theories are teleological in the sense that the goals are typically internal cognitions or representations of future outcomes. We speculate that the dog has an internal representation of catching the cat. In a sense, the dog thinks about catching the cat; it can conceive of doing so.

How do we understand or represent the goal-directed processes? When scientists are puzzled about how a system works, they often develop a model. A model is some familiar system that represents an unknown abstract system. A model attempts to identify the elements of a system and to say how those elements operate. A model is like an analogy; it is not the system itself but rather is a more familiar example that resembles the system in some fundamental way.

Just as the proverbial dog has a goal of catching the cat (as discussed in the text), examples of cooperative and complicated behaviors from the natural environment, such as lions catching a prey, also suggest goal directed behavior.
© *Thomas D. W. Friedman, The National Audubon Society Collection/Photo Researchers*

Historically, models in science have tended to reflect the technology available at the time. The model Descartes used to describe the nervous system, for example, was based on hydraulics because that was the most advanced technology available. In the early part of this century, the prevailing model for the control of behavior by the nervous system was a telephone network, with its many wires and switching channels. Not surprisingly, the current trend uses the digital computer as a model for how the nervous system controls behavior. Like the brain, a computer is tangible. It has wires and transistors, just as the brain has neurons and chemicals. Moreover, the computer behaves according to its software, just as the brain functions according to various rules encoded in the neurons. These rules or programs may represent the cognitive mechanisms by which goal-directed behavior is achieved.

Mechanistic Theories

Mechanistic theories explain behavior not in terms of goals, but rather in terms of the mechanisms that lie behind the process.[24] Behavior is said to be mediated by various mechanisms. By understanding the inputs and knowing the nature of the mechanisms that operate on them, we can predict and understand the behavior.

What are these mechanisms? On the one hand, they may be physiological units, such as neurological structures, neurochemical systems, or hormonal circuits. For example, certain kinds of inputs, such as mild electrical stimulation, are capable of activating various structures in the brain, causing an organism to experience a high degree of pleasure (see Chapter 11).[25] The fact that we can identify these brain structures allows us to better appreciate how behavior is mediated neurologically.

Alternatively, mechanisms may be abstract states or conditions that make no direct reference to neurological structures. Hull (1943), for example, hypothesized that behavior is determined by a variety of mechanisms; the two most important are drive and habit. Drive goads or energizes behavior, whereas habit guides it. Although drive and habit are part of our everyday vocabulary, Hull used them in a more technical sense to describe particular psychological mechanisms that mediated behavior.

Behavior Analysis Approach

The **behavior analysis approach** does not focus on cognitive processes or psychological mechanisms, but rather claims that behavior is selected and strengthened by the environmental consequences of an action. According to this view, to understand behavior, one must focus directly on the relationship between behavior and its consequences.

The most noted psychologist in this area has been B. F. Skinner (see Chapter 11).[26] Skinner and his followers have assumed that behavior is controlled by environmental stimuli. Behavioral control means that the probability that a subject will engage in a certain behavior will increase when the subject is in the presence of appropriate stimuli. The greater the probability of a behavior given a certain set of stimuli, the greater is the behavioral control.

Central to this approach is the belief that cognitive processes and physiological mechanisms are superfluous concepts because they add nothing of scientific value to the description of behavioral control. To say that a behavior is caused by some mechanism does not clarify the causal relationship at all. It merely compels the scientist to explain why the mechanism operates as it does. If, for example, one explained a person's behavior by claiming that it was caused by fear (an internal psychological mechanism), or that it was directed toward the person's goal (a teleological explanation), then before one could really understand the behavior, one must first explain the fear or the goal. No scientific advance is made, according to Skinner, unless the mechanism, or the goal, is explained as well. In fact, the behavior analysis view argues that theoretical constructs are not only unnecessary, they are counterproductive because they distract the scientist from the important and useful task of describing the functional relationships between behavior and its consequences.

What controls behavior if it is not the goals or mechanisms? According to the behavior analysis approach, behavior is selected by outcomes. The parallel between this approach and the theory of natural selection is important in this context. A theory of natural selection says that the characteristics of a species vary from one individual to the next (for example, body size, coloration, or strength), and that the configurations that are more advantageous are, on the average, selected by the environment. They persist, whereas others do not. The same claim is made for behavior. Behavior is variable. Some behaviors are more adaptive than others, in the sense that they are more likely to produce, on the average, beneficial outcomes. These are therefore selected from among all the behaviors.

Resolution

It is difficult to know how to resolve the debate among these theoretical approaches to the study of learning.[27] Perhaps the primary area of contention is the degree to which abstract, theoretical constructs are appropriate.

Arguments Against the Use of Theoretical Constructs.

Many of the arguments raised by Skinner and his colleagues against the use of cognitive concepts and psychological mechanisms deserve considerable respect.[28] Some of the cognitive concepts are admittedly vague and possibly even untestable.[29] In addition, many are contained in our everyday language and thus convey meaning other than what is deserved or intended. An example might be the concept of fear. Because we have a sense, personally and collectively, about what fear means in our everyday lives, we may be seriously misinformed about how these concepts apply to the psychological state of a laboratory animal.

Perhaps the strongest argument against the use of psychological mechanisms in theory is the one cited previously—namely, that unexplained mechanisms cannot provide a useful explanation for behavior. If, for example, we say that someone behaved because that person experienced fear, then, according to Skinner, we must now explain why the fear was present. In a sense, there is an infinite regress of explanations, making it difficult ever to identify with confidence the underlying cause of behavior.[30]

Arguments for the Use of Theoretical Constructs.

There are, however, many scientists who strongly endorse either the cognitive or the mechanistic approach. They suggest that many processes are involved in a behavioral chain, and for the psychologist to avoid speculating about those processes is short-sighted and inappropriate.[31]

These individuals defend the use of theoretical constructs on several accounts. First, the development of theory, whether it be teleological or mechanistic, helps guide future investigations and helps unify our observations. Second, some behaviors are not easily explained except with the use of theoretical constructs. For example, think of sudden emotional outbursts. Behaviorally, these may involve loud shouts, crying, or other obvious and strong behavioral reactions. Yet the paradox is that often such behavioral outbursts are not preceded by stimuli that, on the surface, provide good explanations for such outbursts. How many times do we strike out in a rage, not because we have been provoked by a powerful stimulus but because we have experienced a wholly insignificant stimulus? We say that a person cries "at the least little thing." A faint whisper is often more frightening than a loud shout. What helps in our analysis, therefore, are intervening mechanisms or states, such as anger, sadness, or fear. These help explain behaviors that otherwise are surprising. To say that we should avoid using theoretical states such as anger or sadness to explain the behavior is to beg the question.[32]

Finally, one may justify the use of theoretical speculations by pointing out that the other sciences, including physics and chemistry, do this sort of thing routinely as a shorthand way of referring to the properties of their subject matter. Indeed, the example of chemical volatility discussed previously involves precisely this kind of use of theoretical language.

Multiple Perspectives.

Which theoretical approach, then, is appropriate? It would seem that all perspectives have value; none is entirely adequate, and none is patently inappropriate. Each perspective uses a different language for explaining a common set of behavioral facts, and each focuses on different aspects of the situation. The value of one does not preclude or eliminate the possible value of another. One could claim, for example, that a rat has an objective in mind when it runs to a goal box (goal), or that it has a drive to perform (mechanism), without being concerned at all about the underlying goal or mechanism itself. The goal and the drive are simply names given to a set of orderly behavioral relations. Similarly, one could focus on the stimulus environment and behavior without ever referring to goals or mechanisms, and thereby, one could generate a set of functional relationships between the two.

INTERIM SUMMARY

Three theoretical approaches to the study of learning are reviewed. Cognitive or teleological theories explain behavior in terms of the subject's goals. Mechanistic theories make use of various structures or mechanisms, including physiological mechanisms, such as neurons and neurochemicals, and theoretical mechanisms or states, such as habit and drive. The behavior analysis approach argues that explaining behavior in terms of goals or mechanisms is inappropriate. Rather, behavior is selected and strengthened by the consequences of an action and thus should be explained in terms of the relationship between the action and the consequence. Convincing arguments have been provided for each viewpoint. However, none is necessarily incorrect; each provides a different perspective or language for understanding learning phenomena.

ENDNOTES

1. The ability to control also depends on an understanding of the causal factors, not simply on being able to predict an event.
2. Three excellent and highly readable books dealing with the philosophy of science are by Bechtel (1988); Hempel (1966); and McCain and Segal (1977).
3. Deese (1972) makes this point in arguing that behaviorism, at least the strict and orthodox version first devised by John Watson, is an inadequate approach to the study of behavior. As Deese claimed, "Psychology is the science of behavior only in a trivial sense. It is so in the sense that physics is the science of meter reading and chemistry is the science of observing changes in the color of [litmus] paper . . . . What is of ultimate significance is the fact for which the [behavioral] reaction stands" (p. 12).
4. See Wagner (1959) for a study similar to the example given in the text, and Amsel (1992) for a review of the frustration literature; see also Zaslav and Porter (1974) for an alternative approach.
5. Two kinds of comparisons in running speed have been made—namely, within-subject (speed in the second alleyway, following reward versus no reward in the first goal box) and between-group (speed in the second alleyway for a group that expected reward in the first goal box versus a group that did not).
6. See Daly (1969).
7. Matzel (1985).
8. Gaffan and Keeble (1976).
9. Daly (1970).
10. Sgro (1969).
11. This example is hypothetical. Actual data show a noticeable decline in errors, even for subjects who receive no reward; see Chapter 11.
12. Such an outcome was found in a number of early papers; the phenomenon is called

"latent learning" because learning occurs but is not visible at the time; see Thistlethwaite (1951) and Chapter 11.

13. This example is entirely hypothetical, and, in fact, simple discrimination learning in a T-maze may be better with larger rewards; see Singer (1969).

14. See Hempel (1966).

15. The noted learning theorist Clark Hull was strongly influenced by Newton's work (see Chaplin & Krawiec, 1974, for further details). In his most noted work, Hull (1943) made repeated reference to Newton in an attempt to develop and explain his own theory of psychology. One can sense Hull's admiration of Newton and his wish that scientists in psychology would follow Newton's example in physics. For example, Hull says that "Proper scientific theoretical systems conform exactly to all three of these characteristics [definitions, axioms, proof of theorems]. For example, Isaac Newton's *Principia*, the classical scientific theoretical system of the past, sets out with . . . definitions . . . [of matter] . . . postulates . . . [of the laws of motions] . . . and a hierarchy of . . . formally proved theorems" (p. 7).

16. See Deese (1972); Jaynes (1966).

17. Hempel (1966).

18. Hempel (1966, pp. 74–75).

19. See Deese (1972).

20. See Popper (1959).

21. See Kuhn (1962).

22. Historically, the most notable learning theory in this regard was that espoused by Tolman (1932) (see Chapter 11). In describing his theory, Tolman wrote "To sum up, the complete descriptive identification of any behavior-act per se requires descriptive statements relative to (a) the goal-object or objects, being got to or from; (b) the specific pattern of commerces with means-objects involved in this getting to or from; and (c) the facts exhibited relative to the selective identification of routes and means-objects" (p. 12).

23. Even inanimate systems may be said to serve a goal, although it would be inappropriate to claim that they do so using cognitive processes. For example, a heat-seeking missile has a particular goal—namely, hitting the oncoming aircraft. Its behavior—turning in various ways to track and intercept a plane that is taking evasive maneuvers—is governed by its goal. Each change in behavior is designed to decrease the discrepancy between the missile's current state and the missile's desired final state—namely, hitting the plane.

24. Historically, the most notable mechanistic learning theory was that proposed by Hull (1943) (see Chapter 11). As Hull stated, "Whenever an attempt is made to penetrate the invisible world of the molecular, scientists frequently and usefully employ logical constructs, intervening variables, or symbols to facilitate their thinking. These symbols of X's represent entities or processes which, if existent, would account for certain events in the observable molar world. Examples of such postulated entities in the field of the physical sciences are electrons, protons, positrons, etc. A closely parallel concept in the field of behavior familiar to everyone is that of *habit* [emphasis original]. . . . The habit presumably exists as an invisible condition of the nervous system quite as much when it is not mediating action as when habitual action is occurring" (p. 21).

25. See Hoebel (1988).

26. Skinner has written many books and articles. Two that are particularly illuminating are Skinner (1953, 1963). Those wishing to explore Skinner's theory in depth should see Modgil and Modgil (1987).

27. Some argue that, from a practical point of view, the behavior analysis approach is more fruitful than the mechanistic or the cognitive approaches; see Rachlin (1987). This point, however, has been disputed. For example, physiological investigations, coupled with psychological observations, have helped explain and treat drug addictions and various mental disorders, such as depressions. Theories of memory and interpersonal interactions have helped explain and improve eyewitness testimony.
28. Keat (1972).
29. This has traditionally been one of the strongest arguments leveled at Freudian theory. That is, various Freudian concepts—such as id, ego, and Oedipal complex—are so vague as to defy scientific verification; see Fernald (1979), Robinson (1979).
30. These arguments are made forcefully by Blackman (1983).
31. Killeen (1987).
32. Mineka (1985a).

CHAPTER 3

Basic Procedures in Pavlovian (Classical) Conditioning

PAVLOVIAN (CLASSICAL) CONDITIONING

In Chapter 1, associations were defined as small units of knowledge. Here, the concept of association is developed more thoroughly. According to the British empiricists, if two sensations repeatedly occur together, the mental reactions to those sensations become associated such that when the first sensation or stimulus is given, it triggers the memory of the associated stimulus. Consider this example. Assume that your pet dog has experienced two events in sequence—namely, observing the opening of a can of food and being fed.[1] We presume that each stimulus triggers an associated mental reaction or idea—that is, the dog perceives and reacts to each when presented. The contiguous occurrence of these corresponding ideas produces an association. This is confirmed when the can is opened and the dog shows evidence of anticipating the food. It wags its tail, shows agitated behavior, barks, and drools.

Pavlov's Experiment

Pavlov was studying digestive reactions in dogs when he, almost accidentally, discovered conditioning (for a biographical sketch of Pavlov, see Endnote 2).[2] To conduct his experiments, he surgically isolated the salivary duct so that saliva could be collected in a small flask whenever the dog was given food powder. Pavlov (1927) found, however, that the dogs often salivated merely at the sight of the experimenter entering the room, well before food had been placed in their mouths. He termed these reactions "psychic secretions" because they were caused not by the biological agent of food, but by a stimulus that was observed "at a distance."

In a typical experiment by Pavlov, the dog was restrained in a harness and was presented with two stimuli—for instance, the clicking sound of a metronome and food powder. The first stimulus evoked an orienting reaction, but it did not have the power to elicit salivation. The second stimulus, how-

A portrait of the noted Russian physiologist, Ivan Pavlov
(see Endnote 2 for a biography of Pavlov).
© *Novosti/Science Photo Library/Photo Researchers*

ever, made the dog salivate copiously. After a few sequential presentations of these two stimuli, the dog began to show some evidence of salivation to the metronome alone. After many such pairings, the amount of salivation to the metronome was considerable.

What is important about Pavlov's study is that the salivation response was triggered by the metronome, even though originally the metronome was incapable of triggering the response. This simple demonstration illustrates the acquisition of a unit of knowledge (an association), because the metronome (first stimulus) triggered the anticipation of the food delivery (second stimulus). Evidence for the presence of the association was the salivation to the metronome itself.

Definition of Pavlovian Conditioning

We define Pavlovian conditioning in terms of the procedures used by the experimenter to conduct the study. This is because we cannot observe the association directly, but rather, we must infer its presence from the subject's performance (see Chapters 1 and 2).

Pavlovian conditioning occurs whenever two stimuli are presented independent of the subject's behavior. The exact way in which those stimuli are presented may be complicated (this section of the book elaborates on many variations), but the important thing is that the two stimuli are presented together, regardless of how the animal behaves. Pavlov did not wait until the animal salivated before he presented the metronome or the food powder. He decided ahead of time what the sequence of stimuli would be, and then he gave the animals that sequence whether they salivated or not. The fact that animals *do* salivate under these conditions is a fortuitous reaction that psychologists use to make inferences about the underlying association, but it does not influence the procedure.

Terms

Four major terms apply to a Pavlovian experiment.

Stimuli.

The **unconditioned stimulus (US)** is defined as a biologically potent stimulus, one that reliably evokes an unlearned (reflexive) reaction. In Pavlov's case, it was the food powder. Unconditioned stimuli are highly predictable. They always elicit a reflexive response over which the subject has little control. Pavlov's dogs, for instance, did not choose to salivate. Their reaction was automatic and involuntary. Imagine if someone placed a drop of lemon juice on your tongue. Because the acid in the lemon juice compels you to salivate (a reflex action), the lemon juice qualifies as a US.

This definition of a US poses some problems because one is unable to state ahead of time exactly how large the reaction must be before the stimulus is called a US. Where does one draw the line between powerful and weak, between stimuli that do and do not elicit a reflexive reaction? The usual solution is to use stimuli that are unambiguously powerful. Food, mild electric shocks, water, and loud noises have clear effects in this regard, so they are used routinely in Pavlovian research.

The **conditioned stimulus (CS)** was the first stimulus that Pavlov delivered to his subjects. A CS is an innocuous or biologically weak stimulus. Pavlov actually used many different kinds of conditioned stimuli, including tactile stimuli, changes in temperature, light flashes, odors, whistles, and visual stimuli such as black squares and rotating objects. Although CSs evoke orienting reactions, these tend to be weak responses, in comparison to the reflexes evoked by the US, and these responses subside rather quickly.

Responses.

Two kinds of reactions are observed in Pavlovian experiments. First, the **unconditioned reaction (UR)** is the *un*learned response that is triggered by the US. It is the powerful and reflexive-like reaction referred to previously. Because the UR is biologically linked to the US, the animal does not have to learn to react in this fashion. The UR may actually involve a number of different component reactions. For example, Pavlov's dogs not only salivated when given food, but they also struggled in their harness, turned their heads, chewed, and vocalized. Usually, only one reaction (or perhaps two) is measured during a typical experiment.

The second kind of reaction, the one about which psychologists have the greatest interest, is the **conditioned response (CR).** The CR is elicited by the CS. It represents the learned behavior, the behavioral manifestation of the underlying association between the CS and the US. The CR is learned because initially, the CS was not capable of eliciting any response other than a weak orienting reaction. After sufficient exposure to the CS and US pairings, however, the CS, *by itself,* elicits the CR. The CS gains power or strength that it did not originally have.

INTERIM SUMMARY

Pavlovian (classical) conditioning reflects the development of an association between two stimuli. In Pavlov's original study, the sound of a metronome was paired with food powder. After a sufficient number of pairings, the metronome itself elicited a salivation reaction. Pavlovian conditioning occurs whenever two stimuli are presented independent of the animal's behavior. The stimuli include the unconditioned stimulus (US), a biologically powerful stimulus that reliably evokes a reflexive reaction, and the conditioned stimulus (CS), an innocuous or weak stimulus. Through conditioning, the CS acquires strength, as evidenced by its ability to elicit a response. Two kinds of responses are observed in Pavlovian experiments. The unconditioned response (UR) is the unlearned reaction triggered by the US, and the conditioned response (CR) is the learned reaction elicited by the CS after conditioning.

EXCITATORY CLASSICAL CONDITIONING

Pavlov's original experiment is an example of excitatory classical conditioning. The term excitatory means that the CS is able to excite the CR into being. Procedurally speaking, **conditioned excitation** occurs when the CS presentation is followed by the US presentation.

Appetitive Conditioning

Excitatory–appetitive conditioning occurs when a CS is followed by an appetitive US such as food or water.[3] Common examples of appetitive USs are food, water, sugar solutions, and mild acid solutions.

One important excitatory–appetitive technique is autoshaping.[4] **Autoshaping** studies typically use pigeons as subjects, although other kinds of animals are used, as well. The procedure is virtually the same as that used by Pavlov. A light, placed behind a translucent plastic disk (called a "key"), is illuminated, and, several seconds later, a small container of grain located beneath the floor is raised to a position just under a hole in the floor, so that the pigeon has an opportunity to peck at the grain through a hole. The food automatically evokes a pecking reaction. Pecking small bits of grain and other potential food items is the natural reaction for a hungry pigeon when feeding, just as salivation is the natural reaction of a hungry dog when given food powder. Autoshaping research shows that after a sufficient number of pairings of the key light and the food, the bird pecks the key itself. Such a reaction is a CR because pigeons do not peck the key unless its presentation is followed by food.

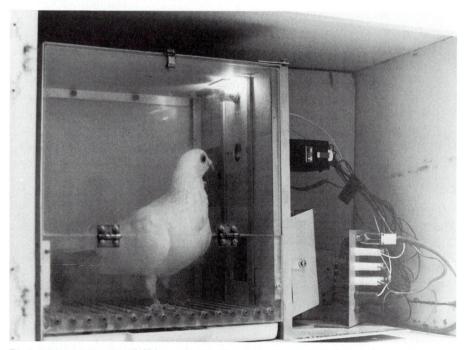

Pigeon in a conventional Skinner box containing a houselight (at the top of the box), a response key behind which colors or geometric targets may be positioned, and a feeding tray (located behind the front wall). In this picture, a horizontal line is projected on the response key.
Author photo

Pigeons not only peck a lighted key, but they also move toward it. Approaching and contacting a CS is called **sign-tracking.**[5] In a study by Wasserman, Franklin, and Hearst (1974), for example, some subjects received only CS presentations, whereas others received the conventional conditioning arrangement (illumination of the response key, followed by 3 seconds of access to food). The experiment was conducted using a box with a floor that tilted back and forth. Thus, the location of the subject could be measured. The average position of the subjects, measured in terms of the time spent on the CS side, relative to the total time spent in the apparatus, is shown in Figure 3-1. Subjects who received CS and US pairings spent a greater proportion of their time on the side of the apparatus containing the key light, relative to the CS-only subjects. Thus, birds not only peck the key (the autoshaping phenomenon), but they also remain physically close to it during most of their time in the apparatus.

Another example of Pavlovian excitatory–appetitive conditioning is the jaw-movement reaction in rabbits.[6] Rabbits are placed in a restraining apparatus similar to that used by Pavlov. The subjects are then given various CSs such as tones or lights, followed by a small amount of water injected directly into their mouth. The water causes an unconditioned reaction—namely, movement of the jaw muscles. After repeated presentations of the CS and US, the rabbit also shows a jaw-movement reaction to the CS alone.

Aversive Conditioning

Pavlovian conditioning is not limited to appetitive situations in which food and water serve as the US. Aversive USs may be used as well. This procedure is **excitatory–aversive conditioning.**

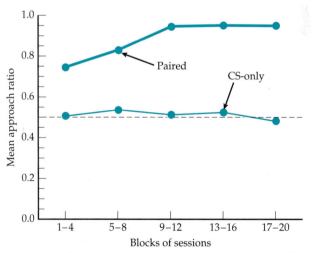

FIGURE 3-1. Mean approach ratio (time spent on the CS side, divided by total time in apparatus), as a function of blocks of training sessions (after Wasserman, Franklin, & Hearst, 1974).

One of the first experiments to demonstrate aversive conditioning was conducted by a contemporary of Pavlov's, Bekhterev (1913). A neutral, tone CS was sounded, and, a few seconds later, a mild electric shock was applied to the forepaw of the dog. The UR to the shock was struggling and paw withdrawal. After repeated presentations of these two stimuli, the tone itself elicited the withdrawal reaction. Experiments of this sort are excitatory because the US follows the CS, and aversive because the animal would terminate or avoid the US if given a chance.

Many kinds of aversive excitatory reactions have been studied. The most common are changes in heart rate or galvanic skin response (GSR) and movement of the rabbit's nictitating membrane of the eye (the US may be either a mild shock or a puff of air to the eyelid, both of which cause a reflexive blinking reaction).[7]

Indirect Tests of CR Strength

All of the aforementioned experiments test the CR directly. That is, they present the CS and the US together, then they measure the positive occurrence of the CR (salivation, eye blinking, changes in heart rate, key pecking, or paw flex). There are, however, indirect ways of assessing the presence of an association. One method is the **conditioned emotional response (CER) technique.** Subjects, such as laboratory rats, are taught to perform a simple behavior, such as pressing a lever to receive a pellet of food. Hungry rats have no trouble learning this behavior, and they will engage in it for long periods of time. Then, independent of the lever-pressing behavior, a Pavlovian study is conducted in which a CS is given (typically a 30-second tone), followed by a mild shock pulse. Initially, the tone CS has little impact on the lever-pressing behavior because it has no meaning or power. The shock, on the other hand, is an aversive US and thus elicits various kinds of URs, including jumping, locomotion, and vocalization. Because the tone and the shock are paired, Pavlovian conditioning takes place such that when the tone is sounded later on, the animal stops lever pressing well before the shock occurs. Anticipating the shock distracts the animal from its current task—namely, lever pressing. The stronger the CR—that is, the greater the anticipation of the aversive shock—the greater is the disruption of lever pressing. In other words, the degree of disruption of an otherwise steady lever-pressing rate by a CS that has been paired with shock is used as a measure of the strength of conditioning.[8]

Disruption of responding in a CER experiment may be quantified in the following manner. The number of lever presses executed during the CS is counted (period "B"), as is the number of lever presses executed during a period of equal duration just prior to the CS onset (time period "A"). If the CS is totally meaningless—that is, if it does not elicit any anticipation of the shock—then, on the average, these two values should be approximately the same. Furthermore, a ratio of the number of presses during the CS (B), relative to the total number of presses (A + B), should equal .5. If, however, the CS has associative power and thus causes suppression of lever pressing, then the ratio will decline toward 0 (the number of presses during the CS will be less than the number prior to the CS). By measuring the strength of the disruption in a quantitative fashion, the **CER ratio** [B / (A + B)] thus expresses the degree to which the CS evokes an aversive reaction.

Here is an example. Assume that an animal presses 30 times during a 30-second tone CS but presses 75 times during the 30-second period just prior to the tone onset. The CER ratio is therefore [30 / (30 + 75)], which is 30/105 or .29. This number indicates that significant suppression occurs during the tone (the ratio is markedly lower than .5). The number, therefore, may be compared with values obtained from another subject. For example, conditioning in one subject is stronger than in another if the average CER ratio is, say, .29 in the former but .5 in the latter subject. In short, a CER ratio of .5 (no suppression) indicates that the CS has virtually no power. As the ratio approaches 0, however, appreciable CR strength may be inferred.

Another indirect test of Pavlovian conditioning, also using an aversive US, is conditioned taste aversion.[9] Taste aversion occurs when a flavor CS is followed by an injection of an illness-inducing substance, usually lithium chloride. Lithium chloride poisons the animal only to the extent that it produces a mild upset or nausea. Because the flavor and the poison are paired, a CR is acquired, causing the subjects to avoid consuming the flavor in the future. Control subjects, who are not given flavor–poison pairings, show no such aversion; their consumption of the flavored substance is unaffected.

INTERIM SUMMARY

Excitatory conditioning occurs when the CS is followed by the US. If the US is appetitive (for example, food or water), then the conditioning is excitatory–appetitive. Autoshaping exemplifies this kind of conditioning. Here, pigeons are given a light, followed by food; their association of the two is shown by their pecking the light. If the US is aversive (for instance, shock), then the conditioning is excitatory–aversive. The CRs are often demonstrated directly. In some cases, however, the CRs are observed indirectly, using the conditioned emotional response (CER) technique. Here, an aversive CS disrupts an ongoing response, such as lever pressing for food. The greater the disruption, the stronger the CR.

BASIC STAGES IN LEARNING

A conditioning study typically involves several stages.

Acquisition

The first stage is **acquisition.** This is the time during which the subject acquires the association (as evidenced by the development of the CR). Presumably, the association is absent at the beginning of acquisition because the subjects have not undergone any training) but present by the end of acquisition (at which point, the effects of the training are evident). The strength of the association that develops during acquisition depends on the particular training conditions used.

A typical acquisition curve is shown in Figure 3-2. The vertical axis illustrates the strength of the CR and, by inference, the strength of the underlying CS–US association. The horizontal axis usually plots training trials—that is, successive CS–US pairings. The growth of the association may take place at various rates, depending on the details of the training sessions.[10]

Extinction

Following acquisition, many experiments use an **extinction** phase. Extinction occurs when the CS is given without a US. As shown in Figure 3-2, the CR strength declines with continued extinction trials.

Does the decline in the CR strength mean that the underlying CS–US association has been eliminated? The answer is no. Despite the fact that the CR declines during the extinction phase of the study, the underlying CS–US association remains relatively intact. It is not obliterated as a result of the extinction procedure, but only suppressed or inhibited.

Disinhibition.

One piece of evidence for such a claim is a phenomenon called **disinhibition.** This occurs when a novel stimulus is given along with the CS during

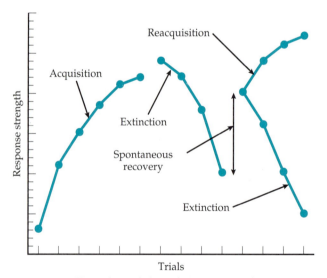

FIGURE 3-2. Hypothetical data showing typical acquisition and extinction curves. The spontaneous recovery curve at the right declines with continued extinction, or increases if additional training trials are given.

extinction, causing the subject to execute the CR immediately. For example, assume that a dog is given a light followed by food during acquisition, and then only the light during extinction. Disinhibition is observed if, during extinction, a novel cue, say a tone, is presented during the light, causing the dog to salivate immediately. The novel stimulus disrupts the process that is currently operating—namely, inhibition—causing the underlying process— excitation—to be expressed. In other words, inhibition is suppressing the expression of the CR, and when a novel stimulus is presented, the inhibition process itself is reduced, allowing the CR to be expressed once again.

Spontaneous Recovery.

The second finding that confirms that extinction merely inhibits the expression of a CR is **spontaneous recovery.** The CR strength recovers, spontaneously, without further training, if a rest interval follows the extinction period (see Figure 3-2). In other words, although CR strength is weak following extinction, it spontaneously recovers to an appreciable level following a rest interval (although perhaps not to the same high level shown at the end of acquisition). Extinction, therefore, must have caused a temporary suppression of the CR, and this suppression dissipated during the rest interval.

A study by Robbins (1990), using the autoshaping procedure, provides a good example of spontaneous recovery. Pigeons were given a blue key light, followed by 5 seconds access to food.[11] As discussed earlier, pigeons peck the key under these conditions (the autoshaping phenomenon). Following acquisition, the blue light was given repeatedly in the absence of food until the animals stopped pecking on 3 out of 4 successive presentations. Different groups of birds were then tested for spontaneous recovery either 15 minutes, 24 hours, 48 hours, or 168 hours later. The results are shown in Figure 3-3.

The recovery ratio measures the recovery from the suppressive effects of acquisition. A score of 0 reflects the absence of spontaneous recovery (behavior is still suppressed from extinction), whereas a ratio of .5 reflects complete recovery (the suppressive effects of extinction are no longer evident). Key-peck behavior, although suppressed during extinction, showed appreciable recovery within 24 hours.

The author's explanation for the spontaneous recovery was similar to Pavlov's theory. According to Pavlov, animals discover that the CS means something important during acquisition (food, in this case); attention to the CS is, therefore, strong. During extinction, the animals recognize that the CS no longer predicts something important, so they eventually stop paying close attention to its onset. After a rest interval, however, their attention is renewed, presumably because they are trying to determine in this new session whether the CS has the strong predictive properties it once had.

CR Renewal.

Finally, a phenomenon called **CR renewal** also indicates that extinction procedures do not abolish the CS–US association. Renewal is observed if extinction of the CS takes place in an environment that is different from the

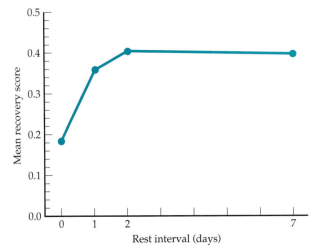

FIGURE 3-3. Mean recovery score on the spontaneous recovery test following extinction after rest intervals of 15 minutes (noted as 0 days), 1, 2, or 7 days (after Robbins, 1990).

one used in acquisition. Although extinction causes the CR to decline in strength when conducted in the extinction environment, the strength is renewed if the animal is tested in the original context.[12]

In a study by Bouton and King (1983), for example, animals were first trained to press a lever for food pellets in each of two environments. Contexts "A" and "B" differed in a number of important ways. One had aluminum sides, a clear plastic top, and thin stainless steel bars for the floor, and it was permeated with a strong odor. The other was a smaller box with plywood floors and walls that were painted flat black, and it contained no odor.

Once subjects achieved a relatively high and stable rate of lever pressing, Pavlovian conditioning was given. Here, all subjects received acquisition with a tone CS and a shock US in context "A."[13] One group ("ext-A") was then extinguished in the same context, whereas a second group ("ext-B") received extinction in a new context, apparatus "B." A third group ("no-ext") did not receive any extinction trials at all.

As shown in Figure 3-4, the suppression of lever pressing during the CS at the beginning of the extinction trials was almost complete. By the end of extinction, however, both groups showed almost complete absence of suppression (CS power had been extinguished). On the test, the no-ext group showed almost total suppression in context "A"; this is not surprising because they did not undergo extinction. The ext A group showed almost no suppression of lever pressing in context A, indicating that when animals are trained and extinguished in the same apparatus, they continue to show the effect of extinction (here, lack of suppression). The interesting result was found in the ext-B group. Although the CS showed virtually no power by the end of

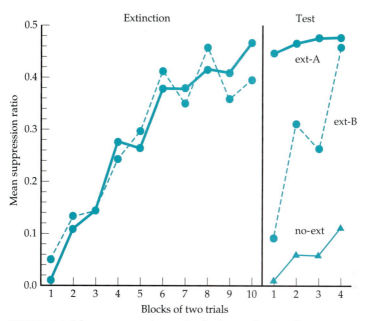

FIGURE 3-4. Mean suppression ratio during extinction (in context A or B) and during the test sessions (in the same or different context) for three groups (after Bouton & King, 1983).

the extinction trials in context B (absence of suppression), suppression was renewed when subjects were tested in the original learning environment (context A). This remarkable finding indicates that extinction of a CS is not permanent; in fact, it is context dependent. When the CS is extinguished in a different context from the one in which it was trained, extinction trials have little effect on CS strength when the subject is tested in the original environment.

INTERIM SUMMARY

Acquisition is the first stage in a conditioning experiment. Here, the CR develops as a result of the CS–US pairings. Many experiments also use a second stage, called "extinction," where the CS is given by itself. The CR declines during this time. The decrease in CR strength during extinction, however, does not mean that the association has been abolished. Three phenomena suggest that extinction produces only a temporary suppression of the CR. Disinhibition occurs when a novel stimulus, presented during extinction, causes the subject to execute the CR immediately. Spontaneous recovery occurs when the CR is observed following extinction, provided the subjects are given a rest interval before the test. The CR renewal phenomenon shows that a CR is restored following extinction if extinction takes place in a different context than the one used for acquisition.

INHIBITORY CLASSICAL CONDITIONING

The work described here on excitatory conditioning involves a CS that precedes, and therefore predicts, the US occurrence. Is that arrangement the only one that leads to learning, however? What would happen if the CS preceded the *absence* of the US? Would conditioning still occur? The answer is yes. In fact, Pavlov himself devoted much of his work to studying just this situation.

A conditioned inhibitor is a stimulus that, through conditioning, acquires properties that are antagonistic to a conditioned excitor (to designate this fact, an inhibitory stimulus is labeled "CS−," in contrast to an excitatory cue, which is labeled "CS+"). From a procedural point of view, a CS becomes inhibitory when it is paired with the absence of a US in the course of normal excitatory conditioning. As a result of this treatment, the stimulus triggers a tendency opposite to that of the conditioned excitor. Specifically, a CS− subtracts from, or cancels out, excitatory processes.[14] The following sections discuss inhibitory conditioning in greater detail.

Measurement of Inhibition

In some cases, conditioned inhibition may be assessed directly—for example, in terms of a subject's physical withdrawal from, or lack of contact with, an inhibitory CS−.

Directed-Behavior Test.

Although the normal strategy for measuring conditioned inhibition is to use one of the indirect tests described below, there is also a direct measure. Here, a subject is given inhibitory training during which its physical withdrawal from, or lack of contact with, the CS− is measured. For example, in a study by Hearst and Franklin (1977), pigeons were tested in a box with a tilting floor. A ratio of the time spent on the side containing the lighted key, relative to the total time that the keys were illuminated gave a measure of approach–withdrawal. A ratio of .5 indicated that the birds' movements were not systematically controlled by the location of the key light, whereas ratios approaching 0 indicated strong withdrawal from the key light. All subjects received 40 key-light illuminations per session, each lasting 20 seconds.[15] For one group, food was negatively correlated with the presentation of the key-light CSs, and thus the key light was expected to become inhibitory.

As shown in Figure 3-5, subjects were initially indifferent to the key light; the light did not systematically affect the position of the animals within the box. However, within about eight sessions, subjects were avoiding the side of the apparatus on which the key light appeared. In other words, the strength of the inhibitory effect of the CS− was revealed by the degree of physical withdrawal from the CS location.[16]

Although a direct test of conditioned inhibition may be used in certain situations, such tests are not available in most others. For example, excitatory conditioning involving salivation or paw withdrawal is directly observable,

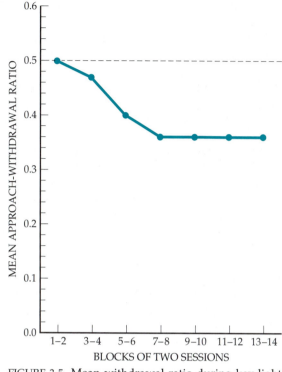

FIGURE 3-5. Mean withdrawal ratio during key-light illumination over successive blocks of sessions for a group that was given food during the absence of the key-light presentation (after Hearst & Franklin, 1977).

but the inhibitory counterpart is not. The tendency to "not salivate" and "not withdraw the paw" are not observable.[17] **Conditioned inhibition,** therefore, poses an interesting dilemma. An association between a CS− and "no US" may exist, but the animal cannot demonstrate that association by performing a lack of a behavior. The solution to the problem is to use an indirect test of inhibitory conditioning.[18] There are two kinds of tests.

Summation Test.

The **summation test** involves the presentation of two stimuli, a CS+ and a CS−, together. The idea is that each stimulus elicits its own associative reaction—excitation and inhibition, respectively—and that each reaction algebraically summates. However, because the two processes are antagonistic, the inhibitory association cancels the excitatory association. This effect is quantified by measuring the strength of the excitatory CS+ by itself, measuring it again in combination with the inhibitory CS−, and then calculating the difference. If a CS− has no inhibitory power, then the full strength of the excitatory reaction is observed in both instances. If, however, the conditioned inhibitor has strength (it elicits a conditioned inhibitory CR), then a reduction in the level of excitation to the CS+ is observed when the stimuli are presented simultaneously. In other words, conditioned inhibition is measured in terms of the degree to which a CS− causes the subject to perform a smaller-than-usual excitatory CR to a CS+.

A good example of the summation technique, by Hammond (1967), used a CER procedure. Rats were taught to press a lever to obtain food. Then, one group ("Group I") was given a tone CS+ followed by a shock (excitatory conditioning) and, on other occasions, a light CS− that was explicitly paired with no shock (inhibitory conditioning). A control group ("Group R") received the excitatory training (tone paired with shock), but the light CS− was presented randomly with respect to shock (thus, no inhibitory conditioning was expected to develop). In other words, both groups received the same amount of excitatory conditioning, but they differed in terms of the inhibitory conditioning. For Group I, the CS− was explicitly paired with no US, whereas for Group R, the light was not consistently paired with any particular event.

The power of the inhibitory association was observed using a summation test. The results are shown in Figure 3-6. Both groups showed strong suppression of lever pressing during the CS+ when it was given by itself (dur-

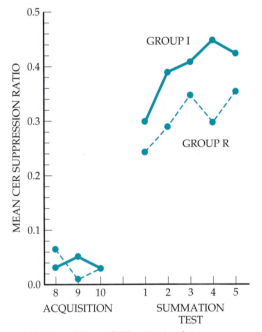

FIGURE 3-6. Mean CER ratio to the tone (CS+) and the tone–light compound (CS+/CS−) on the summation test for the group for whom the light was a conditioned inhibitor (Group I) and for the control group (Group R) (after Hammond, 1967).

ing acquisition, illustrated on the left side of the figure). Conditioned excitation, however, was reduced when the CS+ and CS− occurred together (during the summation test, shown on the right side of the figure). Moreover, Group I showed less suppression to the CS+/CS− combination than Group R because the conditioned inhibition canceled or counteracted the excitation. That is, the combination of CS+ and CS− in Group I produced less disruption (lower net excitation) than it did in Group R.

Retardation of Excitatory Learning Test.

A second way to demonstrate conditioned inhibition is the **retardation-of-learning technique.** Retardation-of-learning experiments involve two phases. First, a CS is used as a conditioned inhibitory stimulus. For example, a CS may be explicitly paired with "no US." Second, the CS is used in a normal excitatory conditioning experiment; that is, the CS is now paired with a US. If the CS had indeed become inhibitory in Phase 1, then it should be more difficult to convert it into an excitor in Phase 2 than to convert a novel stimulus, that had no inhibitory power, into an excitor. In other words, more excitatory training should be needed to convert a conditioned inhibitor into a conditioned excitor than to convert a neutral cue into an excitor.

An interesting demonstration of the retardation test by Tomie and Kruse (1980) used the autoshaping procedure. Pigeons in the experimental group were given two kinds of trials. On one, a green key light was followed by food; on the other, a compound CS (green key light with a white vertical line superimposed on it) was never followed by food. The white vertical line was expected to become a conditioned inhibitor because it was uniquely associated with "no food." A control group was given the same excitatory training (green key light followed by food), but the presentation of a different stimulus (red key light) was followed by "no food."

In Phase 2, all subjects received 60 presentations of the vertical white line on a dark background, followed by food. If the vertical white line had indeed become an inhibitory CS− in Phase 1 for experimental subjects, then it should acquire very little conditioned excitation. However, control subjects should respond to the vertical white line in the usual fashion because, for them, the line was a novel cue, devoid of any associative meaning. As shown in Figure 3-7, the control group, for whom the vertical white line was novel, showed appreciable responding to the stimulus. All eight subjects responded to the cue by the end of training. The experimental subjects, however, showed considerable retardation of learning. For more than 20 trials, none of the eight subjects responded to the CS at all; by the end of the 48 trials, only five of the eight showed any responding.

Procedures that Produce Conditioned Inhibition

Conditioned inhibition occurs when a CS predicts "no US" in the context of excitatory conditioning. There are, however, several different **procedures for creating conditioned inhibition.** These are diagrammed in Figure 3-8.

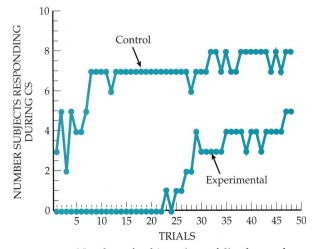

FIGURE 3-7. Number of subjects (out of 8) who made at least one key-peck response to the vertical white line on the retardation-of-learning test (after Tomie & Kruse, 1980).

Procedure name	Types of trials	Involves collateral excitation
Conditional	(a) $CS_E \rightarrow US$ (b) $CS_E CS_I \rightarrow$ no US	yes
Differential	(a) $CS_E \rightarrow US$ (b) $CS_I \rightarrow$ no US	no
Explicitly unpaired	(a) US (b) CS_I	no
Backward	(a) $US \rightarrow CS_I$	yes
Trace	(a) $CS_I \rightarrow$ (gap) $\rightarrow US$	yes

FIGURE 3-8. Chart illustrating five procedures used to generate conditioned inhibition.

Conditional Procedure.

The most common is the **conditional technique.** As shown in Figure 3-8, the conditional method involves two kinds of trials. First, a CS_E (excitatory CS) is paired with a US on excitatory trials. Second, CS_E is given simultaneously with CS_I (inhibitory CS). This compound (double) stimulus is followed by "no US." The CS_I acquires inhibitory properties because it is the unique event that, in the context of an otherwise excitatory trial, signals the absence of the US. In a sense, CS_I cancels the US presentation that is otherwise expected by the subject on the basis of CS_E. Conditioned inhibition in these experiments is tested with the summation and retardation techniques.

Differential Procedure.

The second technique for establishing conditioned inhibition is the **differential technique.** Here, two kinds of trials are also used (see Figure 3-8). Excitatory trials involve CS_E followed by the US. Inhibitory trials involve CS_I followed by the absence of the US. It is more difficult for an animal to learn a conditioned inhibition reaction using this technique (compared to the conditional method) because the predictive validity of the CS_I makes sense only to the extent that the CS_E predicts the positive occurrence of the US. In other words, with the differential conditioning technique, CS_I is associated with "no US," but only within the more general context of excitatory conditioning.

Explicitly Unpaired Procedure.

The third technique involves giving **explicitly unpaired presentations** of the CS_I and the US (see Figure 3-8). Subjects experience both kinds of events—CSs and USs—but they are deliberately scheduled not to occur close together. The CS_I comes neither just prior to nor just after the US but rather is explicitly programmed to occur in the interval between US presentations.

Backward Conditioning.

Backward conditioning involves the presentation of the CS after the US offset. From an informational point of view, the CS predicts the absence of the US, and therefore may be expected to develop conditioned inhibition properties (see also Chapter 4).

Trace Conditioning.

Finally, the fifth technique for generating conditioned inhibition involves a trace design. **Trace conditioning** occurs when the CS offset is given well in advance of the US onset; that is, a temporal gap separates the two stimuli. Conditioned inhibition develops during this gap (see the following discussion; see also Chapter 4 for more details).

Comparison of Procedures.

All of these procedures produce conditioned inhibition.[19] This does not mean, however, that each produces the same amount of conditioned inhibition, or that each necessarily involves the same underlying processes. For example, the conditional, backward, and trace procedures, unlike the differential and explicitly unpaired techniques, involve, paradoxically, the development of *both* inhibition and excitation processes. In each case, the CS_I predicts that there will be no US, but CS_I is also associated with the CS_E (which is excitatory). Eventually, then, CS_I triggers both an inhibitory and an excitatory CR. The excitation elicited by a conditioned inhibitor is referred to in Figure 3-8 as collateral excitation. Such excitation may, in fact, be so strong that it masks or hides the expression of the inhibition. This effect has been demonstrated in studies that extinguished the underlying excitatory associations, thereby revealing the full measure of the conditioned inhibition.[20]

Comparison of Conditioned Excitation and Inhibition

From a methodological point of view, conditioned excitation and conditioned inhibition appear to be mirror-image processes. For excitation, the CS predicts the US occurrence; for inhibition, the opposite is true. From the point of view of overt behavioral reactions as well, inhibition appears to be the mirror image of excitation. The conditioned inhibitory state is antagonistic to excitation, causing both a reduction in excitatory behavior (summation) and retardation of excitatory learning.

However, just as acquisition and extinction are not symmetrical and opposing processes, excitation and inhibition are not mirror-image processes. First, excitatory conditioning takes place more readily than inhibitory conditioning.[21] The likely reason is that the US event is much more salient than the "no-US" event and therefore supports stronger conditioning. Moreover, because animals have had a lifetime exposure to "no-US" circumstances, the salience of, and attention to, that event may be considerably reduced (see Chapter 5).

Second, the presentation of the CS by itself has a pronounced effect on conditioned excitation, but not on conditioned inhibition.[22] In other words, extinction of the CS+ causes the excitatory reaction to decline, but extinction of the CS− does not have the same effect on the inhibitory reaction. This was demonstrated in a study by DeVito and Fowler (1986). Rats were given conditional discrimination training using two kinds of trials. One kind involved tone–shock pairings. The other involved a tone–light compound followed by "no US" (here the light becomes a conditioned inhibitor because it uniquely predicts that there will be "no US"). In Phase 2, the light was given by itself to the experimental subjects; in other words, these animals underwent extinction of the conditioned inhibition. Control animals received the CS− and additional USs delivered in a random fashion. Finally, the strength of the conditioned inhibitor was measured in both groups, using a summation test. More specifically, subjects were made thirsty and were allowed to drink water from a tube during which time the tone CS+ and light CS− were given simultaneously. Suppression of drinking (the number of licks during the 20-second light, divided by the total licks during the cues and the 20-second period prior to the cues) was calculated.

As shown in Figure 3-9, three interesting results were found. First, both groups showed an appreciable suppression to the tone CS+ when it was presented by itself, indicating that conditioned excitation was more or less equally strong in both groups. Second, the control subjects showed suppres-

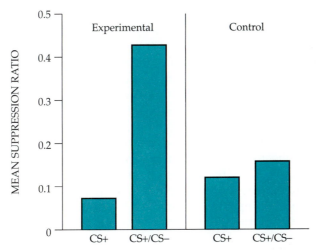

FIGURE 3-9. Mean suppression ratio for the experimental (extinction) and control (no extinction) groups during the excitatory stimulus (CS+) and the compound stimulus (CS+/CS−) (after DeVito and Fowler, 1986).

sion to the conditioned inhibition compound (CS+/CS−). The CS− for these animals was not inhibitory (because the CS− and US had been given randomly) and thus did not affect the suppressive effect of the CS+.[23] Third, the experimental group (the subjects who received CS− extinction) showed virtually no suppression to the CS+/CS− compound. The inhibition elicited by the CS− continued to subtract from, or counteract, the excitation elicited by the CS+, indicating that the presentation of the CS− by itself (that is, CS− extinction) had not weakened the conditioned inhibition. In short, presentation of a CS by itself causes extinction of conditioned excitation, but, as this study shows, presentation of a CS− by itself does not have the analogous effect; conditioned inhibition remains strong.[24]

Not only does the presentation of the CS− by itself fail to eliminate conditioned inhibition, but it may even increase it. For example, DeVito and Fowler (1987) conducted a study very similar to the one just described. The main difference was that the control animals received no treatment during the extinction phase. Again, the strength of the conditioned inhibitor was tested using a summation test, where suppression of licking was used as the measure of conditioning strength.[25] Both groups showed equal suppression to the conditioned CS+, but significant differences were obtained in terms of the suppression elicited by the compound stimulus. Less suppression was observed for the experimental subjects, who received CS− extinction, than for the control subjects. Thus, extinction of the conditioned inhibitor not only failed to eliminate the conditioned inhibition, but it actually increased it.

Why should the presentation of the CS− by itself actually increase conditioned inhibition? Recall that conditioned inhibition training often creates both inhibition *and* excitation. Presenting the stimulus by itself, therefore, sustains the conditioned inhibition (because the CS still precedes the absence of the US) but extinguishes the conditioned excitation. The combination of sustaining the inhibitory function of the CS− but reducing the underlying excitatory reaction causes the expression of the inhibition to increase.

If conditioned inhibition does not decline with extinction, then what procedures reduce it? Research suggests that presentation of the US is required. This was shown by Witcher and Ayres (1984). Here, a tone was always followed by shock, whereas a tone–light compound was never followed by shock. The power of the conditioned inhibitor (the light) was tested using the summation technique. As in the research discussed previously, presentation of the light CS− by itself did not affect conditioned inhibition strength. A random presentation of the CS− and shock, however, did. In other words, presenting the conditioned inhibitor and the US randomly appears to be the appropriate and sufficient procedure for eliminating conditioned inhibition.

INTERIM SUMMARY

In contrast to excitatory conditioning, inhibitory conditioning occurs when the CS is followed systematically by the absence of the US in the course of excitatory training. One technique for measuring conditioned inhibition is the directed-behavior test. Subjects position themselves in the environment close to CS+ and away from CS−. Thus, if a CS− is a conditioned inhibitor, then subjects avoid coming into contact with it. However, because the event "no US" does not always trigger a specific UR, the effects of inhibitory training are usually observed using indirect measures. One is the summation test, where a CS+ and a CS− are given simultaneously. If the CS− elicits conditioned inhibition, which counteracts excitation, then the level of the excitatory reaction, elicited by the CS+, is reduced. A second technique is the retardation-of-learning test. Here, a CS− is paired with a US. If the CS− is a conditioned inhibitor from a previous training phase, then excitatory conditioning takes place more slowly, compared to conditioning with a novel cue. Five procedures for creating conditioned inhibition are discussed. They include the conditional technique (CS_E–US; CS_E/CS_I–no US pairings), differential procedure (CS_E–US; CS_I–no US pairings), explicitly unpaired training, backward conditioning (US–CS_I pairings), and trace conditioning (where an appreciable gap between the CS offset and the US onset is given). Although conditioned excitation and inhibition are mirror-image processes from a procedural point of view, they are fundamentally different kinds of associations. For example, presentation of a CS+ by itself (extinction of the CS+) weakens the excitatory reaction, whereas presentation of a CS− by itself has little effect on the strength of the conditioned inhibitor and may indeed cause the CS_I to become stronger.

THEORIES OF CR PERFORMANCE

Rescorla's Contingency Theory

The previous sections introduced the concepts of excitation and inhibition but said very little about how excitatory and inhibitory stimuli combine to create a measurable CR. One of the simplest and most pervasive theories of CR performance claims that excitation and inhibition involve separate and opposing associations and that excitatory and inhibitory stimuli combine in an additive fashion. Let us examine this notion more closely.

Random CS–US Presentations.

According to an evolutionary perspective (see Chapter 1), Pavlovian conditioning is a mechanism by which subjects predict important future events, such as USs, and thereby behave more adaptively with respect to those events. The implication is that a CS should develop associative strength only when it conveys information about the US occurrence. If the two are not highly correlated, then the CS cannot effectively convey any information about the US occurrence, and the value of the CS, from the viewpoint of adaptive behavior, is reduced. This important idea is the information or **contingency theory of Pavlovian conditioning.**[26] Rescorla (1968) supported this theory directly by demonstrating that conditioning does not take place if the CS and US are given randomly (that is, if the correlation between them is effectively zero). However, if the CS predicts the US, then excitatory conditioning occurs.

Rescorla (1968) used a CER technique. During each 2-hour session, 2-minute tones were sounded every 10 minutes. During the tone, the probability that a subject would receive a shock was always .4. That is, a subject could expect to receive shock on about 40% of the CS presentations. The probability of receiving shock in the absence of the tone CS varied among groups. For one group, the probability of getting extra, unsignaled shocks was 0; all of the shocks were therefore signaled for these animals. For another group, the probability of receiving extra, unsignaled shocks was .4; there were as many unsignaled shocks as there were shocks during the CS. These subjects would therefore be unable to use the CS to predict the US because the US occurred unannounced as often as it occurred during the CS. According to the contingency theory, no conditioning should occur in this **truly random control** group because the CS provided no special information about the US presentation.

Rescorla also had two groups for which the probability of receiving extra, unsignaled shocks was intermediate—namely, .1 and .2. These groups, therefore, reflected an intermediate level of predictability. During the test, no USs were given, so the suppressive effects of the CS should have dissipated over successive extinction sessions as its aversiveness wore off.

The results are illustrated in Figure 3-10. The CER ratio for subjects in the .4 group (the subjects for whom the probability of receiving unsignaled shocks was the same as that for receiving signaled shocks) was near the .5 level; they

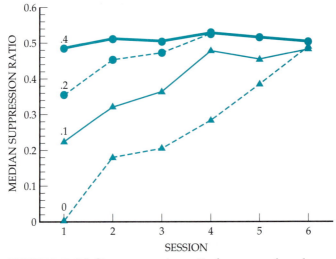

FIGURE 3-10. Median suppression ratio for groups for whom the probability of receiving extra unsignaled shocks was .4, .2, .1, or 0. The probability of receiving a shock US during the CS was .4 for all groups (after Rescorla, 1968).

showed virtually no conditioning to the tone CS. The strongest suppression of lever pressing was in the 0 group, for which shock was always signaled by the CS and never unsignaled. As expected, the strength of conditioning in the other two groups was intermediate.

It is important to note that all of the subjects in this experiment had the same number of CS–US pairings. The strength of conditioning, therefore, cannot be attributed simply to differences in the number of contiguous occurrences of the CS and US. Rather, CS strength depended on its predictive validity. When the CS predicted the US occurrence (and when "no CS" predicted "no US"), conditioning was strong. However, when shocks occurred in the absence, as well as in the presence, of the CS, then conditioning failed to occur, even though an appreciable number of CS–US pairings had actually been presented.

Contingency Space.

According to Rescorla's contingency theory, a CS is originally neutral (has neither excitatory nor inhibitory power), but it becomes either excitatory or inhibitory, depending on the probability that the CS and the US are paired. A good way to represent this theory is by means of a **contingency space** (shown in Figure 3-11). This figure represents the ways in which the CS and the US may be related in an experiment. The vertical axis plots the probability that the US is signaled by the CS. The horizontal axis shows the probability that the US is not signaled by a prior CS. The diagonal line represents a random presentation of the CS and the US. For any given experiment in which CSs and USs are administered, the exact relationship (or correlation) between them may be specified as a point in this contingency space. Experiments that fall

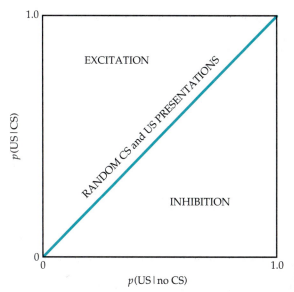

FIGURE 3-11. Diagram of the contingency space in
Pavlovian conditioning. Excitatory conditioning
occurs when the probability of having signaled USs
[p (US | CS)] is greater than the probability of
unsignaled USs [p (US | no CS)] (above the
diagonal line). Inhibitory conditioning occurs when
the probability of receiving unsignaled USs is
greater than the probability of signaled USs (below
the diagonal line).

above the diagonal line are those in which the US is more likely to be signaled than not to be. Here, the CS is excitatory. The farther above the diagonal line, the greater the predictive value of the CS and thus the more excitatory the CS will become.

Experiments in which the US is more likely to be unsignaled than signaled fall below the diagonal line. Here, the preponderance of trials are
inhibitory trials, and thus the CS becomes a conditioned inhibitor. Again, the
farther below the diagonal line, the greater the conditioned inhibition. The
most extreme cases are located at the upper left corner representing maximal
excitation (where all of the USs are signaled, and none is unsignaled) and the
lower right corner representing maximal inhibition (where none of the USs is
signaled by a CS; all of them are unsignaled).

Rescorla's contingency analysis is a simple theory about the production
of the CR. It claims that different kinds of associations develop (excitatory or
inhibitory), depending on the relationship (correlation) between the CS and
the US. Each association has its own corresponding reaction. In the case of
excitation, the reaction is the visible CR; for inhibition, it is the suppression
or inhibition of the CR. The CR that is actually performed is a combination of
the two tendencies.

Problems with the Random Control Procedure.

Rescorla's experiments suggest that a CS fails to acquire associative power when it occurs randomly with respect to the US; it remains essentially neutral. There are problems with such a conclusion, however. First, the animals appear to learn a considerable amount when given truly random CS and US presentations. For example, if CSs and USs are randomly presented and then the CS is later paired with a US, the prior random treatment causes retardation of excitatory learning, relative to what is shown in control subjects who receive no prior training.[27] Excitatory learning should not be retarded if the CS had remained essentially neutral during the random CS and US presentations.

Second, and even more damaging to the contingency theory, measurable excitatory conditioning takes place even when the CS and US are randomly presented.[28] Some researchers claim that excitation results when CS–US pairings occur accidentally early in the training session.[29] This idea is sensible because if training is extended for a long period of time, then accidental CS–US occurrences cease to have much impact.[30] Regardless, these studies demonstrate that some degree of excitatory conditioning takes place when the CSs and USs occur randomly.

Finally, the contingency theory of Pavlovian conditioning cannot explain why different kinds of random presentations have different effects on conditioning. Recall that Rescorla's original experiment involved presenting extra USs. Presenting extra CSs, however, does not have a comparable effect. Hallam, Grahame, and Miller (1992), for example, presented extra CSs to their subjects. All of them, even those for whom only 25% of the CSs were followed by a shock, showed appreciable conditioning. It was only when no shocks were given at all (in a sense, all of the CSs were extra) that conditioning failed to take place readily. In short, giving extra CSs that are not followed by the US does not reduce the amount of conditioning to the CS as much as giving extra USs that are not preceded by the CS.

The truly random control procedure remains an important concept because it highlights the role of CS information in conditioning (see Chapter 5 for more discussion of this point). However, when it comes to specifying the precise treatment or condition that is both necessary and sufficient for the development of an association, the contingency theory seems to be seriously flawed.

Miller's Comparator Hypothesis

Miller and his colleagues have proposed a different theory of CR performance.[31] According to the **comparator hypothesis,** all CSs have excitatory power; there are no separate conditioned inhibitory associations. The strength of performance, however, depends on the relative strength of the various excitatory associations. More specifically, a subject unconsciously compares the excitatory strength of the explicit CS to the excitatory strength of other cues in the situation, such as apparatus cues. When the excitatory strength of the CS is, comparatively speaking, greater than the excitatory strength of the background cues (the so-called comparator stimuli), then the observable CR is strong. If, however, the association between the context and the US is stronger than the association between the CS and the US, then the *relative* excitatory reaction to the CS is weak. A weakened level of excitation is assumed by Rescorla's theory to reflect the presence of inhibition; in Miller's theory, it merely reflects competition between two excitatory reactions.

Let us explain this position further. During normal excitatory training, the US follows the CS, but the US is also being paired with the surrounding background cues, called "comparator stimuli." Two associations therefore develop simultaneously—namely, the CS–US association and the comparator–US association. Because the background cues are also present during no-US periods, they are expected to have weaker excitatory strength than the CS that occurs *only* just prior to the US. Thus, under normal conditions, the CS has stronger excitatory strength than the comparator cues.

Consider, however, how the comparator hypothesis explains the outcome of a typical conditioned-inhibition experiment. The CS that explicitly signals the absence of the US develops exceptionally weak excitatory strength. In fact, the excitatory strength of the CS would be weaker than the excitatory strength of the comparator cues because the comparator cues are not explicitly associated with the no-US outcome. They are paired with both the US and "no-US" events. Relative to the strength of the comparator cues, the CS is weak, and performance thus declines.

US-Preexposure Effect.

The comparator explains a number of interesting and important phenomena. One is the **US-preexposure effect.**[32] This effect occurs under the following conditions. In Phase 1, subjects are given exposure to unsignaled USs; a control group gets no treatment during this time. In Phase 2, both groups get normal excitatory conditioning—that is, CS–US pairings. Typically, conditioning in the experimental group is severely retarded, relative to the control group. The experimental subjects are unable to learn as quickly as the control subjects who did not receive US-only preexposure during Phase 1.

The contingency theory of Rescorla has difficulty explaining this phenomenon. According to that theory, both groups should show about the same level of excitatory conditioning to the CS during Phase 2. After all, how could the preexposure of the US in Phase 1 affect conditioning to the CS in Phase 2?

The comparator hypothesis, on the other hand, explains the US-preexposure effect quite easily. According to this theory, the context (that is, the comparator cues) in Phase 1 gains excitatory strength because it is paired with the unsignaled US occurrences. In Phase 2, subjects compare the developing associative strength of the CS (due to the CS–US pairings) with the already strong associative strength of the context. Because the discrepancy between the two is small, the CS elicits a weaker reaction.

Comparator Stimuli and the Training/Test Context.

The comparator hypothesis makes a second prediction. The strength of the CS, relative to the strength of the comparator cues, should depend on the context in which the conditioned reactions are tested. Consider an experiment by Kasprow, Schachtman, and Miller (1987). Two groups of rats received noise–shock pairings in context "A" (context "A" was a box measuring about 23 cm long × 8 cm wide × 13 cm high, made from clear Plexiglas™, with thin stainless-steel rods running perpendicular to the length of the box). One group also received unsignaled presentations of shock in context "A," whereas the other group received unsignaled shocks in context "B" (context "B" was a box made of nonparallel stainless-steel walls, which formed a V-shape; the bottom of the apparatus consisted of two parallel metal plates separated by a small gap). Finally, all subjects were tested for the ability of the CS to suppress licking in context A (if subjects completed 25 licks of a water tube quickly, they were showing little fear of the noise; if they took a long time to complete the licking, then the CS was considered to have substantial power). Thus, the study examined whether excitatory conditioning to the CS is more evident when subjects are tested in an environment that differs from the one in which they received unsignaled shock (where the excitatory strength of the comparator cues is weak) than when they are tested in an environment that is the same as the one in which they received unsignaled shock (where the excitatory strength of the comparator cues remains strong). The results are shown in Figure 3-12. First consider the group that received unsignaled shocks in context "A." Completion of the drinking took little time, indicating that the CS was not very aversive. According to the comparator hypothesis, the comparator stimuli were

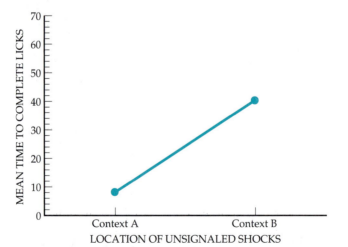

FIGURE 3-12. Mean time to complete 25 licks in context A after the onset of the CS, as a function of the location in which the free unsignaled shock USs were administered (after Kasprow, Schachtman, & Miller, 1987). Note that high scores indicate strong suppression of drinking, whereas low scores indicate that the CS was relatively weak.

strong (because the unsignaled shocks were also given in "A") and thus the relative strength of the CS was low, causing little suppression of drinking.

Now consider the data for the group that received unsignaled shocks in context "B." Because the unsignaled shocks had been given in box "B," the excitatory strength of the comparator stimuli in box "A" was weak. Stated differently, the excitatory strength of the CS was strong, relative to the excitatory strength of the comparator stimuli in context "A", thus causing significant suppression of drinking (completion of the 25 licks took a comparatively long time). In other words, as the subject acquires associative strength to a CS, it also acquires associative strength to apparatus stimuli. For the group that had free shocks in the same environment as the CS–US pairings, the comparator stimuli gained quite a bit of excitatory strength and thus, in comparison, the CS was less powerful (drinking was not suppressed). For the group of subjects that experienced unsignaled shocks in a different environment, however, the cues in context "A" were not strongly excitatory. This means that the excitatory strength of the CS was greater than the strength of the comparator cues, and thus drinking was suppressed substantially on the test.[33]

Extinction of Comparator Stimuli.

A third prediction by the comparator theory is that extinction of the comparator cues reduces their excitatory strength, thus increasing the relative strength of the CS. This was shown by Matzel, Brown, and Miller, (1987).[34] All rats were given six days of exposure to an unsignaled shock US in context "A." In Phase 2, subjects in a no-extinction ("no-ext") group remained in their home cages and were given no further treatment. Subjects in an extinction ("ext") group, however, were placed back in context "A" and given no shock (in other words, context "A" cues were extinguished). This procedure should have weakened the excitatory strength of the comparator cues. In Phase 3, both groups were given CS–US pairings in context "A," and in Phase 4, they were tested for the strength of the CS in context "B." Thus, the study examined whether extinction of the context (comparator-cue strength) prior to conditioning would enhance the strength of the CS. As in the aforementioned study, subjects were allowed to lick a water tube for 25 licks, after which the noise CS was presented. If they completed 25 additional licks quickly, then they were showing little fear of the noise. However, if subjects took a long time to complete 25 more licks, then suppression of the licking was evident; the noise CS was powerfully aversive.

Drinking was completed quickly (after an average of 14.5 seconds) in the no-ext group, indicating that the CS was not strongly excitatory. According to the comparator hypothesis, these subjects experienced the CS–US pairings in the same apparatus as the preexposed shock, and thus the discrepancy between the strength of the CS and the comparator stimuli was relatively small. The subjects in the ext group, who received US preexposure and then extinction of context "A" cues prior to the CS–US pairings, showed substantial suppression of drinking (it took them, on average, about 61.7 seconds to complete their 25 licks of water). The comparator theory claims that the original US-preexposure phase made the comparator stimuli relatively strong, but subsequent extinction of context "A" weakened them. During training, then, when the subjects unconsciously compared the excitatory strength of the CS with the excitatory strength of the comparator cues, the discrepancy was large, and thus the expression of excitatory reaction by the CS was strong. In short, the strength of the excitatory reaction depends on a comparison between the CS–US association and the comparator–US association. When the background cues are extinguished, then the comparator cues are relatively weak, and thus the disparity between the strength of the CS and the strength of the comparator cues is large. Here, the excitatory strength of the CS increases accordingly.

Problems with the Comparator Hypothesis.

The comparator hypothesis has contributed much to our understanding of the rules governing the production of the CR. It argues that the CR merely reflects a discrepancy between two excitatory associations, the CR elicited by the CS and that elicited by the comparator cues. There are problems with the hypothesis, however. First, it is not always clear what the comparator stimuli are. They may be global cues (for instance, the apparatus) or more local stimuli (cues that occur at about the time the CS–US pairings are given.[35] More important, an experiment analogous to the one just discussed, in which the comparator stimuli were strengthened rather than extinguished, did not show decreased excitation to the CS.[36] In other words, presenting an even stronger shock in the context (thus causing the comparator cues to be even more strongly excitatory) did not decrease the excitatory strength of the CS, even though the comparator hypothesis predicts that it should have.

INTERIM SUMMARY

Rescorla's contingency theory claims that excitation and inhibition are separate and opposing kinds of associations, and that the two summate. Excitatory conditioning occurs when the probability of receiving signaled USs is greater than the probability of receiving unsignaled USs. Inhibitory conditioning occurs when the probability of receiving unsignaled USs is greater than that of receiving signaled USs. When signaled and unsignaled USs are equally likely, conditioning fails to occur, indicating that Pavlovian learning is fundamentally based on the predictive value of a CS. Although the contingency theory continues to be an important perspective, several results fail to support it. For example, random presentations of CSs and USs, contrary to the tenets of the theory, often produce conditioning. Miller's comparator hypothesis argues that all CSs develop excitatory strength; there are no conditioned inhibitory associations. When the excitatory strength of the CS exceeds the excitatory strength of the apparatus cues that are also paired with the US (these are called "comparator cues"), then a strong CR is observed. When the comparator cues are strong, however, the excitatory reaction to the CS declines. The comparator hypothesis is particularly good at explaining the US-preexposure effect, where US-only presentations prior to CS–US pairings retard excitatory conditioning.

ENDNOTES

1. The event "opening a can" probably involves many smaller discrete events, such as opening the cabinet to retrieve the can, obtaining the can opener from the drawer, using it to open the can, taking the food bowl, and spooning the food into the bowl.
2. Ivan Petrovitch Pavlov was born on September 26, 1849, in Ryazan, a small rural village in central Russia, the son of a poor village priest (see Gantt's biographical notes in Pavlov, 1928). His father and mother valued education, so despite the rigors of peasant life in Russia at that time, Pavlov learned to read by the age of seven years, and he attended a church school at the age of eleven. A few years later, he and his brothers were enrolled in a theological seminary in Ryazan to be trained for the priesthood. In 1870, at the age of 21, Pavlov left the seminary and abandoned his goal of becoming a priest. He went to the University of Saint Petersburg and began his study of science, particularly chemistry and physiology. Pavlov was a diligent and capable student, and his training under a Professor Tsyon provided the foundation for his life work. In 1875, after an apprenticeship in physiology, Pavlov entered the Military Medical Academy, finishing his degree there in 1879. Becoming a physician qualified him to do a doctoral dissertation in physiology, which he completed in 1883. Several years were spent doing research in Germany, after which Pavlov returned in 1890, to become a Professor of Pharmacology at the Military Medical Academy. The following year, in 1891, he designed and supervised the construction of the first physiological laboratory at the newly founded Institute for Experimental Medicine, the place where he did his most important research. There, he continued his work on the digestive systems. The importance of the work was formally recognized in 1904, with the awarding of the Nobel prize. Pavlov died in 1936.
3. The term appetitive is the adjective form of the word appetite, which denotes a desire to satisfy bodily needs.
4. Brown and Jenkins (1968) discovered autoshaping; see Locurto, Terrace, and Gibbon (1981) for a review.
5. See Hearst and Jenkins (1974).
6. See Gormezano, Kehoe, and Marshall (1983); Smith, DiLollo, and Gormezano (1966).
7. See Patterson and Romano (1987).
8. Many have speculated why responding is suppressed. One factor may be incompatible emotional or motivational states that are aroused by the CS (see Rescorla & Solomon, 1967). Another may be that the CS elicits behavior that is directed at the location of the stimulus itself and thus incompatible with lever pressing. In other words, the subject may cease to press the lever because it is approaching and making contact with the CS, not because lever pressing itself is weakened or suppressed (see Karpicke, Christoph, Peterson, & Hearst, 1977).
9. See Barker, Best, and Domjan (1977).
10. Although the rate of increase in CR strength is important because it reflects the speed of learning, the terminal level of performance, called the "asymptotic rate," is also of interest because it reflects performance factors. Furthermore, conditioning often takes place so quickly, within a single CS–US pairing, that asymptotic performance is a better measure of the variables being studied.
11. See also Burdick and James (1970).
12. See Bouton (1991); Bouton and Bolles (1979); Bouton and Swartzentruber (1991).
13. The groups were actually counterbalanced so that half were trained in "A," the other half in "B."

14. See Fowler, Lysle, and DeVitto (1991); Miller and Spear (1985); Rescorla (1969).
15. The position of the lighted key (whether it occurred on the right or the left side of the box) varied randomly.
16. See also Gaffan and Hart (1981); Jenkins (1985); Wasserman, Franklin, and Hearst (1974).
17. For some behavioral systems, an antagonistic response is, in fact, observable. For instance, the antagonistic reaction to an acceleration in heart rate might be deceleration in heart rate. Similarly, the opposite of paw withdrawal might be paw (or muscle) extension.
18. The utility of the tests was proposed by Rescorla (1969) and has been reassessed by Williams, Overmier, and LoLordo (1992) and by Papini and Bitterman (1993). See Donahoe and Palmer (1988) for an opposing view on the use of indirect tests of conditioned inhibition.
19. Williams and Overmier (1988); see also Matzel, Gladstein, and Miller (1988); see Chapter 5 of this book.
20. Williams and Overmier (1988); see also Miller, Hallam, Hong, and Dufore (1991).
21. LoLordo and Fairless (1985).
22. See DeVito and Fowler (1986, 1987); Witcher and Ayres (1984); Zimmer-Hart and Rescorla (1974).
23. See Witcher and Ayres (1984).
24. This result does not occur when the compound CS+/CS− stimuli are given sequentially, as opposed to simultaneously; see Detke (1991); Holland and Gory (1986); Robbins (1990).
25. This test lasted 2 days and was followed by a retardation-of-learning test. Only the results of the summation test are reported here.
26. Rescorla (1967).
27. Baker and Mackintosh (1979); Matzel, Schachtman, and Miller (1988). Although such subjects eventually learn an excitatory CR after truly random training, they do not reach the same high level of performance as subjects who do not receive the random training; see Brandon and Paul (1987); Tomie, Murphy, Fath, and Jackson (1980).
28. See Papini and Bitterman (1990) for a review; see also Gibbon, Locurto, and Terrace (1975); Jenkins, Barnes, and Barrera (1981).
29. Benedict and Ayres (1972); see also Kremer (1971, 1974); Kremer and Kamin (1971). Another possibility is that the context, which is excitatory, becomes associated with the CS; see Marlin (1983) and Chapter 5 of this book for more discussion.
30. Keller, Ayres, and Mahoney (1977); Rescorla (1972).
31. See Miller and Matzel (1989); Miller and Schachtman (1985a, 1985b) for reviews.
32. See Randich and LoLordo (1979a, 1979b).
33. An interesting aspect of these results was the fact that it made no difference whether the subjects were tested in context "A" or context "B." What mattered was the strength of the comparator stimuli, relative to the strength of the CS, during training, not during testing.
34. See also Schachtman, Brown, Gordon, Catterson, and Miller (1987).
35. See Barnet, Grahame, and Miller (1993a, 1993b); Reilly and Schachtman (1987); Schachtman and Reilly (1987).
36. Miller and Schachtman (1985a, 1985b).

CHAPTER 4

Variables That Affect Classical Conditioning

In Chapter 3, we described the structure of a Pavlovian experiment and many of the basic terms and procedures used for studying classical conditioning. This chapter considers the effects of important variables on strength of conditioning. By exploring the effects of these treatments or variables, along with the Pavlovian phenomena covered in Chapter 5, you will gain a better understanding of the theories of Pavlovian conditioning, which are discussed in Chapter 6.

UNCONDITIONED STIMULUS VARIABLES

Not surprisingly, there are many characteristics of the US that affect the formation and expression of an association. These characteristics include US intensity, duration, and quality.

US Intensity

One of the most reliable and important is the intensity of the US. Conditioning is stronger with more intense USs. This principle holds for a wide variety of responses and species. For example, US intensity affects the amplitude of various skeletal reactions, including eyelid CRs, jaw movements in rabbits, and limb-flex reactions in cats.[1] In an experiment on the flex response in cats by Polenchar, Romano, Steinmetz, and Patterson, (1984), different groups of subjects were given 1-, 2-, 3-, or 4-milliamp shocks to their right hind limb, each shock lasting 25, 50, or 100 milliseconds.[2] The authors measured the percentage of trials on which the subjects gave a limb-flex response, the speed of the response, and the amplitude (measured in millimeters of limb movement).

As shown in Figure 4-1, those that received the weakest shock showed little change in CR amplitude over training. However, the rate of increase in amplitude for the other intensity groups was significantly higher. Thus, both

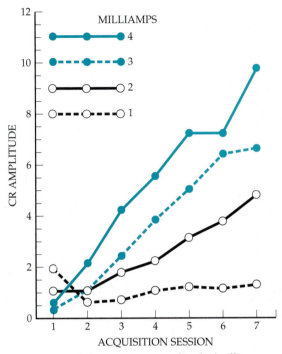

FIGURE 4-1. Mean response amplitude (millimeters of limb movement) for the different US intensity groups (after Polenchar, Romano, Steinmetz, & Patterson, 1984).

the rate at which the CR gains in amplitude and the terminal levels of CR performance are strongly affected by US intensity.[3] Similar relationships between CR strength and US intensity are observed for physiological reactions such as salivation, heart rate, and glycemic changes as a result of insulin injection.[4]

Procedures that measure conditioned strength indirectly also show an orderly relationship between the CR strength and the US intensity. For example, the degree of disruption of lever pressing in a CER experiment is positively related to shock intensity. More intense USs produce stronger reactions and thus greater disruption of lever pressing.[5] Similarly, the extent to which an animal avoids consuming a flavor that had been paired with poison is positively related to the dosage.[6]

Not only do strong USs produce stronger CRs than weak USs, but also two USs given simultaneously may summate to produce a larger CR than either one by itself. In a study by Frey, Maisiak, and Duque (1976), for example, eyelid conditioning in rabbits was studied using a tone CS and a mild shock to the cheek as a US. In addition to the shock, the authors gave a mildly aversive intracranial brain stimulation. (Direct stimulation of various parts of the brain may be aversive or pleasurable, depending on, among other things, the location of the stimulation; see Chapter 11 for more details). The result was stronger conditioning to the tone when both USs were used. The intensified CR was attributed to the greater affective (emotional) impact of the two USs combined. What is interesting is that one US was applied peripherally (the cheek shock), whereas the other was applied directly to the neurons of the brain. Arousal or aversion created internally, therefore, combined with the arousal or aversion created by the external US.

Finally, US intensity has other effects on the CR besides changing its amplitude. Specifically, USs of different intensities may also affect *which* CR is performed. Holland (1979) studied this effect using either a light or tone CS and four levels of US magnitude—namely, 1, 5, 10, or 20 pellets of food. Holland found that early in the CS–US interval—that is, just after the CS onset—subjects performed behaviors that resembled the orienting reaction originally triggered by the CS. These included rearing and exploring when the CS was a light, or startle reactions and jerky head movements when the tone CS was used. The responses that occurred late in the CS–US interval, however—that is, just prior to the US delivery—tended to be food-oriented behaviors. These included approaching the food cup, grooming, and startle reactions when the click of the feeder mechanisms was sounded. Such reactions were similar to the URs that normally occur to food. In terms of US intensity, the study found that strength of the initial CRs (those occurring early in the CS–US interval) declined with larger US quantities, whereas strength of the terminal CRs (those occurring just prior to the US delivery) increased as a function of the quantity of food. It was not simply that a CR became more intense with increases in the US intensity. The distribution of responses actually shifted, indicating that US intensity has a selective action in determining which CRs are performed, not just an amplifying role in determining their size.

US Duration

A second factor concerning the US is its duration. Although there is conflicting evidence, US duration operates much like US intensity: the longer the duration, the larger the CR. Riess and Farrar (1973) paired a light CS with a shock US and measured disruption of lever pressing during the CS. The shock lasted 0.05, 0.2, 0.5, 1, 2, or 3 seconds. The results are shown in Figure 4-2. The 0.05-second shock produced virtually no suppression; when animals received the 1- and 3-second shocks, however, considerable suppression was shown. Comparable results have been found for conditioning of various skeletal reactions. For instance, the hind-limb-flex response in the cat shows stronger conditioning with longer-duration shock US (25, 50, or 100 milliseconds), although little difference was observed between the two longer-duration groups.[7]

One of the problems in determining how US duration affects learning is the fact that as one varies duration, total exposure to the US also changes. When differences in the total exposure become sufficiently large, then the effects of duration itself are obscured. Tait, Kehoe, and Gormezano (1983), for

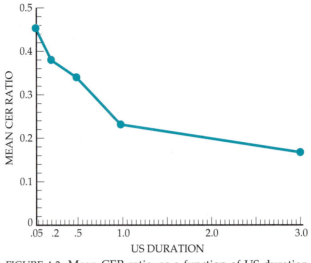

FIGURE 4-2. Mean CER ratio, as a function of US duration (after Riess & Farrar, 1973).

example, studied eyelid responses in rabbits and found an inverse relationship between US duration and CR probability—that is, the longer the US duration (50, 1,500, or 6,000 milliseconds)—the *worse* the animal performed. The total amount of aversion experienced by the 6,000-millisecond group was certainly much greater than that experienced by the 50-millisecond group. To correct for this difference, the authors equated groups for total exposure to shock by giving unsignaled USs during the intertrial interval. Here, the authors found that the probability of making a CR was *positively* correlated to US duration. The study, therefore, demonstrates that US duration affects CR performance in a rather complicated fashion.

US Quality

One of the most important variables that affects conditioning is the quality of the US. This is not surprising, given that the form of the UR is determined largely by which US is used. Consider an obvious case—namely, when USs are shocks versus food. One would not expect to observe an animal salivating to a CS when the US is a shock, and conversely, one would not expect to see a subject perform fear and aversive reactions to a CS when the US is food.

The issue is more complicated, however. For example, in a study by Holland (1979), a tone or a light CS was paired with several kinds of USs. Some animals received a food pellet delivered to a cup that was recessed in the wall of the cage (the subjects had to stick their head through an opening to gain access to the food). Other subjects were given a food pellet in a cup that protruded into the cage. A third group was presented with a sucrose solution in this same cup. The results showed that the type of CR that developed depended to a large degree on which US was used. Conditioned responses that resembled startle reactions (short jerky head movements) were given when the food was delivered into the recessed cup. Reactions that resembled grooming behaviors (the animals would groom their fur or rear on their hind legs) were given when the US was the sucrose solution.

The relationship between the CR and the US quality has also been investigated using an autoshaping procedure. In a study by Jenkins and Moore (1973), a lighted key was followed by either food or water. All of the pigeons learned to peck the key, but the precise form of the peck varied according to the type of US used. Subjects that received the water US made slower reactions, and their pecking was more sustained. Furthermore, as shown in Figure 4-3, their pecks were accompanied by drinkinglike movements of swallowing and licking (left portion). Conversely, animals that were hungry and received the food US made sharp and vigorous pecks at the disk, with their beaks open (right portion of Figure 4-3). If one were to look superficially at the two groups of animals, one might conclude that the CR was equivalent. However, closer examination reveals dramatic differences in the form of the CR.

These autoshaped reactions are part of the innate feeding and drinking mechanism (see also Chapter 12). More specifically, complex appetitive–consummatory behaviors are innately present in the neural circuitry of the brain, but their overt expression depends on the pairing of a CS with a biologically significant US, the role of which is to trigger part of the innate motor system. Thus, pigeons' pecking for food is accomplished by sharp directed pecks, with the beak open, so that the food item can be secured. Drinking, in contrast, more resembles a kind of nuzzling behavior that is typical of the way pigeons drink water.

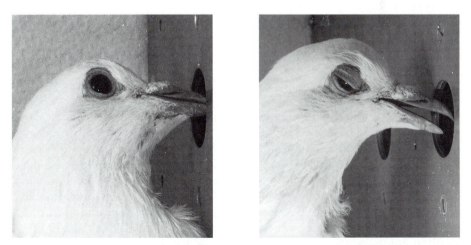

FIGURE 4-3. Photograph showing pigeons pecking keys when receiving water reward (left) or food (right). Pecks to the water-related key included drinking-like movements such as licking. Pecks to the food-related key were made with the beak slightly open, as if to seize a piece of grain.
Photo Courtesy of Bruce Moore

An interesting study that supported this idea was done by Woodruff and Starr (1978). The authors raised newborn chicks by force-feeding them food and water for a few days after birth. Thus, the chicks were not given the opportunity to approach and contact water and food sources on their own. After several days, subjects were given autoshaping sessions. Some received food as the US; others received water. In all cases, the young chicks approached and contacted the CS, and the form of the reaction was appropriate to the kind of US used. For example, chicks who were autoshaped with food performed the feeding response that is characteristic for their species (rapid ballistic pecking motions toward the key, with their beaks open). Subjects who received the water US performed typical drinking reactions (a full extension of the head and neck toward the key, followed by scooping or rapid nibbling motions of the beak during the contact period). All of these reactions were acquired despite the fact that the chicks had never previously contacted food or water on their own and thus could not have learned to perform those reactions prior to the start of the experiment. The study therefore strongly suggests that autoshaped behavior patterns are innate motor sequences triggered by the CS.

The finding that subjects perform CRs that closely resemble the UR is not confined to birds. Jenkins, Barrera, Ireland, and Woodside (1978) found a similar effect in dogs. The dogs were required to position themselves at the start of each trial at a point that was equidistant from two light stimuli (otherwise, the trial would not start). A trial was then initiated. It consisted of either a CS+, followed by the delivery of meat morsels, or a CS−, not followed by food. The dogs' behavior was videotaped and later analyzed.

The results for two subjects are shown in Figure 4-4. Most of the subjects developed consistent and stereotyped reactions toward the CS+. For example, early in the CS period (right frames), a dog walked toward the light when it was on and oriented toward the light. Later in the CS interval (left frames), when the light subsequently went off, the dog approached, sniffed, and even touched the light fixture.

INTERIM SUMMARY

Intensity of the US affects conditioning—the stronger the US, the stronger the CR. This relationship has been shown using a variety of Pavlovian procedures. Intensity even affects the kind of CR that is performed. For example, CRs that resemble orienting reactions are usually performed early in the CS–US interval; these decline in frequency with stronger USs. CRs such as contacting the CS usually occur just prior to the US delivery; these increase with stronger USs. The duration of the US affects conditioning, although duration and total US exposure are often confounded. Finally, the quality of the US is important to the nature of the CR. Water, for example, causes pigeons to perform drinkinglike CRs, whereas food causes them to execute sharp pecks similar to those used in securing small bits of food.

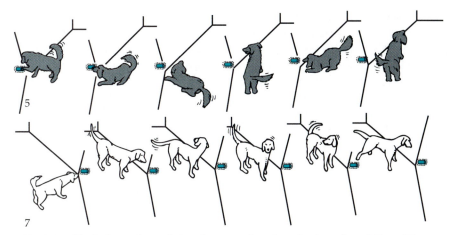

FIGURE 4-4. Typical patterns of signal-centered actions in dogs 5 and 7 on CS+ trials. Frames from right to left represent early to late portions of the 10-second CS+ (after Jenkins, Barrera, Ireland, & Woodside, 1978).

CONDITIONED STIMULUS VARIABLES

Several characteristics of the CS affect the strength and nature of the conditioning processes. These characteristics include CS intensity and CS quality.

CS Intensity

One variable is CS intensity.[8] The general finding is that conditioning increases as a function of CS intensity. The stronger the CS, the stronger the conditioning. The notion that conditioning strength is related to CS intensity makes good sense from an ecological point of view. All animals live in stimulus environments and are constantly being bombarded by CSs of various kinds (visual and taste stimuli, noises, and odors). The more intense a stimulus is, relative to the background—that is, relative to what the subject is accustomed to—the more that cue demands attention and thus is learned. In other words, intense CSs are more easily discriminated from background stimulation than are weak CSs, and thus, they have a greater chance of becoming associated with a US.

The facilitating effect of CS intensity on classical conditioning has been observed in a wide variety of situations. For example, in a CER experiment by Imada, Yamazaki, and Morishita (1981), rats were given a 6-second light CS, followed by a mild shock US.[9] Different groups received CSs of differing intensities. This was accomplished by illuminating a 100-watt electric bulb with different voltages. The group names (0, 30, 45, 65, and 100) refer to the voltage delivered to the light. These corresponded to illumination values of 1.5 (ambient illumination in the testing chamber), 2.6, 8.7, 33, and 133 lux, respectively.

The results, shown in Figure 4-5, reveal a clear effect of CS intensity. The group that received no CS (zero intensity) showed no suppression (after all, those animals could not possibly anticipate the US presentation if no warning signal was given). The other groups, however, showed substantial conditioning over the course of training, and the stronger the CS, the greater the suppression.

Similar effects are observed for taste aversion, although, here, CS intensity has two distinct meanings. On the one hand, more intense CSs may refer to the volume or quantity of flavor consumed; alternatively, CS intensity may refer to the strength of the flavor concentration. Barker (1976) varied both the concentration of saccharin flavor and the duration of access, and found that both factors affect conditioning. Different groups of rats were given a saccharin solution that differed both in concentration and volume. The concentrations were 0.024, 0.12, 0.24 and 1.2% (weight of saccharin per volume of water); and the durations of access were 0 seconds (a control group not given the flavored solution), 5 seconds, 1 minute, or 10 minutes.

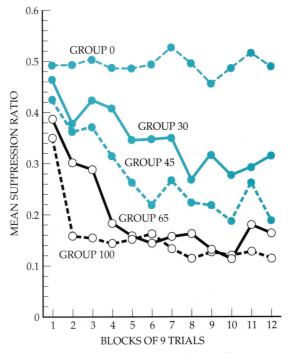

FIGURE 4-5. Mean suppression ratios for five groups of subjects over blocks of nine trials. The numbers refer to CS intensity (voltage) (after Imada, Yamazaki, & Morishita, 1981).

Thirty minutes following the CS presentation, subjects were irradiated with X rays. Such a procedure, although not harmful, produces mild nausea and, as a result, taste aversion to the flavor. The test results are shown in Figure 4-6. The concentration of the saccharin had a strong effect. Average intake was much higher for the weak concentrations than for the strong concentrations. Thus, the reluctance to drink is directly related to intensity of the flavor. Similarly, stronger aversions were observed for animals who were allowed to drink the flavored solution for longer periods of time relative to the subjects given only a brief exposure. This conclusion is best supported when comparing the 1- or 10-minute group to the 0- and 5-second subjects (see Figure 4-6).

CS intensity affects learning in a complicated way because the effects depend on other conditions of the experiment, such as the CS–US interval or the presence of other CSs.[10] For example, a salient or intense CS may overshadow a weaker CS, causing it to gain less strength when paired with a US than it would if given by itself. In a study by Kehoe (1982), rabbits

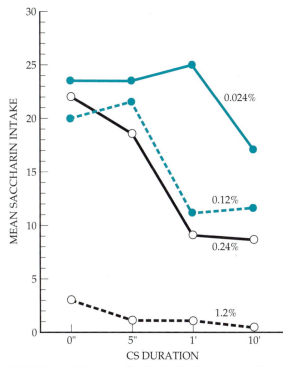

FIGURE 4-6. Mean saccharin intake (grams) on the seventh test day for 16 groups of subjects who had been given a combination of saccharin concentration and drinking duration (after Barker, 1976).

were simultaneously given a light–tone compound CS followed by a shock US. Control subjects received either the light by itself, or the tone by itself, paired with the shock. For the compound-CS subjects, the tone intensity was varied; different groups got 85, 89, or 90 dB. Thus, the intense tones should have overshadowed the light more easily than the weaker tones.

The results confirmed this prediction (see Figure 4-7). The control subjects who did not get the tone showed substantial responding to the light. They were giving CRs on about 95% of the trials, by the third block of trials. The group that got the tone–light compound CS for which the tone was relatively weak (85 dB) showed comparable conditioning to the light. The other two groups, however, showed a reduced level of responding to the light after having previously experienced a more intense tone along with the light. More specifically, when the noise was 89 dB, conditioning to the light varied from about 20 to 70%; when the tone had been 93 dB, the CR to the light remained at an even lower level, between 30 and 40%. Thus, stimuli that occur simultaneously with a CS may overshadow conditioning to that CS.[11] Conditioning depends not simply on the absolute salience or intensity of the CS, but rather on the degree to which it stands out from other stimuli.

CS Quality

It is easy to understand why US quality affects the CR. It is less obvious why the CS quality should affect the CR. A CS, after all, is, by definition, a rela-

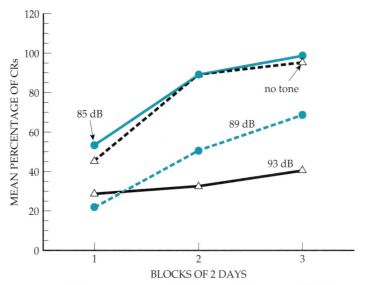

FIGURE 4-7. Mean percentage of trials on which an eyelid CR was given to the light CS, over 2-day blocks of training trials, for four groups that received tones (simultaneously with the light) of an intensity shown on the figure (after Kehoe, 1982).

tively innocuous signal. Furthermore, if its important function is to signal that a US is about to be presented, then *any* sensory event should serve equally well in this regard. Research, however, shows that the quality of the CS has an important bearing on the kind of CR that is performed.

Consider the effects of CS quality on Pavlovian appetitive conditioning in rats. Different CSs actually elicit different kinds of CRs. Holland (1977) showed this using tone and light CSs, followed by food. The form of the CR differed between groups. The tone, for example, tended to elicit head jerks, whereas the light elicited more rearing reactions and investigations of the food tray.

A similar experiment by Holland (1980b) varied the size and location of the CS, using an apparatus in which one entire wall was constructed with translucent plastic. For the diffuse group, the CS was the illumination of the entire wall of the box. Other subjects received the illumination of one quarter of the wall as the CS. A third group experienced only a single small dot of light on the wall as the CS. In all cases, the 10-second CS was followed by a food US. Holland found that the localized CS (the small spot on the wall) evoked inspections of that location. The diffuse CS, on the other hand, evoked behaviors that were directed toward the food tray.

The effect of CS quality and its location was also studied by Bowe, Green, and Miller (1987). These authors demonstrated that animals may process or attend to some kinds of CSs more than to others. Some of the pigeons were given a red light followed by food, and a green light followed by no food. The position of the lights varied randomly; at times the left key light was illuminated, whereas at other times, the right key light was lit. The predictive dimension, therefore, was the color of the stimulus, not its location. Other subjects were given red and green lights, but the position signaled whether food would be delivered. That is, when the left key was illuminated, food followed; when the right key was turned on, no food was given.[12] Here, the position was the relevant factor, not color. Because this was an autoshaping procedure, subjects were expected to peck the key that preceded food. The results are shown in Figure 4-8. Performance was more accurate when CSs differed in color than in location. This finding therefore suggests that pigeons process, or attend to, colors more readily than to the spatial location of the CS.

Color, or light CSs, may have very different effects in other situations, however. For example, in a study of aversive learning in rats by Welker and Wheatley (1977), the CS for one group was an increment in the illumination of the house light. The other group received a decrease in illumination (the overall light intensity in the apparatus was dimmed). Dramatic differences in behavior were observed. As shown in Figure 4-9, suppression of lever pressing during the CS was greater when the CS was an increment in illumination than when it was a decrement in light intensity.[13]

The authors explained their results in terms of the way rats have adapted to their ecological niche over the course of evolution. Rats are nocturnal, so they feed, and are active, during the dark portion of the day–night cycle. Brightness is the less preferred state for these animals; it is associated with daytime activities, during which time the rats are vulnerable to being preyed upon.[14] Thus, brightness is more readily associated with danger than is darkness. Darkness, on the other hand, is associated with the safety of the burrows and is therefore less readily associated with danger.

Such an ecological theory was evaluated by Jacobs and LoLordo (1977), who used a compound CS (noise plus panel light).[15] They found that the tone became powerful when it signaled the onset of shock, but not when it signaled its offset. The opposite was true for the light CS. The light was strong when it signaled no shock but remained weak when it was paired with the onset of shock. The implication is that an auditory signal is more easily associated with danger than is the onset of a light CS.

This result was amplified in a study by Shapiro, Jacobs, and LoLordo (1980). Here, a light-and-tone CS compound was followed by food. Later, the tone elicited conditioned head raising and "prancing," defined as "rapid side-to-side movements, during which the pigeon lifts its feet higher than in normal walking" (p. 588). The light, in contrast, elicited pecking behaviors

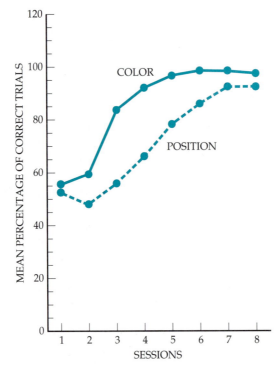

FIGURE 4-8. Mean percentage of correct responses (where at least one peck on the correct key was given and no pecks on the incorrect key were made), as a function of sessions for the groups for which the CSs differed in color or position (after Bowe, Green, & Miller, 1987).

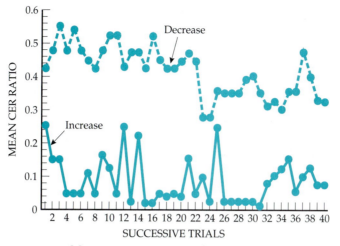

FIGURE 4-9. Mean suppression ratio during 40 trials for the groups receiving an increase or decrease in illumination as the CS (after Walker & Wheatley, 1977).

directed at the key. In other words, both tone and light became associated with food, but the light was associated more rapidly with food than was the tone.[16]

How can we explain the fact that certain CSs seem to be conditioned more easily with specific USs than other CSs? As noted previously, many argue that the ease of conditioning depends on the ecological relevance of the CS (see also Chapters 7 and 12).[17] A CS becomes a releaser of certain classes or systems of behaviors. Which class or system of behavior is affected depends on the US quality and the motivational state of the animal. For example, when the US is food, various food-seeking behaviors are triggered by a CS; when the US is shock or a predator, a different class or system of behaviors is triggered—namely, defensive responses. The precise nature of the CRs that are elicited, therefore, depends on the ecological relationship of the CSs qualities to the behavioral systems themselves. According to this ecological-relevance theory, autoshaping occurs more readily in pigeons because their feeding system normally entails pecking at small distinctive visual objects when hungry; it is a natural part of a pigeon's foraging system. In contrast, rats react to visual CSs by approaching and sniffing them. Here again, a similar kind of process is at work, but the CR differs because the nature of the feeding responses differs (see Chapter 12).

One implication of such a theory is that the nature of the CR depends on the interaction of the CS and US quality. Let us review an important study demonstrating this point. Davey, Phillips, and Witty (1989) used two kinds of CSs. One was a plain retractable metal lever, and the other was a lever covered by an acrylic fabric that resembled synthetic fur. In a cold environment, when the furry lever was inserted into the cage just prior to the delivery of a heat US, the rats approached the lever and showed contact behavior (this resembled the way rats huddle to keep warm). This did not happen with the bare-metal lever. The authors then deprived other groups of rats of food. Again, both kinds of levers were inserted, but this time, the lever insertions were followed by food. Here, subjects tended to press the bare-metal lever, but not the furry lever. In other words, the kind of CR that was performed (thermoregulatory or feeding reactions) depended not simply on the CS quality (metal versus furry lever), or even on the US quality (heat versus food), but rather on the combination of the two. When the CS and the US were ecologically related, then conditioning was strong (the furry lever was more ecologically related to the thermoregulatory system of reactions, whereas the metal lever was more ecologically relevant to the system of feeding behaviors).

INTERIM SUMMARY

CS intensity affects conditioning—the stronger the CS, the stronger the conditioning. This relationship is found in aversive conditioning (for example, in CER studies), as well as in taste-aversion conditioning. However, intense CSs may overshadow other cues, causing the latter to gain less strength than they would if given by themselves. The qualitative nature of the CS also affects conditioning. Tones, for example, elicit conditioned head jerks in rats, whereas light CSs tend to elicit rearing reactions with food USs. Much of the relationship between CS quality and the CR is explained in terms of an ecological theory of learning. For instance, rats associate an increment in illumination with shock more easily than they do a decrement because, in nature, feeding occurs at night. Similarly, lights may be conditioned more strongly than tones when paired with food, whereas the reverse is true for shock USs. The characteristics of the CR, however, depend on the interaction of both the CS and US quality.

TEMPORAL FACTORS IN CONDITIONING

As discussed in Chapters 1 and 3, the British Empiricists speculated that a fundamental unit of knowledge was the association between two sensory events, the presentation of one giving rise to the memory of the other. These philosophers, notably Hartley, attempted to specify the laws by which associations developed. One of the most important was the law of contiguity. According to this principle, stimuli become associated only to the extent that they occur close together in time. Such a law makes good common sense. How could two stimuli become associated if they did not occur close together? Imagine if Pavlov had sounded his metronome and then waited several hours before giving food powder. It is unreasonable to assume that the dogs would have associated the two stimuli, given such a long gap.

Although temporal contiguity is recognized as being central to Pavlovian conditioning, there are various ways to structure an experiment while keeping the two stimuli temporally close. The following section reviews some of these techniques.

Forward (CS–US) Arrangements

Pavlov recognized not only that the CS and US had to be close together in time, but he also confirmed another one of the British Empiricists' laws—namely, that the CS must precede the US. Specifically, Pavlov (1927) noted, "Further, it is not enough that there should be overlapping between the two stimuli; it is also equally necessary that the conditioned stimulus should begin to operate before the unconditioned stimulus comes into action" (p. 27). Again, this law makes good sense from an ecological viewpoint. If the inherent function of Pavlovian conditioning is to enable the animal to predict important future events, such as a US, then the signal surely must precede the event; otherwise, it could not possibly provide any advanced warning of the impending US, and thus, it would not endow the animal with any advantage.

Delayed Conditioning.

There are actually two **forward-conditioning techniques** that involve presenting the CS prior to the US. First, and most common, is **delayed conditioning** (see Figure 4-10). Here, the CS is continued at least until the US is presented. Sometimes there is overlap between the two stimuli, but regardless, the CS remains on until the US occurs.

Trace Conditioning.

Trace conditioning is similar to delayed conditioning, except for one important difference (see Figure 4-10). In the trace procedure, the CS offset occurs before the US onset. There is a temporal gap prior to the US presentation, during which the CS is not being given. This technique is called the "trace procedure" because, for the CS to be contiguous with the US, one must assume that it is the memory of the CS (its so-called trace) that is persisting throughout the gap, not the sensory stimulation itself.

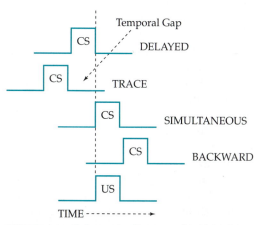

FIGURE 4-10. Schematic diagram showing the temporal relationship of the CS to the US during delayed, trace, simultaneous, and backward conditioning.

Comparison of Delayed and Trace Procedures.

Some investigators have found that the delayed and trace procedures produce identical levels of conditioning.[18] The more usual finding is that delayed conditioning is superior to trace.[19] This issue is somewhat complicated, however, because the advantage of the delayed over the trace procedure depends in part on other characteristics of the experiment, such as the intensity of the US and the overall delay between the onset of the CS and the onset of the US. For example, in a study by Fitzgerald and Teyler (1970), trace conditioning proved to be inferior only when the intensity of the US was high. Here, rats received a 1,000-Hz tone CS followed by a shock. The CS duration for the trace subjects was 1 second, followed by a 6-second gap; the delayed subjects simply had a 7-second CS that overlapped with the US presentation. Conditioned changes in heart rate were measured. When the shock US was weak, the trace and delayed procedures worked equally well. At higher intensities, however, the delayed procedure was significantly superior.

Another factor that influences whether the delayed procedure is superior to the trace technique is the overall CS–US interval. When the interval between the onset of the two stimuli is short, no differences between the two procedures are observed.[20] When the length of the gap increases, however, trace conditioning is inferior to delayed.[21]

Control Procedures

The forward procedures just described comply with the two most important principles noted by Pavlov: (1) that a CS acquires power when it is temporally contiguous with the US *and* (2) that the CS precedes the US. The power is reflected by the presence of the CR. The presence of an overt response, however, does not guarantee that the response is the result of conditioning. We may be fooled into thinking that conditioning has occurred when the behavior, in fact, is due to a process other than conditioning. In other words, a subject may perform reactions that resemble a CR, but if they are not based on forward-conditioning procedures, then they do not qualify as true conditioned responses.

Responses that occur as a result of processes other than conditioning are **pseudoconditioned reactions** (pseudo means "false"). Domjan (1977) provided a good demonstration of this effect. He discovered that rats are reluctant to consume any new flavor, not just those that had been paired with poison, if the subjects are given an illness-inducing drug. In other words, the novel test flavors were never paired with any US, much less an illness-inducing drug, yet they triggered an aversion. In fact, the aversive reactions resembled those shown by animals who had undergone classical conditioning using flavor CSs and poison USs. Because the CSs were thoroughly novel, however, the aversions must have been pseudoconditioned reactions, not true CRs.

How do researchers know whether a given procedure results in, or produces, a true CR or just a pseudoconditioned reaction? There are several kinds of control procedures that are used to provide a means of comparison. Formally speaking, a control group is a group of subjects that receive *all* of the conditions given to the experimental animals *except* the one variable (or treatment) that is affecting the behavior in question. If, for example, a control group shows mild pseudoconditioning, whereas an experimental group (one getting the CS–US pairings) shows an even stronger reaction, then we may say that, although pseudoconditioned reactions are present, a conditioning effect is evident as well.

Simultaneous Conditioning.

Some researchers claim that the simultaneous presentation of the CS and the US provides a good control condition because little conditioned responding is generated (see Figure 4-10).[22] Is this claim accurate, however? Many say "no" on the grounds that **simultaneous conditioning** does, in fact, lead to the development of an excitatory association, although one may require a special test to demonstrate the effect.

In one such study by Burkhardt and Ayres (1978), rats were given one trial of aversive conditioning using a noise CS and a mild shock US.[23] The CS began at exactly the same time as the 4-second shock, but it persisted for various durations, from 0 seconds (no CS was presented) to as long as 2 minutes following shock offset. The power of the CS was then tested on a water-lick-suppression task. Here, thirsty subjects were allowed to drink 100 licks of water, at which point the CS was sounded. The time required for the subjects to complete an additional 10 licks of water provided a measure of conditioning. Whereas the 0-second group took only about 3.2 seconds to complete their 10 additional licks, the 4-second subjects (for whom the CS presentation exactly matched that of the US presentation) took about 94.4 seconds.[24] Thus, simultaneous presentation of the noise and the shock was effective in endowing the CS with excitatory power; it became sufficiently aversive to suppress drinking on the test.[25]

The simultaneous-conditioning procedure leads to excitatory strength, but the levels still do not rival those produced by either of the forward methods. The reason is that even though subjects develop an excitatory association, they cannot perform in a manner that reveals such learning.[26] When special tests are conducted, however, the full strength of these associations becomes manifest.[27]

Backward Conditioning.

Another technique that has been used as a control procedure is **backward conditioning** (see Figure 4-10). As the name suggests, backward conditioning occurs when the US precedes the CS. Historically, it was believed that either the backward procedure did not produce excitatory conditioning, or the effects were only transitory.[28] Such a judgment makes good sense from an evolutionary point of view because if the function of Pavlovian conditioning is to provide the animal with a means of predicting important future events such as USs, then it hardly makes sense that cues that occur after the US would acquire powerful signaling properties.

Is backward conditioning, therefore, a good control procedure? Evidence suggests that it is not because it, too, leads to excitatory conditioning. Some reviewers suggest that the excitatory conditioning occurs only when noxious USs are used, a small number of CS–US pairings are given, and the US itself is rather unpredictable.[29] However, not all experiments that have shown excitatory backward conditioning have contained those features.

For example, Plotkin and Oakley (1975), delivered a mild shock US to a facial muscle near the eyelid, and then, 2 seconds later, a 1,000-Hz tone CS. On occasion, the CS was given by itself to test for a conditioned eye-blink reaction. As shown in Figure 4-11, the forward group showed very marked conditioning from the start of training. Their percentage of responding was nearly 100%. Although the backward group was significantly lower, nevertheless appreciable acquisition was demonstrated. The percentage of responses on which a CR was given was over 50% by the fourth day of training.

A different approach was taken in an experiment by Hearst (1989).[30] On 50% of the occasions, experimental pigeons were given a red key light after food (backward conditioning), whereas control subjects sometimes received the red cue following food, but at other times, they did not. A test for excitatory conditioning was done in Phase 2, when subjects were given the red light followed by the food US. The measure of conditioning was the degree to which the subjects pecked the red key. If the former backward CS had acquired *some* excitatory strength in Phase 1, then in Phase 2, the experimental pigeons should have pecked the key more readily than the control subjects. This is precisely what was found. The mean percentage of trials on which the former backward-conditioned subjects showed pecking behavior to the key was about 56%. In contrast, the control subjects pecked on only about 40% of the test trials. The backward CS, therefore, must have developed excitatory

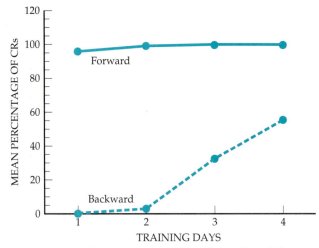

FIGURE 4-11. Mean percentage of conditioned eyelid responses over 4 days of training for the forward and backward groups (after Plotkin & Oakley, 1975).

strength on the original training series because it more easily became excitatory when explicitly paired with food on the test.[31] In conclusion, backward conditioning is a poor control procedure because excitatory conditioning is produced, although the effects are complicated.[32]

Random CS–US Presentations.

Finally, a control procedure that is often used is the random-control procedure, where the CS and US presentations are given randomly. This procedure is important because it involves the presentation of both the CSs and USs, but it avoids establishing a consistent temporal relationship between them. This technique was discussed in detail in Chapter 3.

CS–US Interval

The foregoing discussion dealt with the sequence of stimuli (forward, backward, and simultaneous procedures). Another important variable in classical conditioning is the length of the CS–US interval, usually defined as the time between the onset of the CS and the onset of the US. The reason for its importance is that it embodies the long-standing principle first described by the British Empiricists—namely, the law of contiguity. According to that law, events that are close together in time become associated. If the law of contiguity is central to conditioning, then the temporal interval between the CS and the US should be of paramount importance.

The law of contiguity certainly makes good intuitive sense, and, furthermore, it is consistent with an evolutionary viewpoint. If the CS is essentially a signal for a biologically powerful US, then it cannot occur too early before the US presentation. Imagine, for example, how useless the signal would be if someone yelled "watch out" hours before the threatening event, such as an oncoming automobile, was due to occur! How could the signal, "watch out," possibly serve as an effective warning? In nature, cues are very often contiguous, or nearly so, with the events they signal. The crack of wood is soon followed by the falling branch; the glistening movement in the grass is quickly identified by a bird as an edible worm; a sudden waft of odor signals to a stalking lion that a wildebeest is close by.[33]

Evidence for the Principle of Contiguity.

There is, perhaps, no other principle of learning that has been more strongly supported than the law of contiguity (although there is no complete agreement about the exact time span within which the US must follow the CS). Both the CS–US interval that is optimum for conditioning and the maximum interval that still allows for conditioning to take place vary according to the kind of response being studied. In human eyelid conditioning, for example, the optimum interval is quite short, on the order of about 0.5 seconds.[34] With rabbits, the intervals that prove most successful vary between 0.2 and 0.4 seconds.[35] Fairly poor conditioning is evident with a CS–US interval 0.06 seconds or less or with intervals as long as 0.7 seconds.[36] The conditioning of the jaw-movement reaction in rabbits differs only slightly from the eye-blink data. Here, the optimum interval appears to be between 1 and 4 seconds, 0.5 seconds giving somewhat poorer conditioning.[37] In short, research on conditioning of skeletal movements supports the law of contiguity by showing that the CS must precede the US by as short a time as 0.2 seconds.

A second category of responding involves conditioned autonomic or visceral reactions, such as heart rate, galvanic skin resistance (GSR), or blood pressure. Here again, the law of contiguity is strongly supported, although conditioning is stronger when the CS–US interval is somewhat longer than that found in skeletal conditioning. For example, heart rate in rats is conditioned best when the interval is about 6 seconds.[38] The values are similar for rabbits (2 to 6 seconds), dogs (2.5 to 10 seconds), and humans (13 seconds).[39] Salivary conditioning, also an autonomically controlled behavior, shows similar effects. Effective conditioning occurs when the CS-offset–US-onset interval is 8 seconds, and even some conditioning is found when the interval is 16 seconds.[40] The one exception to this generalization (that visceral conditioning is accomplished with longer CS–US intervals than skeletal conditioning) is that GSR seems to condition best with a 0.5-second interval.[41]

A third category of behavior is autoshaping. Lucas, Deich, and Wasserman (1981) presented a 12-second orange light that terminated 0, 4, 12, 36, or 120 seconds prior to the food presentation. The key-peck responses, averaged over the 320 trials, are shown in Figure 4-12. Little conditioning occurred in the 120-second group.[42] The 0-second group, in contrast, pecked nearly 40 times per

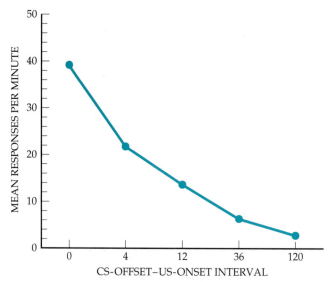

FIGURE 4-12. Mean key-pecking responses per minute in groups that received a 0-, 4-, 12-, 36-, or 120-second temporal gap between the CS offset and food onset. The trace intervals are expressed on a log scale (after Lucas, Deich, & Wasserman, 1981).

minute. The other groups showed an intermediate level of pecking. Thus, Figure 4-12 supports the law of contiguity but shows that the range over which conditioning takes place is even longer than the range for autonomic reactions.

A fourth category of conditioning for which learning occurs at comparatively long CS–US intervals is the CER technique. Often, the light or tone CS lasts between 30 and 120 seconds, although research has shown that the optimum interval is probably closer to 10 seconds.[43]

Finally, a category of classical conditioning that differs from the other forms, in terms of the effects of the CS–US interval on conditioning, is taste-aversion learning. Whereas the CS–US interval for skeletal, autonomic, and autoshaping behavior may be a few seconds long, many studies have demonstrated that taste-aversion learning is possible even when the CS–US interval is several hours long. For example, Kalat and Rozin (1971) gave rats a sucrose-flavored water CS, followed by lithium chloride.[44] Delays between the sucrose and the poison were 0.5, 1, 1.5, 3, 6, or 24 hours. Two days later, the rats were given a choice between plain water and the sucrose.

The results are shown in Figure 4-13. When the poison was administered 6 or 24 hours after the sucrose, consumption did not differ from that of the control animals who were never poisoned at all. However, when the lithium chloride was delayed for 3 hours or less, appreciable aversion developed; the sucrose solution composed only about 40% of their median intake. Although learning occurred in this study with a 3-hour delay, other experiments have shown that flavors become aversive even when the poison US is delayed for as long as 12 to 15 hours.

This vast array of findings leads to several conclusions. First, the US must be presented reasonably soon after the CS for conditioning to take place. For many kinds of CRs, the maximum delay possible is only a few seconds; for

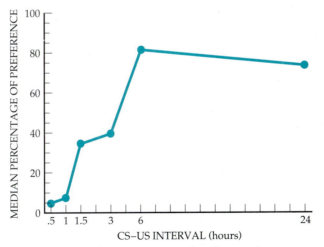

FIGURE 4-13. Median percentage of preference for sucrose solution, as a function of the CS–US interval (in hours) (after Kalat & Rozin, 1971).

taste aversion, it is appreciably longer—namely, hours. Whatever the time scale is, however, the important point is that conditioning is absent if the delay is too long.

Second, understanding the role of the CS–US interval is more complicated than it would appear because the CS–US interval covaries with other dimensions of the conditioning arrangements, such as the CS duration or the gap between the CS offset and the US onset. For example, if one lengthens the CS in order to lengthen the CS–US interval, one is also changing the duration of the CS. If one keeps the CS duration constant and varies the CS-onset–US-onset interval, then one must necessarily create temporal gaps between the CS offset and the US onset.

The third conclusion is that there is no single optimum CS–US interval value. The brain does not require a fixed interval between the CS and the US for all systems. Again, however, certain cautions must be observed. For example, the extent to which a CS and a US are associated may not always be displayed in the performance of the animal. A good example of this was shown by Ginn, Valentine, and Powell (1983). Two responses were measured: leg flex and heart rate. The tone CS, lasting either 0.5 or 4 seconds, was followed by a shock US. The leg-flex response was stronger in the 0.5-second group than in the 4-second subjects. The conditioned heart-rate changes, however, were stronger in the 4-second subjects than in the 0.5-second group. If the experimenters had simply used a 0.5-second interval and had measured only heart rate, then they would have concluded that conditioning is quite poor. Conversely, if they had used only a 4-second CS duration and had measured only leg flex, they would have come to the same conclusion—namely, that conditioning at that interval is poor. If, however, the authors had used a 4-second CS–US interval and had measured heart rate, or a 0.5-second interval and had measured only leg flex, then the opposite conclusions would have been reached. The association between the CS and the US must have been the same, regardless of which measure was used, yet this fact was not demonstrated in the animals' performance. Variations in the strength of the CR, therefore, may reflect differences in performance, not differences in the strength of the underlying association.

Effects of the Interstimulus Interval on the CR.

The foregoing research suggests that conditioning strength is generally weakened when the CS–US interval is lengthened. In addition, other important effects occur as a function of changes in this interval. For example, certain CSs may be strengthened when the CS–US interval is short but other CSs when it is long. Marlin (1981) showed this by placing rats in the black side of a two-compartment apparatus (one side was painted black, the other white) and giving tones followed by a shock. For two groups, the tone offset was simultaneous with the shock presentation. Two additional groups got a 10-second gap between the tone offset and the shock; and two more groups got a 30-second gap. There also were two groups that got only the US (they never received the tone).

On the following day, all subjects were tested. One of the "no-CS" control groups, and one group in each of the 0-, 10-, and 30-second interval conditions was put back into the two-compartment box and was given a spatial-preference test. If the black side was aversive, then they should avoid standing on that side. If, on the other hand, the black side was not aversive, then no systematic preference between the two sides should be evident. The other groups were put into a different apparatus altogether and were given a drinking test. Here, a water tube was presented, and the tone CS came on while they were licking the tube. The measure of aversion was the length of time it took an animal to make 40 licks. If the tone was aversive, then drinking should be suppressed and considerable time should pass before 40 licks are consumed.

The results are shown in Figure 4-14. Consider first the solid line (left vertical axis) of Figure 4-14. A long latency to complete 40 licks reflects a very strong aversion to the tone. The subjects for whom the tone immediately preceded the shock showed great hesitation to drink; they had the strongest aversion. The other groups showed an orderly decline in latency. Thus, in terms of the strength of the tone CS, the typical CS–US interval effect was shown. The longer the interval, the weaker the conditioning. Now consider the dotted line (right vertical axis) of Figure 4-14. The 0-second group showed less aversion to the black side than did the other groups; they spent about 75% of their 5-minute interval on the black side, even though they had previously been shocked there. The subjects who had experienced longer CS–US intervals (or no tone CS at all) showed stronger fear of the black side. In conclusion, variation in the CS–US interval had complicated effects. When the inter-

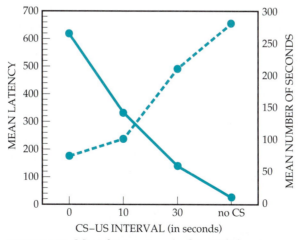

FIGURE 4-14. Mean latency to complete 40 licks, as a function of the CS–US interval (solid lines, left ordinate), and mean number of seconds (out of 300) spent in the white compartment, as a function of the CS–US interval (dotted lines, right ordinate) (after Marlin, 1981).

val was short, subjects became more averse to the tone; when the interval was long, subjects became more averse to the black side of the box. Thus, the length of the interval did not simply determine strength of conditioning overall; it determined which stimulus became the stronger CS.

The CS–US interval may also affect the form of the CR. In a study by Holland (1980a), for example, noise and light CSs were used.[45] Each lasted 5 seconds and was followed by a temporal gap (lasting 5, 10, 30, 60, or 120 seconds) and then food. The reactions to both lights and noises was measured. (Recall from the previous discussion that light and noise CSs elicit distinctly different kinds of reactions. Noises tend to elicit startle reactions and head-jerk behaviors, whereas light CSs tend to elicit CRs such as rearing on the hind legs.) The interesting finding here was that when the CS–US interval was short (5 or 10 seconds), the head-jerk reaction to the noise composed about 60 to 85% of the subjects' total behavior score. With long temporal gaps between the noise and the food, however, as much as 35% of the total behavior count was magazine reactions (defined as standing motionless in front of the feeder cup, or making contact with the cup). A similar effect was found with the light CS. With very short gaps, substantial amounts of walking and rearing on the hind legs was observed. With longer CS–US intervals, the light elicited more magazine behaviors.

According to Holland (1980a), the long CS–US intervals allow more of the US-dominant behavior to occur. These are behaviors, such as food-cup orientation, that are highly associated with food delivery. With very short CS–US intervals, however, orienting reactions to the CS are also performed. (The natural orienting reaction to a noise is a startle or a head-jerk response; the natural orienting reaction to the light, for a rat, is to rear on its hind legs.) When the CS–US interval is very short, the animals engage in these orienting reactions as part of their CR. In a sense, the total CR is a mixture of these shorter orienting reactions, as well as the magazine-dominant behaviors.

Isolation Effect.

Although associations are stronger when the CS and the US occur close together in time, other qualifications need to be made before we accept the principle of contiguity as a full description of a primary condition of learning. The CS–US interval actually operates in conjunction with several other important temporal dimensions of the conditioning experiment. Consider the temporal relationships displayed in Figure 4-15. In both examples, top and bottom, the CS and US are equally contiguous; that is, the CS comes on and then, following a brief gap of time, the US is given. The two examples differ, however, in terms of the interval between the first US presentation and the next CS. In the top example, there is a long interval between those two events; in the bottom example, the interval between the US and the next CS is comparatively short. If the law of contiguity is taken at face value and applied to these two arrangements, we would predict that conditioning would be equally strong in both cases. After all, the CS is equally contiguous with the US in both studies.

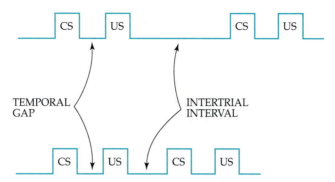

FIGURE 4-15. Schematic showing two kinds of conditioning arrangements. In each arrangement, the CS–US contiguity is the same, but the intertrial interval varies, thus providing, in the top example, greater perceptual isolation of the CS–US pairing.

Many studies have shown, however, that conditioning is not equally strong in these two situations.[46] In one study by Gibbon, Baldock, Locurto, Gold, and Terrace (1977), for example, groups of pigeons were given various combinations of CS duration (the CS-onset–US-onset interval) and intertrial interval (ITI).[47] The ITI is the temporal interval between the US offset and the next CS onset. The ratio of CS duration (1 to 64 seconds) to the intertrial interval (6 to 768 seconds) was varied. The ratios ranged from 2:1 to 96:1. Thus, by combining different absolute ITI values with different CS–US interval values, the authors were able to compare the effects of both the absolute and the relative CS–US interval.[48]

They discovered an **isolation effect.** Conditioning is stronger when the CS–US episode is relatively isolated in time than when CS–US pairings are given closely together. That is, constant ratios of ITI/CS–US intervals produced approximately equal pecking. It is, therefore, not the CS-onset–US-onset interval exclusively that determines strength of conditioning, but rather the *relationship* between that interval and the total duration of the trial. Longer CS–US intervals may be tolerated, provided that the ITI is proportionately lengthened. Stated in the reverse, if the ITI is too short, then the CS–US pairing is not isolated as a singular event, and autoshaping declines.

Let us further explore the implications raised by this work. Consider the procedure used by Kaplan (1984) (see Figure 4-16). Pigeons were given a 12-second green key light, followed by a 12-second gap (trace conditioning procedure) and then the food US. Following this CS–US pairing, an ITI began that lasted 15, 30, 60, 120, or 240 seconds for different groups. Figure 4-16 shows the isolation effect rather clearly. With longer ITI values, the CS–US episode is more isolated, and, as discussed previously, conditioning should be stronger.

However, consider what happens when one CS–US pairing draws closer to the preceding US—that is, as the ITI gets progressively shorter. This is most evident in the 15-second group. The temporal distance between the CS and

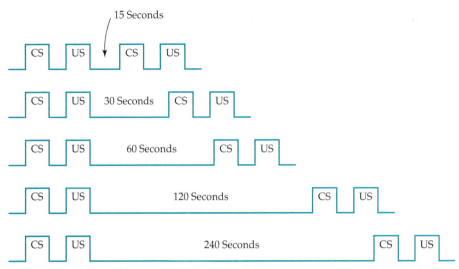

FIGURE 4-16. Schematic diagram of Kaplan's (1984) procedure, showing the isolation effect as a function of the intertrial interval (ITI). For each group, a 12-second CS was followed by a 12-second gap, a 3-second US (food access), and then the ITI (values were between 15 and 240 seconds).

the US becomes virtually the same as that between the US and the next CS. Here, the CS is being paired with the absence of the US as well as the presence of the US. To test for the effect of this procedure, Kaplan measured the amount of time that the birds spent on the key side of the box versus on the nonkey side. The percentage of total time spent on the side containing the illuminated key light is shown in Figure 4-17.

Consider first the behavior of those subjects who received a long ITI— that is, the 120- and 240-second groups. Their mean approach–withdrawal ratio was above 0.5, thus indicating that they preferred to approach the lighted key and to remain on that side. This finding is completely in accord with the isolation effect discussed previously. Excitatory conditioning is stronger when the CS–US interval, *relative to* the ITI, is fairly short.

Now consider the other groups, especially the groups receiving the shortest ITI values (15- or 30-second groups). Those pigeons showed a distinct avoidance of the side containing the lighted key. The point is not simply that conditioning is weak with these time values, but rather that conditioned inhibition (withdrawal from the CS) actually takes place. The CS–US interval was identical for all of the groups, yet there were differences not only in the strength of the excitatory conditioning (based on the isolation effect), but also in the kind of conditioning that took place (inhibitory versus excitatory).

In conclusion, the CS–US interval is important for Pavlovian conditioning, but only with respect to the ITI. A CS becomes an excitor when it is located close to the US *and* when the CS–US episode is relatively isolated in time. As the ITI becomes shorter, thus causing the CS to follow closely the previous US, a transition is shown from excitation to inhibition.

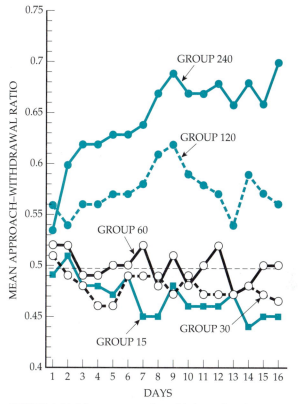

FIGURE 4-17. Mean approach–withdrawal ratios to the CS side, as a function of acquisition sessions for pigeons in the 15-, 30-, 60-, 120-, and 240-second ITI conditions (after Kaplan, 1984).

Facilitation of Conditioning by Intervening Cue.

There is yet another qualification that needs to be raised in connection with the principle of contiguity. Stimuli other than the CS, which intervene between a CS and a US, may have a dramatic effect on the strength of the CS. A CS gains more strength when a second CS, called "CS_2," intervenes between it and the US than it does when the CS_2 is not given, despite the fact that in both cases, the CS–US interval is the same.

An experiment by Rescorla (1982a) demonstrated this effect, using an autoshaping procedure with pigeons. Forty-eight trials were given on 6 successive days. On some trials, one color CS was followed 10 seconds later by food; on others, a different color CS was followed 10 seconds later by the food, but a white light came on during the intervening 10-second CS–US interval.[49] The measure of conditioning strength was the extent to which the pigeons pecked the colored CSs.

The results are shown in Figure 4-18. There was an appreciable increase in responding in all animals over the course of training, indicating that the

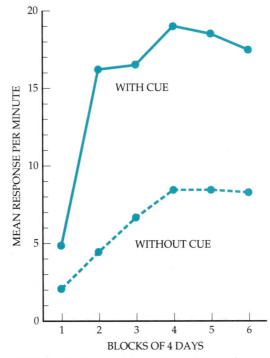

FIGURE 4-18. Mean responses per minute during the color CSs, as a function of blocks of 4 days of training on trials with (solid line) or without (dotted line) the intervening cue (after Rescorla, 1982a).

colored CSs acquired some associative strength. Nonetheless, responding was stronger to the CS that included the intervening white light during the CS–US interval than to the CS that did not. Thus, the presence of the intervening white light facilitated or enhanced conditioning to the colored CS, even though the CS–US interval was the same in both cases.[50]

How does this facilitation work? Perhaps the intervening cue bridges the gap, causing the subject to perceive the US as occurring sooner. This notion cannot be the full story, however. The facilitation effect depends, at least in part, on the associative strength of the intervening cue itself. This was shown in a study of the rabbit's eyelid reaction by Gibbs, Kehoe, & Gormezano, 1991.[51] Experimental animals were given CS_A, then an intervening cue (CS_B), and finally a shock US. Control subjects got CS_A–US trials on half of the occasions and CS_B–US trials on the remaining half (in other words, they did not experience CS_B as an intervening cue between CS_A and shock). In Phase 2, CS_B was given repeatedly by itself, so that its associative strength would decline. In Phase 3, the strength of CS_A was tested.

The results are shown in Figure 4-19. The left panel shows the facilitation effect described previously. Responding is stronger in the experimental sub-

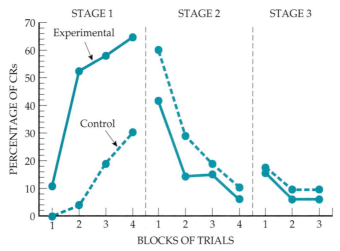

FIGURE 4-19. Percentage of CRs during the three stages of the experiment, as a function of the training block for the experimental group that received serial CS_A–CS_B–US training, and the control group that received separate CS_A–US and CS_B–US pairings. Stage 1 involved 2-day blocks of trials, Stage 2 used 1-day blocks, and Stage 3 involved 20-trial blocks of trials. Note that data in Stages 1 and 3 are CRs elicited by CS_A (after Gibbs, Kehoe, & Gormezano, 1991).

jects, for which CS_B intervened between CS_A and shock, than in the control animals. The middle panel confirms the orderly decline of associative strength to CS_B during the extinction sessions. The test results for CS_A (Phase 3) are shown in the right panel. The experimental subjects showed no facilitative responding to CS_A at all. In other words, once the power of the intervening cue had been eliminated through extinction (in Phase 2), the facilitation effect disappeared. This result, therefore, demonstrates that it is the associative strength of the intervening cue, not just its presence, that facilitates learning of CS_A. Even so, the CS–US interval by itself tells only part of the story in conditioning. Both whether it is isolated and whether other intervening stimuli are present also modulate the effect of the CS–US interval.[52]

Intertrial Interval (ITI)

The foregoing material indicates that the CS–US interval and the ITI jointly affect classical conditioning. However, given a fixed and relatively short CS–US interval, the ITI, by itself, also has an effect, which is consistent with the aforementioned principles. In eyelid-conditioning experiments, for example, using either human beings or rabbits, short ITI values lead to inferior conditioning.[53] The values, however, must be quite short to have such a decrement (from 5 to 20 seconds in humans, and less than 15 seconds in rabbits). Aside from the effect that a long ITI has on isolating the CS–US episode, longer ITI values probably influence the strength of conditioning by giving subjects a longer time in which to rehearse the CS–US pairing.

INTERIM SUMMARY

Pavlov speculated that a CS must precede the US. Such a forward-conditioning arrangement may be structured in one of two ways. Delayed conditioning is when the CS offset is delayed at least until the US onset. Trace conditioning occurs when the CS goes off before the US comes on, thus creating a temporal gap between the two stimuli. Typically, delayed conditioning is superior to trace, although this difference is affected by other variables, such as the CS–US interval. Pseudoconditioned reactions are responses that result from processes other than conditioning. Because pseudoconditioned reactions occur, one may be uncertain as to whether the behavior is learned. To provide an appropriate comparison group, various control procedures have been suggested. Simultaneous conditioning is when the CS and US occur at the same time. Backward conditioning occurs when the US precedes the CS. Although responding is weak in both cases, excitatory conditioning has been found. A final control procedure involves the random presentation of the CS and the US. The CS–US interval is one of the most important dimensions of Pavlovian conditioning because it defines the degree of contiguity between stimuli. Contiguity is essential, but the maximum CS–US interval that still allows for conditioning to take place may vary considerably. For skeletal responses, the CS–US interval must be a second or less; autonomic reactions are conditioned with intervals as long as 15 to 20 seconds; autoshaping occurs with intervals extending a minute or more; and taste-aversion conditioning may occur with intervals as long as 6 to 12 hours. Not only is the strength of conditioning affected by the CS–US interval, but the kind of CR that is performed is also affected. For example, with short CS–US intervals, the rats' head-jerk reactions predominate, but when the temporal gap is longer, food-cup approaches are more prevalent. Conditioning is strong if CS–US episode is isolated in time. In other words, the absolute duration of the CS–US interval is less important than its duration relative to the ITI. Finally, conditioning is increased if intervening cues are given during the CS–US interval. The functional value of the interval is reduced by intervening cues.

ENDNOTES

1. M. C. Smith (1968); Sheafor and Gormezano (1972); Polenchar, Romano, Steinmetz, and Patterson (1984), respectively.
2. Note that each combination of intensity and duration was given to a separate group of subjects.

3. Interestingly, the duration of the shock also changed the magnitude of the CR, with longer durations producing higher CR levels (see subsequent discussion).
4. Wagner, Siegel, Thomas, and Ellison (1964); Fitzgerald and Teyler (1970); Woods and Shogren (1972), respectively.
5. Annau and Kamin (1961).
6. Andrews and Braveman (1975); Nachman and Ashe (1973).
7. Polenchar, Romano, Steinmetz, and Patterson (1984). US duration has also been studied in the context of autoshaping in birds. Although some experiments failed to show a systematic relationship between US duration and autoshaping, others have shown the expected positive relationship; see Balsam and Payne (1979); Lucas and Wasserman (1982).
8. For earlier reviews, see Gray (1965); Grice (1968).
9. See also Kamin (1965); Kamin and Schaub (1963).
10. Deutsch (1978); Kehoe (1983), respectively.
11. Similar results have been found for other conditioning systems, such as taste aversions; see N. W. Bond (1983). These results, however, are probably due to the fact that a flavor, unlike a light, is effectively altered in quality when it is combined with a second flavor.
12. Actually, a third group was tested for which the position of the light was varied, but only a single color was used.
13. Interestingly, in a second experiment, the authors found that the two stimuli did not differ when the US was food. That is, the difference in conditioning was observed only when the two CSs signaled shock.
14. Allison, Larson, and Jensen (1967) showed not only that rats preferred dark areas but also that their preference increased following receipt of a shock.
15. See also Jacobs and LoLordo (1980).
16. See also Shapiro and LoLordo (1982); but for alternative views, see Ayres, Axelrod, Mercker, Muchnik, and Vigorito (1985); Panlilio and Weiss (1993); Sigmundi and Bolles (1983).
17. Davey (1989); Timberlake (1983c, 1993); Timberlake and Lucas (1989).
18. Ross and Ross (1971); Wilson (1969).
19. Fitzgerald and Teyler (1970); Lucas, Deich, and Wasserman (1981); Manning, Schneiderman, and Lordahl (1969); Newlin and LoLordo (1976); Schneiderman (1966).
20. Manning, Schneiderman, and Lordahl (1969).
21. This finding may be explained in terms of inhibition of delay; see also Kaplan (1984).
22. Pavlov (1927).
23. See also Heth (1976); Heth and Rescorla (1973); Mahoney and Ayres (1976); Matzel, Held, and Miller (1988); Sherman (1978); Sherman and Maier (1978).
24. Data are taken from Experiment 2 of Burkhardt and Ayres (1978).
25. One other interesting finding in this study was that conditioning strength to the CS declined if the offset of the CS extended too much beyond the offset of the US. That is, noise CSs that continued for, say, another 4 seconds developed excitatory strength, but the level of strength was significantly below that of a 4-second group for which the CS duration matched the US duration. If the CS extended for a very long period of time following US offset, then conditioning was absent altogether.
26. Matzel, Held, and Miller (1988).
27. The tests performed by Matzel, Held, and Miller (1988) are not described here in detail because an understanding of their method requires knowledge of several important concepts that are covered later in the text (see Chapter 5).

28. See Gormezano and Moore (1969); Hall (1984), respectively.
29. See Spetch, Wilkie, and Pinel (1981).
30. See also Ayres, Haddad, and Albert (1987).
31. Excitatory learning has not always been found with the backward procedure; see Tait and Saladin (1986).
32. See, for example, Keith-Lucas and Guttman (1975); Van Willigen, Emmett, Cote, and Ayres (1987).
33. A signal must not occur too close to the event either. Otherwise, the subject would attend to the more powerful event (the US), and thus fail to notice, or process, the less powerful cue (the CS). The limiting case is when the two stimuli are completely contiguous (simultaneous procedure). Here, the CS event, being relatively innocuous, is barely noticed; it cannot serve effectively as a warning signal under these circumstances.
34. Ross and Ross (1971).
35. Coleman and Gormezano (1971); Smith, Coleman, and Gormezano (1969).
36. Salafia, Lambert, Host, Chiaia, and Ramirez (1980); Millenson, Kehoe, and Gormezano (1977), respectively.
37. Gormezano (1972).
38. Fitzgerald and Martin (1971); Fitzgerald and Teyler (1970).
39. Deane (1965); Black, Carlson, and Solomon (1962); Hastings and Obrist (1967), respectively.
40. Ellison (1964).
41. Prokasy, Hall, and Fawcett (1962); but see Badia and Defran (1970).
42. Nonetheless, pecking did occur to some degree even in those animals. This is interesting, in that other skeletal behaviors, such as eyelid reactions, tolerate US delays of only about a second.
43. Yeo (1974).
44. See also Andrews and Braveman (1975); Garcia, Ervin, and Koelling (1966); Revusky (1977); Chapter 7 of this book.
45. See also Millenson, Kehoe, and Gormezano (1977).
46. See Cooper (1991) for a theoretical discussion.
47. See also Balsam (1984); Terrace, Gibbon, Farrell, and Baldock (1975).
48. For example, to assess the effect of a constant absolute CS–US interval on conditioning, the authors could compare groups that always had, say, a 2-second interval, regardless of the ITI value. To assess the effect of a relative CS–US interval (relative, that is, to the ITI value), the authors could compare groups that always had, say, a 4:1 ratio of ITI value divided by the CS–US interval value.
49. The details of this experiment have been simplified here, for purposes of clarity. In reality, four different color CSs were used, each being followed 10 seconds later by the US. However, the intervening CS (white light) came on for (a) the entire 10-second interval, (b) the first 5 seconds of the interval, (c) the second 5 seconds, or (d) no intervening cue was given. Performance on conditions (b) and (c) was intermediate.
50. Such facilitative effects of an intervening cue have been shown in a variety of other situations; see Kehoe, Gibbs, Garcia, and Gormezano (1979); Kehoe and Morrow (1984).
51. See also Thomas, Robertson, Cunniffe, and Lieberman (1989).
52. See also Egger and Miller (1962); Wickens, Nield, Tuber, and Wickens (1973).
53. Prokasy and Whaley (1963); Spence and Norris (1950), for humans; Salafia, Mis, Terry, Bartosiak, and Daston (1973), for rabbits.

CHAPTER 5

Classical Conditioning Phenomena

Chapter 3 described the basic procedures in classical conditioning, and Chapter 4 discussed many of the important variables that affect conditioning strength. A number of other interesting phenomena have been discovered in the course of studying this form of learning, however. These phenomena are important because they further reveal how Pavlovian conditioning works, thus allowing for the development of a theory of conditioning (see Chapter 6).

SECOND-ORDER CONDITIONING

One of the most important is **second-order conditioning,** also termed **higher-order conditioning.** Second-order conditioning occurs when a new CS (called "CS_2") is paired with an already powerful CS (called "CS_1"). The new CS_2 becomes associated with the CS_1, such that, on a later test, CS_2 also produces a CR, not because it had been paired with a biologically potent US (as the first-order CS was), but because it was paired with an already powerful CS. The existence of second-order conditioning is one reason why the definition of Pavlovian conditioning in Chapter 3 did not mention the need for a US[1].

Second-order conditioning is an extremely important learning ability. Think back over the past 24 hours. How many unconditioned stimuli have you experienced? Surely you have had food, and perhaps you have experienced some unpleasant events. Strong biological events, however, do not pervade our lives so extensively that they account for all the associations we develop. Stated differently, there are so many meaningful and powerful CSs in our lives that it is impossible to imagine that each developed its strength by becoming associated with a US. Many must have gained their strength through second-order conditioning—that is, by becoming associated with other strong CSs, not USs. Second-order conditioning, therefore, is an important phenomenon because it provides a mechanism for the establishment of associations that do not involve a US presentation.

Various techniques are used to illustrate second-order conditioning.[2] One common method, used by Rizley and Rescorla (1972), is the CER technique.[3] The structure of their study is shown in Figure 5-1. During the first phase, the second-order conditioning group (group E) received light–shock pairings (CS–US pairings). In Phase 2, the tone CS_2 was paired with the now-potent light (CS_2–CS_1 pairings). Finally, the tone (the second-order cue) was given during lever pressing, to determine whether it had, indeed, acquired the ability to suppress lever responding.

Several important control groups were used. Group C_1 received the CS_1–US pairings in Phase 1 but random presentations of the tone and light in Phase 2. The purpose of this group was to show that although the light became a powerful CS during Phase 1, the acquisition of strength to the tone depended on the contingency between the tone and the light in Phase 2. Group C_2 received random presentations of the C_1 and the US in Phase 1 but conventional CS_2–CS_1 pairings in Phase 2. Under these conditions, the CS_1 should have failed to develop sufficient strength during Phase 1 because it was not consistently paired with the US. If the CS_1 is not powerful, then presumably it cannot transfer its power to CS_2 during Phase 2.

The results are shown in Figure 5-2. No conditioning was evident in either of the control groups, but strong suppression of lever pressing occurred in Group E. The development of a CR to the second-order stimulus, therefore, requires not only that the CS_2 is paired with the first-order CS_1 (Phase 2 of the study), but also that the CS_1 is paired with the US in Phase 1.[4]

This study used conventional stimuli—namely, lights and tones. The characteristics of first- and second-order stimuli, however, may vary considerably. For instance, either CS_1 or CS_2 may be the context (the apparatus) in which the subjects are trained and tested. In a study by Marlin (1983), subjects were placed into one of two kinds of apparatus and given a shock US. One text box had black plastic walls and a grid floor that was permeated with the odor of peppermint; the other contained two large steel plates for a floor, angled walls,

Phase	Treatment		
	Group E	Group C_1	Group C_2
1	CS_1–US	CS_1–US	Random CS_1, US presentations
2	CS_2–CS_1	Random CS_1, CS_2 presentations	CS_2–CS_1
Test	CS_2	CS_2	CS_2

FIGURE 5-1. Schematic diagram showing the treatments used to demonstrate second-order conditioning.

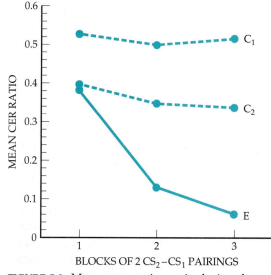

FIGURE 5-2. Mean suppression ratio during three blocks of second-order conditioning trials for the experimental (E) and Control (C_1, C_2) groups (after Rizley & Rescorla, 1972).

and was permeated by a lemon smell. The purpose of this phase was to condition the context as CS_1. In Phase 2, the rats were place in either the same context or the alternative context, and tones were sounded. If the context was the same as the previous shock environment, then the tone should become aversive through second-order conditioning. If the context was the novel environment, however, then the tone should remain neutral.

Aversiveness was tested in a lick-suppression experiment. Here, subjects were put in yet a different environment and allowed to lick a water tube. Beginning with Lick 5, and extending to Lick 40, the CS_2 was sounded. The time it took for the subjects to complete the 35 licks was measured. The results showed that the lick latency was about 74 seconds when the tone (CS_2) had been paired with the previous shock environment (CS_1), but only about 13 seconds when the tone had been given in the neutral box. Thus, the experiment clearly demonstrated that the context or surroundings may easily serve as the first-order CS.

This finding has considerable importance for everyday human behavior. Imagine being in a place that is known to be dangerous or aversive (for humans, who rely so extensively on language, such knowledge is often learned from another person, rather than experienced directly). Marlin's study suggests that new stimuli that are encountered in this context, which otherwise would remain innocuous and neutral, become aversive as well. Objects, events, or even other people, who are not otherwise threatening, may take on a sinister cast because they are encountered in an aversive environment.[5]

Factors Affecting Second-Order Conditioning

Some of the variables that affect the strength of a CS_2 are discussed in the following sections.

Interstimulus Interval.

It is not surprising that the interstimulus interval affects second-order conditioning, given its importance in first-order Pavlovian conditioning. A study that showed these effects was done by Kehoe, Feyer, and Moses (1981), using the eye-blink reaction in rabbits. During first-order conditioning, CS_1 (a light) was paired with a brief and mild shock delivered to the muscle attached to the eyelid.[6] The CS–US interval during this phase was 0.1, 0.14, 0.16, 0.32, or 0.4 seconds; one extra group received unpaired presentations of the CS and US. The second-order conditioning procedure paired a tone CS_2 with the light CS_1. Here, the CS_2–CS_1 interval was fixed at 0.4 seconds. The strength of the CS_2 was then tested.

The results are shown in Figure 5-3. There was an orderly change in CS_2 strength, as a function of the CS_1–US interval. Responding increased systematically over the range of interstimulus intervals tested. This finding is consistent with the information discussed in Chapter 4 concerning the CS–US interval in skeletal conditioning. It indicates that CS_2 strength varies as a function of the strength of CS_1.

The authors also varied the interstimulus interval during second-order conditioning. All subjects experienced a 0.4-second CS_1–US interval during phase 1. During the second-order trials, however, the CS_2–CS_1 interval was

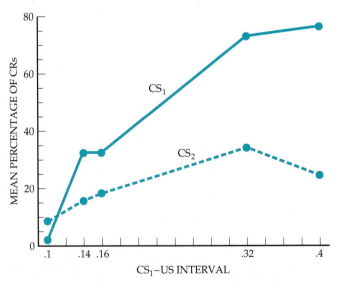

FIGURE 5-3. Mean percentage of trials in which a CR was given to the CS_2 or the CS_1, as a function of the CS_1–US interval (after Kehoe, Feyer, & Moses, 1981).

0.4, 0.8, or 2.4 seconds; an extra group received random presentations of the CS_1 and CS_2. As shown in Figure 5-4, virtually no conditioning was shown in the unpaired group, but substantial conditioning was shown in the other groups, with the strongest conditioning in the group that experienced a 0.4-second interstimulus interval. Overall then, CS_2 is based on CS_1 strength and on the contiguity of CS_2 and CS_1.

Similarity Between CS_2 and CS_1

Another important factor is the similarity of the CS_1 and the CS_2: The more similar, the stronger the conditioning. In a CER study by Rescorla and Furrow (1977), for example, rats were given first-order training with either a tone or a light CS, followed by shock, and then second-order training using the alternative stimulus as the CS_2. Two tones were used—a pulsating 200-Hz tone and a steady 1,800-Hz tone. Similarly, two different kinds of lights were used, a flashing house light and the illumination of a small panel light located on the wall of the cage. The study, therefore, employed four groups ("T" is for tone, "L" is for light). Two T_1–US groups were given second-order conditioning with either T_2–T_1 or L_2–T_1 pairings, and two L_1–US groups were given second order conditioning with either L_2–L_1 or T_2–L_1 pairings.

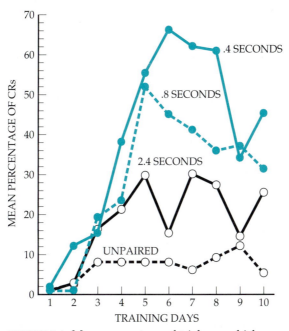

FIGURE 5-4. Mean percentage of trials on which a CR was given to the CS_2, as a function of days of training for groups receiving different CS_2–CS_1 intervals. The unpaired group received random tones and lights (after Kehoe, Feyer, & Moses, 1981).

Stronger second-order conditioning occurred when the CSs were of the same modality. That is, a light CS_2 was better associated with a light CS_1 than it was with a tone CS_1; similarly, a tone CS_2 was more readily associated with a tone CS_1 than with a light CS_1. The cause of this result is not entirely clear. Perhaps the animals more easily attend to the features of two stimuli when they are both from the same modality. In other words, as CS_1 becomes powerful, subjects may attend to its features, and thus when CS_2 is given, attention to that modality, and conditioning, is stronger. Another explanation may be that when confronted with stimuli from the same modality, subjects analyze the sensory differences more closely (to discriminate one from the other) and thus learn about them more thoroughly than when given stimuli from a different sense modality (which are easily differentiated).[7]

Spatial Contiguity.

A third important feature in second-order conditioning is the spatial contiguity between the CS_1 and the CS_2: the closer the stimuli, the better the conditioning. Rescorla and Cunningham (1979) projected an "X" pattern onto the response key and followed it with food. The pattern occurred on either of two keys. One was located on the left side of the cage and the other on the right. In Phase 2, second-order conditioning was given. Here, a green key light, located either on the left or the right side, was followed by CS_1 (the X pattern). Four different conditions were studied: green (left)–X (left); green (right)–X (right); green (left)–X (right); and green (right)–X (left). The measure of conditioning was the probability of pecking the CS_2 key. The autoshaped reaction was acquired more quickly when the key for CS_2 and CS_1 was located on the same side. When the second- and first-order stimuli were given on different sides of the cage, autoshaping proceeded at a much slower rate.[8]

US Magnitude.

As in first-order conditioning, the magnitude of the US affects the strength of second-order conditioning. O'Connell and Rashotte (1982) demonstrated this by training pigeons using the house light or a light located within the food trough itself as CS_1. These stimuli were followed by either 1 or 15 pellets of food. In Phase 2, CS_2 (a key light) was paired with either the house light or the food-trough light. The authors found that key pecking to CS_2 was stronger when the first-order training had used a larger US. This result parallels the findings discussed previously in connection with the CS–US interval. Indeed, the overall conclusion is that treatments that produce strong first-order conditioning carry over to the second-order conditioning phase. In effect, a strong CS_1 leads to a strong CS_2.

Consistency of CS_2–CS_1 Pairings.

Finally, consider an experiment by Rescorla (1979) on the consistency of second-order pairings. During first-order conditioning, both a red and a yellow key light were followed by food.[9] During second-order conditioning, a vertical stripe pattern was used as CS_2. Two groups had consistent pairings. One always had the vertical line followed by the yellow; the other always had the vertical line followed by the red. Another group received inconsistent pairings; the vertical line was sometimes followed by the red, sometimes by the yellow. All of the groups learned, but the subjects that received consistent pairings showed stronger conditioning than those that received inconsistent pairings. In other words, even though all animals always received a powerful CS_1 following the CS_2 presentation, conditioning was better when the same CS_1 was used than when two different CS_1 cues were used.

Level of Training.

There is a striking similarity between the procedure used to establish second-order conditioning and that used in conditioned inhibition (see Chapter 3). In the former, CS_1–US pairings are given prior to the CS_2–CS_1 pairings; in inhibitory conditioning, the same kinds of trials are used, but they are intermixed. In other words, the US is signaled by CS_1, but no US is preceded by CS_1 and CS_2. Is this difference critical in terms of whether CS_2 becomes a second-order excitatory stimulus or a conditioned inhibitor?

The issue was addressed by Yin, Barnet, and Miller (1994). For some of their subjects, the two kinds of training trials were presented sequentially, whereas for other subjects, the two kinds were intermixed. Thus, some of the rats received the CS_2–CS_1 training after the CS_1–US trials (conventional second-order conditioning), whereas others received the CS_2–CS_1 trials intermixed with the CS_1–US training (usual procedure for conditioned inhibition). In addition, the authors varied the extent of training. Specifically, groups received 0, 4, or 48 CS_2–CS_1 trials. The excitatory properties of both CS_2 and CS_1 were tested using a CER procedure, and their inhibitory power was assessed using the summation and retardation tests (see Chapter 3). Interestingly, the order of the training trials made no difference. That is, whether CS_2 became a conditioned excitor or an inhibitor was not affected by whether the CS_2–CS_1 trials followed, or were intermixed with, the CS_1–US training. The extent of training, however, was more critical. When few CS_2–CS_1 trials were given, CS_2 became a second-order conditioned excitor. In contrast, if many such trials were given, CS_2 became a conditioned inhibitor, but only when the two kinds of trials were interspersed.

Theories of Second-Order Conditioning

Much of the contemporary research on second-order conditioning has attempted to understand the nature of the second-order association. Figure 5-5 shows two of the possible links that could occur during second-order conditioning. The CS_2 could become associated with the CR (top portion of Figure 5-5). That is, during second-order conditioning, the CS_2 occurs while the subject is feeling its reaction to the CS_1. This is **stimulus–response (S–R learning.** Second, the CS_2 could become associated with the memory (or mental representation) of CS_1 (bottom part of Figure 5-5). This is an example of

Type of Association

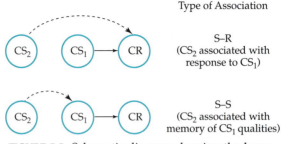

S–R
(CS$_2$ associated with
response to CS$_1$)

S–S
(CS$_2$ associated with
memory of CS$_1$ qualities)

FIGURE 5-5. Schematic diagram showing the hypothetical links or associations that could develop
during second-order conditioning.

stimulus–stimulus (S–S) learning. Contemporary research has provided support for both positions. The arguments and data for each are reviewed in the
following sections.

S–R Association.

One of the earliest and most important findings supported the S–R position. In this study by Holland and Rescorla (1975a), first-order conditioning
was established using a 12-second flashing light followed by food.[10] During
second-order conditioning, a 10-second clicking sound was followed by the
flashing-light CS$_1$. No food was delivered during this time. After CS$_2$ presumably had acquired its strength in Phase 2, CS$_1$ was extinguished for some
subjects but not for others. The final phase tested the strength of CS$_2$. The
important issue was whether CS$_2$ would show any change as a result of the
reduction in strength (through extinction) of CS$_1$. The measure of conditioning strength was an increase in activity given to the CS.

The results are shown in Figure 5-6. The activity elicited by CS$_2$ increased
during Phase 2 and declined during the test phase in both groups. The important finding is that no difference was observed between the group that experienced CS$_1$ extinction and the group that was not given CS$_1$ extinction. In
other words, the decline in strength of CS$_1$ as a result of extinction did *not*
affect the power of CS$_2$. Once CS$_2$ became strong, it no longer depended on,
or was affected by, the continuing strength of CS$_1$.

This finding supports the aforementioned S–R position for the following
reasons (see also Chapter 6). First, a CS that is paired with a US elicits a CR
with a strength that reflects the full power of the US. If the US strength is diminished through habituation, then the CS elicits a weaker CR. Imagine plunging
your hand into a bucket of cold water. A stimulus paired with such a US would
elicit a powerful CR because you experience the US as being intense. Once you
get used to the water, however, the temperature does not seem as severely cold
as it once did. Now, the CS would elicit a much smaller CR.

The same idea is applied to second-order conditioning. If the strength of
CS$_1$ (the so-called power source for conditioning CS$_2$) diminishes as a result
of extinction, and if CS$_2$ elicits the memory, or mental representation, of CS$_1$,

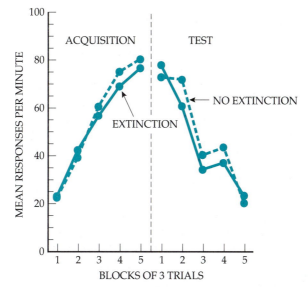

FIGURE 5-6. Mean activity responses per minute to CS_2 during second-order conditioning (Phase 2) and the second-order test (Phase 4) for groups that experienced extinction (vs. no extinction) of CS_1 prior to the test (after Holland & Rescorla, 1975a).

which, in turn, triggers the CR, then one should find that CS_2 elicits a weaker CR. This did not happen. Thus, CS_2 does not elicit the memory of CS_1, but rather becomes associated with the subject's *reaction* to the CS_1 during the second-order conditioning phase. In short, when CS_1 was presented, the subject felt a certain reaction (for example, fear when the US was a shock). The CS_2, being contiguous with this feeling, later was able to evoke the same feeling (see Chapter 6 for more details).

S–S Association.

The aforementioned results were not found by Rashotte, Griffin, and Sisk, (1977), who used a similar approach, except that pigeons, rather than rats, served as subjects, and key pecking, rather than conditioned activity, was measured.[11] The CS_1 was a 6-second white key light, and the CS_2 was a 6-second blue key light. All subjects were given first-order conditioning in Phase 1 and second-order conditioning in Phase 2. Experimental subjects then received extinction of CS_1, whereas the controls got additional CS_1–US pairings during Phase 3. Finally, a test was given in Phase 4. The measure of conditioning was the percentage of trials on which the subjects pecked the key at least once (see Figure 5-7).

During the second-order training sessions, subjects, not surprisingly, pecked the CS_1 on nearly all of the trials (left panel). Furthermore, CS_2 also became stronger during this time (shown in the right panel by the increase in

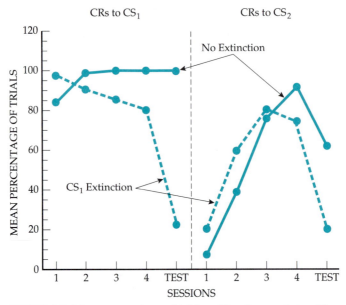

FIGURE 5-7. Mean percentage of trials with a key peck to either CS_1 or CS_2 during second-order conditioning and during the CS_2 test (Phase 4) (after Rashotte, Griffin, & Sisk, 1977).

pecking over the training sessions). The most interesting data are shown on the final test trial for CS_2. The group that continued to have CS_1–US pairings showed appreciable responding to CS_2 on the test, whereas the group that experienced extinction of CS_1 showed a significant decline in responding to CS_2. In other words, unlike the previous study, extinction of CS_1 *did* cause a reduction in responding to CS_2. This result therefore supports the S–S linkage described previously. When CS_2 triggered the memory of CS_1, which, in turn, elicited the CR, the strength of the CR was reduced as a result of CS_1 having been extinguished.

Resolution.

The discrepancy between the two foregoing experimental results naturally stimulated a good deal of research. Although all of the issues have not been fully resolved, some important advances have been made. There are at least two variables that account for the differences. The first concerns the nature of the stimuli used in these studies. Nairne and Rescorla (1981) demonstrated in pigeons that when CS_2 and CS_1 were both visual stimuli, extinction of CS_1 caused a decline in CS_2 strength. When CS_1 was auditory, however, no effect of CS_1 extinction was observed on the strength of CS_2. One theory is that lights are more salient and attention-getting than tones. Birds, therefore, learn less well when CS_1 is a tone. Another is that birds process the properties of two stimuli better when they are of the same modality. Regardless o. the reason for this difference between rats and pigeons, the discrepancies are surely based in part on the methodology used, the responses of birds versus rats, and visual versus auditory CSs.[12]

INTERIM SUMMARY

Second-order (or higher-order) conditioning occurs when a second CS (CS_2) acquires the ability to elicit the CR because it has been paired with an already powerful CS, not a US. The power of CS_2 depends on the contiguous pairings of CS_1 and the US, and of the two CSs. The inter-stimulus interval is an important dimension. Stronger second-order conditioning is achieved through variations in the CS_1–US interval, as well as the interval between CS_2 and CS_1. Furthermore, the similarity and spatial contiguity of the two stimuli, the US intensity, and the consistency of the CS_2 and CS_1 pairings affect second-order conditioning strength. Some theorists argue that second-order conditioning represents the association between CS_2 and the response to CS_1 (S–R association). Others claim, however, that CS_2 becomes associated with the memory, or mental representation, of CS_1 (S–S theory). Evidence for both positions has been obtained.

SENSORY PRECONDITIONING

An important Pavlovian phenomenon, closely related to second-order conditioning, is sensory preconditioning.[13] **Sensory preconditioning** occurs when two CSs are paired. No behavioral reactions are obvious at this time because the two CSs are innocuous stimuli and thus do not evoke such reactions. It therefore appears that no learning takes place. The two stimuli, however, are becoming associated. This fact is evident on a later test, when one of them is paired with a US, and the other is shown to evoke the CR as well.

The structure of the sensory preconditioning experiment is virtually the same as that for a second-order conditioning study, except for the fact that Stages 1 and 2 are reversed (see Figure 5-8). Specifically, the sensory precon-ditioning (experimental) group receives CS_2–CS_1 pairings in Phase 1, receives CS_1–US pairings in Phase 2, and then is tested for the power of the CS_2 in Phase 3. Control subjects are given random presentations of the cues during either Phase 1 or Phase 2. A good example of sensory preconditioning, by Riz-ley and Rescorla (1972), employed three groups of rats, a light as CS_2, a tone for CS_1, and a shock US.[14] The CS_2 was followed by the shock during the test, so the measure of CS_2 strength was the facilitation of learning during this phase, rather than simply whether it triggered a CR.[15] Control group 1 was given unpaired presentations of the light and tone in Phase 1. Because the two stimuli were not consistently paired, the light could not serve as a predictive signal for the tone and thus could not become associated with it. Control group 2 received paired presentations of the two CSs in Phase 1, but unpaired

	Treatment		
Phase	Experimental	Control 1	Control 2
1	$CS_2 - CS_1$	Random CS_1, CS_2 presentations	$CS_2 - CS_1$
2	$CS_1 - US$	$CS_1 - US$	Random CS_1, US presentations
Test	CS_2	CS_2	CS_2

FIGURE 5-8. Schematic diagram showing the treatments given in the stages of a sensory preconditioning experiment.

presentations of the tone and shock in Phase 2. Here, the light and tone became associated, but the tone could not acquire predictive power in Phase 2 (because it was presented randomly with respect to shock), and therefore the light should not elicit a reaction in Phase 3.

The results of the study are shown in Figure 5-9. Although the two control groups showed some response suppression on the first block of test trials, more substantial suppression of lever pressing was shown by the experimental subjects. This comparatively greater suppression was evident throughout

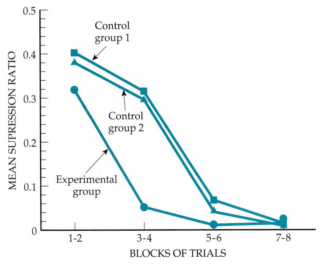

FIGURE 5-9. Mean suppression ratio, as a function of blocks of trials during the sensory preconditioning test phase for the experimental and control groups (after Rizley & Rescorla, 1972).

the entire series of sessions (except for the last block of trials). The reason why the light elicited a stronger reaction in the experimental subjects is because it had associative power, as a result of the prior treatment in Phase 1.

The importance of the sensory preconditioning phenomenon is similar to that for second-order conditioning. An association may develop between two stimuli, even though neither stimulus is a powerful, biologically relevant cue. The contiguous occurrence of *any* two stimuli, even two innocuous CSs, is sufficient to produce an association. Implications for human behavior are far-reaching. Humans have countless associations between words and images that are not based on food, shock, or other biologically related stimuli. Sensory preconditioning demonstrates that associations may develop without the need for reflex-producing USs.

Factors Affecting Sensory Preconditioning

Sensory preconditioning has not been studied as thoroughly as second-order conditioning, but some interesting information has emerged.

Interstimulus Interval.

One important variable is the interstimulus interval, specifically the interval between CS_2 and CS_1 during Phase 1. The optimal interval, at least for some kinds of conditioning arrangements, is about 4 seconds, with strength decreasing at both shorter and longer interstimulus intervals.[16]

A related finding is that the simultaneous presentation of the two CSs in Phase 1 produces a stronger association between them than a successive presentation. Recall from Chapter 4 that simultaneous presentation of a CS and a US typically produces weak excitatory conditioning. Here, however, the effect is reversed. Simultaneous presentation of CS_2 and CS_1 is superior to a forward arrangement.[17] The effect is noticed particularly when using flavor CSs.[18] The most likely explanation is that the subjects represent or process the flavor mixture as a single stimulus. Later, learning about each flavor separately is facilitated because the flavors had been experienced as part of a single, more holist stimulus.[19]

Number of Trials.

A second variable that affects sensory preconditioning is the extent of training. Unlike regular conditioning involving a US, sensory preconditioning reaches its maximum strength within only a few trials. In a study by Prewitt (1967), for example, four pairings of the two CSs were sufficient to produce the maximum effect; additional pairings of CS_2 and CS_1 were superfluous. This occurs because other processes develop with continued training—for example, *habituation*, which is a decline in reactivity to a stimulus. More specifically, when CS_2 and CS_1 are paired, they become associated with each other rather quickly, but because no important biological events occur, the subjects also habituate, or become accustomed to the stimuli. This, in turn, causes the subject to cease paying attention to the CSs (see the following discussion).[20]

Motivational State.

Finally, the subject's motivational state, such as the presence of hunger or thirst, affects sensory preconditioning. Sensory preconditioning is stronger if the subjects are hungry during Phase 1 than if they are satiated.[21] The motivational state at the time of the testing is important, too. For example, if a sudden need for salt is created just prior to the test, then flavors that had previously been associated with salt become preferred, although they are not preferred under normal conditions.[22]

Theories of Sensory Preconditioning

One theory of sensory preconditioning is that it represents a chain of associations. During Phase 1, the two CSs become linked; during Phase 2, the CS_1 and the US become associated; then, during the test, CS_2 elicits the memory of CS_1, which, in turn, elicits the memory of the US and the corresponding CR. In other words, CS_2 evokes the memory of CS_1, which then triggers the expectation of the US and the corresponding CR. In a sense, the second phase of the sensory preconditioning experiment is used only to create some measurable performance. Without such a phase, no overt behavior is available to use as an index of changes in association strength.

Another theory, called the "acquired-equivalence notion," claims that CSs become associated because they share common elements; that is, each stimulus is actually associated with a common third stimulus.[23] This third shared element binds the two CSs together and causes one to elicit a CR following the training of the other. To test this idea, Honey and Hall (1991) varied the degree to which the two CSs shared a common third stimulus. One group of subjects received a weak hydrochloric acid and quinine mixture, which was followed by a sucrose–saline mixture during Phase 1. The other group received the hydrochloric acid plus quinine mixture followed by a sucrose–quinine mixture (the hydrochloric acid and sucrose mixture share a common element—namely, quinine). During conditioning, the hydrochloric acid solution by itself was paired with lithium chloride (poison) for both groups. Finally, the strength of the sucrose was tested. If the sucrose (which had never been paired with the lithium chloride) is associated with the hydrochloric acid because it shares a common flavor element—namely, quinine—then the subjects in the common element group should show a greater aversion to the sucrose than the subjects in the control group. If, however, sucrose and hydrochloric acid are not strongly associated, then the aversion to the sucrose should be relatively weak.

The results of the study showed that consumption was 14.8 milliliters when there had been a shared flavor element. In the control group that did not share a flavor element, consumption of sucrose was 19.2 milliliters, considerably more. Thus, sucrose elicited greater aversion (less consumption) when it was associated with a component that was also included in the hydrochloric acid mixture. This suggests that sensory preconditioning occurs because subjects generalize from one stimulus to the other, based on shared elements.

INTERIM SUMMARY

Sensory preconditioning occurs when two CSs are paired. Behavior is not normally observed at this time. If, however, CS_1 is then paired with a US, thus generating overt performance, CS_2 also has the ability to elicit the CR. Sensory preconditioning thus indicates that the contiguous occurrence of any two stimuli, not just CSs and powerful USs, results in an association. Many of the same factors that affect conventional Pavlovian learning also affect sensory preconditioning, such as the interstimulus interval, the number of training trials, and the motivational state of the animal. The prevailing theory argues that sensory preconditioning represents a chain of associations. The CS_2 evokes the memory of CS_1, which then triggers the expectation of the US and the corresponding CR. The acquired-equivalence theory claims that two stimuli elicit a common CR when they share an association with the same element.

OCCASION SETTING

Chapters 3 and 4 focused on two traditional kinds of Pavlovian associations: excitation and inhibition. Recall that conditioned inhibition occurs when a stimulus signals the cancellation or nonoccurrence of the US. In a typical study, CS_E (excitatory CS) is followed by the US, but on other trials, CS_I (inhibitory CS) accompanies CS_E, and the combination is followed by no US. The subject responds to CS_E when it is presented alone but shows little responding to CS_E when it is accompanied by CS_I. The inhibitor is said to cancel or reduce what would otherwise be an excitatory reaction.

Consider the converse manipulation. On some trials, two stimuli—CS_E and CS_F (facilitator or occasion setter), given either sequentially or simultaneously—are followed by a US. On other trials, the CS_E is given by itself; no US is presented. Rather than signaling the cancellation of the US (as a conditioned inhibitor does), CS_F signals that the US will indeed be presented following CS_E. The CS_F is an **occasion setter** (also termed a **facilitator**). The occasion setter, in itself, does not function as an excitatory stimulus, but rather, it sets the occasion for, or facilitates, the conditioning of another stimulus. The subject responds to the conditioned excitor but *only* if CS_E is accompanied by the occasion setter. The occasion setter, in summary, signals that the conditioned excitor will be followed by the US; without the CS_F occurrence, CS_E will not be followed by the US.[24]

Example of Occasion Setting

A demonstration of occasion setting was shown by Rescorla (1985). Pigeons were given a blue key light followed by an "X" pattern on a white background (each stimulus lasted 5 seconds, and the two were separated by a 5-second white light). On each training session, 12 blue-X-food trials, and 12 X-only trials occurred.[25] If the blue key light becomes an occasion setter—that is, if it modulates the conditioning of the target stimulus ("X" pattern)—then differences in responding to the target pattern should occur, depending on whether the occasion setter (facilitator) is presented. As shown in Figure 5-10, CS_F itself elicited little responding. The occasion-setting role of CS_F, however, is noted in the other two conditions. Responding to the target stimulus was higher when it followed (or was accompanied by) CS_F, than it was when it was presented by itself. Thus, the occasion setter "set the occasion" for, or facilitated, the association between the CS_E and the US.

Properties of an Occasion Setter

The characteristics of occasion setters have been studied in numerous investigations.

Facilitation Versus Excitation.

One interesting finding is that a cue's role as an occasion setter is independent from its role as excitor. Rescorla (1985), for example, gave three kinds of trials over a 16-session period. An orange key light (stimulus A) combined

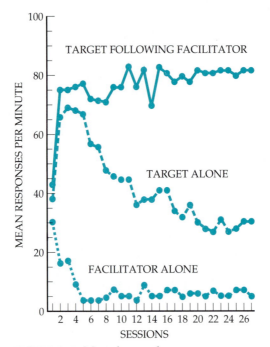

FIGURE 5-10. Mean key-peck responses per minute during the autoshaping sessions to the target stimulus when it was presented alone or following the occasion setter, and to the occasion setter itself (after Rescorla, 1985).

with a hissing noise (stimulus B) were followed by food presentation; the orange key light by itself was followed by nothing; and a house light (stimulus B′) was followed by food. The house light and the orange key light were both excitatory CSs. The noise, however, was an occasion setter because it accompanied the key light and signaled that food would follow. Various tests were then conducted. In particular, Rescorla measured pecking to the orange key light when it was given by itself (A), or when it was combined with either the noise (AB) or the house light (AB′).

The results are shown in Figure 5-11. First, few responses were made to A alone, but appreciable responding was shown to A when it was compounded with the occasion setter (condition AB). Thus, B functioned as a facilitator in promoting substantial conditioning to A. Second, responding to A when it was combined with the other excitatory stimulus B′ was weak, indicating that B′, although a perfectly adequate excitatory stimulus, did not function as an occasion setter. In short, excitation and occasion setting are independent processes. A cue may acquire the ability to elicit a reaction (excitation) without developing the ability to facilitate conditioning to a different CS (occasion setting).

What about the converse case? Do occasion setters develop the properties of an excitor? Rescorla (1985) also examined this question. Subjects were given the same training as described previously (A, AB, and B′ trials). Then a different color key light was presented, followed by the noise (B) or the house light (B′). This procedure is the same as that used to create second-order conditioning (pairing of a novel CS with an already powerful CS). Thus, if either B or

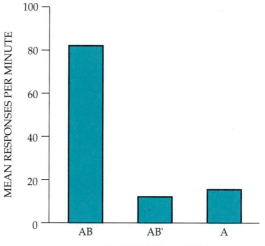

FIGURE 5-11. Mean responses per minute to the orange key light (stimulus A) on the test when given alone (A), or in combination with the noise (AB) or the house light (AB′) (after Rescorla, 1985).

B′ is an excitor, then it should serve as a source of power for the second-order conditioning of the new color key light. If, however, B or B′ does not have excitatory strength, then autoshaped key pecking to the new color should not occur.

The results are shown in Figure 5-12. Rate of key pecking was low when the new key light was paired with the occasion setter (B). Apparently, the occasion setter did not have sufficient excitatory power to cause second-order conditioning to occur. Key pecking, however, increased when the new color was paired with the excitatory cue (B′). Again, facilitation and excitation develop independently.[26]

Transfer of Facilitation.

A second characteristic is that facilitation or occasion setting generalizes from one CS to another.[27] For example, if CS_B facilitates responding to CS_A, it will also facilitate responding to CS_C (a new excitatory CS not previously preceded by the occasion setter) although the strength of facilitation may be reduced somewhat. Moreover, the transfer of facilitation from one CS to another does not depend on the sensory modalities of the CSs. Auditory stimuli facilitate conditioning of light CSs just as easily as they facilitate the conditioning of other auditory CSs.

Temporal Factors Affecting Facilitation.

Occasion setting has been investigated in terms of the temporal relationship between A and B. Again, conventional procedures involving auditory and

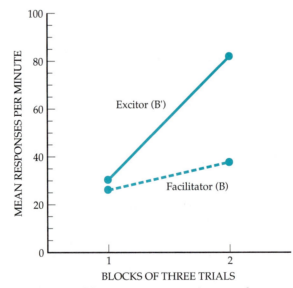

FIGURE 5-12. Mean response per minute to the new color key light, as a function of blocks of three trials when the key light was paired with either the former excitor (B′) or the occasion setter (B) (after Rescorla, 1985).

visual stimuli have been used.[28] First, when A and B are given simultaneously, then B, the occasion setter, actually derives excitatory strength. This is not surprising because both A and B are equally contiguous with reward. Second, when the onset of B occurs prior to the onset of A, then B becomes an occasion setter, not an excitor. The longer the interstimulus interval between B and A, especially if the offset of B occurs prior to the onset of A, the stronger the occasion setter. According to Holland (1986a) "occasion setting is encouraged whenever a perceptual discontinuity in the stream of events occurs" (p. 118).[29] The more that B is perceptually isolated from the A–US pairing, the better it functions as an occasion setter. When B cannot serve effectively as a signal for A–US episodes—for example, when it is given simultaneously with A—then B acquires excitatory strength.

INTERIM SUMMARY

Occasion setters (also called "facilitators") are CSs that set the occasion for, or facilitate, the conditioning of another CS. The excitor and occasion setter together are followed by a US; on alternative trials, the excitor is given by itself. Superior learning is demonstrated by a higher level of responding to a target (excitatory) CS when that cue is accompanied by an occasion setter than when it occurs by itself. Facilitation and occasion setting are independent processes. When a cue is trained to perform one function, the other function does not automatically occur. Furthermore, occasion setters transfer their facilitating power to other CSs.

LATENT INHIBITION

Second-order conditioning and sensory preconditioning show that USs are not needed for associations to develop. Even a CS given by itself may involve learning. **Latent inhibition** (also termed the **CS preexposure effect**) is a process that occurs when CSs are given by themselves prior to conditioning.[30]

Latent inhibition experiments usually have three phases. In Phase 1, the preexposure phase, the to-be-conditioned CS is given by itself to the experimental subjects. Control animals are simply placed in the apparatus but are not given the CS. In Phase 2, excitatory conditioning is given to both groups; that is, the CS is now paired with a US. The strength of the CS is shown either during Phase 2 (in terms of rate of excitatory conditioning) or on a separate test in Phase 3. What is found is retardation of conditioning in the group that experienced CS preexposure.

Latent inhibition has been demonstrated in many organisms, using many different kinds of CSs.[31] A good example is a study by Hall and Minor (1984), using the CER technique.[32] First, the authors trained thirsty rats to lick drops of water from a metal drinking tube. After the licking rate had stabilized, one group was given three sessions in the apparatus, during which a 79-dB, 2,000-Hz tone was presented five times per session. No behavior was recorded, or even evident, at this time.[33] A control group was placed in the apparatus for an equal amount of time, but the tone was never sounded. Following the pre-exposure phase, all subjects were given the tone followed by a brief shock to the foot. Under normal conditions, it requires only one such CS–US pairing to make the tone aversive. Finally, all subjects were tested for the strength of the tone. This was accomplished by placing each rat in the apparatus and allowing it to complete 100 licks of water. After a 1-minute prestimulus period, the tone came on for an additional 1 minute. The suppression ratio was the number of licks made during the tone, divided by the total licks (during and preceding the tone).

The results are shown in Figure 5-13. The group that experienced tone pre-exposure showed virtually no aversion; their CER ratio was close to .5. Apparently, something had occurred during the preexposure phase to cause attenuation of fear conditioning. The control group, in contrast, showed strong suppression of licking, indicating that the tone had become aversive after a single tone–shock pairing.

Latent inhibition is important for the adaptive survival of an organism. Learning allows an animal to form associations between stimuli and their consequences, based on the informational relationship between them. If stimuli are consistently meaningless, however—that is, if they are never followed by any biologically meaningful event—then, from an evolutionary point of view, the stimuli should be ignored. Attempting to learn about them wastes time and energy. A process that causes the animal to discount, or disregard, such stimuli would be highly adaptive. In short, innocuous stimuli that have no important consequences are likely, in nature, to continue to have no important consequences. If, later on, these stimuli reappear, it is advantageous for the animal *not* to process them extensively. This is revealed as a retardation of learning.

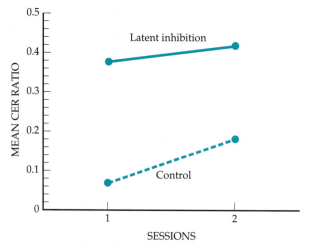

FIGURE 5-13. Mean CER ratio (suppression of licking) on two test sessions for the latent inhibition and control groups (after Hall & Minor, 1984).

Variables That Affect Latent Inhibition

Many of the variables that affect retardation of learning are concerned with the nature of the CS and its mode of presentation.

Number of Preexposures.

One variable that affects the degree of retardation is the number of CS preexposures. The picture is complicated, however. With taste aversions, retardation occurs even with a single CS preexposure.[34] Both the acquisition of an aversion to a flavor, and the retardation of aversion learning with flavor preexposure, occur very rapidly.[35] In contrast, a minimum of about 16 to 20 preexposure trials is normally required to produce a latent-inhibition effect, as measured by the CER technique.[36] Beyond this minimum number, retardation of learning is a graded function of the number of CS-preexposure trials. The greater the number of CS-preexposure trials, the greater the retardation of learning later on.

In a study by Lubow, Wagner, and Weiner (1982), for example, thirsty rats were first taught to press a lever to receive a drop of water as a reward. Groups were then given 0, 20, 40, or 80 preexposures to a tone–light compound CS, followed by 4 classical conditioning trials involving the tone–light compound and a 0.4-milliamp shock. In Phase 3, subjects were tested for their aversion to the CS compound, using suppression of lever pressing as the index of aversion.[37] The suppression ratios for the two tone–light presentations are shown in Figure 5-14. The disruption of lever pressing was quite severe for the 0-preexposure group. However, the other groups showed the CS-preexposure effect to various degrees.[38]

A different picture is seen when considering the conditioning of skeletal responses such as eye-blink reactions. Although the relationship between number of preexposures and retardation is the same, the absolute number of preexposures required to produce the retardation effect is much greater.[39]

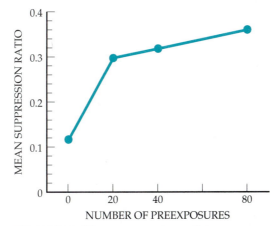

FIGURE 5-14. Mean suppression ratio, as a function of the number of CS preexposures (after Lubow, Wagner, & Weiner, 1982).

CS Duration.

The magnitude of the CS-preexposure effect increases with longer CS durations during the preexposure phase. The problem is that the number of preexposures and the duration are often confounded. The greater the number of CSs given, the longer the total duration of the preexposure. In a study by Domjan (1972), however, a saccharin solution was infused into the oral cavity of a rat, via a surgically implanted cannula.[40] Each subject got a fixed amount of solution, but the rate of infusion differed, thus creating differences in flavor-exposure duration (2.8, 6.7, or 13.3 minutes). In Phase 2, the saccharin flavor was paired with lithium chloride, and a preference test was given. Duration itself has a strong effect. Specifically, aversion learning was attenuated in subjects who received the longer CS preexposure duration, relative to those who were given a short duration of preexposure.

The duration of the CS preexposure, however, interacts with the number of preexposure trials. With few trials, retardation of learning occurs with long CS durations. With many preexposure trials, retardation occurs even with short CS durations. It makes no difference whether the preexposure involves many trials of short duration or few trials with a longer CS duration.[41] What matters is simply the total preexposure time.

A good demonstration of this was an experiment by Ayres, Philbin, Cassidy, Bellino, and Redlinger (1992). Total exposure to a light CS was equated across groups (all subjects got 14,400 seconds of CS preexposure), but the number and duration of exposures varied. Some subjects, for example, were preexposed to many short CSs, whereas others were given fewer long CSs. Following the preexposure sessions, all subjects got four days of CER conditioning, in which the light was paired with a shock, and suppression of ongoing lever pressing was examined.

The results are shown in Figure 5-15. The 0-duration group (no preexposure) showed significant suppression, even on the first test session, confirming that retardation of learning is absent if no CS preexposure is given. The preexposed groups, however, showed a different pattern. No suppression was evident on the first day of testing (conditioning was retarded, relative to the 0-duration control subjects), although aversive conditioning did increase over the next three testing days. The important point is that virtually no differences were observed among any of the preexposed groups. Although both the number of trials and the CS durations affect the strength of the retardation, both factors are entirely subordinate to the more important principle—namely, that retardation of learning increases as a function of total exposure time to the CS.

CS Intensity.

One interesting characteristic of the latent inhibition phenomenon is that it is positively, not negatively, related to the CS intensity: the stronger the CS, the greater the retardation.[42] In a study by Crowell and Anderson (1972), groups were first preexposed to a noise CS that differed in intensity (either 70 or 100 dB).[43] A control group was not given any preexposure to the noise.

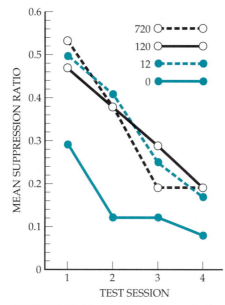

FIGURE 5-15. Mean suppression ratio for groups that got CS durations of 0, 12, 120, or 720 seconds. The total preexposure time was 14,400 seconds for all subjects (after Ayres, Philbin, Cassidy, Bellino, & Redlinger, 1992).

Then, in Phase 2, the noise and a shock US were paired in a separate box. In Phase 3, testing was done in the preexposure apparatus. Suppression of licking was observed in all subjects, but less suppression (weaker conditioning) was observed in the group that received preexposure to the more intense CS. In other words, the stronger the preexposed CS, the more learning is retarded to that CS later on.

Attenuation of Latent Inhibition.

There are two interesting treatments that attenuate the effects of CS preexposure on later learning. The first involves following the CS during the preexposure phase by a second CS. That is, rather than merely preexposing the to-be-conditioned CS by itself, two stimuli follow in rapid succession. Here, latent inhibition fails to develop; conditioning in Phase 2 is not retarded.[44]

The second manipulation that reduces the level of retardation is a change in the context from the preexposure to the training phase. In most studies, preexposure and training are conducted in the same apparatus. If, however, the conditioning takes place in a novel apparatus, then retardation of learning is not observed. The CS preexposure effect is context specific.[45] One experiment by Lovibond, Preston, and Mackintosh (1984), for example, used two environments that differed in terms of their odor (banana versus eucalyptus extracts), visual appearance (continuous overhead lighting versus no light), and the food reinforcement used to establish lever pressing (different flavored food). Preexposure to the CS (tone or flashing light) took place in one environment, whereas the CS–shock pairings were given either in the same context or in the alternative context. A control group did not receive any preexposure to the CS.

The results are shown in Figure 5-16. Retardation of learning was demonstrated in both preexposure groups. That is, suppression was minimal on the first two trials, compared to the suppression in the no-preexposure control subjects. During the last two conditioning trials, however, the group that received conditioning in a novel environment showed greater suppression than the group that received conditioning in the same context. In other words, shifting to a new environment for the training phase reduced the level of retardation.

Theories of Latent Inhibition

Many psychologists have attempted to explain why learning is retarded following CS preexposure.

Conditioned Inhibition.

One of the earliest speculations was that the preexposed CS becomes a conditioned inhibitor during the preexposure phase. After all, the CS is not

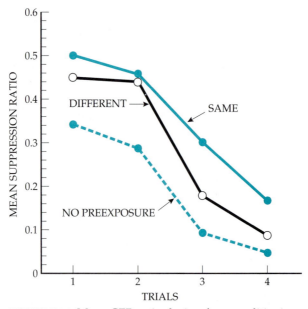

FIGURE 5-16. Mean CER ratio during four conditioning trials for groups that received conditioning in the same or different environment from that used during the CS preexposure phase; controls were not given CS preexposure (after Lovibond, Preston, & Mackintosh, 1984).

followed by a US during the preexposure phase, so it is reasonable to suspect that it develops inhibitory properties. Early research discovered that this was not the case, however.[46] The reason is simple. If the CS is indeed a conditioned inhibitor as a result of the preexposure phase, then conditioning of that cue later on in a conditioned-inhibition experiment should be facilitated, not retarded. Research shows, however, that conditioning of *any* sort, either excitatory *or* inhibitory, is more difficult after CS preexposure.

Habituation.

A second theory is the habituation theory. **Habituation** is a waning of the orienting response (OR) with repeated presentations of a CS. If, say, a light is repeatedly given, the animal initially shows an orienting reaction (pupil constriction, or turning of the head), but with continued presentation, the OR subsides. There is a marked similarity between habituation and the CS preexposure effect in terms of the procedure, but the processes underlying the two are decidedly different.[47]

First, habituation is a waning of the OR *during* the preexposure phase, whereas latent inhibition involves the retardation of conditioning *after* the preexposure phase. Second, only about five presentations are required to eliminate the OR to a tone, but about 25 presentations are needed to retard future learning.[48] If latent inhibition simply involved the decline of the OR, then it should be no harder to produce retardation of learning than to produce habituation to the OR.

The habituation theory was studied directly by Hall and Schachtman (1987).[49] Experimental subjects were given 16 days of CS preexposure (10 presentations of light CS per session). Two control groups of rats were retained in their home cages during this phase. In Phase 2, the experimental subjects now rested in their home cages. Control group 1, however, was given 16 days of light preexposure and control group 2 was simply placed in the apparatus during Phase 2, but not given any preexposure to the light. In all of the sessions, the orienting reaction to the light was assessed in terms of whether the subject brought its snout within a specified distance from the light. On the following day, all subjects were given a test session where the light CS was presented and the ORs were recorded.

Results are shown in Figure 5-17. ORs were observed, but they declined over the course of preexposure. This was observed for subjects in both the experimental group (Phase 1 on the left) and Control group 1 (Phase 2 on the right). Subjects in Control group 2 did not orient toward the light in Phase 2 because they were not preexposed to it (movements of their snout toward the light were assessed at comparable times merely to provide a basis for comparison).

The interesting data occurred on the test session, shown at the right of Figure 5-17. The group that had just previously received preexposure (Control group 1) showed little orientation toward the light. For those animals, the test was little more than an additional preexposure session. However, the experimental subjects, who received preexposure during Phase 1 and then nothing during Phase 2, showed very strong orientation to the light. Thus, the

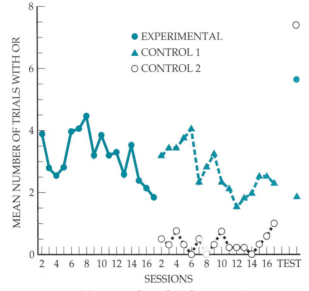

FIGURE 5-17. Mean number of trials per session on which an OR occurred during both stages of the experiment and during the habituation test (after Hall & Schachtman, 1987).

experimental animals showed spontaneous recovery of the OR; the 16-day waiting period in the home cage during Phase 2 was sufficient to restore the habituated OR.

Was the waiting period sufficient to eliminate the retardation of learning due to latent inhibition, however? That question was examined in Phase 3. Here, all subjects were given a conditioning session in which the light was followed by food. The measure of conditioning was the number of times that each subject poked its nose behind the flap that covered the food dish. If the light was a conditioned excitor, then it should elicit the nose-poke reaction. If, however, latent inhibition was still present, the rate of learning the nose-poke reaction should be retarded. No difference in learning was found between the two preexposed groups (experimental and control 1). Conditioned nose poking increased over the five days of training to an equivalent extent. Thus, the experiment demonstrates that groups may differ in terms of the level of habituation of the OR (Figure 5-17, test results), but not in terms of retardation of learning. This implies that habituation and latent inhibition involve different processes. The CS preexposure produces habituation of the OR *and* retardation of learning later on, but the two outcomes are due to different underlying processes.

Information-Processing Models.

Many theorists have explained the CS-preexposure effect in terms of a loss of attention. Simply stated, presentation of a CS normally causes a subject to process that stimulus—that is, to pay attention to it. When the CS is not followed by a US, however, the attention value of the CS declines, and, correspondingly, its ability to become associated in the future declines. Several specific formulations of this theory have been offered and because some of these are discussed more fully in Chapter 6, they are only briefly covered here.

One theory argued that if a CS is a good predictor of its consequences, then it becomes more associable, and its excitatory strength increases.[50] Associable here means that subjects pay greater attention to it and thus mentally process the stimulus to a greater degree. When the CS does not predict the US—that is, when it is preexposed—then its associability (attention value) declines, and future conditioning of that CS becomes more difficult.[51]

Conditioned-Attention Theory.

A similar theory is Lubow's **conditioned-attention theory.**[52] According to this position, animals naturally pay attention to and process stimuli. The strength of such an attention response increases when a stimulus predicts an important consequence but declines when it predicts no consequence. With repeated CS preexposures, attention to the CS declines even further. The theory, however, makes an additional stipulation. The inattention reaction itself may be conditioned to the apparatus or context. Thus, subjects fail to attend to a CS in the future because the context elicits a conditioned inattention reaction. Further, because the subjects are not paying attention to the CS, they fail to learn that it now is followed by a US.

The conditioned-attention theory easily accounts for many of the findings discussed previously. For example, retardation of learning declines if the CS is followed by another CS during the preexposure phase. According to the conditioned attention theory, the added CS is an attention-getting event. It preserves the subject's attention reaction to the first CS and thus eliminates the retardation of learning later on.

A second finding that supports the conditioned-attention theory is the fact that retardation of learning is eliminated when the context is changed.[53] Testing the animal in a new environment (different from the one used during preexposure) eliminates the conditioned-inattention reaction. Attention to the CS, and thus learning, therefore proceed as usual.

Latent Inhibition as Retrieval Failure.

All of the aforementioned theories claim that subjects fail to acquire an association during conditioning because CS preexposure alters their processing of, and attention to, the cue. An interesting series of findings suggests that the retardation effect may not actually be a failure to learn at all. According to Miller's **retrieval-failure hypothesis,** animals learn during the training phase perfectly well, but they fail to retrieve the memory, and thus, they fail to demonstrate the learning during the test (see also Chapter 14).

Consider the following evidence for the retrieval theory, published by Kasprow, Catterson, Schachtman, and Miller (1984).[54] Their experimental design is shown in Figure 5-18. Three groups of subjects were used. The Experimental group was given preexposure to a noise for eight sessions (these were

Phase	Experimental		Control 1		Control 2	
1	CS preexposure		No treatment		CS preexposure	
2	CS–US		CS–US		Random CS and US presentations	
Reminder trial	Yes	No	Yes	No	Yes	No
Test	CS		CS		CS	

FIGURE 5-18. Treatments given to the experimental and control groups in the study on latent inhibition by Kasprow, Catterson, Schachtman, and Miller (1984).

the latent-inhibition subjects). Control group 1 was given no preexposure to the noise; they were simply placed in the apparatus during Phase 1 for an equivalent time period. Finally, Control group 2 was given the CS preexposure (these animals were treated differently later on).

In Phase 2, the latent inhibition and no-preexposure subjects (Experimental and Control 1 groups) were given conventional conditioning involving four noise–shock pairings. Control group 2, which had also received CS preexposure, was given random CS and US presentations. On the day following the conditioning phase, half of the subjects in each of the three groups was given a reminder trial. Here, subjects were placed in a discriminably different apparatus and were given a brief shock. No noise CS was given, so additional learning between the CS and the US was not possible. Presumably the function of the reminder shock was to reinstate the subjects' memory of the previous CS–US pairings. The other half of each of the three groups was simply placed in the apparatus; they were not given any reminder shock.

Finally, in Phase 4, all subjects were placed back into the original apparatus and were given a test. Here, they were allowed to lick a water tube 25 times, after which the noise CS was presented. The time taken to complete an additional 25 licks was measured.

The results are shown in Figure 5-19. First, consider the subjects who did not receive a reminder trial (left panel). The small latency value shown by the latent inhibition group (Experimental) relative to the nonpreexposed subjects (Control group 1) shows the usual retardation-of-learning effect. The CS preexposure had caused retarded learning in the experimental subjects, and thus they showed no suppression of drinking. Subjects in control group 1 took appreciably longer to drink because the CS was aversive and thus caused disruption of drinking. Subjects in Control group 2, who also were preexposed to the noise but were given random CS and US presentations during the conditioning phase, also showed little suppression of drinking on the test. Their deficit, however, could be due to the facts either that they received the CS pre-

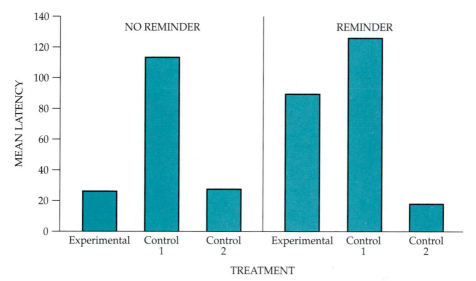

FIGURE 5-19. Mean latency to complete 25 licks in the presence of the noise CS on the test trial, as a function of the treatment during preexposure, conditioning, and reminder phases (after Kasprow, Catterson, Schachtman, & Miller, 1984).

exposure (and thus were expressing the latent inhibition result) or that they received random CS and US presentations in Phase 1 (and thus had not developed an association).

Now consider the results for the subjects who got a reminder treatment (right panel). The preexposed subjects (Experimental group) showed much less of a deficit; their latency to drink was nearly as long as the subjects in control group 1. It was certainly longer than the latency demonstrated by the experimental subjects who did not receive a reminder. The reminder trial, therefore, almost completely eliminated the retardation effect. The preexposed control group 2 subjects (who got random CS and US presentations plus the reminder trial) continued to show the deficit in performance. Thus, the reminder itself was not sufficient to cause the lack of suppression, although it did reinstate the memory for those animals who had been conditioned following preexposure. In conclusion, retardation of learning following CS preexposure may not be due to a deficit in learning ability, but rather to a deficit in memory retrieval.[55] When the animals are reminded of their previous learning, they show almost normal performance despite having been preexposed to the CS earlier.

INTERIM SUMMARY

When CSs are given by themselves prior to conditioning, a phenomenon called "latent inhibition" occurs. Here, future excitatory (or inhibitory) learning to the CS is retarded. Generally, the more preexposures, the greater the retardation of learning. The duration of the CS, however, is important as well. In fact, many preexposures of a short CS are equivalent to a few preexposures of a long CS. Interestingly, the stronger the CS during preexposure, the greater the retardation of learning later on. Latent inhibition is attenuated if the CS is followed by a second cue during the preexposure phase, or if the context is changed between preexposure and conditioning. Such effects support the conditioned-attention theory of latent inhibition, which argues that subjects become inattentive to the CS during preexposure and that the inattention reaction is conditioned to the surrounding context. Thus, after the context changes, or when attention is maintained by the inclusion of a second CS during preexposure, latent inhibition is no longer evident. Other theories include the habituation theory, which links latent inhibition to the declining OR during preexposure, and the retrieval-failure theory, which argues that the inability to learn following preexposure is primarily the result of a failure to remember.

BLOCKING

One of the most interesting and theoretically important Pavlovian phenomena is **blocking.** Recall from the discussion in Chapter 3 that modern Pavlovian theory focuses more on the information value of the CS than on its contiguity with a US. Blocking confirms and extends this principle; moreover, it has provided a testing ground for modern theories of Pavlovian conditioning.

Consider what happens in a conditioning experiment when a compound CS is used (the compound is the simultaneous presentation of two separate CS elements, such as a light and a tone). Pavlovian theory, based simply on the concept of contiguity, suggests that each element in the compound develops an association with the US; after all, both elements are equally contiguous with the US. Under normal circumstances, this is generally true; each element of a compound CS does indeed acquire associative strength.[56] The blocking phenomenon shows, however, that the strength of the association that develops to one element of a compound CS depends very much on the strength of the other element in the compound.

Blocking of Excitation

The blocking phenomenon was first explored by Kamin (1969) using a CER procedure. As shown in Figure 5-20, Kamin's research design involved three phases. The blocking group received normal noise–shock pairings in Phase 1, followed, in Phase 2, by the compound trials. Here, the light–noise CS compound was paired with the shock. The control group was given no treatment in Phase 1 and then the same compound CS training in Phase 2 as that received by the experimental group. All rats were then tested in Phase 3. Here, they were allowed to press the lever for food, during which time the light ele-

	Treatments	
Phase	Experimental	Control
1	CS_A–US	No treatment
2	CS_A/CS_X–US	CS_A/CS_X–US
Test	CS_X	CS_X

FIGURE 5-20. Schematic diagram showing the phases of a blocking experiment.

ment (not the compound) was presented. The measure of strength of the light was the suppression ratio. The crucial issue was whether, during Phase 2, in the blocking group, the strength of the light would be affected by the prior conditioning to the noise.[57]

The results are shown in Figure 5-21. Suppression to the light was strong in the control subjects, indicating that the light had acquired substantial associative strength during the compound conditioning phase. The blocking subjects, however, who received noise–shock pairings prior to the compound conditioning phase, showed virtually no evidence of conditioning to the light. In other words, even though the light had been paired with the US in the

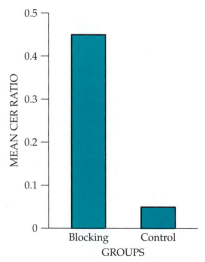

FIGURE 5-21. Mean suppression ratio elicited by the light CS on the CER test for the blocking and the control groups (after Kamin, 1969).

compound conditioning phase just as many times as in the control group, conditioning to the noise blocked conditioning to the light. When one CS became powerful (the noise), it later blocked conditioning to a second CS (the light), with which it was compounded. This blocking phenomenon has been shown in many experiments, using a wide variety of techniques, and in many different species, including human beings.

Blocking of Conditioned Inhibition

The blocking phenomenon is not limited to excitatory conditioning. Inhibitory CSs also may be blocked. Suiter and LoLordo (1971), for example, used a CER procedure to demonstrate this effect. The experimental rats received a light CS that consistently predicted no shock during Phase 1 (light was presented after shock offset). Thus, the light was an inhibitory CS−. The control subjects, on the other hand, received only the shock presentations during Phase 1; no CS elements were involved for those subjects. During Phase 2, both groups of subjects received inhibitory conditioning using a compound CS; specifically, a light and tone predicted the absence of shock. Finally, during Phase 3, the strength of the tone element was tested by pairing it with shock and observing how quickly it acquired excitatory strength (retardation-of-learning test, see Chapter 3).

If the tone had become a strong conditioned inhibitor during Phase 2, then excitatory conditioning should be retarded. If, on the other hand, inhibitory conditioning to the tone had been blocked by the light, then the tone CS should readily acquire excitatory strength during Phase 3. Results showed that excitatory conditioning to the tone took place readily in the experimental subjects. The inhibitory strength of the tone had been blocked by the light during Phase 2, thus allowing it to become excitatory quite easily.

In summary, a stimulus that undergoes conditioning (stimulus A) later blocks (that is, prevents conditioning to) a second stimulus element (stimulus X) when A and X occur simultaneously and are followed by the US. In other words, an added cue X fails to derive associative strength if the other element in the compound is already strong from a previous conditioning treatment, even though X is contiguous with the US during the compound conditioning phase. The important point about blocking, therefore, is that the strength of stimulus X is based not simply on its own relationship with the US (as the law of contiguity would suggest) but also on the strength of the *other* CS in the compound.

Overshadowing and Superconditioning

Overshadowing is a similar phenomenon to blocking. It occurs when one stimulus interferes with the conditioning of another with which it is compounded. As discussed in Chapter 4, a salient CS overshadows a less salient cue. The more intense a CS, the more it overshadows another CS.[58]

A CS element may also overshadow a second CS with which it is compounded because the first is stronger through conditioning. If, for example, one paired a light–noise compound with a US, and intermixed these trials with extra light–US pairings, thus making the light an even stronger excitor, then the tendency for the light to overshadow the noise increases. In other words, blocking is accomplished using a two-phased design (conditioning of CS_A *prior to* the conditioning of the compound). Overshadowing, however, involves only a single phase, during which extra trials (on which one of the elements is followed by the US) are interspersed among the compound trials, causing the one to overshadow the other.

Another important phenomenon related to overshadowing is **supercon-ditioning.** Here, some of the trials are compound trials (a compound CS such as a light–tone combination followed by the US), whereas others involve the presentation of one of the elements—say, the tone—explicitly paired with no US. The result is an inflation of strength of the light. Consider a study by Wagner (1969b).[59] Three groups of rabbits were given eyelid conditioning. Animals in the control group received 112 eyelid trials during which a compound CS (light–tone flashes) was followed by a mild shock. Subjects in Groups E and I received the same treatment (112 compound conditioning trials), but they also got extra trials interspersed among the compound trials. For Group E, the extra trials involved the light element followed by the shock (that is, excitatory training to the light). Subjects in Group I, on the other hand, received extra inhibitory trials to the light (light–no-US presentations). In the second phase, all groups were tested for conditioning strength to the tone.

The results are shown in Figure 5-22. The median percentage of CR elicited by the tone in the control subjects was about 30%. For Group E, CR strength was dramatically reduced; on only about 10% of the trials did the

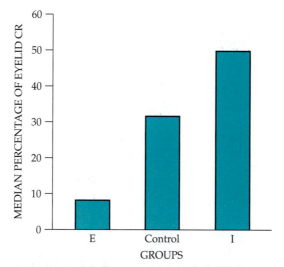

FIGURE 5-22. Median percentage of eyeblink responses to the tone CS by the control group, Group E (extra excitatory trials to the light) and Group I (extra inhibitory trials to the light CS) (after Wagner, 1969a).

tone elicit the CR. This finding demonstrates the overshadowing concept just described. Extra excitatory training to one stimulus (the light) reduced the strength of the target element in the compound (the tone).

The opposite effect was found in Group I. Here, strength of the tone was *enhanced* to about 50% because those subjects received extra inhibitory trials to the light stimulus. In other words, extra trials in which the light stimulus was exposed without the US made the light more inhibitory, thus enhancing the strength of the other element in the compound—that is, the tone. Such an enhancement, called "superconditioning," supports the conclusion made for blocking and overshadowing—namely, that the associative strength of a stimulus element depends not simply on its own relationship to the US, but also on the strength of other CS elements in the compound. If one element gains strength through extra excitatory trials, then the other element is weakened (overshadowing). If, on the other hand, the strength of one element is reduced through extra inhibitory trials, then the strength of the other is enhanced beyond that which occurs from the compound training trials alone (superconditioning). The explanation for superconditioning is based on the concept of overshadowing.[60] If the salience of one CS is reduced to the point that it no longer overshadows a target CS, then the target CS acquires even greater associative power during the compound conditioning phase.

Theories of Blocking

We only briefly review the theories of blocking in this section. A more detailed coverage is contained in Chapter 6, where the modern theories of Pavlovian conditioning are discussed.

Surprise.

Kamin (1968) originally suggested that conditioning occurs only if the animal is surprised by the US. In blocking, the animal learns to expect the US following CS_A in Phase 1. During the compound conditioning phase, the new target CS_X adds no unique information about the US; the animal is able to predict the US occurrence on the basis of the already conditioned CS_A in the compound. As a result, the subject does not process the added CS_X. In other words, during the initial phase of the study, CS_A becomes a good predictor of the US; during the compound conditioning phase, the added element is blocked because it is redundant.

The dependency of conditioning on surprise is perfectly consistent with an evolutionary perspective. Strong biological stimuli such as USs are precisely those environmental events that the subject needs to predict in order to survive and adapt. If a good predictor is already established, then it is wasted time and energy for added cues, which are redundant, to be processed; they do not provide the animal with any added advantage and therefore may safely be ignored.

If informational redundancy is the cause of blocking, then surprise is important for conditioning. Kamin's original work on blocking demonstrated, for example, that when the US is changed from Phase 1 to Phase 2, blocking does not occur. Specifically, if a noise is followed by a weak shock in Phase 1, and the light–noise compound is followed by a noticeably stronger shock in Phase 2 (relative to a group where the intensity of the US does not change), then the light acquires the normal amount of associative strength. The light has informational relevance (it predicts this new, more intense shock) and therefore is conditioned.

Even more compelling evidence has been shown by Holland (1984).[61] Rats were given a light in Phase 1, followed by one or three pellets of food. In Phase 2, compound training was accomplished using a light–noise compound CS, followed either by one or three pellets of food. Thus there were four groups. Two of the groups received the same number of food pellets in both phases of the study (either one or three) whereas the other two groups were shifted to the other magnitude of US (one got a single pellet in Phase 1 but three pellets in Phase 2; the other group got three pellets in Phase 1 and one in Phase 2). Associative strength to the target stimulus was assessed in terms of the number of head jerks elicited by the noise (recall from Chapter 3 that auditory stimuli elicit head jerks and startle reactions in rats in this situation.)[62]

The results of the study are shown in Figure 5-23. When the US was not changed from Phase 1 to Phase 2, little conditioning was found; the control groups show virtually no change in the frequency of head-jerk behavior over the sessions. However, when the US magnitude was changed, blocking was eliminated (conditioning took place). Furthermore, it made no difference

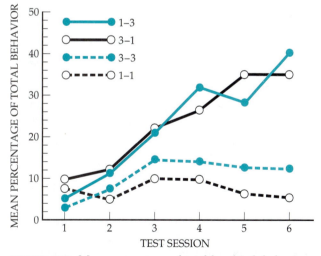

FIGURE 5-23. Mean percentage of total head-jerk behaviors evoked by the light–tone compound during Phase 2, as a function of sessions for experimental subjects for which the US was shifted from one to three or three to one pellets. Control subjects received no shift in US magnitude (after Holland, 1984).

whether the change in the US was an increase in magnitude or a decrease.[63] Animals merely had to be surprised about the amount, relative to what they had previously experienced, to develop a strong association to the noise CS.

The elimination of blocking when the animal is surprised during Phase 2 is **unblocking.** Some suggest that unblocking occurs even when the US is changed in a subtle way—for example, its location.[64] Others disagree, claiming that the US must be changed in a more substantial fashion. For instance, there must be a significant mismatch between the US that is expected and the US that is actually experienced.[65] Regardless, unblocking demonstrates the importance of surprise for conditioning. If the added CS signals a new and surprising condition, such as the presentation of an extra shock or the omission of an expected reward, then blocking does not occur; the added cue gains associative strength.

The aforementioned studies indicated that surprise is necessary for conditioning, but they do not provide any formal model or theory of the blocking phenomenon. The idea of surprise tells us when conditioning will take place, but it does not specify why is does so. We leave that issue to a fuller discussion in Chapter 6.

Retrieval Failure.

Recall from our previous discussion of latent inhibition that the deficit in conditioning observed following CS preexposure may be related to a decrease in the animal's ability to retrieve the memory of conditioning. A similar argument has been made in the case of blocking. Blocking may constitute not so much a lack of associative learning as the inability to remember, or retrieve, that learning.

The role of retrieval failure has been demonstrated in a number of studies. In one by Balaz, Gutsin, Cacheiro, and Miller (1982), subjects in the experimental group received tone–shock pairings in Phase 1 and compound tone–light–shock pairings in Phase 2.[66] Later they were tested for their aversion to the light CS, using a lick-suppression measure (the light was turned on after the 25th lick of the water tube, and the latency to complete an additional 25 licks was measured). Three reminder (control) groups were used. The only difference in their treatment was that they received a brief reminder trial between the compound-conditioning phase and the test. One of the reminder groups was simply put in the apparatus and allowed to remain there for a brief period of time. A second reminder group was given the light CS. A third was given an unsignaled shock.

If the light had indeed been conditioned in Phase 2 but had been forgotten prior to the test, then these reminder treatments should reactivate the memory of the light–US conditioning. This indeed happened, as shown in Figure 5-24. The three groups that received the reminder trial took significantly longer to complete their 25 water licks than did the group that received no reminder trial. Thus, the experimental group showed the greatest blocking (the light stimulus was not aversive, so they completed their licks rather quickly). The groups that were reminded of the compound conditioning train-

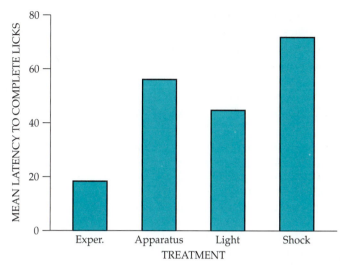

FIGURE 5-24. Mean latency to complete 25 licks during the light. Groups differed in terms of whether the subjects received no reminder trial (exper.), were placed in the apparatus, were given the light CS, or were given the shock US (after Balaz, Gutsin, Cacheiro, & Miller, 1982).

ing, however, showed greater aversion to the flashing light (less blocking). the results therefore suggest that blocking is not a failure of the added CS to acquire associative strength. Rather, blocking is due to a retrieval failure. The added stimulus is conditioned in Phase 2, but the animals fail to remember the conditioning on the test unless reminded.

INTERIM SUMMARY

The phenomenon called "blocking" shows that the associative strength of a CS depends, in part, on the strength of other CSs with which it is compounded. When one CS is conditioned and then is simultaneously presented with a second (added) CS, the added CS does not gain associative strength. Blocking also occurs in conditioned-inhibition studies. A related phenomenon is called "overshadowing." This is demonstrated when one stimulus interferes with the conditioning of another, either because it is more intense or because it has gained strength through additional conditioning. If, however, a stimulus becomes weaker through CS–no-US presentations, then an added stimulus actually gains in strength. This is called "superconditioning." The original theory of blocking argued that conditioning takes place when an animal is surprised. If one CS becomes strong through conditioning, then added CSs are redundant from an informational point of view (the animal is not surprised) and thus are not conditioned. In support of this hypothesis, when an animal is surprised during compound conditioning, blocking does not occur (this is called the "unblocking effect"). An alternative theory of blocking argues that blocking is not a failure to learn, but rather a failure to retrieve. If subjects are reminded of their compound training prior to the test, then blocking is not observed.

ENDNOTES

1. Recall from Chapter 3 that Pavlovian conditioning occurs when two stimuli are paired independently of the animal's behavior.
2. See Rescorla (1980a).
3. See also Szakmary (1979).
4. Second-order conditioning is not confined to excitatory CSs. A CS_2 may become associated with an inhibitory CS_1 such that it, too, will elicit conditioned inhibition; see Rescorla (1976a).
5. A context may also serve as the CS_2. Helmstetter and Fanselow (1989) gave light–shock pairings in one context during first-order conditioning. During second-order conditioning, the light was given in a different context, during which time the subject's freezing behavior was measured. Freezing increased over the course of the second-order training trials indicating that the context itself had become aversive because the fear-inducing CS_1 (the light) was given there. This finding also has important implications for human behavior. Many people become fearful of certain locations, such as buildings or neighborhoods, because the mere presence of stimuli (or people) that are associated with aversive outcomes is sufficient to render the locations aversive as well.
6. Actually, the experiment used a counterbalanced design in which a tone served as CS_1 for some subjects (light was CS_2) and vice versa for other animals. In this discussion, the description of the design has been simplified.
7. The facilitating effects of stimulus similarity on strength of second-order conditioning are even more subtle than those just noted. For instance, in a study by Rescorla and Gillam (1980), green and red colored keys that had horizontal or vertical lines superimposed on them were used as stimuli. Stronger conditioning was found when the CS_2 and the CS_1 both contained horizontal lines or both contained vertical lines. When one had horizontal lines, but the other vertical lines, conditioning was weaker.
8. The reason may be related to the approach behavior elicited by CS_1, which increases the probability that the bird will also peck at CS_2. In addition, note that spatial contiguity does not parallel temporal contiguity. Even the groups for which the two stimuli were not spatially contiguous showed reasonably strong second-order conditioning. Thus, if two stimuli are temporally contiguous, an association develops even when the stimuli are not spatially contiguous.
9. The description of the design of this study has been simplified here for the purpose of clarity.
10. See also Amiro and Bitterman (1980); Rizley and Rescorla (1972); Ross (1986).
11. See also Colwill and Rescorla (1985b); Rescorla (1979); Robertson, Krane, and Garrud (1984).
12. See Rescorla (1982b). Barnet, Arnold, and Miller (1991) have suggested that during second-order conditioning, CS_2 becomes associated with the memory of the US (see also Davey & McKenna, 1983). Groups of rats differed according to whether

first-order conditioning involved simultaneous or forward CS–US pairings. First-order conditioning was stronger in the forward group than in the simultaneous condition; this is exactly what was reported in Chapter 4. Second-order conditioning, however, was equivalent in the simultaneous and forward groups. In other words, the procedure that affected CS_1 did not affect the strength of CS_2. This result disqualifies the S–R hypothesis because if the first-order CR in the forward group was stronger than in the simultaneous group, and yet the CR established in second-order conditioning were equivalent, then second-order conditioning cannot depend on CS_2 being associated with the feeling experienced during CS_1. The experiment revealed another interesting result. Extinction of CS_1 did not affect the strength of the CS_2 in either the forward or the simultaneous groups, suggesting that the S–S interpretation may be discounted as well. This leaves the third hypothesis, that the second-order association forms between the CS_2 and the memory or mental representation of the US.

13. See Thompson (1972).
14. The discussion here focuses on only three of the groups studied in Experiment 4; the original design of the study was more complicated; see also Pfautz, Donegan, and Wagner (1978).
15. See Holland and Ross (1983) for an alternative measure of sensory preconditioning.
16. Lavin (1976); Wynne and Brogden (1962).
17. Rescorla (1980b).
18. Rescorla (1980b).
19. See Matzel, Held, and Miller (1988), however.
20. See Thompson (1972).
21. Adamec and Melzack (1970).
22. Fudim (1978).
23. See Hall (1991).
24. See Holland (1983a, 1985); Ross and Holland (1981).
25. As in most studies, the specific stimuli were counterbalanced across conditions; for the sake of clarity, the description of the full procedure has been simplified here.
26. Rescorla (1986) also examined whether excitatory training affects the ability of the cue to become an occasion setter. The results indicated that the facilitating effect did not occur when the occasion setter (B) had been previously paired with the US. However, if A is given some prior excitatory training, then the ability for B to become a facilitator is enhanced. The general message is that facilitation and excitation are distinct processes that do not substitute for one another, but see Rescorla (1991c) for an important exception. Also, Rescorla (1988) showed that if stimulus A had previously signaled the nonoccurrence of a US (that is, it canceled the US and thus served as a conditioned inhibitor) and then was later followed by the US in the presence of a facilitator, then the facilitation effect was even stronger.
27. Davidson and Rescorla (1986); see also Holland (1989c).
28. Holland (1986a); see also Holland (1989b).
29. See also Holland (1989b).
30. See Lubow (1989) for a thorough review. Although the term latent inhibition may be a misnomer of sorts, the term is still used widely and is thus used here.
31. Lubow (1989) points out that latent inhibition is demonstrated most clearly in mammalian species, including humans; see Lipp, Siddle, and Vaitl (1992). Little evidence is found for latent inhibition in invertebrates or lower vertebrates, including pigeons.
32. See also Siegel (1974).

33. The cessation of orienting reactions could possibly provide a direct measure of the processes involved in latent inhibition, but research has typically suggested that the occurrence (and habituation) of such responses is independent of the latent inhibition process; see Hall and Channell (1985).
34. Siegel (1974); see also Westbrook, Provost, and Homewood (1982).
35. Kalat and Rozin (1973).
36. Lubow (1973, 1989); but see Crowell and Anderson (1972); DeVietti, Bause, Nutt, Barrett, Daly, and Petree (1987).
37. Aversion to each element was also assessed.
38. The difference between the 40- and the 80-preexposure groups was not significant.
39. Lubow, Markman, and Allen (1968).
40. See also Albert and Ayres (1989).
41. See DeVietti, Bauste, Nutt, Barrett, Daly, and Petree (1987).
42. This is interesting because one would expect that strong CSs would maintain the subjects' attention more effectively than would weak cues. Stronger attention, in turn, implies better learning later on. The opposite result is found, however.
43. See also Hernandez, Buchanan, and Powell (1981).
44. Best, Gemberling, and Johnson (1979); Lubow, Schnur, and Rifkin (1976); but see Mercier and Baker (1985).
45. Lubow, Rifkin, and Alek (1976).
46. Reiss and Wagner (1972); Rescorla (1971a); see also Best (1975); Halgren (1974).
47. See Thompson, Groves, Teyler, and Roemer (1973).
48. Domjan and Siegel (1973).
49. See also Hall and Channell (1985).
50. Mackintosh (1975a).
51. For other important information-processing models that apply to latent inhibition, see Pearce and Hall (1980) and Wagner (1976, 1978).
52. Lubow, Weiner, and Schnur (1981); Lubow (1989).
53. Lubow, Rifkin, and Alek (1976).
54. See also Balaz, Capra, Kasprow, and Miller (1982).
55. See also Aguado, Symonds, and Hall (1994).
56. The issue is, however, more complicated than suggested here. As discussed in Chapter 4, the amount of conditioning to an element in a compound depends on several factors, including the relative salience of each element (the more salient CS will overshadow the less salient cue). Moreover, when the CSs are of approximately equal salience, the two elements may overshadow each other. This effect is called "reciprocal overshadowing" (see Mackintosh, 1976).
57. Kamin's study included many more groups than described here. Discussion of them is omitted, however, for the sake of clarity. Moreover, many believe that a more appropriate control is one that receives conditioning in Phase 1 with a novel stimulus. Thus, their treatment would include CS_C–US pairings in Phase 1, CS_A/CS_X–US pairings in Phase 2, and then a test of the strength of CS_X in Phase 3.
58. See Kehoe (1982); Mackintosh (1976).
59. See also Rescorla (1971b).
60. Navarro, Hallam, Matzel, and Miller (1989).
61. See also Dickinson, Hall, and Mackintosh (1976).
62. Actually, Holland used a more elaborate design in which all subjects experienced a change in the US. The added element, however, was either compounded with

the CS and followed by the US, or compounded with an alternative visual CS but not followed by a change in the US magnitude (the control subjects).

63. The unblocking effect found in the three–one group critically depended on the temporal presentation of the three pellets.

64. Stickney and Donahoe (1983).

65. Ganesan and Pearce (1988); Holland (1988); but see Dickinson and Mackintosh (1979).

66. See also Kasprow, Cacheiro, Balaz, and Miller (1982); Miller, Jagielo, and Spear (1990); Schachtman, Gee, Kasprow, and Miller (1983).

CHAPTER 6

Theoretical Perspectives in Classical Conditioning

The previous chapters discussed basic Pavlovian conditioning and described various phenomena that any theory of conditioning must surely explain. This chapter focuses on two major issues. First, the following section examines the nature of the associative connection. During a typical Pavlovian study, a CS is presented contiguously with a US. However, the CS is *also* contiguous with the UR. If Pavlovian conditioning entails the development of an association, then which association is formed? Is it the association between the CS and the US (stimulus–stimulus learning) or between the CS and the UR (stimulus–response learning)? In other words, when a subject is given a CS, does it trigger a memory for the associated stimulus—namely, the US—or does it evoke an associated reaction—the UR?

Second, the remaining portions of the chapter describe various theories or models of Pavlovian conditioning. Understanding *what* is associated during conditioning (as explained in the first section) does not necessarily clarify *why* or *how* an association develops. To accomplish this, researchers have developed formal theories that attempt to explain what happens when an association is formed. They specify the components of this learning system and how the components operate to produce an association. In other words, a full account of Pavlovian conditioning involves knowing what an association is like, and why or how it develops.

NATURE OF THE ASSOCIATIVE CONNECTION

As noted previously, there are two kinds of associations that could develop when a CS is paired with a US and the resulting UR. It could be either an S–R association or an S–S association.

Stimulus–Response (S–R) Associations

The **stimulus–response (S–R) theory of Pavlovian associations** emphasizes the reflexive nature of the conditioning process. According to this theory, the CS, because it has been contiguous with the UR, comes to trigger the reaction directly. A diagram of this theory is shown in Figure 6-1. The larger circles represent the nervous system of the animal in schematic form. The CSs and USs from the external world impinge on the nervous system and activate hypothetical centers or neurological representations (shown as smaller circles). These centers are places in which the external stimuli are represented neurologically in the information-processing system of the animal (but no specific anatomical locations are implied). The US center is directly connected to the UR center, which, in turn, is responsible for activating the response output. The important point is that the US and UR centers are directly—that is, reflexively—linked. According to this theory, then, the CS becomes associated with the UR, so after a number of contiguous pairings has been given, the CS directly activates the response center (right panel of Figure 6-1). Stated differently, because the associative link is between the CS and the response centers, activation of the CS center directly triggers the response.

Evidence Supporting the S–R Theory.

There is impressive evidence favoring the S–R theory. Although much of it was discussed in Chapter 4, a brief summary of some of the more important arguments is provided here. Generally, the S–R position is supported by evidence showing that the CR is nearly identical to the UR. If the CS becomes associated with the UR and thus gains the ability to trigger the UR center directly, then the overt behavior elicited by the CS must be the same as the

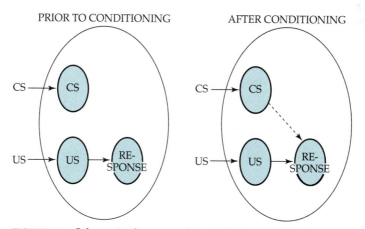

FIGURE 6-1. Schematic diagram of the S–R theory of Pavlovian conditioning. The left panel shows the state of the representation centers prior to conditioning; the right panel shows them after repeated CS–US pairings have been given.

overt behavior elicited by the US. In other words, the S–R theory claims that behavior is triggered by the UR representation and thus should be the same, regardless of whether it was initiated by the CS or the US.

Work on autoshaping in birds provides much support for this theory. Recall that pigeons peck a lighted key when it is followed by either food or water.[1] However, the form of the CR is similar to the reaction evoked by the US. When the US is food, subjects make sharp vigorous pecks at the CS with their beaks opened (the same kind of reaction they exhibit when pecking at solid food items, such as grain). When the animals are thirsty and are given a water US, they make drinkinglike reactions to the CS, such as swallowing and licking. It is as if the subjects are attempting to eat the CS when it is paired with food, but to drink it when it is paired with water.[2]

Perhaps the best example of the CR being the same as the UR was from a study by Davey and Cleland (1982). Hungry rats were presented with levers that were inserted automatically through a slot in the cage. The lever insertion served as the CS. For some of the subjects, when the left lever was inserted, a food pellet was presented 10 seconds later. For other animals, the lever was paired with the presentation of a liquid sucrose solution. Subjects also received occasional presentations of the right lever, but it was never followed by any event (and thus can be regarded as a CS−). The animals were videotaped, and the tapes were later analyzed for the component behaviors demonstrated by the rats.

The results of the study are shown in Figure 6-2. When the lever was followed by a food pellet, subjects tended to sniff, mouth, bite, and paw the lever. However, when the lever was followed by liquid food, the animals tended to sniff, paw, and, more importantly, lick the lever.[3] Virtually no licking of the lever occurred when it signaled a food pellet. The subject's motivational state (hunger) was much less important in determining the CR than was the nature of the UR. The data therefore support the S–R account because the CS elicited a reaction that was virtually the same as that elicited by the US itself, rather than a reaction that, more simply, is given when the animal is hungry.

Evidence Conflicting with the S–R Theory.

Although these studies favor the S–R position, considerably more evidence suggests that the account is inadequate. For example, consider the case of sensory preconditioning (see Chapter 5). Here, one CS becomes associated with another CS; no US or UR is involved. If an association develops between a stimulus and a response, as the S–R theory claims, then how is it possible for two CSs, neither of which evokes a strong or lasting reaction, to become associated?

Other evidence against the S–R position shows that the CR may not resemble the UR; the two may be substantially and qualitatively different. If the CS does not elicit a response that is essentially like the UR, then one cannot argue that the CS center directly triggers the UR output center. The nature of the association must be based on a different notion. Let us review some of these studies.

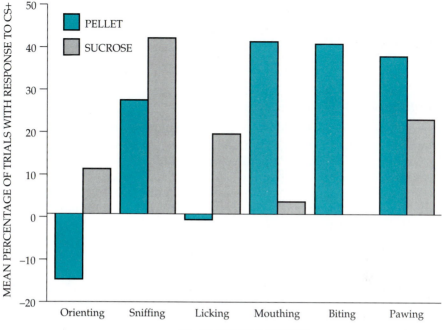

FIGURE 6-2. Mean percentage of trials with a response to the CS+ lever for the various lever-directed behaviors for the pellet (blue bars) and sucrose (grey bars) conditions. Scores represented the percentage of trials with a response to the CS+ less the percentage of trials with a response to the CS− lever. Positive scores, therefore, denote a differential tendency to contact the CS+ lever (after Davey & Cleland, 1982).

One study by Wasserman, Hunter, Gutowski, and Bader (1974) observed differences between the CR and the UR in birds. Chicks were placed in a cold environment and given a key light followed by a short period of heat from a heat lamp. The heat lamp reflexively elicited a UR, called "twittering," which includes fluffing the feathers, and emitting tweeting vocalizations. The CR, however, was not a warmth-related behavior. Instead, the subjects pecked the key.

In a study by Davey, Phillips, and Witty (1989), two kinds of USs were used—namely, a brief period of hot air when the subjects were in a cold environment, or food when they were hungry. In addition, two kinds of CSs were used: a retractable aluminum lever, or a retractable lever covered with a furry acrylic material. Thus, there were four types of CS–US pairings; they were the aluminum lever followed by hot air, aluminum lever and food, furry lever and hot air, and furry lever followed by food. When the US was a blast of warm air, the subjects engaged in thermoregulatory behavior (the animals approached the lever, put their head under it, and huddled near it), but *only* when the furry lever was used. Both conditions were required. When the food US was used, the animals showed food-oriented reactions, but *only* when the

CS was the aluminum lever. In other words, the type of behavior that the subjects engaged in was not determined exclusively by the quality of the US; the nature of the CS also played an important role (see the following section for more discussion).[4]

Stimulus–Stimulus (S–S) Associations

A second theory is the **stimulus–stimulus (S–S) theory of Pavlovian associations**.[5] According to this position, the CS does not become associated with the UR and thus trigger a response directly. Rather, conditioning causes an association between the CS and the US to develop; it is an S–S bond.

The theory is depicted schematically in Figure 6-3. The smaller circles within the larger space signify the neurological representations of the CS, US, and UR (again, no specific neurological sites are implied). The theory assumes that during conditioning, an association develops between the representations of the CS and those of the US. Later, when the CS is presented, it activates the CS center, which, in turn, triggers the US center (not the response center directly). The behavioral output then follows. It is as if the animal remembers the US when it receives the CS; the memory of the US is responsible for evoking the behavior.

Evidence Supporting the S–S Theory.

The evidence supporting the S–S theory is quite compelling. Generally, the theory has been tested by establishing a CS–US association during training and then, independently, altering the subject's memory of the US prior to the test of CS strength. If the CS elicits a response that differs in strength following the alteration of the US memory, then the CS must be triggering a CR

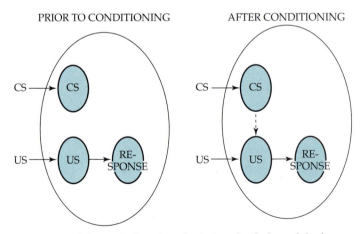

FIGURE 6-3. Schematic drawing depicting the S–S model of Pavlovian conditioning. The left panel shows the state of the representation centers prior to conditioning; the right panel shows them after repeated CS–US pairings have been given.

via the US center. In other words, if a CS becomes powerful through pairing with a US, and then the animal has its memory for the US altered through some manipulation, the strength of the CR should change if indeed the CS activates the US memory center.

Rescorla (1973) used a CER technique to examine this theory.[6] After the rats were experienced in pressing a lever to obtain food, Pavlovian conditioning trials took place. Both groups of subjects were given 3 days of training, consisting of 30-second presentations of a blinking light, terminated by a 2-second 105-dB noise US (a noise this loud is known to be aversive to rats). During Phase 2, one of the groups was habituated to the US. That is, subjects were given three sessions with 24 unsignaled presentations of the loud noise. This procedure was intended to reduce the perceived intensity of the tone. In other words, repeated presentation of an aversive stimulus causes subjects to judge the stimulus to be progressively less aversive.[7] The control subjects were simply placed in the apparatus for an equal period of time. In Phase 3, all subjects were tested for their aversion to the light CS (these trials were extinction trials, so the suppression was expected to diminish progressively.)

The results are shown in Figure 6-4. Both groups suppressed their bar pressing during the light CS in Phase 1, indicating that the loud noise was indeed aversive. The control subjects continued to show marked suppression throughout the entire series of extinction trials. The habituated animals, in contrast, showed appreciable recovery from the suppressive effects of the CS. For those subjects, the light CS was not as aversive as it had been previously.

How does the S–S theory account for these data? Recall that following acquisition, nothing further was done to the CS. Neither additional training nor extinction of the light was ever given until the test. The only treatment

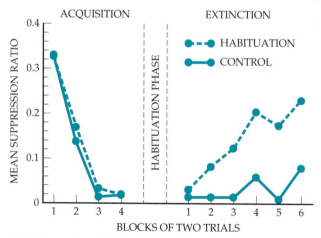

FIGURE 6-4. Acquisition (left) and extinction (right) test trials of conditioned suppression to the light CS in the habituated and control groups. The habituation of the noise US intervened between the acquisition and the test phases (after Rescorla, 1973).

involved the noise. Thus, the fact that the light elicited a weaker CR in the habituated subjects, based on a treatment involving the noise, suggests that the light must have triggered the memory of the US. If it did, the experimental animals had a different memory of the US strength due to the habituation procedure (namely, that it was less intense). Thus, one would expect the resulting CR to be relatively weak. The control subjects, on the other hand, remembered the intensity of the US as being the same as they experienced during acquisition. They did not experience habituation and thus did not undergo an alteration in their memory for the US intensity. When the CS elicited the memory of the US in these subjects, therefore, a strong response, like the one acquired during Phase 1, was elicited.

Rescorla (1974) also used the converse strategy to support the S–S position. Here, the CS was an 1,800-Hz tone, and the US was a 0.5-milliamp shock that lasted 0.5 seconds. As is typically found, lever pressing during the tone CS was dramatically suppressed after only a few days of CS–US pairings. Once the association had been formed between the tone and the shock, the subjects' memory for the US intensity was altered. Three groups were designated; each was given a series of unsignaled shocks with an intensity of 0.5, 1.0, or 3.0 milliamps (the shock intensity value in the latter two groups was higher than that used in the original training). Thus, by the end of this *re*valuation phase, subjects in the 1- or 3-milliamp group should have remembered the US as being more intense than originally experienced during acquisition. Finally, all subjects were tested for their reaction to the tone CS. Again, the animals were not given further training or extinction to the tone, and thus any change in their reaction to it must be attributed to the changes in their memory of the US intensity.

The results are shown in Figure 6-5. Responding was comparatively weak (and thus suppression extinguished most noticeably) in the group that received the same intensity shock on both the acquisition and the revaluation phases (the 0.5-milliamp group). However, reaction to the tone was stronger (suppression was greater) in the groups that experienced the 1- and 3-milliamp shocks during the revaluation phase. According to the S–S theory, the CS elicited the memory of the US, but because those subjects now remembered the US as being more intense than originally experienced, the resulting response, triggered by the US center, was even stronger.

The memory of an event may substitute for the event itself in the formation of new associations. In one interesting study by Holland (1981), two groups of subjects were given pairings of a 1,400-Hz tone and wintergreen-flavored sucrose pellets.[8] The intention of this phase was to endow the tone CS with the ability to evoke the memory of the flavor. Both groups also received presentations of a flashing light CS followed by nothing. In Phase 2, one group was placed in the box, presented with the tone, and then immediately injected with lithium chloride (LiCl). The other group was treated in a similar fashion but was given the flashing light prior to the injection. Finally, both groups were given a 10-minute test of their acceptance of the wintergreen-flavored food. Small dishes containing the pellets were placed in their home cage, and consumption was recorded.

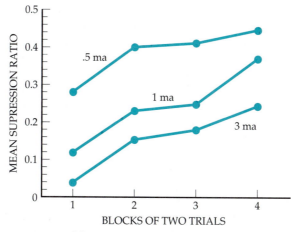

FIGURE 6-5. Mean suppression ratio to the tone CS during the extinction test for the three groups that received unsignaled shocks that were 0.5, 1.0, or 3.0 milliamps (ma) in intensity on the test (after Rescorla, 1974).

The group that received the LiCl following the tone ate, on the average, 71 pellets; the control group, which received LiCl following the light, ate significantly more, about 94 pellets. The explanation for the difference is that the tone in Phase 2 elicited the memory of the food, which, in turn, immediately preceded LiCl. In other words, the food became aversive (as evidenced on the consumption test) not because it was paired directly with the LiCl, but because the animals' memory of the food, elicited by the tone, was paired with LiCl. The control group showed no comparable aversion because they were given the light CS prior to the LiCl, and the light was not capable of eliciting the memory of the food (because it had not been associated with food during Phase 1). In short, if an animal is prompted to remember a stimulus, that memory may become associated with an outcome (here, LiCl) just as easily as if the event itself were presented.

The sensory preconditioning phenomenon (see Chapter 5) may be based on essentially this same notion. Recall that sensory preconditioning involves the pairing of CS_2 and CS_1, followed by the pairing of a CS_1 with a US. The fact that the CS_2 later elicits a CR, despite the fact that it is never directly paired with the US, suggests that it evokes the memory or representation of CS_1, which is itself sufficient to trigger the response.[9] Sensory preconditioning studies, therefore, use a different procedure from the preceding one, but they are consistent with its primary conclusion—namely, that the memory for a US may be nearly as good in promoting conditioning of a new CS as the US itself.

Evidence Conflicting with the S–S Theory.

The foregoing research provides compelling evidence that stimuli evoke representations, and that these representations may become associated. The

S–S theory, however, still gives an incomplete explanation of the form and quality of the CR. Specifically, it does not state precisely what the CR should be if it is not the UR. In other words, although the S–S theory avoids the problem of the S–R position (in that it does not demand that the CR must be identical to the UR), nevertheless it fails by not stating what the CR should be. Presumably, a number of centers are affected when a CS is presented, not just a single UR center. Such a notion must be accepted because, as noted previously, the CR and the UR often differ dramatically (see also Chapter 12).

INTERIM SUMMARY

Pavlovian theory has focused on the nature of the association that develops during conditioning. Because the CS occurs contiguously with both the US and the resulting UR, it is not clear whether the association is between the CS and the US (S–S association), or the CS and the UR (S–R association). Evidence supporting the S–R position is found in the autoshaping literature, where the CR and the UR are virtually the same (a condition demanded by this theory). Many studies, however, show that the CR and the UR are often quite different, thus challenging the S–R position. Additional support for the S–S theory comes from studies in which the memory for the US is altered following conditioning. Here, the CS triggers a CR that is in accord with the new US memory. Such a finding suggests that the CS elicits the memory of the US (S–S association), but because subjects now remember the US as being different from the one originally experienced, the CR is altered as well.

ASSOCIATIVE MODELS OF PAVLOVIAN CONDITIONING

The preceding section argued that a Pavlovian association may best be characterized as an S–S connection. How do S–S associations develop, however? What are the learning mechanisms that are responsible for, or create, an association? Several different classes of theories have been proposed. Each theory focuses on a particular set of processes, and each successfully accounts for a range of phenomena. The following sections describe several of the more influential theories of Pavlovian conditioning.

Good theories of Pavlovian conditioning should be able to account for the effects of important variables on conditioning (discussed in Chapter 4), and the many Pavlovian phenomena (discussed in Chapters 3–5), such as acquisition, extinction, inhibition, and blocking. They do this by specifying the mechanisms of learning—that is, the underlying processes that lead to the development of an association. If the mechanisms are correctly identified, then the workings of the theory should agree with the data derived from laboratory research.

Contingency Theory

The contingency theory was listed as a theory of CR performance in Chapter 3. That discussion claimed that inhibitory and excitatory tendencies combine algebraically to produce a CR. When excitation is greater than inhibition, then an excitatory CR is observed. When the reverse is true, however, no CR is visible because the inhibitory tendency, which rarely involves an overt CR, reduces excitation to a below-zero level.

The contingency theory is actually a theory of learning more than it is a statement about performance. As a theory of learning, it argues that an association is created when a subject develops or assesses the correlation between the CS and a US. For instance, when the correlation between the CS and the US is positive (USs are more likely to be signaled by the CS than not), then an excitatory association occurs. Conversely, when the correlation between the CS and the US is negative (USs are more likely to be unsignaled than they are to be signaled), then an inhibitory association develops. The mechanism for learning, therefore, is simply the assessment of the contingency or correlation between the two stimuli.

The contingency theory was an important starting point for theories of Pavlovian conditioning because it emphasized that conditioning depends fundamentally on the informational relationship between the CS and the US, not simply on their contiguity. As a detailed description of the formation of an association, however, the theory is seriously flawed. For instance, the contingency theory cannot account for blocking. In the blocking design, the added stimulus (CS_X) is correlated with the US to the same degree in both the blocking and the control groups, yet CS_X fails to gain strength in the blocking group because of the prior strength of CS_A. The contingency theory cannot explain why the strength of CS_X depends on the strength of CS_A, rather than simply on the correlation between CS_X and the US.

A second problem for the contingency theory is that it cannot explain why excitation is often observed when subjects are given random presentations of the CS and the US (see Chapter 3). According to the theory, an association should not develop under these conditions, yet excitation often occurs.

A third problem is that inhibition occurs even when the theory predicts it should not. Consider when acquisition is followed by extinction. During acquisition, a CS acquires excitatory strength because it is paired with a US; during extinction, some form of inhibition develops (see Chapter 3). However, for the CS to become inhibitory under these conditions, one must assume that the subject integrates or combines its estimations of the CS–US correlation over many sessions or days, rather than over a series of trials. Such an assumption appears unwarranted. It is unlikely that a subject combines the events experienced during acquisition (positive CS–US correlation) with those experienced during extinction (CS is negatively correlated with the US) to calculate an overall correlation that applies to all sessions. It makes more sense to say that inhibition occurs when a subject expects the US (based on its experience during acquisition) but is not given the US (because of the extinction procedures). The violation of the subject's expectancy for the US accounts for the development of inhibition, not the subject's assessment of the CS–US correlation over the two kinds of training sessions.

US Processing: The Rescorla–Wagner Model

To accommodate many of these criticisms, a new and highly influential model was developed by Rescorla and Wagner (1972). The purpose of the model was to account for various Pavlovian phenomena, particularly blocking and inhibition. For more than 2 decades, the model has proved to be successful in this regard and thus has inspired a great deal of research.

The **Rescorla–Wagner model** claims that the amount of conditioning to a CS—that is, the change in its associative strength—depends on the degree to which the US is processed. According to the model, each US has a certain degree of associative strength that will support conditioning to various CSs, up to a maximum level. The strength of an association is based on the processing of this US strength.

Rescorla and Wagner started with the notion that surprise is essential to conditioning (see the section on unblocking in Chapter 5) and proceeded to develop a mathematical model that explained how this occurred. Surprise is defined as the discrepancy between the US that is expected and the one that occurs. The Rescorla–Wagner model argues that this discrepancy determines the amount of processing, and thus the increment in associative strength of the CS on that trial. If the discrepancy is small, then little surprise is encountered, and the CS–US association is strengthened only slightly. If, however, a large discrepancy between the expected and the actual US occurs, then the predictive element, the CS, becomes associated with the US to a much larger degree. Let us work through a simple problem to illustrate how the model explains the growth of an association during conditioning.

The basic model is given in the following equation.

$$\Delta V_A = \alpha_A (\lambda - V_T)$$

where $V_T = V_A + V_X$

The term ΔV_A is the change or increment in associative strength of CS_A on any given trial when CS_A is paired with the US. The term α_A is a constant; it refers to the associability of the CS—that is, the degree to which the CS is able to enter into an associative relationship with a US.[10] The important part of the Rescorla–Wagner model is the quantity $(\lambda - V_T)$. The term λ is the maximum amount of associative strength that a given US possesses—that is, the maximum amount of conditioning that a US can support. The V_T term is the momentary combined strength of all the CSs present; when any CS increases in associative strength, V_T increases accordingly. The quantity $(\lambda - V_T)$, then, indicates the discrepancy between what the animal expects on a trial (V_T) and the strength of the US that is actually experienced (λ).

Here are some arbitrary values for these terms. Assume that α_A equals .5, and that λ has a value of 100. In this example, because we are concerned with simple excitatory conditioning (rather than conditioning of compound stimuli), we use the notation CS_A to designate the single CS that gets conditioned. The change in strength to CS_A for each CS_A–US pairing is shown in Figure 6-6.

Prior to conditioning, on the first trial, V_T is zero because no CS, including CS_A, has any associative power. As a result of the first CS_A–US pairing, however, V_A increases in value. Specifically, the increment in strength of CS_A on the first trial (ΔV_A) is 50. In other words, given the value of the constant ($\alpha = .5$) and of the maximum associative strength that the US can support ($\lambda = 100$), a single CS_A–US pairing results in 50 units of strength on the first

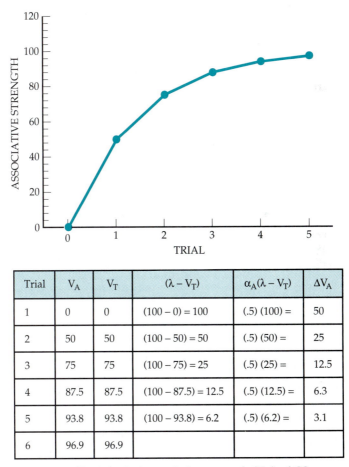

Trial	V_A	V_T	$(\lambda - V_T)$	$\alpha_A(\lambda - V_T)$	ΔV_A
1	0	0	$(100 - 0) = 100$	$(.5)(100) =$	50
2	50	50	$(100 - 50) = 50$	$(.5)(50) =$	25
3	75	75	$(100 - 75) = 25$	$(.5)(25) =$	12.5
4	87.5	87.5	$(100 - 87.5) = 12.5$	$(.5)(12.5) =$	6.3
5	93.8	93.8	$(100 - 93.8) = 6.2$	$(.5)(6.2) =$	3.1
6	96.9	96.9			

FIGURE 6-6. Hypothetical associative strength (V_A) of CS_A following each CS–US training trial. The table provides the trial-by-trial values for V_A, V_T, ($\lambda - V_T$), $\alpha_A(\lambda - V_T)$, and ΔV_A, as computed by the Rescorla–Wagner model. The figure plots V_A at the beginning of each trial.

trial. At the beginning of the second trial, V_T is 50 (the strength that the CS derived on the first trial). The added strength that the CS_A will acquire on this trial will, therefore, be 25 (see Figure 6-6). After two trials, the total strength of CS_A—namely, V_A—is 75. On the third trial, the CS_A gains an extra 12.5 units of strength (V_T now equals 87.5 units), whereas on Trial 4, ΔV_A is 6.25 and on Trial 5, it is equal to 3.125.

The point is that on each trial, the CS_A acquires additional associative strength, the amount of which is a fixed *proportion* of the amount of strength that is still available—namely, the maximum conditioning strength that the US will support minus the strength already used ($\lambda - V_T$). The increment in strength of CS_A declines with each trial because the amount of associative power that remains (namely, $\lambda - V_T$) declines as λ is used up. Thus, the Rescorla–Wagner model clearly predicts the typical learning curve in which each successive increase in strength is smaller than the last.[11] Early in learning, the CS acquires a considerable amount of associative strength on each trial ($\lambda - V_T$ is relatively large), but as the strength of CS_A (and thus V_T) increases, considerably less power is available.

Supporting Evidence.

One of most important findings that supports the Rescorla–Wagner model is the blocking outcome. Let us continue with the problem started in the preceding section, to illustrate this point. After five conditioning trials using CS_A, V_A, and thus the total strength of all CSs associated with the US (V_T), is equal to 96.875. This means that only 3.125 units of strength, from the original 100 units, are available for conditioning on the sixth trial. If a compound stimulus is given on the sixth trial (CS_A combined with CS_X) and is followed by the same US, both elements are conditioned, but only 3.125 total units of strength are available. Assume that the α value for CS_X is the same as the CS_A—namely, .5. On a sixth trial, therefore, the CS_X acquires only 1.55 units of strength.[12] This is a very small change in the associative strength of CS_X (recall that CS_A derived 50 units of strength on its first pairing with the US).

This change is precisely what is meant by blocking; CS_X gains little strength during compound conditioning, even though it is contiguous with the US. According to the model, the reason that the added stimulus, CS_X, gains so little power is that there is so little of the US associative strength remaining after the first five trials; CS_A has used up the available λ. In short, blocking occurs because the pairing of CS_X and the US captures only a small percentage of the total US strength; what was available originally (λ) was used up by CS_A on the first five trials, leaving little strength for CS_X.

In addition to explaining simple acquisition and blocking, the Rescorla–Wagner model also accounts for extinction and conditioned inhibition. Consider the case of extinction. Here, a powerful CS_A causes the subject to expect the US, but because no US is given during extinction, λ is zero. If λ is zero, then the term ($\lambda - V_T$) is negative. This means that the term ΔV_A also becomes negative—that is, inhibitory.

A similar line of reasoning is used to explain inhibition. On the excitatory trials, when CS_A is paired with the US, CS_A comes to elicit the expectation for the US. When CS_A and CS_X are compounded together and followed by the absence of the US, CS_A elicits the expectation for the US, but no US is given, so λ is zero. Therefore, as in extinction, the increment in associative strength to the uniquely informative element—namely, CS_X—becomes inhibitory.

How does the Rescorla–Wagner model explain the development of inhibition when there is a negative correlation between the CS and the US? Here, when the US is presented by itself (that is, when the US is unsignaled), background or apparatus cues are paired with the US and thus acquire excitatory value. On other occasions, when the CS is presented by itself, the apparatus cues generate the expectation for the US delivery, but no US is forthcoming. Once again, this means that λ is zero, and thus the change in associative strength to the CS is negative (inhibitory).

Another phenomenon that the Rescorla–Wagner model explains is superconditioning (see Chapter 5). If the compound CS_A–CS_X is followed by the US, but the CS_A is given by itself on other occasions, then CS_X gains even more strength than it would if given by itself. According to the model, the CS_A–no-US trials cause V_A to become inhibitory, thus reducing the term V_T. Because V_T is lower than it would be without the extra inhibitory trials to CS_A, the term $(\lambda - V_T)$ is larger, and conditioning to CS_X is even stronger.

Finally, a phenomenon that supports the Rescorla–Wagner model is the retardation of learning following US preexposure (see Chapter 3).[13] Recall that when a US is given by itself prior to conditioning, a CS gains little power later on when paired with it. One study that showed this effect quite clearly was done by Baker and Mackintosh (1979).[14] After establishing a baseline of lever pressing for food, rats were given the preexposure treatment. The shock-only group was given eight unsignaled shocks over six sessions. These shocks occurred at irregular times during the session. The placement-only group was put into the apparatus and given essentially no treatment. A third group (light–shock group) was given the same number of shocks as the shock-only animals, but each was preceded by a 1-minute light CS. Following the preexposure phase, all animals were given a CER test. Here, the CS here was a clicker noise that lasted 90 seconds, and the US was the same shock as presented earlier to two of the groups. Over the course of 5 days of CER training, suppression was observed to the clicker.

The results are shown in Figure 6-7. The placement-only and light–shock groups showed considerable suppression. The clicker CS had acquired considerable power by the third day of training. The shock-only group, however, showed significantly less conditioning. Their suppression ratios declined over training, but they were substantially higher than the other two groups. Thus, unsignaled preexposure to shock caused a retardation of learning.

How does the Rescorla–Wagner model explain this effect? The unsignaled shocks in Phase 1 caused the apparatus to become conditioned in the shock-only group. No other predictor of shock was available, so the context or surroundings acquired the excitatory strength. In fact, the context or apparatus

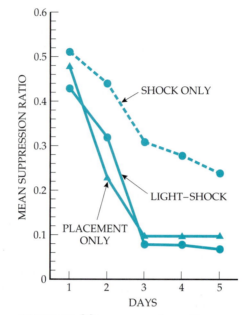

FIGURE 6-7. Mean suppression ratio on daily CER test sessions, as a function of the treatment during a prior preexposure phase (after Baker & Mackintosh, 1979).

acquired strength just as CS_A gains excitatory strength in a typical blocking experiment. When excitatory training was then given in Phase 2 using the clicker, the CS really was a compound stimulus, composed of the clicker *and* the apparatus cues. The clicker–context compound functioned essentially like the CS_A–CS_X compound in a blocking study. Consequently, conditioning to the clicker element (CS_X) was blocked because the context (effectively, CS_A) was already strong from the prior phase. This did not happen in the light–shock group because the light was a good predictor of the shock and therefore overshadowed conditioning to the apparatus cues.

The idea that the context is conditioned during unsignaled shocks and that it later blocks the conditioning to a CS is supported by other research, which shows, for example, that when the context is changed, the retardation is eliminated.[15] Similarly, if the context is extinguished, blocking of the new CS is reduced.[16] In summary, the US preexposure effect appears to occur because a series of unsignaled shocks actually causes the context or apparatus to become conditioned. When a new stimulus, such as a clicker or light, is paired with the US, the now-powerful context causes blocking of the new CS element.[17] The Rescorla–Wagner model predicts this outcome quite easily.

Evaluation of Model.

The Rescorla–Wagner model was an important contribution to learning theory because it provided a formal statement describing the growth of associative strength under a variety of conditions. Given the vast amount of research that it stimulated, it is not surprising that some results have not supported the model. We review only a few of these contradictory findings.[18]

First, the Rescorla–Wagner model cannot easily accommodate latent inhibition (see Chapter 5 for a discussion). Recall that when a CS is presented by itself during Phase 1, the CS does not easily become a good conditioned excitor when paired with a US in Phase 2. Preexposure of the CS results in retardation of learning. The problem for the Rescorla–Wagner model is that the CS should not be acquiring (or losing) any associative strength during the preexposure phase (because change in strength entails processing of the US), yet conditioning later on is retarded.[19]

A second problem with the Rescorla–Wagner model is that, under certain conditions, an already powerful CS can potentiate or facilitate the conditioning of another CS, even though the model suggests that the two should compete for strength. For example, when an odor and a taste are presented as a compound CS and are followed by illness, the odor becomes more strongly aversive than it would have had it alone been paired with illness.[20] The taste, according to the Rescorla–Wagner model, should block or prevent conditioning to the odor, yet, in reality, it does the opposite; it facilitates conditioning.[21]

A third challenge to the model is unblocking (see Chapter 5). Recall that unblocking occurs when a change in the US during the compound conditioning phase eliminates blocking to the added CS. In an experiment by Dickinson, Hall, and Mackintosh (1976), for example, subjects were trained to press a lever and then were given conditioning trials using a clicker CS, followed by two shock USs, the second shock being delivered 8 seconds after the first.[22] During Phase 2, the clicker and a light CS were combined into a single compound; this compound CS was also followed by the shock. One of the groups continued to receive the same double US (one shock followed by a second shock 8 seconds later), whereas the other group was given only a single shock on the compound trials. That is, having received two shocks during the clicker–shock training in Phase 1, these subjects now received only a single shock, following the clicker–light compound. In the test phase, suppression to the light was tested.

The results are shown in Figure 6-8. Substantial suppression (that is, less blocking) occurred in the group for which the US outcome was changed from two shocks to one. The no-change group showed the conventional blocking outcome; their CER ratio was close to .5.

The authors claimed that during Phase 2, subjects in the no-change group experienced blocking because they were not surprised by receiving two shocks. Subjects in the change group, however, were surprised by the omission of the second shock, and therefore, they learned an association to the light. The Rescorla–Wagner model has trouble explaining this result. A reduction in the number of shocks would, if anything, be analogous to reducing λ (the total amount of conditioning that the US will support). Yet if λ were reduced, one would not predict that the added stimulus—here, the light—would gain *more* associative strength. In short, the unblocking phenomenon

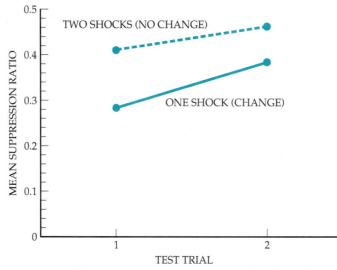

FIGURE 6-8. Mean suppression ratios to the light CS on the test trials. On the compound conditioning trials during Phase 2, the US continued to be two shocks for one group but was changed to one shock for the other group (after Dickinson, Hall, & Mackintosh, 1976).

shows that surprise leads to conditioning even in situations in which the available associative strength (λ) has not been increased (indeed, it may even have been reduced).

Other kinds of manipulations that produce surprise but do not alter the size of λ (and therefore do not alter the magnitude of the associative strength available to the added cue), also eliminate blocking. For example, if the CS–US interval during the compound training is changed from what it was during Phase 1, then blocking is abolished. Again, it makes no sense to say that λ would have increased as a result of a change in the interval.[23] Because the Rescorla–Wagner model focuses exclusively on the available US associative strength—that is, the ($\lambda - V_T$) term—it cannot accommodate this finding easily.[24]

INTERIM SUMMARY

Various theories have tried to specify how Pavlovian associations develop. The contingency theory claims that subjects assess the predictive relationship between the CS and the US over a series of trials, and subjects develop an excitatory or inhibitory tendency based on that correlation. Research shows, however, that an association develops on the basis of the subject's surprise. This fact led to the development of the important Rescorla–Wagner model. According to this US processing model, a change in the associative strength of a stimulus depends on the degree to which the US is processed. Specifically, when there is a discrepancy between the US that is expected and the one that occurs, then the CS gains a fixed proportion of associative strength available on that trial. The Rescorla–Wagner model accounts for many Pavlovian phenomena, including acquisition, extinction, inhibition, and blocking. The model, however, cannot easily explain either latent inhibition or the unblocking effect when the number of USs is reduced from two (during Phase 1) to one (during the compound conditioning phase).

ATTENTION MODEL OF PAVLOVIAN CONDITIONING: PEARCE–HALL MODEL

Miller, Barnet, and Grahame (1995) discuss a number of findings that fail to support the Rescorla–Wagner model. According to these authors, the results cluster around several categories. For example, research from several different areas has challenged the model's assumption that excitation and inhibition are symmetrical but opposite processes. Recall that presentation of an excitatory CS by itself reduces the level of excitation, but the same procedure using a CS− has little effect (see Chapter 3).

Second, a cluster of problems stems from the fact that the conditioning history of a cue affects future conditioning when, according to the Rescorla–Wagner model, it should not. Consider spontaneous recovery. The model predicts that associative strength of a CS will remain low following extinction, yet excitatory strength recovers spontaneously following a rest interval.

A third cluster of problems for the Rescorla–Wagner model concerns the associability of a CS. The model incorrectly assumes that the ability to become associated with a US is fixed over training (that is, α is constant). A variety of results suggests that α, in fact, changes over training. Latent inhibition shows, for instance, that a CS's *ability* to become associated with a US declines following CS preexposure. In other words, it is not merely that the CS lacks strength following preexposure (the V_A term), but rather that it is less able to become associated with a US (α is diminished).

There is another class of models that attempts to accommodate this problem. These models focus on the processing of, or attention to, the CS. They do not hypothesize that a fixed amount of US strength is proportionally used up by CSs over training. Rather, these models argue that as the CS varies in its predictive value, the subjects' attention to, and rehearsal of, the CS changes accordingly. In short, the CS associability itself (α), changes over training.

One of the most successful CS-processing models is the **Pearce–Hall model**.[25] This model is quite consistent with an evolutionary point of view. The theory claims that it is highly adaptive to pay attention to, or process, CSs that, in the future, could become valid predictors of important outcomes such as USs. When subjects encounter a new signal, it is to their advantage to learn what that signal predicts; after all, it could predict an important event such as the occurrence of a US. The model further implies that it is adaptive for subjects *not* to pay attention to, or process, CSs when the important event, such as a US, is already predicted by other signals. It is a waste of time for subjects to invest energy and time rehearsing a CS if they already can predict the US using a different cue.

Given these two premises, the Pearce–Hall model specifically claims that when a subject is surprised, attention to and processing of a CS occur, thus increasing the associative strength of that CS. However, as the US becomes predicted by a CS, and thus is less surprising to the subject, processing declines. The amount of processing—that is, the associability of a CS— changes on each trial, depending on whether the US was predicted.[26] If the US was predicted, then the subject's attention to the CS declines, and associability of the cue (α) is weaker on the next trial. Alternatively, if the US was not predicted, then the subject's attention to that CS (namely, α) increases.

The Pearce–Hall model may be stated more formally in the following way.

$$\alpha_A^N = |\ \lambda^{N-1} - V_A^{N-1}\ |$$

where α_A^N is the associability of CS_A at the beginning of trial N, λ^{N-1} is the strength of the US on the previous trial, and V_A^{N-1} is the strength of CS_A on the previous trial.

The formula shows that when the strength of CS_A is very low, the quantity $(\lambda - V_A)$ is large, and thus the associability of CS_A—namely, α_A—is large as well. The subject is surprised and thus pays greater attention to the CS. However, as the strength of CS_A increases (the subject is less surprised when it gets the US), then the quantity $(\lambda - V_A)$ decreases and α becomes progressively smaller on each trial. What this means is that as the subject learns more and more about how to predict the US (as the subject grows progressively less surprised by the US occurrence), it attends to, and rehearses, the CS_A less; α declines, and additional increments of associative strength are smaller. This idea fits well with other research on attention, which shows that when subjects first encounter a stimulus, they attend to it, but as they learn about it, attention wanes. In short, conditioning in the Pearce–Hall model depends on the size of α—that is, the magnitude of attention to, and processing of, a CS. As the US is better predicted (as the strength of CS_A increases), the attention to the CS declines.

Supporting Evidence

One of the interesting implications of the Pearce–Hall model is that the processing of a CS may be measured directly in terms of the animal's orientation reactions (OR).[27] For example, in a study of Kaye and Pearce (1984b), the No-dipper group received six 10-second presentations of a light per session. The Continuous group was given the same number of light presentations, but each of the presentations was followed by a 5-second presentation of a liquid dipper that contained a drop of condensed milk. The Partial group was given the 10-second light presentations, but the liquid reinforcement followed the light on only 50% of the occasions (determined randomly). All subjects were videotaped. Later, observers rated the subject's ORs to the light. An OR to the light was defined as either rearing in front of or contacting the light with the snout or the paws. If the subject was attending to the cue, then these reactions would be quite obvious.

The Pearce–Hall model predicts that attention to the light will be high initially (subjects have no information as to whether the light is a predictor of some important event), but that the ORs will decline in the Continuous and No-dipper groups. The reason is that as the strength of the CS increases in the Continuous group, the value of α_A decreases; subjects should invest progressively less attention and rehearsal to that stimulus. For the No-dipper group, attention should also be minimum because λ and V_A both equal zero. That is, when no US is given ($\lambda = 0$), CS_A does not acquire any strength, and the quantity ($\lambda - V_A$), and thus α, remain near zero.

The prediction is quite different for the Partial group, for which the CS is an unreliable predictor of the US. This means that the discrepancy between λ and V_A should remain high, thus causing α_A to be strong. The strong attention resulting from the large α value should be manifest in terms of the subjects' ORs to the light.

The results are shown in Figure 6-9. There was a strong OR in the Continuous group initially, but a rapid decline thereafter. Similarly, the No-dipper group showed initial orientation, but rapid decline. The only group that

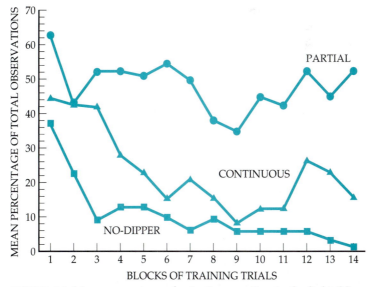

FIGURE 6-9. Mean percentage of orienting reaction to the light CS during 14 sessions for the groups that were given No-dipper presentations, Continuous, or Partial US presentations following the CS (after Kaye & Pearce, 1984).

showed continued orientation toward the light throughout training was the Partial group. This supports the Pearce–Hall model by showing that a stimulus is processed (attended to) when it is not an accurate predictor of its consequences. When the cue is an accurate predictor, as it was for the Continuous subjects, then subjects cease to process the stimulus, and orientation declines. Similarly, when the CS predicts nothing at all, as it did in the No-dipper subjects, then attention and orientation decline. Only in the Partial group, where the CS continued to be a poor predictor of the US, did the subjects continue to invest rehearsal time (as shown by the sustained orientation to the light).

The Pearce–Hall model explains a variety of other phenomena, including blocking. The model makes an assumption similar to that made by the Rescorla–Wagner model—namely, that all CSs combine to predict the US. Thus, attention to a CS_A is affected by how well the US is predicted by all the stimuli on the previous trial, not just by the CS_A itself. If one stimulus, say CS_A, is already strong as a result of a prior conditioning phase, then attention to, and processing of, an added stimulus, say CS_X, will be low because the quantity $(\lambda - V_T)$ is low.

Another phenomenon that the Pearce–Hall model accommodates is unblocking. The explanation is simple. When the subject encounters a US that is not well-predicted by existing stimuli (in other words, when the subject is surprised), the quantity $(\lambda - V_T)$ is large, and the α value increases. Subjects begin to attend to and to rehearse the added CS on the next trial. That is precisely what happens in an unblocking experiment. The conditions of the US change following the initial CS_A–US phase (for instance, the subject is given one US rather than two USs during compound conditioning), thus making the outcome surprising; this causes an increase in attention and processing.

Finally, the Pearce–Hall model, unlike the Rescorla–Wagner model, easily accommodates the latent-inhibition result. As discussed previously, when a CS is presented by itself during a preexposure phase, λ is essentially zero. This means that the α value for that CS (the subject's attention to, and processing of, the CS) declines to near zero. If the α value is low, then in Phase 2, when the CS is paired with a US, conditioning is retarded.

There is a special case of latent inhibition in which the preexposure phase actually entails the use of a weak US. More specifically, when the CS is followed by a weak US during Phase 1, and then, during training, it is followed by a strong US, a latent-inhibition effect is observed.[28] The Pearce–Hall model can accommodate this finding by arguing that α declines over the initial phase, thus causing retardation during Phase 2.[29]

Evaluation of Model

No model of Pavlovian conditioning is entirely sufficient. It is therefore not surprising that various findings challenge the Pearce–Hall model. One is the fact that when subjects are given CS preexposure (the latent-inhibition phenomenon) but then are placed in a different environment during the CS–US training phase, retardation of learning is absent.[30] The Pearce–Hall model cannot explain this because the model focuses exclusively on the attention value and processing of the CS, not on how the α value is affected by changes in the context.

A second problem for the Pearce–Hall model is that random CS and US presentations cause retardation of learning when the CS is later paired with the US.[31] The CS is not predictably followed by the US during Phase 1, and therefore attention to the CS should not decline, yet a retardation effect is observed.

Finally, the Pearce–Hall model claims that the extent of conditioning on trial n depends on the outcome on the previous trial—namely, on trial $n - 1$. However, consider the first compound conditioning trial in a blocking experiment, where CS_A/CS_X is followed by the US. If the added cue (CS_X) has an initial α value based on its salience, then conditioning to the cue should occur on the first trial (although blocking will occur on the second trial, and thereafter, because the cue is redundant). What happens, however, is that blocking occurs even on the first compound trial.[32]

INTERIM SUMMARY

The Pearce–Hall attention model emphasizes that the associability of a CS changes over training. Specifically, attention to the CS is strong at the start of conditioning, when the US is poorly predicted. However, as the CS becomes a better predictor of the US during acquisition, less rehearsal of the CS occurs; its associability declines. The Pearce–Hall model predicts many Pavlovian phenomena, including acquisition, latent inhibition, and blocking. It is also supported by the finding that subjects orient toward novel stimuli and maintain their orientation, provided the stimulus is a poor predictor of the US. Once the stimulus is a good predictor, orientation and processing decline. Like other models, however, the Pearce–Hall model cannot explain certain outcomes, such as the fact that retardation of learning following CS preexposure is abolished if the subject is trained in a novel environment.

MEMORY MODEL OF PAVLOVIAN CONDITIONING: WAGNER'S SOP MODEL

The US and CS processing models discussed in the preceding sections focus on why an association is formed during conditioning. The Rescorla–Wagner model, for example, suggests that an association develops when the outcome of a trial (the US) is not fully anticipated. The Pearce–Hall model, on the other hand, claims that associations develop, and a CS is processed, when the CS is uninformative. Neither theory is concerned with performance, however.

The **SOP model,** developed by Wagner and associates, provides an account of both the information processing that underlies the formation of an association, and the performance of the CR and the UR.[33] The term *SOP* stands for "sometimes opponent process" because the model suggests that there are several opposing memory processes that account for conditioning. The SOP model attempts to explain why associations are formed, under what conditions they are formed, and how they interact to produce behavior based on the activation of various memory centers.

Memory States

According to Wagner, each stimulus has a corresponding hypothetical memory center, called a "node." These nodes, shown schematically in Figure 6-10, are actually a collection of memory elements; each element corresponds to an attribute of the stimulus. Thus, a memory node represents the collective characteristics or features of either a CS or a US. The nodes themselves are part of a larger memory system, and they may become linked or associated through the conditioning process.

The elements in a node may be in one of several states. First, they may be in state I, meaning that they are inactive at the time (not currently being processed in the information-processing system). This is the normal resting state. Second, the elements may be transferred into one of two active short-term memory states. That is, when a stimulus is presented, the elements within the node are transferred to the A1 state. The A1 state means that the elements are in working memory; the elements are actively being rehearsed and attended to.

As soon as the elements of a memory node go into the A1 state, they immediately begin to decay into a second memory state, called "A2." This is depicted in Figure 6-10 by the arrow going from A1 to A2. The A2 state is also a short-term memory state, but the elements of the stimulus are not actively rehearsed during this time.

Finally, as time passes, the elements in state A2 begin to decay back into the inactive state (shown by the arrow from A2 to I).

The model has several important features, shown in Figure 6-10. First, the number of elements that are transferred from I to A1 depends on the characteristics of the stimulus, primarily its intensity. An intense stimulus (such as a US) triggers many elements of a node into the A1 state, whereas a less intense stimulus (such as a CS) causes a smaller percentage of elements to transfer.

Second, although the presentation of a stimulus causes elements to go from the I to the A1 state, activation of a node *by another node* causes the elements to be transferred from the I to the A2 state. This feature of the SOP model, also shown in Figure 6-10, is important because it suggests that one stimulus—for example, a CS—may activate another stimulus node—for example, a US node—causing the elements of the US node to become active in state A2 (see the following discussion for more on this point).

Finally, as shown in Figure 6-10, the system has a response generator. Comparatively little is said about how this generator works. According to Wagner, however, both the A1 and the A2 states trigger corresponding responses; the

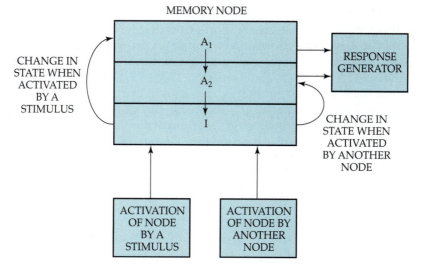

FIGURE 6-10. Schematic diagram of the SOP model, showing that the elements of a given memory node may be in one of three states—states I, A1, or A2. Activation of the node by an external stimulus causes the elements to be transferred into state A1; activation by another node causes them to transfer into state A2. Once in A1, elements spontaneously decay into A2; when in A2, the decay back into the I state (both are shown by the bold arrows). Performance (response generator) is determined by the proportion of elements that are contained in states A1 and A2 at any given time.

final action performed by the subject is the weighted combination of both of these states. In other words, the nature of the performance depends on the relative contribution of A1 and A2 elements. If more A1 elements are present, then the response generator executes a behavior consistent with the A1 state. Alternatively, if the A2 elements are proportionately more numerous, then the response generator causes performance of a response that is consistent with the A2 state (see the subsequent elaborated discussion of this point).

Excitatory Associations

According to the SOP model, an excitatory link between two nodes develops when the elements in each node are simultaneously in the A1 state. Stated differently, the affinity between two nodes increases (one node activates another node more easily) whenever the elements of both are in the A1 state. This can be expressed by the equation;

$$\Delta V^+ = P_{CSA1} \times P_{USA1}$$

This formula means that the change in excitatory strength (ΔV^+) equals the proportion of CS elements that are in the A1 state, times the proportion of US elements that are also in the A1 state.

To clarify how excitatory conditioning takes place under typical conditions (when the CS–US interval is short), consider the left two panels of Figure 6-11. The figure depicts what happens on an acquisition trial when a CS and a US are paired. When the CS is presented, the elements of the CS node are activated into state A1. These elements begin to decay into the A2 state, but before many of them do (that is, after only a brief period of time), a US is presented. Presentation of the US, however, causes the elements of the US node to be transferred into state A1. The proportion of elements that is converted directly into the A1 state is greater for the US node than for the CS node because the US is a more intense stimulus. The point is, however, that the US elements, and most of the CS elements, are primarily in the A1 state at the same time. According to the SOP model, an excitatory linkage develops between the nodes when this happens.

What about the CR that is activated by a CS after several excitatory training trials have been presented? According to the model, when a CS is presented, it not only activates the CS node, but also affects the US node (because

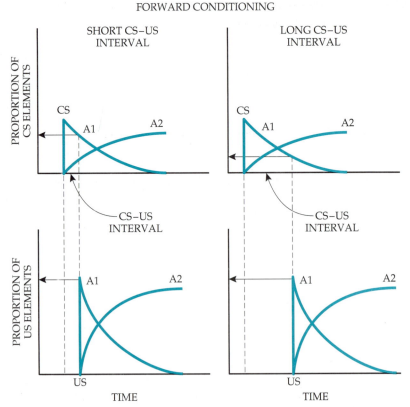

FIGURE 6-11. Schematic diagram showing how excitatory connections develop as a function of the CS and US states during a forward-conditioning trial with a short CS–US interval (left panels) or a longer CS–US interval (right panels).

of the associative linkage between the two). Activation of the elements in the US node by the CS node causes them to be transferred directly into the A2 state. Activation of the response generator then produces a CR in accordance with the US elements—that is, a reaction that is essentially like the UR.

Now consider what happens when the CS–US interval is quite long (see Figure 6-11, two panels on right). Recall from Chapter 4 that excitatory conditioning declines with longer intervals because contiguity is reduced. According to the SOP model, with a longer CS–US interval, most of the elements in the CS node have already decayed from state A1 into state A2 by the time the US is presented. This means that a lower proportion of CS elements is in state A1 when the US elements are transferred into the A1 state. If the strength of the excitatory conditioning on a given trial depends on the proportion of elements from both nodes that are simultaneously in state A1, then weaker conditioning will occur with long CS–US intervals.

Inhibitory Associations

The SOP model also stipulates that an inhibitory linkage develops when the elements of the two nodes are in different states at the same time. In other words, the affinity between two nodes decreases (one node more easily causes an inhibition of the other node) whenever the elements of one node are predominantly in the A1 state, but the elements of the other are primarily in the A2 state. This can be expressed by the equation,

$$\Delta V^- = P_{CSA1} \times P_{USA2}$$

This formula means that the change in inhibitory strength equals the proportion of CS elements that is in the A1 state, times the proportion of US elements that is in the A2 state.

Consider Figure 6-12, which shows the activation of memory nodes during a backward-conditioning trial. When the US is given first, the elements are transferred to the A1 state, but they begin to decay into state A2 immediately. When the CS then follows, the transfer of the CS elements into the A1 state occurs while US elements are in the A2 state. As Figure 6-12 shows, when the CS is given, CS elements are predominately in the A1 state, whereas, at that time, most of the US elements have decayed into state A2. Thus, when two nodes are in different active states, then the connection or linkage between them becomes inhibitory, meaning that the presentation of the CS inhibits the activation of the US node.

Net Associative Strength

The model makes one further stipulation—that the net change in associative strength is a function of both the excitatory and the inhibitory changes. That is, following the presentation of a stimulus, most of the elements will still be in the A1 state, although some will have decayed into A2. This means that *both* excitatory and inhibitory conditioning take place on a given trial. The

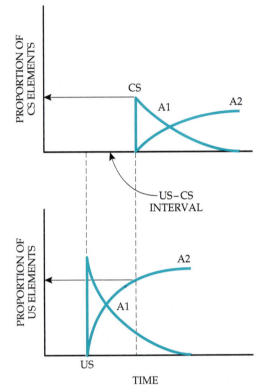

FIGURE 6-12. Schematic diagram showing how inhibitory connections develop as a function of the CS and US states during a backward-conditioning trial.

actual change in strength of the associative connection between nodes is determined by the joint excitatory and inhibitory changes. Specifically,

$$\Delta V^{NET} = \Delta V^{+} - \Delta V^{-}$$

This equation suggests that the net change in associative linkage between two nodes on any given trial is the difference between the change in excitation minus the change in inhibition.

Consider what this means on forward-conditioning trials. As the excitatory linkage between the CS and the US nodes increases over training, an inhibitory reaction also begins to develop. The reason is that on a given excitatory trial, the CS elements are in A1, and the US elements are in A2 (because activation of a node by another node causes the elements of the first to be transferred into state A2). According to the model, an inhibitory reaction begins to develop under these conditions. This inhibitory linkage counteracts the excitatory linkage, causing a gradual decrease in the net excitatory strength on each trial. Such a decrease is evident as the asymptote of learning.

Support for the SOP Model

The SOP model is a sophisticated account of how associations are formed. The model also explains a number of basic phenomena, such as acquisition, extinction, and inhibition, as well as a number of more specific phenomena, including blocking, superconditioning, the effect of the intertrial interval on conditioning, and differences between the UR and the CR. Although the details of how the model explains each of these outcomes is beyond the scope of this text, we briefly review several interesting examples.

The SOP model explains simple extinction in the following way. When a CS that has undergone conditioning is presented by itself, it transfers the elements in the CS node into state A1 and the elements of the US node into state A2. Recall that the model stipulates that when the elements of one node are in A1, but those of the other are in A2, the inhibitory linkage is increased. This is what happens during extinction.

The SOP model also accounts for blocking. Consider what happens when a CS_X is compounded with an already powerful CS_A during the compound conditioning phase. Both CSs activate the elements in their respective memory node, causing them to be transferred into the A1 state. A few seconds later, when the US is presented, the US elements are also transferred into the A1 state. However, because the CS_A node has a strong excitatory linkage with the US node (from the original training phase), CS_A also causes elements in the US node to be transferred into the A2 state. The elements in the CS_X node, therefore, are in the A1 state, whereas the elements of the US node are in both the A1 and the A2 states (A1 because the US itself was given, and A2 because CS_A was given). The linkage between the added stimulus, CS_X, and the US will therefore be both excitatory and inhibitory, and the net change in strength to the added CS_X will be negligible.[34]

Challenges to the SOP Model

Despite its success, there are problems for the SOP model.[35] For example, different conclusions about the strength of an association may be reached when different CR measures are used. In one such experiment by Schneiderman (1972), the nictitating-membrane response and the heart-rate reaction were simultaneously measured in rabbits. These two measures gave very different pictures of conditioning. Certain CS–US intervals that produced strong conditioning measured by one CR led to very weak conditioning measured by the other CR, and vice versa. The SOP model has problems explaining this because, according to the model, variations in the CS–US interval should have changed the strength of each CR but should not have changed them differentially. In other words, the data are inconsistent with the SOP model because the strength of one kind of CR increased with changes in the CS–US interval, whereas the strength of the other kind of CR declined with these changes. The SOP model predicts that a uniform change in CR intensity, as a function of the CS–US interval, should occur for *both* CR measures. To accommodate this problem, as well as other issues, Wagner and his associates have developed a modified version of the SOP model, named AESOP (the AE stands for "affective extension" of the SOP model). Simply stated, the AESOP model contains virtually all of the assumptions of the SOP model, as well as additional principles to account for the emotional effects of the US.[36]

INTERIM SUMMARY

Wagner's SOP memory model not only explains how an association is formed, but also accounts for the CR and UR performance. The term SOP stands for "sometimes opponent process" because the model argues that there are opposing memory processes that are involved in conditioning. Specifically, elements (which correspond to attributes of stimuli) are collected in memory nodes. When a node is activated by a stimulus, its elements are transferred into an active state, A1. As time passes, these decay into state A2, and they remain active but are not rehearsed or processed. Finally, the elements in state A2 decay back into the inactive state, I. When a memory node is activated by another node, the elements are transferred directly into the A2 state. Both the A1 and A2 states have corresponding response generators, such that performance is determined by the joint action of the two. According to the model, when a CS is presented and the US occurs soon thereafter, the elements in both the CS and the US nodes are in the A1 state, and thus an excitatory linkage occurs. If the CS–US interval is long, however, then the elements in the CS node have transferred to state A2 by the time the US is activated. Here, an inhibitory linkage is formed (because the elements of the two nodes are in different states). The net change in associative strength is a function of both the excitatory and the inhibitory changes. Thus, both excitatory and inhibitory conditioning take place on each trial, and the outcome is the algebraic sum of the two kinds of tendencies. The SOP model is a sophisticated account that explains many phenomena, including the facts of acquisition, extinction, inhibition, blocking, and superconditioning.

ENDNOTES

1. Jenkins and Moore (1973).
2. See also Woodruff and Starr (1978). Recall also from Chapter 4 that CR–UR identity is not confined to autoshaping in birds; similar results have been found, for example, in dogs (see Jenkins, Barrera, Ireland, & Woodside, 1978). In addition, Meachum and Bernstein (1990) have shown that a rat's reaction to a flavor CS that had been paired with a poison is the same as its reaction to the poison itself. Both the CS and the US elicit "lying-on-belly" behavior, typically shown by rats when they are ill (but see Parker [1982] and Parker, Hills, & Jensen [1984] for conflicting evidence). Similarly, both coyotes (Gustavson, Garcia, Hankins, & Rusiniak, 1974)

and human beings (Carey & Burish, 1988) have shown conditioned nausea and vomiting to a CS that had been paired with a US that elicited those behaviors unconditionally.

3. Analogous results were found for subjects that were water deprived, although the effects were not noticeable unless the animals were deprived for at least two days.
4. See also Alberts (1978); Peele and Ferster (1982); Timberlake and Grant (1975).
5. See Holland (1990) for a review.
6. See also Holland and Rescorla (1975b); Holland and Straub (1979).
7. This same effect is common in everyday human experience. Imagine jumping into a cold shower. At first it is extremely cold and aversive. However, after getting used to it—that is, after experiencing it for a while—one becomes habituated. The temperature is no longer perceived to be as aversively cold as it was originally.
8. See also Holland (1983b); Holland and Forbes (1982).
9. See Rescorla (1979).
10. There actually is a second constant in the Rescorla–Wagner equation—namely, β. This term refers to the strength properties of the US, but because it does not affect how the model works in this example, discussion of the term has been omitted for the sake of clarity. Note, however, that β accounts for such important effects as the asymptotic level of responding. The larger the β value, the stronger the conditioning.
11. The shape of the learning curve depicted here depends strongly on the values chosen for the α, β, and λ. Curves having different slopes would occur with different values.
12. $\Delta V_X = (.5)(100 - 96.875) = 1.55$.
13. See Baker, Singh, and Bindra (1985) for a review.
14. See also Baker, Mercier, Gabel, and Baker (1981).
15. Hinson (1982).
16. Matzel, Brown, and Miller (1987).
17. However, see Timberlake (1986) for an alternative explanation.
18. See Miller, Barnet, and Grahame (1995) for a review.
19. An important modification of the original Rescorla–Wagner model, by Wagner (1978), was developed to account for findings such as latent inhibition.
20. Bouton, Jones, McPhillips, and Swartzentruber (1986).
21. A similar effect has been observed using other stimuli. For example, a taste that has been paired with poison later will facilitate or potentiate the conditioning of a visual cue with which it is compounded (Jackson & Fritsche, 1989; Westbrook, Harvey, & Swinbourne, 1988). Here again, the Rescorla–Wagner model would argue that the already strong stimulus should block, not facilitate, conditioning to the new added stimulus.
22. See also Mackintosh, Bygrave, and Picton (1977). For the sake of brevity, only two of the groups in this study are described here. Two additional groups were run in Experiment 3. One was given single shocks on both Phase 1 and Phase 2 of the study, whereas the other was given a single shock on Phase 1 and a double shock on Phase 2. The results were virtually the same as the groups reported, but because the arguments against the Rescorla–Wagner model are somewhat less compelling, discussion of these groups has been omitted.
23. Barnet, Grahame, and Miller (1993); Schreurs and Westbrook (1982); but see Ayres and Bombace (1982) for conflicting evidence.
24. Miller, Barnet, and Grahame (1995) list 23 findings that the Rescorla–Wagner model cannot accommodate, and 18 results that the model explains easily.

25. Pearce and Hall (1980); see also Hall and Pearce (1982a); Pearce, Kaye, and Hall (1982). The Pearce–Hall model owes a substantial debt to an earlier version developed by Mackintosh (1975a). In Mackintosh's theory, the associability of a CS increases as that CS becomes a good predictor of the US. This contrasts with the Pearce–Hall model, where the CS associability declines as the CS becomes a good predictor. For the sake of brevity, we discuss the Pearce–Hall model rather than the Mackintosh model because the former provides a useful account of several findings that the latter cannot easily accommodate.

26. Recall that the Rescorla–Wagner model argued that the amount of associability of a CS was fixed at α.

27. Kaye and Pearce (1984a); Pearce and Kaye (1985).

28. See Hall and Pearce (1979, 1982a).

29. Other attention models of Pavlovian conditioning, such as the one proposed by Mackintosh (1975a), cannot explain this finding.

30. Lubow, Rifkin, and Alek (1976); see also Kasprow, Schachtman, and Miller (1985).

31. Baker and Mackintosh (1979).

32. Azorlosa and Cicala (1986); Balaz, Kasprow, and Miller (1982).

33. For reviews, see Mazur and Wagner (1982); Wagner (1981); Wagner and Brandon (1989); and Wagner and Larew (1985).

34. The SOP model also explains some interesting and important findings relating to the differences between the CR and the UR. Recall that the response generator produces behaviors that reflect the relative proportion of elements in the A1 and A2 states. It is well-known that some reactions are biphasic. For example, if a subject is given a foot shock, the immediate response is hyperactivity (subjects jump and move about vigorously), but this reaction quickly gives way to a second response—namely, freezing in place; see Blanchard and Blanchard (1969a); Bolles and Collier (1976); Bolles and Riley (1973); see also Wagner and Brandon (1989) for a more detailed review of this phenomenon. This is not to imply that all URs are biphasic. Indeed, Wagner and Brandon (1989) point out that in some cases, the CR may be complementary rather than antagonistic.

35. See Wagner and Brandon (1989).

36. See Wagner and Brandon (1989).

CHAPTER 7

Conditioning of Biologically Adaptive States

CONDITIONING AND ECOLOGICAL RELEVANCE

Preceding chapters argued that learning in general and Pavlovian conditioning in particular allow animals to cope more successfully with the demands of their environment. Simply stated, many organisms have evolved the capacity to profit from their experience (to learn), so that they may behave more adaptively in the future and thus have a greater chance of reproducing. Most of the preceding chapters focused on the precise way in which animals process information and translate that information into behavior. This chapter considers the way in which Pavlovian learning directly affects an organism's behavior within the ecological niche that the species occupies. This so-called "ecological approach to learning" emphasizes the ways in which learning processes help animals adapt to their environment.[1]

The way that Pavlovian conditioning helps an animal to cope with the demands of the environment was summarized by Hollis (1982). "Consider the difficulties an animal faces if it must actively search for food, water, or for a mate. Where and when can food be found and mates secured? Likewise, where and when will predators most likely strike and rivals appear? For many animals the strategic difficulties of searching . . . would be insuperable obstacles to survival if the environment were a capricious one. But given that an animal could predict where and when food would be available, such information would provide considerable savings in foraging time and energy reserves. And, if an animal could locate predators based upon, say, some sort of warning signal, the danger of a surprise attack would be negated altogether. Pavlovian conditioning is a mechanism for such predictions" (pp. 1–2).

Hollis suggests two important arguments. First, an animal is an information processor, deriving valuable information concerning resources in the environment by means of Pavlovian conditioning. The fact that an animal gathers valid information, not false information, is related to the predictive validity of the signals. CSs become meaningful and powerful when they selectively predict certain important outcomes, usually USs; in the natural environment, these would typically be predators, mates, or nourishment.

Hollis's second argument is that animals not only gather and process valid information, but they also behave adaptively. Classically conditioned reactions are important in this respect because they help subjects cope with their environment in important ways. For example, the CRs may help the subjects to secure mates or food. The general purpose of this chapter is to review a number of the phenomena that illustrate how Pavlovian conditioning contributes directly to the animal's adaptive coping strategies.[2]

INTERIM SUMMARY

Pavlovian conditioning is relevant to an animal's struggle for survival. Classically conditioned CSs serve as signals for important resources, such as food, and for dangerous threats, such as predators. Pavlovian CRs, therefore, prepare an animal to manage its resources, and they facilitate various kinds of survival behaviors, including courtship and copulation, and defensive reactions.

REGULATION OF APPETITIVE BEHAVIOR

One of the most interesting and important areas of research in learning has focused on how animals regulate their diet. This is a crucial problem for an animal if it is to remain healthy and competitive. Individuals who do not receive sufficient nutrients, or those who, for one reason or another, ingest harmful substances, are clearly at a selective disadvantage.

There are numerous strategies for regulating diet. Some species exist perfectly well by specializing in a single food item; for them, diet selection is innate. Other species consume a variety of substances, so they must learn to select which food items are most appropriate. Imagine how maladaptive it would be if such an animal could not learn to identify ahead of time those food items that it could safely eat. Each time it was hungry, the animal would have to sample a food and then wait to see whether the food provided sufficient nutrients (or induced illness). This would be enormously time consuming.

Being able to recognize that a food is healthy and appropriate from its appearance, taste, or odor is a much more adaptive way to deal with the problem. Such learning would endow the animal with great flexibility. Subjects could change their eating habits if the environment no longer contained the food they were used to consuming, they could seek out new kinds of food that were more nutritious than those found in their present diet, or they could learn to avoid harmful foods if they had experienced illness in the past.

Food Aversions

As described in Chapters 3 and 4, an **acquired taste aversion** occurs when a flavor is associated with an illness-inducing outcome—for example, a poison or a deficiency in the diet.[3] In most studies, the subject is given a flavored solution, such as saccharin-flavored water, and then is injected with lithium chloride, which produces nausea. On a later test, the animal shows an aversion to the flavored substance by not consuming it. Control subjects, who receive a placebo during training, drink the fluid quite readily. Flavor CSs thus become aversive when paired with a poison, much as lights or tones become aversive when paired with a shock.[4]

Taste aversions are observed not only in the laboratory but also in natural settings, and for a wide variety of species, including humans.[5] For example, various types of butterflies, especially monarchs, are poisonous because they consume a variety of milkweed and store a toxic substance in their bodies. Blue jays that consume this variety of butterfly become ill and subsequently avoid eating all monarchs (even those that do not eat the poisonous substance). They even avoid eating other species of butterflies, such as viceroy butterflies, that have a similar appearance but are not themselves poisonous.[6] Birds do not even have to experience the illness to learn to avoid a visually distinctive food object. The prey item merely has to taste bitter.[7]

Selectivity of Association.

Most studies on Pavlovian conditioning use arbitrary CSs such as lights and tones interchangeably. It rarely makes a difference which cue is used, because each easily becomes associated with USs such as shock. This practice may have the unfortunate consequence of implying that *all* stimuli become associated in the same way. Research on taste aversion has shown that this is not the case, however. Some stimuli, such as flavors and poison, are more easily associated than others, such as lights and poison.

In a noted experiment by Garcia and Koelling (1966), thirsty rats were allowed to drink a saccharin-flavored solution while a light and a noise were being presented. The authors thought of this compound CS as a "bright, noisy, and tasty" cue. One group of animals was then given a mild poison US; a different group received a shock US. In Phase 2, Garcia and Koelling tested the animals for their acquired aversion. Half the animals that had received the poison US were given the "tasty" solution (the saccharin-flavored solution), whereas the other half were given the "bright noisy" solution (plain water accompanied by the light and noise stimuli). The group that had received the shock US was similarly divided into two subgroups, half being tested with the flavor CS and the other half with the light–noise CS.

As shown in Figure 7-1, drinking of the flavored solution was significantly reduced (that is, conditioning of the flavor component was strong) in the poison condition. Similarly, water drinking during the light and noise components was reduced (conditioning to the light–noise CS was strong) in the shock condition. The other combinations did not produce very strong condi-

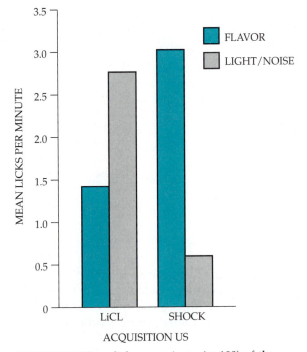

FIGURE 7-1. Mean licks per minute ($\times$ 100) of the "tasty" solution (blue bars) or the "bright, noisy" water (grey bars) for the groups that were injected with poison (LiCl) during training (left) or that were given the shock US (right) (after Garcia & Koelling, 1966).

tioning. The flavor did not become especially aversive when it was followed by shock, and the light–noise CS did not become strongly aversive when followed by poison. In other words, rats easily associated the flavor and the poison, and they were equally good at associating the light–noise and the shock. However, they were poor at learning an association between flavor and shock, and between light–noise and poison.[8]

This dramatic result led a number of theorists to speculate that flavors and poison naturally go together; they belong to the same biological feeding system and thus are especially prone to becoming associated. Flavors and poison are uniquely associable because stomach malaise in the natural environment is almost surely a result of having eaten a harmful substance; it never occurs as a result of receiving a light–noise stimulus. Externally acting stimuli, on the other hand, such as lights and noises, do not belong to internal reactions such as illness; they are essentially irrelevant to one another, so conditioned associations do not occur readily.

The finding that all CSs are not equally associable with all USs provoked the notion that taste aversion is a biologically specialized form of learning.[9] This is an appealing idea from an evolutionary point of view. Animals in the distant past who had a keen ability to identify the flavors of the food that had caused illness were less likely to eat the food again, and thus less likely to be fatally poisoned. These animals had a greater likelihood of surviving and raising offspring. Individuals who lacked this ability were more likely to consume the poison again and thus more likely to die before raising offspring.

If taste aversion evolved as a specialized form of learning, because animals who could better associate a taste with its maladaptive consequence were at a selective advantage, then we should observe other kinds of specialized learning in different species that rely on sensory systems other than taste. For example, if we test an animal whose primary means of locating and procuring food is based on visual appearance, not taste, then these animals should show the opposite result—namely, a stronger association between a visual cue and a poison than between a flavor and a poison.

This issue was addressed in a study by Wilcoxon, Dragoin, and Kral (1971). Both rats and quail were used as subjects. They were given a sour-flavored solution that had been colored blue with food dye. Thus, the animals experienced two types of CSs: an internal gustatory CS (flavor) and an external visual CS (color). Following CS administration, all animals were poisoned with lithium chloride. In the test phase, one group of rats and quail received blue water, whereas another group of rats and quail received a colorless, sour-flavored fluid. The subjects that were given the blue water were being tested for their aversion to the color, whereas those that were given the sour solution were being tested for their aversion to the flavor. The results were striking. Rats showed a strong aversion to drinking the flavored solution but virtually no aversion to drinking the colored water (this result, therefore, replicates the findings of Garcia and Koelling discussed previously). The quail showed a very different pattern of avoidance, however. They demonstrated a strong aversion to drinking the colored solution, but little aversion to the flavored fluid.

By suggesting that rats cannot learn about visual cues (and quail cannot learn a flavor–poison association), these experiments imply that specialized sensory and attentional systems have evolved, and that these systems influence learning. Specifically, smell and taste are important for food procurement in rats; it therefore makes ecological sense for taste to be used more readily as a signal for aversion than color. However, visual stimuli are more important in foraging for quail; for the most part, birds use visual cues to locate and identify food items. Their ability to identify potentially poisonous foods based on visual appearance, therefore, makes sense from an ecological perspective.

However, do these studies prove that taste aversion violates the most fundamental law of Pavlovian conditioning—namely, that CSs and USs become associated when contiguously paired? The answer is far from clear.[10] Indeed, current thinking suggests that although taste-aversion learning may differ from other forms of Pavlovian learning (such as eye-blink or CER conditioning) in some interesting ways, it does not seriously violate the fundamental laws of Pavlovian conditioning.[11] Let us review the evidence.

First, many have argued that taste-aversion learning is essentially like other forms of Pavlovian conditioning because most of the phenomena found in conventional Pavlovian studies are also found in taste-aversion learning research.[12] For example, strength of conditioning depends on US and CS intensity in both taste-aversion and conventional Pavlovian conditioning tasks.[13] Similarly, conditioned inhibition, latent inhibition, sensory preconditioning, second-order conditioning, retardation of future learning following preexposure to the poison US, and blocking are Pavlovian phenomena that have been demonstrated in both conventional and taste-aversion studies.[14]

Second, the **nonequivalence of associability** finding probably results, at least in part, from differences in the nature of the CSs. In an experiment by Krane and Wagner (1975), for example, different groups of rats were given either a saccharin solution (S), a light–tone CS (L/T), or plain water (W), followed by a shock. The shock was delayed for 5, 30, or 210 seconds. This arrangement yielded nine separate groups of rats: S-5, S-30, S-210, L/T-5, L/T-30, L/T-210, W-5, W-30, and W-210. Later, subjects were tested for their consumption of either the saccharin solution or the water accompanied by the light–tone stimulus.

The authors found that conditioning was strong for the light–tone–shock association but only when the CS–US interval was short. The flavor–shock association was also strong, but only when the CS–US interval was long. The other combinations produced weaker CRs. In other words, subjects easily associated the flavor and shock (but *only* if some appreciable delay occurred between them), and light–tone and shock (but *only* if they were contiguous). These results, therefore, do not support the notion of belongingness. Flavors *are* associable with shocks, but the sensory trace of a flavor is longer than that of a light–tone stimulus, and therefore conditioning takes place when the US is delayed. Krane and Wagner claimed that their results "could be generated by conventional principles of Pavlovian conditioning plus the assumption that the stimulus trace occasioned by saccharin consumption is more persistent than that occasioned by exposure to a light–tone compound" (p. 887).[15]

The foregoing study showed that flavors may become strongly associated with shock. The converse finding has also been demonstrated; that is, rats may also develop an aversion to the external characteristics of food when paired with poison. In an interesting study by Domjan and Hanlon (1982), food pellets were placed inside small metal cylinders or sleeves.[16] To eat the food, the rats had to handle the metal sleeves and extract the food from inside; they could not simply break off a piece. The surface of some of the cylinders was smooth, whereas the surface of others was rough-textured.

The results of the study are shown in Figure 7-2. Subjects, for whom the food inside the sleeve was poisoned, were strongly conditioned to the texture of the sleeve, not simply taste. Not only did the subjects hold the poisoned cylinder less time (left side, blue bar), but they also ate significantly less of that kind of food (right side, blue bar).[17]

How do we resolve this dilemma? Are animals such as rats capable of using *any* CS as a signal for illness, or are these subjects relatively constrained in their learning, able to learn only that tastes belong to illness? One set of findings suggests that both possibilities may be true, at least in part. The CS that is most easily conditioned is the cue that the animal actually uses to procure food.

Photograph of a rat in the study by Domjan and Hanlon (1982) in which food was placed in small metal cylinders. Because the subjects had to manipulate the cylinder to extract the food, the surface texture of the cylinder could serve as a conditioned stimulus.
Courtesy of Professor Michael Domjan, University of Texas at Austin

This notion was suggested in an interesting study by Gillette, Martin, and Bellingham (1980). Young chickens were given aversion training using several CSs. Subjects had no trouble forming an aversion to colored food, but they were much worse at learning an aversion to colored water. On the surface, these results appear to conflict with those discussed previously—namely, that birds learn an aversion to the color of water more strongly than to its flavor.

To explain their findings, the authors closely examined the actual behavior of the chickens as they ate and drank. When eating, the bird would position its head inside the feeding trough and maintain visual contact with the food throughout; it had to look at the food in order to peck at it accurately. On the other hand, when the chicken drank from the recessed water trough, it did not really orient visually to the water; rather, it dipped its beak into the trough and immediately retracted its head to allow the fluid to run down its throat. In doing so, the bird did not seem to utilize the visual aspects of the water.

The authors speculated that an aversion to the colored water would occur if the animals actually had to use, or attend to, the color when drinking. In a follow-up study, the authors installed drinking spouts similar to the ones used in previous research and confirmed that the color of the water was, indeed,

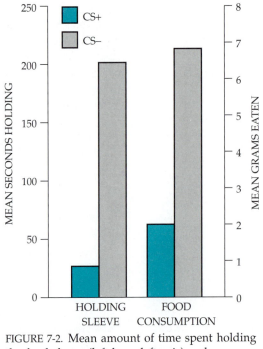

FIGURE 7-2. Mean amount of time spent holding the food sleeve (left bars, left axis) and mean amount eaten (right bars, right axis), as a function of whether the textured sleeve had been followed by poison (CS+) or not (CS−) (after Domjan & Hanlon, 1982).

conditioned more strongly than the taste. This study, therefore, indicates that conditioning is not limited to taste (for rats) or color (for birds) because they are constrained otherwise. The method by which subjects procure food is seemingly more critical.

For many animals, including rats, taste and smell are the most dominant stimulus dimensions in their natural feeding environment. Birds, on the other hand, normally use visual cues in their environment, so there is some selective advantage for color over taste. However, if rats are forced to utilize their nonpreferred sense modality, then learning proceeds quite readily. Similarly, if the situation is structured so that the birds are exposed to the flavor of the water (and other dimensions are less salient), then taste will become conditioned more strongly than visual attributes of the CS. In short, color will not *always* prevail over taste in birds simply because they are visually oriented animals; similarly, taste will not *always* be more salient in rats even though they normally use taste and smell to identify food in their natural environment. Rats and quail may develop aversions to stimuli other than taste and color, depending on which cues they actually use in procuring the CS substance.

A related point was made in a study by Domjan and Wilson (1972). Rats had a small metal tube (called a "cannula") implanted into their cheek so that a taste solution could be infused directly into the oral cavity. All subjects were infused for two minutes with the same amount of taste CS, but they differed in terms of the amount that was actually ingested. That is, by varying the rate at which the solution was infused, the amount that the subject actually swallowed could be controlled. The faster the rate of infusion, the more the solution spilled and thus the less was actually swallowed (some subjects were even given water prior to the conditioning test so that they would not be thirsty and would swallow even less of the taste solution). Twenty-five minutes after the infusion procedure, subjects were injected with lithium chloride. On the following day, they were given a 30-minute choice test between the saccharin solution and the water.

The results are shown in Figure 7-3. Although all of the poisoned groups showed a conditioned taste aversion relative to the unpoisoned control subjects, the weakest aversion was shown in the group that drank the least

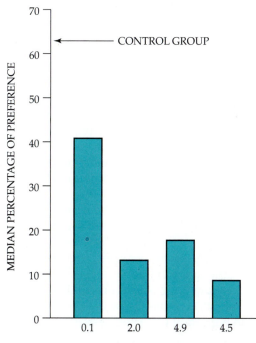

MILLILITERS OF INGESTED CS SOLUTION

FIGURE 7-3. Median percentage of preference for the saccharin solution on the preference test for the groups that differed in terms of the time spent drinking the CS. The amount of drinking in a control group that received no poison US is shown by the arrow (after Domjan & Wilson, 1972).

amount of flavored solution during training. In conclusion, the amount of CS solution that is ingested, not simply attended to, has an important bearing on the strength of the conditioned taste aversion.

Sullivan (1984) reviewed the literature and came to the following conclusions about the selectivity of associations in taste-aversion research. An aversion is learned when the CS is an attribute of the substance that is actually ingested, regardless of the sense modality. When external cues, such as the texture or appearance, are a part of the ingested substance, then they serve perfectly well as CSs in aversion learning. If, however, the cues are not part of the ingested substance, then aversion learning is poor. This resolution makes good sense from an evolutionary point of view. After all, in nature, a substance that is actually swallowed poses a potential threat of poisoning; substances not ingested do not provide such a threat.

Is taste aversion unique with respect to the kinds of associations that develop? The foregoing discussion suggests that the answer is both yes and no. There are certainly many unusual characteristics of taste-aversion learning, but there are also many similarities between taste-aversion learning and other forms of Pavlovian conditioning.

In addition to the argument that taste aversion involves selective associations, there are a number of other distinctive and interesting characteristics of taste-aversion learning.

Potentiation of Conditioning.

Recall from Chapter 5 the discussion of overshadowing. If a stimulus is very salient, then that stimulus may overshadow the conditioning of a stimulus with which it is combined. Given this phenomenon, it is surprising to discover that in the area of taste aversion, the opposite usually occurs. When a taste is compounded with another weaker cue, it actually potentiates or enhances the conditioning of that cue.[18] Such a **potentiation** effect may occur when a taste is combined with odors, the surrounding apparatus cues, or even weaker tastes.[19]

Many theorists have tried to explain why taste, a very salient cue for a rat, facilitates rather than overshadows conditioning of other less salient stimuli with which it is combined. One of the early speculations, based on the belongingness concept discussed previously, was the **sensory channelling theory**.[20] According to this position, because taste belongs to a rat's feeding system, it channels other cues with which it is combined into this feeding system. In a sense, the subject becomes more alert or attentive to a cue that is combined with a taste because the feeding system is called into operation by the taste.

Part of the evidence for this theory is based on a study by Rusiniak, Palmerino, Rice, Forthman, and Garcia (1982), in which rats were given an odor or an odor–flavor compound, followed either by lithium chloride or foot shock. When the CSs were followed by poison, taste was more effective than odor (this is typically found). Moreover, the odor was more aversive when it was combined with the taste than when it occurred alone (this is the potentiation result). The odor did not become more aversive, however, when followed by shock, relative to when it was presented in the odor–flavor compound and followed by shock.[21] Thus, the taste–poison combination was part of the animal's feeding system, and because the odor was combined with the taste, it, too, was channelled into this system, causing better conditioning. When the feeding system was not called into action (when a shock US was used), the potentiation did not occur.

The sensory channelling theory of potentiation has been criticized in other studies. Some investigators found that potentiation occurs primarily when the potentiated stimulus is exceptionally weak, relative to the taste. In other words, a taste potentiates the conditioning of another stimulus, but only if that second stimulus is not at all salient.[22]

An even more serious criticism is the finding that potentiation is not limited to situations involving poison USs. In a study by Westbrook, Harvey, and Swinbourne (1988), for example, two groups of rats were given a sucrose solution for 20 minutes in a novel environment; two other groups received water in the novel apparatus. One group in each of these CS conditions was then given an injection of lithium chloride, and the other was given shock. Thus, there were four groups—namely, sucrose–lithium, sucrose–shock, water–lithium, and water–shock. After several days of training, the subjects were tested for their aversion to water in the conditioning apparatus. The question was whether the sucrose that was given to two of the groups had potentiated the conditioning to the apparatus cues, such that, when the rats were placed back in that environment and given access to water, consumption would be relatively suppressed.

The results on four test sessions are shown in Figure 7-4. First, consider the groups that received the poison US (open circles). There is clear evidence of potentiation. Specifically, subjects that were given sucrose in the novel environment learned an aversion for that environment more strongly than subjects that were given only water. Flavor potentiated conditioning to the apparatus cues. The more interesting data, however, are for those animals that received a shock US during training (closed circles). Potentiation occurred for these groups, as well. In short, subjects that received sucrose in the novel environment, followed by shock, showed a greater aversion to the environment (suppression of drinking) than animals that had merely received water and shock during training. In conclusion, one cannot explain potentiation in terms of the taste cue channelling the apparatus cues into the feeding system, because even animals that had received the shock US showed potentiation.

An alternative theory of potentiation is based on more conventional principles of Pavlovian learning, as discussed in Chapters 5 and 6.[23] The theory claims that three associations actually develop when a taste is combined with another cue and then followed by poison. One is the flavor–poison association; a second is the context–poison association; the third is the flavor–context association. In other words, each of the two combined CSs is associated with the US, but the CSs are also associated with each other. On the test, when the potentiated cue is presented, it elicits the memory of the US (it is directly associated

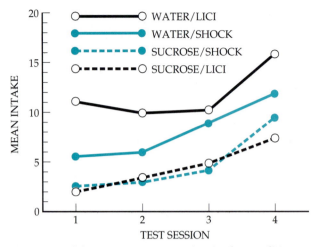

FIGURE 7-4. Mean water consumption in the conditioning environment, as a function of test session, for subjects that received water or a sucrose solution during
training, and a shock or a lithium chloride (LiCl) US
(after Westbrook, Harvey, & Swinbourne, 1988).

with the US), as well as the memory or representation for the taste cue. The
taste cue, in turn, also elicits the memory of the US because of its direct association with it. These two associations therefore summate, producing a stronger
reaction than would otherwise be observed, had the taste not been present.

Interesting support for this theory was shown by Miller, McCoy, Kelly,
and Bardo (1986). Rats were given 15 minutes of access to a flavor–odor combination (saccharin and almond, respectively). Immediately following consumption, one group was injected with a morphine US (a drug that produces
taste aversion), whereas another group was given a saline injection. No conditioning would be expected in the second group of subjects. Following the
training sessions, half of the subjects in each of the two injection groups was
given 15 minutes of access to the saccharin solution by itself, to extinguish the
saccharin–poison association. The other subjects were given only water and
thus did not experience any extinction of the saccharin aversion. Finally, all
subjects were given a test of their aversion to the almond odor.

Consumption during the 15-minute test is shown in Figure 7-5. As
expected, no aversion was shown in the two saline groups. For the morphine-
injected groups, however, the aversion to the almond solution was stronger
in the group that did not receive extinction of the saccharin aversion than in
the group that did. Thus, the saccharin aversion apparently had combined or
summated with the almond aversion. Stated differently, potentiation of the
almond aversion by the saccharin resulted from the summation of the
almond–US and saccharin–US associations because when the saccharin association was reduced through extinction, the summation could not occur, and
thus the aversion to the odor solution was observed to be weaker.[24]

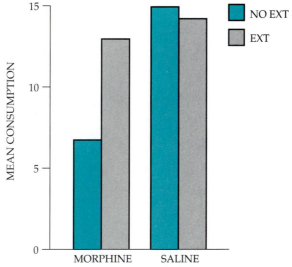

FIGURE 7-5. Mean consumption (in milliliters) of the almond-odor solution by subjects that received an almond–saccharin compound and either a morphine or a saline injection, followed by extinction or no extinction of the saccharin aversion (after Miller, McCoy, Kelly, & Bardo, 1986).

Long-Delay Learning.

Another important characteristic of taste-aversion learning is the fact that the taste–poison association may occur even when the CS and the US are separated by a considerable period of time.[25] In one study by Kalat and Rozin (1971), different groups of rats were given a sucrose solution followed by lithium chloride, which was presented 0.5, 1, 1.5, 3, 6, or 24 hours later. Subjects were tested for their aversion to the sucrose 2 days later, by being presented with a choice between sucrose and water. The results were shown in Figure 4–13 in Chapter 4. They reveal that the percentage of preference for sucrose, the substance the rats normally prefer, increased as a function of the CS–US interval. Thus, a strong aversion was evident in the groups that received lithium chloride within 1 hour following consumption, but no aversion was evident in subjects that were poisoned 6 hours later; they preferred sucrose as much as the 24-hour subjects.

The fact that taste aversion occurs even when the US is delayed for several hours differs from what has been found in studies on, say, conditioned salivation or heart rate, where conditioning fails to occur with CS–US intervals longer than about 10 to 20 seconds. Taste aversion is thus unique in this respect, although some argue that this distinction is really more quantitative than qualitative. That is, the long delay feature violates the usual finding concerning contiguity, but only in the sense that the limits of contiguity are extended by these findings, not refuted altogether.

The **long delay feature of taste aversion** is certainly consistent with an evolutionary perspective. In the distant past, animals that could bridge the long interval between tasting a food item and its poisonous consequence were at a selective advantage; if they survived, they were better able to remember the poisonous substance and to avoid consuming it again (when a second tasting could result in death). In nature, the effects of poisoning typically do not occur immediately upon ingestion of a food, and thus the selective pressure to bridge a relatively long gap was strong.

The fact that taste aversions may be learned when the US is delayed for several hours has intrigued psychologists for nearly 3 decades. One explanation for the effect, the **learned-safety theory,** claims that during a long CS–US interval, animals are actually learning that the flavor is safe.[26] If the interval is long enough—say, 24 hours—the animals show no aversion because they have learned that the CS flavor is safe, not because they have failed to associate the two stimuli.

Let us consider this theory in more detail. It is well known that many animals display **neophobia**—that is, they fear new objects, environments, and, especially, novel flavors.[27] Neophobia is an adaptive reaction to novel objects. If an animal did not show caution when it encountered a new food, it might well consume appreciable amounts. This could be a disastrous mistake because the food could be poisonous. Therefore, animals are born to react warily to new food. At first, they eat only a small portion, but after repeated experience with the food, consumption increases, presumably because the animals have judged the food to be safe. If the animals experience illness prior to the time when they judge the food to be safe, neophobia is reinstated.[28]

Returning to the learned-safety theory, the extinction of neophobia following exposure to a new food is similar to the acquisition of a sense of safety. Extinction of fear of the substance reflects the knowledge of the safety of the substance. The lack of an aversion with a long CS–US interval, therefore, does not mean that an animal failed to associate the CS and the US. Rather, it reflects the absence of neophobia and correspondingly an increase in the animal's sense of confidence in the safety of the CS.

One piece of evidence for this theory is the fact that taste-aversion conditioning is strongest when using novel flavors.[29] Familiar flavors are considered safe and therefore are not judged to be the cause of illness when they are later used in a taste-aversion experiment.

Even stronger support for the learned-safety theory was provided by Kalat and Rozin (1973). One group of rats was given a novel flavor 4 hours prior to receiving the poison US. A second group received the CS only a half-hour before the poison administration. Based merely on the contiguity principle, the second group should demonstrate stronger conditioning to the flavor than the first. The third group was given the CS flavor twice, once 4 hours prior to the poison US and again one half-hour before the US. According to the contiguity principle, this group should be similar to Group 2 because the CS–US interval was only a half-hour in both cases. The learned-safety theory predicts the opposite result, however. The group that received the CS twice should be equivalent to the 4-hour group because both had the same amount of time (namely, 4 hours) in which to discover that the flavor was safe. The results favored the learned-safety theory; Groups 1 and 3 showed approximately the same degree of aversion.

The learned-safety theory has been criticized on several accounts.[30] First, aversions may be conditioned to thoroughly familiar flavors.[31] The learned-safety theory predicts that such conditioning should be exceedingly difficult if not impossible. Second, preexposing a flavor CS reduces the ability of that CS to become a conditioned safety signal.[32] If the animals truly had learned to perceive the preexposed flavor as being safe, then they should show an enhanced *preference* for the preexposed flavor later on. This is not the case, however. A preexposed flavor is not easily converted into a preferred flavor.

Current thinking frames the issue in terms of **learned irrelevance,** rather than learned safety.[33] Such a theory avoids the implication that a special quality called "safety" is conditioned during the delay. The learned-irrelevance theory maintains that animals show a natural wariness or neophobia for new flavors (their genetic programming has made them wary of the possibility of injury or sickness) but, gradually, come to believe that the flavor is meaningless or irrelevant if, indeed, nothing harmful occurs.[34] They apparently do not endow the flavor with any special properties, such as safety, but rather learn that the flavor does not predict an event of any consequence.

Effective Unconditioned Stimuli.

The kind of US that is effective in taste aversion may vary considerably.[35] For instance, some substances that are toxic (lithium chloride or sodium fluoroacetate) produce strong taste aversions, but other substances that are equally toxic (cyanide or strychnine) do not.[36]

Another interesting fact is that certain drugs have dual effects; they may lead to a taste aversion for an associated flavor CS, but at the same time, the drugs themselves may be preferred substances that subjects—humans and rats alike—will self-administer. For example, amphetamine and morphine are both substances that rats will self-administer (they will press a lever in order to have these drugs infused directly into their body through a small cannula), yet these substances, when injected following consumption of a flavor, produce a taste aversion.[37] How can a drug be simultaneously aversive (can lead to taste aversion) and reinforcing (can serve as a positive reinforcer for a simple response that causes self-administration of the drug)?

Part of the answer is that different drugs produce different kinds of aversive reactions. For example, Pelchat, Grill, Rozin, and Jacobs (1983) paired sucrose with one of two kinds of poisons—namely, lithium chloride (which produces discomfort in the upper gastrointestinal tract) or lactose (which produces discomfort in the lower gastrointestinal tract). The authors measured two behaviors—suppression of drinking the sucrose and conditioned nausea. To measure the conditioned-nausea reaction, videotapes were taken during the sucrose test. These were later analyzed for the component behaviors shown by the rats. The classic symptoms of nausea include gaping (subjects draw the corners of the mouth down, to give the mouth an open triangular shape), rubbing the chin on the grid floor, and shaking the head. Both groups avoided drinking the sucrose, but only the lithium-chloride group showed signs of conditioned nausea. This implies that taste aversions, as measured by the suppression of drinking, do not reflect the same underlying process as acquired aversive reactions that involve conditioned nausea.

In a similar study, drugs such as morphine, which serve as positive reinforcers, were compared to other drugs, such as a novel alcohol solution, which do not (rats will not self-administer these substances).[38] Again, both USs produced an aversion to drinking the sucrose-flavored CS, but only the alcohol US caused the typical patterns of nausea to occur. These results suggest that there are two kinds of taste aversions. First, drugs that are positive reinforcers (such as morphine) cause the animal to avoid drinking the CS solution, but they do not cause conditioned-nausea reactions. Animals do not find the associated flavor CS to be distasteful, and thus they do not show conditioned-nausea reactions. However, they use the flavor as a signal for subsequent illness and thus stop drinking the solution for that reason.[39] Second, drugs that do not function as positive reinforcers (alcohol) cause a shift in the palatability of a flavor CS. Subjects find the associated CS flavor to be distasteful and unpalatable, *and* they avoid drinking it.

A third interesting fact about taste aversion is that no UR is needed to produce conditioning.[40] Two kinds of evidence for this idea are available. First, learning occurs even when the UR is neurologically blocked. For example, an aversion may develop when the vagus nerve is severed (the vagus is the main afferent nerve extending from the gastrointestinal tract to the brain).[41] Animals that have had this operation cannot experience the illness because the neural signals are absent, yet they develop a conditioned aversion to the associated flavor. Similarly, subjects learn a taste aversion even when they are anesthetized. This was demonstrated in an experiment by Rabin and Rabin (1984). Rats were given a sucrose solution and then immediately anesthetized with sodium pentobarbital (the anesthesia was maintained for up to about 7 hours). Twenty minutes later, subjects were either injected with lithium chloride or irradiated with X-rays (a treatment also known to produce taste aversions). Control subjects were given a harmless injection of saline. One day later, all subjects were tested for their relative preference for sucrose. The results confirmed that animals who were irradiated or were given lithium chloride while anesthetized learned a strong taste aversion.[42]

The second kind of evidence that questions whether an aversive UR is necessary for taste-aversion learning stems from work showing that other sick animals may serve as a US. In a study by Bond (1984b), a visitor rat was placed into the cage of a host rat for 2 hours; both were allowed to drink a novel saccharin solution.[43] They were then removed, the visitor was injected with a dose of lithium chloride, and then both were returned to the cage for an additional 2-hour period. A second group of subjects was treated in a similar fashion, but neither the host nor the visitor was given an injection. On the following day, all subjects were tested for their preference for saccharin.

The results are shown in Figure 7-6. Control subjects, which had not been injected with poison, drank a good deal of the saccharin; no taste aversion had been induced in these subjects. The injected subjects, however, showed a very strong aversion to the saccharin. Such a result is not surprising, given that those subjects experienced the poison. The interesting data concern the nonpoisoned partners—that is, the rats that drank the saccharin and spent time with the poisoned visitor but that had not actually been poisoned themselves. They showed a significant reduction in the amount of saccharin consumed, relative to the controls. Thus, a taste aversion was induced in those subjects, although no US (or UR) was experienced.[44]

Acquired Taste Preferences

Pavlovian conditioning may play a role not only in teaching an animal to avoid a potentially poisonous food, but also in teaching an animal which food to consume.

Directed Behaviors.

One way in which Pavlovian conditioning affects food selection is in directing the search and recognition processes involved in finding prey. Recall from Chapters 3 and 5 that a CS that is associated with food tends to cause subjects, particularly birds, to orient toward the CS, to approach it, and actu-

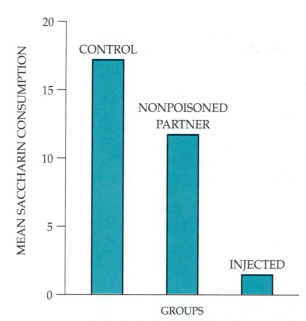

FIGURE 7-6. Mean saccharin consumption (in milliliters) for the no-injection control subjects, the injected partners, and the nonpoisoned partners (after Bond, 1984).

ally to peck it (this is the autoshaping phenomenon). This may be precisely the way some subjects hunt for prey. They recognize and approach CSs that are associated with food items.[45]

Search Images.

A second aspect of cue-directed feeding behavior relates to the concept of **search image.** A search image is a perceptual reaction; it involves selective attention to the characteristics of a prey item.[46] Without such selective attention, subjects often fail to detect a prey item that is cryptic (concealed or hidden among the background patterns of stimulation). If the animals are exposed to the cryptic items, however, their attention shifts toward the characteristics of the prey, and they are successful at foraging for them.[47]

A study by Pietrewicz and Kamil (1979) provides a good illustration of this process. Blue jays were shown photographic slides of moths. Some of the birds were shown slides of several different species of moth, whereas others were shown slides containing only a single, cryptic species of moth. All of the birds could earn food rewards by pecking the slides, provided they contained an image of a moth. The percentage of slides for which the second group of subjects correctly detected the cryptic moth increased as a function of their exposure to the slides. In other words, the birds formed a search image. They selectively attended to the features of the cryptic moth once they had encountered slides containing pictures of it. Birds that were shown slides containing

Photo of the apparatus used by Pietrewicz and Kamil (1979) to study search images in blue jays.
Courtesy of Professor Alan Kamil, Experimental Program to Stimulate Competetive Research, University of Nebraska-Lincoln

different kinds of moths, however, were unable to form a search image for the cryptic variety; they showed no improvement in their detection rate. This problem is similar to a Pavlovian discrimination, where the attributes of the cryptic prey represent the CS+, and the attributes of the surrounding background, which are highly similar, represent the CS−.[48] Once the subjects experience the CS+ stimuli, they are better able to detect them in the future.

Conditioned Taste Preferences.

Research on taste aversion shows that subjects avoid food items that have been paired with a poison. In addition, the opposite phenomenon has been demonstrated, as well. Animals seek out and prefer flavors or food items that are associated with a beneficial consequence. In many of these studies, preference was established by pairing a flavor with an illness-reducing substance—that is, an antidote to the illness. For example, Zahorik, Maier, and Pies (1974) maintained rats on a thiamine-deficient diet, during which time they drank a distinctively flavored water solution.[49] The authors predicted that the flavor would become associated with the vitamin deficiency and therefore be aversive. In Phase 2, the animals were given a different flavor and then were immediately injected with thiamine. Thiamine was, in a sense, the medicine that relieved the deficiency. Because the new flavor was associated with the cure, the authors predicted that subjects would prefer it to, say, plain water or to other flavors. This prediction was confirmed on the test session. The recovery flavor was preferred to all other flavors, including familiar flavors that had been experienced prior to the illness and thus presumably were judged to be safe.

Animals do not have to experience illness, however, to develop a **conditioned taste preference.** Preferences occur simply because flavors are associated with beneficial consequences, such as the intake of calories. This was shown in an experiment by Mehiel and Bolles (1988).[50] Four different sources of calories were used—namely, sucrose (table sugar), polycose (corn starch), ethanol (grain alcohol), and corn oil (a substance commonly used in cooking). Saccharin, a sweet-tasting but nonnutritive flavor, was also used. In a preliminary phase of the study, solutions that contained an equal amount of calories were given to a control group of rats, to confirm that they were more or less equally palatable. Then the experiment began. Rats were given two flavored CS solutions. One flavor, either orange or lime, was mixed with one of the caloric solutions, whereas the other flavor was mixed with the saccharin. On even days of training, animals were given the flavored caloric bottle, and on odd days, they were given the flavored saccharin bottle. This procedure continued for 16 days, after which the subjects were tested for their flavor preference. Here, the two flavors were given by themselves.

The results of the 3-hour preference test are shown in Figure 7-7. In every case, the flavor associated with the caloric solution was preferred to the flavor associated with the saccharin solution, although no differences in preferences occurred for different sources of calories. This work is important because it shows that Pavlovian conditioning may lead to preferences for food items that are of benefit to the animal.[51]

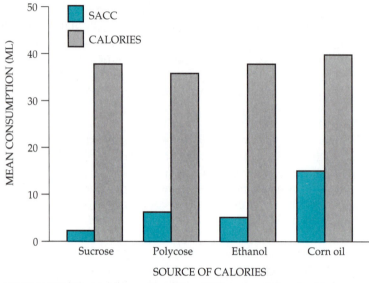

FIGURE 7-7. Mean consumption (in milliliters—ml) for the flavor associated with the saccharin (blue) and the flavor associated with the caloric substance (grey), for groups receiving different sources of calories (after Mehiel & Bolles, 1988).

INTERIM SUMMARY

Pavlovian conditioning is involved in the regulation of diet. One example is acquired taste aversion, where a flavored substance is paired with illness, causing the subject to avoid consuming that flavor in the future. The nonequivalence of associability finding shows that, for rats, some stimuli (flavors and odors) are more easily associated with poison than others (lights and noises). This suggests that taste aversion is a specialized form of learning. However, rats associate external stimuli with poison (and birds associate flavors with poison), provided those are the stimuli used to procure food. Not only are tastes easily associated with poison, but tastes also potentiate the conditioning of other stimuli—for example, apparatus cues or weak tastes. The result is surprising because research in Pavlovian conditioning suggests that a salient cue such as taste should overshadow, rather than potentiate, conditioning of a less salient cue. The potentiation effect may be based on a summation of the taste–poison and the external-cue–poison associations. Taste aversion is unique, in that it occurs even when the CS–US interval is many hours, rather than a few seconds (this may occur because subjects learn that a flavor is safe, or irrelevant, during this time). There are two classes of aversion. Drugs that are positive reinforcers, such as morphine, produce an aversion to drinking an associated flavor. Drugs that are not positive reinforcers, such as alcohol, produce an aversion to drinking, as well as a conditioned-nausea reaction. Taste aversions are interesting because URs are not required (anesthetized subjects, and rats that merely interact with a poisoned visitor, still develop a taste aversion). Animals also learn to select beneficial food through Pavlovian conditioning. A search image, for example, is a perceptual reaction to the visual features of a cryptic prey. A conditioned taste preference occurs when a flavor is paired with an illness-curing substance.

REGULATION OF DEFENSIVE REACTIONS

Pavlovian CRs may also aid an animal in its defense against predators. Clearly this is an important role for Pavlovian learning because defense is a problem that most species confront.

Physiological Reactions

One way in which subjects prepare to defend themselves is by altering various physiological reactions, including heart rate, respiration, and blood pressure, so that they may withstand an attack.[52] For example, an acceleration in heart rate mobilizes energy resources; subjects may be better able to escape predators because their muscles benefit from higher levels of oxygen and heightened levels of glucose utilization when heart rate is elevated. Alternatively, a decrease in heart rate may lead to an increase in the efficiency of an animal's behavior. For example, species such as rats and chickens freeze when encountering a potential predator.[53] These reactions, and their autonomic manifestations such as lowered heart rate, may help the animal to avoid detection and thereby avoid having to risk injury in a fight.

Conditioned Freezing

Behavioral freezing in rodents is a typical reaction to the threat of a predator or to other aversive stimuli, such as shock.[54] Fanselow (1986) placed one group of rats in the test apparatus for 7 minutes but gave no further treatment. A second group was given a 2-second shock immediately upon being placed in the box. A third group was given the same shock, but its presentation was delayed for 2 minutes after being placed in the box. During the last 5 minutes of the test, the behavior of the subjects was visually analyzed. Specifically, the experimenters judged whether freezing was present (freezing was defined as the absence of all visible movement, including movement of the whiskers).[55]

Figure 7-8 shows the results. The no-shock and immediate-shock groups showed virtually no freezing at all. The delayed-shock group, on the other hand, showed freezing behaviors for about 45 seconds out of the 5-minute test period. What accounts for the fact that animals that were allowed to remain in the box for 2 minutes prior to being shocked froze, whereas animals that

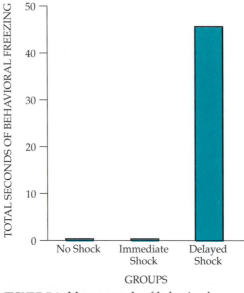

FIGURE 7-8. Mean seconds of behavioral freezing in the no-shock, immediate-shock, and delayed-shock groups (after Fanselow, 1986).

were shocked immediately did not? According to Fanselow, the apparatus constituted a CS that was paired with shock. During the postshock period then, the apparatus elicited a conditioned-freezing reaction. Such a reaction was strong during the 5-minute measurement period in the delayed group but had already extinguished in the immediate group.

This experiment provides no direct evidence that a freezing reaction increases the subject's chances of going undetected by a predator, but the inference is entirely reasonable. For example, in a more naturalistic setting, rats show immobility reactions in the presence of a natural predator—namely, a cat.[56] Because naturalistic reactions such as these may be conditioned, as shown in the Fanselow study, it is reasonable to presume that they would aid in predator defense.

Defensive Aggression

A third example of the way in which Pavlovian CRs may prepare an animal to face an encounter with a predator is in terms of conditioned aggressive responses. In an experiment by Hollis (1984), aggression was studied using a species of fish, the blue gourami, that is known for its territorial defensive behavior.[57] In its natural habitat, a male blue gourami builds a nest (in which a female will later deposit eggs), and then defends it against intruders. The defense involves the nest owner charging to where the intruder enters the territory, giving frontal aggressive displays, and performing aggressive reactions such as biting.[58]

Photograph showing the aggressive display given by blue gourami fish as shown by Hollis (1984).
Courtesy of Professor Karen Hollis, Mount Holyoke College, South Hadley, MA

In Hollis's experiment, two groups of fish were used. The aquarium was divided into two compartments by both a clear piece of plastic and an opaque plastic insert. Over 24 days of training, the Pavlovian conditioned subjects were placed on one side of the aquarium and were given pairings of a 10-second red light and the removal of the opaque door, which revealed another male blue gourami (the two fish, however, were still separated by the clear plastic insert). Thus, the CS was the red light, and the US was the presentation of an intruder fish. A control group of subjects received presentations of the red light CS and intruder fish US, but presentations of these stimuli were separated by about 4 hours and thus were considered to be unpaired.

The acquisition data are shown in Figure 7-9. The red light elicited progressively more frontal aggressive displays directed at the intruder fish in the Pavlovian conditioned fish than in the unpaired subjects. The unpaired animals showed virtually no frontal displays during the red light.

Following training, Hollis tested to see whether the CR would actually help a fish defend its territory against a real encounter with the intruder. During the test, the red light was turned on for 10 seconds, and then both the clear and the opaque doors were removed, thus allowing the subject actually to fight with the intruder. Bites at the intruder were recorded.

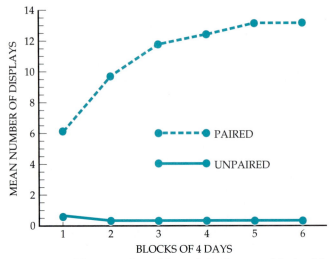

FIGURE 7-9. Mean number of frontal displays per block of 4 days elicited by the CS (red light) in the Pavlovian conditioned (paired) and control (unpaired) groups of fish (after Hollis, 1984).

The results are shown in Figure 7-10. All animals showed an increase in the number of bites that they inflicted on the intruder; this is the animal's natural UR to an opponent. However, the intensity of the fighting (number of bites per minute) was greater in the Pavlovian conditioned group than in the control subjects. Thus, territorial defense was more vigorous in the paired subjects than in the unpaired group (and more vigorous responding is certainly an advantage in terms of fighting off an intruder).

In conclusion, Hollis (1984) argues that "These results suggest an important role for Pavlovian conditioning. In the natural habitat of these fish, Pavlovian conditioning may provide a means whereby territorial males increase the likelihood of successful territory defense. Thus, the function of Pavlovian conditioning seems clear: By means of the conditional aggressive response . . . rivals are confronted at the territory boundary by an already aggressively displaying owner, strategically ready for battle" (p. 422).

INTERIM SUMMARY

Pavlovian CRs help animals in their defense against predators. Subjects prepare to defend themselves through conditioned physiological reactions, such as changes in respiration and heart rate. These help mobilize energy for fighting or fleeing. Similarly, subjects perform conditioned freezing reactions, which help them go undetected from predators, thus avoiding the possibility of injury. A third kind of defense involves conditioned aggressive reactions. If animals are given a CS that had been paired with the opportunity to perform an aggressive display, then the intensity of an encounter with a real predator is increased by the CS presentation.

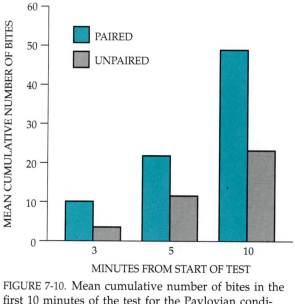

FIGURE 7-10. Mean cumulative number of bites in the first 10 minutes of the test for the Pavlovian conditioned (paired) and control (unpaired) subjects (after Hollis, 1984).

REGULATION OF REPRODUCTIVE BEHAVIOR

In addition to diet and predator defense, a third activity that is central to the survival of most species involves reproductive behaviors. There are many behaviors that are associated with reproduction, including sexual and parental behaviors. Two are discussed in the following sections: courtship and copulation.

Courtship

Many species conduct elaborate courtship rituals to attract a suitable mate. Some of these behaviors are well-known—for example, the elaborate display of the peacock. Research has shown that courtship displays in a number of species are influenced by Pavlovian conditioning. For example, Hollis, Cadieux, and Colbert (1989) used blue gourami fish as subjects. The experimental procedure was similar to the one discussed in the previous section. Pavlovian-trained male and female fish were given a 10-second red light, followed by a 15-second exposure to one another through a clear plastic divider. The light was the CS, whereas the visual encounter was the US. Ten such pairings were given each day for 12 days. Unpaired control subjects received an equal number of CS and US presentations, but they were separated by about 6 hours.

On the test day, all subjects were presented with the red light CS and then both the opaque and the clear plastic dividers were removed, allowing the male and female access to each other. The experimenters measured aggressive frontal displays (the same reaction described previously), as well as a courtship reaction. Here, the male fish assumes a characteristic body angle of about 15 to 60 degrees from horizontal, with all fins in a folded position; often, this display is accompanied by a change in the color of the fish, from pale gray to silver.

The results are shown in Figure 7-11. Pavlovian conditioning led to a reduction in aggressive frontal display behavior (left panel), and a dramatic increase in the courtship display response (right panel). The CS-elicited behaviors were therefore consistent with, and indeed served to promote, the courtship ritual.

Copulatory Behavior

Much work has been done on the Pavlovian conditioning of a second kind of reproductive behavior—namely, copulatory behavior in Japanese quail. In general, the results show that subjects may be conditioned to initiate copulatory and other reproductive behaviors in the presence of suitable Pavlovian CSs. This has been shown in several ways.

First, male subjects approach and contact various inanimate CS objects if those objects were previously paired with copulation (or the opportunity to copulate) with a female. For example, the CS in Holloway and Domjan's (1993)

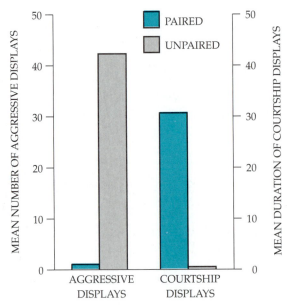

FIGURE 7-11. Mean number of aggressive displays (left) and mean duration of the courtship posture (right) performed on the test by males in the Pavlovian conditioned (paired) and control (unpaired) groups (after Hollis, Cadieux, & Colbert, 1989).

study was a foam block with orange feathers attached to it. The male bird was presented with this CS for 30 seconds, followed by the opportunity to copulate with a receptive female (the US). Other subjects were given the CS but could only make visual contact with the female (a wire screen allowed minimal contact but prevented actual copulatory behavior). Subjects in a third group were shown the CS but were given no opportunity to view or to copulate with the female. On a 5-minute test, all subjects were given the CS and then observed as to whether the subjects spent time near the area that the CS had occupied.

These test results are shown in Figure 7-12. Subjects that had received pairings of the CS and the female quail responded by making contact with the CS on the test; the most contact was shown by the subjects for whom copulatory behavior had been possible during training, although even birds in the exposure-only condition responded to some degree in this fashion.[59] Although the CS was highly artificial in this study, under natural conditions, the CS is actually the attributes of the female.

Will a CS elicit copulatory behavior itself? Domjan, Huber-McDonald, and Holloway (1992) addressed this question and showed that this is indeed possible. Male Japanese quail were given 30 seconds of access to an inanimate object (a terry-cloth pad filled with polyester fiber to which a taxidermic specimen of the head and neck of a female quail was attached). Ordinarily, males do not copulate with inanimate objects, although copulation did take place under these conditions because part of the object—the taxidermically pre-

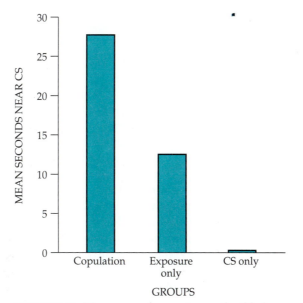

FIGURE 7-12. Mean seconds spent near the CS during the test for the group that could copulate with the female, that received only visual exposure to the female, or that was given only the CS (after Holloway & Domjan, 1993).

Photograph of the stimulus used by Domjan, Huber-McDonald, and Holloway (1992) involving a terry cloth body on top of which was attached a taxidermic specimen of the female quail.
Courtesy of Professor Michael Domjan, University of Texas at Austin

pared specimen—was decidedly similar to a real female quail. Over successive trials, the taxidermic specimen was gradually covered up more and more with a piece of terry cloth, such that after 20 conditioning trials, the entire object was covered. The results were startling. Despite the fact that the CS object looked progressively less like a real female quail, copulatory behavior with the object actually increased over training. Even on the test, when the entire object was covered, copulation attempts were observed. The experiment thus demonstrates that subjects may be conditioned through Pavlovian training actually to copulate with an inanimate object, provided the object had previously been paired with the opportunity to copulate.[60] Again, Pavlovian conditioning plays an important role in this kind of reproductive behavior. Stimuli that elicit approach and copulatory behaviors as a result of a conditioning process increase the adaptive potential of the subject to reproduce successfully.

INTERIM SUMMARY

Pavlovian conditioning helps regulate reproductive behavior. For example, if CSs are paired with the opportunity to copulate, these CSs are later preferred, may elicit courtship displays, and may even trigger copulation itself.

REGULATION OF PHYSIOLOGICAL IMBALANCE

The aforementioned research focused on the role of Pavlovian conditioning in helping animals to behave in an adaptive fashion—for instance, by rejecting or accepting food substances, by mounting an appropriate defense, or by engaging in suitable reproductive behaviors. There is also a vast literature showing that Pavlovian conditioning prepares an animal to cope with the effects of internal changes, such as those brought about by various drugs. Simply stated, CSs associated with the internal consequences of a drug will later elicit an adaptive physiological reaction, even though the drug is no longer physically present.

Conditioning of Drug States

Let us first illustrate how this conditioned drug reaction develops. Woods (1976) showed conditioning of a glycemic reaction as a result of the administration of insulin.[61] Two groups of rats were used. The difference between them was in terms of their injection substance. The experimental animals were injected with insulin, whereas the control subjects were injected with a harmless saline placebo. The training for all subjects involved the following: A subject was removed from its home cage, and a blood sample was taken from its tail while it was confined in a small restraint apparatus. Then, the subject was given an injection of the appropriate substance (insulin for the experimentals, placebo for the controls) and placed for 20 minutes in a training box that was permeated with the odor of menthol. This entire procedure (restraint, blood sample, injection, odor) constituted the CS. At the end of the 20-minute waiting period, all animals were again restrained, and a second blood sample was taken. The purpose of the second sample was to measure any change in blood sugar that had occurred during the previous 20-minute period.

After six such training trials, subjects were given a test. Here, the identical procedure was followed, except that both groups received an injection of the placebo. From a strict biological point of view, none of the animals should have shown a glycemic reaction on the test because none was given insulin.

The results are shown in Figure 7-13. During training, the insulin-injected subjects showed a marked drop in blood sugar on each trial. This is the normal unconditioned effect of insulin—namely, hypoglycemia (lowered blood sugar). The saline control animals, in contrast, showed no such change in blood sugar (actually there was a small increase). The interesting data are those from the test session (right two points). Here, the experimental animals continued to show a hypoglycemic reaction, despite the fact that they were not given insulin. In other words, merely experiencing the CS was enough to cause a conditioned hypoglycemic response.[62]

Compensatory Reactions

The full picture concerning conditioned glycemic reactions is actually much more complicated than the one represented here. Although the unconditioned

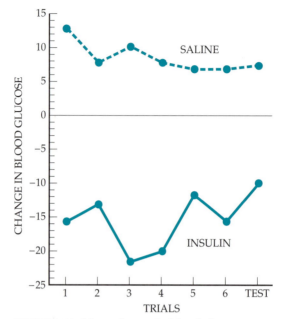

FIGURE 7-13. Mean change in blood glucose over the course of six training and one test trial for subjects that were given insulin or saline during training. Both groups received a saline injection on the test (after Woods, 1976).

effect of insulin seems always to be hypoglycemia, the conditioned effect has been shown to be either the same (hypoglycemia), or the opposite reaction (hyperglycemia, a rise in blood sugar). A study by Siegel (1972) showed this conditioned hyperglycemic reaction.[63] Different groups of rats were put into a restraining apparatus and injected with insulin. A blood sample was also taken at this time. This procedure (restraint, injection, and blood sample) constituted the CS. On each of the four training trials, a second blood sample was taken 5, 10, 20, 30, 50, 70, or 90 minutes later. The change in blood sugar between the first and second sampling indicated the unconditioned effect of the insulin. After training, a test session was then given, where all subjects received a placebo injection rather than insulin. Again, the second blood sample was taken at the same times as during training.

The results are shown in Figure 7-14. During training, when subjects were injected with insulin, blood sugar progressively declined over at least 70 minutes (the unconditioned response to insulin is shown at the bottom of Figure 7-14). However, when injected with the placebo on the test trial, the opposite reaction occurred. Blood sugar increased during the first 20 minutes and then slowly declined for the remainder of the test (dotted line). In short, both hyperglycemia and hypoglycemia were found in these physiological conditioning experiments.

When the CR is opposite to the UR (hyperglycemia versus hypoglycemia), the reaction is called a "compensatory response." It is not entirely clear what

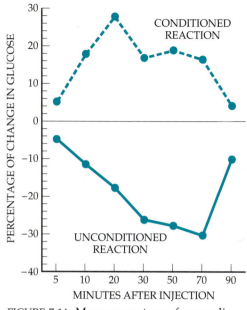

FIGURE 7-14. Mean percentage of unconditioned and conditioned glycemic change, as
a function of time from the injection (after
Siegel, 1972).

is responsible for producing these compensatory reactions. Some suggest that
the form of the CR depends on the procedure, although the precise feature
that produces the UR versus a **compensatory CR** is not clearly understood.[64]
Others have suggested that the form of the CR depends on factors such as
stress arising from the novelty of the conditioning environment and the CS.[65]
Still others have pointed out that many drugs, including insulin, actually have
multiple effects on an animal.[66]

Whatever the precise reason, the existence of compensatory reactions has
proven to be of enormous importance for understanding how individuals
react to various drugs. Furthermore, compensatory reactions certainly make
sense from an evolutionary viewpoint. It is adaptive for the brain to maintain
an internal homeostatic balance. When that balance is disrupted by the presence of a foreign substance such as a drug, the brain should attempt to restore
proper balance. Such a restoration of balance involves, in part, the elicitation
of compensatory reactions, responses in the opposite direction to the unconditioned effects of the drugs.

Drug Tolerance.

Tolerance to a drug develops, or is manifest, when the effect of a given
dose decreases with successive administrations. Many claim that such diminishing effects of a drug are due to some kind of biological adjustment. That
is, the biological receptors on which the drug acts will become progressively

less sensitive over the course of use. For certain drugs, such as morphine or heroin, the mounting tolerance to the effects often cause users to increase their dosage so that the euphoria is maintained in the face of the tolerance.

Research in learning suggests that the tolerance phenomenon is not due to a diminishing sensitivity but rather to the development of a conditioned compensatory response. The argument is based on the aforementioned work. When a drug such as morphine is taken, the body reacts naturally by producing a compensatory reaction. Such a response is an adaptive way of minimizing the disruptive effects produced by the drug. Through Pavlovian conditioning, the surrounding cues become conditioned such that later on, when the drug is given in the same context, the environment elicits the compensatory reaction, which has the effect of counteracting the unconditioned effects of the drug itself. In other words, **drug tolerance** is the development of a conditioned compensatory reaction, a reaction that tends to neutralize or counteract the unconditioned effects of the drug.

Much of the work in this area has been done by Siegel and his colleagues.[67] In one study, Siegel, Hinson, and Krank (1978) gave experimental rats pairings of a CS and a morphine injection.[68] The CS was a complex visual–auditory experience, consisting of a change in the level of lighting and a reduction in the background noise.[69] Unpaired subjects were exposed to the CS and then were given injections of morphine, but the two stimuli were not paired; the morphine injections were made at other times during the day, and they did not include the change in the light and noise intensities. A third group was given the paired presentations of the CS and an injection of a saline placebo substance.

After nine days of training, all animals were tested for their tolerance to morphine. This consisted of presenting the visual–auditory CS, injecting each subject with morphine, and then observing the reactions to a mildly painful stimulus. Specifically, subjects were placed on a hot surface. Normal, untreated rats begin to lick their paws rather soon after being placed there because they find it uncomfortably warm. Animals given morphine, however, typically take much longer before they lick their paws because they do not feel the pain as readily (it is well-known that morphine is an analgesic—that is, it deadens pain).

The results are shown in Figure 7-15. The mean paw-lick latency for the group that had originally received CS–saline pairings during training, but morphine on the test, was very long, indicating that they felt little pain. This group therefore demonstrated the unconditioned analgesic effect of morphine. The unpaired morphine subjects similarly showed a long latency to lick their paws. The morphine was alleviating much of their pain. The paired morphine group, however, showed a comparatively short latency; licking the paws occurred quickly because the pain was intense. In other words, these subjects were not experiencing the analgesic effect of the morphine injection because they were experiencing the opposing compensatory reaction instead. The compensatory reaction elicited by the CS counteracted, and thus reduced, the analgesic effect of the morphine. This is precisely what is meant by the term drug

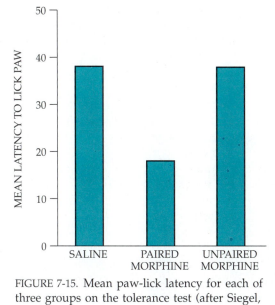

FIGURE 7-15. Mean paw-lick latency for each of three groups on the tolerance test (after Siegel, Hinson, & Krank, 1978).

tolerance. Despite being given the same dose, the morphine fails to have its usual analgesic effect.[70]

The literature on conditioned tolerance has provided a dramatic and powerful explanation for one of society's most vexing problems—namely, the often-reported finding that drug users die from a fatal overdose when the amount of drug actually consumed was no more than their usual amount. According to Siegel's work, if an addict uses morphine in an environment that is distinctively different from the environment in which the person usually takes drugs, then the compensatory reaction is not triggered (because the CS is not present), and the full power of the drug itself is felt. Because the user may have gradually increased over time the dose of heroin or morphine to create the euphoric effect, such an increased dose level, in the absence of the compensatory CR, may be simply too high to tolerate.[71]

Not surprisingly, other points of view concerning tolerance have been expressed. Some suggest, for example, that tolerance to morphine is due to a special form of context-dependent habituation.[72] Others claim that there are several different processes occurring, including a context-specific habituation process and a conditioned-tolerance process.[73] There certainly is evidence for other factors. The fact that the CS is paired in these experiments not only with morphine (or saline) but also with the daily pain test suggests that the body itself could be having a reaction to the pain, and the body thereby becomes conditioned to the surroundings. In short, a CR may be occurring even in the saline-injected control animals because of the contiguity between the CS surroundings and the animal's physiological reaction to pain.[74]

Photograph of two drug addicts. The scene dramatizes the distinctive environment in which many addicts take drugs. Such an environment becomes a conditioned stimulus for a compensatory reaction.
© *Bob Combs/Photo Researchers*

Conditioned Reactions to Pain.

Morphine is an analgesic (it deadens pain). Mammals are endowed, however, with the ability to suppress pain on their own, without taking a drug. When an individual encounters a stressful or pain-inducing event, the brain secretes naturally occurring substances called "endogenous opioids." These biochemicals inhibit the perception of pain. Many people report experiencing such an effect. For example, even though they were severely injured, say, in battle or in an automobile accident, they report that they actually "didn't feel pain" at the time. Later, when the naturally occurring opioids wear off, pain is felt. Such a reaction makes sense from an evolutionary perspective. An individual who is being attacked, or is otherwise under a severe stress, runs the danger of not being able to perform efficiently because of the intense pain. Mechanisms that temporarily suppress pain, so that the individual may act in an organized fashion, have therefore evolved.

Considerable evidence shows that these analgesic reactions to pain and stress may be conditioned. A study by Young and Fanselow (1992) provides a good example.[75] A drug called "naloxone" is known to block pharmacologically the effects of the opioid release, thus reducing their analgesic effect. In this experiment, rats were given an injection of either a placebo or naloxone. They were then put into an observation chamber and given a shock about 3 minutes later. The shock intensity for separate groups was 0, 0.4, 0.6, or 0.8 milliamps (thus, the range was from no shock to a rather intense shock). Freezing behavior was measured during the 3-minute preshock period.

The results are shown in Figure 7-16. The animals that received saline froze significantly less when anticipating shock than did the subjects that received naloxone (neither type of subject froze with a 0-milliamp shock). In other words, the saline-injected animals were less fearful than the naloxone-injected animals. The reason is that the test box (which constituted the CS) elicited the release of the endogenous opioids. These naturally produced analgesic compounds caused the subsequent shock to be perceived as being less intense. If the shock was not perceived to be as intense, then the fear reaction

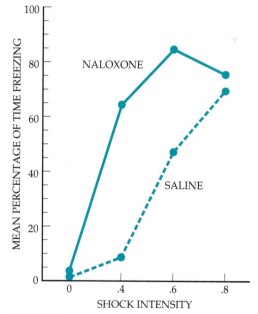

FIGURE 7-16. Mean percentage of time spent freezing, as a function of shock intensity for the saline- and naloxone-injected subjects (after Young & Fanselow, 1992).

(the freezing behavior) would be less intense as well. The naloxone-injected animals, on the other hand, showed considerable freezing, even at the lowest levels of shock. Here, the naloxone pharmacologically blocked the effect of the opioids, thus causing the animals to experience the shock in its full intensity. Their high degree of freezing shows that they experienced a strong aversive reaction to the previous shock.

INTERIM SUMMARY

Animals defend themselves against both external and internal threats. Internal threats are often in the form of a physiological imbalance. When a CS is paired with the injection of a drug substance, a conditioned form of the drug reaction is shown. For example, subjects may show conditioned hypoglycemia following the presentation of a CS on a test trial, even though no insulin was administered. Often, the CR is a compensatory response. These are physiological reactions that oppose, or counteract, the unconditioned effects of a drug. This form of Pavlovian conditioning is used to explain drug tolerance, which is a gradual reduction in the effectiveness of a drug. According to Pavlovian theory, tolerance is due to the development of a conditioned compensatory reaction that neutralizes the unconditioned effects of the drug. Mammals also produce naturally occurring opioids, which have an analgesic effect during stress. These reactions may also be conditioned.

ENDNOTES

1. For an excellent discussion of ecological learning theory, see Davey (1989).
2. The solution offered by Hollis is that the CR helps an animal "to optimize interaction with the forthcoming biologically important event (US)" (Hollis, 1982, p. 3). In other words, the CR is the means by which the organism can better utilize its information and cope with the biologically important USs. Pavlovian conditioning is "nature's way of getting ready" to deal with the upcoming biological event, to make a series of adaptive reactions that will ensure the likelihood that the animal will profit from the outcome as much as possible.
3. See Barker, Best, and Domjan (1977); Garcia (1989); Logue (1979); Milgram, Krames, and Alloway (1977) for reviews.
4. Garcia (1989) points out that the flavor really is more properly thought of as being the US, not the CS, while the poison, or at least the illness that the poison induces, is a form of biological feedback, not a US. However, we use the more conventional terminology here and refer to the flavor as constituting the CS and the poison as functioning as the US.
5. Bernstein (1978) showed that children who undergo chemotherapy for the treatment of cancer may experience taste aversions. Moreover, Bernstein, and Borson (1986) suggested that learned food aversions is a component of anorexia nervosa.
6. Brower (1969); Brower, Ryerson, Coppinger, and Glazier (1968). This is called "Batesean mimicry," in which one species mimics the appearance of another

species to gain certain benefit—here, protection from being preyed upon by blue jays.

7. Gillan (1979) for instance, showed that birds suppress drinking during a visual stimulus when that stimulus signals the presence of quinine (a very bitter flavor); the subjects do not suppress their drinking during other visual stimuli that are not associated with quinine, however. A similar example involves coyotes that readily associate the taste of lamb meat with subsequent illness. When this occurs, their predation on sheep declines; see Ellins, Thompson, and Swanson (1983); Gustavson, Garcia, Hankins, and Rusiniak (1974); Gustavson, Jowsey, and Milligan (1982); and Gustavson, Kelly, Sweeney, and Garcia (1976).

8. Several experiments confirmed Garcia and Koelling's original finding (that subjects demonstrate selective associations) even when using measures other than suppression of consumption; see Miller and Domjan (1981). For example, experiments measuring locomotor withdrawal from the CS show similar selectivity in association. In a study by Miller (1984), subjects that received light–shock pairings tended to freeze during the CS, whereas subjects that received flavor–poison pairings showed a conditioned form of nausea—namely, gaping, head shaking, and chin rubbing; see also Meachum and Bernstein (1990).

9. See Rozin and Kalat (1971); Seligman (1970).

10. As many as eight theories of the nonequivalence of associability are discussed by Domjan (1980).

11. See Kalat (1985).

12. Domjan (1983); Logue (1979).

13. For US intensity, see Andrews and Braveman (1975); Nachman and Ashe (1973); for CS intensity, see Barker (1976); Deutsch (1978); Chapter 4 of this book.

14. Best (1975); Domjan (1972) (latent inhibition); Best, Best, and Mickley (1973); Bond & Harland (1975) (second-order conditioning); Lavin (1976) (sensory preconditioning); Riley, Jacobs, and LoLordo (1976) (US preexposure effect); Taukulis and Revusky (1975) (conditioned inhibition); Willner (1978) (blocking).

15. See also Parker and Smith (1981).

16. See also Revusky and Parker (1976).

17. Domjan (1980) stated, "The fact that nongustatory cues are not as easily associated with toxicosis as novel taste stimuli is not necessarily inconsistent with traditional concepts of Pavlovian conditioning. Differences in the ease of conditioning of various potential CSs is expected if these stimuli differ in intensity, salience, or novelty" (p. 304).

18. See Rusiniak, Hankins, Garcia, and Brett (1979) for one of the original demonstrations of the potentiation effect.

19. Bouton, Jones, McPhillips, and Swartzentruber (1986); Droungas and LoLordo (1991) (odors); Best, Batson, Meachum, Brown, and Ringer (1985); Best, Brown, and Sowell (1984) (surrounding apparatus cues); Bouton, Dunlap, and Swartzentruber (1987); Miller, McCoy, Kelly, and Bardo (1986) (weaker tastes).

20. Garcia, Forthman Quick, and White (1984); Rusiniak, Palmerino, Rice, Forthman, and Garcia (1982).

21. In fact, the addition of the taste to the odor CS actually disrupted conditioning of the odor.

22. Bouton, Dunlap, and Swartzentruber (1987); see also Miller, McCoy, Kelly, and Bardo (1986).

23. See Durlach and Rescorla (1980).

24. See Lett (1984) for conflicting evidence.

25. Andrews and Braveman (1975); Garcia, Ervin, and Koelling (1966); Kalat and Rozin (1971).
26. See Kalat (1977); Kalat and Rozin (1971).
27. Mitchell, Kirschbaum, and Perry (1975); Nachman and Jones (1974).
28. See Rozin (1968).
29. See Ahlers and Best (1971); Revusky and Bedarf (1967); Siegel (1974).
30. See Best and Gemberling (1977).
31. Nachman and Jones (1974).
32. Best (1975).
33. See Baker and Mackintosh (1979). The learned-irrelevance theory of taste aversion is nearly identical to the associative theory of latent inhibition; see Chapter 5 of this book.
34. If they get sick in the meantime, they develop an aversion to the flavor; they do not consider it irrelevant.
35. The issue is important because, by understanding the relationship between drug type and learning, one may better understand the neurological mechanisms that underlie the learning itself.
36. Nachman and Hartley (1975). Unconditioned stimuli other than drugs and irradiation also produce taste aversions—for instance, physical rotation; see Green and Rachlin (1976).
37. Vogel and Nathan (1975); Wise, Yokel, and DeWitt (1976).
38. Parker (1988).
39. See Hunt and Amit (1987).
40. Recall from Chapter 4 that sensory preconditioning occurs when associations develop without the use of a US. The work described here, however, makes a somewhat different point—namely, that stimuli that are ostensibly USs lead to taste aversions, even though the UR reactions are blocked in some fashion.
41. Keifer, Cabral, Rusiniak, and Garcia (1980).
42. Anesthesia extends the interval over which the poison US is effective. Rozin and Ree (1972), for instance, showed that conditioning was possible with a CS–US interval of 9 hours when the subjects were anesthetized, but not if the subjects spent the delay interval awake.
43. See also Coombes, Revusky, and Lett (1980); Lavin, Freise, and Coombes (1980).
44. Rats are capable of transmitting information about the foods they consume, presumably via odors, although the story concerning social transmission of information is more complicated than presented here; see Galef (1986); Galef, McQuoid, and Whiskin (1990). For our purposes, it is sufficient to note that a conditioned taste aversion may occur without the subject experiencing the UR.
45. See Hollis (1982).
46. A. B. Bond (1983); see also D. S. Blough (1993), P. M. Blough (1991).
47. Dawkins (1971); Pietrewicz and Kamil (1981); see also Guilford and Dawkins (1987); Reid and Shettleworth (1992), for alternative views.
48. See Hollis (1982).
49. See also Barker and Weaver (1991); Green and Garcia (1971); Zahorik and Maier (1969).
50. See also Bolles, Hayward, and Crandall (1981); Fedorchak and Bolles (1987); Mehiel and Bolles (1984).
51. Not only do animals prefer flavors associated with calories, but they also develop a preference for flavors that are associated with eating per se; see Capaldi, Sheffer, and Owens (1991).

52. See Hollis (1982).
53. Blanchard, Flannelly, and Blanchard (1986); Suarez and Gallup (1982).
54. See Blanchard and Blanchard (1969a); Bolles (1970).
55. Freezing was also accompanied by shallow and rapid respiration, while the rat was in a crouching posture.
56. Blanchard and Blanchard (1989).
57. See also Hollis, Martin, Cadieux, and Colbert (1984).
58. Frontal displays involve spreading the dorsal, ventral, and caudal fins, while maintaining a characteristic face-to-face posture with the intruder fish.
59. See also Domjan, O'Vary, and Greene (1988). Adkins, Domjan, and Gutierrez (1994) have further shown that approach and contact with the CS varies as a function of the CS–US interval. While that fact, in itself, is consistent with studies on CS–US contiguity using more conventional Pavlovian measures, the interesting result in this study was that the form of the behavior differed with the CS–US interval. Indeed, the authors suggest that the decline in responding one observes with long CS–US intervals may not be due to a failure to associate the stimuli but rather to the fact that different reactions altogether are learned.
60. See also Domjan, Greene, and North (1989).
61. See also Woods and Shogren (1972). The UR to insulin is hypoglycemia, a drop in blood sugar.
62. The conditioned change is dependent on receiving insulin, not actually on experiencing a drop in blood sugar on the training trials. Woods (1976) for example, showed that if the actual change in blood sugar on the training trials was eliminated by the addition of glucose to the injection, conditioned hypoglycemia was still obtained on the test.
63. See also Siegel (1975a).
64. Flaherty, Uzwiak, Levine, Smith, Hall, and Schuler (1980).
65. Flaherty, Grigson, and Brady (1987).
66. See Eikelboom and Stewart (1982) for a theoretical account. According to these authors, a drug that affects the brain only indirectly (by operating at a peripheral site in the body, such as an organ, the effect of which is to produce neural feedback to the brain) produces a different kind of CR than a drug that affects the brain directly. In the former case, the reaction is compensatory. When the brain receives the feedback from the affected organ, it initiates a compensatory reaction to counteract the effects of the drug—that is, to maintain homeostatic balance. A drug that operates directly on the brain, however, produces CRs that are the same as the URs of the drug.
67. See Siegel (1983, 1989) for reviews.
68. See also Siegel (1975b, 1976, 1978); Siegel, Hinson, and Krank (1981) for related studies.
69. Actually, during this 45-minute time period, other events occurred as well, specifically replenishment of the animal's food and water supply, and a change of the cage bedding.
70. Numerous other studies have shown comparable effects with different kinds of drug substances, such as alcohol (Crowell, Hinson, & Siegel, 1981; Mansfield & Cunningham, 1980), amphetamine (Poulos, Wilkinson, & Cappell, 1981), and pentobarbital (Hinson & Siegel, 1986). Conditioned tolerance is also revealed within the context of other Pavlovian phenomena. For example, if the CS complex is repeatedly given by itself, then the tolerance (compensatory CR) extinguishes (Siegel, Sherman, & Mitchell, 1980). Similarly, one stimulus that already elicits a

compensatory CR may block the conditioning of a second added CS (Dafters, Hetherington, & McCartney, 1983). Third, presentation of the environmental cues prior to the drug training trials causes retarded development of conditioned tolerance later on (Siegel, 1977).

71. Siegel (1984); Siegel, Hinson, Krank, and McCully (1982).
72. Baker and Tiffany (1985); see also Poulos and Cappell (1991); Wise and Bozarth (1987).
73. Paletta and Wagner (1986).
74. Schnur and Martinez (1989); Westbrook and Greeley (1992).
75. See also Bolles and Fanselow (1980, 1982); Fanselow and Sigmundi (1986); Ross (1985, 1986).

CHAPTER 8

Basic Procedures in Instrumental (Operant) Conditioning

INSTRUMENTAL (OPERANT) CONDITIONING

The preceding chapters focused on Pavlovian conditioning. There is, however, another kind of learning, equally basic to animal and human behavior: **instrumental conditioning.** Whereas Pavlovian conditioning involves stimulus learning, instrumental conditioning is concerned with response learning.

That humans and other animals learn certain behaviors is, perhaps, so obvious that explicit mention of it seems almost unnecessary. We learn to play games, manipulate toys, and utilize tools. Yet this form of learning lies at the center of virtually all our behavior, even the subtlest action. Most of us, for example, say "please," and "thank you"; we have reasonably acceptable manners; we drive with an appropriate level of courtesy; and we do favors for our friends and family. The list is virtually endless. These behaviors are not inborn, but rather are learned because, as children, we are encouraged and rewarded when we behave in this fashion.

Throughout the history of learning research, theorists have argued that instrumental conditioning is a distinct form of learning, different from Pavlovian conditioning. The essential idea is this. The brain is wired to do many things. It receives visual and auditory information; it controls the various organs of the body; it contains in some fashion the individual's memories (see Chapter 11). It also governs the learning process. This line of reasoning further claims that the neural centers that control the Pavlovian learning processes are distinct from those involved in instrumental conditioning (or at least the overlap is minimal). The laws that govern instrumental learning are, therefore, at least to some degree, different from those that govern Pavlovian conditioning.

The alternative position is that instrumental and Pavlovian conditioning are not separate learning processes, but rather two different manifestations of a single learning process. Although experiments may focus on the learning of stimuli (Pavlovian) or of responses (instrumental), the outcomes are generated by a single learning process. In short, there is only one form of learning, having one set of rules, but it is manifest in more than one way.

Recall from Chapter 3 the everyday example of Pavlovian conditioning. A dog wags its tail and drools (CR) in anticipation of being fed (US) when its owner opens a can of food (CS). The CS (the owner engaged in opening a can of pet food), has special meaning or power because it is associated with the US (subsequent feeding). In contrast, imagine teaching your pet dog to "shake hands." Unlike drooling, shaking hands with humans is hardly something a dog does naturally; it must learn to do so. Typically, one takes the dog's paw, shakes it, and then vigorously rewards the dog with hugs, petting, and perhaps even food. If the dog itself responds (even partially so), one seizes the paw, and proceeds to reward it for making a "good try." Ultimately, the dog not only lifts its paw on its own, but actually directs it toward the trainer in such a way as to "offer it." What has occurred is the conditioning of a simple motor reaction by means of a complicated process involving reward. This is the essence of instrumental conditioning. Just as an animal is able to learn the significance of a stimulus (Pavlovian), it is also able to learn the significance of its own behavior (instrumental learning). Both the details of how this works and the laws that govern instrumental learning are interesting and complex.

The origins of instrumental conditioning are most closely associated with the American psychologist Edward Thorndike.[1] Thorndike's research was not really novel or unique because animal trainers had been using similar kinds of procedures for centuries. However, Thorndike investigated these training procedures systematically and in detail, so the conclusions that he drew about the learning process and the theory that he developed from his observations were important contributions to the science of learning. In retrospect, Thorndike was an innovator not because he discovered a new form of learning or a new learning procedure, but because his experiments provided a broad and systematic framework for investigating the learning process in a scientific way.

THORNDIKE'S EXPERIMENT

In Thorndike's (1898) original work, cats were placed in a small puzzle box such as that shown in Figure 8-1. When the latch on the box was manipulated, the door sprang open, thus allowing the cat access to the food placed nearby. When Thorndike put the cats in the cage for the first time, they thrashed about in an apparently random fashion, as if they were seeking a way to get out. Sooner or later, however, they hit the latch and gained access to the food. Each time this happened, Thorndike placed the animal back into the box and began another learning trial. After many such trials, the cats became more and more efficient in performing the action. For example, they required less time to hit the latch on successive occasions.

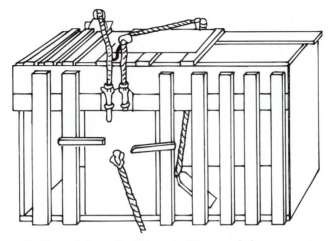

FIGURE 8-1. Schematic diagram of the puzzle-box apparatus used by Thorndike (after Thorndike, 1898).

Results for one cat (#12) are shown in Figure 8-2. Thorndike's cats did not learn an entirely novel behavior. The fact that they had to hit the latch *before* they were released suggests that they were able to perform that reaction all along. The cats, however, did learn to perform this simple motor response in an efficient manner.[2] Because the behavior is instrumental in, or responsible for, securing food, this type of conditioning is called "instrumental conditioning."[3]

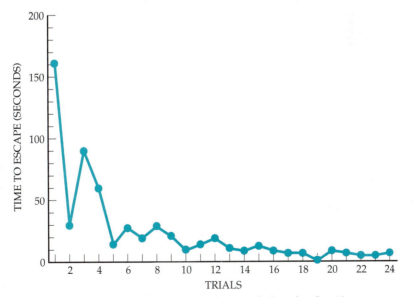

FIGURE 8-2. Time (seconds) to escape the puzzle box for Cat 12, as a function of 24 training trials (after Thorndike, 1898).

Portrait of Edward L. Thorndike, the learning theorist most closely associated with the early study of instrumental conditioning.
The Granger Collection, New York

Definition of Instrumental Conditioning

Thorndike's original study is a prototype for virtually all experiments in this field of research. Because one cannot directly observe the learning process, instrumental conditioning must be defined in terms of the procedures used to strengthen an instrumental response. Formally speaking, instrumental conditioning occurs when the outcome, usually a US, is contingent on the subject's behavior.[4] Unlike Pavlov's dogs, who were given the CS and US whether or not they actually performed the salivation reaction, Thorndike's cats controlled the presentation of the food. They were allowed to leave the box and eat the food only if they hit the latch first. In other words, the food was not independent of the behavior; food was contingent on it. This is an important point, and it provides the essence of our definition of instrumental conditioning.

Terms

The terms used in instrumental conditioning are generally the same as those used in Pavlovian conditioning. There are, however, a few notable differences.

Stimuli.

Unconditional stimuli are used in instrumental conditioning experiments just as in Pavlovian conditioning. The US (or the absence of a US presentation) is the outcome following the response, much as it is the outcome following a stimulus in Pavlovian conditioning. Typically, food, shock, and sweet-flavored liquids serve as outcomes.[5]

Conditioned stimuli are also used in instrumental conditioning experiments. They are relatively innocuous stimuli that have no specific meaning or power, at least at the start of training. Three important points should be stressed, however. First, *explicit* CSs are not necessary. No light or tone was deliberately provided in Thorndike's animals. They simply remained in a general testing context and performed their reactions without regard to any special signals. Such stimuli could have been included, however. For example, Thorndike could have turned a light on to indicate when the subject should hit the latch (turning the light off would have signaled that the response of hitting the latch would no longer open the door). Second, even when explicit stimuli are not presented, stimuli do exist within the testing environment, namely the testing apparatus itself.

Finally, stimuli that serve as CSs in instrumental learning, whether explicit cues such as tones and lights, or implicit cues that are part of the testing environment, play a very different role from that in Pavlovian conditioning. A neutral stimulus that signals when a response may or may not lead to the desirable outcome is a **discriminative stimulus (S_d).** An S_d indicates whether reinforcement is available. It informs the subject when to respond. It sets the occasion for reward. An S_d is therefore quite different from a CS in classical conditioning, where the CS signals the presentation of the US, without regard to any response that the subject may or may not execute.

Discriminative stimuli may have two kinds of meaning. An S+ cue is a stimulus that signals that reward is available—that is, when the subject may respond to produce the desirable outcome. An S− cue is a discriminative stimulus that signals that reward is *not* available—that is, when the subject should withhold its responding. Imagine if Thorndike had used an explicit discriminative stimulus—say, a light. The onset of the light could have signaled when the subject should hit the latch, whereas light offset could have indicated that hitting the latch would not lead to the desired outcome.

A stimulus may actually play two roles simultaneously. First, it may serve as a discriminative signal, as just discussed (it signals when reinforcement is available, pending execution of the correct response). Second, a cue may also become associated with the outcome and thus function as a Pavlovian CS. For example, if a light S_d was turned on (signaling that the subject could earn food by pressing a lever), it would not only signal *when* the response should be executed (its role as an S_d), but also *that* food reward is forthcoming (its role as a CS). This is an important but complicated point. A neutral stimulus in an instrumental-conditioning situation may have the properties of both an S_d and a Pavlovian CS, although researchers typically are more concerned with the former role than the latter.[6]

Responses.

There are two response terms in an instrumental-conditioning experiment. The unconditioned reaction (UR) is, by definition, the massive, reflexive response elicited by the US. Which UR is performed is determined by which US is given. Salivation occurs if the US is food, paw flex for shock. However, researchers are not usually concerned with the UR in instrumental conditioning. They assume that it occurs (for example, the presentation of food causes subjects to salivate), but rarely do they measure it.

The conditioned reaction, more often called the instrumental response, is usually quite unlike the UR. The instrumental, or target, response in most experiments is a relatively arbitrary motor response, such as lever pressing or running down a maze.[7] In Thorndike's experiment, the response was hitting the latch to escape the box.

INTERIM SUMMARY

Instrumental conditioning is concerned with response learning. Processes underlying instrumental conditioning may be different from those involved in Pavlovian conditioning, although many believe that they are merely different manifestations of a single underlying process. Thorndike was an innovator in this field, for systematically investigating instrumental conditioning in detail. In his original experiments, cats hit latches to escape a box and receive food. Although USs are used in instrumental conditioning, explicit CSs are often not present. If a neutral cue is present, however, it is called a "discriminative stimulus" (S_d), and it indicates that the outcome either is available pending a response (S+) or is not available (S−). Although URs are reflexively triggered by the US, the conditioned reaction in instrumental conditioning is usually unlike the UR.

STAGES IN INSTRUMENTAL LEARNING

The stages in an instrumental-conditioning experiment are basically the same as those noted for classical conditioning.

Acquisition

Acquisition is the stage during which the conditioned reaction is acquired. Acquisition provides the visible evidence that a specified response is becoming stronger, due to its relationship with the rewarding outcome. At the start of training, the response is performed at a relatively low level (for example, few lever presses are executed), but, with continued training, the rate increases. The response strength is thus measured in terms of an increase in the probability or frequency of the behavior, a decline in the number of errors committed, a decrease in the time taken to complete the response, an increase in the vigor or speed of the behavior, or a tendency to persist in making the response. A typical acquisition curve is shown in the figure depicting Thorndike's results (see Figure 8-2).

Extinction

Extinction involves the withholding of the outcome following the response. This is analogous to classical conditioning, where extinction involves the withholding of the US following the CS. The result of the extinction procedure is a decline in response strength—that is, a gradual decrease in performance.[8]

The conclusion in Chapter 3, about the permanence of the extinction process, also applies to instrumental conditioning. Extinction produces a decline in the response, but it does not eliminate the response entirely. If the animal is given a rest interval following extinction, spontaneous recovery of the response occurs. In other words, subjects that are trained to make an instrumental response such as lever pressing, and then are given extinction and a rest interval, show at least partial recovery of the original response on a spontaneous-recovery test, despite the fact that performance declined appreciably during the extinction phase. Thus, the response only *appears* to be eliminated as a result of extinction; in reality, it is still relatively dominant among the responses in the subject's behavioral repertoire.[9]

INTERIM SUMMARY

Acquisition is the stage during which the conditioned reaction is acquired. The response increases during this time, as measured by the probability of the response, its speed, the number of errors, and the response's persistence. Extinction occurs when the outcome (for instance, the reinforcer) is withheld. Usually the response declines during this time.

TYPES OF INSTRUMENTAL CONDITIONING

There are four basic instrumental conditioning procedures. Each corresponds to a contingency between an outcome and a response. These procedures are virtually identical to those used in classical conditioning (see Chapter 3). The primary difference is that the contingency in instrumental learning involves a behavior and an outcome, whereas the contingency in classical conditioning involves two stimuli.

A schematic diagram of the basic kinds of instrumental-conditioning procedures is shown in Figure 8-3. The procedures differ along two dimensions. First, the outcome may be either positive and desirable (appetitive) or nega-

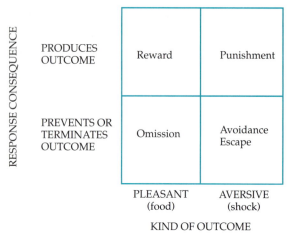

FIGURE 8-3. Schematic diagram illustrating the four basic types of instrumental-conditioning procedures.

tive and undesirable (aversive). Appetitive outcomes include food, water, praise and social contact, sensory stimulation, and warmth. Aversive outcomes include shock, loud noises, and nonlethal poison. The second dimension refers to the nature of the contingency. On the one hand, a response may produce or lead to a particular outcome (either aversive or appetitive). Conversely, a response may prevent or terminate the outcome. The following sections provide a more detailed account of these conditioning procedures.

Reward Conditioning

The most common type of instrumental conditioning is **reward training.**[10] This form of learning is exemplified by Thorndike's original experiment. In reward training, a response produces, or leads to, a desirable outcome, usually food. When such a response–outcome relationship occurs consistently, the response increases in probability.

Omission Training

Omission training is a second instrumental contingency. Here, the outcome following a response is "no appetitive US." That is, although the subject may receive the desirable outcome at other times during the experiment (when it is not engaged in performing the designated response), execution of the response itself leads to the omission of reward on that occasion.[11] The effect of omission training is opposite to that of reward training—namely, suppression of responding.[12]

A good example of the effect of omission training on behavior was shown by Wilson, Boakes, and Swan (1987). Two groups of rats were tested in a wheel-running apparatus similar to those seen in pet stores. During the eight training sessions, both the omission and the control groups occasionally received food presentations if the overhead light was turned off.[13] Occasional food deliveries were also given to control subjects when the light was on, but, in contrast, reinforcer delivery was delayed during this time if the omission subjects were running in the wheel.[14] In other words, if the omission subjects were running in the exercise wheel while the S_d was on, their scheduled food delivery was delayed for as along as 10 seconds; control subjects experienced no such delay.

The results are shown in Figure 8-4. The experimental group had a significantly lower rate of responding during the omission contingency when the light S_d was on than did the control subjects during the same period of time (compare the open circles, solid line and the closed circles, solid line).[15] Moreover, the experimental animals responded at a lower rate during the S_d than they did when the S_d was absent (compare the closed circles, solid line and the closed circles, dotted line). Thus, two kinds of evidence indicate that the rate of running in the exercise wheel is reduced by the omission contingency. First, experimental animals demonstrate a lower rate of response during the S_d, relative to their own behavior during the absence of the S_d. Second, the control subjects' level of responding during the S_d is higher than the omission subjects' rate during the same period of time.

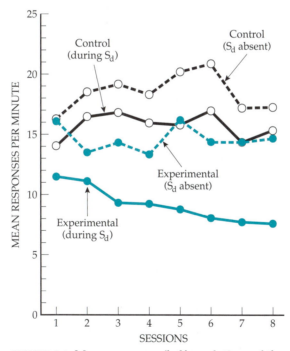

FIGURE 8-4. Mean responses (half-revolutions of the wheel) per minute during the S_d and during the absence of the S_d for the experimental (omission group) and control subjects (after Wilson, Boakes, & Swan, 1987).

Omission training is similar to extinction, in that both procedures lead to the decline in performance. Regardless, the two procedures are distinctly different in several ways. For example, the degree of suppression is markedly different in the two cases.[16] To illustrate, Phase 1 of a study by Uhl and Garcia (1969) involved training two groups of rats to press a lever for food. Following acquisition, extinction was given to one group and omission training to the other. The extinction procedure involved the withholding of reinforcement after each response. Omission, on the other hand, involved not only withholding reward after a lever response, but also presenting food if the subject refrained from pressing the lever for a certain period of time. Thus, omission-trained subjects received food by not pressing the lever.[17]

As shown in Figure 8-5, suppression of lever pressing was less severe for the omission-trained subjects than for the extinction subjects. Stated differently, extinction was more effective in suppressing the behavior than was omission. According to the authors, the reason is that the omission subjects treated the delivery of free food as an S_d for additional lever pressing. After all, during the acquisition phase, food delivery reliably signaled that additional lever pressing was appropriate. Such behavior continued to occur during omission training, even though pressing led to the postponement of food.

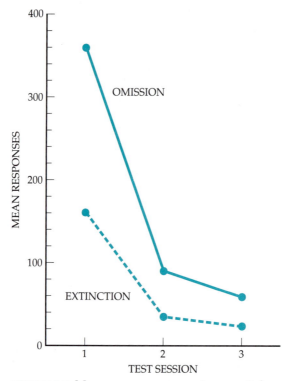

FIGURE 8-5. Mean responses per session over 3 days of testing for the omission-trained and extinction subjects (after Uhl & Garcia, 1969).

There are other ways to conduct the omission-training procedure. Some of them produce important behavioral differences from the one just described.[18] For instance, omission training may lead to more, not less, suppression of the behavior than conventional extinction. In studies showing this effect, reinforcement was presented following a specific alternative response, rather than merely following no response. This form of omission training is **counterconditioning,** because a new behavior that is counter, or antagonistic, to the original response is reinforced. Here, suppression of the target response is greater than what occurs during extinction because not only is it being extinguished (omission contingency), but a specific alternative competing behavior is also being strengthened (reward training for the alternative behavior).

In a study by Rawson, Leitenberg, Mulick, and Lefebvre (1977), for instance, subjects were rewarded with food for pressing Lever 1. During omission, reward was withheld for pressing Lever 1, but food was provided for pressing Lever 2. The results indicated that responding to the first lever declined dramatically, especially when reward was given for pressing the second lever. In short, extinction suppresses a target behavior more readily than omission training, but if a specific alternative response is strengthened at the expense of a target behavior, then omission training suppresses the target response more quickly than extinction. This effect occurs even when the alternative behavior differs markedly from the original response.[19]

Punishment

The third type of instrumental conditioning referred to in Figure 8-3 is **punishment.**[20] Punishment occurs when the instrumental response is followed by an aversive outcome, often shock or loud noise. Not surprisingly, the result of a punishment procedure is a decrease in, or suppression of, the response on which the punishment outcome is contingent. Punishment is the converse procedure from reward training. Furthermore, it is analogous to the excitatory aversive arrangement in classical conditioning (except for the fact that the element preceding the aversive outcome is an instrumental response rather than a CS).

When an aversive stimulus follows a response, the surrounding apparatus cues become aversive. Suppression of the behavior, therefore, results not only from the direct suppression of the response by the punisher, but also from the indirect disruption of behavior caused by these fear-eliciting stimuli.[21] Several studies have shown that these two sources of suppression are separate and distinct. For example, Goodall (1984) first trained rats to press a lever to receive food reward.[22] During each of the 12 test sessions, the subjects responded for food while receiving several presentations of a light and tone.[23] During one of the stimuli, lever pressing was contingently punished with a brief shock.[24] During the other stimulus, the same number of shocks that had been presented during the first stimulus was programmed to occur automatically. These shocks were unrelated to the lever-pressing behavior of the subject.

The results are shown in Figure 8-6. The mean suppression ratios show that when the aversive outcome is not contingent on the response, suppression occurs, but it is relatively minimal. When the shocks are contingent on the response, however, suppression is severe. The results therefore demonstrate that suppression is caused directly by the contingent punishment and indirectly by the fear-provoking CS. However, the contingency between the response and the aversive outcome is the more critical factor.

Although suppression of behavior is the most common result of contingent punishment, other interesting effects occur. For example, alternative behaviors often increase in frequency during punishment. Baker, Woods, Tait, and Gardiner (1986) place gerbils in a cage with a grid floor, a running wheel, an area containing sand for digging, and a food trough.[25] Three kinds of behaviors were measured: eating, digging in the sand, and running in the wheel. In several of their studies, eating was punished with a loud noise, a shock, or the removal of the food. In all cases, eating was suppressed, but an alternative behavior—namely, digging—increased in frequency. The authors claimed that suppression of behavior therefore involves a change in the probability of other behaviors that are in the animal's motivational hierarchy. When the highest-priority behavior in the food-oriented motivational hierarchy (eating) is suppressed by a punisher, then the next strongest behavior related to eating (sand digging) increases.

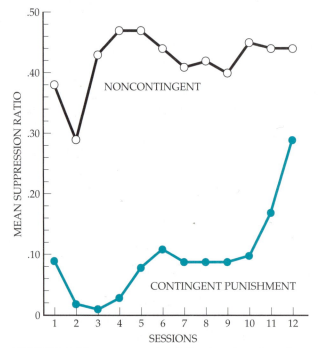

FIGURE 8-6. Mean suppression ratio, as a function of sessions during the response-contingent punishment stimulus and the noncontingent punishment stimulus (after Goodall, 1984).

Escape and Avoidance

In the omission procedure discussed previously, a response leads to the nonoccurrence of a positive US—for example, food. The fourth basic instrumental conditioning procedure, called "escape/avoidance," involves the termination (or nonoccurrence) of an aversive US.[26]

In an **escape** study, the response terminates an aversive US. More specifically, the noxious US comes on (the experimenter determines when) and then goes off after the animal makes the appropriate response. Often a discriminative stimulus such as a tone is given prior to the shock, but this has no effect on the contingency itself. The subject still must wait until the shock is given before it can terminate it.

In a typical **avoidance** study, a rat is placed in a two-compartment box, and a discriminative stimulus, such as a tone, is presented. The S_d signals that responding is appropriate. Specifically, if the animal jumps from one side of the box to the other, shock is omitted for that trial. If the animal fails to respond during the S_d, shock comes on and the animal now must terminate it (that is, the subject must execute an escape response).

Avoidance and escape responses usually are observed in the same experiment. Early in training, when the animal does not know that it is possible to avoid shock, escape behaviors occur. Later in training, however, after the animal has learned to expect the termination of shock following its response, it begins to respond before shock is presented. This constitutes an avoidance

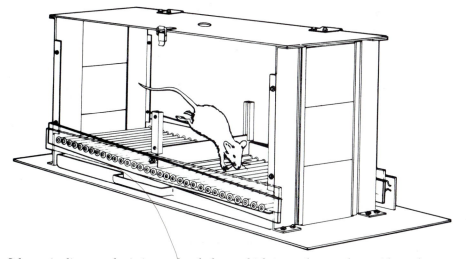

Schematic diagram depicting a shuttle box, which is used to study avoidance learning in rats. On a given trial, an animal avoids shock by jumping over the barrier to the other side of the box during the warning signal; on the next trial, it responds by jumping back to the original side.
Courtesy of Coulbourn Instruments, Lehigh Valley, PA

reaction. In short, before the subject has discovered that responding *prevents* shock, the animal merely escapes the noxious US when it comes on. Once the animal has discovered that a response prevents the US altogether, however, it begins to make avoidance reactions.

Avoidance learning differs from reward training in several ways. First, avoidance involves the termination or prevention of an aversive US rather than the presentation of an appetitive outcome. Second, during avoidance, animals have a limited amount of time during which they may execute the avoidance response. That is, avoidance is usually possible only during the warning signal or S_d. In reward training, on the other hand, no such time restriction is placed on the subject.[27] Despite this difference in methodology, avoidance training, like reward training, leads to the strengthening of the criterion behavior.

There are other techniques for studying avoidance besides the aforementioned use of the two-compartment shuttle box. One is **Sidman avoidance,** in which a subject postpones shock, usually by pressing a lever. Failure to do so means that a brief shock will be delivered shortly, perhaps within 10 or 15 seconds. When the animal responds, however, the timing apparatus is reset and a shock-free interval begins. Thus, if an animal responds at a sufficiently high rate, it may avoid shocks entirely. Unlike the shuttle-box experiment, Sidman avoidance usually does not employ a discriminative stimulus. The animal anticipates the pending shock merely from the temporal spacing of shocks rather than from an external signal.

A third technique used to study avoidance learning is **passive avoidance.** Here, the animal receives the aversive stimulus at a particular place in the apparatus, say, on the black side of a two-compartment box. This causes the animal to escape the shock by running into the safe side of the box. Later, it avoids shock by remaining passively on the safe side.

Historically, many learning theorists have termed the escape/avoidance learning paradigm **negative reinforcement.** According to this terminology, negative reinforcement occurs when an aversive event is terminated, thus producing an increase in the probability of the behavior. Use of this terminology is less common in contemporary learning research, primarily because of the confusion it creates. For instance, negative reinforcement can be a procedure (removal of an aversive stimulus), the product of the method (an increase in the probability of the response), or even the psychological process that is said to occur when the method is used (an increment in the underlying strength of the response). As a result of the confusion in meaning, some have suggested that the term be abandoned.[28] Therefore, rather than using the term negative reinforcement, this text refers to the four kinds of instrumental-conditioning procedures directly by name (reward, omission, punishment, and escape/avoidance).

INTERIM SUMMARY

There are four basic types of instrumental-conditioning procedures. Reward training occurs when a response produces, or leads to, a desirable outcome, often food. Omission training is when subjects receive reinforcers, but execution of the response itself leads to the omission of reward on that occasion. Omission training usually causes response rate to decline less markedly than does extinction, although if subjects are explicitly rewarded for a competing alternative response, then omission suppresses behavior more than extinction does. Punishment occurs when the target response is followed by an aversive outcome—for example, shock or a loud noise. The response is typically suppressed, although nonpunished behaviors may actually increase at this time. In escape learning, the subject terminates an aversive US. Avoidance is similar, but here, the subject responds during an S_d, at which point the aversive US is omitted for that trial. Sidman avoidance is when the subject postpones the next aversive US presentation; usually, an external S_d is not used. Passive avoidance is when a subject positions itself away from the location of the aversive US.

REINFORCER AND RESPONSE SPECIFICITY

Instrumental learning focuses on the relationship between a response and a subsequent reinforcer (or punisher). Both the kind of response that animals are capable of learning and the kind of reinforcers that are effective vary considerably. The following section specifies the reinforcer and the response dimensions in greater detail.

What Is Reinforcement?

It is tempting to think that a reinforcer, or a punisher, is simply a potent biological stimulus, such as food or shock. After all, these stimuli have powerful effects on animals, and they are certainly effective outcomes in conditioning research. Many stimuli that are reinforcing in instrumental conditioning, however, are considerably unlike food, water, and shock.[29] To appreciate this notion, one merely has to recognize the powerful effects that praise and criticism have on behavior.

Definition.

Any definition of a reinforcer must be able to encompass the many varieties of stimuli that are effective in this capacity. Reinforcement, therefore, cannot be defined in terms of the specific physical properties of the rewarding stimulus, but rather in terms of the effect that the stimulus has on behavior. Keeping this in mind, a reinforcer is defined as any outcome or event that, when made contingent on a prior response, increases the probability of that response in the future. A punisher is defined in a similar fashion—namely, as an event that, when made contingent on a prior response, decreases the probability of that response.

In other words, reinforcers and punishers are defined empirically, in terms of their effect on behavior, not *a priori,* in terms of some inherent property or characteristic. If an event causes an increase in the probability of a behavior on which its delivery is contingent, then, by definition, that event is a reinforcer. Similarly, if an event causes a decrease in the probability of a response on which it is contingent, then the event is a punisher. Such a definition encompasses conventional reinforcers such as food and shock, as well as other nonbiological stimuli that also change the probability of the contingent behavior appropriately, such as praise, criticism, good grades, money, and getting the right answer to a problem. By not limiting the concept of reinforcer to biological stimuli, the definition becomes more useful.

One of the problems with this definition, however, is that it is circular. A **reinforcer** is an event that increases the probability of the contingent behavior; any event that increases the probability of a contingent behavior is a reinforcer. The definition cannot predict in advance whether a given outcome or stimulus will function as a reinforcer. Although particular outcomes such as food *do* reliably act as reinforcers, we know this only from having used them in the past, not from the definition of a reinforcer.

Premack Principle.

Several theories attempt to resolve this problem by specifying principles that are critical to the reinforcement relation. A well-known theory of this sort was formulated by Premack (1959).[30] **Premack's principle** involves two assumptions. First, a subject's total activity pattern may be analyzed in terms of component activities. In a given environment, with no restriction placed on the subject's access to the various activities, a subject many engage in each (or at least most) of the activities a certain percentage of the time. For example, in a cage containing a lever, a running wheel, a light, and food, a rat probably would engage in each activity over the course of an observation period. If, however, the rat were in a particular motivational state—for example, if it were hungry—the proportion of time spent performing each activity would be quite different. Here, the subject might eat for a longer period of time, and, accordingly, spend less time engaged in the running or lever pressing.

The implication of Premack's first assumption is that the percentage of time in which the subject engages in a given activity reflects both the probability of that activity and, correspondingly, the preferability of the activity. Preferability does not depend on the number or type of activities, but rather on the rate of performance of the activity *relative to* the available options. For example, a satiated animal may spend 30% of its time eating, 60% running in an activity wheel, and 10% lever pressing. Conversely, a hungry animal may eat for 70% of the observation test, run for 25%, and lever press for 5% of the time. In each case, the percentage values reflect the *relative* preferability of the activity.

The second assumption in Premack's system relates to the reinforcement relationship. Such a relationship always involves two behaviors. A more preferable activity reinforces performance of a less preferable response if access to the preferred activity is made contingent on the execution of the less preferred activity. In the typical situation, eating (a highly preferred activity for a hungry animal) reinforces lever pressing (a much less preferred response) if the subject's access to food is made contingent on executing the lever-press response.

According to Premack's theory, all that is required to predict whether a stimulus (or an activity related to that stimulus) will be reinforcing is to estimate its relative preferability. The problem of the circularity of the definition of a reinforcer is thus solved. A reinforcing activity may be identified in advance by determining that its probability, relative to the probability of the alternative activities, is sufficiently high.

In support of this notion, Premack (1963) observed rats for a series of 600-second sessions, during which the subjects had the opportunity to run in a wheel weighted at either 18 or 80 grams, or to drink a 16%, 32%, or 64% sucrose solution. Premack computed relative time spent performing each activity during the last four sessions. A lever was then placed in the cage, and the rats were required to press it three times to release the brake on the activity wheel or to gain access to the drinking tube. According to the theory, the magnitude of the reinforcement relationship should be determined by the relative preferability of the wheel and the drinking responses.

The results of the study are shown in Figure 8-7. The mean lever responding (on the vertical axis) is a general measure of the power of the reinforcement relationship. The greater the increase in lever pressing, the more potent the reinforcer. Each reinforcer (18- and 80-gram wheel, 16%, 32%, and 64% sucrose solution) was located along the horizontal axis in terms of the prior probability of occurrence. Thus, running in the 80-gram wheel had been the

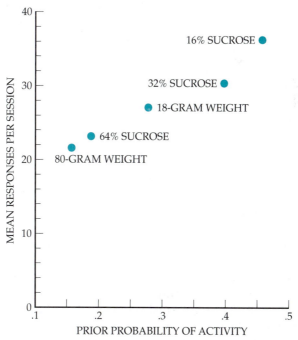

FIGURE 8-7. Mean lever responses per session, as a function of the prior probability of each reinforcing activity (after Premack, 1963).

least preferred activity (occurring only about 18% of the time), whereas drinking the 16% sucrose solution was the most preferred activity (occurring about 46% of the time).

The important point is that the strength of the reinforcement relationship (as indexed by the increase in lever-pressing behavior) was a direct function of the prior probability of the reinforcing activity. The higher the preferability of the activity, the greater its ability to reinforce lever pressing. Thus, although running in a wheel weighted 18 grams was less reinforcing than drinking a 32% sucrose solution, it was more reinforcing than drinking a 64% sucrose solution. The strength of the reinforcement did not depend on the type of activity (wheel running or drinking), but rather on the relative preferability of the activity (see also Chapter 11).

Behavioral Units

In Pavlovian conditioning, the CR is usually similar to the UR. The salivation CR, for example, has virtually the same form as the UR. In instrumental conditioning, this is usually not the case. The target response being conditioned (lever pressing, for example) is very rarely like the UR (salivation).[31]

Discrete Versus Operant Responding.

Most studies of instrumental learning focus on voluntary motor reactions. However, the structure of the experiment, and thus the way in which these responses are performed, may vary. A discrete-response technique involves a single, unitary response (or response sequence) performed only at a certain time. A good example is a typical maze study, where a subject runs from a start box to a goal box to receive food reward. Upon completing that single action, the subject is given the reward, and then, after an intertrial interval, is replaced in the start box. Each response is a discrete action. Although the speed and onset of the behavior are determined by the subject, the experimenter determines when the subject may begin the action (usually by opening the door to the alleyway).

The alternative technique involves free operant responding. Here, the experimenter determines *which* behavior is correct, but the subject determines *when* the behavior will be executed. Studies of lever pressing in rats usually employ this technique. Subjects are placed in the box and allowed to respond at their own pace to receive reward. Whenever they make the necessary response, or complete the appropriate response sequence, reward is delivered.

Studies that combine elements of both the discrete and the operant approaches are also used. Usually, the experimenter determines when the response may be made, but the subject is free to respond at its own speed during that time. For example, an experimenter may turn on a light S_d, at which point the subject responds at its own pace. The responses are freely emitted by the subject, yet there is some control over their execution by the experimenter.

Response Class.

Most instrumental-conditioning studies use voluntary motor reactions such as maze running or lever pressing, but other classes of responding are also used. One involves physiological reactions, such as changes in heart rate or blood pressure. This research is called "biofeedback" because the subject receives reward, or is provided with some sort of feedback, contingent on making a biological response. For human beings, the reward is often praise, money, avoidance of shock, or information concerning the correctness of the behavior. For lower species, various rewards include food, shock avoidance, and pleasurable brain stimulation.

Research on **biofeedback** is important for a number of reasons. First, the mere fact that biological responses may be instrumentally conditioned is theoretically interesting. For many years, involuntary responses of this kind were not considered to be conditionable using instrumental-learning procedures, because an instrumental response must occur prior to the reward, whereas physiological reactions were thought to occur only *after* a biological, reflex-inducing stimulus had been presented. If physiological reactions are controlled by the autonomic nervous system and are thus involuntary, then how could they be performed voluntarily to produce an instrumental reward?

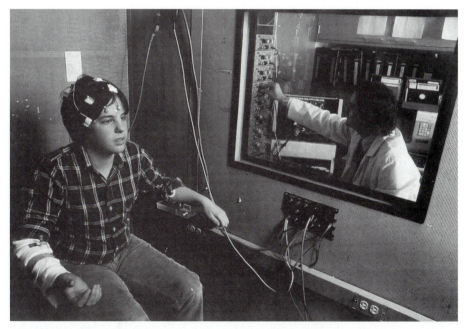

Photograph showing a subject receiving biofeedback training in which various physiological reactions, including electrical brain waves, recorded from the surface of the skull, may be instrumentally conditioned.
© *Pat Lanza Field/Bruce Coleman Inc.*

It is abundantly clear that visceral reactions may be conditioned using instrumental-conditioning techniques.[32] Generally, the process involves waiting until the biological reaction is performed, and then presenting the reward. Consider an example by Kimmel, Brennan, McLeod, Raich, and Schonfeld (1979), who conditioned the skin-conductance response in eight monkeys. The animals were placed in a harness and were given a series of red or green lights. For some subjects, the red light signaled an avoidance procedure. During the light, any change in the skin conductance postponed shock for 40 seconds. The green stimulus, in contrast, signaled a punishment procedure. Here, shock was delivered whenever the animal emitted the skin-conductance response. The authors found that the monkeys learned to respond appropriately within one session. As shown in Figure 8-8, the average response rate during Sessions 2–7 was much higher during the avoidance segments than it was during the punishment segments, indicating that those conditioning procedures had a powerful and predictable effect on the animal's skin-conductance responding.[33]

Instrumental techniques have been used to condition some astonishingly specific patterns of physiological reactions. Schwartz (1972), for example, reinforced some human subjects for changes in heart rate independent of changes

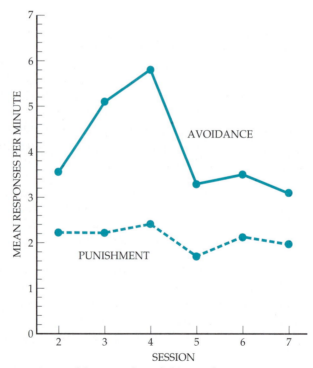

FIGURE 8-8. Mean number of skin-conductance responses per minute, as a function of sessions during the avoidance segments and the punishment segments (after Kimmel, Brennan, McLeod, Raich, & Schonfeld, 1979).

in blood pressure.[34] Others were rewarded for raising (or lowering) both reactions simultaneously. Still others were taught to raise one while lowering the other.[35] The subjects learned readily, indicating that heart rate and blood pressure may be conditioned independently and simultaneously, using instrumental-conditioning methods.

Biofeedback has potential for use as a treatment of certain medical disorders. Researchers, for example, have produced a marked improvement in patients who could not regulate their blood pressure.[36] Unfortunately, many of these patients were unable to maintain control over their blood pressure once they returned to the hectic and rapidly changing world outside the laboratory.[37]

A second unusual response class is verbal behavior. Like motor reactions, verbal utterances are subject to modification by instrumental-conditioning procedures.[38] In a classic experiment by Greenspoon (1955), students were asked to "say all the words you can think of," but not sentences. For some subjects, plural nouns were followed by the experimenter saying "mmm-hm" or "huh-uh." Control subjects were not given this feedback. Greenspoon found that the frequency of speaking plural nouns increased in the experimental subjects relative to the controls. Furthermore, there was evidence that the conditioning took place without any awareness of the reinforcement contingency on the part of the subjects, although subsequent studies disputed that result.[39] Regardless, these studies show quite clearly that instrumental-conditioning procedures are an appropriate means of changing verbal behavior.[40]

Finally, instrumental-conditioning procedures may be applied to larger units of behavior—even complex social behaviors, such as study habits, maladaptive or disruptive actions, and social responses. This area of psychology is known as **behavior modification** or **behavior therapy.** The literature in this field of research is voluminous, so the brief discussion presented here merely highlights the fact that instrumental-conditioning procedures easily affect units of behavior that are larger and more complex than simple motor reactions.[41]

According to behavior therapists, human behavior patterns—including those that are deemed to be highly maladaptive—are acquired (and extinguished) in much the same way that motor behaviors are learned (and extinguished) in nonhuman animal species. To use instrumental-conditioning procedures as a clinical therapy, therefore, one must identify the relevant maladaptive behavior, extinguish it, and then condition a more adaptive substitute behavior pattern.

The process of behavior modification is dramatic and powerful, as shown in a classic demonstration by Ayllon and Houghton (1962). They decreased dependent eating habits in people with schizophrenia—specifically, the need to be brought to the dining hall and spoon-fed. At first, patients could obtain food only by coming to the dining hall during a 30-minute period. Later, the duration was reduced. The success of the program was remarkable. After several weeks of training, virtually all of the patients were showing up to dinner and were feeding themselves appropriately. The procedures were then extended to include the training of social cooperation, a form of behavior that people with schizophrenia often lack. Here, two patients simultaneously had to press separate buttons to be admitted to a meal. For successfully cooperating at this task, each was reinforced by gaining entry to the dining hall. Not only did the patients learn this cooperative behavior, but the frequency of verbal exchanges with nurses and other patients increased as well.

Response Topography.

The foregoing work indicates that a vast range of different behaviors may be conditioned using instrumental-learning techniques. For any given behavior, differences in the form and detail of the response may also be conditioned. For example, reinforcement may affect the timing of a behavior. That is, if subjects are reinforced only when they respond at a relatively low rate, or, conversely, at a relatively high rate, then rate of behavior itself changes accordingly (see Chapter 9 for more details).

Similarly, reinforcement may affect the specific form of the behavior. For instance, Davis and Platt (1983) reinforced laboratory rats for manipulating a joystick. The stick could be moved in any direction. When the animals were rewarded simply for moving the stick, no systematic direction was adopted. When subjects were required to move the stick in a particular direction, however, then a high degree of consistency in direction was shown. In other words, particular characteristics or forms of action, not just the overall action itself, were selectively increased through reward. Finally, reinforcers do not simply affect the general response pattern; they may also alter specific components of the pattern. One example is the effect of differential reinforcement of pauses between lever presses. The pauses themselves may be conditioned by rewarding a response that follows, say, a long pause but not one that follows a short pause.[42]

Another dimension that characterizes holistic response patterns is the variability of the components within the pattern. Variability is conditionable. Subjects may be reinforced not simply for making a response such as pecking a key, but also for doing so in a variable fashion.[43] This was shown by Page and Neuringer (1985). Pigeons earned food by pecking eight times at two different response keys. The eight responses could be distributed in any manner across the two keys. Subjects could alternate between the right and the left key in any fashion they chose, provided they pecked a total of eight times. The only other stipulation was that the exact sequence of right and left pecks could not be repeated for a specified number of trials or runs. If the subjects gave a new sequence, they were reinforced with food, but if they repeated a sequence that had previously been used within a specified number of trials, they were given a brief time-out period and were forced to try again.

Figure 8-9 shows performance as a function of the number of trials without a repetition of any one pattern. Performance was highly accurate. Even when subjects were not allowed to repeat the same sequence for 50 successive attempts, they received reward on about 67% of the trials. The authors therefore concluded that variability of behavior is a dimension of responding that may be conditioned and maintained by a reinforcer, much in the way that other dimensions of a behavior (such as the pacing or location) are affected.

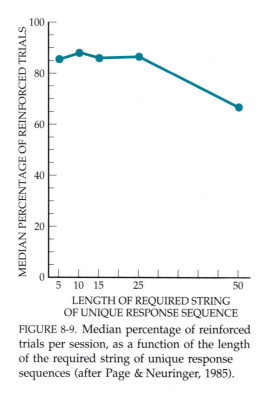

FIGURE 8-9. Median percentage of reinforced trials per session, as a function of the length of the required string of unique response sequences (after Page & Neuringer, 1985).

Variability is not always found in studies on conditioning, however. If subjects are not selectively reinforced for responding in a variable manner, then they may show a high degree of stereotypy.[44] A good example was a study by Schwartz (1980). On the wall of the cage was a matrix of 25 small lights, arranged in five rows by five columns. At the onset of each trial, the upper left-hand light was illuminated. A peck to the right key caused the light immediately below the one currently lit to become illuminated. A peck to the left key caused the light immediately to the right of the one currently lit to become illuminated. In other words, each peck to the right key moved the light down one position, and each peck to the left key moved the illuminated light to the right by one position. When the light at the lower right-hand corner of the matrix was finally illuminated (after a total of four pecks to each key), reinforcement was delivered. The exact sequence of responses made no difference at all; subjects could adopt variable or consistent patterns of responding to the right and left key as they wished. What Schwartz found, however, was that although 70 different successful sequences were possible, pigeons tended to choose one particular sequence and stick with it. Subjects developed a high degree of response stereotypy. For example, one pigeon might peck the left key four times, then the right four times. Another might alternate between the two. Regardless of the between-subject differences in pattern, individual birds were high consistent from one trial to the next.

Creating Behavioral Units Through Shaping

For instrumental conditioning to occur, the subject must execute the desired response prior to receiving the rewarding outcome. The ability to perform the behavior is, therefore, paramount. If subjects cannot, or do not, perform the designated reaction, then reinforcement cannot be forthcoming.

Given this constraint, how does one train a behavior, using instrumental-conditioning procedures, if the subject does not, or cannot, perform that behavior at the time of training? The experimenter appears to have no power to force the subject to perform the correct response. Actually, this is not entirely true. The experimenter does have ways of teaching new behaviors.

The most common technique is **response shaping,**[45] whereby successive approximations to the final target response are reinforced. Consider the task of teaching a rat to press a lever (a response that the rat does not already know). First, the experimenter reinforces only general behaviors that are compatible with the response, such as facing or walking toward the lever. Perhaps these behaviors merely bring the animal into the vicinity of the response. Once those behaviors are firmly established, then the experimenter reinforces a closer approximation to the final reaction. For example, the experimenter may now reward the subject for sniffing or touching the lever, or for positioning its head within a short distance from it. Again, the behavior must be securely established before further steps are taken. In fact, if the subject shows difficulty in learning a behavior, then the experimenter chooses an earlier response in the sequence and resumes shaping from that point. Eventually, the experimenter demands that the subject bite, paw, or even press the lever before reward is delivered.

Shaping therefore creates new behavioral units by reinforcing closer and closer approximations to the final desired action. Subjects may be taught not only simple responses such as lever pressing, but also larger units of behavior, such as elaborate chains of responses. For example, Skinner demonstrated the power of the shaping technique by training two pigeons to play a version of Ping-Pong.[46]

Shaping is extremely important in the area of behavior modification because subjects often do not have the ability to perform the desired reaction. Image training a profoundly retarded individual who has poor motor coordination to use table utensils. These individuals must first be reinforced for touching and holding the utensils, then positioning them correctly on the plate, and finally manipulating them efficiently in bringing food to the mouth. Shaping becomes an invaluable tool in situations such as this.

The basic idea of shaping is to strengthen behaviors that are consistent with, or part of, the desired response by rewarding closer and closer approximations to the final response. Although there are no set rules about which approximations to reinforce, nor any stipulation about when to proceed from one approximation to the next, some investigators have tried to specify the more general rules of shaping.[47] Midgley, Lea, and Kirby (1989), for example, required rats to deposit a small stainless steel ball bearing into a hole in the floor. This kind of behavior is not performed readily by rats, so shaping was

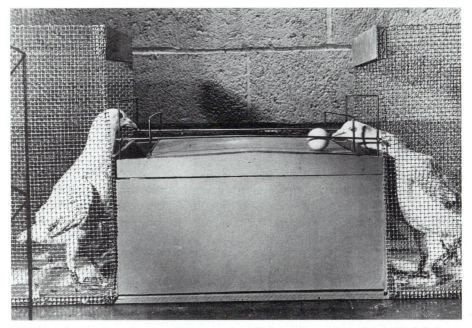

Photograph showing pigeons playing a simplified version of Ping-Pong. Such behavior reflects extensive chains of smaller response units (after Skinner, 1962).
UPI/Bettmann Newsphotos/Corbis

used. Using a computer keyboard, the experimenters recorded several behaviors as they occurred, such as approaching the ball bearing, moving toward the hole, reaching into the hole, depositing a ball bearing, mouthing or chewing on the ball bearing, and touching the ball bearing.

The computer was programmed with a set of rules concerning when to deliver a reward. Initially, a reinforcer was given for approaching and touching the ball bearing. Once the rate of those behaviors increased, reinforcement was given for the next designated approximation. Thus, by varying the rule by which the computer proceeded from one step to the next and then assessing the ultimate success in shaping the response, the experimenters were able to specify the effectiveness of the rule for shaping this behavior. Overall, the procedures were successful, as shown by the fact that 8 out of the 10 rats ultimately learned to deposit the ball bearing in the hole, taking, on the average, only 14.5 15-minute sessions to learn to do so. Although the set of rules or procedures for shaping that these authors used is unlikely to apply in all cases, nevertheless, the study shows that rules may be specified at least for some behaviors.

INTERIM SUMMARY

A reinforcer is an outcome or event that, when made contingent on a prior response, increases the probability of that response in the future. Although food and shock are often used as reinforcers, any event that changes the probability of a contingent response is effective. One problem with this definition of a reinforcer is that it is circular. Premack's principle circumvents this problem by pointing out that a reinforcing relationship involves two behaviors or activities. When a more preferable activity is made contingent on a less preferable activity, then a reinforcement relationship is established, and an increase in the probability of the less preferable activity is observed. Reward may be given either on a discrete basis (only a single unitary response is performed for each reward) or on a continuous basis (the speed and onset of the behavior are determined by the subject). Most instrumental experiments study voluntary motor reactions such as lever pressing, but many other kinds of responses are investigated, too. In biofeedback studies, for example, reward is contingent on executing a biological response such as a change in blood pressure. Highly specific behavioral reactions may be conditioned in this fashion. Verbal utterances and complex social behavioral patterns may also be altered using instrumental-conditioning procedures (complex social behavior is treated in behavior modification, or therapy, settings). Not only may different kinds of behavior be conditioned using instrumental techniques, but also different forms of the response may be altered. For example, reward affects the timing of the behavior and whether the behavior pattern is variable or stereotyped. New behaviors may be created using shaping. Here, successive approximations to the final form of the response are rewarded.

PRINCIPLES OF INSTRUMENTAL CONDITIONING

This section discusses the two principles of instrumental learning that lie at the heart of the conditioning process (see also Chapter 11). The principles are the same as those discussed in connection with Pavlovian conditioning—namely, contiguity and contingency.

Reinforcer Contiguity

Reinforcer contiguity (that is, the immediacy of the presentation of the reinforcer following a response) is a powerful variable in instrumental conditioning. Some theorists have even argued that contiguity is both necessary and sufficient for conditioning. This view was advanced in a classic study by Skinner (1948). Hungry pigeons were repeatedly presented with food after a fixed amount of time had elapsed. The subjects did not have to respond to receive food, but apparent conditioning was nevertheless observed in six out of eight subjects. The form of the CRs, however, was curious. One subject learned to turn counterclockwise about the cage; a second animal thrust its head into an upper corner of the cage in a very characteristic manner; a third subject developed a tossing response with its head. In each case, the behavior appeared just prior to food delivery. The subjects were behaving *as if* their responding caused food to appear (although this was not the case). Skinner claimed that whatever response the subject just happened to have been making just before food delivery was strengthened by the reward, even though the response did not actually cause reward to be delivered. In other words, the subjects were assumed to make a variety of responses, but when any one of them was accidentally contiguous with reward, it was strengthened. Contiguity is all that is needed for instrumental learning to take place.[48]

Researchers have shown that this conclusion is seriously in error. Recall from Chapters 3–5 that the procedure used by Skinner is, in fact, a Pavlovian conditioning procedure (similar to autoshaping), not an instrumental procedure.[49] Food-related behaviors similar to those observed by Skinner are actually Pavlovian CRs, not arbitrary behaviors strengthened by reward.[50] Thus, although Skinner claimed that contiguity is all that is needed for instrumental conditioning to occur, in reality, his experiment does not support such a conclusion.

The failure to show that contiguity is the *only* important factor in instrumental conditioning does not mean that contiguity is not important. Indeed, lack of contiguity (that is, delay of reward), leads to pronounced decrements in instrumental learning (see Chapter 9).[51] Imagine if a subject pressed a lever but did not receive food for several minutes or even hours. Under these conditions, associating the lever press with reward would be extremely difficult unless the subject was able to bridge the delay interval effectively.[52] Such bridging may occur, but without it, learning is very poor when the reward is not contiguous with the response.

Part of the reason that psychologists do not fully understand the role of contiguity is that they often have trouble identifying the exact behavioral unit being performed and thus the extent of response–reinforcer contiguity. If a single lever press is the behavioral unit in question, and reward is delayed for a period of time, then the reinforcer is not contiguous. On the other hand, if the behavioral unit is a larger and more complex sequence of individual components (perhaps several lever presses), then a reinforcer that is delayed after any given component may not necessarily be delayed relative to the larger unit.

Thomas (1981) evaluated this idea experimentally. Rats were given many free reinforcers. In addition, they occasionally earned an immediate reward by pressing a lever, but in doing so, they canceled some of the free reinforcers. In other words, an animal could earn food by responding, but the overall amount of food actually obtained (earned plus free) declined. Although the overall reinforcement rate declined with increasing levels of lever pressing, the rats pressed nonetheless, suggesting that the principle of contiguity was preeminent. Stated differently, the contiguous response–reinforcer relations produced learning despite the fact that overall reinforcement declined. Lever pressing, therefore, cannot have been strengthened simply by the overall consequence of the response (which was a reduction in rate of reinforcement).

Response–Reinforcer Contingency

Research confirms that the contingency between a response and a reinforcer is the more important factor in instrumental conditioning. Learning takes place if and only if the reward presentation depends on the prior execution of the response. Several lines of evidence support this conclusion. First, the previous discussion concerning the effect of reward on response topography provides ample support for this view. Recall that merely presenting a contiguous reinforcer following a response (such as moving a joystick) did not cause the subjects to manipulate the lever in any particular direction.[53] Once a **reinforcement contingency** was established between a specific direction of movement and reward, however, subjects moved the stick consistently in the required direction.

Second, research examining the relationship between the degree of contingency and response strength also provides support. Recall that when a CS and a US are presented randomly with respect to each other, little Pavlovian learning occurs (see Chapter 3). An analogous finding has been shown in instrumental conditioning.[54] For instance, in one study by Hammond (1980), all subjects had a .05 probability of receiving a water reinforcement if they pressed the lever during a given 1-second interval. In more formal terms, $p\{reinforcement/response\} = .05$. If the animal pressed the lever steadily, it therefore would receive a water reward, on the average, once every 20 seconds (5% of 20 is 1). The probability of receiving water without a press during a given 1-second interval was initially .0 ($p\{reinforcement/response\} = .0$); subjects never received unearned water rewards.

During a later stage of the experiment, however, the probability of receiving an unearned water reward was increased to .05. Here, subjects were as likely to receive water during a given 1-second interval for doing nothing as they were for pressing the lever. Reward and pressing the lever were thus random with respect to each other.

The results, shown in Figure 8-10, demonstrate that lever pressing increased as the contingency between lever pressing and water reward increased. When subjects earned water reward at the rate of one reward every 20 seconds, but received no additional free rewards, then the rate of lever pressing was substantial. When the probability of earned and unearned rewards was the same, however, lever pressing declined dramatically. Hammond's experiment is important because it demonstrates that contiguity plays a secondary role in instrumental learning. Lever pressing occasionally resulted in contiguous reward presentations, even when earned and unearned rewards were equally likely. Yet subjects failed to perform the response when responding did not differentially lead to reward. In short, contiguity is important, but the predictive relationship between a response and a reinforcer—that is, the contingency—is more critical.

A related experiment using humans was done by Chatlosh, Neunaber, and Wasserman (1985). College students were given the following instruction: "Your task is to find out whether tapping a telegraph key has any effect on the occurrence of a white light. At any time you may choose to tap the key

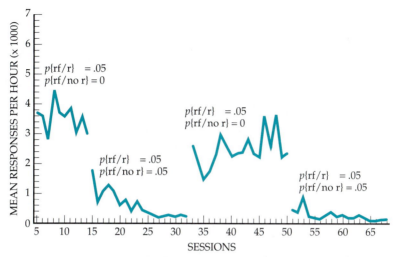

FIGURE 8-10. Mean number of responses per hour, as a function of training sessions where the probability of receiving earned reward ($p\{rf/r\}$) was .05, and the probability of receiving unearned reward ($p\{rf/no\ r\}$) was either 0 or .05 (after Hammond, 1980).

or not tap it.... Each problem will begin when the red light comes on and end when it goes off. After each problem, choose the number between -100 and $+100$ on the rating scale that best characterizes the degree to which your tapping of the telegraph key affected the occurrence of the white light, *from prevents the light from occurring* $[-100]$ to *causes the light to occur* $[+100]$" (p. 7; emphasis original). In other words, the experimenters were primarily interested in determining whether the contingency between tapping the key (response) and the onset of the white light (reinforcer) affected the response rate. Subjects were also asked, however, to indicate their sense of whether a causal relationship existed between the response and the reinforcer, based on the perceived correlation between the two events.

Behavior was sampled at every 1-second interval. The probability of being reinforced for responding (presentation of the white light) during any 1-second interval ($p\{$reinforcement/response$\}$) was varied, as well as the probability of having the white light come on without having had a response during that 1-second interval ($p\{$reinforcement/no response$\}$). The difference between these two probabilities varied from $+.75$ ($p\{rf/r\} = .875$ minus $p\{rf/no\ r\} = .125$) to $-.75$ ($p\{rf/r\} = .125$ minus $p\{rf/no\ r\} = .875$). In the extreme positive case, the probability of receiving the white light, given a response in the previous 1-second period was high, and the probability of receiving a free white light was low. In the extreme negative case, the reverse was true—that is, the probability of receiving a free outcome was high, but the probability of receiving a response-contingent outcome was low. In the middle range, the probability of each kind of event was about equal. Here, subjects were as likely to receive the white light right after making a response as they were right after making no response.

The results are shown in Figure 8-11. Rate of responding increased as a function of the response–outcome contingency. When the white light was contingent on a prior response, and relatively few free lights were given, responding was substantial. When the probability of receiving free outcomes was greater than the probability of receiving response-contingent outcomes, however, responding was very low. Responding was intermediate for the intermediate conditions. These data, therefore, confirm the results found with rat subjects. Instrumental responding increases as a direct function of the magnitude of the response–reinforcer contingency.

What about the subjects' judgments of the causal relationship between the response and outcome? These data are shown in Figure 8-12. The ratings of the degree to which the telegraph tapping was perceived to cause the white light to occur show precisely the same relationship. When the probability of receiving an outcome following a response was high, relative to the probability of receiving free white lights, then subjects perceived their responding to be the cause of the light. As more and more free outcomes occurred, relative to response-contingent outcomes, however, subjects tended to perceive that responding actually prevented the white light from coming on.[55] In conclusion, the most critical underlying principle of instrumental conditioning is the contingency between the response and reinforcer. Although contiguity is nec-

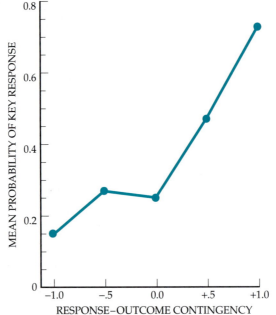

FIGURE 8-11. Mean probability of making a telegraph-key response (during the last six cycles of training), as a function of the response–outcome contingency ($p\{rf/r\}$ minus $p\{rf/no\ r\}$) after Chatlosh, Neunaber, & Wasserman, 1985).

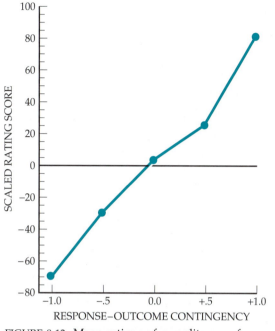

FIGURE 8-12. Mean ratings of causality, as a function of the response–outcome contingency ($p\{rf/r$ minus $p\{rf/no\ r\})$ (after Chatlosh, Neunaber, & Wasserman, 1985).

essary, it is the differential *predictive* relationship between the response and the outcome that supports conditioning.

INTERIM SUMMARY

One important principle of instrumental conditioning is reinforcer contiguity. If reward is delayed, then learning does not take place. The response–reinforcer contingency, however, is an even more important feature of instrumental learning. Even if contiguous reward presentations are experienced, subjects fail to learn if responding does not differentially lead to reward. One reason is that subjects do not perceive causality in these situations.

ENDNOTES

1. Born in 1874, Edward L. Thorndike was one of four children raised in the household of a strict Methodist minister. His early childhood years were characterized by austerity and seriousness of purpose, with a great emphasis on independence and discipline. As a young man, Thorndike entered Wesleyan University in Connecticut,

graduating with a Bachelor's degree in 1895. From there, he went to Harvard University and studied under William James, one of America's greatest psychologists and most notable scholars. Thorndike was originally interested in communication by means of small unconscious gestures and movements, due largely to claims that a German horse, Clever Hans, could do arithmetic. For example, the horse would tap six times with his hoof when asked to multiply 2×3. (As is turned out, the horse was responding merely to the small movements and gestures on the owner's face, which provided a signal for the correct answer; see Candland, 1993, for an intriguing account of this story.) However, when his landlady refused to allow him to raise and study chicks in his bedroom, he turned to his mentor, William James. James failed to secure research space in the psychology facilities but allowed Thorndike to conduct the experiments in James's own basement. After Harvard, Thorndike took a position as a tutor at Columbia University in New York City (bringing his two most educated chicks with him), finally earning his doctorate in 1898. He continued to teach at Columbia until his retirement in 1941. Thorndike died in 1949.

2. The increase in efficiency suggests that instrumental learning involves learning what *not* to do (learning to suppress extraneous reactions) more than learning to perform a specific, new behavior. Although such a notion was suggested formally by Harlow (1959), most theorists think of instrumental learning as the acquisition or strengthening of a specific behavior—namely, the one leading to the desirable outcome, rather than the elimination of competing behaviors.

3. Operant conditioning is a term that many equate with instrumental conditioning. Like instrumental learning, operant conditioning involves the execution of behaviors that operate on the environment. They lead to rewarding outcomes. Historically, the term operant conditioning has been used to refer to experimental situations in which subjects perform at their own pace, as opposed to being given discrete trials. Pressing a lever is a good example. In this text, no distinction is made between operant and instrumental conditioning.

4. Recall from Chapter 3 that Pavlovian conditioning is defined in a similar fashion— that is, in terms of the procedure used to produce a Pavlovian CR. Specifically, Pavlovian conditioning occurs when two stimuli occur independently of the animal's behavior.

5. Reinforcer is the more technical term for the rewarding outcome, although the term reward is often used, too, especially when a food US is used.

6. The fact that an S_d may also serve as a CS does *not* imply that its power as a CS is equivalent to one that has been conditioned using a Pavlovian procedure; see Rescorla (1994).

7. There are exceptions, however. For example, it has been shown that physiological reactions such as changes in heart rate or blood pressure may be instrumentally conditioned, although even here, such responses are arbitrarily chosen by the experimenter as being the correct response.

8. Very often, the onset of extinction leads to a temporary but marked increase in response rate, called the "extinction burst." Some investigators believe such a burst reflects the presence of frustration at not receiving reward. Frustration is certainly known to energize behavior; see Chapter 10 of this book.

9. One factor that influences the degree to which a subject shows spontaneous recovery is the similarity between the training and the test conditions. Procedures that emphasize the similarity between acquisition and a test of spontaneous recovery, while highlighting the dissimilarities between the extinction phase and the test, tend to increase spontaneous recovery; see Holder and Burstein (1981).

10. An alternative name for this type of contingency is positive reinforcement.
11. As later discussed, the food may be delayed, rather than omitted altogether. Furthermore, food given at times other than when the subject is responding actually follows some behavior, although the behavior may not easily be identified. The consistency of the relationship between the other behavior and the reward is rather poor, and thus no single alternative behavior is conditioned. Omission training is also named negative punishment.
12. However, see Sheffield (1965).
13. The authors also used a 2-kilohertz tone for some of the subjects.
14. Thus, the number of reinforcers was equated between groups, but the dependency or contingency between the response and the delay of food differed.
15. The controls, however, showed an unconditioned effect of the S_d—that is, a small but significant reduction in rate of responding.
16. Uhl (1973); Uhl and Gracia (1969).
17. This type of omission training is called a "differential-reinforcement-of-other-behaviors" (DRO) schedule because, in theory at least, the food presentation for "not responding" is really a reward for performing some behavior other than the criterion reaction.
18. See Leitenberg, Rawson, and Mulick (1975); Rawson and Leitenberg (1973); Rawson, Leitenberg, Mulick, and Lefebvre (1977).
19. See Pacitti and Smith (1977).
20. Also termed positive punishment; see Dunham (1971) for a review.
21. Disruption due to a fear eliciting stimulus is the conditioned emotional response (CER) effect discussed in Chapter 3.
22. See also Church, Wooten, and Matthews (1970).
23. These cues were given sequentially, but up to 30 minutes intervened between their presentations.
24. For brevity, the description of the method covers only one group. Goodall (1984) actually employed other groups, which received a different rate and intensity of shocks. The results were similar in all cases.
25. See also Dunham (1978); Dunham and Grantmyre (1982).
26. This kind of contingency is also termed negative reinforcement; see subsequent discussion.
27. There are many situations where a time constraint is used in reward conditioning. The point here is simply that the *typical* reward study does not involve such a constraint.
28. Kimble (1993).
29. Chapters 3–5 suggest a similar message for classical conditioning. Shocks and food are not the only viable USs; outcomes that become associated with neutral CSs may even be other CSs, as shown by the sensory-preconditioning phenomenon.
30. See also Premack (1965).
31. A good exception involves biological responses such as heart rate. Here, the conditioned and unconditioned reactions are similar; see subsequent discussion on biofeedback.
32. See Schwartz and Beatty (1977).
33. See also Miller (1978).
34. See also Schwartz (1975).
35. These results are interesting, in part, because they illustrate differentiation of responding in a system that was thought to lack such differentiation. Specifically, the autonomic nervous system is known to be highly integrated. Elevations in

heart rate, for instance, are usually accompanied by elevations in blood pressure. Because of such interconnections, differentiated actions were thought to be minimal. The fact that precise *patterns* of physiological responding may be instrumentally conditioned, therefore, attests to the power of this technique.

36. Benson, Shapiro, Tursky, and Schwartz (1971).
37. See Fuller (1978); Schwartz (1973).
38. See Holz and Azrin (1966); Williams (1964) for reviews. Vocal responses are conditionable in cats as well; see Molliver (1963).
39. These studies showed that subjects are able to report an awareness of the reinforcement contingency if they are questioned in a more thorough manner; see Verplanck (1962).
40. Conditioning of verbal behavior through instrumental-reinforcement techniques shows many of the same characteristics found in more conventional research. For instance, Lane (1960) and Lane and Shinkman (1963) showed that the frequency of vowel utterances is influenced by intermittent schedules of reward presentation in the same way that skeletal behaviors in animal subjects are affected; see Chapter 9 in this book.
41. For an introduction to this area of psychology, see Masters, Burish, Hollon, and Rimm (1987); Thorpe and Olson (1990).
42. Shimp (1967, 1969); see also Sizemore and Maxwell (1983).
43. See Neuringer (1991, 1993).
44. Schwartz (1980, 1985); Schwartz and Reilly (1983); but see also Wong and Peacock (1986).
45. Another method not discussed is modeling. Here, the experimenter physically molds the behavior and provides a model, which the subject may imitate.
46. Skinner (1962).
47. See Galbicka (1988); Pear and Legris (1987).
48. Skinner (1948) referred to this outcome as "superstitious" responding because the animals behaved superstitiously—that is, as if their behavior produced reward when, in fact, it did not.
49. Recall that autoshaping involves the presentation of light–food pairings independent of the animal's behavior. Normally, pecking is observed.
50. See Staddon and Simmelhag (1971) for a review.
51. Tarpy and Sawabini (1974).
52. See Lett (1973, 1975); Lieberman, Davidson, and Thomas (1985).
53. Davis and Platt (1983).
54. See Scott and Platt (1985) for a theoretical discussion of this area.
55. See also Wasserman, Chatlosh, and Neunaber (1983).

CHAPTER 9

Variables That Affect Instrumental Learning

Chapter 8 provided a general introduction to instrumental conditioning, the basic terms and procedures used to study response learning, and the underlying principles of such learning, including reinforcer contiguity and contingency. This chapter considers the many important variables that affect instrumental learning. Knowledge of how these variables operate promotes an understanding of the various instrumental-learning phenomena (Chapter 10) and theories of reinforcement (Chapter 11).

INTERMITTENT SCHEDULES OF REINFORCEMENT

Most of the work discussed so far has assumed that reinforcement is given each time an animal makes the appropriate response—that is, a subject is rewarded on a continuous basis during acquisition. Reward, however, is rarely like that in most natural environments. Animals, including humans, usually must make several attempts, or wait a particular length of time, before reward is available. Consider the behavior of a small bird foraging for insects on pine cones, a mountain lion chasing rabbits, and a person throwing darts at a target. Each feeding site (cone) may or may not contain a desired prey item; not every chase results in the lion catching a hare; only occasionally does the person hit the bull's-eye. Such intermittency of reinforcement is a common fact of everyday life. How behavior is controlled by **schedules of intermittent reinforcement,** therefore, is an important issue, one that applies to virtually all species.[1]

There are four basic types of reinforcement schedules, as shown in Figure 9-1. For the two kinds of ratio schedules, reward is based on the number of responses that the subject makes. For the two types of interval schedules, a response is reinforced only after a certain period of time has elapsed. Each of these classifications—ratio and interval—are further subdivided according to whether the criterion is fixed or variable. A fixed-ratio schedule is one in which reward is delivered following a specified number of responses; that

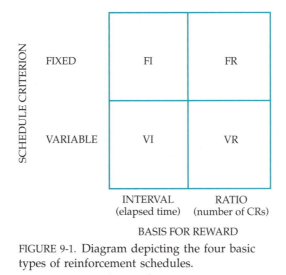

FIGURE 9-1. Diagram depicting the four basic types of reinforcement schedules.

number never varies from one reward to the next. Similarly, in a fixed-interval schedule, reward for a response is delivered following a given length of time; again, the interval is constant. On a variable-ratio schedule, however, although the reward is based on the number of responses emitted, the specific number varies from one reward to the next. Finally, on variable-interval schedules, the response is reinforced after a certain period of time has elapsed, but the precise length of time varies.

The following section considers each of these basic reinforcement schedules in greater detail.

Fixed-Ratio Schedule

Perhaps the simplest intermittent schedule is the **fixed-ratio (FR) schedule.** Under this schedule, the subject receives a reward for executing a fixed number of responses. The overall rate of responding is relatively high (for example, higher than on a continuous schedule), although if the FR value becomes too large, responding deteriorates. This effect, termed scheduled strain, involves long pauses following reinforcement. This was demonstrated by Felton and Lyon (1966), who showed that the length of the pause was directly related to the size of the FR requirement. When pigeons were taught to peck a key 100 times for food (the schedule was therefore FR-100), the animals paused for about 1.5 seconds after each reinforcement. When the response requirement was increased to FR-150, however, the pause lasted nearly a minute.[2]

The **postreinforcement pause** is actually determined by the length of time between rewards, as shown in a study by Killeen (1969).[3] Some of the subjects were trained on an FR schedule, whereas others were forced to wait an equivalent amount of time before being allowed to earn reward. Postreinforcement pausing was identical in both cases. In other words, the length of the pause is affected more by the amount of time to the next reinforcer rather than the number of responses that the FR schedule requires of the animal.

Variable-Ratio Schedule

The **variable-ratio (VR) schedule** is similar to the FR schedule, except that the specific number of responses required to earn reinforcement varies from one reward to the next. A VR schedule is specified in terms of the average number of responses required. For example, if an animal were reinforced after an average of 10 responses, the schedule is VR-10. The actual requirement for each earned reward, however, may be 8 on one occasion, 12 on the next, 7 responses, than 13, and so forth.

Two characteristics of VR schedules are noteworthy. First, a VR schedule produces a higher overall rate of responding than other basic schedules, although, in some cases, VR and FR notes have been shown to be comparable.[4] In fact, the rate on a VR schedule is higher than that on any other basic schedule (later, this chapter offers more discussion of this point). Second, the response rate on a VR schedule is normally very stable. This schedule prevents the animal from acquiring an accurate sense of the number of responses required for reward, thus reducing postreinforcement pausing.

Fixed-Interval Schedule

In the **fixed-interval (FI) schedule,** a subject is rewarded for responding after a fixed period of time has elapsed, the most efficient strategy is to wait until the interval has passed and then to make a single response to earn the reinforcement. Such a strategy allows the subject to expend the minimum amount of energy while capitalizing on all the available rewards. However, subjects do not normally behave in this fashion. Rather, they respond throughout the entire interval, but the rate and pattern of responding vary in a complicated and interesting way.

For example, subjects typically pause for a period of time following reward and then begin to execute the response at an accelerating rate.[5] The longer the FI interval, the longer the animal pauses before resuming its behavior, and the more pronounced the acceleration prior to the next reinforcer. This accelerating pattern of behavior is illustrated in Figure 9-2 for two FI schedules.[6] Acceleration is shown by the fact that the number of responses on each successive 10th of the interval increases.

Why do animals pause immediately after receiving reward and then gradually increase their response rate to a maximum just prior to the next reward?[7] The reason is that animals develop a sense of the temporal interval between rewards; they discriminate the passage of time. Thus, they cease spending effort for a short time because they do not expect to receive another reward immediately. Only after some time has elapsed do they begin to respond in anticipation of receiving the next reward.

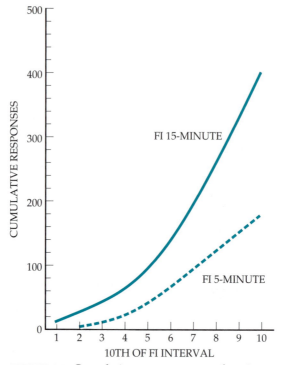

FIGURE 9-2. Cumulative responses, as a function of 10ths of the FI interval for pigeons responding on an FI-15-minute and an FI-5-minute schedule, averaged over 21 sessions of training (after Gentry, Weiss, & Laties, 1983).

Several lines of evidence support this assertion. First, the acceleration in rate is more pronounced when subjects are given extended training. Presumably, their sense of the length of the temporal interval improves with experience.[8] Second, if animals are given external signals that help them discriminate the passage of time, such as a light that increases in intensity throughout the FI period, then they show an even more pronounced acceleration in rate over the interval.[9] Third, merely giving subjects a reward after a fixed interval of time, but not requiring them to respond, causes them to show the typical FI behavior pattern later, when they are required to respond.[10]

The reason that animals pause following reward is that they are temporarily inhibited from responding. If a novel stimulus is presented early in the FI interval (while the animals are inhibited), disruption occurs, causing the subjects to perform the response immediately.[11] In other words, if the animal is distracted, thus removing the inhibition that is temporarily suppressing behavior, then responding is immediately expressed.

Variable-Interval Schedule

The **variable-interval (VI) schedule** is similar to the FI schedule, with one important difference. The interval of time between periods when reinforcement is available varies. The VI schedule is specified in terms of the average interreinforcement time. For example, a 30-second VI schedule (VI-0.5-minute) permits the animal to earn rewards, on the average, every 30 seconds, although the actual intervals experienced by the subject may be 40 seconds, then 20 seconds, 5 then 65, and so forth. The characteristic style of responding under VI schedules is a stable but low rate.

Rate of responding under a VI schedule increases as a function of the rate of reinforcement. Catania and Reynolds (1968) confirmed this using a variety of VI schedules, the average time of which ranged from 12 to 427 seconds. Most of the subjects made about 60 to 100 responses per minute on a VI-0.2-minute schedule (this schedule yielded about 300 reinforcements per hour), but the rate dropped to about 20 to 70 responses per minute for a VI-7.1-minute schedule (which yielded approximately 8.4 reinforcements per hour).

Although rate of responding is fairly stable from one reinforcement to the next, it increases slightly just before the next reward, just as it does on FI schedules.[12] This acceleration is reasonably small, however, because subjects are unable to use the temporal interval to predict when reward is available.

Comparison of Ratio and Interval Schedules

Ratio schedules sustain a much higher level of responding than do interval schedules. The reason is that rate of reward is affected by the rate of responding under a ratio schedule (the faster the responding, the more frequent the reinforcers), but not under interval schedules (no matter how fast the animal responds, reward is available only after the specified amount of time has elapsed).[13]

Does the higher frequency of reinforcement under ratio schedules cause this disparity in rates? The answer appears to be no. Killeen (1969) compared subjects responding on FR and VI reinforcement schedules. A given VI animal obtained reward only when a corresponding FR animal earned its food pellet. In other words, the time it took the FR animal to earn reward became the interval value for the corresponding VI subject. By using this special technique, both animals received the same frequency and pattern of reinforcement. The important differences between them was that the VI subject had to wait until the FR animal completed its required number of responses before it could earn a reward. Killeen found that the response-per-minute averages for the FR animals was higher than for the VI subjects, even though the rate of reward was the same. Thus, the discrepancy in response rate cannot be attributed to a difference in frequency of reinforcement.

A more suitable theory to explain the difference between response rates focuses on the **interresponse time (IRT)**, or pause between each response. Consider the probability of receiving a reward following a given response. On interval schedules, the probability of reward increases with longer interresponse times. That is, the slower the animal responds, the more likely it is that the next response will be reinforced (because the next response is always closer to the end of the time interval). This is not the case for ratio schedules. A low response rate under a ratio schedule does not change the probability that the next response will produce reward. In fact, long interresponse times postpone reinforcement because reward delivery is determined exclusively by the ratio requirement, not by the passage of time.

The explanation for the difference in rate is based on these observations. Reward strengthens the IRT values that are contiguous with reward. With shorter IRTs, a high overall rate of response is generated because the IRTs generalize to other portions of the interval. In contrast, response patterns having long IRT values are selectively strengthened in subjects that tend to respond with such IRTs close to reward; long IRTs translate into a lower overall rate.

This theory has been supported in a variety of ways. Dews (1969) measured the IRTs just prior to reward for subjects responding on interval and ratio schedules, confirming that the IRTs were, on average, relatively long for interval subjects, but short for ratio-schedule animals.

Using a more direct approach, Galbicka and Platt (1986) devised a schedule that reinforced pigeons only if they pecked the key with a specified IRT value; that is, subjects were rewarded on an interval schedule but the reinforcer was withheld unless the IRTs conformed to a specified length. Response rate was controlled by the selective action of reward on the IRT. The more the subjects were required to press with short IRT values, the higher the rate.[14]

Finally, Peele, Casey, and Silberberg (1984) trained pigeons to peck a key on a VI schedule of reward but required them to respond with short IRT values that are characteristic of ratio, not interval, schedules. In Phase 1, food was delivered on a VR-200 schedule when the key was colored, say, green, but on a VI schedule when the key turned red. The actual VI interval was equal to the time it took to earn food under the preceding VR schedule. Thus, the rate of reinforcement was equated for the two schedules. Training conditions were similar in Phase 2 except for one important difference. Reinforcement delivery during the VI component required that the subject peck the key using the same final IRT value that it had used during the prior VR component.

The results are shown for one of the subjects in Figure 9-3. The VR schedule produced a much higher response rate than the VI schedule when no IRT restriction was imposed (left panel). However, when the subject was required to earn food by using the same IRT values that it used on the preceding VR schedule, no rate difference between VR and VI was observed (right panel).

Complex Schedule Arrangement

DRL Schedules.

The preceding section noted that animals may be selectively reinforced for responding with short interresponse times. Animals may also be taught to respond with unusually long interresponse times.[15] This occurs on a **differ-**

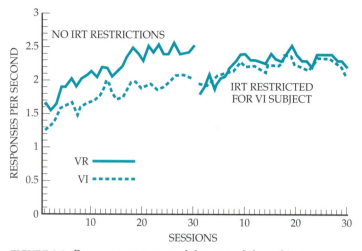

FIGURE 9-3. Responses per second for one of the subjects, as a function of training sessions when the IRT values were free to vary (left panel) or were restricted so that the IRTs during the VI component had to be the same as those given during the VR component (after Peele, Casey, & Silberberg, 1984).

ential reinforcement of low rates of responding (DRL) schedule.[16] Under a DRL schedule, a subject must withhold its response until a certain period of time has elapsed. If it does so successfully, then the next response is reinforced. Otherwise, if a response occurs before the criterion time elapses, the timer is reset and the interval begins again.

Initially, performance under a DRL schedule is inefficient because of the conflict between the need to respond and the need to withhold a response. Efficient responding is possible, therefore, only when two separate response tendencies are strengthened. First, inhibition keeps the subject from responding too quickly. Second, temporal discrimination helps the subject time its responding.[17] With sufficient training, responding on a DRL schedule becomes stable and efficient, although efficiency is negatively related to the size of the DRL value (the higher the value, the worse the performance).[18]

One unique feature about DRL schedules is that subjects engage in collateral or incidental behaviors during the time they are inhibiting the instrumental target response. Some of the animals assume strange and idiosyncratic postures; others nuzzle the food cup, sniff, or chase their tail; some even nibble at their tail.[19] Psychologists are puzzled by this phenomenon, although it seems to be a chain reaction. Each response is an inherent part of a chain and serves as a signal for the next response.

Some researchers argue that **collateral behavior** is, in effect, the animal's way of timing the interval.[20] Others suggest that because these behaviors interfere with the performance of the target response, thus allowing the animals to perform more efficiently, they are reinforced. In other words, animals cannot perform the target response and the collateral behavior at the same time, so a deterioration of the target response, as a result of the subject performing the collateral behavior, is beneficial.[21]

Combined Schedules.

Psychologists are not limited to the four basic schedules discussed previously. More complex arrangements may be established by combining schedules in various ways. For example, when reward is contingent not just on the successful completion of one schedule but on the completion of two distinct schedules, the arrangement is termed a **compound schedule.** One illustration of this is an FI–FR schedule. Here, reinforcement is available only if the subject executes a specified minimum number of responses within a specified time. If both conditions are met, reinforcement is delivered. Normally, behavior under compound schedules reflects the patterns found under each separate schedule. For example, with a compound FI–FR schedule, postreinforcement pauses are evident, and an increase of response rate is shown following the pause (typical of FI schedules), but the response rate just prior to the next reward is higher than would be found under an FI schedule only.

Schedules may also be presented sequentially. Under a **tandem schedule** arrangement, the subject must complete the requirements of two or more individual schedules in succession before reinforcement is delivered. An FI–FR tandem, for example, requires the subject to wait a fixed interval of time and then to execute a fixed number of responses. If each separate schedule is accompanied by an external cue (for instance, one light is turned on during one of the schedules, and a different light during the other), then this is a **chain schedule.**

In a **mixed schedule,** the subject may obtain reinforcement during each of several individual component schedules, but the various schedules are presented in a random order. If each component schedule is signaled by a discriminative cue, then the arrangement is a **multiple schedule.** Here, the rate of responding is determined not only by the component schedule currently in effect, but also by the other component schedules that compose the series.[22]

Reinforcement Schedules in the Human Environment

The importance of studying reinforcement schedules is based on the assumption that behavior in the real world is controlled by reward that is delivered according to various complex reinforcement contingencies. There is little doubt that the behavior of animals, including human beings, is controlled to a considerable degree by reinforcers, and that reinforcers are invariably given on an intermittent basis. Nevertheless, good examples of basic reinforcement schedules in the natural environment, especially that of humans, are difficult to cite.[23]

The clearest example of a basic schedule in the everyday human environment is the payoff for slot machines in gambling casinos. The reward (payoff) is delivered only after a varying number of responses (plays) is made. The

Photograph depicting gamblers in a casino playing the slot
machines. The payoff from slot machines is based on a
variable ratio schedule thus encouraging players to engage
in a high and steady rate of play.
UPI/Bettmann Newsphotos/Corbis

behavior of gamblers (their rate of playing) is therefore maintained at a relatively high and stable level, just as the lever pressing of a laboratory rat is
maintained at a high and stable rate by a VR schedule.

Examples of other basic schedules are less clear. A weekly or monthly paycheck is often cited as an example of an FI schedule, because reward (the pay)
comes after a fixed interval of time. Similarly, payment by commission, called
"piecework," is often claimed to illustrate an FR reinforcement schedule,
because a person receives pay only after completing a fixed amount of labor.
Finally, fishing is cited as an example of a VI schedule. Here, the reward is
achieved after a certain period of time has elapsed, although the exact time
varies from one catch to the next.

Part of the reason it is difficult to identify unambiguous examples of basic reinforcement schedules in the real world is that we often cannot identify the relevant behavioral unit. Reinforcement may be contingent on a complex unit of actions consisting of many components rather than a single, easily identified action. Consider fishing. What behavior is being reinforced? Casting the line? (If so, the rewards might better be described as under the control of a VR schedule). Waiting patiently and watching for signs of a catch? (If so, our analysis breaks down because waiting is not the behavior that catches fish). Consider the example of a monthly paycheck. What precisely is being reinforced? It is not an individual unit of work because there is no contingent relationship between pay and work. Pay is given at the end of the month, regardless of how many units of work the person completed.[24]

In conclusion, the study of reinforcement schedules continues to be an important focus in learning research, but we must be cautious in applying our knowledge to the real world, especially the everyday human environment, because it is often difficult to identify the behavior that is reinforced and thus the schedule that is in effect. The caution expressed here only applies to identifying *unambiguous* examples of *basic* schedules in the natural environment. It is much more likely that complex schedules do occur routinely in nature, although they may be hard to identify precisely because they are complex.

Comparison of Human and Animal Schedule Performance

Many learning psychologists believe that behavior is powerfully affected by schedules of reinforcement, and, furthermore, that the effects of a schedule on behavior are the same for both humans and other animal species. In other words, one may generalize the effects of reinforcement schedules on animals to humans.

The findings on this issue are complicated. They do not permit any simple conclusions about the similarities in performance between humans and other species. Humans often do not show the same behavioral patterns under schedule control as other animals.[25] For example, when responding on FI schedules, animals show the characteristic response pattern—namely, a pause after reward and then a gradually accelerating response rate until the next reward is delivered. Humans rarely show this acceleration behavior, and, furthermore, the rate of responding is often not affected by the length of the FI interval.[26] Instead, humans either have a high and steady rate throughout the FI interval, or they give only one or two responses toward the end of the interval. Similar discrepancies are found for responding on an FR schedule. For example, humans do not show the pause-and-run behavior that is typical of rats, nor is their rate of responding affected by the size of the FR requirement.[27]

It is not clear why these differences exist, given that the testing situations are comparable. Catania (1981) suggested that the instructions provided by the experimenter exert a powerful influence on human performance.[28] Instructions are necessary because humans are under a different motivational state than rats. Whereas animals are hungry and thus eager to respond to earn food, humans must be encouraged to perform for unessential rewards such as praise or small amounts of money. As a result, human behavior is guided by *both* factors—namely, the reinforcement contingency (the demands of the schedule itself) and the instructions (which invariably suggest to the subject a strategy for achieving reward).

A second and related theory was expressed by Lowe (1979). According to this position, humans invariably formulate their own rules and descriptions of the reinforcement contingencies. In a sense, humans talk to themselves, generating their own understanding of what produces reinforcement. Presumably, rats and pigeons do not engage in this kind of self-instructional process. For them, the reinforcement schedule is the single and most powerful factor.

INTERIM SUMMARY:

In the natural environment, reward is almost always delivered according to schedules of intermittent reinforcement. There are four basic reinforcement schedules. Under an FR schedule, reward is given after a fixed number of responses is made. Often, the subjects pause after a reinforcer before resuming their responding. On a VR schedule, reward is delivered following a series of responses, but the exact number varies from one reinforcer to the next. Reward on an FI schedule occurs for responding after a fixed period of time has elapsed. Typically, subjects pause following reward and then begin to respond at an accelerating pace. VI schedules are similar, except that the time period varies from one reward to the next. Ratio schedules sustain a much higher level of responding than do interval schedules because short interresponse times are differentially reinforced on ratio schedules, whereas long interresponse times are selectively reinforced on interval schedules. More complex reinforcement schedules are also possible. DRL schedules reward animals for withholding their responses until a certain time period has elapsed. Often, animals perform collateral behaviors, which help them time this interval. Compound schedules reflect two basic schedules operating jointly. Tandem schedules provide reward after two basic schedules, presented sequentially, are satisfied (if each component schedule is signaled by an S_d, then it is called a "chain schedule"). Mixed schedules present two or more basic schedules in random order (if each component schedule is signaled by an S_d, then it is called a "multiple schedule"). Unambiguous examples of basic schedules in the human environment are not easily cited, partly because the actions that earns the rewards are not obvious. Although humans are affected by schedules of reinforcement, their behavior patterns differ from those shown by nonhuman animals in laboratory experiments, because unlike rats, humans develop response strategies based on the instructions provided by the experimenter.

REINFORCER CHARACTERISTICS

A second major factor in instrumental conditioning deals with the character-istics of the reinforcer. The following sections discuss several of the more important dimensions of reward, such as reinforcer magnitude, immediacy, and quality.

Reinforcer Magnitude

The magnitude of the reinforcer is an important factor in instrumental learn-ing. The larger the reward, the better the learning. This notion is consistent with an evolutionary perspective. Animals invest time and energy to gain food. Any strategy that maximizes food intake, relative to the time and energy invested, should, therefore, be advantageous. In fact, the more food the ani-mal receives, the healthier it is, relative to its competitors, and thus the more adaptive its food-gathering strategy.[29] The relationship between instrumental learning and US magnitude, however, is complex. Although it has been shown to influence behavior, there are many inconsistencies.[30]

One problem in understanding how reinforcement magnitude affects learning is in defining reinforcer magnitude. Most researchers define it in terms of the amount or quantity of food or the intensity of shock, but some define magnitude in terms of the concentration of the reinforcer. Maze per-formance, for example, is affected by the sweetness of the sucrose reward.[31] Concentration and magnitude often affect behavior in quite different ways, however, adding to the uncertainty about the effects of reinforcer magnitude on learning.[32]

Another problem in assessing the effects of reward magnitude on behav-ior involve the measurement of learning. The conventional approach assesses learning in terms of response rate (say, number of lever presses per minute) or increases in response speed. These performance measures, however, are not always consistent with each other, suggesting that each measures a different underlying processes.[33] For instance, the speed of running down an alleyway may be affected by motivational factors (such as the degree of hunger) more than rate of lever pressing. On the other hand, the response rate in a lever box may reflect the strength of the strength of the response—outcome association more than does speed.[34]

Reward Training.

Nowhere is the complexity and uncertainty of the effects of reinforcer magnitude on learning more evident than in the area of reward training. Many studies suggest that learning is positively related to the size of the reinforcer, but this is true for speed of running in an alleyway more than for rate of responding in a lever box.[35] Consider alleyway performance. Both rate of improvement and terminal performance levels are positively related to reward magnitude, as shown in a study by Roberts (1969). Five groups of rats were trained to run down a straight alleyway for food. Subjects received 1, 2, 5, 10, or 25 reward pellets in the goal box. Figure 9-4 shows that speed during the final 10 acquisition trials was positively related to the number of reward pellets in the goal box.

A similar finding was obtained by Ratliff and Ratliff (1971). Here, rats were rewarded with 2, 4, 8, or 16 reward pellets for running down an alleyway to a goal box. Both running speed and, more important, rate of improvement over training were positively related to reward magnitude. As shown in Figure 9-5, the learning rate (a specialized mathematical measure, which reflects the trial-by-trial improvement in running speed and hence the rate of learning) increased with reward size.

The picture is less clear when it comes to rate of lever pressing. The relationship between reward magnitude and the rate of responding may be positive, negative, both, or neither.[36] Skjoldager, Pierre, and Mittleman (1993), for example, tested rats in a lever box, using a progressive FR schedule of reinforcement. Under this schedule, subjects first receive reward according to, say, an FR-5 schedule, but then the requirement is increased to FR-10 following reward; once another reward has been earned, the ratio is again increased. When the FR requirement gets to be too large, subjects cease responding altogether (this is called their "break point"). Groups differed in terms of the magnitude of reward, receiving either one or three pellets of food. Reinforcer magnitude did not affect the rate of response, latency to initiate a lever press, or

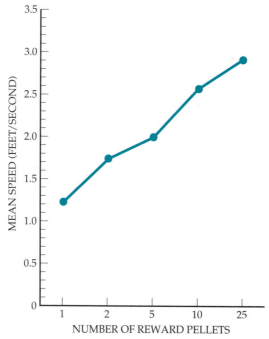

FIGURE 9-4. Mean speed (feet per second) during the final 10 trials, as a function of the reward magnitude (after Roberts, 1969).

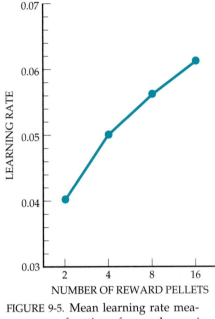

FIGURE 9-5. Mean learning rate measures, as a function of reward magnitude (after Ratliff & Ratliff, 1971).

time taken to retrieve the food from the food cup. The break point, however, was affected by reinforcement magnitude. The persistence or effort of responding in the face of an increasing FR requirement increased with larger rewards. In other words, reward magnitude in a lever box may not affect some measures of learning, but it does affect the animal's persistence. Animals persist longer for a large incentive (a motivational effect of reward), but they do not learn the task any better.[37]

One reason why reinforcer magnitude has such varied effects on rate of performance in a lever box is that magnitude interacts with the kind of schedule employed. For example, Reed (1991) studied rats using a multiple VR–VI schedule.[38] A multiple schedule contains two separate schedule components, each signaled by a different S_d. Increases in reinforcer magnitude, from one to four pellets, caused an increase in rate when the subjects were responding on the VR component. In contrast, increases in magnitude caused a decline in response rate when the subjects responded on the VI portion of the schedule. Reed hypothesized that the reinforcer selectively enhanced short IRT values typical of VR schedules, thus causing an increase in rate. On the other hand, larger reward magnitudes enhanced long IRT values commonly found on VI schedules, thus causing response rate on those schedules to decline. Thus, the change in the rate of behavior as a function of reward magnitude may simply be a by-product of the change in the distribution of IRT values.

Another factor that influences how reinforcer magnitude affects response rate is whether the subjects are required to earn all of their daily food in the experimental chamber (this is a **closed-economy experiment**) or are returned to their home cage after the test session and given supplementary food. Collier, Johnson, Hill, and Kaufman (1986) studied this issue. Their rats earned their entire daily food ration by pressing a lever on a ratio schedule of reinforcement. Reward magnitude was defined in terms of the length of time subjects were given access to the feeder. Rats maintained a constant level of consumption, regardless of their duration of access to food. When access was short, subjects compensated by responding faster and thus earning a meal more often. In other words, response rate was *inversely* related to reward size. This finding contradicts the conventional notion that the larger the reinforcer, the stronger the response.

Punishment.

Because punishers typically suppress behavior, response rate should be an inverse function of US intensity. The greater the punisher intensity, the more the response is suppressed. This appears to be the case.[39] In many experiments, a graded relationship between response suppression and shock intensity has been found, even for avoidance reactions.[40] Moreover, punishers other than shock (for example, loud noises or temperature changes), show the same relationship between responding and intensity.[41]

The effect of punishment on rate of responding may be quite specific. In a study by Sizemore and Maxwell (1985), rats pressed a lever to get food on a VI-40-second schedule. They also received a shock if the interval between responses (the IRT) was longer than 8 seconds.[42] Shock punishment selectively suppressed the long IRT values (over 8 seconds) and thus, at the low-intensity shock level at least, produced an increase in the response rate. Such an increase in the response rate as a result of receiving punishment confirms that shock selectively suppressed responses involving long IRTs.

Escape and Avoidance.

The US intensity has also been studied in connection with escape/avoidance learning. For escape conditioning, studies show that the stronger the US, the greater the improvement in escape performance. Most of these studies used shock USs, but the relationship between US intensity and performance has also been observed using escape from cold water, loud noise, and intense light.[43]

Figure 9-6 illustrates the results of a study by Franchina (1969). Rats were placed in a white start box and given shock that they could terminate by jumping into an adjoining safe compartment painted black. Shock intensity was 20, 50, or 80 volts. Speed of responding was directly related to intensity: the higher the shock, the faster the escape response.[44]

The effect of US intensity on escape behavior, however, is not really analogous to the effect found in reward or punishment training because the tasks differ significantly. For escape learning, both the outcome of the response *and* the initial motivational level of the subject are affected by US intensity. The

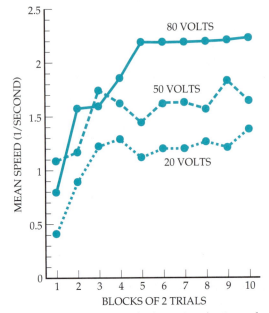

FIGURE 9-6. Mean speed of running (reciprocal latency), as a function of blocks of two escape-training trials for groups receiving 20-, 50-, and 80-volt shocks (after Franchina, 1969).

stronger the shock, the more motivated the animal is, and the faster the subject performs. This is not the case for reward and punishment.[45] Faster performance on escape trials may therefore have less to do with better learning than with stronger motivation.

Like escape responding, avoidance training is also influenced by US intensity, but the effects are more complicated. Several studies have shown that lever-pressing avoidance behavior is positively related to shock intensity.[46] For example, Riess and Farrar (1972) trained rats to postpone a 0.15-second shock for 20 seconds by pressing a lever. Failure to press the lever resulted in shock being delivered every 3 seconds. Different groups of subjects received shock intensities of 0.25, 0.5, 1.0, 2.0, or 4.0 milliamps. The rate of lever pressing increased as a function of shock intensity. Although few lever presses occurred at the lower intensities, performance increased with higher shocks.[47]

Shock intensity also affects passive avoidance learning. Pearce (1978) showed that intensity and performance are positively related, but only when naturalistic reactions of the animal are involved. Rats were shocked when they stepped off a safe platform onto the grid floor. Later, they were tested to see whether they would passively avoid shock by remaining on the platform. When the safe platform was located at the center of the apparatus, the rats jumped off the platform quickly, showing little passive avoidance. The reason was that the rat's natural inclination to jump off and run toward the wall of the box interfered with its avoidance learning. When the safe platform was located near the periphery of the apparatus, however, the conflict between passively staying on the platform and jumping off was not present. Here, passive avoidance learning increased as a function of shock intensity.

Finally, the relationship between US intensity and avoidance learning has been studied using a more conventional apparatus—namely, the shuttle box. Shuttle-box avoidance learning occurs when an animal runs from one side of the box to the other to avoid shock, and then, on the next trial, runs back to the original side to avoid shock once again. Several investigators found that shuttle-box avoidance is inversely related to shock intensity. The higher the US intensity, the worse the avoidance performance.[48]

Such a finding is, on the surface, paradoxical because higher shock levels should increase the animal's motivation for avoidance and thus increase avoidance performance, just as it does in the other avoidance settings discussed previously. The inverse relationship actually occurs because, as Theios, Lynch, and Lowe (1966) argue, shuttle-box avoidance conditioning involves two conflicting tendencies. The first is the avoidance reaction itself—namely, moving away from the place where shock is presented. The second is the passive-avoidance tendency—that is, refraining from returning to where shock had occurred on the previous trial. According to these authors, the subject is in a state of conflict. It has an inclination to flee from its present location, but, at the same time, a tendency to be wary of the other side of the box. After all, shock was presented there on the previous trial. Responding is therefore slower with increasing shock intensity because the higher the shock intensity, the greater the passive avoidance for the previous shock side. In support, one-way avoidance learning is positively related to shock intensity. In one-way learning, subjects always begin in the same start box and run to a discriminably different goal box. The animals are then re-placed in the starting area for the next trial. Such a procedure, like shuttle-box avoidance, involves running away from shock, but it does not involve the conflicting passive-avoidance tendency.[49]

Other theories for the inverse relationship between shock intensity and shuttle-box avoidance have been offered. One contends that the chamber to which the animal must return elicits freezing, which competes with the active-avoidance learning.[50] Another claims that shuttle-box avoidance learning involves a lower overall magnitude of reinforcement than other forms of avoidance conditioning.[51] More specifically, reinforcement occurs when the animals run from the fear cues they are experiencing at the moment to a safe place (the more safety cues obtained, the greater the reinforcement). Because the side to which the animal runs in a shuttle box is also fear-provoking, the overall reward level is low.[52]

Immediacy of Reward

Contiguity between the CS and the US is necessary for a Pavlovian association to develop. The same claim is true in instrumental conditioning. For a response–outcome association to form, the response and the reward must occur close together in time. If an appreciable delay of reward occurs, then performance declines markedly.[53] Delay interferes with learning new behaviors, as well as with the performance of well-established reactions.[54]

Reward Training.

The debilitating effect of reward delay is one of the most reliable findings in modern learning research. For example, Dickinson, Watt, and Griffiths (1992) trained rats to press a lever on a continuous-reinforcement schedule.[55] Different groups were given reinforcement delays of 0, 2, 4, 16, 32, or 64 seconds.[56] Figure 9-7 shows the relationship between lever pressing and the experienced delay (that is, the time between the last response and the reward delivery). The figure depicts the so-called delay-of-reward gradient. Performance declines with increasing delay, in a graded fashion.

Delay of reinforcement may selectively change the nature of the response unit being performed. This was shown by Arbuckle and Lattal (1988). They trained pigeons to peck a key for food on a VI-60-second schedule; the delay of reward in one part of the study was 0.5 seconds. Such a short delay had no effect on the overall rate of responding, but it did affect the distribution of IRTs. Long IRT values, which are characteristic of interval schedules, were selectively suppressed. When the delay value was increased to 5 seconds, the reverse occurred. These longer delays caused an *increase* in the frequency of long IRT values.[57]

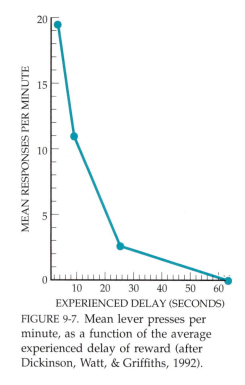

FIGURE 9-7. Mean lever presses per minute, as a function of the average experienced delay of reward (after Dickinson, Watt, & Griffiths, 1992).

Studies show that learning is possible with short delays, but not with longer delays. Is there a limit to which a reward may be delayed and still allow for learning to take place? Little agreement as to an answer has been reached. Studies by Lett and others show that rats are able to learn the correct turn in a T-maze even when the food reward is delayed for 1 minute.[58] Other experiments suggest that the maximum permissible delay is merely 5 seconds.[59] The fact that little agreement has been reached on this matter implies that factors other than the delay itself are also important.

One such factor is the extent to which external cues occur during the delay interval. Not only do external delay-related stimuli facilitate performance, but they also virtually eliminate the deficit caused by the delay. Consider an experiment by Schaal and Branch (1990).[60] Pigeons pecked a green key for food on a VI-60-second schedule. Reward was delayed for 27 seconds following the operative key peck. During this delay period, the color of the response key changed from green to red. The duration of the red light varied systematically, between 0.5 and 27 seconds (the signal, therefore, occupied from about 2% to 100% of the delay interval).

The results for one of the pigeons are shown in Figure 9-8. Performance was exceedingly low when no delay signal was provided. As signal duration increased, relative to the delay interval, however, performance improved dramatically. Thus, although delay of reinforcement profoundly retards learning, receiving an external cue during the delay period virtually abolishes that

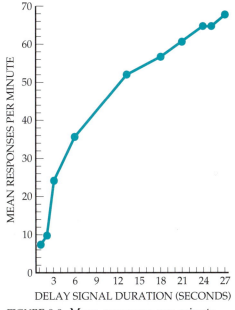

FIGURE 9-8. Mean responses per minute during the last five sessions of training, as a function of the signal duration (after Schaal & Branch, 1990).

deficit. Moreover, cues that occupy a greater percentage of the delay interval facilitate performance more than cues that occur only briefly at the beginning of the interval.

Why does an external cue improve performance in this situation? This is not an easy question to answer, but various suggestions have been made.[61] One hypothesis is that the external cue itself functions as a reinforcer (see Chapter 10). That is, the cue itself takes on reinforcing properties because it is followed by, and thus associated with, reinforcement.[62] When the cue is given immediately following the response, the subject is receiving two rewards. One reward is the food; the other is the cue, the power of which is derived from the fact that it is paired with food reward. In short, an external cue that occurs during the delay interval functions as a reward because of its association with food and thus augments the overall reward level that the subject experiences.[63]

An alternative theory about how an external cue facilitates delayed-reward learning is the **marking hypothesis.** The initial purpose of the experiments by Lieberman, McIntosh, and Thomas (1979) was to examine the claim that subjects learn the correct turn in a T-maze, despite having an extended delay of reward.[64] The apparatus used to study marking, shown in Figure 9-9, consisted of a start box and a choice box (both painted gray). At the far end of the choice box were two doors, one leading to a black alleyway and the other to a white alleyway. At the end of each of the alleyways was a door leading to a gray-painted delay box. Finally, the delay box had a door leading to the goal box.

At the start of a trial, a subject was placed in the start box and was allowed to choose one of the two alleyways. The white alley was define as being correct for all subjects. Three groups were designated.[65] Immediately after the subjects in the light group made their choice (regardless of whether they chose the correct alley), they received a 2-second light and then were allowed to proceed into the delay box. Subjects in the noise group were treated in the same fashion, except that they received a 2-second noise rather than a light. Animals in the control group were not given any stimulus. They went directly into the delay box following their choice. Once in the delay box, all animals were confined for 2 minutes, after which the door to the goal box opened and the subjects were allowed to enter. Food reward was given, but only if the subject had previously chosen the white side. In short, all subjects were sub-

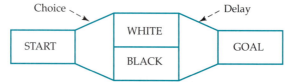

FIGURE 9-9. Schematic view of the discrimination apparatus used by Lieberman, McIntosh, & Thomas (1979).

jected to a 2-minute delay of reward following a correct response. Groups differed in terms of what happened immediately after choosing. Some animals received a tone or light; control subjects received no cue at all.

The results are shown in Figure 9-10. All subjects started out performing at about the 50% point (they were as likely to choose the black side as the white side early in training). However, the light and noise groups learned the discrimination by the end of training. Performance in those groups was over 90% correct on the last block of training trials. In contrast, performance in the control group remained at the chance level; they failed to learn to choose the correct side.

Why did the light and tone improve discrimination learning? According to the authors, the cues helped to mark the choice response in memory. That is, after making a choice and receiving a tone or light, the subjects more effectively rehearsed, and thus remembered, the choice they had just made. When reward was given later on, their memory for their previous choice was stronger. In the words of the authors, "The most plausible explanation for this effect [the facilitation of learning as a result of having received the light or noise following the choice response] seemed to be that [the cue] was marking the preceding choice response in the rats' memory so that they were more likely to recall this response when they were later rewarded."[66] In other words, an unexpected and salient event (the light or the noise) immediately

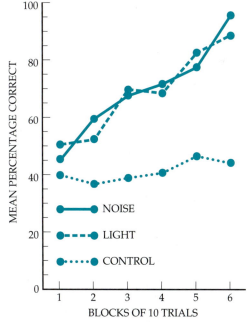

FIGURE 9-10. Mean percentage of correct responding, as a function of blocks of 10 trials for the light, noise, and control subjects (after Lieberman, McIntosh, & Thomas, 1979).

after a choice response, causes better rehearsal, and hence memory, of the choice response. When later reinforced, subjects are better able to associate their previous correct choice with food reward.

Aversive Conditioning.

Not surprisingly, delay of reward affects instrumental aversive conditioning in the same way as it affects reward learning. For instance, Fowler and Trapold (1962) trained rats to terminate shock by running down an alleyway. Once in the goal box, the offset of the shock was delayed for various amounts of time. Learning was inversely related to delay. Immediate offset led to the best acquisition scores; delays of 8 or 16 seconds retarded escape learning.

Cues that intervene between the response and the reward facilitate aversive conditioning just as they do reward conditioning. Tarpy and Koster (1970) showed that even a 3-second delay of shock offset precluded learning of a lever-press escape response. If, however, a light was given during the delay interval, learning was not affected; subjects performed at the same level of proficiency as a no-delay group.

Finally, the effect of a delay in the delivery of a punisher is a reduction in the degree of response suppression. That is, punishment is less effective when delayed.[67] A reduction in the suppressive effects of punishment is precisely the result one would expect to see if the punisher is delayed.

Does Reinforcement Affect Learning or Performance?

Research on reinforcer magnitude and immediacy suggests that the predominant effect of a reward may be on performance rather than on learning.[68] Reward causes performance to be more energized, but it does not change the degree to which the animal learns about the response–outcome relationship. Stated differently, instrumental reward does not affect what an animal learns but rather changes its motivation to perform. High-reward subjects, according to this view, are more eager to receive the reinforcer than are low-reward subjects.

One phenomenon that supports this point of view is **incentive contrast.**[69] Consider the classic experiment on this topic by Crespi (1942). Three groups of rats were given 20 training trials on which they could run down an alleyway for food. One group was given a large reward in the goal box (64 pellets), the second was given a medium-sized reward (16 pellets), and the third group received a small reward (4 pellets). In Phase 2, the reward level was switched for two groups. Specifically, subjects in the large (64 pellets) reward group were shifted to the 16-pellets condition, and subjects in the 4-pellets condition also received 16 pellets. The design therefore compares the performance of subjects who were switched to 16 pellets (from a larger and a smaller amount) to those who received 16 pellets throughout training. If current reward magnitude alone affects behavior, then the three groups should perform at about the same rate during Phase 2 because all were receiving the same magnitude of reward. If, however, some other factor affects behavior during Phase 2, such as memory for the previous reward level, then behavior should differ between groups.

Behavior differed. As shown in Figure 9-11, the group that was shifted to a smaller reward magnitude (the 64–16 subjects) actually ran much more slowly in Phase 2 than did the group that had been given the 16 pellets throughout. Conversely, the group that was shifted from low to medium reward (the 4–16 animals) ran even faster than did the 16–16 group. The former phenomenon is **negative contrast** because the behavior is deflated below the level shown by the unshifted group. The second result is **positive contrast,** because when the reward conditions suddenly get much better, animals overshoot and perform at an even higher level than subjects who have had that reward size from the start of training.[70] Positive and negative contrast indicate that behavior is not controlled simply by the conditions that exist currently. Performance is also influenced by previous reward conditions.[71]

How does Crespi's experiment confirm that reward magnitude affects performance by changing the animal's motivation to perform rather than its learning? Two aspects of the data are important in this regard. First, the changes in performance following the shift in reward magnitude were so sudden that it is unlikely that the animals' learning was being affected. If a higher level of

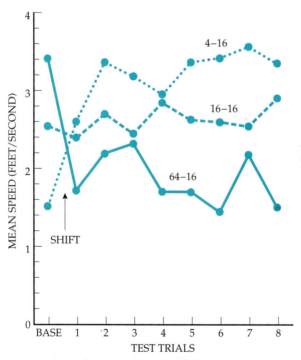

FIGURE 9-11. Mean running speed (feet per second) during the final preshift trial (base) and the eight postshift test trials for subjects for which the number of reward pellets was shifted from 64 to 16 or 4 to 16. Subjects in the 16–16 group received the same number of reward pellets in both phases of the study (after Crespi, 1942).

reward was causing the subjects to learn more, then logic suggests that they would have shown a gradual improvement in performance (similar to the improvement shown in Phase 1). Instead, the change in performance in the 4–16 group was almost instantaneous, suggesting that the larger reward was a more valued incentive, so the animals were more eager to reach the goal box.

The second aspect of Crespi's data that supports this argument was the decline in performance in the 64–16 group. Those animals could not have suddenly unlearned their response; their knowledge about the response and its relationship to reward was not weaker following the shift in magnitude. The more plausible explanation is that those animals were less eager to receive a smaller reward after having been accustomed to receiving the large reward in Phase 1.

Reinforcer Quality

Many kinds of reinforcers support instrumental conditioning. This fact is easily forgotten because so many studies in animal learning use food, water, and electric shock. A reinforcer, however, is *any* event that increases the probability of a contingent response (see Chapter 8). Three unusual types of reinforcer are discussed in this section: sensory reinforcement, odors, and social reinforcements.

Sensory Reinforcement.

Sensory reinforcement is a change in sensory input, in which the presentation of a light or a noise is contingent on a behavior, such as lever pressing.[72] The sensory change serves as an effective reinforcer. In a study by Glow and Winefield (1978), for example, rats received a 3-second response-contingent light following a lever press. During the light, an additional response caused an ongoing noise to be turned off for 3 seconds. Animals that could turn the light on responded at a higher level than control subjects that could not. Subjects that could turn the light on *and* turn the noise off responded at an even higher level.

Sensory reinforcement occurs primarily when animals have not recently experienced changes in the light or noise patterns, that is, when the animals have undergone a period of sensory deprivation.[73] If they are exposed to such changes, then the sensory reinforcement effect is diminished markedly.[74]

Odors.

Many studies focus on the naturalistic learning patterns of animals (see Chapter 12). Most indicate that animals are extraordinarily sensitive to naturalistic stimuli, odors being among the most salient for rodents. Furthermore, they indicate that these powerful odors may serve as punishers or reinforcers in conventional instrumental-learning tasks. For example, the odor emanating from the urine of dominant mice is aversive to other mice and may serve as a punisher for an instrumental response.[75] Similarly, naïve rats approach a so-

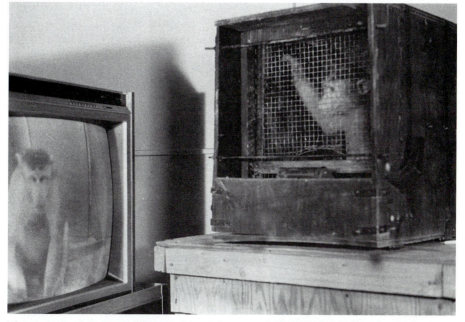

Photograph of the apparatus used by Schwartz and Rosenblum (1980) in which bonnet monkeys were reinforced for pressing a lever in order to view various images on the TV monitor. The most powerful visual reinforcer was a film of a moving conspecific bonnet monkey.
Courtesy of Professor Karyl Swartz, Lehman College, NY

called reward odor left by animals that are given food reward, and they avoid frustration odors left by animals that experience nonreward.[76] These findings are not surprising, given that rats have such a highly developed sense of smell, which they use in procuring food and avoiding predators.

Social Reinforcement.

Finally, social stimuli may serve as reinforcers in instrumental learning. A study by Swartz and Rosenblum (1980) provides a good illustration. Bonnet macaques (monkeys belonging to the genus *Macaca*) were given access to a lever that turned on a color television (the television display was presented for the duration of the lever press). Four 15-minute videotapes were given during a testing session in a counterbalanced order, and the number of seconds that the subjects viewed each tape was recorded. One of the videotapes showed another bonnet (conspecific—same species) macaque in motion, the second showed a moving nonconspecific monkey (a female pigtail monkey), the third film was taken of a still photo of bonnet monkey, and the fourth videotape was of the empty chamber that housed the monkeys.

The scores are shown in Figure 9-12. The subjects responded to all of the videotapes, but the moving conspecific female elicited the strongest reaction. Subjects were less interested in viewing a nonconspecific monkey, a film of a

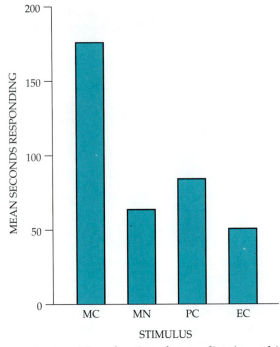

FIGURE 9-12. Mean duration of responding (seconds) for each stimulus: MC = moving conspecific (bonnet) female; MN = moving nonconspecific (pigtail) female; PC = still picture of conspecific (bonnet) monkey; EC = empty chamber (after Swartz & Rosenbaum, 1980).

still photo of a conspecific monkey, or the empty chamber. The fact that each stimulus reinforced lever pressing is consistent with the sensory reinforcement phenomenon described previously. The fact that the most powerful reinforcer was the film of the moving conspecific monkey, however, indicates that social reinforcers do not affect behavior merely by elevating the overall level of sensory stimulation. They are reinforcing in their own right.

Primates find videotapes of their own species more interesting then neutral pictures. Many animals find social interaction with other species reinforcing as well. In one interesting study by Davis and Perusse (1988a), two groups of rats were taught to press a lever. Each time contact with the lever was made, the experimenter reinforced the animal by reaching into the cage and physically petting it for about 5 seconds. The experimenter also gave verbal praise, such as "good rat," or "way to go."

Subjects were separated into two groups. One was given 25 half-hour preexposure sessions during which the rats interacted freely with the experimenter. The control animals spent an equivalent amount of time in their home cage and thus lacked prior contact with human beings. None of the control subjects acquired the lever response, but 4 of the 8 preexposed (experimental) rats did. Not only did these animals show appreciable contact with the lever during the training session, but they also showed significant extinction when the social reinforcer was withdrawn.[77]

Pattern of Reward Magnitude

The pattern of reward magnitude strongly affects instrumental learning. Consider an experiment by Hulse and Dorsky (1977), who trained rats to run down a straight alleyway to get food. For the experimental animals, the reward magnitude in the goal box systematically decreased over a series of trials, from 14 pellets to 0 pellets (the specific magnitudes were 14, 7, 3, 1, and 0 pellets on successive runs). Control animals were given the same reward magnitudes but in a random order across trials. The experimental subjects ran more slowly as they got closer to the end of the series—that is, on the last two trials on the 14–7–3–1–0 sequence.

This finding is shown in Figure 9-13. The subjects were therefore anticipating reward magnitude. Additional subjects, for which the pattern of diminishing reward magnitude was not as consistent as for the experimental rats (their series involved declining magnitudes 14–1–3–7–0), showed a similar anticipation of the last 0-pellet trial, but the effect was much smaller. Thus, the more prominent the pattern, the better the animals anticipated the magnitude on the next trial and responded accordingly.[78]

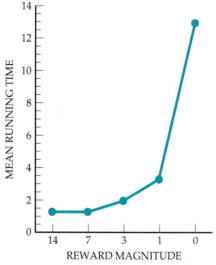

FIGURE 9-13. Mean running time (seconds), as a function of the reward magnitude. Note that the values on the X axis represent a series of decreasing reward magnitudes (after Hulse & Dorsky, 1977).

These results were expanded in an interesting study by Fountain and Hulse (1981). Training was essentially the same as that just described, except that subjects received only a four-run sequence (14–7–3–1 pellets on successive trials). After 13 days of training, the rats were given a test. Here, they received the same pattern, but it was modified to include five, rather than four, runs. On the fifth run, subjects were given no food in the goal box. Control groups received a weakly declining series of magnitudes—either 14–5–5–1, or 14–3–7–1. During the training phase, subjects in the experimental group ran much more slowly on the 1-pellet trial, indicating the same kind of anticipation as described previously. On the test, however, these animals anticipated the 0-pellet quantity (although they had never experienced this no-food condition previously) and ran even slower. Their mean running time on this test dropped from about 3.0 to 8.5 seconds. Such anticipation was not found in the other two groups.

Thus, animals trained with a strongly declining pattern of reward magnitudes showed more anticipation on a fifth trial involving 0 pellets than did the subjects for which the reward patterns were not as clearly declining. The result suggests that the rats learned a rule—namely, that each successive trial involves fewer reward pellets than the previous trial. Using such a rule, the animals then extrapolated to the fifth trial, thus anticipating 0 pellets. The fact that they ran unusually slowly on the fifth trial supports the notion of a response rule. If subjects were responding from memory rather than by applying this response rule, then they would not have performed in that fashion, because they never experienced 0 pellets following the 1-pellet trial and thus could not have a memory of it.[79]

INTERIM SUMMARY

Reinforcer magnitude is an important factor in instrumental conditioning, although the effects are complicated. Speed of running in an alleyway is positively related to reinforcer size; rate of lever pressing does not necessarily change with reward magnitude, but persistence may be affected. One reason is that rate is strongly affected by reward schedules. If subjects earn all of their daily rations in the test environment (called a "closed economy"), then response rate is inversely related to reward size. The more intense the punisher, the more the response is suppressed. Escape learning, passive avoidance, and one-way avoidance are positively related to US intensity. For shuttle-box avoidance, however, learning is inversely related to shock intensity. The reason is that subjects develop two tendencies. One is to flee from the present location because of impending shock, and the other is passively to avoid the goal area because it is associated with previous shocks. Under these conditions, increasing shock intensity causes a deterioration in performance. Reward immediacy is an important characteristic of reward. Even short delays preclude learning, although external cues that occur during the delay interval virtually eliminate the deficits caused by delay. These cues may function as rewards, or they may mark the behavior in memory. Both reward magnitude and immediacy affect performance, rather than learning. Studies on incentive contrast, for example, show that current behavior is affected by current reward levels, as well as by previous reward conditions. Receiving a lower level of reward causes negative contrast; being given a higher level of reward causes positive contrast. Many kinds of reinforcers are used in instrumental conditioning, including sensory reinforcement, positive and negative odors, and social reinforcement (for instance, observing videotape pictures of other animals or having direct contact with human experimenters). Finally, the pattern of reward is important, in that subjects anticipate reward levels based on the pattern of reward experienced over a series of trials.

RESPONSE CHARACTERISTICS: ECOLOGICAL RELEVANCE

Recall that the form of a Pavlovian CR is usually determined by the US. This is not the case in instrumental learning, however, where the target response is defined by the experimenter. Indeed, the response could be a food-related reaction, such as inspecting a food cup; a motor response, such as lever pressing or running down an alleyway; a physiological reaction; or even a vocalization. In short, many kinds of reactions may be designated as correct in an instrumental-conditioning study. Are the response characteristics important, however? Are some responses more easily associated with reinforcers than others?

Research suggests that the answer is yes. Not all responses are conditionable to the same degree, even though an appropriate reinforcer is used.[80] This section reviews some of this work, as well as the theory about instrumental learning from an ecological perspective (see Chapters 11 and 12 for additional discussion).

A noted experiment on this topic was done by Breland and Breland (1961).[81] In one part of their study, the authors tried to teach a pig to pick up large wooden "coins" and to deposit them into a piggy bank. Normally, pigs condition quite easily, but Breland and Breland developed problems getting the animals to do this particular task.

In their own words, "At first, the pig would eagerly pick up one dollar, carry it to the bank, run back, get another, carry it rapidly and neatly, and so on, until the ratio [schedule] was complete. Thereafter, over a period of weeks, the behavior would become slower and slower. [The pig] might run over eagerly for each dollar, but on the way back, instead of carrying the dollar and depositing it simply and cleanly, [the pig] would repeatedly drop it, root it, drop it again, root it along the way, pick it up, toss it up in the air, drop it, root it some more, and so on."[82] There was no indication that the reinforcement was inappropriate, or that the animals were incapable of making the response, yet the animals resorted to their instinctual food-oriented behavior patterns. That is, the pigs tossed and rooted the tokens as if the tokens themselves were food. This unwanted behavior was termed a **misbehavior.**[83]

Reward Training

The inability of certain responses to be learned effectively has been studied extensively since the work by Breland and Breland. Much of our knowledge stems from the work of Shettleworth, who studied a number of naturalistic behaviors in the golden hamster. The behaviors investigated were walking, sniffing various objects, rearing on the hind legs in the open area of the cage, rearing on the hind legs while touching the wall of the cage, scrabbling (scraping the forepaws against the wall while standing erect, sometimes hopping up and down), digging in the sawdust, pushing sawdust backward with the hind feet, gnawing, standing motionless, marking with their scent glands, face washing, grooming the fur, and stretching. This is not an exhaustive list, but it provides a good account of some of the many simple action patterns performed by these animals. These behaviors are neither fixed reflexes nor are they entirely arbitrary. Rather, they are naturalistic action patterns that occur in the animal's own environment but also are subject to change, depending on the experience of the animal.

One of Shettleworth's (1975) main tasks was to investigate whether these action patterns are affected to the same degree by food reward. The specific behaviors that were reinforced included scrabbling, digging, rearing in the open, marking, washing, and scratching. As shown in Figure 9-14, the first three behaviors showed large and immediate increases in rate, as a function of a contingent food reinforcer. The latter three action patterns showed weak effects.

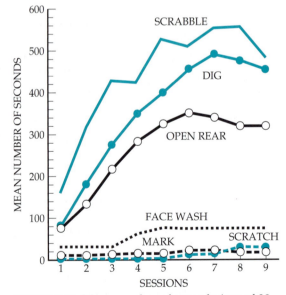

FIGURE 9-14. Mean number of seconds (out of 20 minutes), as a function of reinforcement sessions during which the food-reinforced actions patterns were performed (after Shettleworth, 1975).

The implication is that some responses (scrabbling, digging), but not others (scratching, face washing) are more relevant to, or influenced by, food reward. This finding is consistent with an evolutionary perspective. Specifically, it is adaptive for a hungry hamster to engage in behaviors such as scrabbling and digging because they increase the chance of coming into contact with food. Similarly, it makes sense from an ecological point of view that these same behaviors have an affinity for food reinforcement. In other words, response patterns that are relevant to, and performed in anticipation of, food are more susceptible to the effects of food reward than patterns that are not (see also Chapter 12).

Aversive Conditioning

Shettleworth (1978) also studied the effect of punishment on these action patterns. The general finding was that response-contingent shock suppressed scrabbling to a substantial degree; little recovery was observed once punishment ceased. Face washing was also suppressed, but not permanently so. Shock was least effective at suppressing rearing in the open part of the cage.[84] The pattern of suppression caused by shock was, therefore, different from the pattern of response increase caused by food. Punishment suppresses behavior, but the action patterns that are affected differ from those that are affected by food reward.

Theory of Effects of Rewards and Punishers

Shettleworth's work does not show whether the response–outcome association failed to develop for those reactions that were poorly learned, or whether some other factor had affected performance. Are subjects constrained in the kind of response–reward association they form, or are they simply unable to express these associations? Stated differently, do these failures illustrate a lack of learning, or just a lack of performance?

This issue is not easy to resolve, but both learning and performance factors may be involved (see Chapter 11 for a more complete discussion). Evidence for the performance-deficit hypothesis comes from a study by Charlton (1983), who investigated grooming in golden hamsters (a behavior that is known to be hard to condition). In one study, hamsters that were continuously reinforced with food for grooming showed a decline in the average duration of the behavior. The reinforcement schedule was then shifted to a fixed-interval schedule. Here, a reliable increase in the rate of grooming occurred, suggesting that the hard-to-condition response was not impervious to the effects of reward after all.

Why did the rate of grooming increase under an FI schedule but not with continuous reinforcement? According to Charlton, the most likely reason is that, when feeding, hamsters perform a series of individual behaviors. Grooming is one, and it invariably occurs early in the series, at a time when the animals are not directly engaged with the reward. With continuous reward, therefore, the hamsters generally were restricted to performing behaviors that occur near the time of reward, such as approaching, eating, and so forth. Under the FI schedule, however, behaviors that occur at a more temporally remote time, such as grooming, were more likely to be performed and thus were more likely to be influenced by the reinforcer.

The author concluded; "To be sure, differences between various responses do exist, as can be seen in the differences between open rearing and grooming obtained in [these] experiments. These differences in conditionability do not, however, represent species-specific or response-specific constraints that are beyond the level of a general process analysis. Instead, the existence of differential conditionability among various responses is more likely the result of unforeseen interactions between schedule contingencies and differing response topographies. It is the opinion of this author that these differences in conditionability represent only differences in degree, rather than qualitative differences among classes or types of behavior."[85] In other words, according to Charlton, the fact that behaviors, such as grooming, are hard to condition reflects a performance deficit, not an inability to learn.

The problem in conditioning a given behavior may also reflect an inability to associate the behavior with reward. Morgan and Nicholas (1979) supported this position by giving rats the opportunity to press a lever for food reward after face washing, rearing on their hind legs, or scratching. The reinforcer increased the rate of each of these behaviors, although scratching appeared to be much less susceptible to reward than was rearing or washing.

This experiment also had an additional feature, however. Not only were the subjects allowed to press a lever for food following one of these behaviors, but the behaviors themselves were also used as discriminative stimuli. That is, subjects had to choose between the right or the left lever, based on which behavior they had just performed. If, for example, scratching occurred, subjects had to press, say, the left lever to obtain food; pressing the right lever would not give a reward. If, however, they had just face washed, then subjects had to press the right lever for food; pressing the left lever gave nothing.

The results showed that scratching served as a poor discriminative stimulus. Subjects were not accurate in their choice of lever when scratching served as the S_d. In other words, although scratching was acquired as an instrumental response, it was much harder to condition than rearing and washing, *and* it was less effective as a discriminative stimulus. The experiment therefore shows not only retarded levels of instrumental conditioning (when using scratching as the response), but also that the behavior itself is not very salient. Thus, the deficit suggests a lack of associative learning.[86]

In conclusion, evidence indicates that the failure to condition a given response may be due to either performance factors or a failure in associative learning.[87] Whichever position eventually proves to be the more valuable, the ease of conditioning reflects the appropriateness of the behavior to the motivational state of the subject. This point was made clearly in the work by Shettleworth described earlier. The action patterns that were strongly affected by food reinforcement were those that were displayed by hungry animals near feeding time.[88] Similarly, behaviors displayed by hungry animals are more susceptible to the effects of food reward than are the behaviors that are unrelated to feeding activities.[89]

INTERIM SUMMARY

Not all responses are learned with equal facility during instrumental conditioning; some behaviors are learned with great difficulty. Response patterns that are relevant to, and performed in anticipation of food are more susceptible to the effects of food reward than patterns that are not. Similar results have been shown for aversive conditioning. Such variation in learning reflects performance deficits, as well as deficits in learning itself.

ENDNOTES

1. See Schoenfeld (1970) for a review of theories of schedules of reinforcement; see also Zeiler (1984) for a dissenting view on the importance of research on schedule control.
2. It is perhaps surprising that animals pause following reward on an FR schedule; after all, the postreinforcement pause merely delays the process of completing the next block of responses and thus delays receipt of the next reward.
3. See also Neuringer and Schneider (1968).
4. Crossman, Bonem, and Phelps (1987). Postreinforcement pauses, however, may also develop on a VR schedule if the VR requirement is exceedingly high; see Ferster and Skinner (1957).
5. Schneider (1969).
6. The acceleration in rate described in the text and shown in the figure is actually averaged over several sessions. An examination of this phenomenon on a response-by-response basis has confirmed that the acceleration in rate is, in fact, not at all gradual. Rather, early in the FI interval, subjects alternate between having short and long gaps between their responses (called "interresponse times," or "IRTs"); as the FI interval elapses, the short IRT values tend to predominate; see Gentry, Weiss, and Laties (1983) for a discussion.
7. See Hanson and Killeen (1981) for a theory.
8. Caplan, Karpicke, and Rilling (1973).
9. Auge (1977); Kendall (1972).
10. Kello (1972).
11. Singh and Wickens (1968).
12. Harzem, Lowe, and Priddle-Higson (1978); Leslie (1981).
13. However, the reinforcement rate declines if the subject delays its response after the interval has expired.
14. Galbicka and Platt (1986), however, also showed that the rate of response was controlled to a significant degree by the reinforcement rate, although such an effect was not found by Dawson and Dickinson (1990); see also Capehart, Eckerman, Guilkey, and Shull (1980).

15. See Shimp (1967). Schedules involving the deliberate reinforcement of short IRT values are called "differential reinforcement of high rates of response (DRH)" schedules.
16. See Kramer and Rilling (1970) for a review.
17. Gage, Evans, and Olton (1979).
18. Lejeune and Jasselette (1986).
19. Laties, Weiss, Clark, and Reynolds (1965).
20. Laties, Weiss, and Weiss (1969).
21. See Hemmes, Eckerman, and Rubinsky (1979); Schwartz and Williams (1971).
22. See Wanchisen, Tatham, and Mooney (1989); Williams (1979).
23. Most schedules in nature are complex schedules involving the interaction of many simpler schedules. Thus, the fact that unambiguous examples of a simple, basic schedules are difficult to cite does not mean that schedules do not operate in the natural environment.
24. There are situations where this probably would not be the case, for example, where a person must keep up with the pace of an assembly line, or where productivity is routinely assessed. Nevertheless, the point still holds. Typically, the size or delivery of one's monthly paycheck is not contingent on one's actual work behavior.
25. See Lowe (1983) for a review.
26. Lowe (1979); Lowe and Wearden (1981).
27. Lowe (1983).
28. See also Shimoff, Catania, and Matthews (1981).
29. Subjects certainly do prefer bigger rewards; see Killeen, Cate, and Tran (1993).
30. See Bonem and Crossman (1988) for a review.
31. Kraeling (1961).
32. Bradshaw, Ruddle, and Szabadi (1981); Bradshaw, Szabadi, and Bevan (1978).
33. Bonem and Crossman (1988).
34. Perone and Courtney (1992).
35. See Bonem and Crossman (1988).
36. Bonem and Crossman (1988).
37. See Killeen (1985) for a model of incentive. Osborne (1978) also showed that increases in reward magnitude affect the activity levels (arousal) of both rats and pigeons, but not the rate of response itself. Bonem and Crossman (1988), however, pointed out that responding on concurrent schedules is positively related to reward magnitude. Here, when animals have a choice between larger and smaller rewards, they tend to respond more rapidly for the larger choice. Such a result has been found by many investigators.
38. See also Reed and Wright (1988). Recall that on a multiple schedule, each sequential component is signaled by an external stimulus, such as a light.
39. Camp, Raymond, and Church (1967); Church, Raymond, and Beauchamp (1967); Powell (1970).
40. Smith, Misanin, and Campbell (1966).
41. The duration of punishment is also an important parameter. Campbell, Smith, and Misanin (1966), for example, showed that response suppression is positively related to the duration of a shock.
42. In the second experiment, the IRT values had to be between 8 and 12 seconds.
43. Bolles and Seelbach (1964) (noise); Franchina (1969); Kaplan, Jackson, and Sparer (1965) (light); Staveley (1966); Trapold and Fowler (1960) (shock); Woods, Davidson, and Peters (1964) (cold water).

44. Franchina (1969) also showed that animals that received all of the shock intensities in a varied order showed even faster performance at each level of shock. That is, performance was faster at, say, the 50-volt level if subjects received all three intensities than if the subjects received only the 50-volt intensity.
45. Incentive motivation, however, is affected by reward magnitude (see subsequent discussion).
46. Boren, Sidman, and Herrnstein (1959); Myers (1977); Riess (1970); Riess and Farrar (1972).
47. Souza, Moraes, and Todorov (1984) showed that this positive relationship between shock intensity and rate of lever-pressing avoidance actually may be an all-or-none phenomenon.
48. Bauer (1972); Levine (1966); Moyer and Korn (1964); Theios, Lynch, and Lowe (1966).
49. For additional support of this theory, using a different approach, see Freedman, Hennessy, and Groner (1974).
50. Blanchard and Blanchard (1969a, 1969b); Bolles and Collier (1976).
51. Modaresi (1978); see also McAllister, McAllister, and Dieter (1976); McAllister, McAllister, and Douglass (1971).
52. However, see Masterson, Crawford, and Bartter (1978).
53. See Tarpy and Sawabini (1974) for a review.
54. Reed and Reilly (1990).
55. See also Lattal and Gleeson (1990).
56. The authors also had control groups of subjects that could earn reward every time the experimental animals earned reward. The purpose of these control subjects was to equate for rate of reinforcement, so that the effects of delay could be more easily determined.
57. The authors claimed that the longer delay changed the functional unit of behavior from a single response to multiple key pecks.
58. D'Amato and Buckiewicz (1980); Lett (1973, 1974, 1975); but see Roberts (1976).
59. Grice (1948).
60. See also Schaal and Branch (1988).
61. Spence (1947); see also Tarpy and Sawabini (1974).
62. Presumably, the principles by which a cue acquires reinforcing properties are those of Pavlovian conditioning.
63. Schaal and Branch (1990).
64. See also Lieberman, Davidson, and Thomas (1985); Thomas, Lieberman, McIntosh, and Ronaldson (1983); Thomas, Robertson, and Lieberman (1987).
65. In Experiment 4, the authors also included a group that got handled (rather than receiving a noise or a light). A discussion of this group has been omitted for the sake of brevity.
66. Lieberman, McIntosh, and Thomas (1979), p. 241.
67. See Baron (1965); Baron, Kaufman, and Fazzini (1969); Camp, Raymond, and Church (1967); Randalll and Riccio (1969).
68. This hypothesis is plausible because the animal already knows how to perform the response in an instrumental task (if it did not know how to perform the response, then reward would never have been earned in the first place).
69. See Flaherty (1982) for a review. Two other forms of contrast have been identified. Behavioral contrast is most easily observed when experimental subjects are given a mixture of high and low reinforcement rates—for example, high- versus low-

yield reinforcement schedules or large versus small reward magnitude. Control subjects receive only one level of reward. Subjects that get both types of reward conditions perform at more extreme levels than do control subjects; see Dougan, Farmer-Dougan, and McSweeney (1989); Williams (1991). Anticipatory contrast is observed when a subject responds at a faster rate, or consumes a greater amount of food, in anticipation of receiving a reduced level of reward later on; see Capaldi and Sheffer (1992); Flaherty and Rowan (1985, 1986).

70. Crespi called negative contrast "depression" and positive contrast "elation."

71. Contrast effects are found not only with shifts in reward magnitude, but also with changes in the delay, quality, or schedule of reinforcement, and the motivational level; see Flaherty (1982) for a comprehensive review.

72. See Eisenberger (1972); Kish (1966).

73. Fowler (1967).

74. Russell and Glow (1974, 1976).

75. Jones and Nowell (1974).

76. Mellgren, Fouts, and Martin (1973).

77. However, see Candland, Horowitz, and Culbertson (1962).

78. See also Couvillon, Brandon, Woodard, and Bitterman (1980).

79. Capaldi, Verry, and Davidson (1980), however, provide evidence for an alternative view. They argue that such results can be better explained in terms of how memory for reward and nonreward trials affects subsequent responding; see Chapter 14 of this book, and Capaldi, Verry, and Nawrocki (1982).

80. See Hinde and Stevenson-Hinde (1973); Seligman (1970); Shettleworth (1972) for early discussions of this point.

81. See also Timberlake, Wahl, and King (1982), the discussion of Timberlake's work in Chapter 11, and the discussion in Chapter 12.

82. Breland and Breland (1961, p. 683).

83. Breland and Breland described this shift in behavior in terms of a concept called "instinctual drift."

84. The results, however, were somewhat different when punishment was given on a noncontingent basis. Free shock did not affect many action patterns, such as digging or gnawing; in fact, it increased some—for example, scent marking, standing motionless, and urinating. One conclusion was that various action patterns differed in their responsiveness to shock.

85. Charlton (1983), p. 34.

86. See also Pearce, Colwill, and Hall (1978) for an alternative account.

87. A third position is that certain actions are poorly learned because they have occurred many times in the past without ever having been followed by the reward in question, and thus the response–reinforcer relationship is effectively ignored by the subjects. Consider the fact that food was a relatively ineffective reinforcer for scratching. Surely, scratching has occurred in the past but in situations quite unrelated to eating. If scratching had occurred but was never reinforced with food in the natural environment, then it follows that it would be hard to condition scratching in the laboratory because subjects would find food irrelevant to scratching. Such a claim is similar to the one made for the latent inhibition effect found in Pavlovian conditioning (see Chapter 5).

88. An evolutionary perspective claims that such behaviors have been selected for throughout evolution because of their adaptive value to an animal whose existence is threatened by hunger.

89. See also Walters and Glazer (1971).

CHAPTER 10

Instrumental-Conditioning Phenomena

Chapter 8 introduced instrumental conditioning, and Chapter 9 discussed several variables that affect learning. Learning research, however, has studied many phenomena that extend well beyond the simple action of certain variables on learning. These phenomena represent interesting and complex situations in instrumental learning, and many have great relevance to everyday human behavior. The following sections describe four major phenomena that occur primarily in the context of instrumental learning (although many of them involve classical conditioning, as well).

CONDITIONED REINFORCEMENT

One important concept in basic learning research is **conditioned (secondary) reinforcement.** A secondary reinforcer (denoted as S_r) is an innocuous stimulus that acquires the properties of a primary reinforcer, such as food or water, through consistent pairings with the primary reinforcement. On subsequent occasions, the secondary cue by itself reinforces behavior. Stated differently, a secondary reinforcer is a Pavlovian CS (it has been paired with either an appetitive US or the offset of an aversive US) that serves as a reinforcer in an instrumental-learning context.

Secondary reinforcement is important because humans and other animals respond not only for biologically important reinforcers, but also for secondary reinforcers. The process of reward is not necessarily linked inextricably to the subject's biological well-being, although a secondary reinforcer is, at least initially, related to such an outcome (see Chapter 11).

Tests of Secondary Reinforcement

The power of a cue to serve as an instrumental reinforcer in its own right may be demonstrated in several ways: response maintenance (extinction technique), chaining technique, and acquisition technique.

Photograph of a noted study in which chimpanzees deposited tokens (secondary reinforcers) to obtain a primary food reward.
Courtesy of the Yerkes Research Center of Emory University, Atlanta

Response Maintenance.

One means of showing secondary reinforcement is the extinction technique. Presentation of a conditioned reinforcer during extinction maintains the behavior on which the cue in contingent. That is, subjects that are given the secondary reinforcer following the target response typically show a more sustained level of responding during extinction than subjects that are not.[1] Similarly, secondary reinforcers maintain behavior during acquisition under conditions that otherwise would cause a deficit in the behavior. For example, a delay of reward causes a significant reduction in the rate of responding (see Chapter 9).[2] However, if a brief cue is given during the delay, no such decline in response rate is observed because the S_r acts as a reward.

Chaining Technique.

The **chaining technique** has been widely used to demonstrate conditioned reinforcement.[3] During training, a subject experiences two kinds of outcomes following its behavior. A response produces no reward in the presence of S_2 but leads to reward during S_1. On a later secondary-reinforcement test, responding during S_2 produces S_1; responding during S_1 then produces the reward. If the behavior during S_2 is sustained, then S_1 must be a reinforcer because responding during S_2 is not followed by primary reinforcement but by the presentation of S_1, the conditioned reinforcer. There are various control conditions. The most common involves the presentation of a new stimulus, S_3, contingent on the completion of the first schedule. Because S_3 was never paired with reward (or with nonreward for that matter), it cannot serve as a reinforcer for responding during S_2.

A good example of the chaining technique was a study by Kelleher and Fry (1962). Pigeons had three FI components, each designated by a separate color. At the start of a trial, the key light was white, but after a fixed interval of time, a response changed the color from white to green. Again, after a fixed amount of time had elapsed, a response turned the color to red. Finally, responding during the red light produced food reward on an FI schedule. Responding was rather slow during the white component, and pauses were frequent. Thus, the green stimulus was a weak reinforcer for responding during the white component.[4] Responding accelerated noticeably, however, during the green and red stimuli, especially during the red stimuli where response rate was at its maximum. Responding during the green light was maintained by the red cue, which was a conditioned reinforcer.[5]

Acquisition Technique.

Finally, a technique that provides an even more compelling demonstration of conditioned reinforcement is the acquisition procedure. In Phase 1 of a study by Hyde (1976), the secondary-reinforcement subjects were given a 3-second auditory stimulus (tone or clicking noise) followed by food reward. Here, the auditory stimulus should become a conditioned reinforcer because it is paired with food. One control group received random presentations of the auditory stimulus and food.[6] Two additional control groups received the food presentations, but not the auditory CSs.[7] During the test phase, a lever was inserted into the cage for the first time. One of the groups that had received food-only presentations in Phase 1 received nothing following a lever press (they were included to provide a baseline of responding against which to compare performance in the other groups). The other groups were given a 3-second presentation of the auditory stimulus following each lever press (for the other food-only group, such a cue was novel).

Mean responding over the eight test sessions is shown is Figure 10-1. There was appreciable responding in all of the groups, relative to the no-cue group, but the auditory stimulus that had previously been paired with food had the strongest effect on lever pressing. Mean number of lever presses during the first session was nearly six times the level of the no-cue control group.[8]

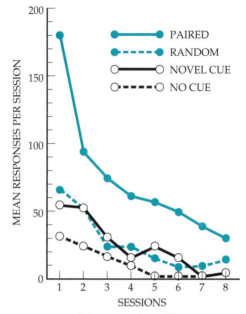

FIGURE 10-1. Mean number of lever responses per session, as a function of test sessions for the groups that received the auditory stimulus and the no-cue control condition (after Hyde, 1976).

Not only does a conditioned reinforcer sustain behaviors that have already been learned (response maintenance and chaining techniques) and increase the frequency of new behaviors (acquisition technique), but it also affects the rate of learning itself. For example, Williams and Dunn (1991) trained rats to make a conditional discrimination. Subjects were reinforced for pressing one lever during a noise but a different lever during a light. A correct response was followed by both a tone and food. The tone facilitated discrimination learning; indeed, the tone substituted for the food, indicating that its role was the same as the primary reinforcer.

Theories of Secondary Reinforcement

Several theories have been proposed to account for secondary reinforcement. Actually, there are two important questions. First, what is the source of power for a secondary reinforcer? What process accounts for a cue becoming a powerful reinforcer? The section immediately following addresses this issue.

Second, why does a secondary reinforcer affect behavior in the manner described above? Why is behavior maintained so effectively when a conditioned reinforcer follows its execution? There are two possible mechanisms of action. A cue may affect behavior on a secondary-reinforcement test, by serving as an S_d. If operating in this capacity, presentation of the cue evokes additional responding. Alternatively, the cue may have reinforcing properties in its own right because it has been paired with a rewarding outcome.[9] If functioning in this fashion, presentation of the cue on the secondary-reinforcement test strengthens the response on which it is contingent. The second section following discusses which of these functions—evocation by an S_d or reinforcement from an S_r—is the more important.

Acquisition of Strength.

Many believe that a secondary reinforcer derives appreciable power through its association with reward, that is, through Pavlovian conditioning. Several results support this claim by showing that the principles for generating strong secondary reinforcement are precisely those used to train strong Pavlovian CSs. For example, secondary reinforcement strength is a positive function of US magnitude and immediacy.[10] Moreover, secondary reinforcement is strong when the CS is paired with the US but virtually nonexistent when it is given randomly with respect to food.[11] This is precisely what research on Pavlovian conditioning has found with respect to CS strength (see Chapter 3).

Function of the Cue.

The second theoretical issue concerns the function of the cue. According to the discriminative-stimulus hypothesis, a secondary stimulus acts primarily as an S_d. Behavior on a secondary-reinforcement test is maintained at a relatively high level because each presentation of the cue triggers further responding.[12]

Some early work supported this hypothesis. For example, Dinsmoor (1950) trained rats to press a lever for food in the presence of a light (S_d) and to avoid pressing it its absence.[13] Subjects then were divided into three groups and were given extinction. For one group, the light came on and remained on until the subject made a lever press; here, the light preceded the press and thus served as an S_d for the behavior. For a second group, the light was given following the bar press. A third control group received no light at all. Dinsmoor showed that the light was equally effective in maintaining the lever response in the two cue groups, relative to the no-cue control animals. Because the cue had been an S_d for lever pressing during the initial training phase (the two experimental groups did not differ from one another in this respect), then the outcome on the test must have been a result of the cue acting as an S_d even when it came after the response. That is, the cue presented after the response during the secondary-reinforcement test evoked additional responding.

Although the S_d functions of a cue may be important in various experimental settings, the response-cue contingency is more critical for the effects observed in studies on conditioned reinforcement than the cue-response relationship.[14] Part of the evidence for this claim comes from studies that have simultaneously measured both the S_d and the S_r properties of the cue. For example, Ratner (1956) trained thirsty rats to drink from a water dipper when a clicker sounded. Here, the click presumably functioned both as a reinforcer and as an S_d for approaching the dipper. Later, a lever was inserted into the cage, and lever presses produced the clicking noise for some subjects but not for others. Both lever responding and the approaches to the dipper were measured. A strong secondary-reinforcement effect was found. The group that received the click contingent on a lever press emitted more lever presses than the controls. However, there was no difference between the groups in terms of the number of dipper approaches. Thus, the stimulus affected a response by virtue of its reinforcing value, without simultaneously affecting the behavior in its role an an S_d.[15]

INTERIM SUMMARY

A conditioned (secondary) reinforcer (S_r) is a CS that acquires the properties of a primary reinforcer with which it is paired. Many behaviors are learned or maintained through secondary reinforcers. The strength of a secondary reinforcer is demonstrated in terms of response maintenance (in which the contingent presentation of the cue maintains behavior), response chaining, and response acquisition (where a new behavior is acquired using a contingent secondary, rather than primary, reinforcer). An S_r derives its reinforcing properties from its association with food reward, and it functions primarily by providing reinforcement for the contingent response rather than as an S_d.

CHOICE BEHAVIOR

The study of instrumental conditioning involves understanding of the principles that control the development and maintenance of behavior. Instrumental behaviors, however, are never performed in a vacuum; they always involve a choice. For example, responding to earn food often involves a choice between different paths. Even in a highly restricted environment, an instrumental behavior represents a choice between responding and not responding.

Matching Law

One of the most celebrated principles describing choice behavior is the **matching law.** The matching law is a mathematical statement describing the relationship between rate of responding and rate of reward[16]: Animals match their rate of responding to the rate at which that action is reinforced.

Reinforcement Frequency

Herrnstein (1961), who originally developed the matching formulation, trained pigeons to peck either of two keys for food. Each key was associated with a different VI schedule. This is called a "concurrent VI–VI schedule" because both schedules are given simultaneously, and the subject has a choice between them. Common sense, not to mention ethological considerations, suggests that the subject's interest is best served by pecking the key associated with the more favorable reinforcement schedule. However, Herrnstein found that the subjects matched their responses on a given key to the relative frequency of reinforcement for that key. That is, the number of pecks to key a, relative to the number of pecks to key b, matched the number of rewards earned on schedule a relative to the number earned on schedule b.

In more formal terms, the matching law is defined by the following equation:

$$\frac{R_a}{(R_a + R_b)} = \frac{F_a}{(F_a + F_b)}$$

Equation 10-1

The terms R_a and R_b stand for number of responses on schedule a and b, respectively, and the terms F_a and F_b stand for the number (or frequency) of reinforcers received as a consequence of responding on schedules a and b, respectively.

Let us substitute some arbitrary numbers into the equation to demonstrate how it works. Assume that schedule a is a VI-1-minute schedule, whereas schedule b is a VI-2-minute one. This means that, over an hour, schedule a would yield twice as many rewards as schedule b if the subject responded at a steady rate on both. Specifically, the VI-1 schedule would yield 60 rewards per hour, whereas the VI-2 would give 30 rewards. The relative rate of reinforcement for schedule a then would be 0.67 (this figure is derived from the right-hand side of Equation 10-1; 60 divided by [60 + 30] equals 0.67). Herrnstein found that the number of pecks to key a matched this ratio. That is, the number of responses to key a, divided by the total number of responses (left-hand term in Equation 10-1) was 0.67 as well. In short, when confronted with the choice between two schedules that differed in terms of the frequency of reinforcement, animals did not simply respond to the better of the two (namely VI-1). Rather, they divided their responding in such a way that the relative number of pecks to key a matched the relative number of reinforcers for that schedule.

A more general statement of the matching law is shown in Figure 10-2. This figure depicts more or less the same data that Herrnstein found in his original study of matching. The horizontal axis represents the proportion of rewards programmed by schedule a; the vertical axis shows the proportion of pecks to key a. The diagonal line plots the values predicted by the matching law. It makes no difference what the specific VI schedule values are; the *relative* rates of responding should match.

Other Reward Characteristics.

If the relative reward rate is the essential reinforcing value of option a (the greater the number of rewards per hour, the greater the value), then other dimensions of reward—such as amount, quality, and immediacy—which also affect the overall value of a reward, should also influence choice behavior in

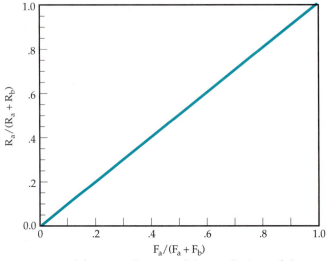

FIGURE 10-2. Schematic diagram of the predictions of the matching law, showing proportion of responding on schedule a, as a function of the proportion of reinforcement on schedule a.

a similar fashion. This has been found in many studies. For example, in terms of reward magnitude, the matching law may be restated in the following way:

$$\frac{R_a}{(R_a + R_b)} = \frac{A_a}{(A_a + A_b)} \qquad \text{Equation 10-2}$$

Relative response rate matches relative reinforcer amount.[17]

Let us again consider some hypothetical data. Assume that the amount of reward earned on schedule a is 1 gram, whereas the reward amount on schedule b is 3 grams.[18] According to the matching formula, the relative rate of reinforcement for schedule a is 0.25 (1 over [1 + 3] equals 0.25). In other words, rats and pigeons do not merely respond on the schedule that yields the larger reward. Rather, they allocate their responses to both options in such a way that some are made to the less desirable option—here, schedule a.[19]

The matching law also describes choice behavior when rewards differ in terms of immediacy.[20] For delay of reward, the matching formula is stated by the following equation:

$$\frac{R_a}{(R_a + R_b)} = \frac{\dfrac{1}{D_a}}{\left(\dfrac{1}{D_a} + \dfrac{1}{D_b}\right)} \qquad \text{Equation 10-3}$$

Immediacy is defined as the reciprocal of delay; as the delay increases, the immediacy declines. Assume that schedule a yields a reward that is delayed

2 seconds, whereas schedule b produces a reward that is delayed for 3 seconds. The matching law predicts that the relative reinforcement value of schedule a would be 0.6. Here is how the formula is solved.

$$\frac{R_a}{(R_a + R_b)} \ = \ \frac{\frac{1}{2}}{\left(\frac{1}{2} + \frac{1}{3}\right)} \ = \ \frac{\frac{3}{6}}{\left(\frac{3}{6} + \frac{2}{6}\right)} \ = \ \frac{3}{5} \ = \ 0.6$$

In short, when two equal VI schedules are presented to a subject, each yielding the same magnitude of delayed reward, subjects respond more to the schedule giving the more immediate reward. However, they also respond to the less favorable option, at least some of the time. The proportion of responding to each schedule is describe by the matching equation.

These results suggest that the matching law applies to the quantitative value of a reinforcer, regardless of whether that value is determined by the frequency of the reward, its amount, or its immediacy. Matching also occurs, however, when reinforcers differ qualitatively. In a study by Holland and Davidson (1971), rats responded on one of two VI schedules.[21] One schedule controlled the rate of food presentation, and the other controlled the rate of pleasurable brain stimulation. It is widely known that the application of minute electrical impulses to certain areas of the brain, called "pleasure centers," is reinforcing (see Chapter 11). How could one possible compare the reinforcing value of two reinforcers that differ so dramatically in quality? Holland and Davidson argued that the matching law provided an answer. They measured the number of food pellets per reward that was necessary to offset a brain-stimulation reinforcement. In other words, they adjusted the schedule values until matching occurred. Here, they could say with confidence that a certain number of food pellets was equivalent in its reinforcing value to a given number of brain stimulations.

Aversive Conditioning.

The matching formula applies to situations involving aversive, as well as appetitive, outcomes. In a study by Baum (1973), for example, rats could stand on either side of a cage; shock was programmed to occur on both sides.[22] A time-out from shock was occasionally given, but the frequency of time-outs differed, depending on which side of the cage the subject was in at the time. Subjects matched their relative time spent on side a to the relative frequency of time-outs on that side.

Experiments have also examined how punishment affects choice. In a study by de Villiers (1980), rats were allowed to earn food reward on a concurrent VI–VI schedule.[23] Lever pressing was also punished by mild shock, according to a concurrent VI–VI schedule (the food and the shock schedules were thoroughly independent of one another). Both the frequency of shock and the frequency of food were varied. The relative rate of responding on side a was described by the following equation:

$$\frac{R_a}{(R_a + R_b)} = \frac{F_a - P_a}{(F_a - P_a) + (F_b - P_b)} \qquad \textit{Equation 10-4}$$

The terms R_a, R_b, F_a, and F_b represent the number of responses and the number of reinforcers for schedules a and b, respectively; P_a and P_b refer to the frequency of punishment on schedules a and b, respectively. The equation suggests that the suppressive effects of punishment subtract from the excitatory effects of food reward. That is, the net reinforcing value of side a equals the value of the positive reward minus the value of punishment. Using those terms to estimate the relative value of each schedule outcome, de Villiers found that the relative response rate matched the proportion quite precisely.[24]

The matching law is an important contribution to our understanding of choice behavior because it helps to specify the quantitative relationship between reinforcement value and responding. Since its formulation by Herrnstein, many studies have confirmed that the equations generally hold for a wide variety of conditions (but see the subsequent discussion). Moreover, Herrnstein has expanded the law to include not only the proportion of responses made on schedule a relative to b, but also the rate of responding on a single schedule a relative to not responding at all.[25]

Finally, the matching law gives a good description of choice behavior in the natural environment. Houston (1986), for example, analyzed the foraging of pied wagtails and found that the matching law fit their behavior quite closely.[26] Similarly, Graft, Lea, and Whitworth (1977) investigated the foraging strategies of five rats housed together. The rats had access to four different levers, each of which was associated with a different VI schedule. Collectively, the rats matched their response rate on each lever to the relative frequency of reinforcement.

Self-control.

Imagine the following dilemma. You are studying for a very important exam; doing well on the exam means that you will probably earn a good grade in the course and thus improve your chances of securing the job of your choice following graduation. Thus, the reward for studying is high, although its benefits will not be felt until much later, when the grades are issued or even when you search for a job. Your friends drop into your room to ask you to accompany them to the movies. This, too, represents a valued activity, although many would claim that its value is lower than receiving a good grade in a course. Which option would you choose—the immediate but smaller reward (going to the movies), or the delayed but more significant reward (good exam grade)?

Many studies of **self-control** show that rats and pigeons act impulsively; they choose the more immediate but smaller reward option.[27] Such impulsiveness is also observed in human beings, particularly children.[28] Apparently, the value of a delayed reward is perceived by most animals (including humans) to be less than the value of the same reward given immediately.[29]

Let us examine how the matching law accounts for the impulsive choice.[30] Assume that a pigeon is given a choice between responding on schedule a or schedule b. Schedule a involves a large but delayed reward (4 grams, delayed for 4 seconds). Schedule b, on the other hand, involves a smaller reward (2 grams), but the delivery occurs much sooner (1 second). Would the subject delay gratification by choosing the larger reward despite the delay, or would the animal be impulsive and choose the smaller, more immediate reinforcer?

According to the matching law, a subject matches rate of responding to the rate of the *combined* effect of amount and immediacy. The formula describing this relationship is the following:

$$\frac{R_a}{(R_a + R_b)} = \frac{\dfrac{A_a}{D_a}}{\left(\dfrac{A_a}{D_a} + \dfrac{A_b}{D_b}\right)}$$

Equation 10-5

The terms R_a and R_b refer to the number of responses to schedules a and b, respectively. The terms A_a/D_a and A_b/D_b refer to the reward size divided by the delay for schedules a and b, respectively. Equation 10-5, therefore, is simply the combination of the two previous equations dealing with the size and the immediacy of reward separately. Substituting the arbitrary values used previously into this formula gives the following prediction:

$$\frac{R_a}{(R_a + R_b)} = \frac{\dfrac{4}{4}}{\left(\dfrac{4}{4} + \dfrac{2}{1}\right)} = \frac{1}{3} = .33$$

Thus, the matching formula predicts that only 33% of the responses will be devoted to schedule a, the large delayed reward option. Here, the animal behaves impulsively 67% of the time.

Although delay and amount are important determinants of choice, the situation is more complicated than it appears based on these factors.[31] Several factors cause subjects to exert greater self-control than suggested by the matching formulation. First, stimuli that are given during the delay interval just prior to reward delivery decrease the detrimental effects of delay (see the foregoing discussion on secondary reinforcement and Chapter 9). This means that a signaled reward is not devalued as much as a reward that is not signaled. Second, adult humans often show greater self-control than, say, pigeons or children, because they develop rules concerning the requirements for earning rewards.[32] Children do not have an ability to create such rules and thus tend to behave more impulsively in these situations.[33]

Third, whether an animal demonstrates impulsiveness or self-control depends, in part, on the activities in which the subject engages during the delay interval. If the rewards are salient, then animals tend to be impulsive.[34]

If, however, the temptation of the immediate reward is reduced (that is, the salience of the reward is reduced), and the subject is allowed to engage in other kinds of distracting behaviors during the delay period, then a greater degree of self-control is demonstrated even by pigeons.

Fourth, self-control may be maintained by omitting the delay at first but later increasing it gradually over training. For example, Mazur and Logue (1978) trained pigeons to choose between a large delayed reward (6 grams, 6 seconds) and a small delayed reward (2 grams, 6 seconds). The animals reliably preferred the larger reward. Then the authors gradually shifted the delay for the small reward to a shorter value—namely, 0.5 seconds—giving subjects a choice between a large delayed reward and a small immediate reward. Here, the pigeons continued to choose the larger delayed reward; that is, they showed self-control. In other words, if one reward condition is gradually shifted to another, then subjects may show appreciable self-control.

Fifth, the degree of self-control is affected by the experience of the subject. In an interesting study by Eisenberger, Weier, Masterson, and Theis (1989), rats were trained to run down an alleyway to a goal box and back again to receive food. The continuous reinforcement (CRF) animals received reward for each complete round trip. The fixed ratio (FR) subjects had to make as many as five complete round trips to receive food reward.[35]

In a subsequent phase, all rats were given eight choice trials per session, where they could run to one of the goal boxes and press a lever. Operating one of the levers required that subjects use 85 grams of force, and the reward was two food pellets. Operating the other lever required only about 32 grams of force, but only a single pellet was delivered. In this situation then, effort was used as a deterrent to responding rather than delay of reward. Animals were expected to prefer to operate the easy lever (smaller reward) rather than exerting more energy by pressing the hard lever (large reward).

The results are shown in Figure 10-3. The group that had been forced to respond five times per reward in the alleyway pressed the more effortful lever more than the group that had been rewarded after making one round trip in the maze. In other words, having been forced to run five round trips per reward in the maze, as opposed to one, caused the FR subjects to exert greater self-control later on.

Finally, impulsiveness is avoided when subjects make a commitment to the large delayed reward prior to the choice point.[36] This was shown in a study by Rachlin and Green (1972). A flowchart depicting their procedure is shown in Figure 10-4. Subjects could peck either the left or the right key (both illuminated with white light). If the pigeons pecked the left key 15 times, a 10-second delay was given (all the lights were turned off), after which the key turned green, and a single peck yielded a 4-gram reward, delayed for 4 seconds. If, however, they pecked the right key 15 times, then a 10-second delay was given, after which the subject had a choice between pecking either a green or a red key. Here, the options were the same as those described earlier. Specifically, pecking the green key yielded a 4-gram reward, delayed for

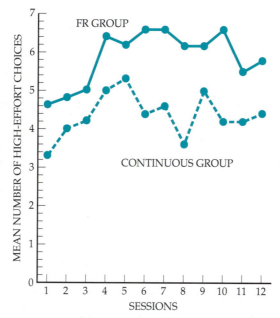

FIGURE 10-3. Mean number of times out of 8 that
the subjects chose to press the difficult lever, as
a function of 12 test sessions for the FR group
(had to make five round trips in the alley) and
the continuous group (rewarded in the alley
after only one round trip) (after Eisenberger,
Weier, Masterson, & Theis, 1989).

4 seconds, and pecking the red key gave a 2-gram reward, delayed for only
1 second.

Recall that when confronted with this choice, pigeons act impulsively,
choosing the red key (small immediate reward) more than the green key (large
delayed reward). What does the added 10 seconds delay do to choice, however? Here is what the matching law predicts:

$$\frac{R_L}{(R_L + R_R)} = \frac{\frac{4}{14}}{\left(\frac{4}{14} + \frac{2}{11}\right)} = .61$$

According to the theory, the percentage of the responses to the left key should
be 61%. This is precisely what is found in such a situation. The subject is more
likely to choose *not* to have a choice later on; the subject responds mostly on
the side that precludes a choice. In short, if one makes a commitment in
advance which eliminates having to confront the tempting choice later on,
then self-control increases. To return to the previous example, a student may

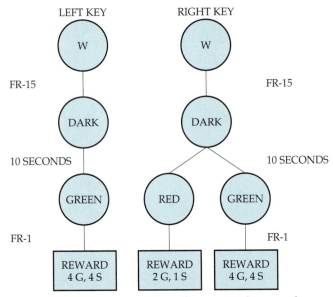

FIGURE 10-4. Schematic diagram illustrating the procedure used by Rachlin and Green (1972) to study self-control. (G is grams of reward; S is seconds).

avoid the temptation of the small, immediate reward (going to the movies) by earlier in the day electing to study for the important exam in the library where movie-going friends are unlikely to venture.

Evaluation of Matching Law.

The matching law provides an accurate description of choice behavior in many situations, but serious problems have been documented. One challenge, posed by Logue and Chavarro (1987), focused on whether the absolute values of immediacy, amount, and frequency of reward were important for matching. The matching law predicts that the same choice will be made whenever the *relative* values of these parameters remain the same; the absolute values should not matter.

For example, the matching law predicts that subjects will make the same choice when the reward magnitudes are 5 versus 3 as they do when the reward magnitudes are 10 versus 6 (or 100 v. 60). The same argument holds for immediacy and frequency. Using pigeons as subjects, the authors varied the absolute values while keeping the ratio of amount (or delay, or frequency) constant. Specifically, the relative ratio of these reward parameters was always 3 to 1, but the absolute values ranged form low to high. According to the matching formulation, the number of responses made to the left key relative to the right key should be the same for every combination of reward values. The authors found, however, that the proportion of responses devoted to the better choice declined as the absolute values of the reward increased, despite the fact that the ratio stayed the same. This is a serious problem for matching because the formula predicts that the proportion should remain the same, provided the relative reinforcement parameters do not change.

A second problem with the matching law is that it does not always predict choice behavior accurately. According to Baum (1974), there are three systematic errors that subjects tend to commit in choice situations: bias, overmatching and undermatching.[37] **Bias** is shown when the subject has a special affinity or preference for one of the choices. For example, some subjects may prefer, say, the right lever or key; others may have a preference for a particular color. If such a bias exists, then the allocation of choice responses is not controlled primarily by the parameters of reward.

Two other systematic errors are over- and undermatching.[38] **Overmatching** is a higher rate of response for the better of the two schedules than what the matching formula predicts. Overmatching occurs when it is costly for a subject to switch to the less preferred side. Such a high cost exists when the time-out period that is normally imposed for switching from one schedule to the other is relatively long. **Undermatching,** on the other hand, occurs when the subject responds less than predicted on the preferred or advantageous schedule.

To accommodate theses systematic errors in matching, Baum developed the generalized matching law. This equation is similar to Herrnstein's original formula, but it includes additional mathematical terms that correct for bias, overmatching, and undermatching. According to Baum, matching is described by the following equation:

$$\frac{R_a}{R_b} = b \left(\frac{F_a}{F_b}\right)^s$$

Equation 10-6

where R_a, R_b, F_a, and F_b refer to the responses and frequency of reinforcement on schedules a and b, respectively, b is a constant representing the response bias, and s is an exponent that adjusts for the sensitivity of the subject to the two schedules (overmatching occurs when s is greater than 1.0; matching obtains when s equals 1.0; and undermatching occurs when s is less than 1.0).

Because deviations from strict matching are so widespread, this formulation has become the preferred expression of the matching relationship.

There is a third problem with the matching law. Imagine that the choice offered to the subjects is between two VR schedules, rather than between two VI schedules. For example, assume that schedule a is VR-10, and schedule b is VR-5. The original matching formula predicts the following:

$$\frac{R_a}{(R_a + R_b)} = \frac{F_a}{(F_a + F_b)} = \frac{10}{(10 + 20)} = .33$$

The percentage of responses given to schedule a should be 33.3%. This is not found. Subjects do not match response rate to relative reinforcement rate when given a choice between two VR schedules. Rather, they respond exclusively on the better schedule. Why do animals match their response rates on concurrent VI schedules, but not on VR schedules?[39] To understand this issue, a clearer understanding of the theories of matching is needed.

Theories of Matching

Matching is a description of behavior; it attempts to predict how choices are allocated between two options. The matching law, however, does not say *why* a subject behaves in this fashion. Several interesting theories have been advanced about the underlying nature of matching.

Maximization.

One theory claims that matching occurs because subjects attempt to maximize the rate of reinforcement. According to the **maximization theory of matching,** animals have evolved to perform in a manner that yields the greatest rate of reinforcement.[40] Let us examine how matching behavior on concurrent VI-VI schedules actually maximizes reward.

When an animal works on one VI schedule, time progresses for the other schedule as well. Because both schedules run simultaneously, time is expiring for schedule b, as well as for schedule a, even though the animal devotes its attention at any given moment to schedule a. Once the interval has expired for schedule b, the reinforcer is saved or stored until a later time when the animal finally switches and makes the single response necessary to collect it. By momentarily switching from a to b, the animal collects the reward that has been stored on b. It is thus advantageous for a subject to respond on both schedules, even though one of them is, by itself, less generous than the other.

Storing rewards for future collection does not occur on a concurrent VR-VR schedule, however. Here, the only thing that produces a reinforcer is the completion of the ratio requirement. An animal gains no opportunity or advantage on schedule b when responding on schedule a. If the subject switches to schedule b, it still must complete the required number of responses stipulated by that schedule before reward is delivered.

In conclusion, the maximization theory of matching argues that subjects match on concurrent VI-VI schedules because such a strategy maximizes reward, but not on concurrent VR-VR schedules, because switching between schedules has no effect on reward rate. Although this theory makes good intuitive sense, the maximization interpretation has not been universally supported.[41] Thus, uncertainty still exists about whether subjects are, in fact, maximizing reinforcement when they engage in matching behavior. In fact, some investigators have even argued that a critical test of the maximation theory may be impossible to achieve.[42]

Melioration.

A second theory of matching is **melioration.**[43] To meliorate is to "make better." According to this view, matching behavior occurs because the subject is continuously choosing the more promising option—namely, the schedule with the momentarily higher rate of reinforcement. In other words, subjects switch from one choice to another because the probability of reinforcement changes with time on interval schedules. Subjects are continuously attempting to better their current chances of receiving reward by switching to the other choice. As with the maximization theory, both supportive and conflicting evidence has been found for the melioration view, thus suggesting that a resolution is still pending further research.[44]

INTERIM SUMMARY

The matching law describes a mathematical relationship between the rate of responding and the rate of reward. When subjects choose between either of two VI-VI schedules that occur simultaneously (a compound schedule), they divide their responses between both schedules, so that the relative rate of response on a given schedule matches the relative rate of reinforcement for that schedule. Matching also occurs when rewards differ in terms of amount, quality, and immediacy, and in aversive situations. Matching has been applied to the issue of self-control, where subjects impulsively choose a small reward delivered immediately rather than a larger reward given at a later time. Several procedures minimize impulsive behavior, such as using signaled delayed reward, developing self-instructions concerning response strategies, performing distracting behaviors during the delay period, changing the delay values gradually, experiencing effortful responses prior to the self-control test, and making commitments to avoid a choice early in the sequence. Although the matching law accurately describes choice behavior in many situations, some problems have been noted. For example, the absolute reinforcement values affect choice behavior, even though the matching law focuses exclusively on relative reinforcement values. Second, the matching law is not always accurate. Subjects may show a bias (preference for one of the choices), or they may over- or undermatch. These problems led to the development of the generalized matching law. Finally, the fact that matching does not occur for concurrent VR-VR schedules poses a problem for the matching law. The maximation theory of matching claims that matching behavior is actually a maximizing strategy, according to which subjects gain more reward per unit time by matching than by simply focusing on the more profitable schedule. The melioration position argues that subjects switch from one option to another to avail themselves of a momentarily higher rate of reinforcement.

PARTIAL-REINFORCEMENT EFFECT

The partial-reinforcement effect has perhaps received more attention than any other phenomenon in the area of instrumental learning.[45] It is defined as an increase in resistance to extinction that results when animals receive intermittent (rather than continuous) reinforcement during acquisition. Stated differently, if an animal is reinforced on only a portion of the acquisition trials, then the speed and persistence of responding during extinction is increased, relative to subjects that receive reward on every trial during acquisition.

Historically, the **partial-reinforcement effect** was considered to be a paradox. If reward strengthens a response, then continuously reinforced animals should persist longer during extinction than partially reinforced animals, because the more the reward, the stronger the response (as measured by the subject's persistence when reward is no longer forthcoming). The partial-reinforcement effect is no longer viewed as a paradox, however, because significant advances in theory have occurred in the past few decades. Before describing those theories, an account of how several factors affect persistence during extinction is provided.

Factors That Affect Persistence

Many of the variables that affect acquisition also influence the animal's persistence during extinction.

Reward Magnitude.

One variable is the magnitude of the reward during acquisition. Large rewards, when given on each acquisition trial, decrease later resistance to extinction. When given intermittently during acquisition, however, they increase resistance to extinction. Consider an experiment by Ratliff and Ratliff (1971).[46] Rats were trained to run down an alleyway for food. During acquisition, groups received 2, 4, 8, or 16 food pellets in the goal box. The animals in each of the magnitude conditions were further subdivided on the basis of percentage of reward. Specifically, the percentage of trials on which subjects received reward in the goal box was 25%, 50%, 75%, or 100%. The experiment therefore combines four levels of reward magnitude with four levels of partial-reward training. Figure 10-5 illustrates the performance during extinction (the numbers on the vertical axis show extinction performance, relative to acquisition performance; the lower the value, the faster is the extinction).[47] Resistance to extinction decreased as a function of reward magnitude for the continuously reinforced subjects (100% reward). For the 2-pellet condition, the extinction index was about .91, but for the 16-pellet group, the value dropped to about .83. The effect of magnitude on resistance to extinction for the partially reinforced subjects differed dramatically, however. Here, persistence was greater when the reward magnitude was large (for example, 16 pellets) than when it was small (2 pellets). The changes are particularly noticeable for the 50% and 75% subjects. In short, reward magnitude affects behavior differently, depending on, among other things, the schedule of reinforcement. Resistance to extinction is low following continuous large reward, but high following partial large rewards.[48]

Number of Training Trials.

Similar results are found when varying the number of training trials. Resistance to extinction decreases as a function of the number of continuously

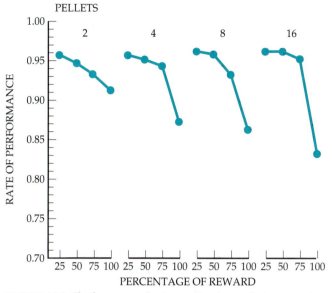

FIGURE 10-5. Performance during extinction, relative to prior acquisition performance, as a function of reward magnitude and percentage of rewarded trials during acquisition (after Ratliff & Ratliff, 1971).

reinforced trials but increases with a larger number of partial-reinforcement trials.[49] In a study by Hill and Spear (1963), for instance, five groups of rats were given partial-reinforcement training for 8, 16, 32, 64, or 128 trials. During extinction, running speed in the alleyway was a positive function of the degree of training. Subjects that received 128 trials continued to run fast during extinction, whereas subjects that received fewer trials were slow.[50]

Patterns of Reward During Acquisition.

A third factor that influences extinction behavior is the pattern of reward during acquisition. An alternating sequence of reward and nonreward during acquisition produces less resistance to extinction than a random pattern of reward and nonreward trials, even though the same number of rewards is used.[51] One theory is that the random animals persist during extinction because they cannot distinguish the conditions that exist during extinction from those that were experienced during acquisition. The alternating subjects, however, do not persist because the conditions experienced during extinction (namely, no reward) are sufficiently distinct from the strictly alternating pattern of reward and no reward experienced during acquisition.[52]

This speculation was supported in a study by Rudy (1971), using three groups of rats. The random and alternation groups showed the same result as just noted (a pattern of alternating reward and nonreward trials during acquisition decreases later resistance to extinction, relative to a random sequence of reward and nonreward). A signaled group was also given the random sequence, but a light was turned on in the alleyway during the nonrewarded trials. Rudy hypothesized that the light should help those subjects discriminate reward from nonreward trials. Then, during extinction, these animals should extinguish as readily as the alternation subjects because the extinction trials are clearly identified as involving no reward. The result confirmed this speculation. When the alternating pattern of reward and nonreward was easily differentiated from no reward, or when a cue was provided that helped subjects to discriminate reward and nonreward trials, then extinction took place quickly.

Another important pattern that affects extinction is the order of schedules. Resistance to extinction is greater when partially reinforced trials are given *after* continuously reinforced trials than when the order is reversed. In a study by Dyal and Sytsma (1976), for instance, some animals received partial-reinforcement training during acquisition, whereas others received continuous reinforcement.[53] In Phase 2, half of each of these groups continued with this same training procedure, whereas the other half was switched to the opposite reinforcement condition. Thus, the procedure involved four groups: P–P, C–P, C–C, and P–C (where "C" means a series of continuous trials, and "P" means partially rewarded trials). All animals were then extinguished in Phase 3.

The usual partial-reinforcement effect was demonstrated. Group P–P was more persistent during extinction than was group C–C. However, the group that received partial reinforcement after the series of continuous trials (group C–P) was more resistant to extinction than the group that received continuous reinforcement following partial reward training (group P–C). This result suggests that a block of continuous reward trials is more easily distinguished from extinction than a block of partial reward trials. Stated differently, the switch from continuous reward to no reward is more apparent than from partial reward to no reward, and thus, the decline in behavior is faster.

Theories of the Partial-Reinforcement Effect

Many theories have been proposed during the past 50 years to explain the partial-reinforcement effect. The two most successful, and, most fully developed, are the frustration and sequential theories.

Frustration Theory.

The **frustration theory** has been studied most extensively by Amsel and colleagues.[54] To appreciate how frustration theory explains the partial-reinforcement effect, let us first consider what frustration is and how it affects behavior in general.

According to the frustration theory, subjects come to expect reward during acquisition. During extinction, when no reward is given, they experience an unconditioned reaction called "frustration" (R_F). This feeling of frustration energizes behavior; that is, an animal's ongoing behavior becomes more vigorous when it experiences frustration. In a demonstration of this effect by Zaslav and Porter (1974), rats were required to press the left lever 18 times.

After a brief delay, the right lever was inserted into the cage, and the rats had to press it 18 times.[55] Subjects in Group 100 were always given reinforcement for completing the response sequence on the left lever. Subjects in Group 50, on the other hand, received reward only 50% of the time for responding on the left lever; they were given nonreward on the other trials (the sequence of rewarded and nonrewarded trials was random). All subjects were rewarded for completing the 18 responses on the right lever.

The measure of performance was the speed with which subjects initiated responding on the right lever once it was inserted. According to frustration theory, Group 50 would experience frustration following a nonrewarded trial on the left lever. If frustration energizes behavior, then their speed of response to the right lever should therefore be high.[56] Following rewarded trials to the left lever, however, these subjects should respond slowly to the right lever. Group 100, on the other hand, would never experience frustration, so their speed to initiate responding on the right lever should be low.

As shown in Figure 10-6, Group 100 animals were relatively slow in initiating their responding to the right lever. Moreover, Group 50 rats were relatively slow following a rewarded trial on the left lever, but not following nonreward. According to the theory, frustration at receiving no reward on the

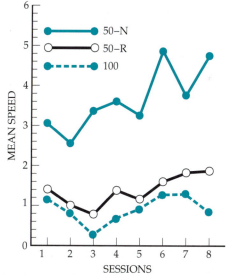

FIGURE 10-6. Mean speed to initiate responding on the right (second) lever for Group 100 (continuous reward on the left lever) and Group 50 (partial reward on the left lever). For Group 50, open circles show speed following a rewarded trial to the left lever; closed circles show speed following a nonrewarded trial to the left (after Zaslav & Porter, 1974).

left lever energized behavior, causing the subjects to initiate responding sooner when the right lever was inserted. Frustration is therefore a motivational state that energizes behavior; it results when animals expect reward but are not given reward.[57]

As a consequence of energizing behavior, frustration may disrupt an ongoing instrumental response. Imagine feeling frustrated after losing coins in a soda machine. Under these circumstances, one is hardly inclined to continue to insert coins into the machine, much less increase the rate of doing so. Rather, one is more likely to kick the machine or storm off in anger.

Frustration-induced behaviors of this kind help explain the behavior of continuously rewarded subjects during extinction. During acquisition, these subjects expect to receive reward on every trial. When confronted with no reward during extinction, they experience a significant amount of frustration. In fact, they continue to feel frustration when placed in the start box at the beginning of the next trial. The unconditioned reaction to the frustration competes or interferes with the instrumental response taught during acquisition— namely, running down the alleyway in a direct and efficient manner.

The effect of reinforcer magnitude and number of acquisition trials on resistance to extinction following continuous reinforcement supports this theory. Subjects feel greater frustration during extinction when acquisition involves large rewards than when it involves small rewards because the discrepancy between the subjects' expectations and what they actually receive is larger. Greater frustration means more disruption and thus faster extinction.[58] Similarly, if subjects are given extended training during acquisition, then their expectation for reward increases and, when they receive no reward during extinction, their frustration is enhanced. Again, more frustration means greater disruption and thus less resistance to extinction.[59]

Frustration theory makes an additional and important assumption. Through classical conditioning, the stimulus resulting from the frustration reaction becomes conditioned and later serves as an S_d for the instrumental response. This is an important point because it explains why resistance to extinction is greater for partially reinforced subjects.

During partial-reinforcement acquisition, subjects occasionally experience nonreinforcement, but because other trials involve reward, the overall tendency to execute the response increases. When the animals experience frustration on a nonrewarded trial, the feedback stimulation, called "S_F," generalizes to the start box. That is, the subject experiences S_F when placed back into the start box for the next trial. If the subject proceeds to make the response in the presence of the S_F, and receives reinforcement on that trial, then the association between S_F and the reward is strengthened. In other words, the frustration stimulus, experienced in the start box following a nonrewarded trial, becomes an S_d for the instrumental response. The subject is being reinforced for responding in the presence of frustration cues. The frustration stimulus becomes part of the animal's discriminative-stimulus complex. Then, during extinction, when no reward is given, the frustration stimuli that were conditioned during acquisition continue to evoke the running behavior. Resistance to extinction is strong.

Sequential Hypothesis.

The frustration theory of the partial-reinforcement effect emphasizes the emotional aftereffects of nonreinforcement. The **sequential (aftereffects) hypothesis** is similar in many respects, but it claims that animals have memories of the outcomes of previous trials that are not necessarily emotional in nature.[60] Animals remember the consequence of responding on previous trials.[61] In some cases, those trials were rewarded (R), so the memory aftereffect is for reward (S_R).[62] In other cases, the trials were nonrewarded (N), so the aftereffect is for nonreward (S_N).

A second claim of the sequential theory is that the aftereffects of reward and nonreward become part of the array of stimuli that the animal experiences on the next trial in the start box. During acquisition, when the animal receives reward on every trial, the consistent aftereffect is S_R. This memory becomes one of the discriminative stimuli that elicit the behavior on the next trial. During extinction, S_R is absent (because the animal no longer receives reward), and S_N is now salient. Such dramatic changes in the array of discriminative stimuli constitute a major disruption of the stimulus complex, and thus a reduction in the degree to which these stimuli elicit the behavior.

In other words, the controlling stimuli in the start box are noticeably different during extinction, because S_R is now absent (the subject does not remember receiving reward on the previous trial), and S_N is included (during acquisition, S_N was not present, and therefore, its inclusion in the array of stimuli during extinction is disruptive). When the stimulus complex changes dramatically from acquisition to extinction, then the instrumental response is not elicited. Such a decline in behavior is viewed as response extinction.

Many studies show that a disruption of the stimulus complex during extinction hastens the course of extinction. For example, if subjects are given an extinction trial, but they experience food in a different cage during the intertrial interval, then the aftereffect in the start box on the next trial is S_R, rather than S_N. Here, extinction is retarded.[63] Similarly, extinguished behaviors recover if the animals are given food-related cues prior to the test.[64] Such a procedure facilitates performance by restoring the cues that were present during the original acquisition training. A third finding is that if cues are changed between acquisition and extinction, thus causing even greater deterioration of the stimulus complex than what is produced simply by the omission of reward on the extinction trials, then extinction is even more rapid.[65]

Like the frustration theory, the sequential theory readily explains the effect of reward magnitude and the extent of acquisition on extinction. The greater the magnitude, the more salient the aftereffects of reward during acquisition. During extinction then, omission of a salient S_R produces a greater deficit in the discriminative stimulus complex than omission of a weak S_R. Similarly, the memory for the reward aftereffects is strong after extensive training.

During extinction, when reward is no longer given, the deficit produced by the absence of the S_R, and the disruption produced by the inclusion of S_N, is therefore even greater.[66]

The sequential theory explains the partial-reinforcement effect in the following way. During partial reinforcement acquisition, two kinds of memories are being formed—namely, S_R and S_N. When a subject experiences S_N in the start box but is subsequently given reward for running to the goal box on that trial, the S_N becomes part of the stimulus complex, because running in its presence is followed by reward. In other words, partially reinforced animals are rewarded for responding in the presence of S_N. Partially reinforced animals have S_N built into their discriminative stimulus complex during acquisition and thus tolerate extinction more readily than continuously rewarded animals.

The sequential theory accounts for many of the other effects noted previously. Large rewards during partial-reward acquisition condition S_N more strongly than do small rewards. Similarly, the more partial-reward acquisition trials a subject is given, the more S_N, is built into the stimulus complex, and thus the greater the resistance to extinction later on. In conclusion, the frustration and sequential theories explain the effects of reward magnitude and number of training trials for continuous versus partial reward in a similar fashion. For continuous subjects, the changes that occur during extinction are more drastic with large rewards than they are with small rewards, and thus, disruption of responding is more extensive. For partially reinforced animals, however, the effects are the reverse because S_N (or S_F) is conditioned during acquisition.[67]

INTERIM SUMMARY

The partial-reinforcement effect is an increase in resistance to extinction, following acquisition with intermittent, rather than continuous, reward during acquisition. Large rewards and extended training cause faster extinction after continuous reinforcement, but the reverse occurs after partial reinforcement. Extinction is also affected by the patterns of rewards, for instance, alternating patterns of reward (R) and nonreward (N) lead to faster extinction than do random patterns. The frustration theory claims that subjects experience frustration when they expect reward but do not receive it. Following continuous-reinforcement acquisition, frustration during extinction disrupts responding. During partial-reinforcement training, stimuli associated with the frustration generated on N trials become part of the stimulus complex when they are reinforced on R trials. These conditioned-frustration stimuli continue to elicit behavior during extinction, thus causing greater resistance to extinction. The sequential hypothesis is similar, except that the aftereffects of N and R trials are memories rather than emotional reactions. When there is a disruption in the stimulus complex, then the elicitation of behavior declines. This occurs during extinction following continuous reinforcement. However, during partial-reinforcement acquisition, N aftereffects become part of the stimulus complex and thus continue to elicit the behavior during extinction.

LEARNED HELPLESSNESS

Recall that the critical factor on which instrumental conditioning depends is the contingency between the response and the reinforcing outcome (see Chapter 8). If the animal's response and reward occur randomly with respect to one another, then learning fails to take place. Is this observed effect really the case, however? When the response and reward are independent, does learning fail to occur, or does the animal learn something about their independence? Research on learned helplessness suggests that learning does occur in such a situation. In particular, subjects learn that their behavior is independent of reward. Furthermore, such learning has disruptive effects on future learning.[68]

Examples of Learned Helplessness

The finding that future learning is retarded if the animal previously received uncontrollable outcomes is **learned helplessness.**[69] The phenomenon has been demonstrated in a variety of settings.

Aversive–Aversive Transfer.

In one of the earliest studies, Seligman and Maier (1967) used three groups of dogs. Animals in the escape group were restrained in a hammocklike device and were given unsignaled shocks to their hind feet. However, they were allowed to terminate the shock by pressing either of two panels, located on either side of their snout. Subjects in the yoked group were also placed in the hammock and given the same number and pattern of shocks as the escape animals, but the yoked subjects could not control shock by pressing the panels. They merely received shock whenever the escape animals were shocked. Finally, the no-shock subjects were placed in the restraining hammock and were given no treatment during this phase.[70]

In Phase 2, all animals were treated alike. They were put into a two-compartment shuttle box and taught a normal escape/avoidance reaction. The dogs could avoid the shock by responding during a 10-second warning light, or escape the shock once it came on by jumping to the other side of the box. If the subject did not respond within 60 seconds, the light and the shock were terminated for that trial, and the subject was awarded the maximum response latency of 60 seconds. Thus, the experiment tested whether the prior inescapable shock affected later escape/avoidance learning.

The results are shown in Figure 10-7. Both measures of learning—mean latency to escape (left panel) and mean number of failures to escape (right panel)—showed the same pattern: The escape group learned the new task as easily as the no-shock subjects, but the yoked group showed marked impairment in learning the new escape/avoidance reaction. This deficit in learning is the learned-helplessness phenomenon.[71]

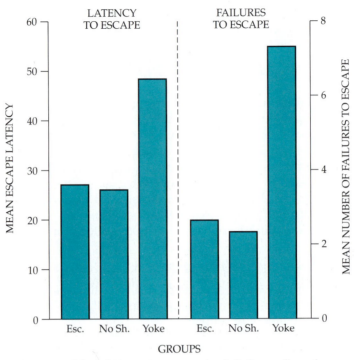

FIGURE 10-7. Mean latency to escape shock (left panel), and mean number of failures to escape (right panel), for the escape (Esc.), no-shock (No Sh.), and yoked (Yoke) groups (after Seligman & Maier, 1967).

The specific design used in this study is important because it equated the escape and yoked groups for shock. Thus, failure by the yoked subjects to learn the new task in Phase 2 cannot have been due simply to having received shock in Phase 1. The escape group received the same pattern of shock, yet they learned the new response easily. The yoked group's failure to learn must have been due to their inability to control shock in Phase 1. No matter what response they performed, behavior was unrelated to the offset of shock. This lack of control, according to the authors, led to the development of the general expectation that behavior is irrelevant to the shock offset. The expectation of lack of control, in turn, transferred to the new situation, causing retardation of learning. In short, the yoked animals performed in Phase 2 as if they were helpless because they developed such an expectation in Phase 1 when they, indeed, were helpless to control shock.[72]

Appetitive–Appetitive Transfer.

According to the theory expressed above, the independence of the behavior and the shock offset produces a general expectancy that the behavior is irrelevant to reward. The consequence of this expectancy is expressed as negative transfer on the learning test (Phase 2). If this is true, then one should observe similar effects in an appetitive conditioning situation. Generally, the same kind of negative transfer, **learned laziness,** has been observed.

For example, in a study by Job (1988), rats were placed in a box and given one of four treatments.[73] The response-contingent animals received continuous food reward for pressing a lever in Phase 1. Subjects in the yoked group received the same number and pattern of food presentations, but the presentations were delivered entirely randomly with respect to the subjects' behavior. The en masse control group received the same number of pellets as the contingent and yoked subjects, except that all of the pellets were placed in the food cup at the start of the session. Finally, a no-reward group was placed in the apparatus but was not given any food. During the test phase, all subjects were trained to make a nose-poke response to earn food. The question was whether the noncontingent delivery of food pellets earlier would cause retardation of learning the nose-poke reaction.

The results are shown in Figure 10-8. Although the contingent, en masse, and no-reward groups showed appreciable learning, the yoked group did not. Thus, failure to control the delivery of food during Phase 1 negatively transferred to Phase 2, when rewards could indeed be earned.[74]

Cross-motivational Transfer.

Some have suggested that the impairment in learning is not due to the transfer of an expectancy, but rather to the fact that the animal undergoes a change in general activity as a result of uncontrollable shock. If, for example,

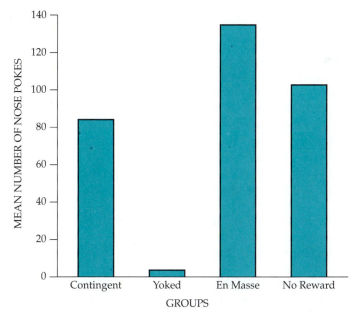

FIGURE 10-8. Mean number of nose pokes on the test for the response-contingent, yoked, en masse control, and no-reward groups (after Job, 1988).

activity declined following uncontrollable shock, then the inferior performance of the yoked subjects may actually be the result of a general decline in activity rather than an expectancy of remaining helpless. The evidence for a decline in general activity, or reactivity to shock, is compelling.[75] Indeed, the more inactivity a subject shows in Phase 1, regardless of the treatment received during that phase, the more the activity declines in the test phase.[76]

There is, however, reason to believe that more is occurring than simply a change in activity. First, studies show negative transfer between appetitive and aversive situations involving markedly different kinds of response tasks. An experiment by Rosellini, DeCola, and Shapiro (1982) provides a good example.[77] They first trained rats to expect food delivery following a light–noise CS (the purpose of this stage was simply to prepare the animals for a discrimination test later on). Two groups of subjects were then formed. One was given inescapable shock, whereas the other was merely placed in the apparatus and given no shock. Finally, in Phase 3, discrimination training was given. Here, a light CS was turned on behind one of two small holes in the front wall, and the subject's task was to poke its nose into the correct hole to earn food. This provided an interesting test of the activity and helplessness hypotheses, because even though a reduction in activity might occur as a result of the inescapable shock, such a change should not affect how well the subjects learned to discriminate between the right and the left holes. The inescapable-shock subjects were unable to learn this simple discrimination. The no-shock subjects, in contrast, readily learned.

The opposite strategy has also been employed—namely, giving subjects noncontingent food presentations and then observing whether they have greater difficulty in learning an aversive task. In several studies, negative transfer has been shown. For instance, Sonoda, Okayasu, and Hirai (1991) used three groups of rats.[78] The response-contingent subjects pressed a lever to receive 100 pellets of food per day.[79] The yoked subjects received food delivery whenever the response-contingent subjects earned a reward. Subjects in the en masse control group were given their entire daily allotment of 100 pellets at the start of each session. Following pretraining, subjects were placed in a shuttle box and allowed to escape shock by running to the other side of the box and back again. Failures to escape were assigned the maximum latency of 60 seconds.

The results are shown in Figure 10-9. The yoked subjects showed virtually no escape learning in Phase 2; their mean latencies were nearly at the maximum. The contingent and en masse groups, however, showed an orderly decline in response latency, indicating effective learning of the escape response.[80]

One of the most interesting demonstrations of the learned-helplessness effect was by Rosellini, DeCola, Plonsky, Warren, and Stilman (1984). Rats in three groups were first trained to poke their nose through a small hole in the wall to receive a food pellet. The escape group was then given 80 trials in which they could escape shock by running to the other side of a shuttle box and back again. The yoked subjects experienced the same shock, but their

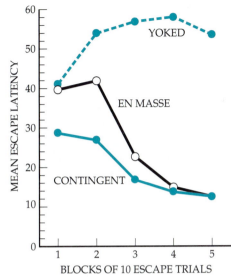

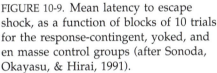

FIGURE 10-9. Mean latency to escape shock, as a function of blocks of 10 trials for the response-contingent, yoked, and en masse control groups (after Sonoda, Okayasu, & Hirai, 1991).

behavior was irrelevant to the shock offset. The no-shock group was simply placed in the apparatus during this phase.

Finally, all subjects were given three test sessions during which a food pellet was delivered randomly about every 10 seconds. Because the nose-poke behavior was no longer needed to produce reward, subjects generally ceased to make the response during this time. The authors predicted that the yoked (helpless) animals should show faster learning of the response-reward independence than the escape animals, because of their persistent expectation that their behavior and the reinforcing outcomes are independent. The other subjects, however, should continue to make the same nose-poke response, thus behaving as if their responding still caused reward to be delivered.

Results of the first test session are shown in Figure 10-10. All of the groups showed a decline in responding over the six time periods, meaning that subjects were learning that the food pellets were delivered without respect to their behavior. However, the yoked (helpless) group showed a greater decline in nose-poking behavior than did the others. This result confirms that inescapable shock affects behavior in an appetitive learning situation and that helplessness is revealed not only by a deficit in learning that behavior controls reward delivery (the conventional demonstration of helplessness), but also by an enhancement in learning that behavior and reward are independent.

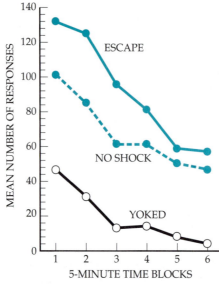

FIGURE 10-10. Mean number of responses over six 5-minute time periods for the prior-escape, yoked, and no-shock groups (after Rosellini, DeCola, Plonsky, Warren, & Stilman, 1984).

Principles of Learned Helplessness

In investigating the learned-helplessness phenomenon, a number of interesting effects have been shown.

Immunization.

One is that subjects may be immunized, or protected, against the effects of inescapable shock by being given prior escapable shock. That is, uncontrollable reinforcers do not impede later learning if subjects experience controllable rewards prior to the helplessness phase.[81] The immunization effects occur even when the response during the **immunization** phase differs from the response during the test phase.

For example, in a study by Williams and Maier (1977), the immunized rats were put into a box containing a small wheel that protruded into the cage and were allowed to terminate shock by turning the wheel a quarter turn. Subjects in the yoked and no-shock groups were merely placed in the apparatus at this time. In Phase 2, subjects in the immunization and helplessness groups were restrained in small plastic tubes and given 80 inescapable 5-second shocks delivered to their tail. The no-shock group was merely restrained in the tubes for about 1.5 hours but did not receive shock. Finally, all subjects were given 30 trials of escape/avoidance training in a shuttle box 24 hours later. Rats could either avoid shock by responding during a 5-second tone, or terminate shock if it came on.

Results of the study are shown in Figure 10-11. The helpless group showed significantly longer latencies than the other groups, indicating that retardation of learning occurred in this task. This is the normal helplessness outcome. The immunized subjects performed essentially no differently than the no-shock control subjects, indicating that exposure to prior escapable shock immunized them against the deleterious effects of the inescapable shock, even when the response used during the immunization phase (wheel turn) differed from that used on the test phase (running).[82]

Learned Mastery.

Experiencing control over the delivery of reinforcers not only eliminates deficits in learning caused by helplessness training (immunization effect), but it also causes animals to be unusually persistent in various learning tasks. This is the **learned-mastery** phenomenon. A good example was shown by Volpicelli, Ulm, Altenor, and Seligman (1983).[83] One group of rats was given 4 days of escape training, in which two lever presses terminated shock.[84] A yoked and a no-shock group were also included. Subjects were tested 24 hours later in a shuttle box. Inescapable shocks were given during each of the four test sessions. Here, the subject could not avoid or escape the shocks, and thus, attempts to do so were expected to decline over time.

The data are shown in Figure 10-12. A decline in performance is seen in the no-shock and yoked groups. The escape subjects, in contrast, continued to

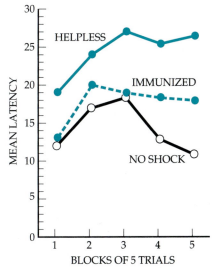

FIGURE 10-11. Mean latency in seconds on the shuttle box escape/ avoidance training, as a function of blocks of five trials for the immunized, helplessness, and no-shock groups (after Williams & Maier, 1977).

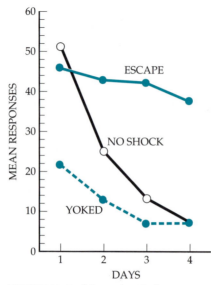

FIGURE 10-12. Mean shuttle-box responses, as a function of 4 days of testing for the escape, yoked, and no-shock group (Volpicelli, Ulm, Altenor, & Seligman, 1983).

respond on the shuttle box test even though their behavior had nothing to do with the offset of shock. Such behavior cannot be explained in terms of the persistence of the original lever-press reaction, because lever pressing competes with shuttle-box avoidance. Lever pressing requires the subject to remain at one location and focus on the lever itself, whereas responding in a shuttle box requires the subject to move from one place to another. Thus, the mastery of the lever-press response did not physically enhance the shuttle-box response. Rather, the animals developed a counterexpectancy during the initial training (that behavior did indeed control the offset of shock), which transferred to the new situation.

As the authors stated, "It follows logically from the Learned Helplessness Theory that experience with controllable events should lead to an expectation of 'there is something I can do to escape.' In new situations, this expectation should: (1) increase motivation to find an escape response, and (2) increase ability to associate responses and outcomes."[85]

Reversibility.

A third finding concerning helplessness—**reversibility**—is that the condition may be corrected. In a study by Seligman, Rosellini, and Kozak (1975), three groups of rats received inescapable shock in Phase 1. All groups showed retardation of learning when later tested on a lever-press escape response. Animals in one of the groups were then forcibly dragged by the shock electrode wires attached to their tails to the area where the bar was located. This had a therapeutic effect, in that these animals eventually learned to press the level more quickly than the animals that did not receive this treatment. Forced responding helped subjects overcome the learning deficit caused by inescapable shock.

Theories of Learned Helplessness

Several theories of learned helplessness have been suggested.

Learned-Helplessness Hypothesis.

The original theory focused on the subject's lack of control over the reinforcing outcomes. According to this position, when the outcomes are independent of the animal's behavior, the subject develops a state of learned helplessness, which is manifest in two ways. First, there is a motivational loss, indicated by a decline in performance and a heightened level of passivity. Second, the subject has a generalized expectation that its behavior will continue to be independent of the reinforcing outcomes. This persistent belief is the cause of the future learning deficit.

The **learned-helplessness hypothesis** has been challenged by studies showing that it is not the lack of control that leads to the learned-helplessness outcome, but rather the inability to predict the US.[86] Two specific findings are relevant to this issue. First, receiving predictable inescapable shock is significantly less damaging to future learning than is receiving unsignaled (unpredictable) shock. In other words, if the inescapable shock is signaled, then the deficit in learning is virtually eliminated.[87]

Second, the presentation of stimuli following the offset of inescapable shock eliminates the learned-helplessness deficit. For example, in a study by Jackson and Minor (1988), rats in the escape group received 100 unsignaled escape trials in which the shock was terminated when they turned a small wheel 360°.[88] Two yoked groups received shock whenever the escape subjects were shocked. For the yoked–feedback group, the house light was turned off for 5 seconds whenever the shock went off. Subjects in the yoked–no-feedback group, on the other hand, experienced the house light throughout the session; they were given no feedback stimulus signaling shock offset. Finally, a no-shock control group was used. Twenty-four hours after the initial treatments, the rats were tested in a shuttle box, where they ran to the other side of the box and back again to terminate shock.

The results are shown in Figure 10-13. The escape and no-shock groups performed better than the yoked–no-feedback group, thus showing the typical helplessness effect. The yoked–feedback subjects, however, learned as well as the escape and the no-shock animals. In other words, receiving a feedback stimulus following shock offset eliminated the deficit in learning that is normally caused by inescapable shock.

Anxiety Hypothesis.

The **anxiety hypothesis** was developed by Overmier, Minor, and their colleagues, as an alternative to the learned-helplessness hypothesis. It claims that

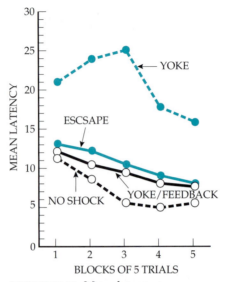

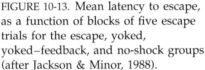

FIGURE 10-13. Mean latency to escape, as a function of blocks of five escape trials for the escape, yoked, yoked–feedback, and no-shock groups (after Jackson & Minor, 1988).

animals who receive inescapable shock become chronically anxious, and that such a stressful experience causes them to learn poorly later on.[89]

Helpless animals develop a chronic state of anxiety because the shock is unpredictable and inescapable. There are virtually no periods of time when the animal feels relief from the stress. Not only does inescapable shock engender chronic fear, but it also induces various biochemical abnormalities that may explain why animals that are experiencing chronic anxiety show a deficit in learning later on.[90]

Although subjects recover from the effects of inescapable shock, there is also a more permanent form of the condition based on the odor from the stress, as shown in a study by Minor and LoLordo (1984). Rats were given either escapable shock, inescapable shock, or no shock, in an apparatus containing a small wheel. The escape animals terminated shock by turning the wheel 360°. The yoked subjects received the same shocks, but they had no control over them. The no-shock control subjects were merely placed on the apparatus for the same length of time.

A day later, all rats received 40 escape trials, in which shock could be terminated by pressing a lever three times. For half of the subjects, the same odors were present in both the training and the test phases. This is the dirty condition because the soil trays under the apparatus were not cleaned between phases. For the other half of the subjects, in the clean condition, the apparatus was thoroughly cleaned with a disinfectant and deodorizing agent and was sprinkled with a potent-smelling after-shave solution before being used.[91]

The results are shown in Figure 10-14. The helplessness effect was evident only in the dirty condition. Specifically, the yoked–dirty subjects took significantly longer to respond than either the escape or the no-shock groups. The performance deficit was not shown in the clean condition, however, suggesting that if stress odors are removed, then no learned-helplessness effect is shown. Later experiments confirmed that merely exposing animals to the odor of stressed subjects did not impair performance on the test. A deficit in learning was observed only when the animals received inescapable shocks *and* experienced the stress odors on the test.

Why do stress odors induce helplessness? The answer is not entirely clear, but some believe that the odors trigger a conditioned depletion of neurochemicals, and thus reinstate the stress experienced earlier.[92] Minor, Dess, and Overmier (1991) summarized the anxiety theory in the following way: "Subjects [that] are unable to discriminate between dangerous and safe periods during exposure to unsignaled inescapable shock . . . remain chronically afraid throughout the pretreatment session. . . . [such] Chronic fear has two immediate effects that contribute to later performance deficits. First, odors in the pretreatment environment become strongly associated with inescapable shock and serve as critical retrieval cues during later testing.

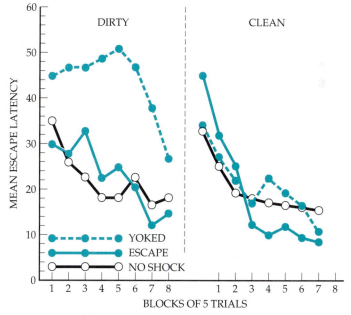

FIGURE 10-14. Mean lever-press escape latencies, as a function of blocks of five trials for the escape, yoked, and no-shock groups, tested with the stress odor (dirty) or without the stress odor (clean) (after Minor & LoLordo, 1984).

Second, excess time in fear has nonassociative effects, as exemplified by enhanced neophobia."[93]

Chronic fear is critical to the learned-helplessness effect, and signaling of relief eliminates helplessness. Does this mean that feedback signals cause a decrease in the level of chronic fear? The answer is yes. For example, Mineka, Cook, and Miller (1984) trained rats to press a lever to terminate a shock that had been preceded by a tone.[94] A light was turned off for 3 seconds following shock offset for the yoked–feedback group, but not for the yoked–no-feedback subjects. Over 3 test days, fear of the warning signal was measured in terms of freezing behavior, both prior to and during the tone.

Results are shown in Figure 10-15. Little freezing was evident in any of the groups prior to the tone (left panel). During the tone, however, the yoked–no-feedback group showed considerable freezing, whereas the yoked–feedback group did not (right panel). Thus, the study confirms that a feedback stimulus attenuates chronic fear.[95]

This result supports the anxiety hypothesis. Escape animals show less fear (and no learning deficit) because the internal stimuli that are created by movement of the muscles constitute feedback signals. In other words, escape subjects produce their own response-produced feedback signals when they escape shock. Yoked animals, in contrast, do not produce their own feedback signals,

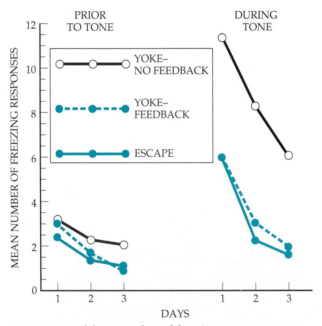

FIGURE 10-15. Mean number of freezing responses per day prior to and during the tone CS for the escape, yoked–feedback, and yoked–no-feedback groups (after Mineka, Cook, & Miller, 1984).

although if the subjects are given external feedback cues, then fear declines and the learning deficit is reduced.[96] In short, the anxiety hypothesis suggests that when a signal predicts shock offset, the animals feel less fear. With less fear, then the odor-mediated fear does not produce the helplessness effect later on.[97]

The anxiety hypothesis highlights the role of stress odors as mediators of the learned-helplessness effect. Chronic anxiety is established during inescapable shock, unless subjects are given feedback stimuli. Such anxiety, which is mediated by odors that are present during the learning test, causes a deficit in learning. The anxiety hypothesis, however, does not clearly specify how odors mediate the learning deficit. One possibility is that they elicit a conditioned depletion of norepinephrine, an essential brain neurochemical.[98] Another is that excessive fear in the inescapable group causes a reduction in activity (or even freezing) on the test. The reduced level of activity is incompatible with performance of the learned reaction.[99]

The anxiety hypothesis accounts for several facts. For example, anxiety is stronger following inescapable shock than after escapable shock, feedback reduces anxiety, and odor-mediated anxiety triggers a learning deficit. The theory, however, cannot explain the fact that anxiety itself may be unnecessary for the learning deficit to occur.

Such a result was shown by Maier (1990).[100] On the first day of training, each of the rats was restrained in a small plastic tube, and a shock electrode was attached to each rat's tail. Two groups received inescapable shock; two groups did not. One day later, subjects were measured for their fear (freezing) reactions during a 10-minute period and then were given an escape-learning test in a shuttle box.[101] Prior to the test, one of the two inescapable groups and one of the two no-shock groups was given an injection of the drug diazepam, which is a well-known sedative that reduces fear.[102] The other inescapable and no-shock groups were given an injection of a harmless placebo substance.

If anxiety is responsible for the learning deficit, then the inescapable–drug animals should show both freezing and a learning deficit. If, however, the diazepam reduces fear in these subjects (less freezing), but they still show the learning deficit, then the learned-helplessness outcome cannot be based exclusively on anxiety. This result was found. The freezing data are shown in Figure 10-16. Freezing was very low in the two no-shock groups, and in the inescapable–drug group that had received diazepam. This finding confirms the claim that diazepam reduces fear. Predictably, fear was high in the inescapable shock group that was given a placebo.[103]

Performance on the escape task is shown in Figure 10-17. *Both* inescapable-shock groups showed considerable elevation in their latency scores, indicating poor learning of the escape response, despite the fact that the inescapable-shock–drug animals had earlier demonstrated little fear on the freezing measure. The learned-helplessness phenomenon, therefore, cannot be fully explained in terms of the continued presence of anxiety. Although anxiety is present in inescapable-shock animals under normal conditions, the anxiety itself is not necessary for producing the learning deficit.

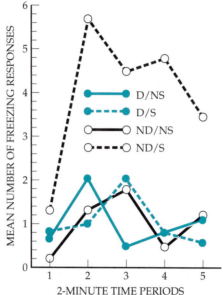

FIGURE 10-16. Mean number of freezing responses, as a function of 2-minute time periods on the initial fear test for the inescapable-shock–drug (D/S), inescapable-shock–no-drug (ND/S), no-shock–drug (D/NS), and no-shock–no-drug groups (ND/NS) (after Maier, 1990).

Cognitive-Processing Theory.

According to the **cognitive-processing theory of learned helplessness,** subjects that receive inescapable shock change the way in which they later process information.[104] Helpless animals learn less efficiently, regardless of their anxiety state. This was shown in a study by Jackson, Alexander, and Maier (1980).[105] Two groups of rats were given inescapable shock to the tail (the intensity was 1.0 milliamps) while being restrained in a plastic tube. Two no-shock control groups were simply restrained for an equal period of time. On the test, escape learning was given in a Y-maze. Here, the subject's task was to run from a start box to a goal box, but shock was terminated only if the subject entered the left alleyway.[106] The purpose of this study was to determine whether the subjects would show a deficit in discrimination learning, independent of whether they show a decline in running speed (which most studies of learned helplessness use as evidence for a learning deficit). The shock intensity in the Y-maze test was the same as before (1.0 milliamp) for

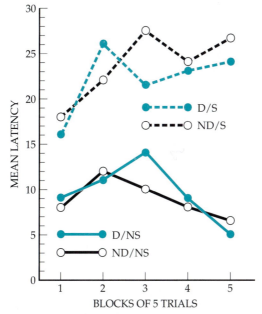

FIGURE 10-17. Mean latency to escape shock
on the test, as a function of blocks of five
training trials for the inescapable-
shock–drug (D/S), inescapable-shock–no-
drug (ND/S), no-shock–drug (D/NS), and
no-shock–no-drug groups (ND/NS) (after
Maier, 1990).

one of the inescapable-shock and no-shock groups, but shock was increased
to 2.0 milliamps for the other two groups.[107]

The latency to respond is shown in Figure 10-18. Learned helplessness was
evident only when the weaker shock was used (left panel). When the shock
intensity was increased, no group differences were found (right panel). These
data, therefore, suggest that the higher shock level reduced the motivational
deficit normally shown by the helplessness animals. Stated differently, the
more intense shock caused the helpless animals to run as fast as subjects in
the no-shock group.

The choice behaviors are shown in Figure 10-19. The no-escape subjects
tested with the 1.0-milliamp shock showed an orderly decline in errors, but
the inescapable-shock animals showed appreciable errors throughout the
test (left panel). This difference reflects the effect of inescapable shock on
discrimination learning. When the more intense shock was used, the no-
shock animals performed as poorly as the inescapable-shock animals.
Increasing the shock intensity therefore eliminated the deficit, as measured

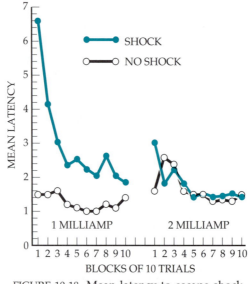

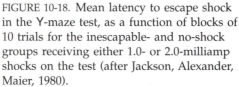

FIGURE 10-18. Mean latency to escape shock in the Y-maze test, as a function of blocks of 10 trials for the inescapable- and no-shock groups receiving either 1.0- or 2.0-milliamp shocks on the test (after Jackson, Alexander, Maier, 1980).

by running speed (Figure 10-18), but did not change the deficit, as measured by discrimination accuracy (Figure 10-19). Stated differently, the inescapable-shock animals showed an inability to solve the discrimination problem, regardless of the intensity of shock, although they ran faster with the more intense shock. Inescapable shock caused a cognitive deficit. Helpless subjects were unable to learn the discrimination effectively, even though they were able to run as fast as the controls with the higher shock level.[108]

What cognitive abilities do helpless animals lack? One possibility is a lack of attention.[109] Minor, Jackson, and Maier, (1984), for example, showed that inescapable-shock rats are more susceptible to the disruptive effects of irrelevant cues than are escape or no-shock subjects. In one of their experiments, two groups were given inescapable tail shock, and two no-shock groups were simply restrained in the plastic tubes. One day later, all groups received 100 escape trials in a Y-maze. For one inescapable-shock and one no-shock group, however, irrelevant and distracting light cues were presented during the learning task. Specifically, one of the alleyways in the apparatus was illuminated for the duration of the trial, and the order of illumination was randomly determined. For the other inescapable-shock and no-shock groups, no such distracting cues were given. The learned-helpless-

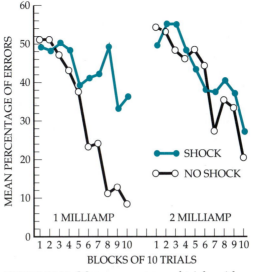

FIGURE 10-19. Mean percentage of trials with one or more errors, as a function of blocks of 10 Y-maze escape trials for the inescapable- and no-shock groups receiving either 1.0- or 2.0-milliamp shocks on the test (after Jackson, Alexander, Maier, 1980).

ness effect was observed only when the distracting cues were present. According to the cognitive-processing theory, the inescapable-shock animals were distracted by the irrelevant lights, making correct performance more difficult to achieve.[110]

INTERIM SUMMARY

Learned helplessness occurs when a subject's behavior and the USs are independent. In the typical learned-helplessness design, an escape group is allowed to escape shock, a yoked (helplessness) group receives the same number and pattern of shocks but is unable to control them, and a no-shock group receives no shocks. Later, all groups are given a learning test—for example, an avoidance task. The yoked group shows retardation of learning (the manifestation of learned helplessness). Similar results are found in appetitive situations, and when the pretreatment is one (either aversive or appetitive), but the learning task is the other. Subjects may be immunized against the effects of inescapable shock by being given prior escapable shock. Learned mastery is shown by the escape animals, who continue to perform an escape reaction as if it were still effective. Helplessness is reversed when the animals are forced to respond once escape has become possible. The learned-helplessness theory argues that subjects develop an expectancy that their behavior lacks control, and this belief persists on future learning tasks. The anxiety hypothesis argues that retardation of learning occurs because inescapable shock causes chronic anxiety. The anxiety is mediated by stress odors that occur during the inescapable-shock phase. If anxiety is reduced, for example, by the use of feedback cues, then retardation is diminished. The cognitive-processing theory says that subjects that receive inescapable shock change the way in which they process information. Specifically, they are more susceptible to the disruptive effects of irrelevant cues.

ENDNOTES

1. Miles (1956).
2. Schaal and Branch (1988).
3. See Kaufman and Baron (1969); Schuster (1969) for reviews.
4. If the red stimulus was a secondary reinforcer, then it would be proper to call the green stimulus a "tertiary reinforcer"—that is, a conditioned reward twice removed from primary reward.
5. The chaining technique has also been used with conditioned stimuli, based on shock offset. Dinsmoor and Clayton (1963), for instance, trained rats to press a lever during shock. The lever response produced a noise lasting 30 seconds, after which a different response (pushing against a response key with their nose) terminated both the noise and the shock. The noise was paired with shock offset and thus was a secondary reinforcer. The results confirmed that subjects pressed the lever when it resulted in the onset of the noise. When lever pressing no longer produced the noise, the frequency of pressing declined.
6. Recall from Chapter 3 that such a truly random control procedure leads to little Pavlovian conditioning of the CS.
7. Hyde (1976) studied an additional treatment, the CS condition, but discussion of this group is omitted for the sake of brevity.
8. Studies have also used the acquisition technique to demonstrate secondary reinforcement, based on the pairing of the CS with shock offset. Kinsman and Bixenstine (1968), for example, trained rats to escape shock by running to the opposite side of the cage during a flashing light (S_1); see also Murray and Strandberg (1965). Immediately following the response, a buzzer (S_2) was given for 0.5 seconds. The buzzer was expected to become a conditioned reinforcer because of its association with shock offset. To test that possibility, a lever was inserted into the cage, and subjects were given 0.5 seconds of either S_1 or S_2 following each lever-press response. The group that got S_2 showed the higher frequency of lever pressing, indicating that the stimulus had become a positive secondary reinforcer through its association with shock offset.
9. These properties accrue even though the delay between the onset of the cue and the reward may, at times, may be appreciable.
10. Butter and Thomas (1958) (magnitude); Bersh (1951) (immediacy).
11. Hyde (1976).
12. See Schuster (1969).
13. Dinsmoor (1950).

14. See Hendry (1969).
15. The reinforcing and signaling properties of a cue have been separated using a chaining technique. For example, Ferster (1953) trained pigeons to peck a key during S_2 to produce S_1. During S_1, however, the pigeons were required not to peck. If the subject refrained from pecking for 1 minute, it was rewarded; otherwise, a peck reset the timing mechanism, and food was delayed. Under these conditions, pecking was maintained during S_2, presumably because S_1 was a secondary reinforcer. The finding does not support the discriminative-stimulus hypothesis because S_1 was not an S_d for pecking; in fact, it was an S_d for *not* pecking.
16. See Davidson and McCarthy (1987) for a review.
17. Brownstein (1971); but see Logue and Chavarro (1987); Todorov (1973).
18. In many studies using pigeon subjects, reward magnitude is often specified in terms of access time to the feeder because, unlike rat experiments, no discrete amount of reward is dispensed.
19. Similar effects have been found for reinforcers that differ in quality—for example, different kinds of grain that pigeons find differently attractive; see Miller (1976).
20. Chung and Herrnstein (1967); but see Logue and Chavarro (1987) and Snyderman (1983) for discrepant results.
21. See also Miller (1976).
22. See also de Villiers (1974).
23. See also Farley (1980).
24. The model supported by de Villiers was not the only theory tested. The reward for a given response a might also equal the quantity $(F_a + P_b)$. This represents the appetitive outcome for that response (namely, F_a) plus the reinforcement derived from *avoiding* the punished response b (which is P_b). The additive and subtractive models make different quantitative predictions about choice behavior; de Villiers's data supported the subtractive model.
25. de Villiers and Herrnstein (1976); Herrnstein (1970, 1974).
26. The equation used by Houston (1986) was Baum's generalized matching formula (see subsequent discussion).
27. See Ainslie (1974, 1975).
28. See Logue, Forzano, and Tobin (1992).
29. Rachlin, Logue, Gibbon, and Frankel (1986); but see Sonuga-Barke, Lea, and Webley (1989).
30. Ainslie (1974).
31. See Logue (1988); Logue, Forzano, and Tobin (1992).
32. Recall that humans often do not show the same response patterns on reinforcement schedules as rats and pigeons because of their ability to generate self-instructions concerning the schedules (see Chapter 9).
33. Logue (1988).
34. Grosch and Neuringer (1981).
35. The authors also had two control groups, which were fed at the same time as these experimental subjects but were not required to make the running response.
36. Rachlin and Green (1972); see also Logue and Pena-Correal (1984).
37. See also Baum (1979); McSweeney, Melville, and Whipple (1983).
38. Wearden and Burgess (1982) show that undermatching is, by far, the more common error; it occurs in a preponderance of studies on matching.
39. The behavior on a concurrent VR–VR schedule is predicted by the matching formula, but only in a trivial sense. Subjects that devote 100% of their responding

to, say, the VR-5 side would be complying to the matching law (20 divided by [0 + 20] equals 100%). The problem is that the same prediction is made with reference to the less preferred lever, the VR-10 choice. Here, 10 divided by (10 + 0) also equals 100%.

40. See Rachlin, Battalio, Kagel, and Green (1981); Rachlin, Green, Kagel, and Battalio (1976); Staddon and Motheral (1978).
41. Baum (1981); Heyman and Herrnstein (1986); Rachlin, Green, and Tormey (1988); Williams (1985).
42. Rachlin, Green, and Tormey (1988).
43. See Herrnstein and Vaughan (1980); Vaughan (1981).
44. See Williams and Royalty (1989).
45. See Robbins (1971).
46. See also Capaldi, Lanier, and Godbout (1968); Leonard (1969).
47. See Anderson (1963).
48. Sytsma and Dyal (1973) furthermore showed that variability of reward magnitude affects resistance to extinction. Two groups were trained in two alleyways. One received 10 pellets in both goal boxes; the other always got 10 in one, but 1 or 10 in the other. Having received variable reward magnitude caused these latter subjects to persist longer than the first group in the constant-amount alleyway (see later in this chapter for more discussion of reward-magnitude patterns).
49. Bacon (1962); Hill and Spear (1963); Wilson (1964).
50. Partial-reinforcement subjects are more resistant to extinction than continuously reinforced animals, even after experiencing only a few acquisition trials; see Capaldi and Deutsch (1967).
51. Capaldi (1958).
52. Interestingly, with a small number of training trials, this principle is reversed; that is, an alternating pattern leads to greater resistance to extinction than does a random one (see Capaldi & Hart, 1962).
53. See also Mellgren, Seybert, and Dyck (1978).
54. Amsel (1958, 1962, 1972, 1992); see also Daly (1991) and Daly and Daly (1982).
55. See also Hughes and Dachowski (1973), but see Matzel (1985). The demonstration by Zaslav and Porter (1974) used a lever box to show the energization effect of frustration on behavior. It was meant to serve as an operant analog to a study by Amsel and Roussel (1952), who first demonstrated the effect in a double alleyway; see Scull (1973) for a review.
56. Sgro (1969) showed that the frustration effect is also found when reward is delayed following completion of the first response requirement, but see Sgro, Glotfelty, and Moore (1970).
57. To this extent, frustration resembles fear (see Bertsch & Leitenberg, 1970; Daly, 1970; Linden & Hallgren, 1973, Wagner, 1969a; but also see Fallon, 1971). That is, subjects escape from conditions of frustration just as they escape from fear situations; see Daly (1970).
58. Brooks (1975); see Bower (1962), Daly (1968), Peckham and Amsel (1967).
59. Senkowski and Vogel (1976); Stimmel and Adams (1969); Yelen (1969).
60. Capaldi (1966, 1967, 1992, 1994).
61. Capaldi and Spivey (1964).
62. In earlier versions of the aftereffects hypothesis, by Sheffield (1949), aftereffects of reward were thought to be the lingering taste of food on the animal's tongue.
63. Capaldi, Hart, and Stanley (1963).
64. Homzie (1974).

65. Capaldi and Spivey (1963); Welker and McAuley (1978).
66. Capaldi (1964).
67. See Capaldi and Capaldi (1970).
68. The case is the same for Pavlovian conditioning. For example, Baker and Mackintosh (1979) showed that random CS and US presentations lead to future retardation of excitatory conditioning. Their theory is that an animal learns that the CS is irrelevant to the US occurrence and thus, later on, has difficulty in learning that the two are, indeed, correlated.
69. See Maier and Seligman (1976); Maier, Seligman, and Solomon (1969); Seligman, Maier, and Solomon (1971) for reviews of the early literature.
70. The term yoke is derived from the idea of an oxen yoke, which ties the animals movement together, such that movement by one causes a similar movement by the other. Here, subjects are yoked, or tied, in terms of the patterns of shock.
71. Animals that receive noncontingent shocks show deficits in later learning, even though a vastly different kind of response and reward are involved. Altenor, Kay, and Richter (1977), for example, gave rats inescapable shock in Phase 1 and found that it interfered with learning to escape from water.
72. Learned helplessness has been shown many times in humans, as well as in other animal species (see Hiroto & Seligman, 1975), and has served as the basis for a theory of human depression, although the principles are more involved than described here; see Peterson and Seligman (1984).
73. See also Job (1987); Tomie, Murphy, Fath, and Jackson (1980); Wasserman and Molina (1975); Wheatley, Welker, and Miles (1977).
74. Job (1988) actually conducted a more complicated experiment than described here, showing that the negative transfer occurred only when the nose-poke hole was present during Phase 1 and the lever was absent from the apparatus in Phase 2.
75. Anisman, deCatanzaro, and Remington (1978); Rosellini and DeCola (1981). Furthermore, Drugan and Maier (1982) have shown that the reduction in activity as a result of inescapable shock is not due to adventitious reinforcement of a freezing reaction.
76. Balleine and Soames Job (1991).
77. See also Caspy and Lubow (1981).
78. See also Goodkin (1976). Rosellini (1978) found that the negative transfer occurred only when the appetitive instrumental response was rather difficult.
79. The schedule involved continuous reinforcement on Day 1, FR-5 on Day 2, and FR-20 on Day 3.
80. Negative transfer as a result of inescapable aversive stimulation, or noncontingent food delivery, has even been shown using a Pavlovian learning task in Phase 2. For example, Baker (1976) demonstrated that rats are deficient in learning to suppress their lever pressing in a CER task if they received inescapable shock previously. If inescapable shock merely causes subjects to be less active (and such inactivity is mistaken for poor learning on the test), then, if anything, lever-press suppression should be more pronounced, not weaker, following inescapable shock. Similarly, Dess, Raizer, Chapman, and Garcia (1988) showed that inescapable shock later causes the retardation of a conditioned taste aversion. Again, if the transfer is due merely to inactivity, then better, not worse, taste avoidance should be observed.
81. See Seligman, Rosellini, and Kozak (1975). Troisi, Bersh, Stromberg, Mauro, and Whitehouse (1991) showed that immunization effects are absent if subjects receive extended exposure to inescapable shock. The reason may be that subjects

discriminate periods in which shocks are escapable from those in which shocks are not.

82. The immunization effect has also been demonstrated in terms of how easily subjects learn that behavior and rewards are independent; see Ferrandiz and Pardo (1990).

83. See also Sonoda and Hirai (1993).

84. On the first two days of training, each lever press terminated shock.

85. Volpicelli, Ulm, Altenor, and Seligman (1983, p. 218).

86. See Overmier (1985).

87. Overmier (1985); Overmier and Wielkiewicz (1983). Overmier (1985, Experiment 2) also demonstrated that the lack of predictability of a shock caused interference with learning a Pavlovian reaction. Such a deficit was abolished when the inescapable shocks were signaled.

88. See also Volpicelli, Ulm, and Altenor (1984).

89. See Minor, Dess, and Overmier (1991).

90. Dess, Linwick, Patterson, Overmier, and Levine (1983); Weiss, Goodman, Losito, Corrigan, Charry, and Bailey (1981).

91. Furthermore, the cages were washed in an acid solution and a sodium hydroxide solution prior to being rinsed thoroughly in water.

92. Minor and LoLordo (1984) showed that an artificial odor, such as peppermint, which was present during the inescapable-shock phase and the test, was sufficient to produce this condition of helplessness.

93. Minor, Dess, and Overmier (1991, p. 101).

94. See also Overmier (1985).

95. Mineka, Cook, and Miller (1984) also showed that even when the shock was not signaled, reduced fear reactions to the apparatus were made by subjects that were given feedback.

96. See Mineka, Cook, and Miller (1984); Jackson and Minor (1988), respectively. However, the decline in fear with feedback stimuli does not always occur. As shown by Rosellini, DeCola, and Warren (1986) the effect is found only when a relatively long intertrial interval is used. Some suggest that different mechanisms are operating in the decline in fear with feedback stimuli and in the effect of control. DeCola, Rosellini, and Warren (1988), for example, showed that feedback following shock offset did not affect how persistent a subject was during a noncontingent food test. The subjects that could control the shock, however, were more persistent during such a test. The study therefore suggests that feedback from shock offset and control over shock, although both eliminate later retardation of learning, do not necessarily have the same effect for persistence of behavior on a noncontingent food test.

97. Minor, Trauner, Lee, and Dess (1990) also showed that the deficit is eliminated if the offset of shock, as opposed to the onset of the no-shock period, is signaled. This is called "cessation training."

98. Weiss, Goodman, Losito, Corrigan, Charry, and Bailey (1981).

99. Anisman, deCatanzaro, and Remington (1978).

100. See also Maier (1989).

101. Subjects were actually then given two escape trials and an additional 20-minute observation period prior to the more extended learning test. These data showed essentially the same pattern of results as those reported in the text.

102. Dantzer (1977).

103. Maier (1990) also included subjects that were given the opiate antagonist, naltrexone hydrochloride, which reduces the learning deficit but not the fear. For the sake of brevity, these results are not included in this discussion.
104. This position actually represents a revised version of the learned-helplessness theory.
105. See also Maier and Jackson (1979).
106. Because the start box changed from one trial to the next, the left alleyway was not a single location, but rather a left turn.
107. In Experiment 3, an intermediate value of shock, 1.6 milliamps, was also used.
108. Rosellini, DeCola, and Shapiro (1982) showed a similar finding using appetitive conditioning.
109. Barber and Winefield (1986).
110. Another possibility is that the subject's response is not salient. As shown by Maier, Jackson, and Tomie (1987), if responding is accompanied by a signal, then learning is normal. According to those authors, the stimulus draws attention to the escape response, thus allowing the response to become more strongly associated with the reinforcing outcome—namely, shock offset.

CHAPTER 11

Theoretical Perspectives in Instrumental Conditioning

As discussed in previous chapters, one of the most important concepts in instrumental learning is the notion of reinforcement contingency. When a reinforcing outcome, such as the presentation of food or the termination of a shock, is contingent on a response, then the probability of that behavior increases accordingly.[1] The concept of a reinforcement contingency itself implies very little about the underlying nature of reward or the way in which a response and a reward become associated. There are, however, various theoretical perspectives that address this issue (see Chapter 2). These perspectives include the cognitive, mechanistic, and behavioral-regulation viewpoints. The purpose of this chapter is to describe specific theories that fall into these major classifications.

PHYSIOLOGICAL MECHANISMS OF LEARNING

Neural structures represent one kind of behavioral mechanism. Many argue that learning involves a structural or chemical change in the nervous system. This is an appealing idea. In fact, it is impossible to imagine how behavior, in theory at least, could be initiated without some physiological mechanism being involved. Research on the neurophysiology of learning therefore provides a valuable perspective on the nature of the learning process.

Biological Substrates of Memory

One important focus in this area of research is the neurological basis for memory. Because memory is a unit of acquired behavior that persists through time, it makes sense that memories are encoded neurologically at specific sites in the brain.[2]

Early Research.

Some of the earliest research was carried out by Lashley (1929). Lashley's strategy was to damage or remove selected areas of the brain and then to conduct tests of learning. Usually, the test determined whether the subject could learn to negotiate a complicated maze (examples are shown in Figure 11-1). If the subject did not learn, then Lashley concluded that the area of the brain that had been damaged was the neurological basis of learning. Generally, Lashley's results were quite surprising. The destruction of as much as one half of the cortical tissue had very little effect on the learning of simple mazes, although performance in more difficult mazes was affected to some degree.

Lashley formulated two principles to account for these results. First, the principle of **equipotentiality** claimed that other areas of the brain take over the functions of a damaged area; no one part of the cortex is more important than another for learning tasks such as these. Second, the principle of **mass action** asserted that the cortical areas of the brain are not specialized. Efficiency of performance declines as a function of the total mass of tissue destroyed, but the deficits are not selective.

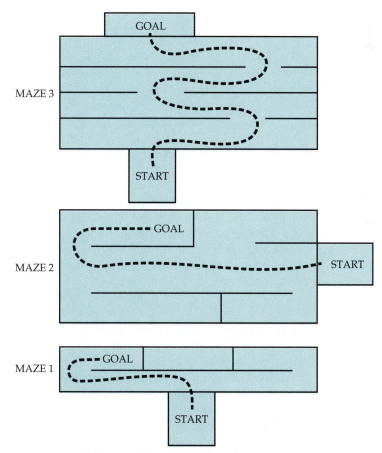

FIGURE 11-1. Schematic diagram of several mazes used by Lashley to investigate the neurological basis of learning (after Lashley, 1929).

Lashley's work was important in stimulating an interest in the neurological basis of learning, but it produced little support for the notion that memories are encoded at specific sites in the brain. Later work by Penfield and colleagues, however, did provide a more encouraging picture.[3] As a neurosurgeon, Penfield operated on severely epileptic patients to remove areas of the brain that were susceptible to seizure. To identify these areas, Penfield stimulated brain tissue and then determined whether the area was susceptible to seizures by observing the patient's behavior. Here, the patient needed to be awake and thus able to behave in a revealing manner.[4]

Penfield's remarkable finding was that stimulation of particular areas of the brain often caused the patient to express vivid memories. At certain times, the patients felt emotions such as fear; at other times, they had flashbacks to specific events. One patient, for example, reported, "That music, from the stage hit 'Guys and Dolls' . . . I was listening to it."[5] Another said, "Now I hear people laughing—my friends in South Africa . . . yes they are my two cousins, Bessie and Anne Wheliaw."[6]

Modern research has disputed whether these results actually demonstrate localization of specific memories. Many responses were more like dreams or hallucinations than like detailed memories.[7] Nevertheless, Penfield's results supported the notion that memories reside in specific anatomical locations.

An influential theory of the neurological foundations of learning was proposed by Hebb (1949). According to this theory, when several neurons are repeatedly stimulated in succession, structural changes at the synapse occur. Knobs or buttons develop on the axon. As Hebb noted, "when one cell repeatedly assists in firing another, the axon of the first cell develops synaptic knobs (or enlarges them if they already exist) in contact with the soma [cell body or nucleus] of the second cell."[8] After developing knobs, clusters of neurons form larger functional units, termed **cell assemblies.** If one neuron in the cell assembly is activated, then others are also triggered. Groups of cell assemblies, in turn, form even larger collections of neurological material, termed **phase sequences.** Thus, although not identifying the location of the neurological units, Hebb argued that, in theory, memories are based on an interconnecting web of cell assemblies.[9]

Contemporary Research.

Considerable progress has been made in recent years in demonstrating the importance of various anatomical locations, or biochemical substances, for memory formation. For example, memory may be related to changes in brain ribonucleic acid.[10] It also may be affected by various hormones, such as brain catecholamines, pituitary hormones, and peptides.[11] Some argue that memories result from changes in the synaptic efficiency in neural pathways.[12] These changes are the by-products of protein synthesis (proteins regulate the production or uptake of neural transmitters that are responsible for communication between nerves) or changes in the receptivity of the neurons. If mice are given a substance that inhibits the synthesis of a protein called "cycloheximide," for example, retention is unaffected for about 15 minutes but deteriorates by about 3 hours.

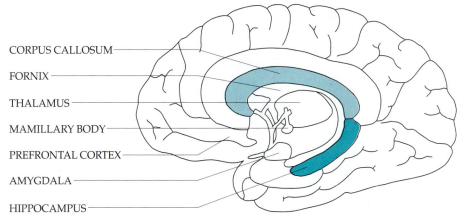

CORPUS CALLOSUM

FORNIX

THALAMUS

MAMILLARY BODY

PREFRONTAL CORTEX

AMYGDALA

HIPPOCAMPUS

FIGURE 11-2. Schematic drawing of some of the important structures in the brain that have been shown to be involved in memory processes.

In terms of anatomical locations for memory, the **hippocampus** has been identified as being important.[13] As shown in Figure 11-2, the hippocampus is a large bilateral structure; each half is shaped like a cashew nut. It is neurologically interesting because of its unique interconnections and its special role in the memory process.[14] Damage to the hippocampus produces impairment in short-term memory formation.[15] Humans who have suffered damage of this sort show marked impairment in the formation of new memories, particularly spatial memories, although older memories are not affected.[16]

One important characteristic of the hippocampus is that it develops **long-term potentiation,** which is an enduring increase in the postsynaptic responsivity following a period of stimulation. In other words, for several weeks following stimulation, various neural circuits in the hippocampus show greater sensitivity to new stimulation (as much as a 200–300% increase). Such long-term potentiation of neural activity may be involved in the formation of memory.[17]

Neurological Mechanisms of Reinforcement

In addition to theories dealing with the neurological basis of memory, several theories focus more directly on the physiological mechanisms that underlie the learning process itself—specifically, the anatomical and biochemical basis for reward.

Electrical Self-stimulation.

Olds and Milner (1954) made a remarkable discovery when they showed that rats, fitted with thin wire electrodes that terminated in the septal area of their brain, pressed a lever to deliver themselves a small electrical current.[18] In the original experiment, subjects were stimulated with weak electrical impulses.[19] Stimulation continued as long as the lever was pressed.

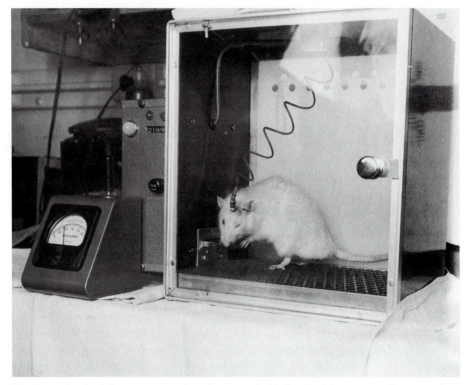

Photograph of a laboratory rat administering itself electrical brain stimulation. Whenever the rat presses the lever, a minute electrical current is delivered to various "pleasure" centers in the brain. Such reward maintains lever pressing.

On average, subjects that received septal stimulation pressed on 85% of each successive 30-second period. Subjects that had electrodes placed in other areas of the brain pressed much less. In fact, most of them pressed less than 6% of the time.[20]

Another noted study, by Delgado, Roberts, and Miller (1954), showed that stimulation of other parts of the brain may have quite different effects. Specifically, subjects in these studies pressed levers to terminate brain stimulation. Such a result suggests that the stimulation was aversive.[21]

Since the time of its discovery, the self-stimulation phenomenon has been replicated in countless experiments involving many different species, including humans.[22] Two implications are derived from this work. First, the anatomical sites that support self-stimulation constitute a kind of **pleasure center.** Stated differently, subjects that receive electrical stimulation in those areas press the lever because they find the stimulation pleasurable or reinforcing.[23] Second, stimulation of these areas by artificial means (that is, with an electrical stimulator) may initiate the same processes that occur when an animal is reinforced in its natural environment. Stated differently, reward in the natural environment may eventually stimulate the same neural pathways as those studied in these experiments.[24]

Anatomy of Reward and Punishment.

Researchers have tried to specify the exact location of the pleasure and punishment centers.[25] Although a number of interconnected structures sustain self-stimulation—including the amygdala, the hippocampus, and the septum—the predominant area that constitute the pleasure center is the **medial forebrain bundle.** As shown in Figure 11-3, this is a tract of nerve fibers that runs longitudinally in the brain, extending forward to the septal and lateral hypothalamic areas, and backward to the central gray, ventrotegmental area, and the reticular formation.

The primary punishment system is the **periventricular tract.** This is a set of nerve fibers that runs parallel to the medial forebrain reward system but closer to the center axis of the brain. The system originates in the forward part of the brain, near the periventricular and supraoptic nuclei, and extends through the thalamus and posterior hypothalamus to the tectum in the posterior part of the brain.

According to Vaccarino, Schiff, and Glickman (1989), the reward system is represented schematically by the diagram shown in Figure 11-4. The medial forebrain bundle neurons descend from the lateral preoptic area, transversing through the hypothalamus, to enervate three distinct circuits. First, an output circuit (shown at the left in Figure 11-4) goes through the pedunculopontine nucleus and spinal cord. This system is responsible for the expression of species-specific behaviors.

Second, fibers enervate the ventral tegmentum and then ascend through the nucleus accumbens to the substantia innominata and lateral preoptic areas. This ascending system of fibers, called "system I," is primarily responsible for

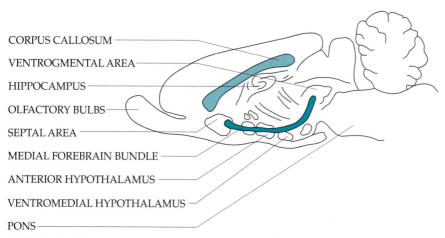

CORPUS CALLOSUM

VENTROGMENTAL AREA

HIPPOCAMPUS

OLFACTORY BULBS

SEPTAL AREA

MEDIAL FOREBRAIN BUNDLE

ANTERIOR HYPOTHALAMUS

VENTROMEDIAL HYPOTHALAMUS

PONS

FIGURE 11-3. Schematic diagram showing some of the structures involved in the reward system, including the medial forebrain bundle.

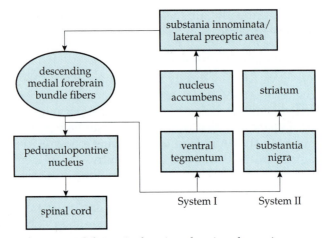

FIGURE 11-4. Schematic drawing showing the various pathways included in the reward system (after Vaccarino, Schiff, & Glickman, 1989).

the motivational effects of reinforcement. Subjects not only press levers to receive electrical stimulation in these areas, but they also show species-specific behaviors, such as feeding reactions.

Third, medial forebrain fibers form an ascending tract called "system II." This system extends from the substantia nigra to the striatum. System II facilitates memory formation. For example, memory for a passive-avoidance response is enhanced if stimulation of these fibers occurs following the learning phase.[26]

Even though both system I and system II are part of the so-called pleasure center, they play different roles in the reinforcement process. First, lever pressing for stimulation to the striatum (system II) involves highly stereotyped behaviors. Destruction of the striatum causes a decrease in behaviors such as running back and forth in the text box or biting the lever. Second, the behavioral topography when pressing for stimulation to system I includes components of species-specific behaviors, such as feeding reactions.[27] Moreover, feeding behaviors that are elicited as a result of stimulation of system I are affected by variables such as the level of food deprivation or the incentive value of the food reward. This is not the case for system II. System I, therefore, unlike system II, is involved in the motivational aspects of reward.

The foregoing model forms the basis for the **consummatory response theory of reinforcement.**[28] According to this theory, reinforcement represents "the facilitation of activity in neurons which underlie the expression of behaviors that are important for the survival of the organism."[29] In other words, performance of life-sustaining, species-specific behavior is precisely what subjects find reinforcing. When animals are engaged in those behaviors, they are experiencing reward. These behaviors include feeding, drinking, exploration, sexual behaviors, and hoarding. Most of these behaviors may be elicited via direct stimulation of the brain, notably the hypothalamus. These same anatomical sites sustain reward self-stimulation. In short, species-specific survival behaviors and rewarding brain stimulation are mediated by the same neural circuits.

Neurochemistry of Reward.

Research has also focused on the biochemical nature of reinforcement. Studies show that the reward system involves catecholamine neurons—that is, nerves in which norepinephrine and dopamine are the primary transmitter substances.[30] In contrast, the aversive periventricular (punishment) system is a cholinergic system, for which the primary neuronal transmitter is acetylcholine.[31]

The evidence for this position is compelling. Destruction of the system I dopamine neurons (or a blocking of their receptors) attenuates the self-administration of catecholamine drugs such as cocaine or amphetamine, and it reduces the reinforcement effects brought about by the electrical stimulation of those areas.[32] Moreover, the action of various dopamine antagonists resembles the effects obtained when a reduction in the magnitude of a conventional reward is given.

For example, Ettenberg (1989) trained two groups of rats to run down a straight alleyway. During acquisition, one group was reinforced on every trial, whereas the other was given food on only 20 of the 30 trials. As expected, the partially reinforced animals were more resistant to extinction than were the continuously rewarded animals (see Chapter 10). Two additional groups of animals were used. Each was given continuous reinforcement during acquisition, but on 10 of the trials (the same days as the partial subjects were not rewarded), one was injected just prior to the trial with haloperidol (a dopamine antagonist), and the other was given a harmless placebo substance. During extinction, the haloperidol subjects performed just like the partially reinforced animals.

In other words, the dopamine antagonist increased resistance to extinction. Reducing the levels of dopamine in this fashion had an effect analogous to giving no reward. Because the extinction session occurred well after the effects of the drug had worn off, increased resistance to extinction in the drugged animals must have been due to a reduction of the impact of reward on those trails, rather than simply a direct, detrimental effect of the drug itself on motor performance.

In a similar study, Nakajima (1989) administered a dopamine antagonist that acted only on the dopamine neurons in system I. The same result was obtained—namely, a reduction in reinforcement—on a variety of tests, such as running down an alleyway to receive brain stimulation, and pressing a lever to obtain food, water, saccharin, or a heroin injection. Thus, the underlying physiological mechanism for reward is a well-defined series of structures and tracts that contain catecholamine neurons.[33] Given this view of reinforcement, it is not surprising that certain kinds of psychoactive drugs, such as heroin, are highly reinforcing.[34]

INTERIM SUMMARY

The learning process may be investigated from a physiological point of view. Although early research found equivocal support for this view, contemporary research has discovered that specific anatomical locations and biochemical substances are important for learning and memory formation. For example, long-term potentiation (enhanced sensitivity to new stimulation) occurs in the hippocampus, a structure associated with memory. The neurological basis for learning began with the discovery of the pleasure center, located primarily in the medial forebrain bundle, and of areas mediating aversion, located in the periventricular tract. Generally, the reward system contains two major fiber tracts. System I involves species-specific behaviors such as feeding reactions; system II involves stereotyped behaviors. Reward centers contain catecholamine nerves, in which norepinephrine and dopamine are the primary transmitter substances. When those substances are depleted or blocked, the effect of reward declines; when those substances are enhanced, reward value increases. The primary transmitter substance involved in aversive centers is acetylcholine.

MECHANISTIC (S–R) THEORIES OF LEARNING

The preceding material focused on the physiological mechanisms that mediate behavior. Mechanisms may be hypothetical rather than physical, however. Recall from Chapter 2 the discussion about inferring hypothetical states of a system. The example, taken from chemistry, involved how the volatility of a chemical may be assessed from its tendency to evaporate when heated. Volatility is not a physical property, but rather a hypothetical state or characteristic that mediates the chemical's behavior. Analogous hypothetical mechanisms that mediate animal behavior have also been proposed.

Hull's Neobehavioristic Theory

The best known, and historically most influential, mechanistic theory of behavior was developed by C. L. Hull (1943).[35] Hull's system is a hypothetico-deductive system because it involves formal postulates and theorems.[36] Postulates are general statements about behavior. Theorems, logically deduced from the postulates, are propositions that may be tested directly. If the outcome of the test is predicted by the theorem, then support for the postulate is gained. If the experiments do not verify the theorem, then the postulate is revised.

Hull's theory is mechanistic, in the sense that it proposes the use of intervening variables. Intervening variables refer to the states or characteristics of animals that mediate their behavior. Consider the following example: Assume that one animal is deprived of water for 24 hours, another is given a diet containing a high level of salt, and a third is put into an extremely hot environ-

Photograph of Clark L. Hull.

ment. These animals may perform any of several behaviors. For example, they may drink copious amounts of water, press levers to obtain water, or cross an electrified grid to reach a water source. To explain these diverse acts, researchers use a simple and unifying mechanism that links or relates the independent variables (water deprivation, salt, heat) and the dependent variables (drinking, pressing levers, crossing electrified grids). The mechanism is called "thirst." Thirst, in this case, is a motivating state arising from the biological need for water. It comes between the stimuli that impinge on the organism (sight of the drinking spout or lever, for instance) and behavior (drinking from the spout, pressing the lever). It is a hypothetical mechanism that is measured in terms of an animal's behavior, rather than physically. Hull employed hypothetical mechanisms of this sort, arguing that they help to explain the regularities of behavior.

Hull's formal theory contained 16 major postulates. Several made important assumptions about psychological processes. For example, stimuli that impinge on an organism are effective for some period of time following their offset, in the form of a stimulus trace (postulate I); sensory impulses interact (postulate II); and an organism, at birth, is able to perform many unlearned responses (postulate III). Postulates IV through IX, however, are more critical to the present discussion.

Postulate IV: Drive Reduction.

Hull claimed that organisms have basic biological needs, such as the need for food, water, air, and sleep. These give rise to one of Hull's most important concepts, **drive.** Need is a biological state that produces unlearned behaviors designed to reduce the need. Drive on the other hand, is a psychological state corresponding to, and covarying with, the biological imbalance. Hull further argued that reinforcement involves drive reduction. According to postulate IV, "whenever an effector activity [a response] and a receptor activity [a stimulus] occur in close temporal contiguity . . . and this [contiguity] . . . is closely associated with the diminution of a need . . . there will result an increment to a tendency ($\Delta_S H_R$) of that afferent impulse on later occasions to evoke that reaction. The increments from successive reinforcements summate in a manner which yields a combined **habit strength ($_S H s_R$)** which is a simple positive growth function of the number of reinforcements (N)."[37] In other words, whenever a subject experiences a certain stimulus–response sequence, followed by a reduction in its drive state, then the habit ($_S H_R$), which is the tendency to perform that reaction in the presence of that stimulus, is increased.[38]

Habit is an intervening variable. It reflects the strength of the S–R connection. The strength of the habit is a function of the number of times that the S–R sequence has been followed by drive reduction. Formally speaking, the rate of increase in the strength of habit is equivalent to

$$_S H_R = 1 - 10^{-.0305N} \qquad \qquad Equation\ 11\text{-}1$$

where N equals the number of reinforcements.

This relationship between the number of reinforced trials and habit is shown graphically in Figure 11-5. The greater the number of reinforced trials, the stronger the animal's habit.[39] In summary, Hull hypothesized that an intervening variable, called "habit," results when a subject's behavior, in the presence of a given stimulus, is followed by reinforcement—namely, drive reduction. With an increase in $_S H_R$, the probability that a subject will perform the given reaction in the presence of the appropriate stimulus (rather than some other reaction, the habit strength of which is weaker) increases.

Postulate VII: Reaction Potential.

Postulate VII deals with the performance of a subject. Habit is translated into overt performance only when a subject is motivated. Thus, performance, according to Hull, occurs when habit and drive are both present. This is expressed by Hull's most famous equation:

$$_S E_R = {}_S H_R \times D \qquad \qquad Equation\ 11\text{-}2$$

Excitatory potential ($_S E_R$) predicts the subject's performance, $_S H_R$ is habit, and D is drive. According to this equation, performance occurs when the subject

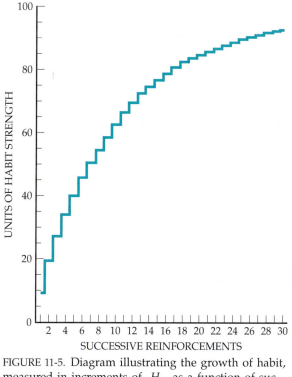

FIGURE 11-5. Diagram illustrating the growth of habit, measured in increments of $_SH_R$, as a function of successive reinforcements (after Hull, 1943).

had developed a habit ($_SH_R$) *and* when the organism is in a drive state. Both are necessary.[40]

Hull's basic formulation makes good intuitive sense, and it is strongly supported by research. Consider the example of a rat that is placed in the start box of a complicated maze. Will it run to the goal box quickly and efficiently? It can do so only if two conditions are met. First, the animal must know how to reach the goal box; that is, the habit for making the correct turns must be present (the $_SH_R$ term). If such knowledge is absent, then the subject will make incorrect turns as often as it makes correct turns. Second, the subject must be motivated (the D term). If, for example, the subject is not hungry, then it has no motivation to perform. It may know *how* to reach the goal box, but it may not care to do so. In short, performance occurs only when both habit and drive are present.[41]

The multiplicative relationship between drive and habit was demonstrated by several of Hull's colleagues.[42] In these studies, hungry rats responded to obtain food. Groups differed in terms of the number of training trials (number of reinforcements) and the degree of food deprivation. Thus, the various combinations of drive level and habit were investigated. The joint effect of habit strength and drive level on performance was measured in terms of resistance to extinction.

Several important concepts were revealed. First, drive (hours of food deprivation) and habit (number of reinforcements) jointly affect performance, but they are distinctly different intervening states. In the case of drive, the relationship between performance and drive is approximately linear; number of responses during extinction increases proportionately with hours of deprivation. In the case of habit, the effect is not linear; resistance to extinction increases as a function of number of reinforcements, but the increase showed diminishing returns (see Figure 11-5). Habit and drive therefore combine to produce performance, but the two states affect behavior in a markedly different fashion.

Second, the relationship between habit and drive is multiplicative. An increase in drive, say from 6 to 22 hours of food deprivation, does not simply add a constant amount of excitatory potential; the increase magnifies $_sE_R$. Stated differently, excitatory potential increased with changes in drive or habit by a multiple, rather than by a constant fraction.

Postulates VIII–IX: Reactive and Conditioned Inhibition.

Subjects grow tired during a training session even though they are reinforced. **Reactive inhibition (I_R)** is essentially the fatigue that builds up as a result of responding. Reactive inhibition subtracts from excitatory potential.

Conditioned inhibition ($_sI_R$) is based on the reduction of reactive inhibition. Behaviors that remove or reduce an unpleasant state are reinforced. More specifically, reactive inhibition is aversive, so the behavior that causes the dissipation of reactive inhibition—or fatigue—namely, "no responding," or is strengthened when the animal stops responding. In other words, as the subject grows tired (experiences reactive inhibition), it becomes increasingly motivated to stop performing because the state of reactive inhibition is aversive; cessation of performance itself is reinforced because it dissipates the aversive reactive inhibition. Furthermore, like $_sH_R$ and $_sE_R$, reinforcement takes place in the context of a stimulus, and thus subjects are conditioned to cease responding.

Conditioned and reactive inhibition combine with drive and habit to produce performance. Formally, this is expressed in the following equation:

$$_s\bar{E}_R = {}_sH_R \times D - (I_R + {}_sI_R)$$

Equation 11-3

The term $_s\bar{E}_R$ is effective, or net, excitatory potential. The equation states that performance is energized by the combination of habit and drive but reduced by the animal's momentary fatigue (I_R), as well as by its conditioned tendency to stop responding when tired ($_sI_R$).

Status of Hull's Theory

It is difficult to exaggerate the influence that Hull's theory had on learning research. During the 1940s, as many as 70% of the studies published in the relevant American Psychological Association journals made reference to

Hull's work.[43] The theory was successful because it was both comprehensive and, more important, capable of being tested. At a time when many were still arguing the relative merits of introspectionism and behaviorism, Hull's theory provided an inspired extension of the scientific method to the problem of behavior.

Criticisms.

There were, however, many criticisms of Hull's theory and, indeed, the details of his system have not survived to the present. First, many faulted Hull's molecular view of behavior, according to which an animal's behavior is explained in terms of muscle movements rather than more molar concepts, such as goals.

Second, the mathematical precision in Hull's theory, although a strong point in many ways, proved to be a problem because the psychological concepts on which the mathematical terms were based were subject to direct test and thus disproof. Consider Equation 11-1. The exponent in the right-hand term gives the precise rate of change for $_sH_R$, as a function of number of reinforcements. Research shows, however, that learning curves are highly variable. Many factors influence the rate of growth, including minor variations in procedure. To specify the growth of habit in such a precise fashion was to invite attack.

Finally, not all of the concepts developed by Hull have survived close examination. For example, consider the concept of drive.[44] Hull believed that drive was based on biological need, thus implying that only those behaviors that led to a reduction in the need state would be reinforced. Many behaviors, however, are learned, even though no drive or need reduction is involved.[45] Saccharin reduces no biological need, yet it is highly rewarding; exploration serves no obvious biological need, yet subjects learn behaviors simply for the opportunity to explore their environment (see Chapter 9).[46] In fact, some theorists explicitly disavow the notion that need reduction plays a major role in learning, arguing instead that animals, even rats, are motivated by curiosity more than by biological imbalance.

Neo-Hullian Theory.

Although the details of Hull's theory are no longer held in high regard, the fundamental approach, and many of the underlying concepts, continue to influence learning theorists. Perhaps the best example of the explicit use of Hullian theory is shown in the work of Amsel on the partial-reinforcement effect (see Chapter 10).[47] The central features of Amsel's theory are drawn directly from Hullian theory, particularly Hull's $r_g - s_g$ mechanism. For example, Amsel's most important intervening variable is frustration. When a subject expects a reward but receives none, it experiences an aversive motivational state called "frustration." This state is not unlike reactive inhibition, in that it is aversive and motivates the subject to seek ways of reducing it. The success of Amsel's approach attests to the enduring relevance of Hull's ideas to contemporary learning theory.

INTERIM SUMMARY

Mechanisms for learning may be hypothetical, rather than physical. Hull's theory of behavior is the best example of such a mechanistic approach. Hull claimed that animals have basic biological needs, and that habits that reduce these needs are reinforced. Habit combines with drive to produce performance (called "excitatory potential"). Performance is also affected by reactive inhibition (comparable to fatigue) and conditioned inhibition, which is a conditioned form of inactivity. Although initially influential, Hull's theory is no longer supported because many of the concepts, and most of the mathematical detail, have been challenged.

COGNITIVE (R–S) THEORIES OF LEARNING

Cognitive theories of learning contrast with the aforementioned mechanistic theories (see also Chapter 2). They are centered on the notions that subjects are goal-oriented (their behavior is directed toward some goal), and that subjects develop mental representations of their behavior, not that subjects have particular mechanisms that directly mediate behavior.

Tolman's Cognitive Behaviorism

One of the first, and most noted, cognitive-learning theorists was E. C. Tolman (1932).[48] Tolman used terms such as purpose and cognition, arguing that the goal of behavior was to reach some final goal (reaching the goal demonstrated the subject's purpose). In other words, a subject has a purpose in reaching a goal and is able to think about and behave with respect to that goal.

Expectancies and the Role of Reinforcement.

A central tenet of Tolman's theory is that animals derive general knowledge about their environment, and they form expectancies about the consequences of their behavior (rather than performing in a mechanistic S–R fashion). The implication is that reinforcement is unnecessary for learning, only for performance.

This notion was illustrated in Tolman's study of **latent learning** (also discussed in Chapter 2).[49] Tolman and Honzik (1930) trained rats to run through a maze that contained 14 choice points. Animals in the reward group always received food in the goal box. Subjects in the no-reward group never were given food in the goal box but were removed after a fixed period of time and fed in their home cage. Rats in the shifted group were treated like the no-reward subjects for the first 10 sessions of the study. However, beginning on Day 11, these subjects were given reward in the goal box.

The results are shown in Figure 11-6. First, consider the behavior of the

Photograph of Edward C. Tolman.

reward and the no-reward groups. In the former case, mean number of errors declined gradually and systematically over training. The no-reward subjects, however, showed only a slight improvement in performance; their error rate remained at a relatively high level throughout training. This difference, based on whether on the subjects were given a reward in the goal box, is not surprising. It suggests that reward in the goal box is necessary for learning to occur.

Second, consider the behavior of the shifted subjects. Those rats showed little evidence of learning during the first 10 training sessions.[50] Once a reward was provided in the goal box (starting on Trial 11), however, they showed a sudden and dramatic improvement in performance. In fact, the shift in performance was so sudden that the logical conclusion is that the animals had

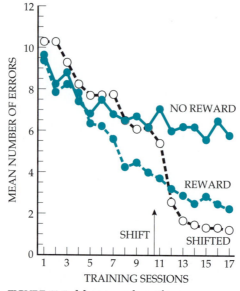

FIGURE 11-6. Mean number of maze errors, as a function of daily sessions for the reward, no-reward, and shifted groups (after Tolman & Honzik, 1930).

learned the maze all along but simply were not performing in a manner that revealed their learning. If these subjects had not learned the maze during the first 10 sessions, then one would expect them to show only gradual improvement beginning on Trial 11. The latent-learning experiment, therefore, suggests that animals do not need reinforcement to develop a cognitive map of their environment. Reward is unnecessary for learning; it is only required for stimulating efficient performance.

Cognitive Maps.

According to Tolman, rats develop expectancies about the outcomes of their behavior, and they develop mental or **cognitive maps** of their environment. They do not, as Hull suggested, simply perform a sequence of muscle movements. These two opposing hypotheses—making specific muscle movements versus developing cognitive maps—were evaluated in a number of experiments, including one by Tolman, Ritchie, and Kalish (1946). The authors used a maze such as the one depicted in Figure 11-7. Rats were first reinforced for running from the start location to the goal box. The route involved several turns. According to Hull, the animals were being taught to make a specific series of right and left turns. For Tolman, the rats were learning to go to a particular place contained within their cognitive map (near the desk lamp, as shown in Figure 11-7).

Once this behavior was well-learned, the subjects were tested. Here, many radiating alleyways were available, but the original route was blocked. If the

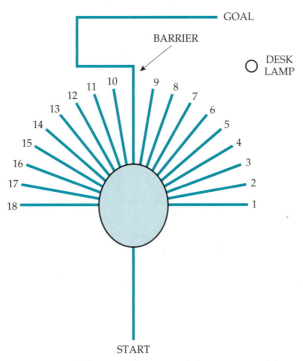

GOAL

BARRIER

DESK
LAMP

START

FIGURE 11-7. Schematic diagram of the maze used by
Tolman, Ritchie, and Kalish (1946).

rats had learned to go to a particular location, as Tolman asserted, then they
should choose alleyway 6, because that route led to the same location. If, however, the animals had learned to make a series of muscle movements, as Hull
contended, they should attempt to use the original route (or choose one close
to it).

The results, shown in Figure 11-8, support Tolman. Subjects chose alleyway 6 more often than the other routes, even though it was not the alleyway
used in original learning. Thus, the study suggests that rats develop a cognitive map of their environment, including the location of important landmarks
(see Chapter 15 for a more detailed discussion of cognitive maps).

Criticisms of Tolman's Theory.

Cognitive-learning theory, at least as espoused by Tolman, has been criticized on several accounts. First, behavior does not always seem to be goal
directed. For example, subjects often perform merely to explore their environment. Imagine puppies engaging in rough-and-tumble play, or monkeys
pressing levers to look outside their cage.[51] Although one could hypothesize
that exploration is an essential need, and therefore that these behaviors are
goal directed in fulfilling that need, the argument is not entirely compelling.

Second, animals often engage in behaviors that are highly goal directed
but hardly can be called purposive. Does a moth have a purpose in flying

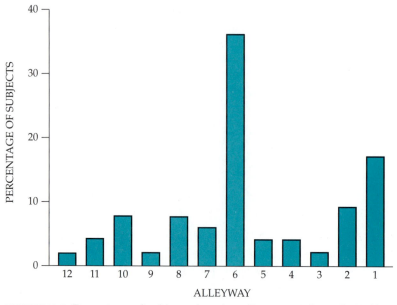

FIGURE 11-8. Percentage of subjects choosing alleyways 1 through 12 (the original path to the goal, between alleyways 9 and 10, was blocked) (after Tolman, Ritchie, & Kalish, 1946).

toward an electrical light bulb? Does a squirrel have a purpose when it buries a hazelnut? The concept of purpose, therefore, is problematic because it implies that the subject has some conscious insight and self-knowledge about the goal of its behavior.

Perhaps the most important criticism of Tolman's theory is that it says little about which behaviors an animal will execute. Imagine a rat pressing a lever to obtain food. Tolman would claim that it has a purpose and a goal for doing so, yet precisely what behavior will the animal engage in? Pressing the lever with its paws or its hind legs, biting the lever, or jumping on it? Each of these behaviors causes the lever to be pressed, but they are different kinds of reactions. Biting the lever, for example, is a more aggressive reaction than simply pressing it; jumping on the lever may suggest that the animal is trying to escape from the box; pressing the lever with the hind legs may mean that the subject simply stumbled onto the lever accidentally. Thus, claiming that an animal seeks a goal does little to specify the kind of behavior that is likely to be learned.

Associations in Instrumental Learning

The other aspect of Tolman's theory is the claim that animals develop mental representations of their own behavior. This issue relates to the contemporary research on Pavlovian conditioning. As discussed in Chapters 3, 5, and 6, modern Pavlovian theory is cognitive, in the sense that animals process information and form mental representations of the relationships among stimuli. The power and meaning of a CS depends on, among other things, its information value. Instrumental conditioning is now viewed in the same light as Pavlovian conditioning. Subjects are information processors not only with respect to stimuli (Pavlovian), but also with respect to their own behavior (instrumental).[52] A subject's responding, like a Pavlovian CS, is part of a larger network of associations. Animals, in other words, develop representations of goals and associate them with representations of their own behavior.

There are three major components in a typical instrumental-learning situation. They are discriminative stimuli (which set the occasion for reward by signaling when reinforcement is available, pending the response), the response, and the outcome (a reinforcer or punisher). Associations develop among each of these elements. The discriminative stimulus becomes directly associated with the response (S–R association), as well as with the outcome (S–O association.)[53] The response becomes associated with the outcome (R–O association).

R–O Associations.

The most extensive research program demonstrating that responses become associated with outcomes has been conducted by Rescorla and colleagues.[54] One experiment, by Colwill and Rescorla (1985a), trained a subject to earn an outcome by making a given response, changed the animal's memory of that outcome by pairing it with lithium chloride (LiCl, a poison), and then tested the strength of the response.[55] If the animal had associated the response and the outcome but now remembers the outcome as being aversive (because it had been paired with LiCl), then responding should decline.

More specifically, Colwill and Rescorla trained rats to make two responses. On some days, they were required to press a lever to obtain one outcome (either a sucrose-flavored solution or a food pellet). On other days, they could tug on a thin metal chain hanging from the ceiling of the cage to obtain the other outcome (the lever-pressing and chain-pulling reactions are referred to as R_1 and R_2; the food and sucrose-solution outcomes are referred to as O_1 and O_2). Thus, for some subjects, lever pressing produced sucrose, and chain pulling yielded food; for others, lever pressing produced food, whereas chain pulling was followed by sucrose. As suggested by Figure 11-9,

Training	Devaluation	Test
R_1–O_1 and R_2–O_2	O_1–LiCl and O_2–nothing	R_1 and R_2

FIGURE 11-9. Schematic diagram showing the conditions used in the Colwill and Rescorla (1985a) study.

the subjects were presumably developing two different response–outcome associations—namely, R_1–O_1 and R_2–O_2.

In Phase 2, some subjects received LiCl following O_1, and, on alternate days, nothing following O_2. Here, their memory for, or representation of, O_1 was being devalued through poisoning. Subjects should therefore recall O_1 as being aversive when later tested. The other subjects were given LiCl following O_2, but, on alternate days, nothing following O_1. For these animals, the memory of O_2 was made aversive. Finally, on the test day, all subjects were given a 20-minute extinction session, with both responses available. They could either press the lever or pull the chain, although neither outcome was given at this time. The authors predicted that if one response evoked the memory for a devalued (aversive) outcome, but the other did not, then the response rate for the former should decline, but the rate for the latter should not.

The results are shown in Figure 11-10. It made no difference whether the poisoned outcome had been associated with the lever-press or the chain-pull response. Similarly, it made no difference whether the poisoned outcome was sucrose or food. Thus all groups are combined in this figure. When a reinforcer was devalued by being paired with poison, the response that produced

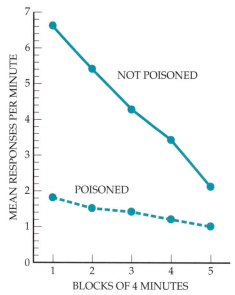

FIGURE 11-10. Mean responses per minute, as a function of blocks of 4 minutes on the test for (a) the response for which its previous outcome had been devalued through LiCl administration, and (b) the response for which its previous outcome had not been devalued (after Colwill & Rescorla, 1985a).

the reinforcer declined in rate. The reason is that subjects later remembered the reinforcer as being aversive and therefore devalued the response with which the reinforcer was associated. The response that led to the other reinforcer remained strong. These results confirm the notion of a response–outcome association.[56]

Much is known about **response–outcome associations.** For example, when subjects develop an $R–O_1$ association, that association is not affected if a different outcome, O_2, follows the response. The original $R–O_1$ association remains intact.[57] Second, the R–O association continues to develop throughout the course of extended training.[58] Finally, the R–O association persists despite the fact that interfering treatments are given. For example, an extinction procedure causes the response to decline, but the original R–O association remains intact.[59]

Overall, research on the formation of response associations indicates that instrumental conditioning, like classical conditioning, involves the development of associations. The research therefore supports the cognitive view of instrumental conditioning, in that a subject functions as an information processor, developing associations between the response and the goal object. Memory for, or the representation of, the goal object is crucial for the execution of the response.[60]

S–O Associations.

Like Pavlovian CSs, discriminative stimuli become associated with outcomes. This was shown by Colwill and Rescorla (1988a). The design of the experiment is shown in Figure 11-11. The study used two S_ds (noise and light), four responses (nose poke, handle pull, lever press, and chain pull), and two outcomes (food pellet and sucrose solution).[61]

In Phase 1, subjects performed R_1 in the presence of S_1 to obtain O_1, and R_2 in the presence of S_2 to obtain O_2. If S_ds become associated with USs, then

S_d training	Response training	Test
$S_1–R_1–O_1$ $S_2–R_2–O_2$	$R_3–O_1$ $R_4–O_2$	$S_1–R_3$ vs. R_4 $S_2–R_3$ vs. R_4

FIGURE 11-11. Schematic diagram of the basic experimental design used by Colwill and Rescorla (1988a). Note that S_1 and S_2 were a light and a noise, R_1 and R_2 were a nose-poke and a handle-pull response, R_3 and R_4 were a lever-press and a chain-pull response, and O_1 and O_2 were a food pellet and a sucrose solution. During the test, both the lever and the chain were available during S_1 and, on alternate sessions, during S_2. Note also that S_1 and R_3 shared O_1, whereas S_2 and R_4 shared O_2.

S_1 should become associated with O_1, whereas S_2 should become associated with O_2. In Phase 2, two new responses were taught—namely, R_3 (which was followed by O_1) and R_4 (which was followed by O_2).[62] Finally, in the test phase, subjects were presented with both S_1 and S_2 and were allowed to perform either R_3 or R_4.

The question was whether the stimuli would facilitate the response rate of a new behavior for which the stimuli had not previously served as an S_d, based on the fact that the behavior and the S_d shared a common outcome. In other words, S_1 and S_2 were not discriminative stimuli for R_3 and R_4, but they did previously lead to the same outcome. For S_1 and R_3, the outcome was O_1; for S_2 and R_4, the common outcome was O_2. The discriminative stimulus, therefore, should facilitate making the response with which it shares an outcome.

As shown in Figure 11-12, the predictions were confirmed. The discriminative stimulus more easily facilitated making a new response when the stimulus and the response shared a common outcome. The S_d therefore must have become associated with the outcome because its ability to set the occasion for the response was stronger when its outcome and that of the response were the same.[63]

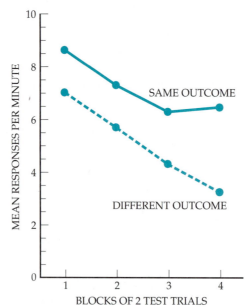

FIGURE 11-12. Mean responses per minute, as a function of blocks of two test trials during the discriminative stimuli for the response that shared the same outcome as the S_d and the response that had involved a different outcome from the one associated with the S_d (after Colwill & Rescorla, 1988a).

Hierarchical Associations.

The preceding research shows that subjects associate surrounding stimuli with eventual outcomes, and they associate their own behavior with those outcomes. A subject's knowledge involves more than simple associations between two elements, however. A subject also forms a hierarchical network of associations in which stimuli become associated with the relationship between a response and its outcome (an S–[R–O] association).

A good demonstration of hierarchical associations was provided by Rescorla (1990b).[64] Recall from Chapter 3 that a CS is powerful only when it reliably predicts a US. When the CS provides no reliable information about the US occurrence, then conditioning is weak. The same idea was applied to the learning of a **hierarchical association.** Here, a sucrose solution and food pellets were used as the outcomes (O_1 or O_2), lever pressing and chain pulling were the responses (R_1 or R_2), and a noise and a light were used as the discriminative stimuli (S_1 or S_2).

The training procedures are shown in Figure 11-13. During S_1, one set of response–outcome relations was available. Specifically, during S_1, a subject could perform R_1 to obtain O_1, and R_2 to obtain O_2. During the other discriminative stimulus, S_2, the opposite relations were in effect. That is, during S_2, subjects could make R_2 to obtain O_1 and perform R_1 to get O_2. The two discriminative stimuli did not differ in terms of their relationships to the responses or outcomes. Both S_1 and S_2 signaled R_1, R_2, O_1, and O_2 an equal number of times. The two S_ds did differ, however, in terms of the *relationships* between the responses and the outcomes. The combinations of R_1–O_1 and R_2–O_2 followed S_1, whereas R_2–O_1 and R_1–O_2 followed S_2.

One additional feature of the training was important. During the intertrial interval when no S_d was present, the same response–outcome combinations were available as during S_1. That is, subjects could respond with R_1 to obtain O_1, and R_2 to get O_2. The S_1 stimulus therefore predicted R_1–O_1 and R_2–O_2, but those two response–outcome combinations were *also* available when S_1 was not present. Thus, S_1 was unreliable, or uninformative, with respect to whether R_1 would produce O_1, and R_2 would yield O_2. The S_2 stimulus, on

Training	Test
Kinds of trials	
1. S_1–[R_1–O_1]	
2. S_1–[R_2–O_2]	S_1–R_1 vs. R_2
3. S_2–[R_1–O_2]	
4. S_2–[R_2–O_1]	
Intertrial events	S_2–R_1 vs. R_2
1. R_1–O_1	
2. R_2–O_2	

FIGURE 11-13. Schematic diagram showing the treatments used by Rescorla (1990b).

the other hand, was highly informative about the response–outcome relations. Only when S_2 was present could the subjects produce O_2 by making R_1, and O_1 by making R_2.

The strength of the two discriminative stimuli was tested during an extinction phase. Four 30-second presentations of each stimulus were given with both the lever and the chain available. The results are shown in Figure 11-14. The more powerful S_d was the cue that reliably predicted the response–outcome combinations—namely, S_2. The S_1 stimulus, which unreliably predicted the R–O relations, was much weaker. The experiment, therefore, shows that subjects not only form associations between single elements of a learning situation, but they also form hierarchical associations, anticipating on the basis of a discriminative stimulus which *combination* of response and outcome is available.

The work on hierarchical associations is consistent with a cognitive approach to learning because the goal (that is, the outcome) is embodied in the representation or memory developed by the subject. Furthermore, the hierarchical association is analogous to a cognitive map. Rather than representing the spatial arrangements within an environment, the hierarchical association represents the functional or contingent relations. "Cognitive maps are internal representations of instrumental properties. A rat guided by a cognitive

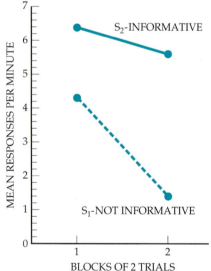

FIGURE 11-14. Mean responses per minute, as a function of blocks of two trials on the test for the discriminative stimulus that was informative of the response–outcome relations (S_2), and the stimulus that unreliably signaled the response–outcome relations (S_1) (after Rescorla, 1990b).

map does what is appropriate in the environment represented by its map."[65] Here, a subject's behavior in the presence of a discriminative stimulus is guided or determined by a mental representation of the relationship between its behavior and the outcome.

INTERIM SUMMARY

Cognitive approaches to learning, first developed by Tolman, argue that animals have goals and representations of their own behavior. Latent learning shows that animals learn without receiving reinforcement, suggesting that reward stimulates efficient performance but is unnecessary for learning. In contemporary research, the ability to develop mental representations of behavior is best exemplified in the work of Rescorla. Associations form between discriminative stimuli, responses, and outcomes. For example, an animal develops representations of the goal or outcome and then associates these representations with representations of its own behavior. Moreover, animals develop hierarchical associations in which a discriminative stimulus signals the relationship between a response and its outcome.

THEORIES OF BEHAVIORAL REGULATION

In contrast to the mechanistic and cognitive approaches to learning, the behavioral-analysis view focuses exclusively on the conditions that regulate behavior; it does not speculate about internal mechanisms or associations. Several approaches are discussed in this section: Skinner's behavior-analysis approach, the response-deprivation hypothesis, and behavioral economics.

Skinner's Behavior-Analysis Approach

The most noted psychologist in the behavior-analysis tradition was B. F. Skinner. Because Skinner's view was discussed in Chapter 2, only a brief review of several of the more important arguments is provided here.

Skinner claimed that theories (or mechanisms) of learning are unnecessary.[66] Explanations of behavior involving physiological or behavioral mechanisms do not substantively add to our understanding of behavior. To say that a response is evoked by a stimulus because of the existence of an internal mechanism (for example, drive), does not explain the response because the internal mechanism itself is not explained. If one claims that a rat makes an avoidance reaction because of fear, then one must explain why the fear state exists before it can serve as an explanation for the response.

Rather than relying on internal states to explain behavior, Skinner focuses on the concept of reinforcement contingency. According to Skinner, a reinforcement contingency has two important effects. First, it selects behavior. An organism has many responses in its repertoire, and only those that are followed by a rewarding event survive.[67] Behaviors that are not followed by reward, or that are followed by punishers, decrease in probability. Thus, the

Photograph of B. F. Skinner.

selection of one behavior from many potential behaviors is the result of differential reinforcement.

Reinforcers have a second function—namely, maintaining behavior. It is the maintenance, or regulation, of behavior that has become the dominant focus in this area of research. This strengthening of a response by reinforcement is termed the empirical law of effect. The law is not an explanation of behavior, but rather a description of the fact that behaviors that are followed by reinforcers increase in probability.[68]

Response-Deprivation Hypothesis

Reinforcement contingency plays a central role in the behavior analysis approach. One formulation or expression of this concept was the Premack principle (see Chapter 8). According to the Premack principle, a reinforcement effect is based on the differential probability of two activities. First, one observes the probability or preferability of two separate activities when the subject is not constrained. For example, for a thirsty rat, the probability of drinking is invariably higher than the probability of pressing a lever or running in an exercise wheel. Second, a reinforcement relation is established when the execution of a more probable response is made contingent on first executing a less probable behavior. This is analogous to saying, "you may watch TV [high-probability behavior] only after you have finished washing the dishes [low-probability behavior]."

Allison's (1989) **response-deprivation hypothesis** is a theory of behavioral regulation that disputes the claim of the Premack principle.[69] According to this account, the predictable change in the rate of an instrumental behavior does not result because of a special consequence called a "reinforcer," but rather because the subject is deprived of the activity on which the instrumental behavior is contingent.

Assume that a subject is given access to two activities for 60 minutes, without any constraint being placed on its behavior. The subject will probably engage in both behaviors. The combination of the two activities that the subject prefers is its **bliss point.** This point is shown in Figure 11-15 for a hypothetical subject.

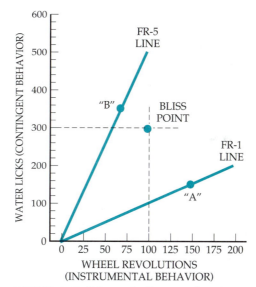

FIGURE 11-15. Schematic diagram showing the combination of two activities or commodities (wheel running and water licks) preferred by a given subject. This preferred or baseline value, established during a session when no constraints are placed on the subject's behavior, is called the subject's "bliss point." Under two schedules, shown by the FR-1 and FR-5 schedule lines, a subject's behavior is constrained, resulting in its obtaining the combination of commodities shown at points "A" and "B," respectively.

For example, assume that the two activities are running in an exercise wheel and licking a water tube. Figure 11-15 shows that the subject will perform 100 wheel-turn responses for every 300 licks. Now, however, assume that we constrain the animal by forcing it to perform according to a fixed ratio (FR-1) schedule. Specifically, it must run in the exercise wheel one revolution for every lick of water it chooses to consume. The animal does not have free access under these conditions and thus cannot engage in the two activities at its preferred rate. Rather, the rates will be confined to a point along the FR-1 schedule line shown in Figure 11-15.

After 1 hour, assume that the subject would have had 150 revolutions and thus received 150 water licks (shown at point "A" in Figure 11-15). The subject obtained far *fewer* licks than it would have if it were not constrained by the schedule. Furthermore, the subject performed many *more* wheel revolutions than it would have chosen to perform on its own. Thus, wheel running increased under the schedule conditions, relative to baseline conditions, but licking the water tube was reduced, relative to the bliss point. According to Allison (1993), the increase in wheel running would not be due to the reinforcing consequence of drinking, but rather to the fact that the schedule deprived the subject of water. What produced a reinforcement effect was the constraint on behavior imposed by the schedule, not a special outcome called a "reinforcer."[70]

This formulation is preferred over the Premack principle because the reinforcement relationship depends on constraining the more probable activity, relative to the bliss point. Imagine that drinking water is more probable than running in the wheel, but the subject must engage in drinking in order to gain access to the wheel. For example, the subject must take five licks of water for every one revolution in the wheel. This reverse FR-5 schedule is also shown as the FR-5 schedule line in Figure 11-15. The subject's combination of licking and running could be at any point along that line, but assume that over a 1-hour period the subject performs 350 licks and 70 revolutions. This combination is shown at point "B" in Figure 11-15. Here, the amount of drinking is *above* the level of the bliss point and the number of wheel turns is *below* the bliss point level. Drinking is still more probable than wheel running, yet the increase in drinking occurred because the subject was deprived of access to the wheel. In other words, the conditions responsible for an increase in an instrumental response involve response deprivation. If the constraints of a reinforcement schedule deny or restrict access to a particular behavior, then subjects engage in other behaviors above their preferred baseline rate to try to perform that restricted activity as close to the bliss point as possible.[71]

According to this model, the strength of a reinforcement effect depends on the discrepancy between the behavior that is permitted by the schedule and the bliss point. As the discrepancy between the obtained result and the bliss point increases, the instrumental behavior increases as well. This explains why large incentives produce a stronger reinforcement effect than do small incentives (see Chapter 9). If sucrose were added to the water, then the subject would initially show a higher baseline of drinking than if the water contained no sugar; the animal's bliss point would be higher than shown in Figure 11-15. A reinforcement schedule would therefore result in a relatively larger response-deprivation effect, and the instrumental behaviors that must be executed for access to the sucrose would be correspondingly higher.

Behavioral Economics

Many investigators within the behavior analysis tradition have found that the concepts and language of economics provide a powerful way in which to describe the laws of behavior. Although a complete discussion of this area of theory is beyond the scope of this book, a brief account of several important findings is given here.[72]

Economic Principles.

An economic analysis of behavior begins with a set of assumptions about motivation, called the "axioms of demand."[73] These notions are, in a sense, a theory of animal motivation. They claim, among other things, that organisms have essential needs, which create demand for the goods that satisfy those needs. In securing these needs, however, animals inevitably pay a certain price or cost. Goods, therefore, may be described as providing a benefit to the organism, but, at the same time, as incurring a cost. For example, food provides needed nutrition for an individual, but it is secured only after the individual pays a cost, either in terms of the time and effort needed to find and secure the food, or the money needed in exchange for it.

The laws of supply and demand suggest that as the cost of a good increases, the demand for that good declines. This relationship between cost and benefit is shown in Figure 11-16. A good example of this cost–benefit relationship would be the number of videocassette recorder (VCR) movie rentals purchased in an average week, relative to their cost. When the cost is very low, people are more inclined to use this kind of entertainment. As the cost increases, however, the average number of movie rentals per week declines; people favor other forms of entertainment. Indeed, there is, in theory at least, a high cost, above which people would simply not rent VCR movies at all.

In studying animal learning and behavior, a demand function of this sort is established by a fixed-ratio (FR) schedule. Here, the animal must pay a certain cost (a specific number of lever presses) to obtain a desired reinforcer (usually a pellet of food). By varying the FR schedule, one demonstrates the relationship between cost and derived benefit in laboratory subjects.

The demand for a reinforcer varies not only with its cost, but also with the degree to which that good is an essential commodity. Goods that are essential for survival, such as food or water, do not show as sharp a decline in demand with increasing price as goods that are not essential. In other words, demand for VCR rentals declines with higher prices because rental movies are not essential to survival. Demand for essential food items, such as bread or milk, do not show this same decrease with higher prices. When their price is raised, demand diminishes only slightly, because people still need to consume

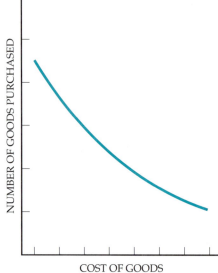

FIGURE 11-16. A hypothetical curve showing the relationship between the number of items purchased (benefit) and the price (cost) of each item.

bread and milk. With nonessential items, demand is said to be elastic; demand declines noticeably with increases in price. When the demand stays reasonably stable over a relatively wide range of prices, then the demand is said to be inelastic.

A good example of **elasticity of demand** in laboratory animals was a study by Hursh and Natelson (1981).[74] Rats lived in a two-compartment box; each side contained a lever. One lever yielded a small electrical current to the brain, which the subjects found pleasurable (see previous discussion on physiological mechanisms of reward). The other lever provided food pellets. The authors varied the cost of each of these goods (the required FR ratio), measuring both the number of lever presses and the number of reinforcers earned.

The data are shown in Figure 11-17. The consumption of food remained relatively constant, despite the changes in the FR ratio. Demand for food was, therefore, inelastic. In contrast, the demand for electrical brain stimulation was high when the cost was low, but it declined dramatically at higher FR ratios. Thus, demand for brain stimulation was elastic. In short, subjects responded at a faster rate when the price increased, to maintain a relatively constant supply of food, but they did not increase their response rate when the cost of brain-stimulation reinforcement increased.

Another factor that affects demand **is substitutability.**[75] Individuals may substitute one commodity for another when the price increases. For example, in a study by Rachlin, Green, Kagel, and Battalio (1976), rats had continuous access to two levers, but they were permitted to make only a certain total

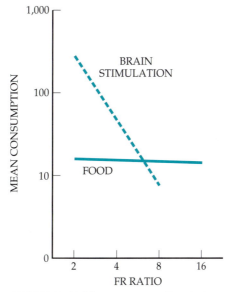

FIGURE 11-17. Mean consumption (reinforcers per hour), as a function of the
price (responses per reinforcer) for the
food reinforcement and the brain-stimulation levers (after Hursh & Natelson,
1981).

number of lever presses during a 24-hour period. Each lever was associated
with a different commodity, and each varied in terms of the cost required to
earn the commodity. When the reinforcers were substitutes for each other, then
demand was very elastic. For example, when the number of lever presses
required to obtain a drop of root beer increased, subjects responded more on
the lever that yielded a drop of Tom Collins mix. The two reinforcers were
substitutes. However, when the two reinforcers were not substitutes (for
instance, one produced food and the other water), such a trade-off was not
observed. As the cost of food increased, subjects were willing to pay the higher
price to keep the supply relatively constant; they were unwilling to substitute
the other commodity.

Demand may be expressed in terms of a choice between two different
commodities. An economic analysis of behavior assumes that every action
reflects an outcome of a choice on the part of the subject.[76] When we choose
to go to dinner, we are deciding not to engage in some other activity, such as
going to the movies; when we order pizza, we decide not to order hamburg-
ers. Even when the alternative outcomes are not obvious, responding for one
reinforcer is in lieu of not responding at all.

Choice between two objects may be described in terms of an indifference
curve, as shown in Figure 11-18. An **indifference curve** plots a series of points,
each of which represents an equally valuable combination of products. For

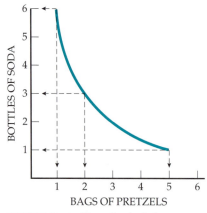

FIGURE 11-18. Hypothetical data showing an indifference function for bottles of soda and bags of pretzels.

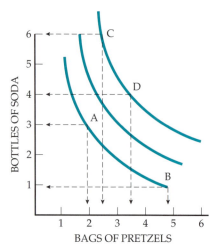

FIGURE 11-19. Hypothetical family of indifference curves. Points "C" and "D" are equally preferable, but both are more preferable to points "A" and "B."

example, the hypothetical person depicted in Figure 11-18 is indifferent between having six bottles of soda and one bag of pretzels, or three bottles of soda and two bags of pretzels. Having fewer of one item means that the person demands more of the other. The person, for example, is willing to have only a single bottle of soda, provided that he or she has, in this example, five bags of pretzels.

The indifference curve shown in Figure 11-18 is actually only one of a family of curves (see Figure 11-19). The axioms of demand argue that a person, although indifferent to any two points along a single curve, prefers to be at the outermost curve, because that is where she or he has the highest absolute level of goods. Thus, in Figure 11-19, points "A" and "B" are equally preferred (because they fall on the same indifference line), but both points are less preferable than points "C" and "D" (because the latter points are on a higher indifference curve). A greater absolute amount of goods is represented at points "C" and "D."

The family of indifference curves shows the combinations of goods that a subject finds equally acceptable. Which indifference curve actually holds for a given individual, however, is determined by the individual's budget. Although a person may wish to have 6 bottles of soda and 2½ bags of pretzels (point "C" in Figure 11-19), that person's budget may not permit such an expenditure.

Budget lines are shown in Figure 11-20. In the case of budget line 1, a person could buy 5 bottles of soda and 0 bags of pretzels, 0 bottles of soda and about 4½ bags of pretzels, or any other combination, provided that it falls

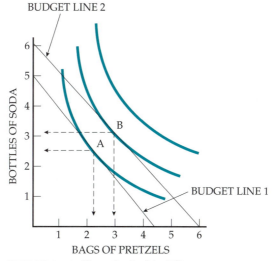

FIGURE 11-20. Hypothetical indifference curves with two budget lines. The indifference functions plot preferences for the two goods; the budget lines indicate the combination of goods that can be afforded; the intersection of the two functions shows that particular combination of commodities that the person purchases.

on the budget line. The combination actually purchased by a person with this budget would be at point "A." This equilibrium point is the junction between the person's indifference function and that person's budget line. In other words, the number of bottles of soda and bags of pretzels that are affordable is shown by the budget line; the combinations of goods that the individual prefers are shown along the indifference curve; and the number actually purchased is shown at point "A" (about 2½ bottles and 2½ bags), which is the intersection or single point of agreement between the two functions.

If the budget line changes, then a new equilibrium point is established.[77] A new budget line 2 is also shown in Figure 11-20. Here, six bottles of soda and zero bags of pretzels, zero bottles of soda and six bags of pretzels, or any other combination along the budget line, may be purchased. The new equilibrium point is shown at "B" (three bottles of soda and three bags of pretzels).

Optimal Behavior Plans.

An economic approach to behavioral regulation does not focus on physiological or behavioral mechanisms of behavior; nor does it focus on the relationship between a subject's behavior and its goals (other than to assume that individuals have a demand for various goal objects in accordance with the axioms of demand). The approach's primary objective is to describe how a subject's behavior is regulated by the laws derived from the study of economics, such as those just briefly discussed. By managing or regulating its behavior with respect to costs and benefits, an individual may obtain the maximum benefit from its efforts.

In other words, animals maximize the benefit–cost functions through adaptive behavior. To perform in a less-than-optimal fashion is to jeopardize one's success in coping with environmental demands. Thus, according to this line of reasoning (termed **optimality theory**), various behavior plans reflect an unconscious decision to maximize the benefit, relative to the costs.[78] Let us consider one example in detail—namely, foraging for food.

Food is unevenly distributed within the environment in areas called "patches." The first problem for an individual, therefore, is to find a patch and to begin to forage for food. The selection of an appropriate patch is an important decision because patches vary considerably in how much food they contain. At times, a patch may contain many food items; at other times, it may not. One strategy is to sample several patches to determine which is the best, and then to feed from the more profitable one exclusively.

Krebs, Kacelnik, and Taylor (1978) examined this strategy in small songbirds. The birds could hop onto one of two perches to produce food. Each perch was reinforced according to different variable-ratio (VR) schedules; thus, the two response options represented different feeding patches. When the two VR schedules were quite similar, subjects sampled both patches, taking a long time to determine which was the more profitable. When the schedules differed, however, subjects sampled both patches for only a short time before beginning to exploit the more profitable patch.

Furthermore, the sampling behavior was nearly optimal. Subjects spent just enough time discovering which patch was better before beginning to exploit the more favorable patch. Spending too little time evaluating the patches could have resulted in the subjects making an error in judgment—namely, exploiting the less profitable patch. Conversely, taking too long to sample the alternative patches would have wasted time. The length of time actually taken to sample the two options, on the average, was optimal, in that it yielded the greatest amount of food in the time available.

Zeiler (1987) showed that sampling occurs not only when subjects are faced with two patches differing not only in the number of responses required to earn food, but also in the probability that reward will be delivered once the schedule requirements are completed. Pigeons pecked either of two keys (blue or green); each was scheduled to give food reward after 30 pecks (FR-30). The probability that reward would be delivered following completion of the FR requirement, however, varied across the 12 sessions. On some days, the probabilities were equal (.5 in each case). On other sessions, the probabilities differed to varying degrees (0 versus 1.0, .1 versus .9, .2 versus .8, .3 versus .7, or .4 versus .6).

The data for one subject are shown in Figure 11-21. The subject sampled the two alternative patches, and the degree of sampling reflected the uncertainty of the outcome. When the probability of reward on the red key was

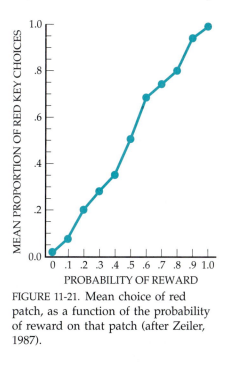

FIGURE 11-21. Mean choice of red patch, as a function of the probability of reward on that patch (after Zeiler, 1987).

low, little effort was devoted to that key. Conversely, when the probability of receiving reward on the red key was close to 1.0, the subject pecked that key almost exclusively. For the intermediate values, where the probability of receiving reward on the two keys was similar, the bird showed less preference for the better patch. Indeed, responding to each key was the same when the two probabilities were .5.

Finding a suitable patch is the first critical problem faced by a foraging animal. Deciding when to leave the patch after feeding for a period of time is the second important decision. How long should an animal stay at a location before venturing off to find another patch? According to optimal-foraging theory, the point at which a subject should leave a patch depends on a variety of factors, including the rate of energy intake within the patch, the time it takes to travel from one patch to another, and the time required to search for and prepare a prey item.

One formulation, shown in Figure 11-22, was developed by Charnov (1976). Assume that an animal begins its foraging behavior at time "A," travels to a patch, and then begins to eat at time "B." Initially, the rate of energy intake is high because food is relatively plentiful. However, as the food begins to run out, the rate of energy intake (food per unit of time) declines. This is shown in Figure 11-22 as a gradual flattening of the cumulative energy curve (solid line). Each additional period of time yields less and less energy because fewer prey are remaining, and thus it takes the subject progressively longer to find each one.

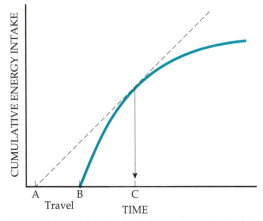

FIGURE 11-22. Graph depicting a hypothetical forager that gains energy as a function of continued feeding in a patch (solid line) but leaves the patch at time "C" (see text for explanation).

When should the subject leave to find another patch? If it leaves too soon, it is sacrificing food that is still available in that patch. If the animal stays too long, then the number of remaining food items continues to diminish, causing the intake of food per unit of time to decline even more. In other words, staying too long means that the subject experiences diminishing returns for its effort; leaving too soon means that it forfeits food that is readily available there. The optimal time to leave is shown in Figure 11-22 at point "C." Here, the total available energy per unit of time is at its maximum value.[79] Several studies have supported this model, although not all of its predictions have been upheld.[80]

If leaving a patch depends on gauging the rate of energy intake per unit of time, then what is the time period over which a subject assesses rate of intake? How long will an animal persist without being fed before it abandons its current patch? So-called **time horizons** were studied by Timberlake, Gawley, and Lucas (1987). The box used for testing the rats was divided by a partition, thus creating two separate patches. Each contained a lever. The schedule in one patch was called a "progressive schedule" because the number of responses required to obtain the next food pellet increased by one after each reward. For example, a subject might be required to press five times for the first food pellet, six for the next pellet, then seven, eight, and so forth.

After a fixed time had elapsed, the schedule in the other patch became available.[81] Here, responding was continuously reinforced. The time between when the animal started responding on the progressive schedule and when the continuous-reward schedule in the other patch became available (called the "time horizon") was 4, 8, 16, 32, or 64. The rats foraged at a high rate in the progressive patch when access to the continuous patch was delayed more than 16 minutes. Stated differently, if subjects could begin foraging in the continuously rewarded patch within 16 minutes, they showed a decline in responding in the low-yield progressive patch. However, if access to the high-yield (continuous) patch was more than 16 minutes away, then subjects did not show a decline in response rate in the progressive patch.

These data are shown in Figure 11-23. When the continuous patch was available within 16 minutes, less than 100% of the baseline number of pellets was earned in the progressive-ratio patch. Subjects suppressed their behavior in favor of the more profitable patch, which they expected to enter within 16 minutes. However, when access to the profitable patch was delayed for 32 minutes or longer, subjects did not show such a decline; they continued to work on the low-yield (progressive) schedule. The experiment, therefore, shows that animals are sensitive to the rates of food intake in the current patch, relative to future patches, but that there are certain time limitations over which the comparison takes place.

The third major issue addressed by optimal-foraging theory is diet selection. From the point of view of costs and benefits, an animal must be selective in what it eats. Eating prey items that are too small yields little energy, compared to the cost of finding and preparing the items. Larger prey items

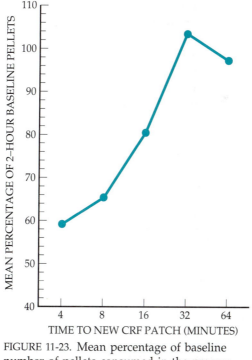

FIGURE 11-23. Mean percentage of baseline number of pellets consumed in the progressive-ratio patch, as a function of the time prior to access to the continuously rewarded patch (after Timberlake, Gawley, & Lucas, 1987).

are better in this regard, but they are less plentiful and thus take an even longer time to find and prepare.[82]

According to an optimality model developed by MacArthur and Pianka (1966), diet selection should follow the principles shown in Figure 11-24. Assume that a forager chooses from among eight prey items that vary in size. As shown in the upper solid line of Figure 11-24, the energy afforded by the prey item increases with size. At the same time, however, each prey item differs in terms of the amount of time required to find and prepare it. As shown in the lower solid line, prey items 1–5 are quite plentiful (time required to find them is short), but the larger items are less so; they require considerably more time to find.

An animal's strategy should not simply be to take the largest available prey item, but rather the most profitable prey item—that is, the one that yields the highest energy per unit of time. The energy per unit of time is shown by the dotted line in Figure 11-24. Thus, even though prey item 8 affords the greatest amount of energy, it also takes the most time to find. Its *relative* energy is not as high as for other prey items. For example, the energy for prey item 4 is somewhat lower than for prey item 5, but the time required to secure it is less, making the energy per unit of time greater.[83] Animals follow a strategy of this kind in choosing which items to eat.[84] The exact strategy, however, may be more complicated, especially when the cost of recognizing edible prey from nonedible items is appreciable.[85]

An example of the selective choice of prey items was Zach's (1978) study of the feeding behavior of northwestern crows.[86] These birds feed on whelks, a form of shellfish found among the rocks during low tides. After securing a whelk, the crow flies in the air and releases the whelk over a rock to crack

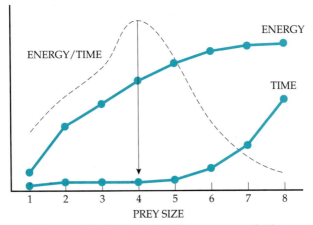

FIGURE 11-24. Model depicting the energy available from prey items that vary in size, the time required to secure and prepare the prey item, and the energy per unit of time that each prey item represents.

the shell and secure the meat. According to optimal-foraging theory, the crow has an optimal strategy that evaluates the costs and benefits of its action. Smaller whelks are more plentiful, but less energy is gained, and they are harder to break because their shells are more pliable. Larger whelks are less plentiful, but they afford more energy, and they are easier to break because their shells are more brittle.

In terms of the costs of breaking a whelk, flying too high wastes energy and risks scattering the prey on the rocks, at least for whelks with brittle shells. Flying too low expends less energy but risks not breaking the whelk, thus requiring the bird to try again. The predicted height, based on the cost of flying and the energy gained, was calculated to be 5 meters. In reality, the crows were observed to drop the whelk from an average height of 5.2 meters.

Foraging optimally is only one consideration for a hungry animal; another is whether the subject is at risk from a predator. Foragers must balance foraging, vigilance, and predator defense. A fourth area of behavioral regulation addressed by optimality theory, therefore, is the trade-off between foraging behavior and predator defense.

Several experiments show that when the threat of a predator is low, foraging occupies more of the subject's time than when the threat of a predator is high.[87] For example, in a study by Helmstetter and Fanselow (1993), rats lived in a two-compartment box and had to earn all of their food by pressing a lever. One side contained the lever; the other contained a nesting area filled with sawdust, where the animal could spend time when not foraging. To begin a meal, a subject was required to press 50 times; after that, a reward pellet was delivered for each additional press. Thus, a subject could control both when it foraged for food and the size of each meal.

For the first 7 days, the subject's normal meal pattern was measured. For the next 7-day period, shocks were delivered randomly whenever the subject was on the food side of the box. The number of shocks per day varied between 12 and 96. This meant that the subject had to make a decision. It could earn food at any time, but it also risked receiving shock.[88] Should it ignore the shocks and earn all of its daily rations, or should the subject reduce its food intake to avoid receiving shock?

The results showed that meal size increased and meal frequency decreased when the rats were given the low and medium intensity shocks. Subjects ate fewer meals, but each meal was larger. Using such a strategy, subjects were able to maintain approximately the same daily intake of food even when receiving frequent shock.[89] In short, subjects visited the foraging site less often (thus exposing themselves to less risk and aversion), although, when there, they ate longer meals. The rats demonstrated a trade-off between feeding time and exposure to aversion.

INTERIM SUMMARY

The behavior-analysis approach to learning, shown in the work of Skinner, does not explain behavior by making use of physiological or behavioral mechanisms, nor does it appeal to goals and behavioral representations. Rather, the approach focuses primarily on the reinforcement contingency and the functional relationships between behavior and outcomes. The response-deprivation hypothesis argues that instrumental behaviors are not learned because of a special consequence called a "reinforcer," but rather because the subject is deprived of an activity on which a response is contingent. If constrained by a reinforcement schedule, subjects engage in one behavior above its baseline rate in order to have access to another activity that has been restricted. A second important focus within the behavior analysis tradition is behavioral economics. According to this view, animals have essential needs that are met with regard to the laws of supply and demand. If the cost of the good increases, then demand diminishes. The extent to which demand declines, however, depends on how critical the commodity is for survival. Important items show inelasticity of demand, meaning that demand diminishes only slightly with increases in price. Substitution between two commodities also influences demand. An indifference curve plots a series of points that represent equally valuable combinations of two commodities. The combination actually purchased is shown at the intersection of the budget line and the indifference function. Within the economic approach to behavioral regulation, research has focused on how behavioral plans maximize benefit, relative to cost. For a foraging animal, food is unevenly distributed in patches, so the first task is to find a suitable patch. This involves sampling. The second decision involves leaving the patch. This occurs when the food per unit of time begins to decline. The subject's estimation concerning when other more desirable patches become available also influences the decision to leave the patch. A third issue is diet selection. Finally, optimal-foraging theory has focused on issues such as the trade-off between foraging efficiency and vigilance for predators.

ENDNOTES

1. Recall that the Premack principle defined a reinforcement relationship in terms of two activities, one more preferable or probable than the other, rather than in terms of a response and a stimulus such as a US (see Chapter 8).
2. See Donegan and Thompson (1991) for a historical discussion and evaluation of research strategies.
3. See Penfield and Jasper (1954); Penfield and Perot (1963).
4. The brain itself has no pain receptors, so this can be accomplished using only local anesthesia.
5. Penfield and Perot (1963, p. 653).
6. Penfield and Perot (1963, p. 654).
7. Halgren, Walter, Cherlow, and Crandall (1978); Loftus and Loftus (1980).
8. Hebb (1949, p. 63).
9. Hebb explicitly avoided suggesting that cell assemblies could be physically located. These were functional units of neurological material, not necessarily adjacent and segregated clusters of neurons.
10. Dunn (1980).

11. See Martinez, Schulteis, and Weinberger (1991); McGaugh (1983) for reviews.
12. Davis and Squire (1984); see also Brinton (1991).
13. Some suggest that cortical tissue, specifically the perirhinal and entorhinal areas that lie beneath the hippocampus, is actually more critical; see Petri and Mishkin (1994); Zola-Morgan, Squire, Amaral, and Suzuki (1989).
14. See Teyler (1991).
15. Barr, Goldberg, Wasserstein, and Novelly (1990).
16. Milner, Corkin, and Teuber (1968).
17. See Morris (1994); Teyler (1991).
18. See also Milner (1989) for a historical account of this contribution. Animals fitted with these brain electrodes behave normally in virtually every respect. The electrode is fixed to a plastic plug, which, in turn, is secured to the skull; the electrodes are then attached to the stimulator via wires.
19. These impulses were just above threshold; they varied between about 1.4 and 4.8 volts.
20. Because of the unusual way the data were recorded, exact response rates cannot be determined, but informal analysis shows that only one of the nonseptal animals responded during the stimulation period, relative to nonstimulation periods, at levels approaching those of the septal animals.
21. This finding, although important in terms of establishing a neurological basis for punishment, is more intuitively plausible than the discovery by Olds and Milner (1954) of a positive reward system. That is, given that electrical shock is usually aversive, the fact that it produces a punishing effect when applied directly to the brain is not as surprising as the finding that direct stimulation to the brain may be highly rewarding.
22. See Heath (1963).
23. Indeed, rats find the stimulation so compelling that they have been known to starve themselves of food to continue pressing for brain stimulation; see Routtenberg and Lindy (1965).
24. Although Lenzer (1972) discussed differences between the effects of natural rewards and those involved in brain self-stimulation (but see Gibson, Reid, Sakai, & Porter, 1965), it is more widely held that the reward system and appetitive motivational centers are inextricably linked; see Panksepp (1982).
25. See Panksepp (1986); Routtenberg (1978).
26. Mondadori, Ornstein, Waser, and Houston (1976); see also Carr and White (1984).
27. Vaccarino, Schiff, and Glickman (1989).
28. Glickman and Schiff (1967); Vaccarino, Schiff, and Glickman (1989).
29. Vaccarino, Schiff, and Glickman (1989, p. 120).
30. See Panksepp (1986).
31. Wise, Berger, and Stein (1973).
32. Lyness, Friedle, and Moore (1979); Wise (1978).
33. However, see Gray (1985).
34. See Wise (1989).
35. See also Hull (1952).
36. For an excellent account of theories of learning, see Malone (1991).
37. Hull (1943, p. 178).
38. Drive reduction in Hull's system was always closely associated with biological need reduction. However, Hull also recognized that stimuli that had been associated with need reduction are also capable of reducing drive. For example, a stimulus that had been paired with food (which reduced the primary need) is itself capable of reducing drive and thus reinforcing an S–R connection.

39. Although the figure depicts $_sH_R$ as a function of the number of reinforcers, habit is also affected by the size of the reinforcer. Events that are more need reducing constitute stronger reinforcement than those that reduce the subject's need to a lesser extent.

40. This general formulation (performance = learning × motivation) is important not only for learning research, but also for theorists in social and motivational psychology.

41. Performance of an incorrect response may be observed if the subject is, say, hungry but does not know how to execute the correct response. What is meant here by performance, therefore, is really performance of the correct response, relative to other incorrect reactions.

42. See Perin (1942); Williams (1938).

43. Spence (1952).

44. See Bolles (1975) for an excellent discussion.

45. See Harlow (1953).

46. Butler (1953).

47. Amsel (1992).

48. See also Tolman (1948).

49. The latent-learning outcome was used in Chapter 2 to illustrate the learning-versus-performance distinction. Here, we provide the details of Tolman and Honzik's experiment.

50. Critics have argued that learning actually did take place in the first phase for the shifted and no-reward subjects. The small but systematic decline in latency scores is used as evidence. Whether this is true, however, is irrelevant to the larger issue raised here—namely, that the relative change in performance for the shifted group, following the introduction of food reward, was large and dramatic (thus illustrating the fact that changes in reward magnitude affect incentive motivation).

51. Butler (1953).

52. See Bolles (1972).

53. In some sense, the message from the research on S–O associations is similar to that described for S–S associations in Pavlovian conditioning (see Chapter 6), although discriminative stimuli and Pavlovian CSs have been shown to function in a decidedly different fashion; see Rescorla (1994).

54. See Rescorla (1991b) for a review.

55. See also Adams (1982); Adams and Dickinson (1981); Bolles, Holtz, Dunn, and Hill (1980); Rescorla (1990b).

56. A different kind of association could also be formed during instrumental conditioning—namely, an O–R association. According to such a position, when the S_d is turned on, the subject anticipates receiving the outcome (S–O association), which, in turn, causes it to remember the associated response (O–R association). Research has not supported this alternative theory, however; see Rescorla (1992); Rescorla and Colwill (1989).

57. Rescorla (1991a).

58. Colwill and Rescorla (1988b).

59. Rescorla (1993a); see also Rescorla (1993b).

60. Mackintosh (1983) suggests that the performance is based on propositional reasoning. Specifically, "The association between instrumental response and reinforcer should be regarded as an expectation or proposition about certain relationships, which, when combined with other premises, can be used to derive instructions to perform or withhold that response. . . . Instrumental performance is thus the con-

sequence of an instruction inferred from an association, rather than being directly elicited by an association" (Mackintosh, 1983, p. 111).

61. The handle pull involved tugging upward on the handle portion of an L-shaped rod that extended up through the grid floor.

62. These responses were a lever press and chain pull.

63. The discriminative stimulus could actually have two functions: (1) signaling that reinforcement is available, pending execution of the appropriate response (its discriminative function; and (2) signaling that reinforcement will follow (its Pavlovian function). This question was addressed by Rescorla (1994); see also Holman and Mackintosh (1981). In Rescorla's study, subjects could respond to S_1 to obtain O_1, but during S_2, they automatically received O_2. Thus, S_1 functioned as an S_d, and S_2 was a Pavlovian CS. Transfer tests were then performed. The S_d augmented a response with which it shared an outcome more than did a Pavlovian CS. Rescorla concluded, "These results suggest that instrumental training endows a stimulus with information about the outcome that goes beyond the simple Pavlovian S–O association. A conventional view that an instrumental discriminative stimulus simply has an embedded Pavlovian relation does not appear to capture the present results" (p. 48).

64. See also Colwill and Rescorla (1990); Gaffan & Gowling (1984); Rescorla (1990a).

65. Ringen (1993, p. 9).

66. Skinner (1950a); see Modgil and Modgil (1987) for a thorough assessment of Skinner's theory.

67. The intended analogy here is with natural selection. Skinner argued that just as the morphological characteristics of a species are selected for by outcomes in the environment, behaviors, too, are selected for by their consequences.

68. The circularity of Skinner's notion of reward is most noticeable when describing the empirical law of effect. Empirically, a behavior increases when followed by a reinforcer; if it does not increase, then the event that followed it cannot, by definition, have been a reinforcer. The empirical law of effect, and the concept of reinforcement on which it is based, are, therefore, not contestable in this sense.

69. See also Allison (1993); Allison and Timberlake (1974, 1975); Timberlake and Allison (1974).

70. See Allison, Buxton, and Moore (1987).

71. See Hanson and Timberlake (1983); Rachlin and Burkhard (1978); Staddon (1979).

72. See Allison (1983); Green and Kagel (1987); Hursh (1984); Lea, Tarpy, and Webley (1987); van Raaij, van Veldhoven, and Wärneryd (1988) for general reviews of economic psychology.

73. See Lea (1978).

74. See also Hursh (1984); Lea and Roper (1977).

75. See Green and Rachlin (1991); Rachlin, Green, Kagel, and Battalio (1976); Rachlin, Kagel, and Battalio (1980).

76. Awareness of the choice is not necessary.

77. For example, the subject may have more money to spend, due to a raise, or less money because of an increase in taxation.

78. Excellent reviews of optimal-foraging theory have been written by Kamil, Krebs, and Pulliam (1987); Kamil and Roitblat (1985); Kamil and Sargent (1981); Lea (1981); Pyke, Pulliam, and Charnov (1977); and Stephens and Krebs (1986).

79. The total time spent foraging is represented on the horizontal axis by the distance from "A" to "C"; the total energy derived is given by the vertical axis at point "C."

80. Cowie (1977); Killeen, Smith, and Hanson (1981); Krebs, Ryan, and Charnov (1974); also see Iwasa, Higashi, and Yamamura (1981); McNamara (1982) for alternative models.
81. Small lights in the box signaled the availability of the schedules.
82. Two assumptions are relevant here. First, a prey requires time to grow. Larger prey are thus invariably older. Second, the longer a prey lives, the greater the probability that it will be killed and eaten. Thus, it follows that larger prey are less plentiful.
83. The model predicts that if the environment suddenly changes, and many more large prey items are available (and thus the time required to find them is less), then the optimum prey item in the diet would shift.
84. See Goss-Custard (1981); Krebs, Erichsen, Webber, and Charnov (1977).
85. See Erichsen, Krebs, and Houston (1980).
86. See also Zach (1979); Zach and Smith (1981).
87. See Fanselow, Lester, and Helmstetter (1988); Milinski and Heller (1978).
88. Shock, much like a predator, represents an aversive cost to foraging.
89. With high densities of shock, however, total food intake was suppressed.

CHAPTER 12

Adaptive Specializations in Learning

Chapter 7 introduced the concept of adaptive specializations in Pavlovian conditioning. The analogous claim may be made for instrumental learning—namely, that animals display adaptive, species-specific learning processes in the context of response learning. The assumption is that throughout evolution, individuals that were born with the capacity to make a slightly more advantageous response (for example, to secure more food or to avoid predators more effectively) were at a selective advantage, relative to other members of their species, which were not. On the average, the former individuals were more likely to survive and successfully reproduce than were individuals that were not endowed with this behavioral advantage.

The primary goal of this chapter is to review the research and theories pertaining to species-typical response learning. Two cautions are in order. First, instrumental responding depends on the stimuli present at the time of the behavior. That is, the response–reinforcer relationship cannot be divorced from the stimuli that trigger the response. In fact, this notion is part of the claim made by the behavior systems approach, which is discussed in detail later in this chapter. Second, the distinction between Pavlovian and instrumental conditioning is based primarily on procedural differences. In terms of mechanisms, the distinction between these processes is less compelling. Indeed, as discussed in Chapters 6 and 11, many of the generalizations that pertain to Pavlovian conditioning, such as the development of an association between a CS and a US, also apply to instrumental conditioning.[1]

Thus, learning is discussed in this chapter from an instrumental viewpoint, but the distinction between the two forms of conditioning is largely a procedural one. Given these warnings, the general argument is that if subjects have evolved biologically specialized forms of Pavlovian learning (as discussed in Chapter 7), then they should have evolved biologically specialized behaviors in the context of response learning, as well.

PHASE-SPECIFIC LEARNING

A characteristic of species-typical response learning is that a reinforcer often is not necessary or even obvious. Individuals perform an act, but they do not receive any obvious reward for doing so.[2] Furthermore, several forms of species-typical learning are phase-specific, meaning that they occur only, or at least most strongly, during a certain period of time in the animal's life.[3] Such periods, or phases, are referred to as critical periods.[4] Two forms of **phase-specific learning** considered here are song learning in birds and imprinting in various animals.

Song Learning

Birdsong, for many species of bird, such as the alder and the willow flycatcher, is innate.[5] For others, however, songs are learned.[6] Although the songs are not learned through conventional instrumental or Pavlovian conditioning processes, nevertheless, many species learn them as a result of critical feedback from the environment.[7] If individuals are isolated early in life, then they develop abnormal songs, compared to other members of their species, which are not isolated. Song learning in birds is a widely studied and important topic in behavioral development.[8]

Constraints on Song Quality.

Some researchers believe that birds are constrained in terms of the kind of song they are able to learn. This view is the **template theory.**[9] According to this position, birds are born with a pattern, or template, that is responsible for shaping the details of their song. The template is, in a sense, a kind of filter. Evidence favoring this position shows, for example, that males that are raised in isolation develop abnormal songs.[10] They sing when reaching adulthood, but the characteristics of the song (for example, the number of syllables, the patterns, and the sequence of notes) do not resemble the song of normal white-crowned sparrows. Exposure to the appropriate song between 10 and 50 days of age, however, results in normal song development. Similarly, exposure to the songs of other species has no effect on the development of the appropriate white-crowned sparrow song. The template excludes songs from other species.

Let us consider these results in greater detail. Marler and Peters (1977) studied two species of sparrow—swamp and song sparrow—that live in the same area of the country but sing dramatically different songs. The two kinds of songs are shown in Figure 12-1. The photos in Figure 12-1 are sound spectrograms of the songs performed by these two species. A spectrogram is a visual depiction of song. It plots tone frequency on the vertical axis and time on the horizontal axis. Thus, lines that move upward depict notes that are rising in pitch; the steeper the line, the sharper the rise. To the human ear, the swamp sparrow's song consists of only one part—namely, the repetition of a single syllable. The song sparrow, in contrast, sings a two-part song, consisting of a number of short notes, followed by a trill near the end.

Swamp sparrow   Song sparrow

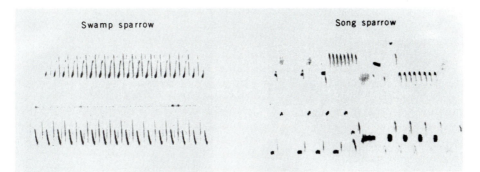

FIGURE 12-1. Sound spectrograms of the songs demonstrated by swamp and song sparrows (after Marler & Peters, 1977).
Courtesy of Professor Peter Marler, Animal Communications Lab, University of California, Davis

The authors cut and spliced sections of a tape recording of both swamp and song sparrow songs to create a series of 22 different artificial songs. Some of them were swamp-sparrow-like; that is, they contained only one part. Other songs were distinctly song-sparrow-like; they contained two parts. Songs also varied in terms of whether the pitches were rising, steady, or falling, and whether the changes in pitch were fast or slow.

The swamp sparrow subjects had been either hand-reared in acoustical isolation or reared by foster parents (canaries). They were given 30 days of training, during which they heard all of the 22 artificial songs. These birds exhibited extremely selective learning. They developed songs that contained swamp sparrow syllables, rejecting songs that contained song sparrow syllables, even when the syllables were presented in a fashion that resembled the song of the swamp sparrow (that is, even when the song had only one part). In short, the subjects were unable to learn songs that contained inappropriate syllables, causing the authors to conclude that a template for one's own species-typical song is involved in song learning.

Although the template theory accounts for some results, it does not account for others. For example, some birds learn about, and respond to, songs that they themselves never sing.[11] Petrinovich (1985) studied isolated white-crowned sparrows, giving them a range of tape-recorded songs. The songs were recorded from various species, including the Mexican junco. The sparrows were able to learn components of the song of the alien species.[12] Thus, song learning is more flexible than suggested by the strict template theory. According to Petrinovich, "It seems likely that factors other than stimulus filtering or genetically tuned templates have a profound influence on the acquisition of song."[13]

Sensitive Period.

Many researchers assert that in addition to possible constraints on song type, there is a sensitive period during which the song must be learned.[14] In its strictest sense, this notion implies that song learning cannot take place

Photograph of the swamp (top) and song (bottom) sparrows used to study different bird song dialects.
© *Thomas W. Martin, The National Audobon Society Collection/Photo Researchers*
© *Allan D. Cruickshank, The National Audobon Society Collection/Photo Researchers*

before or after a **critical period.** There is evidence that a sensitive period exists for many species of birds, although the length of the period varies. White-crowned sparrows develop their song between 10 and 50 days of age.[15] Indigo buntings, on the other hand, have a much more extended sensitive period.[16] Zebra finches have yet a different sensitive period, from 35 to about 60–80 days of age, a period of time that roughly marks the point at which birds become independent from their parents, and sexual maturity is reached.[17]

Eales (1985) demonstrated the sensitive period in zebra finches. Young male subjects remained with both parents until they were 35 days old, at which point the mothers were removed. Subjects then remained with their fathers for an additional 0, 15, 30, or 85 days (until age 35, 50, 65, and 120 days, respectively). After about 4 months, the songs of these young birds were analyzed.[18]

Normal zebra finch males sing a song that contains anywhere from 2 to 11 discrete elements or syllables. These syllables are strung together in a sequence or song bout. It was thus possible to determine how many of the father's elements were present in the young male subjects. Figure 12-2 shows the percentage of the father's song that was performed, as a function of age at isolation. All of the subjects that were isolated at 35 days of age showed an abnormal song; the song structure did not resemble the father's song. Subjects that had 15 days or more of tutorial from their fathers, however, showed about 70% or more overlap. By age 65 days (30 days of tutorial), matching was virtually perfect.[19] In short, the proportion of the shared elements between father and son increased over time, suggesting that zebra finches develop their song between the ages of 35 and 65 days.

Is this sensitive period rigid? Do subjects learn before the age of independence from their parents (35 days), and, conversely, do they learn after age 65 days if they had been isolated prior to that? The general conclusion is that the sensitive period is not fixed. Song learning may occur prior, and subsequent, to the critical dates.

First, consider the learning that occurs during the first 35 days. Clayton (1987) took young zebra finch males away from their parents at 35 days of age and placed them with Bengalese finch male foster tutors. They learned rather poorly from their tutors. They continued to produce songs heard during their first 35 days of life despite having a male tutor present during the so-called sensitive period, between age 35 and 60 days.

Clayton's study indicates that male zebra finches learn during the first 35 days of age, but such learning does not preclude additional learning from a tutor during the sensitive phase. This result was demonstrated by Eales (1987b). Young male zebra finches were raised by their mothers, in isolation from the adult male song, until the age of 35, 50, or 65 days. At that point, the fathers were returned to the environment, thus allowing the young males to hear the male song.

The results are shown in Figure 12-3. When a young subject was exposed to the adult male song at 35 days of age, all of its subsequent song, measured 4 months later, overlapped with the father's song. Delaying exposure to the father by even 15 days considerably reduced the extent of overlap. Only about

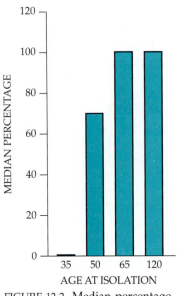

FIGURE 12-2. Median percentage of their father's song that was learned by the young male subjects, as a function of age when they were removed from the father (days) (after Eales, 1985).

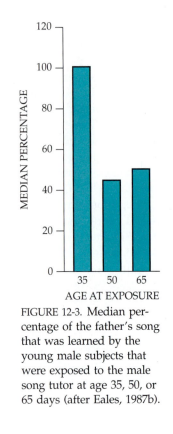

FIGURE 12-3. Median percentage of the father's song that was learned by the young male subjects that were exposed to the male song tutor at age 35, 50, or 65 days (after Eales, 1987b).

40–45% of the song elements for subjects exposed at 50 or 65 days of age were the same as those found in the father's song.

Thus, if an adult male's song becomes available after approximately 35 days of age, then the subjects not only have no difficulty learning the song, but this song actually replaces any song that may have been learned from the mother. Young males use the female call notes (which differ from the male song), but only on a temporary basis. If the male song is heard afterward, they adopt that song. Eales's study therefore shows that young zebra finch males do not need to experience song during the first 35 days of age, but they must hear the song beginning at about that time if they are to learn it accurately. Furthermore, subjects discard female call notes that may have been learned during the first 35 days in favor of the male song.

Zebra finch males are also capable of learning their song after the critical period. Eales (1985), for example, isolated males at age 35 days but placed them with normal adult tutors 6 months later. These subjects learned the appropriate song even though they had been isolated during the critical period. This is shown by the spectrograms in Figure 12-4. The overlap between songs was very poor after 4 months, prior to being given the tutor, but the match was very good when measured after 1 year.

Thus, the sensitive period is not fixed. Although males that are isolated at 35 days of age develop an abnormal song, they develop an appropriate song

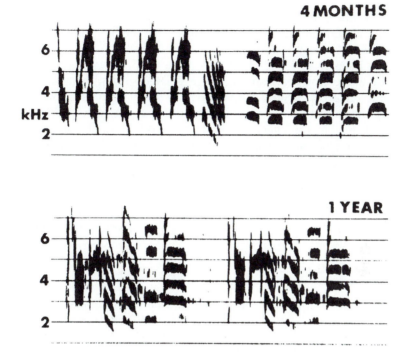

FIGURE 12-4. Spectrograms showing tutor's song (on left) and subject's song (right) after 4 months (top) and 1 year (bottom). Subject had been isolated between 35 and 120 days of age (after Eales, 1985).
Courtesy of Academic Press, London
(By Ms L. A. Eales published as figure 4 on page 1296 from "Song Learning in Zebra Finches" pp. 1293–1300 of Animal Behaviour, *vol. 33, 1985)*

when allowed to hear it at 6 months of age. "As far as song learning is concerned, normally raised males tend to reproduce songs heard at around 35 to 65 days of age. Birds can be deprived of appropriate experience at this time by not letting them hear adult song, by not allowing them to interact visually with a song tutor, or by giving them only a tutor belonging to a different species from the male that reared them. In these circumstances our experiments have shown that young males may produce elements from songs heard *before or after* this time [emphasis added]."[20]

Social Factors.

The preceding quote suggests that the opportunity to interact socially with another bird is an important factor in song learning. This was shown by Eales (1987a), who placed young male zebra finches with a Bengalese finch and showed that the zebra finch learned the song adequately from this foster father. Later, however, when the zebra finch was allowed to interact with another zebra finch, and contact with the foster father was restricted, so that only visual and auditory contact was possible, then the new zebra finch influenced the subject's song.

Another interesting experiment was done by Baptista and Petrinovich (1984). Male white-crowned sparrows were isolated during their first 50 days of age. Some birds remained isolated, whereas others were then placed with a tutor. The subject could see and hear its tutor but was confined to a separate compartment in the cage. Some of the tutors were the subject's own species, some a different subspecies of sparrow, and others were an alien species—namely, a strawberry finch. All of the subjects learned the song that was produced by their tutor, despite the fact that they were past the so-called critical age. Moreover, subjects heard songs from an alien species that could not have conformed to their template, yet, given the appropriate social interactions, they learned the tutor's song effectively. Thus, social contact may overcome learning deficits created by isolation.

Imprinting

It is reasonable to assume that the ability for a newborn animal to recognize a member of its own species is innate. Species identification in many animals, however, at least in terms of preference, is learned by means of a phase-specific learning process called "imprinting."[21]

Imprinting is most readily observed in birds that are relatively well-developed at birth and thus are able to utilize their motor abilities nearly to their full extent.[22] In the natural environment, the imprinting process takes place readily. Usually the mother, say, a duck hen, vocalizes recurrently and then slowly walks away from the brood. The chicks follow within a short period of time. This following behavior is evidence for the imprinting process.

Young chicks not only follow their mother, they follow virtually any moving object soon after birth. In laboratory demonstrations of imprinting, for example, chicks are placed in a testing arena and exposed to an imprinting object such as a geometric shape, toy train, tennis ball, watering can, foam-rubber doll, stuffed animal, or even a human being.[23] Once following is observed, the chick is then put into a choice apparatus and allowed to approach either the preexposed object or a novel object. Inevitably, the bird demonstrates the effects of imprinting by approaching the preexposed (imprinted) stimulus. Indeed, the animal will show a strong and lasting preference for the imprinted object over the animal's own natural mother.

Critical Period.

Early research suggested that imprinting is a unique form of learning, quite unlike classical and instrumental conditioning.[24] There were several lines of evidence. First, imprinting was thought to be irreversible. If a bird was imprinted to an inanimate object, such as a revolving cardboard disk, then its preference would be permanent; it would be impossible to substitute a dif-

Photo showing ducklings following the woman to which the ducklings had become imprinted. In the natural environment, of course, the object on which ducklings imprint is the mother hen.
© *Clyde H. Smith/Peter Arnold, Inc.*

ferent object for that imprinted stimulus later on.[25] Second, imprinting could only occur during a critical period of time. This was suggested in studies of imprinting by Hess (1959b). Ducklings were imprinted at various ages after hatching. The task was to follow a duck decoy around a circular alleyway for a period of 10 minutes. Hess found that imprinting increased to a maximum at about 13–16 hours of age and then declined. In other words, the subjects imprinted on the decoy only during a particular time. If the animals failed to be imprinted during this sensitive period, then the opportunity was lost, and imprinting was difficult to achieve.

Although imprinting continues to be regarded as a phase-sensitive learning process, research has challenged the notion that it is confined to a critical period of time. For example, researchers have shown that even 5- to 10-day-old ducklings may be imprinted.[26] Granted the older birds must be given more exposure to the imprinting stimulus, but nevertheless, imprinting does occur. The earlier belief—that imprinting is restricted to a few hours after birth—was based on experiments using short exposure periods.

Imprinting is also reversible. With a long enough exposure to a second imprinting object, subjects shift their attachment to a new stimulus.[27] The shift represents a true change in preference because the occasional presentation of the first imprinting object retards the switch.[28] However, the switch occurs only when subjects are passively exposed to the original imprinting object.[29]

If ducklings are allowed to follow the original object, then they are resistant to change when exposed to a second object that differs in color and shape. The reason is that when animals actively follow the original imprinting object, they learn its characteristics in greater detail. Subjects that only observe the object from a distance do not.

Critical Features of Imprinting Stimuli.

Many studies of imprinting have attempted to specify the critical characteristics of the imprinting stimulus. One factor is whether the imprinting object is inanimate. Although birds may imprint on many kinds of inanimate objects, they treat them differently than they do members of their own brood. For example, Gaioni and Ross (1982) housed Peking ducklings in two kinds of environments 10 to 20 hours after hatching. Some were housed with 12 companion ducklings. Others were housed with 12 foam-rubber blocks that were hung from the frame of the apparatus in such a way that they could move about. On the seventh and eighth days, all ducklings were given a test. Here, they were placed in a testing arena along with 0, 1, 2, 3, 4, 5, or 12 of the original imprinting objects. The subject's distress calling was measured (subjects that are deprived of an imprinting object will show distress and will engage in distress-calling behavior).

The data are shown in Figure 12-5. When none of the original imprinting objects was present, both groups of subjects showed considerable distress. The

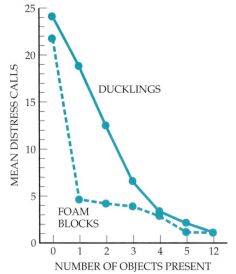

FIGURE 12-5. Mean number of distress calls on the test, as a function of the number of imprinting objects present during the test, for groups that had been imprinted on 12 conspecific ducklings or 12 moving foam-rubber blocks (after Gaioni & Ross, 1982).

ducklings that had been housed with other ducklings showed a graded relationship between number present and distress calling. The fewer objects present, the more distress the ducklings showed. Subjects imprinted on the foam-rubber blocks, however, showed little distress, even when only a single foam block was present. Perhaps the difference is due to the fact that live conspecifics are more reinforcing than are inanimate objects. Alternatively, live ducklings may provide more social contact or warmth, and thus their loss is more distressing than is the loss of inanimate objects (see the following section for a discussion of the reinforcement theory of imprinting).

A second factor that influences imprinting is whether the imprinting stimulus moves. In the preceding study, stationary foam blocks were much less effective in producing imprinting than were moving blocks. Other research has supported this finding more directly. For example, Klopfer (1971) compared decoys that moved within the apparatus to projected movie images of the same decoys rotating. More specifically, 6 hours after hatching, ducklings were exposed to either a moving three-dimensional decoy or a rear-projected image of the same decoy rotating. Twenty-four hours later, they were given a 20-minute preference test on which their approach and following behaviors for two targets were recorded. The behavior on the test depended on whether the subject *and* the imprinting object moved during training. Subjects that were given the opportunity to approach the decoy showed much more filial behavior later on. Furthermore, the moving decoys were more effective in eliciting imprinting than were the two-dimensional images. Thus, movement of both the imprinting object and the subject is critical.[30]

A third important dimension is the sound that the imprinting object emits. Although many mallard ducklings appear to have an innate preference for the maternal call, exposure to their own vocalizations, which resemble the maternal call in a fundamental way, are critical for imprinting.[31] Furthermore, appropriate responding to the maternal call after hatching depends on experiencing the highly specific patterning of the call during embryonic development.[32] In short, a response to the species-specific duck call depends on the auditory experience of the duckling during embryonic development, and on hearing their own vocalizations prior to being exposed to the maternal call.

How does the maternal duck call affect a subject that has already been imprinted? This question was addressed in an interesting study by Johnston and Gottlieb (1981). Twenty-four hours after hatching, mallard ducklings were imprinted on a stuffed mallard decoy that was suspended over the circular arena. A photograph of the apparatus is shown in Figure 12-6. The model rotated around the periphery of the apparatus at about 9 centimeters per second. Furthermore, the model contained a small tape recorder that emitted the species-typical call of the mallard hen during the first minute of each 5-minute training period. A 10-minute choice test was given 48 hours later.[33] Here, the mallard decoy and a red-and-white striped wooden box were suspended on opposite ends of the crossbar of the apparatus. These stimuli are shown in Figure 12-7. Subjects were scored in terms of (a) the latency to approach either the decoy or the box, and (b) the duration of their following behavior.

FIGURE 12-6. Photograph of the apparatus used by Johnston and Gottlieb (1981) to study imprinting in ducklings. Here, the duckling is following a taxidermic specimen of the mallard hen.
Courtesy of Professor Gilbert Gottlieb, Center for Developmental Science, University of North Carolina, Chapel Hill

A compilation of the results is shown in Figure 12-8. When neither the decoy nor the box emitted any sound, subjects strongly preferred the decoy, and the latency to approach the silent decoy was much shorter than that to approach the silent box (Figure 12-8, left). When the decoy was silent, but the box emitted the mallard duck call, preference dramatically shifted. Here, the ducklings approached the box within a short period of time (Figure 12-8, mid-

FIGURE 12-7. Stimuli used during the test session (after Johnston & Gottlieb, 1981).
Courtesy of Professor Gilbert Gottlieb, Center for Developmental Science, University of North Carolina, Chapel Hill

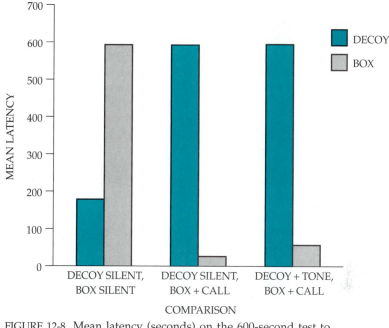

FIGURE 12-8. Mean latency (seconds) on the 600-second test to approach the mallard decoy or the red box on three different comparisons (after Johnston & Gottlieb, 1981).

dle). The same was true when the decoy emitted pure tones; subjects showed an overwhelming preference for the wooden box that emitted the natural mallard call, moving toward it quickly, rather than toward the decoy (Figure 12-8, right).

The species-typical maternal call, therefore, is extremely important in eliciting filial behavior. Although young ducklings follow moving objects, the maternal call virtually assures that the filial response will be made. Apparently, the call arouses the duckling's attention, so that it imprints onto the visual characteristics of the object. The maternal call continues to enhance the preference for the stimulus even after the imprinting process has taken place.[34]

Theories of Imprinting.

Researchers do not entirely agree about the theoretical mechanisms underlying the imprinting phenomenon.[35] One speculation is that imprinting is based on perceptual learning.[36] Mere exposure to the imprinting stimulus produces familiarity and preference. As the imprinting object becomes more familiar, novel objects tend to elicit fear reactions.

A second option is the **conditioning theory of imprinting,** proposed by Hoffman and Ratner (1973). The theory makes three claims. First, precocial birds are innately disposed to respond to certain kinds of stimulation— namely, moving objects. Animals find this stimulation reinforcing and therefore show filial behavior toward the object. Furthermore, through Pavlovian conditioning, the visual appearance (and perhaps sound) of the imprinting object acquires the capacity to elicit the filial behavior, as well. That is, the mere sight of the object is sufficient to elicit the imprinting reaction.[37]

A second assumption is that precocial birds develop fear of novel objects as they grow older.[38] Initially, they do not fear them (in fact, they find them reinforcing), but within a day or so after hatching, the birds become more and more frightened by novel objects.[39] An older subject, therefore, requires a longer period of exposure before an imprinting stimulus is reinforcing than does a younger animal.[40]

The final claim of the conditioning theory is that behavior is a resolution of the two competing tendencies aroused by the imprinting stimulus—namely, the filial or approach tendency and the fear reaction. The animal follows an object if it learned about the visual characteristics through Pavlovian conditioning, but the animal avoids the object and shows distress if the object was not exposed previously. The degree to which the animal follows or avoids is a combination of the two tendencies.

Hoffman and Ratner's theory explains many findings in the imprinting literature. For example, filial behavior is restricted to the exposed stimulus because that stimulus is familiar and rewarding; other stimuli that are presented later in training are novel and aversive. Similarly, older animals require a longer period of time to become familiar with a particular object, but once familiarity is achieved, then the novelty-induced fear reactions subside.

Some theorists do not agree with the reinforcement model of imprinting, claiming that precocial birds identify their species on the basis of species-typical auditory calls, rather than a conditioning process (see previous discussion).[41] Furthermore, the conditioning model makes various predictions that have not been supported. For instance, when subjects are repeatedly exposed to the visual aspects of an imprinting object, then, according to the conditioning model, extinction should occur (a decline in attachment should take place). Such an effect has not been found.[42] A third problem for the conditioning model is that, under some conditions, young birds become imprinted to static environmental cues or to stationary objects.[43] This finding is inconsistent with the conditioning theory because the theory assumes that moving objects are innately preferred by, or reinforcing for, young chicks.[44]

INTERIM SUMMARY

Some forms of species-typical learning are phase-specific, meaning that they occur only, or at least most strongly, during a certain critical period. Song learning for some species of bird is such an example. According to the template theory, birds are born with a pattern or template for a particular song, such that exposure to the appropriate species-typical song during the critical period results in normal song development. Some birds, however, learn songs from other species. Moreover, birds learn songs prior to, and after, the critical period. Social interaction with song tutors also affects song learning. Another example of phase-specific learning is imprinting, a process by which an individual learns species identification. Evidence for imprinting is the filial behavior shown to the mother (in nature) or to inanimate objects (in laboratory demonstrations). Early research suggested that imprinting was limited to a critical period, but contemporary evidence shows that imprinting may occur after the critical period. Factors that affect imprinting include the type of object (for instance, whether it is inanimate), the movement of the object and subject, and the sound that the object emits. The conditioning theory of imprinting claims that birds are innately disposed to respond to moving objects, and that through conditioning, the visual appearance of an object acquires the capacity to elicit the filial behavior. The theory also assumes that birds develop a fear of novel objects as they grow older, and that the following behavior is a resolution of the approach and fear reactions.

PREDATOR DEFENSE AND AVOIDANCE LEARNING

Many theorists argue that avoidance learning and predator defense, like certain phase-specific behaviors, constitute specialized forms of learning. Defense from predators or other harmful stimuli is an important activity related to survival. Therefore, from an evolutionary perspective, it is reasonable to assume that many species have evolved specialized means for defending themselves against predators. Some may be morphological characteristics, such as camouflage (protective coloration), or threatening characteristics; others may involve special sensory and motor capacities such as exceptionally keen eyesight or swift legs. Learning potentials related to avoidance or predator defense may also have evolved in specialized ways.

Bolles (1970) claimed that avoidance behaviors are innate defensive reactions that are specific to a given species; they are, therefore, **species-specific defense reactions (SSDRs).**[45] Many SSDRs evolved because, according to Bolles, survival from predators is too important to depend on a gradual learning process. If an animal had to learn to avoid its predators, it would probably not survive long enough to raise offspring. Effective avoidance, therefore, must have evolved as an innate behavioral capacity and thus should reflect the specialized sensory and motor abilities of a particular species.

As Bolles stated, "The parameters of the natural environment make it impossible for there to be any learning of defensive behaviors. Thus, no real-life predator is going to present cues just before it attacks. No owl hoots or whistles five seconds before pouncing on a mouse. And no owl terminates his hoots or whistles just as the mouse gets away so as to reinforce the avoidance response. Nor will the owl give the mouse enough trials for the necessary learning to occur. What keeps our little friends alive in the forest has nothing to do with avoidance learning as we normally conceive of it or investigate it in the laboratory."[46]

According to Bolles' theory, each species possesses a hierarchy of SSDRs. When confronted with a threat, the animal first performs its preferred SSDR. If that particular response is not effective, then the subject performs its next most probable SSDR. For example, rats easily learn to run down an alleyway to avoid

Defense against predators takes many forms. Some species have various morphological characteristics for predator defense. One of the most noted are spines of the
porcupine.
© *Jen & Des Bartlett, The National Audubon Society Collection/Photo Researchers.*

shock because the experimental procedures allow them to perform their preferred SSDR, which is running. In lever-press avoidance studies, in contrast,
where the preferred SSDR is not permitted, learning is very poor. To perform
efficiently, the rat must suppress its natural inclination—running—in favor of
an unnatural defense reaction—lever pressing. In short, bar-press avoidance is
not the rat's natural reaction to aversive cues such as shock, so the response is
learned either not at all or only after very protracted training experience.[47]

The following discussion deals with avoidance learning and predator
defense from an evolutionary viewpoint. The theme of this chapter—that conventional reinforcement is ineffective in some cases and superfluous in others—is consistent with the SSDR position.

Avoidance Behavior

Is reinforcement necessary for avoidance learning, or are avoidance behaviors
reflexive? The following is a discussion of several forms of avoidance behaviors
from an evolutionary, or species-specific, point of view (see also Chapter 8).

Active Avoidance.

The SSDR theory is supported by the finding that rats may be selectively bred for good or poor avoidance behavior.[48] Bond (1984a), for example, trained two strains of rats. One had been selectively bred for their good avoidance. Some subjects from the high and low strains could avoid shock by responding during a 5-second tone; others were given classical conditioning (that is, they received a 5-second tone followed by shock, regardless of their behavior).[49] The task made no difference in terms of the latency to respond. The high-avoidance strain performed better than the low-avoidance strain, regardless of the training condition.

In other words, subjects that could avoid the shock (the avoidance groups) were no faster to respond to the tone CS than subjects that could not (the Pavlovian groups).[50] According to the SSDR theory, the Pavlovian CS induces a reflexive-like reaction. In the case of the high-avoidance strain, the response is more likely to be fleeing because freezing had been bred out of the subjects. For the poor avoiders, the reaction is a freezing response because fleeing has been bred out of them. Regardless, the CS induced a reflexive-like reaction (either fleeing or freezing). Behavior was not controlled by the avoidance contingency.[51]

Another revealing study supporting the SSDR theory was done by Blanchard and Blanchard (1971). Two groups of rats were placed in a small wire cage that was located inside a larger wooden test box (see Figure 12-9). For the experimental subjects, a cat was placed in the corner of the larger box after a 2-minute baseline period. Control subjects were treated in the same way, but no cat was used. During the next 10 minutes, all subjects were rated according to the extent to which they were mobile or immobile (that is, showed freezing behavior).

The results are shown in Figure 12-10. Both groups were active prior to the test. Once the cat was introduced into the test box, however, the experi-

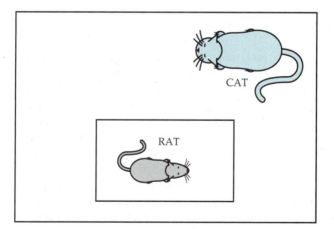

FIGURE 12-9. Schematic diagram of the apparatus used for testing freezing behavior (after Blanchard & Blanchard, 1971).

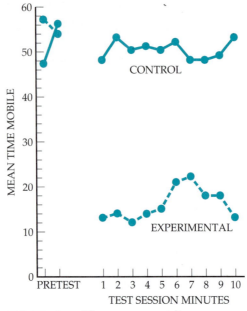

FIGURE 12-10. Mean movement time, as a function of minutes on the test session for the experimental and control rats (after Blanchard & Blanchard, 1971).

mental rats showed an immediate and strong suppression of their movement, suggesting that the freezing response is reflexive.

In a second study, an apparatus similar to that shown in Figure 12-11 was used. Here, experimental rats were placed in one corner of the test arena, and a cat was positioned in the other corner. Control subjects were put in the box, but no cat was used. All rats could escape the test box by running down the alleyway, across an electrified grid floor. The intensity of the shock was increased over trials, from 0.0 to 4.0 milliamps.

The average time it took for them to reach the entry of the alleyway is shown in Figure 12-12. All subjects ran quickly toward the exit when there was no shock. Latency increased, however, when shock was present on successive trials. Here, the control rats showed considerable reluctance to enter the alleyway, even with a relatively mild shock intensity of 0.4 milliamps. Rather than receiving shock, they stayed in the apparatus. The experimental rats, in contrast, persisted in escaping quickly, even when shock intensity was high. They were running from the cat, despite being shocked in the alleyway.

These studies therefore support the SSDR theory by showing that subjects adopt a naturalistic response without being taught to do so, and that the response may be either fleeing or freezing, depending on the circumstances. When the contingencies prevent fleeing, rats freeze in the presence of a preda-

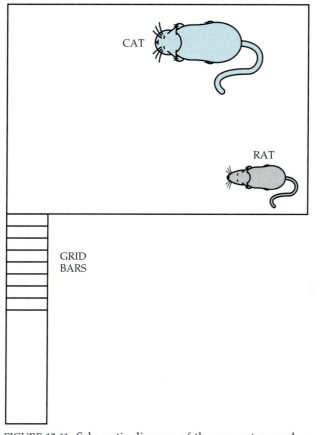

FIGURE 12-11. Schematic diagram of the apparatus used for testing fleeing behavior (after Blanchard & Blanchard, 1971).

tor. When conditions permit fleeing, rats choose that form of unconditioned defense reaction.[52]

As noted earlier, the SSDR theory speculates that lever-press avoidance should be difficult to learn because it is an unnatural reaction. Normally, this is the case. However, a challenge to the SSDR theory was posed by Crawford and Masterson (1978), who showed that lever-press avoidance may be learned quite easily, provided that the appropriate reinforcer is used.[53] Rats were tested in a two-compartment box containing a shock chamber (which had a response lever) and a safe compartment (which was separated from the shock side by a small door). A 10-second warning signal was given prior to shock.

The run group could avoid shock by pressing the lever during the signal, at which point the signal was turned off and the door to the safe chamber was opened, allowing them to run into the safe chamber.[54] The carry group could also press the lever, but they were then lifted out of the shock chamber

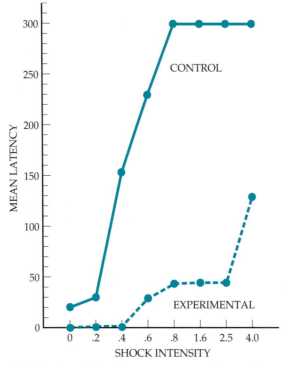

FIGURE 12-12. Mean latency to enter alleyway for experimental and control rats, as a function of shock intensity (milliamps) in the alleyway. Note that shock intensity increased over trials (after Blanchard & Blanchard, 1971).

and placed into the safe box. In other words, these subjects experienced the safe chamber but were not allowed to run there on their own. Finally, the lifted group could avoid shock, but they were lifted out of the shock compartment and then immediately replaced back into the shock chamber.

The results are shown in Figure 12-13. The run and the carry groups showed good lever-press avoidance behavior, whereas the lifted subjects did not. Thus, the data indicate that access to a safe area, whether or not the subject is permitted to run there on its own, strongly reinforces lever pressing. These data challenge the SSDR theory by showing that non-SSDRs, such as lever pressing, may be learned, provided that suitable reinforcement—namely, access to a safe area—is used.

Is learning a lever-press avoidance response difficult because subjects execute SSDRs, or because a suitable reward is rarely used? An experiment by Modaresi (1990) helps to answer this question.[55] Subjects could avoid shock by pressing a lever that was located 17 centimeters above the grid floor. The elevation of the lever is important because it forced the rats to "climb and

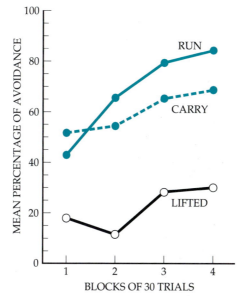

FIGURE 12-13. Mean percentage of avoidance response, as a function of blocks of 30 trials for the run, carry, and lifted groups (after Crawford & Masterson, 1978).

scratch" rather than to freeze. Climbing and scratching at the wall are consistent with fleeing from the compartment, whereas freezing is not. When the lever was pressed, one of the walls was retracted by a motor, giving access to a safe platform. Two groups differed in terms of where the lever was located in the cage. For the same-wall group, the elevated lever was located on the same wall as the safe area. For the opposite-wall subjects, the lever was positioned on the opposite wall from where the safe area emerged.

According to Modaresi, when the lever was on the same wall as the platform, climbing and scratching at the lever would cause it to be depressed. Furthermore, such a reaction was consistent with jumping onto the safe platform. When placed on the opposite wall, however, pressing the lever and proceeding onto the safe platform were incompatible.

The results are shown in Figure 12-14. Both groups learned the lever-press avoidance reaction, thus confirming that access to a safe area is a powerful reinforcer for lever-press avoidance. However, performance in the same-wall group was superior. Thus, when the lever response is compatible with, and, indeed, part of, the SSDR reaction of fleeing, then learning is better than when the avoidance task is incompatible with the SSDR tendency. In short, lever pressing is easily acquired as an avoidance reaction, provided that it is made congruent with the rat's natural defense strategy, *and* that it is appropriately reinforced by giving the subject access to a safe area.[56]

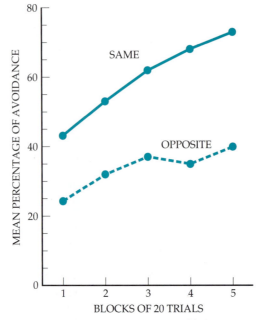

FIGURE 12-14. Mean percentage of lever-press avoidance responding, as a function of blocks of 20 trials for the same and opposite groups (after Modaresi, 1990).

Passive Avoidance.

Similar conclusions were reached in studies on passive-avoidance learning. Pearce (1978), for example, trained rats to avoid shock passively by staying on a wooden safe platform rather than stepping down onto an electrified grid floor.[57] The platform was located in the center of the cage for some of the subjects, but in the corner of the cage for others.

As shown in Figure 12-15, both groups stepped down quickly on the first trial. They could not have known that shock was going to be delivered on the grid floor and thus showed no fear of stepping down. On the second trial, however, both groups showed passive avoidance, but the corner group showed better passive avoidance than the center group. The explanation is that thigmotaxis (the tendency to run to the periphery and stay close to the walls) was incompatible with the passive-avoidance response in the center group. In other words, although the center group had a tendency to avoid shock by staying on the platform, they also had a tendency to flee to the edge or periphery of the cage because of their thigmotaxis. The two response tendencies were incompatible. For the corner group, however, remaining on the platform and being at the periphery of the box were compatible. The general conclusion, therefore, is that avoidance tasks that are compatible with a subject's SSDRs are learned more readily than those that are not.

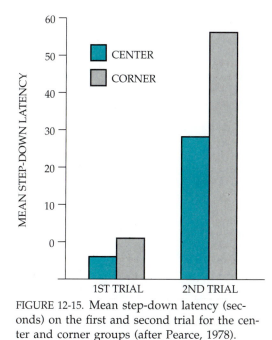

FIGURE 12-15. Mean step-down latency (seconds) on the first and second trial for the center and corner groups (after Pearce, 1978).

Defensive Reactions

The SSDR theory stipulated that a rat's defensive reactions were primarily fleeing and freezing. Rats and other species, however, also use burying and aggression when confronted by aversive stimuli.

Burying.

Pinel and Treit (1978) showed that burying an object is a defensive response. Rats were placed in a test box containing 5 centimeters of bedding material. The shock subjects received a mild shock when they touched a wooden prod that had been wrapped with bare wire. The prod subjects were treated in the same fashion, but no shock was delivered. Finally, the no-prod control animals were placed in the box, but they received neither the prod nor the shock. All subjects were removed and then replaced in the box for a 15-minute test that was given 10 seconds, 5 minutes, 5 hours, 3 days, or 20 days later. Both the time spent burying the prod under a mound of bedding material and the size of the pile of bedding were measured.

Figure 12-16 shows the duration of burying, as a function of the test interval. Subjects that received no shock (prod and no-prod groups) spent little time burying the prod. The shock subjects, in contrast, spent considerable time burying it, and they developed a significantly higher pile of material. These subjects treated the prod as an aversive object; they defended themselves against future aversion by burying it under the bedding.[58] In subsequent

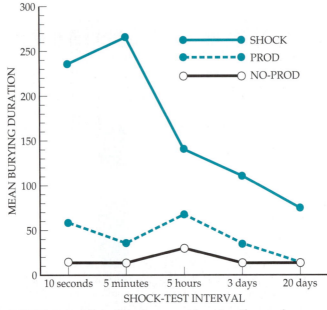

FIGURE 12-16. Mean duration spent burying the prod, as a function of the shock-test interval for the shock, prod, and no-prod groups (after Pinel & Treit, 1978).

experiments, Pinel and Treit showed that the **defensive-burying** response occurs even when subjects are tested in a different environment, that burying occurs when the shock is delivered from a grid floor rather than from the prod itself, and that the burying response is directed toward a prod that actually delivers a shock rather than toward a second prod that does not.[59]

Defensive burying is not limited to prods that deliver a shock. Jackson, Garbin, and Hollingsworth (1984) presented rats with various flavored solutions in drinking tubes. Following consumption, they were given an injection of lithium chloride (control animals were given a saline placebo injection). Later, a drinking tube containing water and one containing the flavored solution were placed in the test box, along with bedding material. Subjects that had been poisoned pushed bedding material from the floor so that it covered the flavor tube.[60]

Is the burying reaction a true defensive response? According to several studies, the answer is yes. Peacock and Wong (1982), for example, tested animals in a two-compartment box. For some subjects, bedding was located in the prod compartment, whereas for others, it was located in the other compartment.[61] Various behaviors were measured, including burying the shock prod, burying a control (no-shock) prod, spreading bedding but not over the prod itself, freezing, and grooming. The burying response did not occur if escape to the alternative apartment was available. Burying did occur, however, when the bedding was located on the shock side of the box, although subjects tended to escape first and then, about 10 to 17 seconds later, return

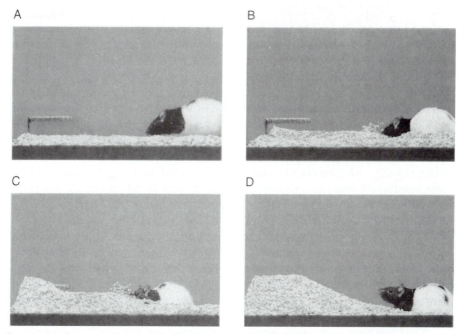

Sequence of scenes showing the burying of a shock prod by a rat. In panel A, the rat approaches the metal rod. In panel B, the rat is seen pushing sawdust toward the prod. In panel C, the rat continues to push sawdust toward the prod, which is nearly buried. In panel D, the entire prod is buried under the sawdust.
Courtesy of Allyn & Bacon, (From page 128 of Biopsychology, *Professor John P. J. Pinel, used with permission)*

to the shock side to bury the prod. Thus, the initial reaction to shock is escape, but if the potentially threatening stimulus is still there, then other defensive behaviors are performed, including burying.

Moser and Tait (1983) also tested the notion that defensive burying is an SSDR by determining whether burying emerges when fleeing and freezing are also available. A large wooden box was divided into two chambers. The shock prod was located on one side, above a bed of sawdust. After being habituated to the apparatus, subjects were exposed to the prod and then shocked. During the 15-minute test, their escape, freezing, and burying behaviors were measured. Freezing took place almost immediately and lasted for more than one third of the test. Escaping to the safe box, on the average, was executed within about 10 to 20 seconds following shock. Burying did not emerge until several minutes later. Freezing and escape behaviors were therefore more dominant SSDRs than burying. Fleeing and freezing are the first lines of defense, but when those reactions do not remove the source of aversion, then defensive burying takes place.

The aforementioned work suggests that subjects have priorities concerning which SSDR they execute first. An interesting extension of this notion was shown by Pinel, Petrovic, and Hilton Jones (1990). Lactating female rats and their young pups were presented with a wire-wrapped prod in the nest compartment of a two-compartment box. Two groups of females were shocked by the prod, and two others were not. For one of the shock and one of the no-shock groups, the prod was taken away 2 seconds after shock. For the other two groups, however, the prod was left in the nest compartment. The authors measured three kinds of defense reactions—namely, burying, relocating of the pups into the safe chamber, and relocation of the entire nest into the safe area.

Subjects that were shocked, and for which the prod remained in the nest area, tended to relocate the nest and the pups into the safe area more than did the other three groups. The other groups did not differ from each other in this respect. All subjects showed some defensive burying, but they did not differ appreciably on this measure.[62] Thus, when a lactating female has pups, burying occurs, but removal of the nest and pups takes priority.

Many species do not demonstrate burying behavior, at least not as readily as rats and mice. Gerbils, for example, bury shock prods, but only when tested in circular chambers (the shape of the apparatus reduces the frequency of competing escape responses, such as digging in the corner, that occur in rectangular boxes).[63] On the other hand, Whillans and Shettleworth (1981) showed that hamsters do not engage in defensive burying even when tested in a variety of conditions.[64]

What accounts for this species difference in burying? According to Whillans and Shettleworth, rats are social animals; they live together in large colonies. Hamsters, on the other hand, are solitary creatures; they live alone and, typically, they are hostile toward one another. Burying, therefore, may have evolved in rats as a form of inherited altruism. Rats bury aversive objects so that their colony mates will not encounter them. Such an altruistic act, however, did not evolve in a nonsocial animal such as the hamster.[65]

Aggression.

Aggressive behaviors are another form of instrumental defense.[66] Blanchard, Kleinschmidt, Fukunaga-Stinson, and Blanchard (1980) investigated the aggressive behavior of male and female rats that were restrained in a plastic tube and shocked on their tail. For 2 seconds, just prior to and following the shock, an anesthetized male rat was held 1 centimeter below the subject's snout. Shock intensity increased over the series of trials from 0.2 to 5 milliamps. Both male and female rats bit the target animal's snout, and biting increased dramatically as a function of shock intensity. Males and females differed, however. The female rats did not inflict wounds on the target animal, whereas the male rats did.

In a second study by these authors, an anesthetized cat was held near the subject's nose. Here, females tended to bite the cat even before shock was delivered and with a greater degree of severity than had been directed toward the rat. This pattern was not shown by the male rats; males bit the cat only as a result of receiving shock. These data, therefore, suggest that an attack is a defensive strategy but only under certain circumstances. For the male rats, attacks are the same, whether the object is a conspecific rat or a predator cat.

For the females, aggression is a form of preemptive attack designed to guard young pups and thus only occurs when challenged in this manner.

The attack behaviors described here were given in response to an unavoidable aversive stimulus. In a sense, the animals had no alternative defense than to attack. Blanchard, Flannelly, and Blanchard (1986), however, showed that, like burying, attack behaviors may be only one in a series of defensive reactions that a rat executes, depending on the circumstances.[67] Here, rats were placed at one end of a hallway. The human experimenter then entered the other end of the hallway through a door. The experimenter approached the subject 1 meter at a time, resting 10 seconds between each step. For some of the rats, the experimenter moved a square white card mounted on a rod back and forth in rapid succession during these pauses.

The subjects' behavior was assessed on a 5-point scale, in terms of freezing, startle reactions, jumps, vocalizations, and attacks. The initial reaction of the rat was to freeze when the stimulus was still far away. That is, rats froze between 6.75 and 9.13 seconds of the 10-second period when the experimenter was between 2 and 5 meters away. Freezing, however, gave way to vocalization and jump/attack behaviors when the experimenter was within 2 meters or less. In fact, subjects attacked as much as 86.7% of the time when the experimenter, or the moving cardboard stimulus, was about 0.5 meters away. Thus, attack behaviors tend to be a defense of last resort. Flight is the preferred defensive strategy, freezing next. If those fail to terminate the threat, then attack becomes an option.

INTERIM SUMMARY

An evolutionary perspective suggests that many species evolved specialized means for defending themselves against predators. The species-specific defense-reaction (SSDR) hypothesis claims that survival is too important to rely on a gradual learning process. Rather, species possess a hierarchy of defense reactions. In an aversive situation, the preferred SSDR is performed; if that fails to cope with the threat, then responses lower on the hierarchy are selected. Research on active avoidance supports the SSDR theory. When contingencies permit, fleeing is performed readily; when conditions do not, rats freeze. Although some research suggests that non-SSDRs are learned, provided an appropriate reinforcer is given (access to a safe chamber), other research suggests that such a reward is effective only when animals can also perform reactions compatible with their SSDR tendencies. Passive avoidance is facilitated when the response is compatible with the animal's natural defense tendencies. Other kinds of defensive reactions occur, including defensive burying of objects that are aversive. Defensive burying is subordinate to fleeing and freezing. Aggression is a fourth form of defensive reaction. Rats attack each other when experiencing aversive shock, or they show preemptive forms of attack against animals that potentially pose a threat to the young. Attack behavior is a defense of last resort.

BEHAVIOR SYSTEMS APPROACH

Is it possible to resolve traditional learning theory with the findings from these species-specific learning studies? One promising approach involves the notion of a behavior system. In the following section, the behavior systems approach is compared to traditional learning theory.

Traditional Approach

One of the central tenets of instrumental conditioning is that reinforcement causes learning to occur and performance to take place. This view is a causal theory, in that reinforcement is considered to be the cause of, or explanation for, behavior.

Causal Model.

The causal model is diagrammed in Figure 12-17. Reinforcement is represented by the feedback portion of this sequence. The feedback from the reinforcing outcome strengthens the behavior, or the R–O link between the response and the outcome.[68]

Challenge to Reinforcement Model.

Much of the work described in this chapter (as well as in Chapter 7) challenges this simple reinforcement model. According to Timberlake (1993), the reinforcement model fails to take into account all of the critical links shown in Figure 12-17, especially the stimulus-input phase. Rather than focusing on a single event (namely, reinforcement), Timberlake suggests that a more profitable approach is to view the animal's behavior as part of an integrated functional behavior system, which has (1) an initial starting value (stimulus input), (2) behaviors that are appropriate to those starting values (responses), and (3) the capability of being modified by the consequence (feedback).

By viewing an organism's behavior as a functional system, the behavior systems approach accounts effectively for many outcomes that conventional learning theory has difficulty explaining, as well as for those results that are consistent with the species-specific learning argument. The following sections review the behavior systems approach and provide an account of how the approach explains the species-typical behaviors described earlier in this chapter.

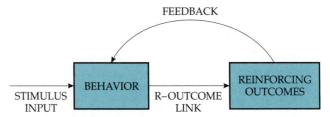

FIGURE 12-17. Schematic diagram depicting a theory of behavior based on reinforcement.

Behavior Systems and Learning

According to traditional learning theory, the responses typically used in learning research are relatively arbitrary. Indeed, the arbitrariness is often cited as a strength of the learning theory approach, because the laws depicting how animals learn about any one arbitrary response ought to generalize to other responses as well. According to this argument, if special or unique responses were studied, then one could never be sure that the laws of learning governing those responses are universal laws.

What Are Behavior Systems?

According to the **behavior systems approach,** responses and stimuli appear arbitrary to the experimenter, but they are certainly not arbitrary for the subject. The subject's behaviors, and its perceptual reactions to the stimuli, are preorganized into functional units. The experimenter may give a subject a stimulus it has never encountered in the past, but the subjects reacts to the stimulus according to an existing, preorganized framework or set of perceptual reactions. Similarly, the experimenter may require a subject to perform a new response, such as pressing a lever, but the act of lever pressing is integrated into an existing set of behavioral capacities. Lever pressing, rather than being arbitrary, is consistent with, or similar to, other forms of behavior that the animal already has in its repertoire, such as grasping, inspecting, or biting.

The behavior systems approach thus claims that learned behavior is preorganized.[69] Animals have various motivational processes, perceptual–motor systems, and response sequences that are organized into functional units. These units are organized in a hierarchical fashion, and they are organized around, or integrated with respect to, a single function, such as feeding. As Timberlake and Lucas (1989) noted, "A behavioral system is a complex control structure related to a particular function or need of the organism, such as feeding . . . , reproduction . . . , defense . . . , or body care . . . . The critical features of a behavior system are: (1) motivational processes that prime other structures and help organize and maintain the sequence of their expression, and (2) perceptual–motor structures . . . that relate specific stimulus sensitivities to particular response components."[70]

Behavior Systems, Evolution, and Learning.

The behavior systems approach is closely linked to an evolutionary perspective of learning. As various species developed through evolution, behavioral repertoires that met environmental demands, such as feeding or defense, were selected for their flexibility. An individual did not survive because of arbitrary behaviors that were strengthened by their consequences. Rather, an animal was born with certain behavioral repertoires, and the capacity to learn evolved with respect to those behavioral systems. For example, changes in the way an animal avoids or defends itself against a predator evolved with respect to the animal's existing defensive strategies. Animals therefore evolved sequences, or streams, of behavior that led them away from dangerous stimuli and toward beneficial stimuli.[71] Such strings of behavior have survived because they increased the probability of survival and reproduction.[72] Learning modifies these strings by adapting them to novel environments or by reorganizing them to meet new environmental challenges.[73]

Behavior-Systems Components

A schematic view of a behavior system for feeding in the rat is shown in Figure 12-18.

System.

The most inclusive level is the **system level;** this is the general function that the system serves. The system identifies the collection of perceptual and motor behavioral units that serve a particular function in an integrated fash-

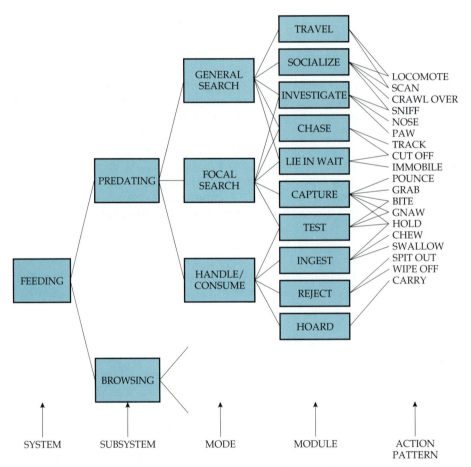

FIGURE 12-18. Example of some of the components involved in the feeding system in the rat (after Timberlake & Lucas, 1989).

ion. The example shown in Figure 12-18 is for feeding, but others exist as well, such as drinking and sexual or mating functions.

Subsystem.

The **subsystem** is the next most general level of organization. The subsystem refers to "coherent strategies that serve the general function of the system."[74] Whenever a given subsystem is called into action, particular stimuli become salient for the animal, and certain behavior streams are initiated. For example, as shown in Figure 12-18, given one kind of input, the predation subsystem is triggered; the animal becomes sensitized to moving objects. In contrast, given another kind of input, the subsystem governing browsing behaviors is activated; the animal becomes sensitized to other kinds of environmental stimuli, such as stationary objects. Depending on which subsystem is activated, particular behavior streams then follow. Thus, the subsystem controls different global strategies or perceptual and motor patterns related to the overall function represented by the system.

Mode.

According to Timberlake and Lucas (1989), a **mode** is "a motivational substrate related to the sequential and temporal organization of action patterns with respect to terminal stimuli in the system."[75] In other words, a mode is a motivational unit, a substrate of the subsystem, that coordinates specific behavioral streams. For example, in the feeding system of the rat (Figure 12-18), prey that are spatially and temporally distant from the organism activate the general search mode and trigger the appropriate behavioral stream. Prey items that are closer in time and space cause the subject to go into a new mode—namely, a focal-search mode. Here, the behavioral stream differs from that executed when the subject was in the general search mode. Finally, when the prey is close at hand, the subject goes into yet a third predatory mode—namely, handling and consuming. Again, the subsequent behavioral stream differs from those triggered by previous modes, in that it includes ingesting, hoarding, and rejecting. The point is that the mode reflects different motivational and behavioral strategies. These strategies are part of the predatory subsystem, and each triggers an appropriate and unique stream of behavior.

Module.

Modules are "predispositions to respond to particular stimuli with particular response components."[76] Modules represent more specific, or further refined, kinds of behavioral actions. They also provide a kind of stimulus filter in which environmental cues trigger some modules but not others. For example, as shown in Figure 12-18, when an animal is in its general search mode, it will travel, socialize, investigate, and chase. These are specific behavioral streams that occur when the prey item is still located at a distance from the animal. However, when the subject is in the handle-and-consume mode (that is, the prey item is close at hand), the specific behavioral streams engaged in (the module) involve testing, ingesting, rejecting, and hoarding the prey.

Modules are not physiologically localized in any particular part of the brain, but rather, they represent functional units of behavior, or behavioral streams.

Modifications to behavioral systems that occur as a result of Pavlovian or instrumental learning procedures take place between and within modules. For example, when Pavlovian conditioning is conducted, CSs that initially were innocuous trigger a given module because they are associated with the US that activates that module. Similarly, instrumental responses cause certain outcomes to occur, such as gaining food, which, in turn, activate the appropriate modules.

Action Pattern.

Finally, the most basic unit of output is the **action pattern.** These are the specific movements and motor reactions that are executed in a stereotyped fashion. They are the component behaviors of the modules or behavioral streams. Locomotion and scanning are two examples that are part of the travel module (which, in turn, is the behavioral stream engaged in while the subject is in the general search mode). Specific action patterns may be part of more than one module. As indicated in Figure 12-18, a subject may gnaw on a prey item while ingesting it (gnawing is part of the testing stream of behavior) or when the subject is capturing the prey item (gnawing is also part of the capture module).

Behavior Systems and Integrated Behavior

The behavior systems approach explains a number of phenomena that conventional learning theory has difficulty explaining.

Misbehaviors.

One is the performance of misbehaviors instead of the target response for which reward contingencies are available. Recall the noted study by Breland and Breland (1961), which attempted to condition members of various species to perform circus tricks (see Chapter 9). In a series of studies using pigs, raccoons, and chickens, the authors found that the animals often had difficulty in learning an instrumental response, despite the fact that the reinforcement contingency appeared to be suitable. Rather, the subjects performed species-specific behaviors that seemed to interfere with learning.

For example, the researchers tried to teach a raccoon to deposit tokens in a metal box to obtain food reward. The animal had no problem with this task when it was given only one token. However, when the raccoon was required to deposit two tokens, the response was poorly learned. Instead of releasing the tokens into the box, the raccoon performed misbehaviors—namely, rubbing the coins together, often dipping them into the opening, only to pull them back out again.

As the authors state, "Raccoons condition readily, have good appetites, and this one was quite tame and an eager subject. We anticipated no trouble. Conditioning him to pick up the first coin was simple. . . . Then the metal container was introduced, with the requirement that he drop the coin into the container. Here we ran into the first bit of difficulty: he seemed to have a great deal of trouble letting go of the coin. He would rub it up against the inside of the container, pull it back out, and clutch it firmly for several seconds.... The rubbing behavior became worse and worse as time went on.... The examples listed we feel represent a clear and utter failure of conditioning theory."[77]

Misbehaviors pose a serious problem for reinforcement theory because animals perform the species-specific feeding reactions rather than the simple target behaviors for which reinforcement is provided. A behavior systems approach, however, provides a coherent explanation of misbehaviors. According to this approach, misbehaviors occur because the subject's natural feeding system is activated by the stimuli. When the raccoon dips the tokens into the slot and rubs them together, it is responding to the tokens as it would respond to food items, such as a small crustacean. The action patterns associated with feeding are automatically triggered by these stimuli, making reinforcement irrelevant.

Interesting support for this claim was found by Timberlake, Wahl, and King (1982).[78] Rats were placed in a rectangular metal box. A special mechanism dispensed a small stainless-steel ball bearing through a hole at the base of one wall. The cage was tilted in such a way that the ball bearing would roll to the other side of the box and exit through a hole in the floor. It took

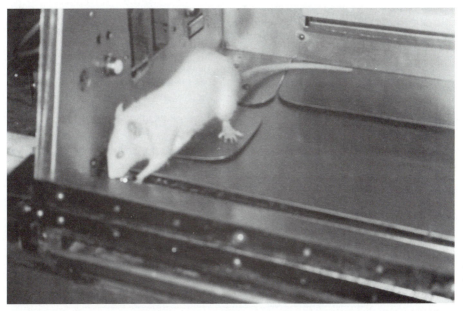

Photograph of a rat manipulating a ball bearing in the study by Timberlake, Wahl, and King (1982). Approaching and contacting the ball bearing were part of the natural sequence of feeding behaviors.
Courtesy of Professor William Timberlake, Department of Psychology, University of Indiana, Bloomington

approximately 5.2 seconds for the ball bearing to travel the full distance. Subjects in the exit group received food after the ball bearing had left the box through the exit hole. If they interfered with the ball, then food delivery was delayed until the ball bearing had disappeared. The random group was given food and the ball bearing independently.[79] The experimenters observed the animals during this time and recorded whether they engaged in any of a variety of behaviors directed at the ball bearing, including orienting to the bearing, approaching it, contacting it with its nose or mouth, nosing or pawing the ball bearing, carrying it in its mouth, releasing and then grasping the bearing and chewing it.

The results for orienting, approaching, and contacting are shown in Figure 12-19. Presenting the ball bearing just prior to food, independent of the animal's behavior, increased the contact with the bearing. That is, the exit group oriented, approached, and contacted the ball bearing, but the random group showed no such behavior. Contingent reward, therefore, is not necessary for contact to occur; approach and contact were part of the natural behavior stream in which rats engage when feeding. These results therefore resemble those found in the study on misbehaviors discussed previously, in which raccoons engaged in feeding behaviors independent of reward. Here, contact

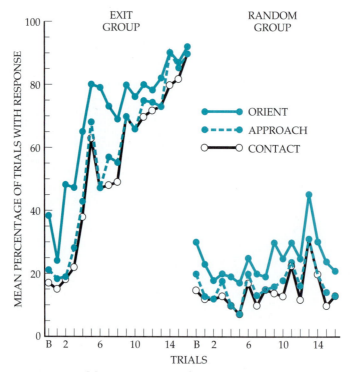

FIGURE 12-19. Mean percentage of trials with an orienting approach, and contact response, as a function of baseline (point B) and conditioning trials for the exit and random groups (after Timberlake, Wahl, & King, 1982).

behavior with the ball bearing occurred despite the fact that contingent reinforcement was not provided.

How does reward affect these behavior streams? The researchers
addressed this question in a subsequent experiment, in which rats were reinforced for contacting the ball bearing. The reinforcement contingencies
affected the contact behavior, but the effects were complex. A contingency that
delayed delivery of food did not eliminate the contact behaviors, but if food
delivery occurred during contact with the ball bearing, then the animal tended
to stop its contact behavior and to retrieve the food. In other words, early contact with the moving object resembled modules associated with search behaviors, but once the contact was made, the handle-and-consume modules were
triggered.

To illustrate how the rat progressed through different motivational modes
and behavioral modules, the authors compared three groups of rats. The exit
group received food once the ball bearing exited the box (as described above).
The before-exit group was presented with food approximately 1.6 seconds
after the ball bearing had entered the chamber (the food was delayed as long
as the rats manipulated the bearing). A third group, the after-exit group, was
given food reward about 2.5 seconds *after* the ball bearing had exited the box.

The mean percentage of trials with contact of the ball bearing is shown in
Figure 12-20. Little contact was shown in the before-exit group. That is, the

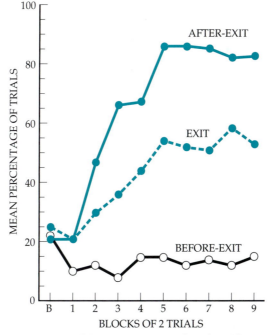

FIGURE 12-20. Mean percentage of trials with at
least one contact response to the ball bearing by
the after-exit, exit, and before-exit groups (after
Timberlake, Wahl, & King, 1982).

delivery of food caused the subjects to switch from one stream of behavior (investigation, contact, orientation) to another (consummatory). The highest level of contact was shown by the after-exit group. When food was delivered very late in the search mode (when animals were in the handle and consume mode), then they continued to show the misbehaviors.

Maze Running.

A behavior systems approach has also been applied to maze running. According to Timberlake (1983a), running to the end of a maze is not governed by the instrumental consequence because animals run down alleyways even when no reward is provided. Rather, the running behavior resembles action patterns that are typical of animals that live in burrows. Thus, running is facilitated when the alleyway is long and/or dark, but disrupted by lights and novel odors. This is precisely the kind of action pattern that one would expect to see in animals that live in burrows.

Shaping.

The strengthening of a response through successive approximation (shaping) was discussed in Chapter 8. Recall that shaping is usually given as evidence for the powerful effects of contingent reinforcement on behavior. New behaviors, such as lever pressing in rats, are taught by rewarding closer and closer approximations to the final behavior. Reinforcement strengthens each individual component behavior until the final response is executed.

A behavior systems approach, however, views shaping in an entirely different light. According to this account, the behaviors in which a rat engages during the shaping procedure reflect elicited, species-specific, appetitive reactions that are part of the overall feeding system. In fact, Timberlake and Lucas (1989) point out that experimenters go to great lengths to encourage and increase the frequency of these reflexive action patterns.

For example, they first allow rats to find food in the food cup, thus activating the feeding system and the action patterns associated with it. They present food delivery at a fairly high rate so that subjects continue to explore the food cup, and, because the lever is usually located nearby, the area in which the lever is located. They invariably deliver food when the rat contacts or investigates the lever. These contact and orienting reactions are part of the behavioral stream associated with the focal search mode of the feeding system.

Shaping is therefore similar to autoshaping, in that food delivery automatically activates portions of the feeding system. As the authors note, "Like predisposed and constrained learning, shaping appears based on a combination of the experimenter's manipulations with the rat's particular stimulus sensitivities, response components, and motivational processes. In behavior system terms, shaping activates the food system, instigates a combination of general and focal search modes primarily focused on the area of the food tray, and links modules related to food capture or handling to the movement of the lever."[80]

Defensive Behaviors.

The SSDR theory of avoidance learning argues that organisms are geneti-cally endowed with behaviors that are appropriate for coping with predators and other aversive threats. A behavior systems approach argues that the behaviors executed in threatening situations involve behavioral streams that are elicited by the relevant environmental stimulus. For example, when the threatening stimulus is far away, the animal engages in preparatory defense strategies. However, as the threat draws closer in time and space, other actions ensue, such as fleeing, freezing, or fighting.[81]

One behavior systems approach to the problem of defensive behavior was described by Fanselow (1994).[82] The components, or motivational modes of action, of this defense system are shown in Figure 12-21. They include preen-counter modes of behavior, postencounter modes, and circa-strike modes. Let us illustrate these behaviors with a phenomenon called the "immediate shock deficit" (see also Chapter 7).

Fanselow (1986) compared the freezing behavior of three groups of rats.[83] Some were given 2 minutes to explore a test box before being given a shock. Others were shocked immediately upon being placed in the box. A third group received no shock. The data were presented in Figure 7-8. The immediate-shock and no-shock groups showed virtually no freezing. Rats that were given delayed shock, however, showed considerable freezing.

According to Fanselow, a behavior systems approach is an appropriate way to account for these data.[84] The approach argues that a rat's defensive strategy has three modes—namely, preencounter, postencounter, and circa-strike modes (see Figure 12-21). These modes are activated by different kinds of environmental stimuli. The preencounter mode is activated when the ani-mal is placed in a potentially threatening situation; no aversive threat has been encountered, but the animal is wary that such a threat could occur. The post-encounter mode is triggered when the animal actually encounters the aversive threat and now must cope with it. Finally, the circa-strike mode is activated whenever there is direct sensory contact with the predator or threat itself. Thus, the rat's naturalistic behavior stream, which results from these different modes of action, depends on the environmental stimulus that the animal encounters.

As shown in Figure 12-21, when the animal is in the preencounter mode, various kinds of behavior modules are activated. One is an alteration in the animal's feeding pattern. Recall from Chapter 11 that when a rat is allowed to feed on one side of the cage but is also given shock there, then it shows a trade-off between foraging efficiency and increased vigilance by altering its feeding patterns. Specifically, the animal decreases the number of feeding ses-sions but lengthens the duration of a given meal.[85] When the animal is in the postencounter mode—that is, when it actually encounters the aversive threat—the predominant module is freezing.[86] Finally, the circa-strike mode activates two kinds of modules: locomotion away from the predator and jump/attack or aggression. These are behaviors of last resort. That is, once the animal comes inevitably into direct contact with the predator, its last-resort defensive reaction is to attack or to jump away.

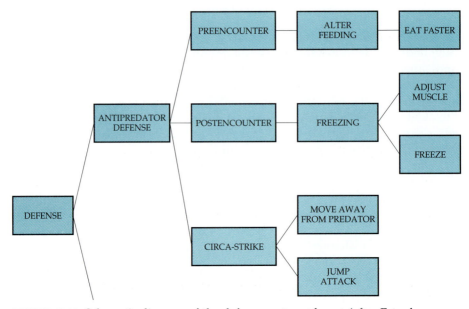

FIGURE 12-21. Schematic diagram of the defense system of a rat (after Fanselow, 1994).

INTERIM SUMMARY

The causal or reinforcement model of learning suggests that behaviors are strengthened by their consequences—namely, reinforcers. The behavior systems approach, in contrast, views an animal's behavior as part of an integrated and functional behavior system. According to this argument, animals have various motivational processes, perceptual–motor systems, and response sequences that are organized. Responses are executed within the context of these larger, preorganized behavioral units or systems. Stimulation from the environment triggers the components of those systems, causing a behavioral stream to be executed. Systems exist for various functions, such as feeding, drinking, and reproduction. The subsystems are the larger behavioral strategies embedded in the functional system. Modes are motivational substrates related to the organization of behavior. A mode coordinates the behavioral stream that is ultimately executed. The mode represents the behavioral strategy by which the subsystem is served. Modules are predispositions to respond to particular stimuli with certain response components. Modifications to behavior systems occur primarily at the level of the module. For example, a Pavlovian CS comes to trigger a module because it is associated with the US that activates that module. The smallest unit of output is the action pattern. These are specific movements that compose the component behaviors of the module. A behavior systems approach has been used profitably to explain misbehaviors (situations in which behaviors occur without respect to the reinforcement contingencies), maze running, shaping, and defensive behaviors.

ENDNOTES

1. The integration of Pavlovian and instrumental processes is also found in the area of biological adaptations. A good example is autoshaping. On the one hand, autoshaping is viewed as a Pavlovian phenomenon because the visual CS acquires the power to elicit pecking reactions simply as a result of being paired with a US (see Chapter 3). In this sense, a pigeon's pecking to a visual stimulus that is followed by food is analogous to a rat's salivating to a visual stimulus that is followed by food. On the other hand, key pecking in pigeons may be viewed in an instrumental context, in that the behavior is dramatically influenced by contingencies of reinforcement. Indeed, autoshaping was once claimed to be a species-specific, *instrumental* response, so easily conditioned that it was not analogous to prototypical instrumental responses such as lever pressing (Seligman, 1970, pp. 411–412; but see Burns & Malone, 1992).
2. This does not deny that feedback loops may provide reinforcing value.
3. See Immelmann and Suomi (1981).
4. Under normal conditions of development, phase-specific learning takes place during the critical time period, but the system is flexible. Learning also occurs prior to, and following, these developmental periods.
5. Kroodsma (1984).
6. See Slater, Eales, and Clayton (1988) for a review of song learning in zebra finches.
7. See Marler (1984).
8. See Slater (1981) for a discussion of the evolutionary significance and ecological function of birdsong.
9. See Marler (1976).
10. Marler (1970).
11. McGregor and Avery (1986).
12. This result was not found by Marler (1970).
13. Petrinovich (1985, p. 28).
14. See Kroodsma (1978).
15. Marler (1970).
16. Payne and Payne (1993).
17. Immelmann (1969).
18. After this tutorial period, subjects were taken from their fathers and were placed with a different adult male. Here, the subjects were in groups of about 6 to 10 individuals. They were separated from their new tutor by a wire mesh, but they could see and hear the tutor.
19. These data also reflect the pattern found when measuring the percentage of subjects that learned from the father. None of the birds that were isolated at 35 days of age copied their father's song; about 80% of the 50-day subjects sang the appropriate song.
20. Slater, Eales, and Clayton (1988, p. 22); but see Immelmann (1969).
21. Imprinting is an important process from an evolutionary point of view. By staying near the hen, chicks maintain their security. Furthermore, they learn to identify,

and associate with, members of their own species. Such learning may facilitate appropriate mate selection later on.

22. Imprinting is not restricted to precocial birds, however. Many species—including human beings (Bowlby, 1969), infant monkeys (Mason, 1970), and sea lions (Schusterman, Hanggi, & Gisiner, 1992)—show imprinting.
23. Lorenz (1937).
24. Hess (1959a).
25. From an evolutionary viewpoint, such a belief makes sense because it would be highly maladaptive for a newborn animal to alter its filial behavior once imprinted onto its mother.
26. Eiserer (1978); Gaioni, Hoffman, DePaulo, and Stratton (1978). Moreover, Eiserer (1980) showed that ducklings retain their ability to form filial attachments to novel objects after the so-called critical period has expired, but chickens do not.
27. Hoffman, Ratner, and Eiserer (1972); Zajonc, Marcus, and Wilson (1974).
28. Eiserer and Hoffman (1974).
29. Kertzman and Demarest (1982).
30. Imprinting reactions are not demonstrated for stationary objects, but if the object moves for a prolonged period of time, then various species—including chickens, turkeys, quail, and ducks—demonstrate filial reactions to the visual characteristics of the object when presented as stationary; Eiserer and Swope (1980); see also Hoffman, Eiserer, and Singer (1972).
31. Gottlieb (1980b).
32. Gottlieb (1979, 1980a).
33. A second test, given at 72 hours, showed essentially the same results.
34. Bolhuis and Honey (1994); see also van Kampen and Bolhuis (1993). The former study, for example, showed that exposure to the auditory component before or after exposure to the compound visual/auditory object reduced the preference for the visual characteristics when presented alone.
35. See Rajecki (1973).
36. Bateson (1966).
37. The presentation of an imprinting object may even be used as a reinforcer for responses such as pecking (Bateson & Reese, 1969), and its withdrawal may be used to suppress these behaviors (Hoffman, Stratton, & Newby, 1969).
38. Hoffman, Ratner, and Eiserer (1972).
39. In fact, if the birds are deprived of viewing their environment, by the use of special goggles that preclude patterned light from reaching their eyes, then the age at which the birds begin to show this fear reaction is increased (Moltz & Stettner, 1961).
40. Gaioni, Hoffman, DePaulo, and Stratton (1978).
41. See Bolhuis, de Vos, and Kruijt (1990).
42. Eiserer, Hoffman, and Klein (1975); Hoffman (1978).
43. Eiserer (1980).
44. Although these findings pose a problem for the theory, research has provided some countersupport for the conditioning approach. For example, Pavlovian blocking occurs in an imprinting context; that is, exposure to an imprinting object blocks filial attachment to a second object; see de Vos and Bolhuis (1990); Chapter 5 of this book.
45. See also Crawford and Masterson (1982).
46. Bolles (1970, pp. 32–33).
47. See D'Amato and Schiff (1964); Delprato and Holmes (1977); Giulian and Schmaltz (1973).

48. See Brush, Froehlich, and Sakellaris (1979). Moreover, the range and intensity of natural defensive behaviors of domesticated rat strains are substantially reduced from those of wild rats; see Blanchard, Flannelly, and Blanchard (1986).

49. If these subjects responded during the tone, then the tone was terminated, and a brief shock was given immediately.

50. This result conflicts with the historically famous study by Brogden, Lipman, and Culler (1938), which showed that an avoidance contingency led to better motor performance than did a classical contingency.

51. See also Walters and Glazer (1971).

52. However, see Fanselow, DeCola, and Young (1993) for an alternative explanation.

53. See also Crawford and Masterson (1982); Crawford, Masterson, and Wilson (1977).

54. When these subjects entered the safe chamber, they were immediately picked up and replaced in the safe chamber, to control for handling effects.

55. See also Grossen and Kelley (1972); Modaresi (1989).

56. Analogous findings have been shown in the case of key-peck avoidance responding in pigeons. Under normal circumstances, key-peck avoidance is poorly learned, but if subjects are allowed to avoid shock by making a response that is more compatible with their natural defense strategy—namely, wing flapping—then learning occurs readily (Rachlin, 1969).

57. See also Grossen and Kelley (1972).

58. Results of a study by Modaresi (1982) argue against this position. Rats do not necessarily bury an object, although they may displace bedding material toward the front wall of the cage where the object is often located.

59. Arnaut and Shettleworth (1981) confirmed that the burying response occurs when subjects are shocked through the grid floor, but only if the rats are shocked in the presence of the prod, not in its absence. If the prod is present, but the floor shock is delayed for more than 1 minute following contact with the prod, then burying does not take place.

60. The result found by Jackson, Garbin, and Hollingsworth (1984), however, depended on the solution having a distinctive odor. Defensive burying did not take place for tubes containing a saccharin or salt solution.

61. A third group of animals had bedding on both sides.

62. In those groups for which the prod was removed, burying around the hole that had contained the prod was measured.

63. Davis, Moore, Cowen, Thurston, and Maggio (1982). Tsuda, Ida, and Tanaka (1988) showed that substantial differences in the burying reaction occur even between different strains of rats. Albino rats generally show less burying behavior and more freezing behavior than hooded rats do.

64. Subsequent research showed that the hamsters developed a fear reaction to the prod but did not engage in burying.

65. For a discussion of the evolution of altruism, see Trivers (1971).

66. The distinction between Pavlovian- and instrumental-conditioning procedures is really arbitrary in this example. When fish are given a red light CS that had previously been paired with the opportunity to confront an intruder fish, they are better able to defend their territory during a real aggressive encounter than are fish that have not undergone the Pavlovian training; see Hollis (1984; Chapter 7 of this book). In other words, the natural SSDR of the fish—namely, aggression—was enhanced by the Pavlovian CS. This section considers studies that focus on the species-specific aggressive behaviors themselves, and the outcomes that they provide, rather than on the influence of Pavlovian cues.

67. See also Blanchard, Blanchard, Takahashi, and Kelley (1977).

68. According to Timberlake (1993), this is a backward causal model, where the outcome of the sequence actually causes the response or initial portion of the sequence to occur. The more usual conception of a causal sequence is where the initial event causes a subsequent event to occur, not the reverse. Timberlake uses the example of two billiard balls colliding. When one ball strikes another, the first ball is said to be the cause of the second ball's behavior. According to Timberlake, however, the reinforcement model represents the reverse notion. The second event in the sequence (the reinforcement) is said to be the cause of the first event (the behavior).
69. See Timberlake (1994).
70. Timberlake and Lucas (1989, p. 241).
71. Timberlake (1994).
72. See Timberlake (1994).
73. See Shettleworth (1994).
74. Timberlake and Lucas (1989, p. 244).
75. Timberlake and Lucas (1989, p. 244).
76. Timberlake and Lucas (1989, p. 245).
77. Breland and Breland (1961, pp. 682–683).
78. See also Boakes, Poli, Lockwood, and Goodall (1978); Timberlake (1983b).
79. Two additional groups were used. One was given only the CS—namely, the ball bearing—and the other was given food just before the ball bearing was scheduled to exit the box, about 5.1 seconds after its appearance.
80. Timberlake and Lucas (1989, p. 262).
81. As Fanselow (1994) points out, one of the drawbacks of the SSDR theory is that it claims that an animal executes its preferred SSDR when threatened, but if that response does not effectively remove the stimulus, then the animal suppresses the SSDR in favor of the next most preferred action. As noted in the text, a behavior systems approach argues that different behavior streams are elicited at different points in the temporal sequence, rather than that ineffective SSDRs are suppressed.
82. Fanselow's work has focused on the neurological and biochemical substrates of these defensive behaviors. Masterson and Crawford (1982) were among the first to describe a defense motivational system. They argued that "The defense motivation system selectively potentiates or primes a set of innate defensive reactions that includes fleeing, freezing, fighting, and defensive burying. . . . Each innate reaction is most likely to occur in the presence of a specific set of environmental cues" (Masterson & Crawford, 1982, p. 664).
83. See also Fanselow, DeCola, and Young (1993).
84. See Fanselow and Lester (1988).
85. See Helmstetter and Fanselow (1993).
86. Freezing, however, simultaneously adjusts the animal's muscle tone so that it is primed for a startle reaction.

CHAPTER 13

Generalization and Discrimination

Previous chapters described how CSs and S_ds gain strength through Pavlovian and instrumental training. Responding, however, is not restricted to the stimulus used in training. Other stimuli that are similar to the original cue may also elicit reactions. This phenomenon is stimulus **generalization.** The degree to which these novel cues elicit responding depends largely on the degree to which they resemble the original CS or S_d. The more similar the cues, the greater is the conditioned reaction on the generalization test.[1] Usually, stimulus similarity is based on a physical characteristic, such as intensity, wavelength, or size. However, generalization takes place along other kinds of stimulus dimensions, as well. For example, if a human being is given a word, then the person might also generalize to novel words that are not physically similar to the original word, but that resemble it in general meaning.[2]

Generalization involves responding in the same way to two different stimuli because of their similarities. **Discrimination** is the opposite process—namely, responding differently to two stimuli on the basis of their apparent differences. Formally speaking, an animal discriminates when it performs the response to the S+, but not to the S−.[3]

Although discrimination and generalization are complementary processes, they are discussed separately in this chapter. Furthermore, no distinction is made between CSs and S_ds. Subjects respond similarly (generalize) or differently (discriminate) to two or more stimuli, regardless of whether their responding is elicited by a Pavlovian CS or enabled by an instrumental S_d.

One way to think about generalization and discrimination is in terms of stimulus control. Responding that is elicited by a CS, or occurs in the presences of an S_d, is said to be controlled by one or more attributes of the cue. A tone CS, for example, may be characterized in terms of its pitch and intensity. By presenting various tones that differ either in pitch or intensity (that is, by conducting a generalization test using stimuli that differ from the original cue along either one of those dimensions), one may discover which stimulus dimension actually controls behavior. If responding is observed to novel tones that are similar in pitch but not in loudness, then the frequency of the tone controls behavior. On the other hand, if intensity were the controlling dimension, novel tones similar to the original CS in loudness (but not pitch) would elicit a generalized response. In summary, **stimulus control** simply refers to the fact that some dimensions of a stimulus are relevant (and thus elicit behavior), whereas others are not. A generalization test reveals the extent to which one dimension, but not another, elicits behavior.

GENERALIZATION GRADIENTS

One striking aspect of generalization is the orderly relationship between the strength of the response to the generalized stimuli and the similarity of those stimuli to the original CS or S_d. This graded relationship is the **generalization gradient.**[4]

Measures of Generalization

Several methods are used to demonstrate generalization gradients. Each has certain advantages and disadvantages.

Multiple Stimulus.

The multiple-stimulus technique involves conditioning a target S+ and then, during an extinction session, presenting the original stimulus plus numerous others that are similar (all in a random order) and observing the subject's reaction to each. The advantage of this technique is that each subject experiences all of the generalized stimuli. The disadvantage is that responding to one stimulus may affect a subject's reaction to other stimuli along the continuum.

Single Stimulus.

The single-stimulus technique involves training subjects with the original stimulus, and then testing them with only a single generalized cue. The ability for each generalized stimulus to evoke responding is assessed through group comparisons. Although this approach may be more time consuming and costly, the advantage is that the subject's reaction to one generalized stimulus is not affected by exposure to other stimuli.[5]

Maintained Generalization Procedure.

A third approach is to reinforce a subject continuously for responding to the original S+, usually on an intermittent schedule of reinforcement, but periodically to give test trials during which a generalized stimulus is presented without reinforcement.[6] Over the course of several sessions, all of the generalized stimuli are presented several times in a random order. The advantages here are that subjects experience each generalized stimulus and that the strength of responding to the S+ is maintained throughout the test. The disadvantage is that subjects eventually discriminate the original S+ from the generalized stimuli, and thus the gradient may become artificially steep.

Types of Generalization Gradients

Generalization occurs for both excitatory and inhibitory stimuli.

Excitatory.

Generalization gradients for excitatory S_ds were demonstrated in a classic experiment by Guttman and Kalish (1956), using pigeons. A light was placed behind the response key; by using chromatic filters, the color of the light could be controlled accurately. Four groups of animals were used, the only difference among the groups being the wavelength of the S+. One group received an S+ with a wavelength of 530 nanometers; other groups were given a 550-, 580-, or 600-nanometer S+. During the 60-second S+ periods, food was available on a VI-1-minute schedule of reward (during the S− periods, key pecks were not reinforced). On the generalization test, the original S+ plus 10 other stimuli that were both higher and lower on the color spectrum were presented for 30 seconds. Each set of 11 stimuli was repeated 12 different times. No food rewards were delivered during these test sessions.

The results are shown in Figure 13-1. Mean total number of responses to each stimulus is plotted separately for the four groups. Maximum responding in each group was, not surprisingly, elicited by the original training S_d. However, the generalized stimuli also elicited pecking, the magnitude of

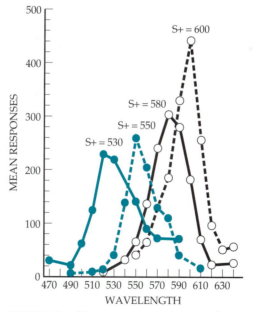

FIGURE 13-1. Mean responses given to the S+ and the generalized stimuli by groups for which the wavelength of the original training stimulus was 530, 550, 580, or 600 nanometers (after Guttman & Kalish, 1956).

responding being a positive function of the similarity between the training and the test stimuli.[7]

Inhibitory.

Gradients for generalized inhibition have also been demonstrated.[8] One technique (the summation approach) involves training both an S+ and S−, and then presenting the S+ along with cues that are similar to the S−. The generalized S− stimuli subtract from the excitatory power of the S+; the more similar a stimulus is to the original S−, the more it reduces the excitation elicited by the S+.

A study by Weisman and Palmer (1969) provides a good example of generalized conditioned inhibition.[9] Pigeons were given discrimination training in which pecking a green key was reinforced (S+), whereas pecking the green key with a vertical white line projected onto it was not rewarded (S−). After training, each subject was given a generalization test, consisting of the S+ (green background), over which one of seven white lines was superimposed—namely, the original S− (0° from vertical), or a line that departed from the vertical by −90°, −60°, −30°, +30°, +60°, and +90°.

The generalization gradient for one of the pigeons is shown in Figure 13-2.[10] Number of responses to each generalized stimulus is shown as a function of the stimulus. Responding to the green S+ key by itself is shown along the top of the figure. The original S− elicited the greatest conditioned inhibi-

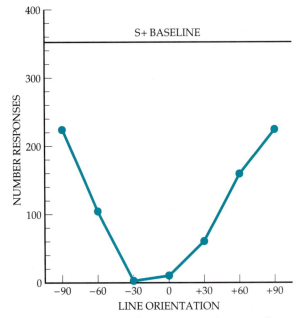

FIGURE 13-2. Number of responses to the green S+ key (S+ baseline) and the S− inhibitory cues by one pigeon subject (after Weisman & Palmer, 1969).

tion; responding was most depressed when that stimulus was presented. The other stimuli also elicited conditioned inhibition, at least to some degree, and the degree of suppression was related to the similarity between the S− and the generalized cues.[11]

Excitatory–Inhibitory Interactions: The Peak Shift.

When original training involves discrimination between an S− and an S+ cue, and then generalization is assessed on a test phase, an interesting effect, termed the **peak shift,** occurs. The peak shift is defined as a displacement of the peak of the excitatory gradient away from the original S+, in the direction opposite to that of the S−.[12] This was demonstrated in a study by Hanson (1959). Pigeons earned food by pecking a key during the S+ stimulus (a colored light with a wavelength of 550 nanometers). Different groups were then given discrimination training for which the S+ continued to be the 550 light and the S− was 555, 560, 570, or 590 nanometers in wavelength. A fifth control group did not receive discrimination training. In Phase 3, a generalization test was given, using 13 different stimuli, ranging from 480 to 600 nanometers.

The results are shown in Figure 13-3. First, the peak of the responding in the control group was, predictably, at the original S+, and an orderly decrease in responding was observed to the various generalized stimuli. In

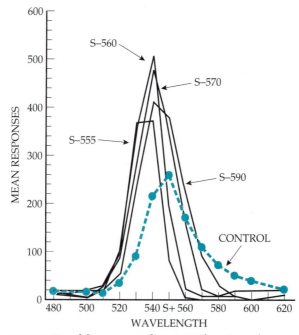

FIGURE 13-3. Mean responding, as a function of wavelength, for groups receiving a 550-nanometer S+ and a 555-, 560-, 570-, or 590-nanometer S− cue (controls did not receive an S− cue) (after Hanson, 1959).

the discrimination groups, however, the peak of the curve was not at the original S+, but rather was displaced away from the S+ in a direction opposite to that of the S−. For example, subjects that received the 570-nanometer S− cue showed the highest rate of responding to the 540-nanometer, not the original 550-nanometer S+ stimulus.[13] Furthermore, the amount of displacement was a function of the difference between the S+ and the S− cues. The closer the S− was to the S+, the greater was the peak shift. For instance, when the S− cue was located farther away from the original S+, as in the group that received the 590-nanometer S−, then animals did not show as great a shift in the peak of their responding.[14]

What explains the fact that maximum responding during generalization is not to the original S+ cue? Spence (1937) argued that postdiscrimination generalization gradients are derived from the interaction of the excitation and the inhibition gradients.[15] More specifically, each generalized stimulus elicits *both* generalized excitation and generalized inhibition. Responding to a given stimulus is the algebraic sum of the separate excitatory and inhibitory tendencies for that stimulus. If the excitatory and inhibitory gradients are measured separately and the algebraic sums are computed, then the resulting gradient shows a peak shift away from the S+.[16]

To illustrate, consider the following hypothetical case. Assume that subjects are reinforced for responding to a stimulus labeled as 0 (the S+) but not reinforced for responding to a stimulus labeled as −2 (the S−). Assume further that both the excitatory and the inhibitory generalization gradients are plotted separately, using arbitrary strength units. The gradients might resemble those shown in the top portion of Figure 13-4 (top). By subtracting each value on the inhibitory gradient from the corresponding value on the excitatory gradient, one derives the combined, or net, gradient (Figure 13-4, bottom). Here, the peak of the combined gradient is not located at the S+ value, but rather is displaced away from the S+ value on the side opposite to that of the S− value.[17]

INTERIM SUMMARY

Generalization is the process by which novel stimuli that are similar to a training CS or S_d elicit a conditioned response. The opposite process is discrimination—namely, responding differentially to two stimuli, based on their perceived differences. The graded relationship between the response and the similarity of the cues is called the "generalization gradient." There are several ways to demonstrate the gradient. Following conditioning to a single S+, many, or only one, generalized stimuli may be given on the generalization test. Generalization gradients occur in both excitatory and inhibitory conditioning. The peak shift shows an interaction between excitatory and inhibitory gradients. The peak shift is a displacement of the peak of the excitatory generalization gradient following discrimination training. The shift is away from the original S+ in a direction opposite to that of the S−.

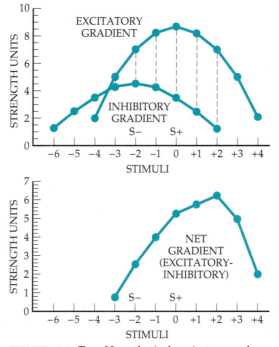

FIGURE 13-4. Top: Hypothetical excitatory and inhibitory generalization gradients. Differences between the excitatory and the inhibitory values are shown by the dotted lines. Bottom: Net generalization gradient derived by subtracting the values for the inhibitory gradient from those of the excitatory gradient (after Spence, 1937).

THEORIES OF GENERALIZATION

Several theories of stimulus generalization are reviewed in the following section.

Generalization as a Primary Process

Pavlov.

One of the earliest theories was proposed by Pavlov (1927). According to Pavlov, generalization is a primary neurological process. When an area of the brain is activated by a CS+, there is a spread of electrical activity to other nearby areas of the brain, thus triggering the neurological centers for other stimuli as well.[18]

Hull.

Hull (1943) also suggested that generalization is an inherent and fundamental process in learning, not a secondary by-product of some other process.

More specifically, a response is conditioned to a zone of stimulus values, not to a single stimulus value. The reason is that the nervous system that senses a stimulus, unlike a scientific instrument, is in a constant state of oscillation or flux; the brain registers several stimulus values when it senses a cue, not a single value. During a generalization test, new stimuli evoke the response because some of their sensory values are the same as those conditioned earlier. In this respect, dissimilar stimuli are weaker than cues that are close to the original S+ because fewer of their values lie within the zone of values for the original cue.[19]

Generalization as a Failure to Differentiate

A more widely supported theory, proposed by Lashley and Wade (1946), suggests that generalization is a result of a subject's inability to differentiate among the stimuli.[20] The **Lashley–Wade theory** makes two claims. First, subjects are confused during the generalization test. That is why they respond to stimuli they have never encountered before. The more similar the stimulus is to the original S+, the greater the confusion and thus the greater the generalized responding. In this sense, generalization is the inverse of discrimination. Second, a subject learns about the dimension along which generalization takes place. Subjects initially do not know the basis on which two stimuli differ (and thus they generalize from one to the other), but they attend to, and thus learn about, the relevant dimension. Such learning occurs as a result of experiencing a variety of stimulus values, either prior to the test or during the generalization test itself.

Inverse Hypothesis.

The claim that generalization is a failure to discriminate is known as the **inverse hypothesis.** If subjects cannot discriminate, they generalize. If they discriminate between stimuli, then generalization is minimal and the gradient is steep.

A direct test of the inverse hypothesis was conducted by Blough (1972), using pigeons.[21] The S+ values ranged from 480 to 630 nanometers. During the generalization test, various stimuli, spaced 4 nanometers apart, were given. As shown in Figure 13-5, the generalization gradients at the low end of the spectrum (S+ equal to 480 nanometers) were relatively broad. Here, the discriminability among colors is relatively poor. Lack of discrimination, according to the inverse hypothesis, should lead to flat generalization gradients. The generalization gradients were quite steep, however, in those areas of the spectrum where pigeons are highly sensitive to color—namely, around 600 nanometers. Birds easily differentiate between colors at that point in the spectrum and thus do not generalize between them. The generalization gradients therefore closely reflect the subjects' ability to discriminate among colors.[22]

Attentional Factors.

The involvement of attentional processes in generalization is shown by the fact that prior discrimination training affects generalization.[23] Discrimination draws the subject's attention to the relevant dimension of the stimulus,

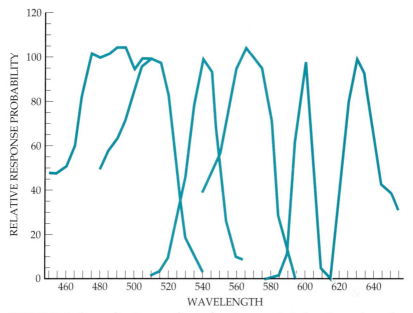

FIGURE 13-5. Generalization gradients for pigeons at six locations along the spectrum (after Blough, 1972).

thus causing less confusion among stimuli (and less generalization) later on. In some cases, attention is due to the salience of the cues and thus specific to the stimuli used in the discrimination task.[24] In other cases, the attentional effects transfer to stimuli not involved in the discrimination.

For example, in a study by Honig (1974), several groups of pigeons were first trained to discriminate between vertical and horizontal black stripes.[25] In Phase 2, the true discrimination group discriminated between a blue S+ and green S−.[26] The pseudodiscrimination group received both the green and the blue key lights, but reward was given for responding to each key on 50% of the occasions. These subjects, therefore, were not differentially reinforced for responding to one key or the other. In Phase 3, a generalization test was given in which the vertical lines were now tilted to various degrees. The issue was whether the true discrimination training with the blue and the green colors would affect stimulus control by the vertical black lines.[27]

The data are shown in Figure 13-6. The generalization gradient for the true discrimination group was significantly steeper than for the pseudodiscrimination subjects. This is an interesting finding because those two groups of subjects had received exactly the same discrimination training in Phase 1 with the vertical and horizontal lines, yet because the former animals were given discrimination training with a *different* dimension, attention to the vertical/horizontal stimuli was stronger.

In other words, discrimination with the colors in Phase 2 maintained the animals' general attention and consequently caused stronger control by the vertical black lines in Phase 3.[28] In summary, discrimination training affects

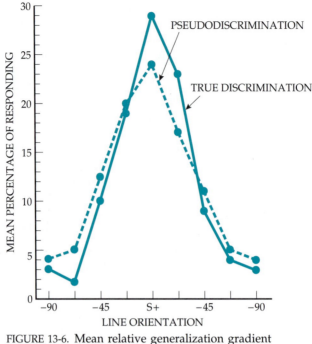

FIGURE 13-6. Mean relative generalization gradient (percentage responding), as a function of line orientation for the true and pseudodiscrimination groups (after Honig, 1974).

generalization by enhancing attention.[29] These results support the Lashley–Wade theory because they suggest that the tendency to generalize is, in part, due to the subject's inability to discriminate, which, in turn, is a function of the subject's lack of attention to the relevant stimulus dimension.

Information-Processing Models of Generalization

Many contemporary theorists believe that learning involves information processing. This viewpoint was emphasized in earlier chapters dealing with both Pavlovian and instrumental conditioning (see especially Chapters 6 and 11). Several models suggest that generalization also involves the processing of information.

Blough Model.

Blough's (1975) model of generalization is similar to the Rescorla–Wagner model of Pavlovian conditioning (see Chapter 6). The Rescorla–Wagner model measures strength of a response in the presence of a CS; **Blough's model of generalization** includes generalized stimuli.[30] It provides a quantitative description of how generalized excitatory and inhibitory reactions develop.

The model specifically claims that the presentation of a reinforcer modifies the probability of a response to the training CS and to other generalized CSs that share elements or characteristics with the training CS.

According to Blough, stimuli such as lights or tones are represented by their elements or characteristics. When a stimulus is presented, a set of elements or characteristics is activated. Each element or characteristic is capable of gaining associative strength through pairing with a US (the associative strength of element i is given by the term v_i). These summate across all elements, creating the overall associative strength of the stimulus (designated by V_s).

Blough also assumes that elements may be shared by two stimuli, depending on their similarity. If the elements of one stimulus gain associative strength by being paired with a US, then a generalized stimulus, which shares elements or characteristics with the training CS, also gains strength. The strength of the generalized elements are weighted according to the degree to which they are shared. Those characteristics or elements that are shared are weighted more heavily than those that are not. The strength of a stimulus (V_s) is, therefore, the sum of the strength of the individual elements (v_i), weighted by a generalization factor (γs_i).

Formally speaking, the strength of a stimulus is given by the following equation:

$$V_s = \Sigma \; \gamma s_i v_i \qquad\qquad \textit{Equation 13-1}$$

This equation asserts that the strength of a generalized stimulus (V_s) is the sum of the strengths of the i elements of the stimulus (v_i) weighted by a similarity factor for each i element (γs_i).

The model further asserts the following.

$$\Delta v_i = \Sigma \; \gamma s_i \beta (\lambda - V_s) \qquad\qquad \textit{Equation 13-2}$$

where V_s is the associative strength of stimulus S (given by Equation 13-1), Δv_i is the change in associative strength of element i, γs_i is the generalization weighting factor, β is a learning-rate parameter that, in part, determines how steeply the learning curve rises, and λ is the asymptotic or maximum associative strength that V_s may obtain.

The generalization factor (γs_i) increases with the physical similarity between stimuli. Knowing the similarity, therefore, allows one to predict the change in strength of an element on any given trial. Blough simulated these equations on the computer, using arbitrary values for the different factors, and found them to predict actual generalization data quite accurately.

Pearce Model.

In contrast, Pearce (1987), having found Blough's model lacking in several respects, developed a model that assumes that animals have a memory buffer containing the pattern of stimulation currently being experienced by the subject.[31] When a CS is presented, the hypothetical memory buffer contains representations of its elements plus elements from other cues in the environment, such as the apparatus. When the US follows, the CS representations in memory, in their entirety, gain associative strength. However, the contents of the memory buffer change when a new generalized stimulus is presented. A response is evoked by a generalized stimulus to the extent that the elements it activates already possess associative strength derived during original training. In short, the current stimulus environment (the CS and apparatus elements) is represented as a set of elements in memory. Generalization occurs when elements that were conditioned previously are activated by the generalized stimulus. The magnitude of the generalized response is determined by the proportion of elements common to both the original and the generalized cues.

Pearce uses $_AS_{A'}$ to represent the degree of similarity of the contents of the buffer for two different stimuli, CS_A and $CS_{A'}$. If two stimuli are similar, then $_AS_{A'}$ is close to 1.0; if they are not, the value of $_AS_{A'}$ is close to 0.[32]

Pearce's model of generalization is formally stated by the following equation:

$$e_{A'} = {_AS_{A'}} E_A \hspace{4cm} \textit{Equation 13-3}$$

where the term E_A is the excitatory strength of CS_A; $_AS_{A'}$ is the proportion of elements that CS_A and $CS_{A'}$ share; and $e_{A'}$ is the excitatory strength of the generalized stimulus—namely, $CS_{A'}$.[33]

A generalized stimulus activates elements contained in memory; the greater the similarity between CS_A and $CS_{A'}$, the more that common elements are activated and, therefore, the higher is the generalized excitation ($e_{A'}$).

Generalization as Relational Responding

The preceding theories all argue that generalization in inversely related to the physical similarity between the training and the test stimuli. As the number of shared elements between the two stimuli declines, the generalized reaction declines as well. There is a different way of viewing generalization, however. According to a relational approach, generalized responding is not based on the absolute physical differences between stimuli but rather on their relative differences.

Central-Tendency Effect.

An example of relational responding, the **central-tendency effect,** was shown by Thomas and Jones (1962).[34] Human observers were given a green light of 525 nanometers for 60 seconds and were instructed to "keep this color in mind because you will be asked to identify it later. After 1 minute this color will be turned off and you will place your finger and press down on the telegraph key in front of you. I will give the signal 'ready' and a few seconds later a color will again be presented. You must decide whether this is the original color shown you at the start of the experiment. If it is, lift your hand as rapidly as you can from the key."[35] Subjects were tested with the original color and four generalized stimuli. Five groups of subjects differed only with respect to which set of generalized stimuli they were given. Some subjects received generalized stimuli, all of which had lower wavelengths than the original color—for instance, 485 through 515 nanometers. Others got generalized stimuli, all of which had higher wavelengths—for example, 535 through 565 nanometers. Still other observers received two generalized stimuli that were lower (505 and 515 nanometers) and two that were higher (535 and 545 nanometers) than the original color. Responses on the telegraph key were recorded for each stimulus.

The generalization gradients are shown in Figure 13-7. All subjects were trained only with a single color value as the CS, so the generalized gradients should be symmetrical about the 525-nanometer value if generalized responding is based on the absolute physical similarity of the original cue to the generalized stimuli.[36] For instance, subjects should display the same generalized reaction to the 515-nanometer stimulus as they do the the 535-nanometer cue because, from the point of view of physical similarity to the original color, both cues are equally dissimilar. Figure 13-7 shows that this was not obtained, however. The group that was given the symmetrical generalization test (heavy line with filled circles), showed a symmetrical gradient, but the other groups did not. The peak of their gradients shifted away from the original value in a direction toward the test stimuli.

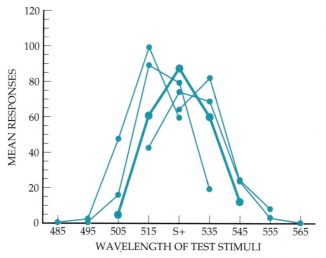

FIGURE 13-7. Mean responses to the S+ and generalized stimuli by five groups of humans, who differed in terms of which series of generalized stimuli they received (after Thomas & Jones, 1962).

Thomas's Adaptation-Level Effect Model.

A model that accounts for this phenomenon was proposed by Thomas (1993).[37] According to Thomas's model, subjects judge stimuli against a stored referent, or subjective representation of the average value they encounter. If subjects experience only one value of a stimulus, then that value becomes the referent. If they experience multiple values of a stimulus, then they develop an adaptation-level referent, or memory representation, of the average value of all the stimuli. Generalized stimuli are judged in terms of this adaptation-lever referent, not in terms of the S+ value alone.

Thomas's adaptation-level effect model explains the central-tendency effect by claiming that subjects who experience generalized stimuli below the S+ develop a subjective representation of the average value of the stimuli that is also below the S+ value. Their responding is based on this averaged value. Similarly, subjects who experience only stimuli above the S+ value develop a memory representation of the average value of stimuli that is higher than the S+.

Thomas formally expressed the model in the following terms:

$$Y(t) = \Sigma\ w(i)\ f[X(i)] \qquad\qquad Equation\ 13\text{-}4$$

where $Y(t)$ denotes the average subjective value that occurs after t presentations of all the stimuli, $w(i)$ is a parameter that weights the value of stimulus i, and $f[X(i)]$ represents the perceived values of the generalized stimuli.

The equation therefore implies that the subjective adaptation-level value of the entire set of stimuli is a function of the value of each generalized stimulus, times the weighted values of the original S+.

To explain this model, let us arbitrarily assume that a subject is given an S+ and 4 generalized stimuli, all of which are more intense.[38] If the original S+ is weighted 1 and is given 5 times during original training, and the generalized stimuli are subjectively scaled as 2, 3, 4, and 5, respectively, then the average subjective representation of the entire set of stimuli (original training and one repetition of all the stimuli on the test) is 2.0.

This is calculated from Equation 13-4 by summing the 5 original training trials (5 trials times a weight of 1 = 5), and the 5 test trials (weights for the test cues are 1, 2, 3, 4, and 5; each is multiplied by 1 trial, thus giving 15), and then dividing the total by the number of cues experienced (20/10 = 2). If the test series is given twice, then the adaptation-level shifts away from the S+ value even more, to a value of 2.33 (sum of the weights times trials for original training = 5; the sum of the weights times trials from two presentations of the generalized stimuli = 30; the average = 35/15 or 2.33). If the test series is presented three times, then the subjective average is even higher—namely, 2.5 (50 divided by 20). Thus, the response tendency shifts away from the S+ value of 1.0 as more exposure to generalized stimuli, which are higher in intensity, is given.

The precise quantitative predictions (which depend on how the various stimuli are weighted) are less important for the present purposes than the essential idea of the model, which is that generalization is a relational process in which subjects judge the value of generalized stimuli, not on the basis of the absolute physical dissimilarity to the S+, but rather in terms of an averaged subjective representation of all of the stimuli experienced. The contribution of the original S+ training to a subject's reaction to an array of stimuli is certainly recognized by Thomas's model, but the values of the generalized stimuli contribute to the subjective average, as well.[39]

Peak Shift Revisited.

Thomas's relational theory of generalization relates to a variety of phenomena, including the peak-shift phenomenon. This was shown in a study by Thomas, Mood, Morrison, and Wiertelak (1991). Forty university students viewed a white light projected onto a viewing screen. Eleven different light intensities were then used (noted as stimuli 1 through 11). The subjects were told to press a button if the light being presented was the same as the original light. However, subjects also received discrimination training. The S+ (original light intensity) was stimulus value 2 and the S− was stimulus value 4.[40] The experimenter said "correct" when the subject correctly responded to the S+ , but "no, it is different" if the subject incorrectly claimed that the light being presented was the same as the original light, or "no, it is the same" if the subject incorrectly failed to identify the light being presented as being the one given previously. Immediately following discrimination training, subjects were shown six generalized stimuli.

Before discussing the results, let us review the theoretical predictions. According to Spence's theory, discussed previously, subjects should show a shift in the peak of responding away from the S+ in a direction opposite to the S− cue, because the peak of the excitatory gradient at stimulus 2 should be reduced by the generalized inhibition for 2 (see previous discussion). The adaptation-level model, on the other hand, predicts that the peak of responding should shift away from the S+ but *toward* the S− cue, not away from it. The reason is that subjects experience generalized stimuli that are more intense than the original training S+, so their subjective representation of the average value of all stimuli, and thus their peak of their responding, should be higher than the S+, not lower. The results are shown in Figure 13-8. The peak of the generalization gradient is at stimulus 5. Such a shift in the peak supports Thomas's relational model of generalization. Exactly why pigeons show a peak shift whereas humans do not is yet to be determined.

INTERIM SUMMARY

Several theorists, including Pavlov and Hull, claimed that generalization is a fundamental process in learning, not a by-product of some other process. The Lashley–Wade theory is more widely supported. It claims that generalization results from a failure to discriminate. The relationship

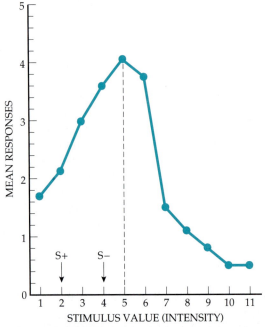

FIGURE 13-8. Mean responses, as a function of stimulus value (light intensity), following discrimination in which the S+ was stimulus 2 and the S− was stimulus 4 (after Thomas, Mood, Morrison, & Wiertelak, 1991).

between discrimination and generalization is called the "inverse hypothesis." Several information-processing models of generalization have been proposed by Blough and Pearce. According to Thomas's relational theory, generalized responding is not based on the absolute physical difference between stimuli, but rather on their relative difference. This theory explains the central-tendency effect, which is a shift in the peak of responding toward an averaged, subjective value for all stimuli experienced.

FACTORS AFFECTING THE GENERALIZATION GRADIENT

Many factors affect generalization. Several are discussed in this section. Bear in mind that a steep generalization gradient reflects little generalization; even stimuli that are quite similar to the original S+ evoke only a marginal response. Flatter gradients, on the other hand, reflect greater generalization; even stimuli that are rather discrepant from the training S+ evoke considerable generalized responding.

Degree of Training

Generalization is influenced by the amount of training given to the S+. The more extended the training is, the less is the generalization (the gradient becomes sharper). One study by Hearst and Koresko (1968) taught pigeons to peck at a vertical line on a colored key (S+). Groups received 2, 4, 7, or 14 50-minute sessions of training. Generalization was measured for six stimuli that differed from the S+ in terms of the slant of the line.

The results are shown in Figure 13-9. The overall height of the generalization gradient increased as a function of training level, but the gradients were steeper with more training; that is, a larger *proportion* of the responses was given to the S+, and a smaller proportion was given to the generalized stimuli.[41] These findings therefore support the Lashley–Wade position. As subjects become more familiar with the dimension on which the stimuli differ, then discrimination is stronger, and, correspondingly, generalization is weaker.[42]

Training-Test Interval

Generalization increases with time, not because the subject responds less to the original S+ cue, but because the more discrepant generalized stimuli, which did not originally elicit strong generalized responding, exert greater

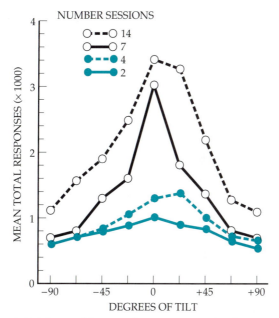

FIGURE 13-9. Mean total responses to the S+ (0 degrees of tilt) and generalized stimuli (differing in their tilt), as a function of number of training sessions (after Hearst & Koresko, 1968).

control as time passes. This has been observed using both appetitive and aversive learning tasks.[43] For instance, Thomas, Windell, Bakke, Kreye, Kimose, and Aposhyan (1985) trained pigeons to peck a key displaying a vertical white line.[44] Generalization testing—administered 1 minute, 1 day, or a week later—consisted of presenting the training S+ and six other generalized stimuli. These other cues were lines that deviated from the vertical by 15°, 30°, 45°, 60°, 75°, or 90°. Although all the animals received the same original training, the degree of generalization varied. As shown in Figure 13-10, subjects that were tested immediately showed a steep gradient. The generalization gradient was much flatter after 1 day and 1 week, however. Here, the relative number of responses to generalized stimuli, even those quite discrepant from the S+, was substantial. Such a finding suggests that the details of the particular stimulus are forgotten with time.[45]

Context

Although the passage of time flattens the generalization gradient, a change in the general context has the opposite effect. When animals are tested in a box that differs from the one used in original conditioning, a steeper gradient (less generalization) is observed. The claim is that the details of the original train-

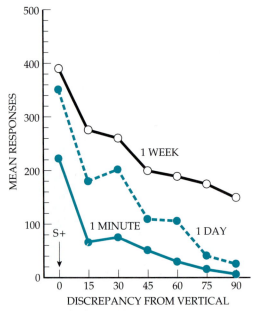

FIGURE 13-10. Mean responses to the S+ and to six generalized stimuli that deviated from the verticals, as a function of the training–test interval (after Thomas, Windell, Bakke, Kreye, Kimose, and Aposhyan, 1985).

ing context are distorted, thus causing a failure in memory retrieval (see Chapter 14).[46]

The joint effect of context change and training–test interval was demonstrated in a study by Gisquet-Verrier and Alexinsky (1986).[47] Rats were initially trained to run down an alleyway to obtain food. They were then tested 1, 3, 5, or 7 days later (variation in the training–test interval). Half of the subjects were tested in a different alleyway, whereas the other half were not (variation in the context).[48] At the end of the training–test interval, subjects were given 12 retraining trials, and latency to respond was measured.

The data for the 1- and 7-day groups are shown in Figure 13-11. A change in context disrupted performance. This effect is evident in the 1-day groups. Such disruption was counteracted, however, by the increase in the training–test interval. This is shown by the lack of group differences at the 7-day interval. Thus, subjects generalize less when the context is changed but generalize more as time passes.[49]

Prior Discrimination Training

When a subject is given discrimination training followed by a generalization test, the gradient is sharper than if the subject is not given discrimination training.[50] One example of this phenomenon was a study by Hanson (1961).[51]

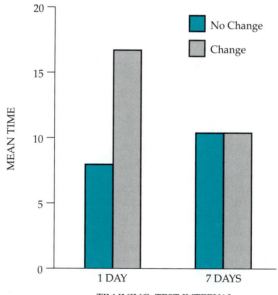

FIGURE 13-11. Mean running time for the 1- and 7-day groups that experienced either a change or no change in the context (after Gisquet-Verrier & Alexinsky, 1986).

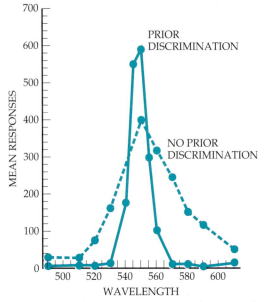

FIGURE 13-12. Mean responses, as a function of the wavelength (nanometers) of the S+, S−, and generalized stimuli, by the prior-discrimination and no-discrimination groups (after Hanson, 1961).

Pigeons were trained to peck a key for food that was delivered on a VI schedule. The S+ was a colored key light (550 nanometers). After 5 days of acquisition, the control subjects continued with this same treatment, while experimental subjects were given discrimination training, consisting of the S+ and two S− cues (lights of 540 and 560 nanometers). After reaching a criterion of discrimination, both groups were tested with the S+, both S− stimuli, and eight other generalized stimuli.

As shown in Figure 13-12, both groups of subjects showed a generalization gradient, but the gradient for the no-discrimination subjects was relatively flat, compared with the gradient for the prior-discrimination animals. Discrimination training therefore produced not only a higher rate of responding to the S+, but also a steeper gradient.[52] These results support the Lashley–Wade theory of generalization. To discriminate between two stimuli, a subject must learn about the relevant stimulus dimensions involved in the discrimination. In doing so, the subject becomes less confused about the stimuli and thus shows less generalization.

INTERIM SUMMARY

Generalization is influenced by the extent of original training. The more training is given, the less generalization occurs (the steeper the gradient). Generalization increases (the gradient flattens) as the interval between training and testing increases, probably because the details of the training stimulus are forgotten over time. A change in the context between training and testing has the opposite effect. It sharpens the generalization gradient because the details of the training context are distorted, and thus the elicitation of the response is reduced. Prior discrimination training also sharpens the generalization gradient, presumably because a subject's attention is drawn to the relevant stimulus dimension during the discrimination training, thus causing less confusion among stimuli on the generalization test.

DISCRIMINATION TRAINING: TYPES OF DISCRIMINATION

As noted previously, discrimination training involves the presentation of reinforcement following a response to one stimulus (the S+), but the withholding of reinforcement following a response to a different stimulus (the S−).[53] The fact that the animal responds differently to the two stimuli indicates that certain salient properties of the stimuli control behavior.

There are several ways to conduct a discrimination experiment. In each case, the rate or probability of responding to the S+ increases over training but decreases to the S−.

Simultaneous

For the simultaneous technique, S+ and S− are presented at the same time, usually using two different response keys. If the subject perceives a difference between them and is under stimulus control, then responding to the S+ is higher than responding to the S−. An inability to differentiate between the stimuli, or a lack of stimulus control, causes the subject to respond to the two patterns more or less at the same rate.

Successive

Another technique is to present the S+ and the S− successively. The measure of discrimination is whether the subject responds differentially. A special version of the successive task is called "go/no-go discrimination." Here, the S+ is the presence of a cue, and the S− is its absence. The subject must "go" with its behavior during the cue's presence but show "no-go" during its absence. Successive discriminations are typically harder to solve than simultaneous discriminations.[54]

Schedule Discrimination

The simultaneous- and successive-discrimination techniques contrast a rewarded and nonrewarded condition. However, the schedule of reward may also vary during the S+ and S− presentations. An example of a simultaneous discrimination between schedules is the concurrent schedule, where the subject chooses between two response options (see Chapters 9 and 10). Responding to the left key is reinforced on one schedule, say, a VR-5, whereas responding to the right key leads to reward on, say, a VR-10.

An example of discrimination of reward schedules using a successive approach is called a "multiple schedule." Subjects earn reward during, say, a green key light, according to a VI-1-minute schedule, but when the discriminative stimulus turns red, then reward is obtained according to a different reinforcement schedule, say, a VI-2-minute one. The signaled components occur sequentially in time. The evidence for discrimination is the differential rate of responding during each component.

Conditional

A **conditional discrimination** is when a subject performs R_1 in the presence of S_1, but a different response—namely, R_2—in the presence of S_2. In other words, the correct response is conditional, or dependent, on which stimulus is presented. The S_1 cue is the S+ for R_1, but the S− for R_2.

Conditional discrimination is essentially the same as conditioned inhibition and occasion setting in Pavlovian conditioning (see Chapters 3 and 5). Recall that during Pavlovian inhibitory conditioning, CS_E is followed by the US, whereas the compound stimulus $CS_E CS_I$ is followed by no US. The cue CS_I becomes inhibitory because it is the informative element that signals no US presentation. Performance is essentially a conditioned discrimination, because in the presence of CS_E, performance of the CR is appropriate, but in the presence of the compound $CS_E CS_I$, no CR is appropriate. The same argument is used in the case of occasion setting, where $CS_E CS_F$ is followed by the US, but CS_E, by itself, is not. Again, the differential responding is based on the differential stimulus pattern.

INTERIM SUMMARY

Discrimination training involves the presentation of reinforcement following a response to the S+, but withholding of reward following a response to the S−. The two stimuli may be presented either simultaneously or successively. Subjects also show discrimination between schedules of reinforcement. A conditional discrimination is performed when a subject executes R_1 in the presence of S_1, but R_2 in the presence of S_2.

THEORIES OF DISCRIMINATION

The two major theories of discrimination learning, noted previously, were developed by Hull (1943) and Spence (1936), and by Sutherland and Mackintosh (1971).[55]

Hull–Spence

The Hull–Spence theory makes three assumptions. First, reinforcement leads to conditioned excitation to the S+. Second, nonreinforcement leads to conditioned inhibition to the S−. Finally, excitation and inhibition generalize to other stimuli, and, more importantly, these conflicting tendencies algebraically summate for any given stimulus. In other words, an S+ has predominantly excitatory strength, but it also has some inhibitory strength because it is a generalized stimulus to the S−. Similarly, the S− stimulus is predominantly inhibitory, but it also has some excitatory strength because excitation generalizes from the S+ to the S−. The same argument is made for any other stimulus along the dimension. Each is similar to both the S+ and the S−, and therefore, each evokes both a generalized excitatory and a generalized inhibitory reaction. Whether a subject performs a reaction when presented with a given stimulus depends on the relative strength of the generalized excitatory and inhibitory tendencies for that stimulus. Performance is observed when the excitatory tendency is greater than the inhibitory tendency.

The **Hull–Spence theory of discrimination** has been supported in a number of experiments.[56] The strongest support comes from studies of the peak-shift phenomenon discussed previously.

Sutherland–Mackintosh

A schematic diagram of the **attention theory of discrimination** formulated by Sutherland and Mackintosh is shown in Figure 13-13. According to the theory, discrimination learning involves two separate processes. First, attention itself is affected when a subject is reinforced. More specifically, the brain has **analyzers** that receive and process sensory information. Each dimension that characterizes a particular stimulus is represented by a separate analyzer. In the example shown in Figure 13-13, the stimulus is characterized by its size, brightness, and orientation. At the start of training, the strength of a given analyzer is related to the strength of the incoming signal. If a stimulus has a salient feature, such as its brightness or its color, then the subject's attention is drawn toward that dimension. This accounts for the fact that stimuli that are stronger evoke greater attention and thus are conditioned more easily.

If the animal pays attention to a particular stimulus dimension and receives reward following its response, then the attention response, the analyzer, increases in strength. For example, if the tilt of a line were correlated with food, but brightness and size were not, then the strength of the orientation analyzer would increase, but the strength of the brightness and size analyzers would decrease.

The second process identified by the attention theory involves the acquisition of a response. This is shown in Figure 13-13 as a choice response. A bond or attachment develops between a specific response and an analyzer. For example, the analyzer for line orientation may become attached to a specific response, such as choosing the horizontal rather than the vertical stimulus.

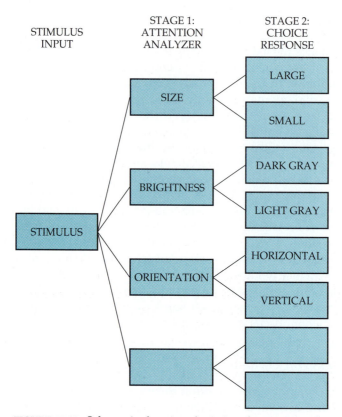

FIGURE 13-13. Schematic drawing depicting the attentional processes involved in discrimination learning. In this example, the stimulus is defined by three dimensions—specifically, size, brightness, and orientation.

Support for Attention Theory.

Direct support for the attention theory was obtained by Waller (1973a). Two groups of rats ran down an alleyway and received reward in the goal box on every trial. Two other groups were rewarded on only 50% of the trials. For one group in each of the preceding conditions, the alleyway was painted gray, whereas for the other group in each condition, it was covered with black and white vertical stripes. Thus, Waller's four groups received 100% reward, gray; 100% reward, stripes; 50% reward, gray; or 50% reward, stripes.

In Phase 2, all subjects learned to choose between two goal boxes for food reward. [57] One goal box was covered with stripes that slanted 45° to the right, the other with stripes slanting 45° to the left.

The attention theory makes several predictions. First, the 50%-stripe group should learn the discrimination more slowly than the 100%-stripe group, because line orientation was rewarded only 50% of the time, and thus they should have a weaker analyzer for line orientation than the 100% group has. Second, the two groups that were trained in the gray alleyway during Phase 1 should learn equally well during the discrimination phase, because those subjects never experienced stripes, so their attention to line orientation (the analyzer strength for orientation) should be about equal.

As shown in Figure 13-14, subjects that were trained in the gray alleyway during Phase 1 learned to discriminate between the two striped patterns at approximately the same rate. Discrimination learning, however, differed between the 100%- and the 50%-striped groups. The 50%-striped subjects took more trials to reach the discrimination criterion in Phase 2 because they had not developed sufficient attention to line orientation. Subjects in the 100%-striped group, on the other hand, learned better because they had developed a strong analyzer for orientation in Phase 1.[58]

Attention Measurements.

The attention response itself has been measured in a variety of situations, including studies that use a method called "matching-to-sample" (see also Chapter 14).[59] An example of this approach is a study by Lamb and Riley (1981).[60] Pigeons were first given a white key located in the center of the front wall. A peck to this key caused a sample stimulus to be presented. The sample could be one of two types. First, element samples contained either a small square of color (red or orange) or parallel black lines (oriented either vertically or horizontally). Second, a sample could be a compound stimulus con-

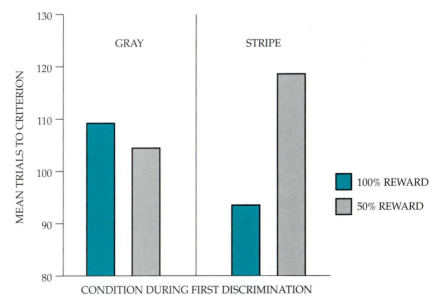

FIGURE 13-14. Mean trials to the discrimination criterion by groups that had original discrimination training with either gray or striped stimuli and that had been rewarded on either 100% or 50% of the trials (after Waller, 1973a).

taining both a color and a set of lines—for example, a patch of red located just above horizontal lines. Once the bird pecked the sample, two test stimuli were illuminated on either side of the front wall. Here, each key contained an element that had been part of the sample stimulus.

For example, if a red patch had been presented as a sample, then one test key would contain a red patch, and the other test key would have an orange patch. Similarly, if a compound sample had been presented, then the test stimuli would be either two keys, each containing a color patch, or two keys, each containing a set of lines oriented horizontally or vertically.[61] Examples of single and compound element trials are shown in Figure 13-15. If the subject pecked the correct test key, then it was rewarded with grain. If, however, it pecked the key that did not match an element on the sample stimulus just experienced, then it experienced a 5-second period of darkness, at which point a new trial was initiated.

According to the attention theory, subjects attend to the dimensions represented on the sample and respond accordingly when given a choice between the test keys. However, the theory also stipulates that subjects cannot attend to two dimensions simultaneously. If they receive a compound stimulus involving both a color patch and a set of lines, then attention to one dimen-

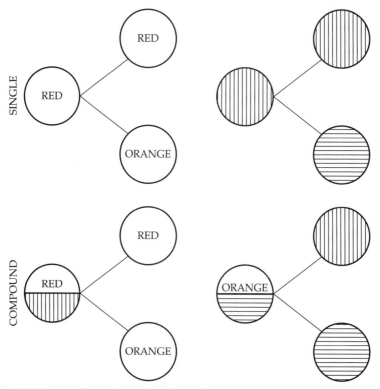

FIGURE 13-15. Examples of single- and compound-element stimuli used by Lamb and Riley (1981).

sion—say, line orientation—precludes or diminishes attention to the other dimension (in this case, color). Thus, the accuracy of the matching performance for the poorly attended-to dimension should be less than for the strongly attended-to dimension. For instance, if subjects on a compound trial attend to the orientation, then matching performance for two test stimuli containing color patches should be poorer than matching performance for two test stimuli containing sets of lines.

The results are shown in Figure 13-16. Subjects matched the sample more accurately when the sample was a single element (either a color patch or a set of lines) because no conflict between attending to two dimensions was experienced, and thus all of the subject's attention could be directed toward the relevant dimension. However, when a compound stimulus was presented, matching was less accurate, because, on the average, subjects attended to the wrong dimension on half of the trials.

For instance, if they had attended to the orientation dimension and then were tested with two color patches, performance was less accurate than if they were tested with two sets of lines. In short, the pigeons' ability to match a sample just seen depends critically on having attended to the correct dimension. When only a single element is presented during the sample, attention is easy, and good matching occurs. When a compound stimulus is presented, however, attention is divided, and matching performance declines accordingly.

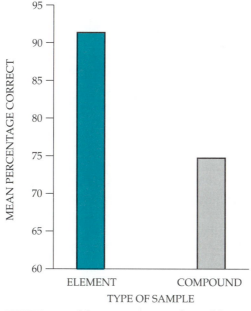

FIGURE 13-16. Mean percentage of matching performance following samples that were elements or compounds (after Lamb & Riley, 1981).

INTERIM SUMMARY

The Hull–Spence theory of discrimination assumed that reinforcement leads to conditioned excitation to the S+, nonreinforcement leads to conditioned inhibition to the S−, and the excitatory and inhibitory gradients summate. The peak shift supports the Hull–Spence position. The attention theory of discrimination claims that discrimination learning involves two processes. Reinforcement strengthens a subject's attention to the relevant dimensions; the attention reaction is called an "analyzer." The second process involves the acquisition of the choice response. Many studies support the attention theory.

FACTORS AFFECTING DISCRIMINATION

Discrimination learning is affected by many factors. Several are discussed in the following sections, including problem difficulty, prior discrimination, stimulus information, and differential outcome.

Problem Difficulty

Discrimination learning occurs more rapidly when the S+ and the S− stimuli are easily distinguished from one another than when they are not.[62] For example, rats that must choose between one of two alleyways painted black and white learn faster than animals that must choose between two alleyways painted different shades of gray.[63] The same finding has been shown for color and line tilt.[64] For instance, Thomas, Windell, Bakke, Kreye, Kimose, and Aposhyan (1985) found that pigeons took approximately 76 trials to learn a discrimination between a line tilted 0° (S+) and one tilted 30° (S−), but only about 26 trials when the S+ was tilted 0° and the S− was 90°.[65]

Prior Discrimination

Prior experience with one discrimination problem affects how well a subject learns a second. This effect, the **easy-to-hard effect,** was first shown by Lawrence (1952).[66] Rats were trained to choose one of two goal boxes on the basis of brightness. Animals in one group were given 80 trials with a very difficult discrimination. Here, each goal box was a different shade of gray. Subjects in a second group were treated in the same fashion, but they had first been given 30 trials with goal boxes that were easily contrasted (one black, the other white). The study found that mastering the easy discrimination problem facilitated performance on the more difficult problem.

Lawrence's explanation was that animals more easily attend to the relevant stimulus dimension during an easy task, and that such an attention reaction later facilitates the more difficult discrimination.[67] Stated differently, an animal first learns about the relevant stimulus dimension (here, goal box brightness); performing the correct response is easy when the two stimuli are highly discriminable. Performance on the difficult task is then facilitated because the subject must attend to the same dimension to solve that problem.

A related theory of the easy-to-hard effect maintains that the facilitation of discrimination stems from an improvement in the subject's general ability to solve discrimination problems, not simply from attending to one relevant dimension, such as brightness. According to this position, experience with any discrimination problem, regardless of what stimulus dimension is used or how difficult it is, promotes general problem-solving skills that aid the organism when it later confronts the difficult problem.

Seraganian (1979) tested this hypothesis. Pigeons were trained to make a difficult discrimination between a line pattern oriented 30° from one oriented 60°.[68] Prior to that time, subjects were given experience either with a single stimulus (an amber light served as both S+ and S−), or a discrimination problem involving an orange (S+) and an amber (S−) key light.[69]

The mean proportion of responses given to the S+ are shown in Figure 13-17. During Phase 1, the single-stimulus group, not surprisingly, performed at about chance level. The color group performed at a much higher rate. Performance for the two groups in Phase 2, however, shows a clear superiority

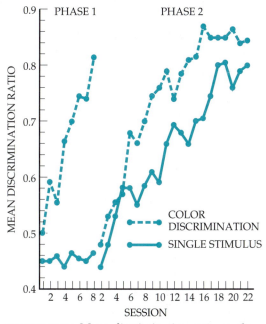

FIGURE 13-17. Mean discrimination ratio on the difficult line-orientation problem during Phase 2 for subjects given only a single stimulus during Phase 1 and subjects trained during Phase 1 to discriminate two colors (after Seraganian, 1979).

for the group given the prior discrimination training. Experience with the color-discrimination problem facilitated discrimination training on the more difficult line-orientation problem,

Stimulus Information

The information value of an S_d affects discrimination learning, as shown in a noted study by Wagner, Logan, Haberlandt, and Price (1968). The experimental design is shown in Figure 13-18. The correlated group earned food by pressing a lever during a compound S+; the cue was a light combined with one of two tones (referred to as LT_1).[70] The S− compound for the correlated group was the same light, presented simultaneously with a different tone (namely, LT_2). The uncorrelated group of rats was given the same stimulus compounds, but subjects could earn food 50% of the time whenever either LT_1 or LT_2 was presented.

The important thing about this design is that the light element was followed by food on 50% of the trials in *both* the correlated and the uncorrelated groups. Subjects were trained until the correlated subjects reached a criterion of discrimination.[71] The uncorrelated group, being unable to respond differentially to the S+ and the S− stimuli (because neither was a reliable predictor of reward availability) was given the same amount of training. Finally, all subjects were tested for the strength of the respective elements—namely, L, T_1, and T_2.

The results are shown in Figure 13-19. First, consider the correlated group. When subjects have good predictive stimuli (the two tones), then an added

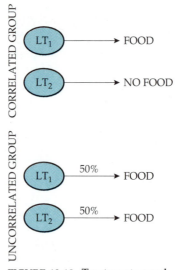
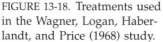

FIGURE 13-18. Treatments used in the Wagner, Logan, Haberlandt, and Price (1968) study.

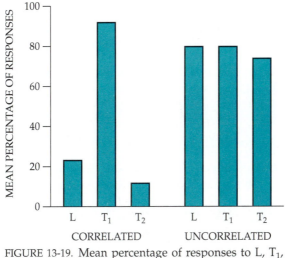

FIGURE 13-19. Mean percentage of responses to L, T_1, and T_2 during the test session by the correlated and uncorrelated subjects (after Wagner, Logan, Haberlandt, & Price, 1968).

element in the compound (the light), which is redundant from an informational point of view, derives little strength (see also Chapter 5). Figure 13-19 shows that T_1, which was consistently followed by food, elicited stronger responding than did either T_2 or L.

Now consider the results of the uncorrelated group. The light elicited as strong a response as did the tones. None of the three cues was a good predictive stimulus because reinforcement was available on 50% of the trials, regardless of which compound was presented. The study, therefore, confirms that an S_d gains strength as a result of its *relative* validity. The light was paired with the food on precisely the same number of trials in both groups, yet when the light was as predictive as the tones, it gained strength, but when it was *relatively* less predictive, it did not. These results support the attention theory of discrimination, which argues that subjects attend to the relevant or predictive stimuli in order to solve the discrimination problem.

A similar study by Wasserman (1974) expanded on these results.[72] Wasserman used two response keys, one illuminated with a white light, and the other illuminated with either a red or a green light. The white key (W) was lit on both S+ and S− trials. In the correlated condition, the other key was lit with color 1 (C_1) on the S+ trials, but with color 2 (C_2) on the S− trials. In other words, two separate keys served as the S+, one lit with W and the other lit with C_1. The joint presentation of W and C_2 was the S−. In the uncorrelated condition, the same joint stimuli were presented (W/C_1, and W/C_2), but reward was presented on 50% of the trials for both compounds.

The primary difference, therefore, between this design and the one used by Wagner, Logan, Haberlandt, and Price is that the compound stimuli comprised two illuminated keys rather than a light and tone combination. This difference was important because it allowed Wasserman to measure the subject's selective attention directly by counting pecks to each individual key. The results were very similar to those found previously. For the correlated subjects, responding to the unique predictive key of the S+ combination increased, relative to the other keys. The uncorrelated subjects, however, showed a comparable level of key pecking (attention) to all stimuli.

Differential-Outcome Effect

Another condition that affects discrimination learning is the degree to which the response leads to a unique outcome. Responding differentially to S_1 and S_2 (by performing R_1 and R_2, respectively) occurs more readily when R_1 leads to O_1 (one outcome), but R_2 results in O_2 (a different outcome). The outcomes must differ in some significant way—for example, in terms of the magnitude, delay, or quality of the reward.[73]

An experiment by Peterson, Wheeler, and Armstrong (1978), for example, studied the **differential-outcome effect.** A center key was illuminated with either green or red light. If the pigeons pecked it, two side keys were illuminated. One had vertical lines, the other horizontal. If green had been presented first, then the vertical target key was appropriate; if the red had been presented, then the horizontal side key was correct.

Animals were run under two kinds of reward conditions. In the consistent condition, the green–vertical sequence was reinforced with 3 seconds of access to food and the red–horizontal sequence was rewarded with 0.2 milliliters of water. Thus, there was a differential or unique outcome for each S–R sequence. In the inconsistent condition, both food and water rewards were used for each type of trial. That is, no unique relationship between the stimulus–response sequence and the type of reward was employed. Discrimination was more accurate in the consistent condition. When only a single type of reinforcer was used for both reactions, or when two reinforcers were used but in an inconsistent fashion, performance was significantly lower.

Animals learn a conditional discrimination more easily even when the differential outcomes are two different sensory events rather than two different kinds of reward. For example, Fedorchak and Bolles (1986) trained rats to make R_1 in the presence of S_1, and R_2 in the presence S_2. The same water reward followed each response. In addition, one group was given a 0.5-second light flash following one of the correct responses.[74] A second group was given the same number of flashes, but they occurred on a random 50% of the trials. A third group of animals received no light stimulus.

The results are shown in Figure 13-20. Although all subjects learned the S_1–R_1 versus S_2–R_2 discrimination, the most proficient animals were in the differential-outcome group. Consistently receiving a light flash, along with the water reward, caused subjects to discriminate more effectively between S_1–R_1 and S_2–R_2.

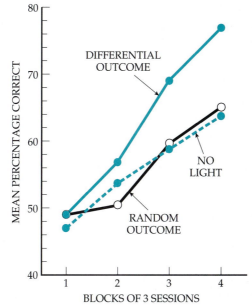

FIGURE 13-20. Mean percentage of correct responding, as a function of blocks of training sessions for groups for which their reward was accompanied by a differential outcome (light flash), a random outcome, or no light (after Fedorchak & Bolles, 1986).

Fedorchak and Bolles explained the facilitated discrimination learning in terms of reinforcer representation. Specifically, "rats learned to anticipate the light flash's presence or absence during the [appropriate discriminative stimulus] and that these specific expectations served to enhance the discriminability of the two stimulus–response chains."[75] In other words, differential outcomes make it easier of the subject to develop an expectancy for what follows the S–R sequence.[76]

INTERIM SUMMARY

Discrimination learning occurs more readily when the S+ and the S− stimuli are easily distinguished from each other. A difficult discrimination problem is learned more easily if the subject first masters an easy discrimination problem; this is called the "easy-to-hard effect." The attention theory argues that the subject's attention to the relevant dimension is strengthened during the easy problem, thus making it easier to solve the more difficult problem later on. The information value of a stimulus affects discrimination learning; a stimulus gains strength as a result of its relative validity. The sequences in a conditional discrimination—S_1–R_1 and S_2–R_2—are learned more readily if R_1 and R_2 lead to differential outcomes. The outcomes may be different types of reinforcers or the same reward, accompanied by different sensory events.

DISCRIMINATION PHENOMENA

Numerous phenomena have been discovered in the course of studying discrimination learning. These phenomena demonstrate many of the ways in which discrimination works and thus form the basis for the theories of discrimination. Several phenomena are discussed in the following sections: overlearning–reversal effects, learning sets, transfer, and feature learning.

Overlearning–Reversal Effect

Consider the following experiment by Mackintosh (1969).[77] Two groups of rats were reinforced for choosing between a black and a white goal box (half were rewarded for running to the black box, the other half to the white). Ten noncorrection trials were given per day until subjects were performing correctly on 9 out of 10 choices per session.[78] After all the animals learned the discrimination, rats in the overtraining group were given 100 additional training trials. Rats in the control group remained in their home cage during this period. Finally, all subjects were given reversal training. Here, they were rewarded for choosing the alternative goal box (if they had been rewarded for choosing black, they now were rewarded for choosing white; if they had learned to go to white, then black was now correct). Reversal training continued until all subjects had met the same criterion of discrimination—namely, 9 out of 10 correct choices on a given session.

The results are shown in Figure 13-21. According to Spence's theory of discrimination, subjects that were overtrained should reverse much more slowly than those that were not, because overtraining should have strengthened the original habit, making it more difficult to reverse the choice. Figure 13-21 shows that this did not happen. The group that received the extra training learned the reverse discrimination more readily than did the control group.[79]

The **overlearning–reversal effect** is a reliable phenomenon, although it is obtained only when a rather difficult discrimination problem is used and when a large reward is given for the correct response.[80] The effect is usually not observed for spatial-discrimination problems, such as turning left and right in a T-maze (which rats find easy to learn).[81] If the spatial problem is made more difficult, however, or if very extended training on the original discrimination is provided, then the overlearning–reversal effect is found.[82]

The most successful theory of the overlearning–reversal effect is the attention theory.[83] According to that theory, attention to the relevant dimension on which the discrimination is based strengthens an attention response, the analyzer. The theory further assumes that discrimination occurs without the subject's attending exclusively to the relevant stimulus dimension.

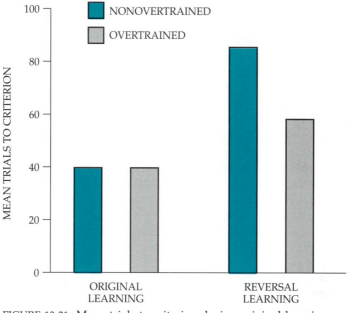

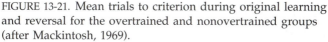

FIGURE 13-21. Mean trials to criterion during original learning
and reversal for the overtrained and nonovertrained groups
(after Mackintosh, 1969).

In other words, although the subject must pay attention to the relevant
dimension to some degree, analyzers for other dimensions still may be present when the original discrimination criterion is met. Overtraining continues
to strengthen the analyzer for the relevant dimension while reducing the
strength of attention analyzers for irrelevant dimensions. During reversal
learning then, animals that were trained only to the normal criterion are not
giving their maximum attention to the relevant dimension. The overtrained
subjects, on the other hand, maintain stronger attention to the relevant dimension during reversal learning. Other analyzers do not compete for their attention because they have been weakened during the overtraining trials.

The attention theory of the overlearning–reversal effect has been further
supported in several ways. For example, if an irrelevant stimulus dimension
is added for the first time during reversal learning, the behavior of the normally trained subjects is disrupted. This treatment does not affect speed of
reversal learning in the overtrained subjects, however.[84] According to the
attention theory, nonovertrained subjects do not attend exclusively to the
appropriate dimension at the end of the original learning, so the new dimension, by competing for attention, disrupts performance. Added extraneous
dimensions do not affect the overtrained animals because they solidified their
attention to the relevant dimension during overtraining.

The attention theory also accounts for the fact that a difficult problem
must be used in order to demonstrate the overlearning–reversal effect. Most
spatial discriminations, such as choosing the right and left turns in a T-maze,

are so easy for rats that attention to this dimension (the analyzer strength) is maximum within a few trials. As the discrimination problem becomes more difficult, however, more trials are needed to develop a strong analyzer, and thus overtraining has a greater impact on reversal behavior.

Although the attention theory provides a successful account for the overlearning–reversal effect, the theory has been challenged.[85] Several investigators suggest that animals are better at solving problems *in general* as a result of overtraining, not that their attention to a specific stimulus dimension has increased.[86] Purdy and Cross (1979), for example, taught rats to discriminate between horizontal and vertical striped targets. Experimental subjects received extra training trials using a single gray card. Attention to the horizontal–vertical dimension could not have increased during this period, and thus the overtraining should not have affected reversal. The overtraining experience, however, did produce the overlearning–reversal effect. Reversal of the horizontal–vertical line discrimination was facilitated by having experienced additional practice with a single, gray stimulus.

Learning Sets

Discrimination between novel objects is improved if prior discrimination training using other stimuli is given beforehand. Specifically, exposure to many different discrimination problems produces a dramatic improvement in the ability to learn new problems. This phenomenon is a **learning set.**[87]

The classic study on learning sets was done by Harlow (1949), using rhesus monkeys as subjects. The apparatus, shown in Figure 13-22, consisted of a tray with two food wells, over which various stimuli, such as blocks or other objects, could be placed. The monkey's task was to choose one of the stimuli. If the monkey chose correctly, it was allowed to eat the reward concealed beneath the object. If it chose incorrectly, however, the opaque screen was lowered, causing both objects to be withdrawn from the monkey's view. The objects were then rearranged and presented once again for another trial. From 6 to 50 trials were given for each pair of objects. Once the animal mastered the discrimination for one set of objects, a different set was used. This procedure continued until a total of 312 different discrimination problems had been presented.

The results are shown in Figure 13-23. The percentage correct is plotted for each of the first 6 trials. Learning on each of the first 100 problems was somewhat slow; performance on the second trial was only about 80% correct. However, as the animal experienced more and more problems, the rate of learning improved. For instance, for problems 257–312, animals were correct almost 97% of the time on the second trial. Such an improvement in the ability to learn discrimination problems occurs in many species, including other kinds of monkeys, as well as minks, cats, dolphins, rats, and birds. It also occurs when training involves avoidance of unpleasant stimuli, rather than the receipt of positive rewards.[88]

Harlow's work demonstrated an important principle in learning—namely, that the ability to solve problems, the ability to learn itself, may be influenced by previous learning experiences. Too often, psychologists study learning in

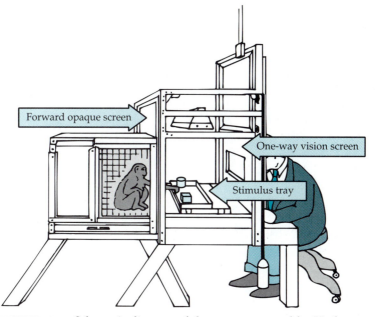

FIGURE 13-22. Schematic diagram of the apparatus used by Harlow (1949) to study learning sets in monkeys (after Harlow, 1949).

subjects that have had limited experience. The animals are born and raised in laboratories, without having much chance to learn anything. Animals in their natural environment are very different in this respect. They are constantly faced with discrimination problems in their struggle to survive, and thus, their ability to solve any one problem is likely to be quite different from the ability of subjects in the laboratory.[89] Certainly, the investigation of learning sets provides an added dimension to the study of learning that is particularly relevant to organisms in their natural environment.

Another issue raised by Harlow's research was the possibility that learning sets provide a measure of a species' general intelligence level. According to this notion, the ability to utilize previous experience to solve problems is related to the evolutionary complexity of the organism. Monkeys should show greater improvement from one problem to another than, say rats; humans should show even better learning–set performance than monkeys do.[90]

Although several investigators favored this idea, contemporary research has not provided much support for it. On the one hand, learning–set performance may differ in two closely related species of monkeys, merely because of differences in methodology.[91] On the other hand, some species show poor learning–set performance when using certain stimuli, but good performance when using others. Rats, for instance, are relatively poor in their learning–set formation when visual stimuli are used, although when odors are used (a stimulus dimension to which rats are extremely sensitive), learning–set performance is comparable to that reported for primates.[92] It is therefore erroneous to conclude that monkeys are more intelligent than rats because if the

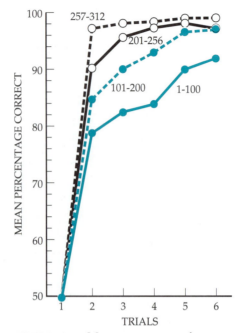

FIGURE 13-23. Mean percentage of correct
responses on trials 1–6 during discrimination problems 1–100, 101–200, 201–
256, and 257–312 (after Harlow, 1949).

appropriate stimulus dimension is used, to which rats are sensitive, then no
difference is found. In short, learning–set formation provides valuable information about the learning capacities of various species, but it does not provide a simple measure of general intelligence.

Harlow's (1959) theory of learning–set formation claimed that a subject
learns what not to do. A subject's tendency to make an incorrect choice gradually is inhibited during the extended training. Harlow's theory stemmed
from the observation that animals committed specific errors during training.
Some continued to choose the incorrect stimulus following nonreward because
of innate or acquired preferences. Others responded to the right or left side,
regardless of which object had been placed there.

A more developed theory of learning–set performance was proposed by
Levine (1975), who claimed that animals develop, and then test, hypotheses
about the discrimination problems.[93] Discrimination learning, according to
this approach, is not a slow, gradual increase in excitation for the correct
response and inhibition for the incorrect reaction, as claimed by Spence.
Rather, subjects have strategies for solving the problem; these are confirmed
or disconfirmed, depending on the outcome of the trial. For example, a
hypothesis might be "respond to the left." If such a strategy is successful, then
a subject continues performing in that fashion. However, discovering that such

a strategy does not consistently lead to reward, the subject, according to the theory, abandons this hypothesis and forms a different strategy altogether.

The strategy that animals follow most closely in learning–set formation is this: Win—stay with object; lose—shift to other object. If the subject is correct on the first trial, then it continues to choose that object. If, however, the first choice is incorrect, the animal immediately switches to the alternative object.

Research supports Levine's theory.[94] For instance, Behar and LeBedda (1974) examined the win–stay and lose–shift strategies separately.[95] Two groups of rhesus monkeys were given extensive pretraining with as many as 240 problems prior to being tested on a 400-problem learning–set task. During pretraining, the win–stay group was rewarded for continuing to choose the same object that it had on the first presentation. If it switched to the other object, then the problem was terminated. The lose–shift group was rewarded on the second trial (and every trial thereafter) for choosing the object other than the one it first chose; choosing the same object terminated the problem. During the final learning–set training, the second trial performance was recorded.

The results are shown in Figure 13-24. Both groups showed excellent transfer of their respective strategies. That is, the behavior of the win–stay group, after being correct on the first trial, was over 70% correct on the second trial. Similarly, the behavior of the lose–shift group, after being incorrect on the first trial, was nearly 75% correct on the second trial. Performance differed, however, in the other two conditions. The win–stay subjects eventually

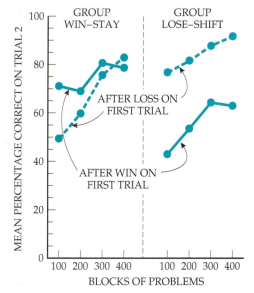

FIGURE 13-24. Mean percentage of correct responses on the second trial, as a function of the problem set for the win–stay and lose–shift groups (after Behar & LeBedda, 1974).

learned to shift to the alternative object after being wrong on the first trial. The lose–shift subjects, in contrast, did not learn to stay with the same object after winning on the first trial. Even after 300 problems, they were inappropriately switching to the alternative object about 65% of the time, after having been correct on the first trial. The lose–shift strategy persisted throughout the learning–set test. The authors therefore concluded that the win–stay and the lose–shift strategies are inseparable. Efficient learning–set performance requires a balance of the two.

Transfer Following Discrimination

Learning–set research shows that experience with discrimination problems transfers to new problems, making them easier to solve. Does the facilitation occur only when the old and new problems use the same stimulus dimension (**intradimensional shift**), or does facilitation also occur when the new discrimination problems involve a different stimulus dimension (**extradimensional shift**)?

In one study by Mackintosh (1964), rats were trained to respond to one of two targets for food. For one group of subjects, the targets were either black-and-gray squares or white-and-gray squares. For a second group, the choice was between a square and a diamond shape (each stimulus was painted black or white, but the shape, not the brightness, was the relevant dimension). In Phase 2, all subjects were trained to make a brightness discrimination. Here, the stimuli were squares, and they were painted either black or white. During Phase 2, therefore, the first group of subjects made an intradimensional shift, because the same stimulus dimension—namely, brightness—was relevant. The second group, in contrast, made an extradimensional shift discrimination in Phase 2, because the appropriate dimension changed from shape to brightness.

The results showed that the intradimensional subjects took 45.6 trials to master the new discrimination, but the extradimensional animals required about 61.2 trials. Learning a second discrimination, therefore, was easier when the initial problem involved the same stimulus dimension than when it involved a new dimension.[96]

The difference between intradimensional and extradimensional transfer is easily explained by the attention theory. This theory argues that the analyzer for the relevant stimulus dimension is strengthened in the first phase of the study. After the shift in Phase 2, the intradimensional subjects already possess a strong attention response to the appropriate dimension. The extradimensional subjects, in contrast, have to suppress their attention to the formerly relevant dimension and have to learn to attend to the new dimension.[97]

Feature Learning

Discrimination is strongly affected by the predictive value of the S_d. In a typical discrimination task, however, both the S+ and the S− cues are informative and unique. Which is more critical to learning the discrimination? Do subjects use the information contained in the S+ display to make the discrimination, or do they use the S− cue as a guide? This question was addressed by Hearst and Wolff (1989).[98] One group of pigeons was reinforced for pecking a green key when a small white square was superimposed on the green fields. If the key was solid green, pecking was not rewarded. Another group was rewarded for pecking at the plain green key. The S− contained the white square. Because the white square was equally predictive, the issue then was whether discrimination is better when the distinctive feature is added to the S+ display or is added to the S− key. The measure of discrimination was the ratio of key pecks during the S+ to key pecks during the S−. The data are shown in Figure 13-25. The addition of the distinctive feature to the S+ key led to better discrimination learning than did the placement of that feature on the S− display.[99]

A related phenomenon is the **feature-positive effect.**[100] This occurs when the single predictive feature that distinguishes the S+ from the S− is physically part of the S+ display. Sainsbury (1971) trained pigeons to peck two keys that were physically divided into four quadrants, each illuminated by a red or a green circle, projected from behind. The S+ and the S− displays looked exactly the same, except for one quadrant on one of them, which had the opposite color. This distinctive feature was located on the S+ key for some animals, but on the S− display for others. The basic question was whether

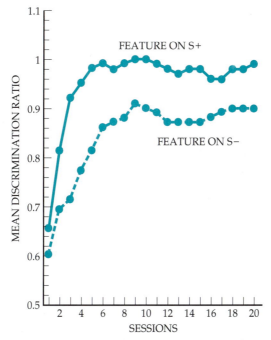

FIGURE 13-25. Mean discrimination ratios when the distinctive feature was on the S+ or S− (after Hearst & Wolff, 1989).

discrimination learning is better when the distinctive feature is located on the S+ or the S− target.[101] Sainsbury found that discrimination learning is better when the distinctive feature is located on the S+ key than when the distinctive circle is part of the S− display.[102]

The explanation for both these results uses two different concepts. First, responding is related to attention. To make the correct response, the animals must attend to the distinctive element. When the distinctive element is part of the S+ display, attending to that element is rewarded immediately; this further strengthens the subject's attention response. If the animals attend to the distinctive feature when it appears on the S− stimulus, however, reward never follows immediately, so attention to the element itself is not strengthened.

Second, performance may be related to sign tracking (see Chapter 3).[103] Sign tracking refers to the motor reactions directed toward (or away from) stimuli that are associated with reward (or nonreward). Recall that birds and other species position themselves close to, and even peck at, signals for food. Similarly, they move away from cues that are associated with nonreward. In terms of the feature-positive effect, animals literally peck at, or respond to, the distinctive element.[104] They come into physical contact with the very element that differentiates the S+ from the S−. When the feature is part of the S+ display, discrimination learning is facilitated because the reaction is rewarded immediately. Subjects are not rewarded, however, for coming into contact with the distinctive feature when it is located on the S− display.

INTERIM SUMMARY

If two groups of subjects are trained to make a discrimination to the same criterion of proficiency, and then one of them is given extra practice at performing that discrimination, then the reverse discrimination is more easily learned by the latter group than the former. This is called the "overlearning–reversal effect." Overlearning strengthens the analyzer for the relevant dimension, thus facilitating the reversal of the choice response. Exposure to many discrimination problems produces an improvement in the ability to learn. This is called a "learning set." Subjects accomplish this by adopting hypotheses or strategies, such as "pick the same object following an correct choice" or "but pick the other object following an incorrect choice." Transfer between discrimination problems may occur when the same stimulus dimension is altered (intradimensional shift) or when a new discrimination problem is used, which involves a different stimulus dimension (extradimensional shift). Normally, intradimensional shifts are more easily accomplished than extradimensional shifts because the analyzer for the relevant dimension is not altered. The feature-positive effect occurs when the single predictive element that distinguishes the S+ from the S− is physically part of the S+ display. Here, subjects learn more readily than when the distinctive feature is part of the S− display. The reason is that subjects attend to the distinctive element and are immediately rewarded for doing so.

ENDNOTES

1. Generalization allows animals to behave adaptively in their environment. It would be an ecological calamity if subjects were able to respond only to those stimuli explicitly learned about during training. In the natural environment, for example, individuals would be unable to identify sources of food when exploring new locations that were similar to the ones that previously contained food.
2. See Lacey, Smith and Green (1955).
3. The ability to react differently to stimuli is highly adaptive. Without it, organisms would be unable to solve problems, to differentiate among stimuli, or to make necessary response adjustments based on a changing environment.
4. See Kalish (1969). Historically, generalization has been considered to be a continuous process or function. That is, a continuous relationship exists between the stimuli and the response, such that the more similar the generalized stimulus is to the original S+, the stronger the reaction. A different view, called the "quantal interpretation," suggests that control by a given stimulus is on an all-or-none basis, and that fluctuations in response strength reflect momentary control by other stimuli that are inadvertently measured, along with the stimulus in question (see Bickel & Etzel, 1985, for a review).
5. Kalish and Haber (1963) directly compared the single- and multiple-stimulus methods and found that the gradients obtained with the two techniques differ substantially (but see Hiss & Thomas, 1963). In particular, the slope of the gradient is much steeper with the multiple-stimulus method (rate of responding to the S+ is higher, whereas responding to adjacent generalized stimuli is lower). The authors claimed that experiencing all the generalized stimuli help subjects to differentiate among them, thus generalizing less from the S+ to the various generalized stimuli.
6. See Blough (1969b, 1975).
7. Guttman and Kalish (1956) obtained reasonably symmetrical generalization gradients. The rate of decline for generalized stimuli that had a higher wavelength than the original S_d was about the same as the rate of decline for stimuli with lower wavelength. Such symmetry is rarely observed, however.
8. See Hearst, Besley, and Farthing (1970); Rilling (1977) for a discussion.
9. See also Hearst, Besley, and Farthing (1970); Hiss and Thomas (1963); Jenkins and Harrison (1962).
10. The gradient shown by this subject (#1363) was like all but one of the other five subjects.
11. An interesting study was done by Wilkie (1974), who trained pigeons to obtain food on an FI-3-minute schedule (one subject actually received an FI-6-minute schedule). The S+ was a vertical line, and the S− cues were lines that departed from vertical by either ±22.5° or ±45°. Recall that FI schedules typically produce a scallop effect—namely, a low rate of responding during the early portion of the interval, but a high rate toward the end (see Chapter 9). Here, the early portions of the FI interval exerted an inhibitory effect on the subject's responding (few responses per minute), whereas the later portions of the fixed interval exerted an excitatory effect (high rate of response). Such differential control by the temporal interval was expressed in Wilkie's experiment in the generalization gradients established during the first, second, and third portion of the fixed interval.
12. See Honig and Urcuioli (1981); Purtle (1973) for a review.

13. A negative peak shift has also been observed in several experiments. Here, the peak of the inhibitory gradient (that is, the point of minimum responding) shifts away from the S− in a direction opposite to that of the S+ (see Blough, 1973).

14. The same result has been shown for dimensions other than physical continua. For example, Honig and Stewart (1993) demonstrated that pigeons can discriminate a visual array that contains an equal number of red and blue elements from another that contains an equal unequal number. Then, during a generalization test, where the proportion of red and blue elements is varied, the subjects generalize on the basis of numerosity, and they demonstrate the peak-shift phenomenon.

15. See the later section on Spence's theory as it applies to discrimination; see also Marsh (1972).

16. Another theory is that the inhibitory gradient represents an emotional reaction. The S− becomes aversive during discrimination training because it is associated with no reward. During generalization testing, when the aversive S− is presented, the subject tries to avoid that cue as much as practical. This avoidance tendency results in overshooting the S+. Moreover, the closer the S− is to the S+, the greater the tendency to overshoot the S+. This emotional theory of the peak shift has been supported in a variety of ways. For instance, Lyons, Klipec, and Steinsultz (1973) gave a tranquilizing drug to their subjects during the generalization test. It was predicted that the tranquilizer (chlorpromazine) would reduce the emotional reaction to the S− and, therefore, would eliminate the peak shift. This prediction was confirmed.

17. Marsh (1972) showed that the generalization gradient following discrimination training may be derived from the excitatory and inhibitory gradients. However, the derived gradient, and its theoretical peak, depend on the shape of the excitatory and inhibitory gradients, which cannot always be assumed to resemble those shown in the figure (because many factors influence their shape). Another problem is that the peak of the gradient shifts only if the S+ and S− cues are given in some alternating fashion. Honig, Thomas, and Guttman (1959), for instance, found that the peak remained at the S+ when massed extinction to the S− was given for up to 40 minutes, but shifted appropriately when the S+ and S− were alternated (see also Ellis, 1970).

18. The spread of activation was compared to the ripples created when a stone is thrown into a still pond. The neurological energy, like the ripples, spread in radiating circles from the original point of activation. Although this theory is no longer taken seriously, some neurophysiological evidence provides support. For example, the noted neurophysiologists Hubel and Wiesel (1979) recorded electrical activity from single cells in the brain while simultaneously presenting targets to the cat's visual field. Certain cells fired only when the cat was presented with a 45° line. Furthermore, when lines slanted either 35° or 55° were given, generalized responding was observed. That is, the individual cells fired but at a slower rate than when the original 45° line was presented.

19. Hull's theory has received only limited support; see Hovland (1937).

20. This issue raises a more general point—namely, that failure to discriminate between two stimuli does not necessarily mean that subjects cannot, or have not, differentiated between them. Differentiation may take place without subjects performing in a manner that demonstrates such differentiation. Hearst (1987), for example, showed that pigeons that engage in a feature-negative discrimination task (see subsequent discussion in text) may show no signs of discrimination and

yet later give evidence of having engaged in learning about the feature-negative stimulus earlier on.

21. See also Jitsumori (1978). Some earlier studies directly supported the inverse hypothesis as well. For example, Kalish (1958) found that generalization in humans could be predicted on the basis of previous information dealing with discrimination of colors. Similarly, Kalish and Haber (1965) taught pigeons to peck an S+ of 550 nanometers and then gave a generalization test with stimuli ranging from 490 to 550 nanometers. Other subjects were given training with the same S+, as well as discrimination training using a 540-nanometer S− cue. The ratios of responses to the S− relative to the S+ for the discrimination subjects were nearly identical to the ratios of responding to the generalized stimuli relative to responding to the S+ for the generalization animals.

22. The study by Guttman and Kalish (1956), discussed previously, failed to support the inverse hypothesis. Marked differences between discriminability and the slope of the generalization gradients were obtained. According to earlier determinations made by Hamilton and Coleman (1933), stimuli with wavelength of approximately 530 nanometers are hard to discriminate from one another, whereas stimuli with wavelengths of about 580–600 nanometers are easily discriminated. The inverse hypothesis predicts that generalization gradients should be flat for the former kinds of stimuli (because they reside in the difficult-to-distinguish part of the spectrum), but steep for the latter kind of cues (because they are located in the area of the spectrum where the pigeon's acuity is good). Although Guttman and Kalish failed to show such a correspondence between discrimination abilities and the slope of the generalization gradients, they unknowingly used faulty information concerning the discriminative abilities of pigeons (see Honig & Urcuioli, 1981). When more contemporary (and accurate) data are consulted, then the correspondence is much greater (see Wright, 1972, 1974).

23. See Honig and Urcuioli (1981) for a discussion of attentional mechanisms.

24. Newman and Baron (1965); see also Blough (1969a).

25. See also Hall (1975); Rodgers and Thomas (1982).

26. The pigeons were trained until 90% of their responses were given to the S+.

27. This is an extradimensional paradigm because the vertical black lines and the colors are independent dimensions.

28. Honig (1974) also ran a group that was not given any discrimination training during Phase 2; they simply remained in the home cage during this time. Their generalization gradient was comparable to the gradient shown by the true discrimination subjects. The author concluded that pseudodiscrimination actually caused a loss of stimulus control by the vertical line, whereas true discrimination maintained the subjects' general attention.

29. See Mackintosh (1977) for an alternative theory.

30. See Rescorla (1976b) for the application of the Rescorla–Wagner model itself to the issue of generalization; see Rescorla and Wagner (1972) for a description of the Rescorla–Wagner model.

31. For example, Pearce (1987) argues that the Rescorla–Wagner and Blough models incorrectly predict that overshadowing between two stimuli will not occur on the first trial on which the compound is followed by a US.

32. However, the contents of the memory buffer also contain all of the stimuli currently in the environment, including elements from static cues such as those of the apparatus. Thus, even if an entirely new stimulus is given (for example, a tone

is substituted for a light), then the elements in the memory buffer do not change completely.

33. Pearce (1987) argues that the intensity of the stimulus determines the relative space that it occupies in the memory buffer, and thus that the $_AS_{A'}$ term is related to the perceived intensity of the two stimuli (see Pearce, 1987, p. 65 for details).

34. See also Thomas, Mood, Morrison, and Wiertelak (1991); Thomas, Strub, and Dickson (1974); Thomas and Thomas (1974). Relational responding in other contexts has been shown by Gonzalez, Gentry, and Bitterman (1954); Lawrence and DeRivera (1954).

35. Thomas and Jones (1962, p. 78).

36. Shifts in the peak of the generalization gradient occur when an excitatory and an inhibitory gradient summate. Here, only an excitatory gradient is present.

37. Thomas's (1993) model is based on work by Capehart, Tempone, and Hébert (1969) and draws heavily from the adaptation-level theory of Helson (1964).

38. This example, taken from Thomas (1993, p. 661), is essentially like the study by Thomas and Jones (1962) on the central-tendency effect. Thomas (1993) assumes "a one-to-one correspondence between physical stimuli and subjective experience, and . . . that the psychological averaging process is arithmetic" (p. 660). Thomas claims that these assumptions are unwarranted, but that they allow useful tests of the model to be made.

39. See Thomas (1993) for the application and limitations of the model.

40. The values were 1.28 and 3.04 footlamberts, respectively. Actually, the experiment used two groups. The one not discussed here received the stimulus 4 cue as S+ and the 2 stimulus as the S−. Both Thomas's model and Spence's theory predict that the peak of responding should shift away from the S+ value in a direction opposite to the S−. That is exactly what Thomas, Mood, Morrison, and Wiertelak (1991) found. Because this group does not distinguish between the two theoretical positions, discussion of it has been omitted for the sake of brevity.

41. See also Brown (1970); Friedman and Guttman (1965).

42. These results are also predicted by the Spence (1937) and Hull (1943) theories. According to those positions, continued training should increase the strength of responding to all stimuli in the conditioning zone. However, because the zone of values constantly oscillates, more dissimilar stimuli (those least central to the zone of stimulus values) will be strengthened proportionately less than more similar stimuli (those that are more central to the zone of values, the S+ being the most central of all).

43. Burr and Thomas (1972); Desiderato, Butler, and Meyer (1966); see Riccio, Ackil, and Burch-Vernon (1992); Riccio, Richardson, and Ebner (1984) for reviews.

44. This study was essentially a replication of an earlier experiment by Thomas and Lopez (1962).

45. See Riccio, Ackil, and Burch-Vernon (1992).

46. See Steinman (1967).

47. The study of Gisquet-Verrier and Alexinsky (1986) was a replication and extension of the original finding by Perkins and Weyant (1958); see also Riccio, Richardson, and Ebner (1984).

48. One alleyway was painted white, whereas the other was painted with vertical white and black stripes.

49. Gisquet-Verrier and Alexinsky (1986) performed a second experiment in which they provided a reminder cue (exposure to the start box and presentation of a

reinforcer) prior to the test. Here, the cuing treatment alleviated the performance deficit created by the training–test interval, but not by the change in context. Thus, the authors argued that these treatments operate by means of different mechanisms; but see Riccio, Ackil, and Burch-Vernon (1992); see also Chapter 14 for a more complete account of memory retrieval.

50. This is an extension of the peak shift described earlier.
51. See also Friedman and Guttman (1965); Jenkins and Harrison (1960, 1962); Thomas (1962).
52. The effect of discrimination training on generalization occurs not only when the discrimination training involves the same stimulus dimension (as in Hanson's study), but also when the discrimination stimuli and the generalization dimensions are entirely different. Mackintosh and Honig (1970), for example, showed that discrimination training using tilted lines as the stimuli later influenced the generalization gradient for wavelength. The gradient for wavelength was steeper for subjects that were given prior line-tilt discrimination training than for subjects that were not.
53. On some occasions, responding to the S− may result in punishment or a lower magnitude of reward than is given following a response to the S+.
54. See Bitterman, Tyler, and Elam (1955).
55. Krechevsky (1938) formulated an earlier attention theory; see also Riley (1968) for a discussion of the earlier literature.
56. See Spiker (1970). Wolford and Bower (1969) also provided evidence for Spence's position; but see Turner and Mackintosh, (1970).
57. The criterion of learning was making at least 15 correct responses in a run of 16 trials.
58. See also Waller (1971).
59. See Blough (1969a) for an alternative approach.
60. For an elaboration of this study, see Lamb (1988); see also Leith and Maki (1975, 1977).
61. Various kinds of compound samples were actually used. Superimposed compounds had the two elements overlapping, far compounds had the elements separated spatially, and unified compounds consisted of line elements that were colored either red or orange. For the sake of brevity and clarity, only two sample conditions (element sample and compound sample in which the two elements are adjacent) are discussed.
62. See Thomas, Durran, and Russell, (1988) for an example.
63. Lawrence (1952).
64. Kraemer (1984), moreover, has shown that pigeons learn to discriminate a target containing two dots from one containing three less well than they discriminate two dots from five.
65. The same result was found with wavelength. Both groups were given an S+ of 538 nanometers. The subjects for which the S− was 555 nanometers took longer to master the discrimination than did those for which the S− was 606 nanometers.
66. See also Haberlandt (1971).
67. See also Mackintosh and Little (1970).
68. Marsh (1969), however, did not support this hypothesis. Facilitation of discrimination occurred only when the stimuli on both the easy and the difficult problems were from the same category. For a different theory of the easy-to-find effect, see Turney (1976).

69. Although the actual design of this experiment was more complicated, only two groups are discussed here.
70. Tone 1 was 1,000 Hz; tone 2 was 2,500 Hz. The tone that served in the S+ condition was counterbalanced across subjects.
71. The criterion was responding on at least 90% of the S+ trials, but 50% or less on the S− trials.
72. See also Williams (1984).
73. Carlson and Wielkiewicz (1976); Carlson and Wielkiewicz (1972); Brodigan and Peterson (1976), respectively; but see Reed (1993).
74. For half of the subjects in this group, the light flashed following the S_1-R_1 sequence; for the other half, it followed the S_2-R_2 sequence. The authors found no preference for either sequence by either group.
75. Fedorchak and Bolles (1986, p. 127).
76. The authors dismissed the idea that the light flash had become a secondary reinforcer and thus enhanced the effectiveness of the water reward. The differential-outcome subjects showed no preference for the stimulus−response sequence that led to the outcome. That is, S_1-R_1 and S_2-R_2 sequences were performed with equal facilitation, regardless of which sequence led to the light flash; see also Trapold (1970).
77. See also Denny (1970), Sperling (1965a, 1965b), for early reviews of this phenomenon.
78. A noncorrection procedure is where an animal is not allowed to retrace its steps following an incorrect response, but rather is removed from the goal box after a fixed period of time, here 10 seconds.
79. A related effect, called the "overtraining−extinction effect," occurs when extinction takes place more readily following many discrimination-learning trials than after few trials; see Traupmann (1972). Although it was believed that this effect is not found when measuring free operant behaviors, such as lever pressing in rats, Senkowski (1978) has shown that it does occur, at least under certain conditions.
80. Hooper (1967); Mackintosh (1969); Theios and Blosser (1965).
81. Mackintosh (1965a, b, 1969).
82. Richman and Coussens (1970); Richman, Knoblock, and Coussens (1972).
83. Lovejoy (1966); Mackintosh (1969).
84. Mackintosh (1963).
85. See Nakagawa (1992) for additional findings that are inconsistent with the attention theory.
86. See Hall (1973a, 1973b, 1974); Waller (1973b).
87. See Medin (1972); Reese (1964) for early reviews of this problem.
88. Stoffer and Zimmerman (1973).
89. See Kamil, Lougee, and Shulman (1973).
90. Warren (1965).
91. Devine (1970).
92. Slotnick and Katz (1974). However, Fagan and Olton (1987) and Zeldin and Olton (1986) have shown that spatial learning sets may be acquired by rats.
93. See also Levine (1959).
94. Schrier (1974); Schusterman (1964); but see Medin (1972).
95. See also Ricciardi and Treichler (1970).
96. Similar results have been observed for pigeons (Mackintosh and Little, 1969), rats (Shepp and Eimas, 1964), and nonhuman primates (Roberts, Robbins, and Everitt, 1988; Shepp and Schrier, 1969).

97. A direct test of the attention theory was performed by Whitney and White (1993).
98. See also Hearst (1971).
99. Hearst and Wolff (1989) point out that this phenomenon, possible an example of stimulus salience, may not occur with very intense or very weak stimuli.
100. See Jenkins and Sainsbury (1970).
101. The feature-positive effect is the same issue as discussed in Chapter 5 in connection with occasion setting. Recall that when a cue signals the occurrence of a Pavlovian CS–US pairing, it becomes an occasion setter. Furthermore, the occasion setter has certain properties that differ from those of a conventional Pavlovian excitatory CS. In this section, the emphasis is not on the properties of the occasion setter itself (see Ross & Holland, 1981), the temporal relations between the occasion setter and the CS (see Holland, 1986a, Nakajima 1993), or how the power of the occasion setter may or may not transfer to new stimuli (see Holland, 1986b, 1989a, 1989b; Holland & Coldwell, 1993; Lamarre & Holland, 1987). Rather, the concern here is for the properties that affect the ease of learning the instrumental discrimination.
102. The superiority of feature-positive discrimination, versus feature-negative discrimination, has also been demonstrated using escape and avoidance procedures; see McCoy and Yanko (1983).
103. See Hearst (1978); Hearst and Jenkins (1974).
104. Crowell and Bernhardt (1979); Looney and Griffin (1978)

CHAPTER 14

Memory

To study learning is to study memory. Learning would be impossible without memory because each execution of a learned reaction requires memory of the previous trial. Studies that focus directly on memory, however, typically assess the permanence of a learned reaction, rather than its formation.

GENERAL NATURE OF MEMORY

Before discussing the research and theory relevant to animal memory, the stages and general theoretical approaches to memory are described.[1]

Stages of Memory

An item in an individual's memory is said to go through at least three stages, shown in Figure 14-1.[2] First, the learning stage is where information becomes encoded. Here, the memory is formed. Second, the retention or storage phase is where the information or knowledge persists over time. In some cases, the storage phase may be quite short. Short-term memories, for example, last only about 15 to 20 seconds. In other cases, storage may last throughout an individual's entire life. These are called "long-term memories."[3] Third, the retrieval or performance stage is where the individual recalls the information and performs the response, thus giving evidence of having learned earlier. If performance is good, relative to the levels shown in acquisition, then forgetting is minimal. However, if performance has declined significantly, then forgetting has occurred.

General Theories of Forgetting

A major challenge for psychology is to understand why memories persist once they are encoded, or, alternatively, why forgetting takes place following learning. There are several general theoretical approaches.

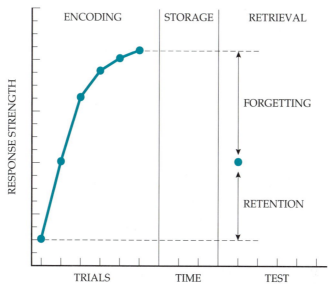

FIGURE 14-1. Hypothetical data showing the three memory stages—namely, learning (encoding), retention (storage), and recall or performance (retrieval). Forgetting and retention levels are shown on the right panel.

Storage Theories.

Storage theories of forgetting focus generally on what happens to information during the storage phase. The decay theory, for example, claims that forgetting occurs because memories grow weaker, or decay in strength, during the retention interval, much as footprints on a sandy beach slowly fade over time. Although some evidence supports this point of view (see the following discussion), few contemporary theorists describe forgetting in terms of memory decay.

The interference theory claims that forgetting occurs because competing memories develop during the retention interval.[4] For example, acquisition of new memories may cause an individual to forget an older memory (this is **retroactive interference**). Similarly, the presence of existing memories may interfere with the expression of a newly formed memory (this is **proactive interference**).

Retrieval Theories.

Retrieval theories of memory generally claim that forgetting results from a failure to retrieve information during the performance stage. That is, a memory survives the retention interval, but the subject simply cannot gain access to the memory. A good analogy would be looking for a library book that has been misplaced on the shelves. The book is in the library (the memory is intact), but it cannot be found (the subject fails to retrieve the memory). Much of the contemporary research on memory supports this viewpoint.

INTERIM SUMMARY

Individual memories are said to go through at least three stages. The encoding stage is where the information is first learned; the retention or storage phase is where the information persists over time; the retrieval or performance phase is where the individual recalls the information and performs the response. Storage theories of memory claim that memories grow weak during the storage phase, or that they are interfered with by more recently acquired memories (retroactive interference) or by memories formed prior to the learning phase (proactive interference). Retrieval theories argue that forgetting occurs because subjects cannot gain access to memories during the retrieval phase.

SHORT-TERM MEMORY: DELAYED MATCHING-TO-SAMPLE

The most common procedure for investigating **short-term memory** in nonhuman animals is a technique termed **delayed matching-to-sample.**[5]

Basic Processes in Delayed Matching-to-Sample

The basic procedure in a delayed matching-to-sample experiment involves the same stages noted previously—namely, encoding, retention interval, and retrieval.

Types of Delayed Matching-to-Sample Tasks.

An animal, usually a monkey or a pigeon, is placed in a box containing three response keys capable of projecting different colors or geometric shapes.[6] When the trial begins, the center key is illuminated, showing the sample stimulus, such as a red color.[7] Subjects demonstrate that they recognize the sample by responding appropriately. A delay period (retention interval) is then given, after which both side keys are illuminated. One side key contains the same stimulus that was just presented on the center key (the red sample), whereas the other presents a different stimulus, say, a green color.[8] The animal's task is to demonstrate its memory for the sample by choosing the correct comparison stimulus, the red key. If the animal matches the sample, then it receives reinforcement; if the animal is incorrect, it receives no reward.[9] Performance invariably declines as a function of the delay interval. The longer the animals have to remember the characteristics of the sample, the less accurate they are on the matching task.[10]

In the typical delayed matching-to-sample experiment, colored patches or geometric figures are used as the sample and the comparison stimuli. A more complex task involves so-called conditional matching. Here, matching is based on an arbitrary association between the sample and the comparison, rather than on a physical similarity. For instance, a subject might be given a red key as the sample and be required to match it by choosing a triangle (rather than a circle). Similarly, the animal might receive a vertical line as the sample and be required to choose a dot pattern (rather than a green-colored patch).

A study by Bowers and Richards (1990) demonstrated two kinds of conditional delayed matching, one based on the visual appearance of the stimuli, the other on the stimulus duration. Pigeons were given red or green key lights that lasted either 5 or 30 seconds.[11] Following a retention interval of 0.5, 1, 2, 4, or 8 seconds, two comparison stimuli were presented; a yellow and blue key light. The pigeons for which the color of the sample was the relevant dimension were required to perform a conditional matching response based on the color. For instance, if the sample was green, the correct comparison was yellow; if the sample was red, the correct choice was blue. Subjects for which the temporal duration of the sample was the relevant dimension had to peck yellow if the sample lasted 30 seconds (regardless of color), but blue if the sample lasted 5 seconds.[12]

Figure 14-2 shows the average performance. Performance declined as a function of the retention interval for both the visual and the temporal groups. This is the typical finding in delayed matching-to-sample studies. The visual delayed matching-to-sample performance, however, was more accurate than the temporal matching, suggesting that birds process visual information more easily than temporal information.[13]

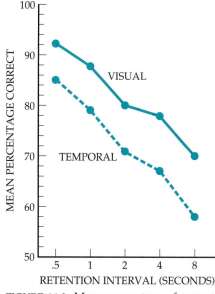

FIGURE 14-2. Mean percentage of correct responses for the visual and temporal groups, as a function of the retention interval (after Bowers & Richards, 1990).

Evidence for Rehearsal.

Rehearsal is an important part of the short-term memory process. This was shown in an interesting study by Grant (1981).[14] In Phase 1, a group of pigeons was trained on a delayed matching-to-sample task.[15] Here, the purpose was simply to train subjects to peck a key that matched the sample, but not a key that did not. Thus, on some trials, the comparison color matched the sample color (red or green key light), and subjects had to peck the correct comparison key to earn reward. On other trials, the comparison and sample colors differed (matching was impossible), so the comparison key simply remained lit for 5 seconds, after which a new trial began.

In Phase 2, a sample was always followed by a 1-second memory cue (either a horizontal or a vertical black line projected onto a white key). Trials on which the vertical line was given were called "remember trials"; trials on which the horizontal line was presented were called "forget trials." On the remember trials, subjects were tested for their matching performance, just as in Phase 1. In other words, the vertical line indicated that subjects would be given a comparison stimulus that either did or did not match the sample. On forget trials, however, subjects were not tested for matching; rather, the horizontal line indicated that they would receive an entirely irrelevant stimulus (a black dot) and that key pecks would be ineffective.

In summary, subjects were given a sample and then a second (memory) stimulus that informed them whether they would be given an opportunity to match the sample. On remember trials (vertical line), they were given the relevant comparison stimuli, and matching was possible. On forget trials (horizontal line), they received an irrelevant stimulus that did not match the sample.[16]

Subjects were tested in Phase 3. This phase was conducted exactly like Phase 2, except for two differences. First, the delay interval between the sample and the comparison varied across trials. Second, some of the forget trials were probe trials. Here, the forget cue was delivered, but the comparison cues were presented rather than the irrelevant dot stimulus. In other words, subjects were given the correct comparison stimuli (to determine whether they remembered the sample color), even though the memory cue had instructed them that this particular trial would not involve a memory test. The issue, therefore, was whether the subjects, having been instructed to forget the sample, would, nevertheless, remember it when asked to do so.

The results are shown in Figure 14-3. The measure of discrimination was the number of matching responses executed when the correct comparison was presented, divided by the total number of responses executed on matching and nonmatching trials. Good matching, therefore, is indicated by values greater than .5. Performance was extremely efficient for the trials on which subjects were instructed to remember the sample. Discrimination ratios ranged between .8 and .9. However, performance was significantly reduced on the probe trials, suggesting that subjects had ceased to rehearse the sample following the onset of the forget cue.[17]

The study therefore suggests that pigeons actively process or rehearse the sample characteristics during the retention interval unless instructed not to do

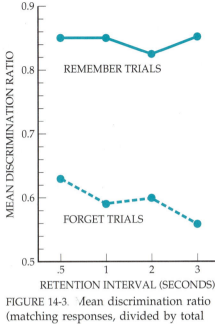

FIGURE 14-3. Mean discrimination ratio (matching responses, divided by total responses), as a function of retention interval on the remember and forget trials (after Grant, 1981).

so by a forget cue. Subsequent studies indicate that the forget cue actually reduces rehearsal or processing, as opposed to the remember cue increasing the level of processing, relative to what occurs when no memory cue at all is given. Thus, subjects are automatically inclined to rehearse and process a sample stimulus unless they are informed that their memory will not be assessed, in which case rehearsal ceases.[18]

Trace Theory of Delayed Matching-to-Sample

One of the most thoroughly evaluated theories of delayed matching-to-sample performance is the **modified trace theory,** proposed by Roberts and Grant (1976).

Theory Postulates and Evidence.

According to this theory, presentation of the sample creates a neural trace that fades over time. The trace is analogous to the aftereffect experienced when viewing the sudden discharge of a flashbulb. Initially, the image is vivid, but with the passage of time, it gradually fades. The theory further stipulates that subjects perform the delayed matching-to-sample task by literally matching the remnants of the fading neural trace with the sensory characteristics of the comparison stimuli. If the trace has faded to a considerable degree, a match becomes difficult, and delayed matching-to-sample performance declines. If, however, the trace is still sufficiently vivid when the comparison is presented, then good matching is possible. The theory also claims that subjects are relatively passive in this process. The sensory characteristics of the sample and comparison stimuli activate neurological centers, but no active rehearsal is involved.

The trace theory makes a third assumption—namely, that the strength of the original memory trace increases as a function of the exposure to the sample. The longer the exposure to the sample, the stronger is the trace.[19] This assumption was needed to explain the fact that delayed matching-to-sample performance is positively related to the duration of the sample.[20] In a study by Roberts and Grant (1974), for example, pigeons were given a red or a green sample lasting 0.5, 1, 2, 4, or 8 seconds. After a delay of 1 second, the subjects chose between the sample and an alternative comparison stimulus.[21] As shown in Figure 14-4, mean percentage correct on the delayed matching-to-sample task increased as a function of the sample duration. Whereas a sample that lasted only 0.5 seconds produced about 57% correct choices, performance was more than 80% correct with a sample lasting 8 seconds.

Criticisms of Theory.

The trace theory accounts for the effect of sample duration on matching accuracy, but it has several serious limitations.[22] Four kinds of evidence are presented. They all show that subjects are not passive agents in the memory

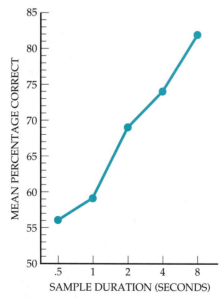

FIGURE 14-4. Mean percentage of correct responses on the delayed matching-to-sample task, as a function of the duration of the sample stimulus (in seconds) (after Roberts & Grant, 1974).

process. Rather, subjects actively rehearse information during the retention interval. First, as discussed previously, if subjects are instructed by a forget cue not to rehearse, then accuracy of matching declines. This result suggests that rehearsal is critical to short-term memory.

Second, if the sample contains both a geometric form and a color, but the subject is required to match only on the basis of the geometric form, then performance is worse than when the sample contains only one dimension. In the former condition, the animal must share its attention between two dimensions. Because attention cannot be shared easily, performance suffers.[23] Again, this suggests that subjects actively rehearse information during the retention interval.

Third, delayed matching-to-sample performance suffers if a disruption in rehearsal occurs during the retention interval (this is called "retroactive interference").[24] Disruption may be produced from the illumination of a diffuse house light, or illumination of a more localized light, such as a key light or a ring of light surrounding the sample.[25] The more intense the intruding illumination, the greater the disruption.[26] The onset of the house light is more disruptive than its offset.[27] Illumination during the delay interval disrupts delayed matching-to-sample performance because it provides the subject with the opportunity to rehearse other stimuli—namely, the intrusive light itself.[28] Such a finding cannot be explained by the trace theory.

Finally, an important phenomenon, called "proactive interference," contradicts the trace theory. Proactive interference occurs when a stimulus that is given prior to the sample interferes with the subject's processing or rehearsal of the sample, causing a reduction in delayed matching-to-sample accuracy later on. A good example was a study by Grant (1982a).[29] Control pigeons were given a color sample for 4 seconds; a retention interval of 0, 1, 3, or 6 seconds; and then a choice between two comparison colors. Experimental birds were given the same task, except that the sample stimulus was preceded by a 4-second interfering stimulus (which was the color to be used as the incorrect comparison). For example, if the sample was green, and the comparison stimuli were green and red, the interfering stimulus was red.[30] Such an interfering stimulus caused a reduction in matching accuracy.

As shown in Figure 14-5, performance was worse in the experimental subjects that received the incorrect comparison color just prior to the sample than in the control animals. Thus, stimuli that occur before the sample cause proactive interference with the rehearsal of the sample.[31] Subjects are information processors engaged in rehearsal, not passive agents in a trace-decay process.[32]

Temporal-Discrimination Hypothesis

A second theory of delayed matching-to-sample performance is the **temporal-discrimination hypothesis**.[33] According to this hypothesis, declining performance as a function of the retention interval reflects a kind of confusion. Animals are exposed to a limited number of sample stimuli on these tests, so their challenge is not remembering the characteristics of the sample, but rather recalling, on any given trial, which sample was presented. The animals do not

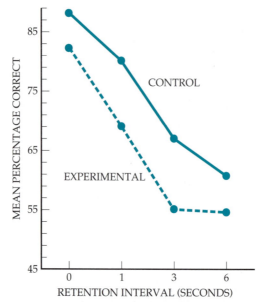

FIGURE 14-5. Mean percentage of correct matching, as a function of the retention interval for the control (no prior interfering cue) and experimental (interfering cue given prior to the sample) pigeons (after Grant, 1982a).

forget the color; they are simply confused about which color was most recently used.

This theory accounts for some important facts. First, animals show relatively better delayed matching-to-sample performance with extended training. One monkey tolerated only 9 seconds delay between the sample and the choice when first trained, but after several years of training, and many thousands of trials, matched correctly after a delay of 9 minutes. The trace theory cannot explain this result because it argues that the intensity of the stimulus trace is based on the intensity and duration of the sample and thus should not change as a function of training.

A second finding that supports the temporal-discrimination hypothesis is that the use of many samples, rather than just a few, improves delayed matching-to-sample performance.[34] With a greater variety of stimuli, animals find it less difficult to remember which one was presented most recently. Confusion occurs more readily when only a few stimuli are used.

Information-Coding Theories

The more successful theories of delayed matching-to-sample focus on retrospective and prospective rehearsal processes. The following sections elaborate on the nature of these information-processing strategies.[35]

Retrospective Coding.

During delayed matching-to-sample, subjects reflect back on, or rehearse, the characteristics of the sample and code them into memory. The more extensive the retrospective coding, the better the memory, and thus the better the matching performance when given the comparison stimuli.[36]

Evidence for **retrospective coding** was provided by Urcuioli and Zentall (1986).[37] Pigeons were given a delayed matching-to-sample task in which highly discriminable stimuli (colors) and less discriminable stimuli (vertical and horizontal black lines) were used. Following the presentation of the sample, two comparison side keys were lit. As usual, pecking the comparison that matched the sample produced reinforcement, whereas pecking the comparison key that did not yielded an equivalent time-out period. The comparison stimuli were always the horizontal and the vertical lines, but the sample stimulus was a hue (red or green) for some subjects, but a line (vertical or horizontal) for others. Thus, the former received a color sample followed by two line comparisons; the latter subjects got a line sample followed by the two line comparisons.

The results are shown in Figure 14-6. At very short retention intervals, both groups showed excellent matching. As the retention interval increased,

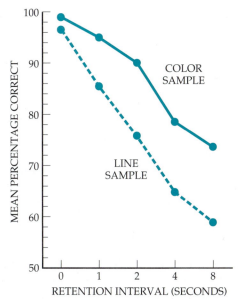

FIGURE 14-6. Mean percentage of correct responses, as a function of retention interval (seconds), for groups that received the color or the line samples (note that all subjects were given vertical and horizontal lines as comparison stimuli) (after Urcuioli & Zentall, 1986).

however, the group that received a color sample showed superior short-term memory. Given that the comparison stimuli were the same for both groups, the difference in delayed matching-to-sample performance must have been due to differences in the way subjects encoded or rehearsed the sample. It is well-known that birds find colors more discriminable than lines.[38] Thus, the study shows that subjects retrospectively rehearsed the samples, and that the color samples were more strongly encoded into memory than the line samples.

Prospective Encoding.

Prospective encoding involves the rehearsal of the to-be-presented comparison stimuli rather than retroactive reflection on the sample. Subjects think ahead to the to-be-presented comparison stimuli and develop a set of instructions about their future responding. For example, if the sample is a green color, then the animal might encode an implicit instruction such as "respond to the green comparison."

Three kinds of evidence for prospective encoding have been offered.[39] First, subjects perform conditional or symbolic discriminations following the retention interval. Recall that a conditional delayed matching-to-sample task involves matching S_1 with C_1, and S_2 with C_2, where the sample and the comparison stimuli are physically dissimilar. To accomplish this task, subjects need to encode the comparison stimuli prospectively, rather than to rehearse the characteristics of the sample.[40]

Second, a subject's memory is affected by the amount of information it must process. This was shown by Zentall, Jagielo, Jackson-Smith, and Urcuioli (1987). The logic of the study was as follows. If a subject codes retrospectively—that is, if it reflects backward in time during the retention interval—then increasing the number of sample stimuli should strain its information-processing capacities. Increasing the number of comparison stimuli, however, should not. On the other hand, if a subject codes prospectively—that is, it develops a set of instructions concerning the to-be-presented comparison stimuli—then increasing the number of comparison stimuli should strain its capacity to rehearse. Varying the number of sample stimuli should not. In this study, the authors varied both the number of samples and the number of comparison stimuli to assess the retrospective and prospective effects.

Vertical and horizontal lines, as well as circle and triangle shapes, were used as stimuli. Subjects in the 2–2 group were given two sample and the same two comparison stimuli. Pigeons in the 2–4 group had two possible samples, but four comparison stimuli. For example, a subject might receive either vertical or horizontal lines as a sample, and then either vertical and horizontal lines, or a circle or triangle shape, as comparison stimuli. Birds in the 4–2 group had four possible sample stimuli, but only one pair of comparison stimuli. Finally, birds in the 4–4 group received four sample and four comparison stimuli.[41] During the 25 test sessions, the retention interval was 0, 1, 2, or 4 seconds.[42]

The results are shown in Figure 14-7. Not surprisingly, delayed matching-to-sample performance declined overall as a function of the retention interval. The more interesting outcome was that the 4–2 and the 2–2 groups performed

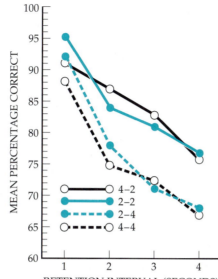

FIGURE 14-7. Mean percentage of correct responses, as a function of retention interval (seconds) for the four groups that differed in terms of the number of sample stimuli (first number) and the number of comparison stimuli (second number) (after Zentall, Jagielo, Jackson-Smith, & Urcuioli, 1987).

significantly better at all retention intervals than did groups 2–4 and 4–4. Thus, the number of sample stimuli was irrelevant to the accuracy of delayed matching-to-sample performance. Only the number of comparison stimuli affected the outcome. This result suggests that prospective encoding occurred because a subject's memory-processing capacity was taxed more when it was confronted with 4 comparison stimuli than when confronted with 4 sample stimuli. Subjects are, in a sense, thinking ahead, encoding the comparison stimuli during the retention interval.

A third result that confirms prospective encoding is the finding that subjects that are given a differential outcome show superior short-term memory (see Chapter 13). An experiment by DeLong and Wasserman (1981) demonstrated this effect.[43] Pigeons were rewarded for matching sample S_1 with comparison C_1, but, on alternative trials, they were to match S_2 with C_2.[44] Groups differed on the basis of whether they received the same outcome for each successful match or a different outcome. For the differential outcome group, S_1–C_1 matches resulted in reward only 20% of the time, whereas correct S_2–C_2 matches always were followed by reward. Those that got the nondifferential outcome earned reinforcement on 60% of the trials for a correct match to either

S_1 or S_2. Thus, the two groups had identical training except for a difference in the probability of reward following a correct match. In one case, the probability of reward was the same, regardless of which sample had been given; in the other group, the probability of receiving a reward differed for the two samples.

The results for the last 30 days of training are shown in Figure 14-8. Matching accuracy was measured in terms of the responses on matching trials, divided by total responding. The differential treatment produced good delayed matching-to-sample performance across the entire range of retention intervals. The nondifferential treatment did not.[45] These differences in performance cannot be attributed to differences in the amount or strength of retroactive rehearsal of the samples because the samples were identical for both groups. Rather, the differential outcome must have facilitated the proactive encoding of the comparison stimuli.

Joint Processing.

The retrospective-encoding hypothesis claims that subjects rehearse the sample during the retention interval. The prospective-encoding hypothesis suggests that animals rehearse what to do next. Several experiments showed that both kinds of processing take place in the same situation, although whether the two processes occur simultaneously or sequentially has not been resolved.

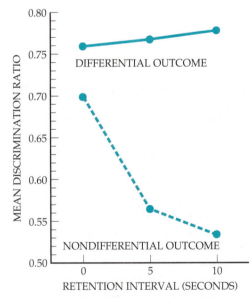

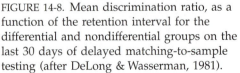

FIGURE 14-8. Mean discrimination ratio, as a function of the retention interval for the differential and nondifferential groups on the last 30 days of delayed matching-to-sample testing (after DeLong & Wasserman, 1981).

In a study by Cook, Brown, and Riley (1985), for example, spatial short-term memory was studied. Here, a maze containing 12 alleyways was used, each arm or alleyway radiating from a central starting point. The rat's task was to secure the food at the end of each arm. Visiting goal boxes that had been visited previously was an error because such visits reduce the overall rate of food intake. Typically, rats make few errors in this situation (see the following section on spatial memory), indicating that they remember which arms they visited previously. How they accomplish this feat was the issue addressed here. There are two strategies. Rats may avoid returning to previously visited arms by retroactively rehearsing those alleyways already visited. Alternatively, they may focus on encoding the yet-to-be visited alleyways, making sure they do not duplicate ones already visited. They also may follow both strategies, either simultaneously or successively.

In this experiment, rats were placed in the maze and allowed to visit 2, 4, 6, 8, or 10 baited goal boxes before being removed. On some trials, the animals were immediately placed back into the maze and allowed to continue their search for food. On other trials, they were given a 15-minute delay before being returned to the maze. The rationale was that if subjects are interrupted late in the sequence—that is, after completing many trials—their retrospective-encoding task becomes more difficult and complex; thinking back over many arms visited is more difficult, from an information-processing point of view, than retroactively rehearsing only a few arms. However, if they are interrupted early in the sequence, the prospective encoding is more complex and difficult; planning ahead is more difficult when many arms have yet to be visited than when only a few unvisited arms remain. Errors in performance (revisiting an alleyway) on the delay trials were expressed relative to performance on the no-delay trials. The higher the number, the more revisits occurred, relative to performance on the no-delay condition.

The data are shown in Figure 14-9. The disruptive effect of delay was greatest when the subjects were interrupted after completing 6 visits (out of 12 total arms). The ability to avoid previously chosen alleyways on the post-delay test improved when subjects were interrupted after making only 2 or 4 choices, or after making 8 or 10 choices. In other words, the delay was most disruptive when it was given in the middle of the choice sequence.

According to the authors, the increasing portion of the curve (from 2 to 6), indicates the use of retrospective encoding; the declining portion of the curve (from 6 to 10) shows the subjects' use of prospective encoding. The authors assume that a correspondence exists between the number of arms and the amount of information that must be retained in memory, and that the disruptive effect on memory is greater when more information is being retained than when less information is being processed. Thus, as subjects visit more and more alleyways in the initial part of the session, and if they are retrospectively encoding the arms that they have already visited, then the amount of information contained in their retrospective-encoding process increases with more arms visited. Delay would have an increasingly disruptive effect on the retroactively encoded memories. In contrast, if subjects are

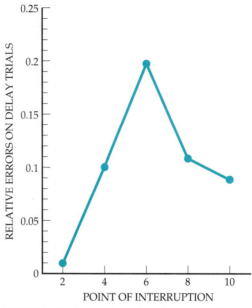

FIGURE 14-9. Mean deviation from control, as a function of the trial after which the interruptive delay condition was imposed (after Cook, Brown, & Riley, 1985).

proactively encoding the to-be-visited arms of the maze, then the amount of information they must retain in memory over the delay interval declines as they visit more and more arms. Disruption late in training, therefore, is less severe than disruption earlier in training. This is precisely what the results show. Further, delay is most disruptive when it is given in the middle of the 12-response sequence. Retrospective *and* prospective rehearsal take place simultaneously.

INTERIM SUMMARY

The most common procedure for studying short-term memory in non-human animals is the delayed matching-to-sample task, where the sample is presented, and, after a retention interval, two comparison stimuli are given. Subjects demonstrate their memory by choosing the correct comparison. Similar results have been found for spatial memories, and for conditional matching, where performance is based on arbitrary association between the sample and the comparison rather than a physical similarity. Rehearsal occurs during short-term memory. However, if subjects are given a stimulus that informs them that their memory will not be tested later on, then rehearsal ceases. The trace theory of delayed matching-to-sample performance stipulates that subjects match the remnants of a fading neural trace with the sensory characteristics of the comparison stimuli, and that the strength of the neural trace increases as a function of the duration of the sample. The theory has been criticized on four accounts, all of which suggest that subjects actively rehearse information during the retention interval, rather than remaining passive agents. The temporal-discrimination hypothesis claims that performance on a delayed matching-to-sample task is a function of confusion. Animals do not forget the sample; they are simply confused about which one was most recently used. Information-coding theories focus on retrospective and prospective rehearsal processes. Retrospective encoding occurs when subjects reflect back on the sample and rehearse its characteristics. Prospective encoding occurs when subjects think ahead and encode implicit instructions concerning the comparison stimuli. Both kinds of encoding occur simultaneously.

FORGETTING AND LONG-TERM MEMORY

Comparatively little is known about the **long-term memory** of nonhuman animals. There are reports of pigeons remembering discrimination stimuli years after training, and anecdotes concerning the keen memory of elephants are legendary.[46] What little is known about animal memory is interesting because it provides a means of comparison to data derived from studies of human memory. Moreover, long-term memory capacity in nonhuman species is interesting because animals, unlike humans, cannot code visual images using verbal labels (a strategy that aids considerably in recognition memory in human subjects).[47]

Long-Term Memory Duration and Capacity

Most literature on human memory considers memory to be long term when the information is retained for as long as 24 hours, although there is nothing special about that particular time period.[48] A second characteristic of human long-term memory is that it appears to be unlimited in its capacity; the amount of information it may contain is unlimited. Only a few studies have systematically studied long-term memory capacity in nonhuman animals, however. Vaughan and Greene (1984) trained pigeons to peck at photographic images projected onto a small screen inside the cage. If the image had been presented previously, then pecking was reinforced. Pecking so-called negative cases was not reinforced; the slide was simply presented for 15 seconds.[49] In one experiment, 160 slides containing randomly drawn squiggles were given. In a second study, 320 slides of various outdoor scenes were used (houses, trees, cars, and flowers). Overall, accuracy approached a high level in both studies. The pigeons remembered not only that they had seen the slides, but also that each slide was a positive (rewarded) or negative (no reward) instance.[50] More significantly, memory was good even after a retention interval of 751 days.[51] The capacity of long-term memory was not exceeded by any means. The birds recognized stimuli from hundreds of example over more than a 2-year period of time.

Although these findings suggest that a pigeon's memory for visual stimuli may last several years, other research has shown forgetting within a much shorter period of time. For example, Schreurs (1993) studied the long-term retention of a Pavlovian conditioned eyelid response. Adult rabbits were given 80 presentations of a 100-Hz tone CS, followed by a brief shock to the eyelid. Memory was tested 1, 3, or 6 months later.[52]

Performance is shown in Figure 14-10. During acquisition, all of the subjects performed at a high level of proficiency. During the memory test, however, memory for the CS was present in the 1- and 3-month groups but was nearly absent in the 6-month subjects. These results challenge the notion that forgetting is exclusively the result of interference during the retention interval. Here, subjects remained in their home cages and received no further treatment, suggesting that the memory traces had decayed in some fashion.

The duration and capacity of long-term memory is very difficult to specify. First, subjects remember not only the current significance of a stimulus,

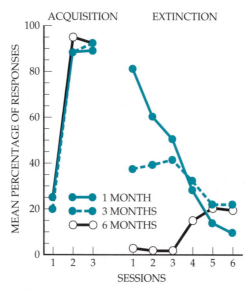

FIGURE 14-10. Mean percentage of conditioned responses during acquisition and extinction (memory) sessions for the eyelid CR in rabbits, by groups that were tested after a 1-, 3-, or 6-month retention interval (after Schreurs, 1993).

but also past associations.[53] Second, and more important, different measures of memory do not always agree, even though all of them presumably reflect the endurance of a single item of information contained in the long-term memory store. If a memory for a certain stimulus exists, then evidence of retention should be revealed, whatever measure is used. For example, the memory of an aversive CS may last for a month when measured by means of a conditioned suppression or enhanced startle response.[54] Comparable fear stimuli, however, are not remembered well when measured in terms of avoidance relearning.[55] Thus, one cannot be sure whether a forgetting function reflects the impermanence of the memory or simply differences in performance at the time of testing.

Conditions Affecting Long-Term Memory

A detailed account of all the factors that affect long-term memory is beyond the scope of this book.[56] Research on animal memory, however, has revealed several important factors that are worth reviewing briefly.

Retroactive Interference.

Retroactive interference plays an important role in long-term memory, just as it does in short-term memory processes. If a subject experiences a traumatic event after learning a response, then the event may retroactively disrupt memory for the learned reaction.

The most commonly used agent, or traumatic event, is electroconvulsive shock.[57] **Electroconvulsive shock** is used by clinicians to treat sever depression in humans. It is administered to humans and laboratory subjects by means of electrodes attached to the cranium. When given electroconvulsive shock, the subject typically loses consciousness and experiences a seizure. The seizure lasts only a few minutes, however, and the subject appears to have fully recovered within 24 hours. No one knows precisely how electroconvulsive works, but its apparent therapeutic effects are somehow caused by the massive firing of brain neurons.[58]

Electroconvulsive shock disrupts memory; it interferes with memory retroactively. One study showing this was done by Quartermain, Paolino, and Miller (1965).[59] Experimental rats entered one side of a two-compartment box and were given a 2-second electric shock to the foot. Then, after a delay of 0.1, 1, 2, 5, 7.5, 15, 30, or 60 seconds, the rats were given an electroconvulsive shock, as described previously. Two control groups were used. One was given only the foot shock; the other received neither the foot shock nor the electroconvulsive shock. Retention for the fear of the shock compartment was tested 24 hours later, using a passive-avoidance measure. Here, subjects were allowed access to the shock compartment. If they declined to enter the larger compartment within 180 seconds, then they were said to have retained the fear reaction to the foot shock. Subjects that walked back into the former shock compartment, on the other hand, showed forgetting.

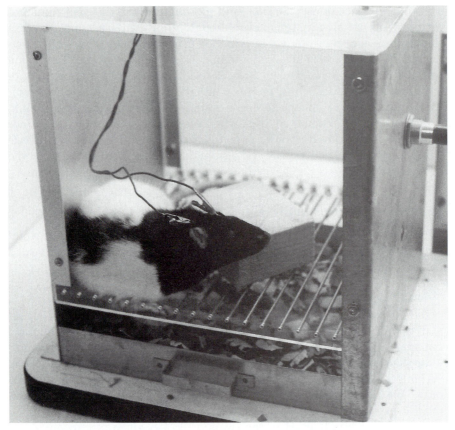

Picture of a rat positioned to receive an electroconvulsive shock via the wire electrodes attached to the ears.

The percentage of subjects in each experimental group that stepped back into the shock compartment is shown is Figure 14-11. Control subjects that had experienced neither the foot shock nor the electroconvulsive shock showed no fear of the compartment; 100% of them stepped back into the former shock area within the 180-second test period. Not surprisingly, all of the control rats that had been given foot shock but no electroconvulsive shock showed strong passive avoidance; none ventured back into the shock area. The experimental animals that were given foot shock and electroconvulsive shock showed both patterns of behavior, depending on the delay interval between the two events. Substantial forgetting was observed when the electroconvulsive shock was given soon after the foot shock. Even when the delay was as long as 15 seconds, more than 40% of the subjects entered the shock area. With a longer delay between the foot shock and the electroconvulsive shock, however, better memory of the foot shock was observed; fewer animals were willing to return to the shock compartment. In short, the longer the time between foot shock and electroconvulsive shock, the better was the memory.

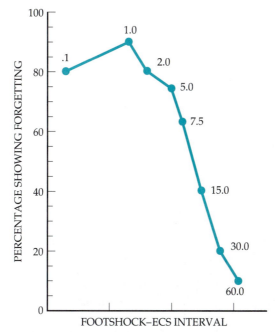

FIGURE 14-11. Percentage of subjects in each group, which showed forgetting by stepping into the former shock area, as a function (log scale) of the foot-shock–electroconvulsive shock (ECS) interval (in seconds) (after Quartermain, Paolino, & Miller, 1965).

One explanation for the effect of electroconvulsive shock on memory, proposed in an important paper by McGaugh (1966), is the **consolidation theory of memory.** According to this position, memories must undergo a period of consolidation if they are to endure. Memories become fixed during this consolidation time; the neural trace established during learning becomes permanent. Thus, memories are like impressions in wet concrete. After the impression is first made (the learning phase), a certain period of time must elapse before the impression is permanent. If something interrupts the consolidation process—much as if water is splashed on the impression in concrete—then the impression fades and recovery is impossible. According to consolidation theorists, electroconvulsive shock affects memory much like the splash of water affects the impression in concrete. It scrambles the brain neurons in such a way that the neural trace established during learning fails to become consolidated or fixed. The more time one allows for the consolidation process, however, the stronger the memory. That is, the longer the learning–electroconvulsive-shock interval, the greater the consolidation and, therefore, the stronger the memory.

Many theorists now believe that the consolidation theory is inaccurate. Forgetting does not reflect the prevention of memory formation, but rather the inability to retrieve the memory at the time of the test.[60] The evidence to support such a retrieval theory is discussed in a later section of this chapter (see the section on "Retrieval Theory").

Proactive Interference.

The more important source of interference with long-term retention comes from events or conditions that occur prior to original learning. As mentioned previously, this is called "proactive interference."[61] Formally speaking, proactive interference occurs when performing task "B" prior to task "A" interferes with the memory for task "A."

A good example was a study by Kraemer (1984).[62] Six groups of pigeons were trained to discriminate between two target stimuli.[63] One was a pattern of three green dots, the other a pattern of two green dots (one stimulus served as S+, the other as the S−). Once the pigeons reached the learning criterion, (at least 9 out of 10 pecks to the S+ display), subjects were given a memory test after a retention interval of 1, 10, or 20 days. Three other groups were taught the reverse discrimination from what they had learned originally. For example, if the three-dot pattern had been the original S+, now the two-dot display was the S+ and the three-dot pattern became the S−.

After mastering the reversal problem to the same level of proficiency, these animals were given a 1-, 10-, or 20-day retention interval, and a retention test. Here, the subjects were required to perform the most recently learned discrimination. The issue was whether the original learning would interfere with the retention of the reversal problem for those subject that had experienced reversal, relative to those that had not. Groups were matched on level of proficiency and length of the retention interval.

The data are shown in Figure 14-12. The measure of retention was the number of responses made to the S− display. The more the animal responded to the S−, the less accurately it remembered the most recently acquired discrimination. As Figure 14-12 indicates, all subjects showed significant forgetting as a function of time. The longer the retention interval, the less accurate was the performance. Performance, however, was significantly inferior for the groups that had to recall the reversed discrimination. Thus, although the reversal animals had learned this most recent discrimination to the same level of accuracy as the nonreversal subjects, and had the same retention interval, their memory was inferior. The logical explanation is that the original discrimination had proactively interfered with their memory for the more recently acquired reverse discrimination.

Age.

One factor or condition that affects long-term retention is the subject's age at which the memory is formed. Conventional wisdom suggests that traumas experienced at an early age have a disproportionate effect on adult behavior. They are unusually potent and long-lasting. Research, however, has failed to confirm this notion.[64] Memories learned early in life are, in fact, forgotten

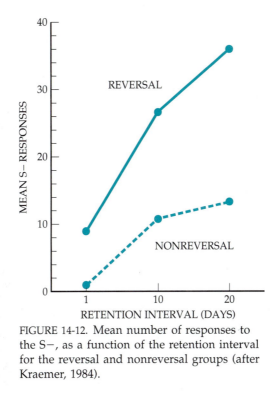

FIGURE 14-12. Mean number of responses to the S−, as a function of the retention interval for the reversal and nonreversal groups (after Kraemer, 1984).

more easily than memories formed during adulthood.[65] This is the **age-retention effect.**

In an experiment by Coulter, Collier, and Campbell (1976), rats were placed in a box and were given four tone–shock pairings.[66] Control subjects received the same treatment, except that the tone and the shock were presented randomly. Training took place at various ages. Some animals were trained when they were 11 to 13 days of age, others experienced training at 14 to 16, 17 to 19, or 20 to 22 days of age.[67] The animals were then returned to their home cage and allowed to mature for about a month. At this point, they were taught to press a lever to get food. Forty-two days after the original training, the rats were given a fear test. Fear was measured in terms of the suppression of lever pressing (see Chapter 3 for a discussion of the CER ratio). The greater the fear, the greater was the disruption of lever pressing.

The subjects that received unpaired tones and shocks during original training showed no fear of the CS on the test trials; their CER ratios remained near the .5 level. The data for the conditioned rats are shown in Figure 14-13. Various degrees of fear of the CS were shown, and the amount of fear changed as a function of the age at training. Animals that experienced fear training at a very early age (11 to 16 days) showed little suppression; that is, they forgot completely. Fear retention was evident, however, in the older groups. The best

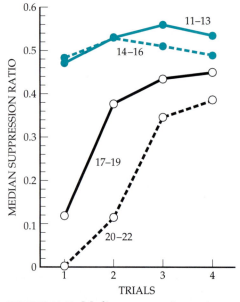

FIGURE 14-13. Median suppression ratio on the four extinction test trials for groups trained at 11–13, 14–16, 17–19, and 20–22 days of age (after Coulter, Collier, & Campbell, 1976).

retention was shown by the oldest subjects (20 to 22 days at original training). Here, suppression was nearly complete on the first test trial and never recovered, even after four extinction trials.[68] In summary, memory performance increases with age. Although young animals are capable of learning various responses, they have trouble remembering them.[69]

Memory Organization.

One of the most important factors contributing to the permanence of long-term memory is its organization and cohesiveness. The amount of information that may be retained increases when subjects organize the information into hierarchical chunks or memory units. Often, this is based on the perceptual characteristics of the information. For example, the letters, "m," "e," "m," "o," "r," and "y," are discrete units of information, but, when perceptually clustered together, they form a coherent and organized chunk—namely, the word "memory." It is easier to encode the word memory into long-term memory than it is to retain the letters as separate, individual items of information.[70]

Analogous findings have been shown for nonhuman animals. Units of memory may be larger and more complex than lever presses, right–left turns, and key colors. Individuals chunk information together, thus forming organized and holistic memory units. Chunking of information increases memory capacity and allow an animal to predict reward more effectively. That is, by chunking information together, an animal is better able to understand the regularities in its environment and thus more likely to earn a reward.[71]

Much of the work on memory chunking has been done by Capaldi and associates.[72] Capaldi identifies three kinds of memory chunks: trial chunks, series chunks, and list chunks. **Trial chunks** refer to the aggregate of individual responses that are organized in a meaningful way. For example, if a subject is required to press a lever five times to produce a reward (an FR-5 schedule of reinforcement) then the five responses taken as a single, holistic unit is a trial chunk.

The second kind of memory chunk is a **series chunk.** Here, the subject chunks together a number of individual actions. For instance, Capaldi and Verry (1981) trained a group of rats to run down a straight alleyway to receive a food reward. On some occasions, the animals were given an RNNNN series of trials (where R is a rewarded trial and N is a nonreward trial). On others, the subjects experienced the sequence NNNNR. Both series were given repeatedly, in an irregular order.

It is well-known that if a subject anticipates receiving reward, it will run faster than it it anticipates receiving nonreward. The results on the last three blocks of trials on sessions 10 to 12 are shown in Figure 14-14. The rats ran very quickly on the first trial, regardless of the sequence. The reason is that they had no way of knowing whether that particular sequence of trials was the RNNNN of the NNNNR series. If the first trial was an R trial, then speed dropped considerably and stayed low on the remaining trials of the sequence.[73] However, if the subjects were given no reward on the first trial (the NNNNR sequence), speed dropped on the second trial but increased

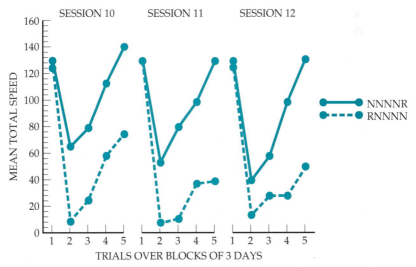

FIGURE 14-14. Mean total speed (centimeters per second) for each of the five trials on the last three blocks of three training days for the NNNNR (solid line) and the RNNNN (dotted line) conditions (after Capaldi & Verry, 1981).

dramatically over the next few trials until a maximum speed was reached on the last sequence. In other words, by the fifth trial of the sequence subjects were remembering not merely what had happened on the previous trial, but also what had happened four trials earlier. The results of this experiment therefore demonstrate that subjects have memories that extend back several trials. Capaldi calls this a series chunk of information. Animals process the events and outcomes not simply one trial at a time, but rather as a series of trials.[74]

Finally, the third kind of information chunk is a **list chunk.** This is a hierarchy of several series chunks. When a subject anticipates which of two series of trials will occur, then it has combined the series into a list chunk. For example, Capaldi, Miller, Alptekin, and Barry (1990) gave rats pairs of R and N sequences.[75] In one case, the series involved an RN series followed by another RN sequence. On other occasions, the series included an RRN followed by another RRN pattern. In all cases, the larger patterns of trials were separated by 15 minutes, but the individual trials were separated by only 15 seconds. The authors were interested in whether subjects could anticipate reward or nonreward on the second trial of the second pattern in each pair. The first trial gave no information as to whether the second trial would be rewarded. Only by remembering which entire pattern had occurred 15 minutes earlier could a subject know whether the second trial in the pattern involved reward or nonreward.

The results on the 13th block of repetitions are shown in Figure 14-15. Subjects ran much more slowly on the second trial of the second RN series than they did on the second trial of the second RRN series. The explanation is that the subjects were able to anticipate that the current second trial was N, having received an RN pattern 15 minutes earlier. However, when subjects were performing the RRN pattern for the second time, they anticipated being reinforced on the second trial of the series because they remembered having received an RRN pattern 15 minutes earlier. Anticipation of events in the future was based not simply on the previous trial, or even a successive number of trials, but on the entire series of trials experienced earlier.

Retrieval Theory

The notion that forgetting is due to retrieval failure has been supported extensively in recent years.[76] According to the **retrieval theory of memory,** a response is elicited by a network or complex of stimuli. Any manipulation that changes the network alters the degree to which the network elicits the memory.

The theory makes three specific predictions. First, when new stimuli, resulting from either internal or external sources, are added to the stimulus complex, then the complex differs from the one that existed during original learning, and forgetting occurs, because the altered stimulus context no longer elicits the response in question. Failure on the part of the stimulus complex to elicit a response is precisely what is meant by retrieval forgetting. Second,

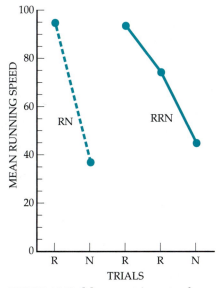

FIGURE 14-15. Mean running speed (centimeters per second) on the last two blocks of six repetitions of each series for the RN (solid line) and RRN (dotted line) series (after Capaldi, Miller, Alptekin, & Barry, 1990).

if salient stimuli that were part of the original complex are suddenly omitted, then the complex is similarly disrupted, and the extent to which it is able to elicit the learned reaction declines. Third, if stimuli that were part of the stimulus complex during acquisition are reinstated at the time of recall, then retrieval failure is alleviated.[77]

These predictions, and the kinds of stimulus alterations that affect memory retrieval, were discussed by Spear (1973). "This view of memory retrieval . . . simply restates the ancient principle that learning is evidenced [that is, remembered] to the extent that the circumstances of testing are similar to those of training . . . . Forgetting . . . is viewed as a consequence of a variety of events that accompany increasing retention intervals. These events modify stimuli that define the context of testing compared to that of training and may include . . . (a) the relatively rapid dissipation of the sensory consequences of training . . . (b) changes in the external environment that may be rhythmic [for example, the seasons] . . . or irregular [such as the weather] . . . (c) changes in the internal environment that may be progressive [aging] . . . or cyclical [such as hormonal variations] . . . (d) the acquisition of different memories having some attributes in common with the memory to be retrieved . . . and (e) changes . . . in the idiosyncratic response patterns . . . that immediately precede testing."[78]

Retroactive Interference Explained.

Much of the contemporary research on memory has focused on these predictions. Studies on retroactive interference, stemming from maturation or electroconvulsive shock, support the retrieval theory. For instance, Gordon and Mowrer (1980) trained rats to avoid shock by running from a white to a black compartment during a 5-second flashing light.[79] After making three consecutive avoidance responses, the experimental subjects were given electroconvulsive shock; control subjects were not. Approximately 72 hours later, half of the experimental and half of the control animals were given a reminder treatment, consisting of a single extinction trial. Here, they were placed in the white chamber for 60 seconds with the flashing light on, but the door to the black side was closed. The other subjects were not given this reminder.

The retention test consisted of five trials similar to acquisition. Results showed that subjects that were given electroconvulsive shock but no reminder trial responded slowly on the first test trial. That is, they showed forgetting of the original active-avoidance response. Experimental subjects that were given the reminder trial, however, responded quickly on the test, indicating that their forgetting had been alleviated. This study therefore confirms that electroconvulsive shock interferes with long-term memory, but that the forgetting may be alleviated by giving subjects a reminder treatment.

The **reminder treatment** does not have to be identical to the treatment given during acquisition. For instance, Springer and Miller (1972) trained rats to swim to a platform in an ice-cold water bath.[80] Once the rats had climbed onto the platform, they were given electroconvulsive shock. As predicted, these subjects showed no memory for the location of the platform. Subjects that were given a mild shock in a different apparatus before being tested, however, recalled their previous water-immersion experience and swam to the platform with no difficulty. Memory retrieval was facilitated by a reminder trial, even though the reminder experience was altogether different from the original learning conditions. Apparently, the fact that both experiences were highly aversive was sufficient to jar the animals' memory.

The theory for the age-retention effect focuses on retrieval factors and is therefore similar to the one that explains forgetting after electroconvulsive-shock treatment.[81] Although young animals learn at a normal rate, the changes that are experienced during maturation cause a dramatic and substantial change in the network of stimuli that control behavior. When the animals are tested as adults, forgetting is observed because the stimuli that were present during infancy have changed. Because the stimuli are so radically different, the memory cannot be retrieved effectively.[82]

Many studies of infantile amnesia support the retrieval theory quite directly. For example, Parsons and Spear (1972) used environmental enrichment as a source of interference. They trained young and old rats to make an active avoidance response. During the retention interval, experimental subjects were placed in a special cage containing various items, such as a platform with a ladder, a running wheel, other rats, and a food dish. Control animals were retained in their home cage. After 60 days, all animals were tested for retention of the avoidance reaction. The young animals did, indeed, forget their avoidance, and more important, the enriched living conditions enhanced the forgetting.

Memories formed during infancy are not always forgotten. According to the concept of reinstatement, first developed by Campbell and Jaynes (1966), if the organism is periodically reminded of the original learning during the retention interval, then there is little forgetting.[83] The reinstatement procedure involves placing the animal back into the apparatus and occasionally giving it a reminder trial. The reminder treatment itself is not sufficient to teach the animal the original response. Control subjects that receive only the reminder trials do not develop a memory for the originally learned behavior. The periodic rehearsal, however, does reduce the amnesia normally observed after a maturational time period has elapsed.[84]

Warm-up Decrement.

If an animal is tested each day at approximately the same time, it typically performs poorly at the beginning of each session, but shows improvement thereafter. This **warm-up decrement** phenomenon supports the retrieval theory of memory. In a demonstration of this effect by Spear, Gordon, and Martin (1937), rats were trained to avoid shock. The average number of seconds required to relearn this response 24 hours later was 554.1. However, if the animals were placed in a different apparatus and were given a brief shock just prior to the test, then they required only 413.8 seconds to relearn the response.[85] Even after a single day, animals took appreciable time before they were able to perform efficiently; they required a warm-up period before performing efficiently. If they were reminded of their previous training, however, then the initial decrement was eliminated.[86]

Reactivation and Retrieval.

Many studies show that reactivation treatments restore otherwise forgotten memories. One interesting study was done by Deweer and Sara (1984). Hungry rats were tested in a relatively complex maze consisting of six choice points. Subjects were given five training trials in which the rewarded sequence was either LRRLLR or RLLRRL (L for left, and R for right). Twenty-five days later, they were tested for their memory of the right–left sequence. Control subjects were placed directly into the start box and allowed to run the maze. The reminded groups, however, were placed in a wire-mesh cage next to the start box and given a 90-second exposure to the room cues. One of the reminded groups was tested immediately, another after 1 hour, and a third 24 hours later.

The errors in performance are shown in Figure 14-16. The control subjects showed considerable forgetting of the correct sequence of turns. Groups given a reminder treatment, however, demonstrated significantly fewer errors. The best performance was shown by the group given the reminder treatment and tested immediately. Thus, reminding subjects of the original environmental context during acquisition alleviated forgetting. The reminder effects are

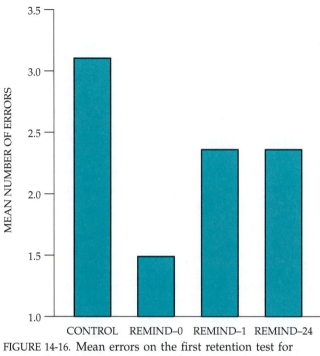

FIGURE 14-16. Mean errors on the first retention test for groups that were given no reminder treatment (controls) or were given reminder treatments 0, 1, or 24 hours prior to the test (after Deweer & Sara, 1984).

relatively short-lived, however, because animals tested 1 or 24 hours later showed some forgetting.

Memory that is reinstated through a reminder treatment may actually be stronger than original memory. This curious result was shown by Spear, Hamberg, and Bryan (1980). Rats were given 25 fear-conditioning trials consisting of a flashing light CS, followed by a 2-second foot shock. Four groups of animals were tested. One group was tested immediately (actually, 3 minutes later), and the others were tested 1, 3, or 7 days later. Four other groups were placed in their home cage for 27 days, given a reminder treatment (consisting of 25 nonshock trials in the original acquisition apparatus), and then tested 3 minutes later or 1, 3, or 7 days after the reminder treatment. The essential difference between these sets of groups, therefore, was that memory was tested following original learning in some, but after a reminder trial in others.

The results of these groups are shown in Figure 14-17. Considerable forgetting was evident even within 24 hours in the groups that received no reminder treatment. However, animals given the reminder treatment and then tested 3 minutes, 1 day, 3 days, or 7 days later showed good retention. Speed of response remained high for 3 days, dropping somewhat after 7 days. The study, therefore, shows not only that a reminder treatment reinstates memory,

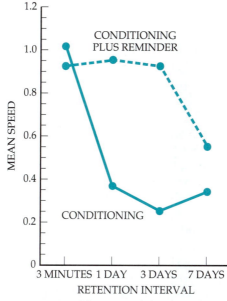

FIGURE 14-17. Mean speed (reciprocal latency) on the fifth block of five test trials, as a function of the retention interval for groups that were tested following acquisition, and groups that received a reminder treatment 27 days following acquisition (after Spear, Hamberg, & Bryan, 1980).

but also that performance of the memory following the reminder treatment remains strong for several days, even though performance of the same memory in subjects not given the reminder declines over the same period of time.

Why does a reactivation treatment given well after original learning do more than alleviate forgetting? Why is memory actually better after a reminder treatment than it is after original learning itself? Although researchers are not entirely certain, the reactivation effect appears to enhance original learning; it adds to the strength of the memory acquired during acquisition.[87] Subjects process the original memory during the reminder treatment, thus strengthening it further.

Finally, the effectiveness of a reminder treatment depends on when it is presented. In an interesting study by Hars and Hennevin (1990), rats were trained to run down a complicated maze involving six choice points.[88] All subjects had been implanted with small wire electrodes. Some electrodes were located in the neck muscles, others in the cortical area of the brain. The cortical electrodes were used for recording electrical brain activity during sleep and wakefulness, whereas the intramuscular electrodes were used for delivering a small electrical impulse to the neck muscles.

Subjects explored the maze until they reached the goal box where reward was located. If, however, the animals in the stimulated group entered a blind alleyway, they were given a small electric current delivered to the neck muscles. Subjects in the nonstimulated group were not given such a treatment.

Following acquisition, subjects were placed in their home cages for a 25-day retention interval and then were given either a reminder treatment or no reminder treatment prior to the memory test. The reminder treatment consisted of stimulating the neck muscles. In summary, stimulated groups received electrical stimulation to the neck for entering a blind alleyway (other animals did not receive this treatment). Furthermore, some of the stimulated, and some nonstimulated, subjects were given a reminder treatment prior to the memory test; the others were not. Finally, one additional manipulation was used. Some reminder subjects were given their treatment while they were awake, whereas others were given the reminder while they slept.[89]

The reminder improved memory of the right–left sequence, but only if it had been administered while the animals were awake. When the reminder treatment was given during sleep, forgetting occurred. Thus, the study implies that memories may be recovered through reminder treatments, but that the animal's state of vigilance is an important factor. Reactivation of memory alleviates forgetting, but only if the animal is able to attent to and rehearse the memory. When such an ability is not possible—for example, when subjects are sleeping—then the reactivation treatment has little effect on memory.[90]

Role of Context.

The evidence just reviewed here supports the retrieval theory of memory by showing that memories that apparently have been forgotten may be reactivated if subjects are given the appropriate reminder treatments prior to the test. Critical to the retrieval theory is the notion of the environmental context. The context is which an animal is trained and tested plays a major role in both learning and memory processes.[91] Indeed, context is a unifying concept, linking the processes of conditioning and remembering.[92] As such, context helps to explain a variety of phenomena covered in the chapters on Pavlovian and instrumental conditioning.[93] As Spear (1978) stated, "a memory will be manifested to the extent that the circumstances at testing match those at training. Hence, manipulations of contextual stimuli are expected to alter manifestation of prior learning . . . through mechanisms responsible for memory retrieval."[94]

Bouton (1993) offered three general principles of long-term memory concerning how context affects memory retrieval. The first and most important is that context stimuli guide memory retrieval. According to this theory, a subject stores the memory of the CS, the US, and the context at the time of training. Memory is retrieved when the representations of both the CS and the context are activated. If either one is missing or deficient, then retrieval failure occurs.

A study illustrating this principle was done by Peck and Bouton (1990).[95] In Phase 1, rats were given tone–shock pairings in one of three contexts: A, B, or C. Each context was a distinctive environment, differing in terms of size, construction of the grid floor (for example, size, spacing, and orientation of the grid bars), presence of odor cues, and wall construction (plastic vs. aluminum). In Phase 2, all subjects were given tone–food pairings in context A. Thus, the appetitive and aversive conditioning contexts were the same for some of the animals, but different for others. Normally, when a CS is conditioned using shock, and then the same CS is later paired with food, the appetitive conditioning is retarded. Here, a change of context in Phase 2 reduced this retardation effect. For example, as shown in Figure 14-18, subjects in the B and C groups performed the appetitively motivated CR (head jerk) without appreciable interference. Subjects in group A, however, showed significant retardation of learning when given appetitive training in context A after having previously received fear training in the same apparatus. The experiment, therefore, demonstrates that retrieval of the appropriate response is based on the similarity of the context in which that response was trained and the context in which it was retrieved.[96]

A related point was made by Hall and Honey (1990). Rats were given fear conditioning in two contexts: A and B. The environments differed in several respects, including a difference in odor and in visual appearance (plain aluminum versus black-and-white checked walls). One CS was the offset of a light

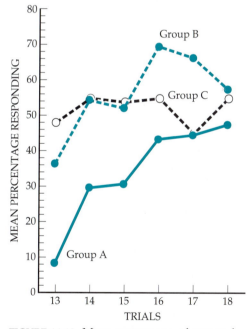

FIGURE 14-18. Mean percentage of responding on the appetitive head-jerk task in context A, on trials 13–18 for groups that had previously received aversive conditioning in contexts A, B, or C (after Peck & Bouton, 1990).

for 30 seconds; the other CS was the presentation of a series of clicks. Subjects got one CS followed by shock in context A, but the other CS followed by shock in context B.[97] In the test phase, some of the subjects were tested for the strength of the two CSs in the same context as that used in acquisition, whereas other subjects were tested in the alternative context. In essence then, the study examined the effect of a change in context on the strength of a Pavlovian CR. The measure of retention was the degree of suppression of lever pressing (see Chapter 3 for a discussion of the CER technique).

The results are shown in Figure 14-19. Because there were no differences between the light offset and the click CS conditions, those data are combined in the figure. Rats that were tested in the same environments had greater fear of the CSs than subjects tested in the alternative contexts. Performance was not affected by differences in the strength of the CSs or of the context, but rather by the match or synchrony between the learning and the testing environments. The experiment thus confirms Bouton's (1993) theory that activation of *both* the context and the CS memories are needed for good retrieval.

Finally, the phenomenon called "CR renewal" also confirms Bouton's (1993) principle (see Chapter 3 for further discussion of the renewal phenomenon). The CR-renewal phenomenon shows that memory for acquisition and memory for extinction are highly context dependent. For example, Brooks and Bouton (1994) trained subjects in one context and then extinguished them in

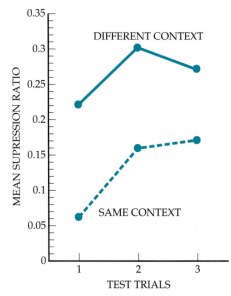

FIGURE 14-19. Mean CER suppression ratio, as a function of three test trials for groups that were tested either in the same environments as those used in training or in a different context (after Hall & Honey, 1990).

a different context.[98] If subjects were subsequently tested in the original context, considerable responding was observed (this is the renewal effect). However, if they were placed in the original context but given a cue that was associated with the extinction context, then the renewal effect was cancelled.

In other words, the extent to which an animal performs the CR depends critically on the context in which it is tested. If tested in the original acquisition context, the CR is retrieved; if reminded of the extinction context, then the CR is not retrieved. These results suggest that when subjects form memories, they encode representations of both the CS and the surrounding environment. Activation of these representations combine at the time of retrieval. If the context changes, then memory is not effectively retrieved.[99]

Bouton's (1993) second principle is also critical to an understanding of the memory process. Bouton claims that the passage of time itself causes a change in context.[100] In other words, forgetting occurs because the subject's stimulus context, both internal and external, changes with the passage of time. This is essentially the theory for the age-retention phenomenon discussed earlier. Juvenile subjects learn readily, but forgetting occurs because the internal context changes over the maturational processes.

Bouton's (1993) last principle concerning context and memory is that forgetting occurs at the time of retrieval.[101] If the representation of the context becomes encoded at the time of learning, and if the retrieval of the memory depends on the match between the learning and the retrieval contexts, then it is logical to conclude that forgetting is the inability to retrieve memories at the time of the test.

How does the environmental context affect retrieval at the time of testing? The answer to this question has been widely debated.[102] Some researchers suggest that the context becomes associated with the US during training, and thus its excitatory effects summate with those of the CS during the retention test. Others argue that the CS is not merely the representation of the nominal stimulus presented to the subject, but rather a combination of the nominal CS plus the surrounding context. More likely, both the context and the CS get encoded during learning, and their joint presentation during the memory test is critical to retrieval.[103]

INTERIM SUMMARY

Long-term memory has been studied less thoroughly in nonhuman animals, but studies show significant retention after several years. Long-term memory is affected by retroactive interference. One agent is electroconvulsive shock, which disrupts memory. If subjects are given foot shock followed immediately by electroconvulsive shock, they show little fear of the place at which the received the foot shock. The consolidation theory of memory explains this in terms of an interference with the consolidation process. Long-term memories are affected even more so by proactive interference. A third factor is age. Although young animals learn various responses as well as adult animals do, the young animals show inferior memory. This is called the "age-retention effect." Greater information may be retained if subjects organize material into hierarchical memory chunks. Three kinds have been studied: Trial chunks refer to an aggregate of individual responses that are organized into one holistic unit; series chunks reflect sequences of actions—for example, multiple trials—that are organized as a series; and list chunks are a hierarchy of several series chunks. The retrieval theory of memory claims that information is not lost during the retention interval but rather is not performed on the memory test. It makes three predictions. First, when new stimuli are added, the stimulus complex differs from original training, and forgetting occurs. Second, if salient stimuli that were part of the original stimulus complex are omitted, them memory declines. Third, if animals are given reminder treatments, then the original memories are reinstated. All of these predictions have been confirmed. Memory that is reinstated through a reminder treatment may actually be stronger than the original memory. The role of context also supports the retrieval theory by showing that performance of a memory is context specific. If both the original memory item and the original context in which it was learned are not provided during retrieval, then forgetting occurs.

SPATIAL MEMORY

The discussion of memory thus far has focused primarily on short-term and long-term processes. Historically, these two kinds of memory have been differentiated in terms of their duration and capacity. Although treating animal memory in terms of these two categories may be convenient, it may not accurately portray all of the processes that are relevant. For example, Sherry and Schacter (1987) suggest that multiple memory systems have evolved as specialized adaptations. Each system is specialized to a certain degree, and each is relevant to particular functions that are important for survival. Two distinct kinds of memory systems include song learning and imprinting (see Chapter 12). A third involves orientation (for instance, the migratory behavior of birds or salmon) and spatial memory (navigation in the natural environment), Sherry and Schacter (1987) claim that selective pressures have made these memory systems different from one another. Given this point of view, spatial memory is treated in this chapter as a distinct category of memory, even though it was discussed briefly in connection with short- and long-term memory processes.

Radial Arm Maze

One experiment that kindled an interest in **spatial memory** was done by Olton and Samuelson (1976).[104] Rats were tested in an apparatus called a "radial arm maze," which contained eight different alleyways radiating from a central starting position (see Figure 14-20). First, food reward was placed in each goal box. Then a given subject was placed in the central part of the apparatus and allowed to wander freely for up to 10 minutes, or until it had ventured down 16 alleyways, whichever came first. Over 10 days of training, the mean number of different arms chosen in the first 8 attempts was 7.7. If the animals had no memory for the arms they had previously visited, then one would not expect such consistent behavior. Rather, one would expect the animals to choose old and new paths with the same relative frequency. Indeed, a conventional learning approach, emphasizing the power of a contingent reinforcer, suggests that animals should return to the alleyway in which they had just received reward, rather than picking a new path. Subjects did not perform in this fashion, however; they consistently chose an alleyway not previously visited.

The results suggest that a subject's memory for alleyways previously visited determined its choice. Other factors were irrelevant. For instance, a subject did not choose a path simply by following is own odor trail left over from previous trials. This was confirmed by giving subjects 3 days of training, during which time after-shave lotion was generously sprinkled throughout the maze. If the subjects were leaving an odor trail, which helped them determine which alleyway they had visited and thus which arm to avoid on future trials, then such a masking odor should reduce the accuracy of performance. Although the odor disrupted performance somewhat on the first day of testing (some subjects, for instance, were hesitant to run at all), no change in the accuracy of the choice was observed on subsequent days.

Use of surrounding environmental stimuli is critical to the accuracy of this behavior. When the alleyways are covered, so that each resembles a tunnel

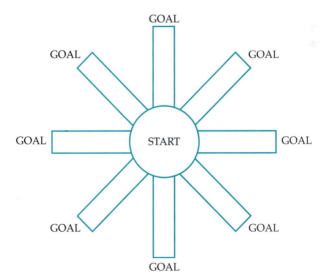

FIGURE 14-20. Schematic diagram of the radial arm maze used to study spatial memory (after Olton & Samuelson, 1976).

rather than an open platform, performance declines to about chance level.[105] Conversely, when subjects are allowed to inspect the environment visually, then radial-arm-maze accuracy increases.[106] Finally, the length of the alleyways, the brightness of the maze, and the slant of the arms also affect performance by changing the subject's willingness to revisit previously chosen arms rather than by changing the animal's memory for those arms.[107]

The radial-arm-maze study is important not only because it demonstrates that animals have a memory for spatial locations, but also because it helps to explain a rat's natural foraging strategy.[108] In their natural environment, where rats typically deplete a food source before moving to a new location, avoiding previously visited locations makes good ecological sense. The reason is that by consistently choosing new paths, animals maximize their potential intake of food over the long run.

Cognitive Maps

Rats develop a **cognitive map,** or internal model, of the spatial characteristics of the environment, which allows them to negotiate the radial arm maze.[109] An elegant demonstration of the use of cognitive maps in a different context was done by Morris (1981). A schematic diagram of the apparatus is shown in Figure 14-21. The testing arena was a circular aquarium about 1.3 meters in diameter, filled with milky-colored water to a height of about 0.4 meters. Two kinds of platforms were used. The top of the black platform stood about 1 centimeter above the surface of the water; the top of the white platform was about 1 centimeter below the water's surface.[110] Rats were given 8 escape trials for 3 days. The starting point varied over each block of four trials; that is, subjects were started from the north, east, south, and west positions on a random basis on successive trials. Morris measured both the time to reach a platform and the distance traveled to reach it.

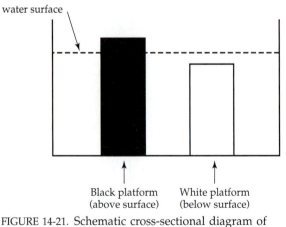

FIGURE 14-21. Schematic cross-sectional diagram of the apparatus used to demonstrate cognitive maps in rats (Morris, 1981).

There were four groups. Subjects in the visible–fixed group swam to the black platform, which was always in a fixed location in the aquarium (locations differed across subjects, but for a given animal, the location was the same on every trial). Subjects in the hidden–fixed group escaped to the white platform, which was always located in the same position. Because the water was cloudy, however, the surface of the white platform was invisible. These subjects could respond effectively only by remembering the location of the platform, relative to the cues in the surrounding environment. Subjects in the visible–random group swam to the black platform, but its location in the aquarium varied randomly from one trial to the next. The only way these subjects could locate the platform, therefore, was to make visual contact with it. Finally, subjects in the hidden–random group swam to the white (invisible) platform, but its position was varied randomly over trials. Presumably, these subjects would not be able to locate the platform effectively, either by direct sighting or by remembering its spatial location.

The results confirmed that the hidden–random group took considerably longer to escape than did the other subjects, and they traveled a much greater distance on each trial. This is graphically shown in Figure 14-22. These lines represent the paths taken by four subjects on the last four trials. The subjects were started at different locations on each of these trials, and yet for the visible–random, visible–fixed, and hidden–fixed groups, the paths to the platform were more or less direct. Behavior of the visible–random group shows that, given the opportunity, rats are able to navigate by direct visual sighting.

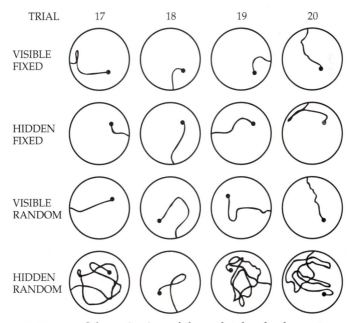

FIGURE 14-22. Schematic view of the path taken by four rats (one in each group), as a function of the last four escape trials (after Morris, 1981).

Behavior of the hidden–fixed subjects indicates that animals are able to construct a mental map of their environment and thus to perform on the basis of their memory of the location. The behavior of the hidden–random group, however, demonstrates that efficient escape behavior was virtually impossible when the rats could neither see the platform nor learn its location.

Cache Sites in Birds.

The implication of the research on cognitive maps is that spatial memories are used in an animal's natural environment.[111] This has been demonstrated in various species of birds that hoard food items in caches. Some species, for instance marsh tits, make good use of a temporary abundance of food when available, by retrieving food items, storing them in caches, returning for more food, and so forth until the source of food is depleted. The birds later return to the caches to retrieve the food and eat it.[112]

Shettleworth and Krebs (1982) demonstrated that they accomplish this by developing spatial memories for cache sites.[113] Marsh tits were tested in a large aviary containing 12 artificial trees. Each tree had from 7 to 9 holes drilled in it; each hole was covered by a small flap of cloth, stapled to the wood. A perch was located in the center of the aviary, on which a bowl of water and a bowl of hemp seeds was placed. A given bird was deprived of food for about 2 hours and then permitted to fly into the aviary to store 12 seeds. After a 2- to 3-hour retention interval, the bird was placed back in the aviary for 12 minutes, during which time it could recover its stored seeds. The bird was also given test trials on which the seeds had been moved to 12 randomly chosen holes. Here, the subject could not retrieve the seeds by memory. The authors recorded the number of cache sites inspected and the number of stored seeds retrieved (an error was defined as visiting a hole that did not contain a seed).

Generally, when the seeds were left undisturbed, subjects made few errors for each seed recovered. However, when the seeds had been relocated, many errors occurred. This is shown in Figure 14-23. The number of incorrect visits to cache sites was low when the bird could retrieve seeds from locations it had used previously. However, on test trials where the locations had been changed, many errors occurred. The birds therefore do not use the seeds (or their odor) as a cue for retrieval, but rather develop a memory for the location within the aviary.[114] Apparently, the birds navigate by developing a cognitive map of the individual cache sites.

Sherry (1992) demonstrated that hoarding birds are also sensitive to global landmarks. In this study, the general location of an artificial tree within the aviary was identified by a large colored target (for example, a yellow circle, a red triangle, a purple rectangle, or a colored poster). Individual cache sites on each tree were identified by local cues—namely, small colored cards placed near the holes. Removal of these local cues did not disrupt the search pattern of birds when retrieving stored seeds. However, removal, or rotation, of the global cues significantly reduced the accuracy of the birds' search.

If cognitive maps are developed in species that hoard food, then spatial memory probably differs among species of birds, depending on their ecological

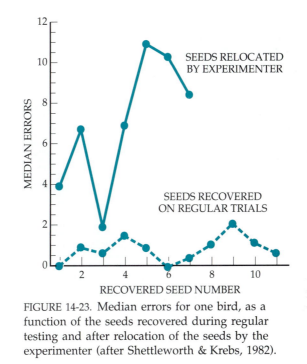

FIGURE 14-23. Median errors for one bird, as a function of the seeds recovered during regular testing and after relocation of the seeds by the experimenter (after Shettleworth & Krebs, 1982).

niche. This was demonstrated by Brodbeck (1994).[115] Two species of birds were compared: black-capped chickadees and dark-eyed juncos. The former stores food, but the latter species does not. The aviary housed blocks of wood that contained holes drilled into them that could be covered with black cloth. Each block was located along one of the walls, varied in size, was painted in a distinctive color, and covered with various patterns (for instance, stripes or designs). During training, the holes in each block were uncovered. A bird entered the aviary and stored a food item in one of the holes. Thirty minutes later, the bird was placed back in the aviary, where it encountered the same feeders, although now each was covered with a piece of cloth. The spatial location, furthermore, was changed randomly on some trials, thus providing a test of spatial memory.

The chickadees responded to the spatial cues more than to the color or pattern. The nonstoring juncos, on the other hand, responded more to the visual appearance of the blocks than to their spatial location. These behaviors are consistent with natural feeding strategies. Juncos typically feed on the ground, and thus the spatial location of a food source is less critical than its appearance. Chickadees, on the other hand, are storing birds, and they use three-dimensional space as a means of locating their caches.

Cognitive Maps in Bees.

The development of cognitive maps is by no means confined to so-called higher-order species. Invertebrates—for example, honey bees—also appear to develop such maps.[116] This was shown by Gould (1986). The experimental

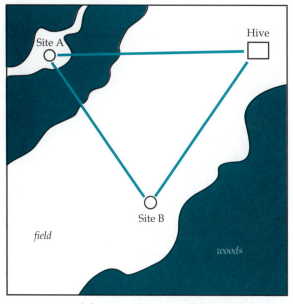

FIGURE 14-24. Schematic diagram of the environment
used to test cognitive maps in bees (after Gould, 1986).

arrangements are shown in Figure 14-24. Bees learned to find food by flying
from their hive to the food source located at site A. Individuals were then cap-
tured upon leaving the hive, transported in a dark container to site B, at which
point they were released. The direction of their flight was measured. The bees
could not travel to site A simply by viewing it from site B because a ridge
between the two sites blocked their view. If, however, they had developed a
cognitive map of the environment, then they should proceed more or less
directly to site A when released from site B, rather than fly at right angles to
the correct flight direction.

The vast majority of bees did, in fact, fly directly toward site A, suggesting that they had oriented themselves within the environment. Control subjects, which were transported to site B but then back again to the hive before
being released, flew in the familiar orientation. Although some of the work
by Gould has not been replicated, much of the evidence suggests that even
invertebrates may proceed to an unseen destination from a novel location
based, at least in part, on their knowledge about the general landmarks.[117]

INTERIM SUMMARY

Theorists suggest that multiple memory systems have evolved as specialized adaptations. Spatial memory is an example. For instance,
research using a radial arm maze shows that rats develop a keen sense
of the goals already visited by constructing a cognitive map of their sur-

roundings. When challenged to find a goal, rats use both direct sighting and an internal cognitive map of the area. Various species of birds make use of spatial cues in creating caches of food. They retrieve seeds by using both local cues and global landmarks. Even invertebrates, such as honeybees, appear to develop cognitive maps. If individual bees are taken to a new location, they fly toward the direction of the food source, suggesting that they have a mental map of the surrounding area.

ENDNOTES

1. For excellent reviews of memory research, see Kendrick, Rilling, and Denny (1986); and Spear and Riccio (1994).
2. These stages refer not only to the basic processes in memory, but also the way in which psychologists investigate memory. That is, memory experiments involve learning, retention, and retrieval phases, just as memories themselves are said to progress through these stages.
3. The question as to whether stored memories are affected during this phase, or whether this is essentially a passive stage, has been debated for many decades (see subsequent discussion for theories of forgetting).
4. Interference is actually not confined to the storage phase of memory. Information may be disrupted by interference during any of the three phases.
5. See D'Amato (1973); D'Amato and Cox (1976); Roberts and Grant (1976); Roitblat (1984a, 1984b).
6. Many delayed matching-to-sample studies employ stimuli that are more complex than simple colors and shapes. These may be shapes of various sizes or orientations, or shapes that differ in color from their background (see text for more examples). Subjects have also been shown to perform delayed matching-to-sample using auditory stimuli; see Kraemer and Roberts (1984). Furthermore, short-term memory may be assessed in terms of a subject's *non*matching accuracy; see Roitblat and Harley (1988); Roitblat and Scopatz (1983); van Haaren and van Hest (1989).
7. In most procedures, this is preceded by a white ready light, the response to which starts the trial and initiates the sample stimulus.
8. The position of the two stimuli is randomly varied across trials.
9. A successive delayed matching-to-sample task involves the presentation of the sample and then, after a retention interval, only one of the comparison stimuli by itself. If the comparison matches the sample, then responding is rewarded; if it does not, then no reinforcement is forthcoming. Performance is assessed in terms of response rate during the comparison stimuli, rather than by percentage choice of the matching comparison; see Nelson and Wasserman (1978). Generally, choice and successive matching do not differ appreciably, but see Spetch and Grant (1993).
10. Striking differences, however, are observed between different species of animals. For instance, monkeys and dolphins match the sample even with delays as long as 2 minutes. For one monkey, D'Amato (1973) showed that delayed matching to sample was possible even with a delay of 9 minutes. Pigeons, on the other hand, match the sample with delays of only 10 to 15 seconds. Moreover, matching performance declines if the retention interval is fixed over a series of blocks of trials, rather than being variable; see White and Bunnell-McKenzie (1985).

11. All four combinations were given 10 times each during the training session, in a random order.
12. The intertrial interval was also varied systematically (5, 10, or 30 seconds), along with the retention interval. The data reported here are for the 30-second intertrial-interval condition only.
13. Detailed analysis showed that these differences tended to decline toward the end of training.
14. See also Grant (1988a,b); MacDonald and Grant (1987). The focus of the latter paper was on the effect of signals that informed the subject of the retention interval length rather than of the nature of the matching test. Comparable effects have been shown in rats (Grant, 1982c) and monkeys (Roberts, Mazmanian, and Kraemer, 1984).
15. Actually, two groups were used. On the forget trials, the no-test group was given no stimulus, rather than the irrelevant stimulus. Their results were identical to the other subjects and so are not reported here.
16. On half of the forget trials, reinforcement was given on a noncontingent basis to equate the overall rate of reward with the remember trials.
17. Stonebraker and Rilling (1981) showed that the effectiveness of the forget cue to reduce rehearsal of the sample depends critically on its temporal location. Matching accuracy declines more when the cue occurs at the beginning of the retention interval. Such a finding suggests that the effect of a forget cue is to cancel rehearsal, not to interfere with the performance of the memory at the time of matching; see also Maki, Olson, and Rego (1981).
18. Santi (1989), however, has not supported the notion that rehearsal is automatic.
19. This aspect of trace theory is unconventional, in the sense that earlier trace theories assumed that the sensory impression created by a stimulus did not grow with duration of the exposure. Sensory activation was thought to be at full strength throughout the presentation of the stimulus, decaying appropriately with stimulus offset.
20. See Devine, Jones, Neville, and Sakai (1977); Herzog, Grant, and Roberts (1977); Roberts and Grant (1974).
21. A 0-second delay condition also showed the same relationship between matching performance and sample duration.
22. See also Reynolds and Medin (1979).
23. Maki and Leith (1973); Maki, Riley, and Leith (1976); see Riley (1984) for a review. Two alternative hypotheses have been proposed. One asserts that subjects develop an implicit set of instructions to be followed when the comparison stimuli are presented; see Grant and MacDonald (1986). Another hypothesis, called the "stimulus-generalization-decrement hypothesis," claims that when the sample contains two elements or dimensions, but the choice stimuli contain only one dimension, performance may decline because the overall stimulus complex has changed; see Cox and D'Amato (1982); Roberts and Grant (1978b).
24. D'Amato and O'Neill (1971) were the first to observe that delayed matching-to-sample performance improved if the lights in the apparatus were turned off during the delay interval. This is called "retroactive interference."
25. Grant and Roberts (1976); Wright, Urcuioli, Sands, and Santiago (1981). Kendrick and Rilling (1984) reported that the presentation of cues associated with extinction, variable interval schedules, or differential reinforcement of other behavior schedules (see Chapter 9), also interfered with delayed matching-to-sample performance. They concluded that these manipulations interfere with baseline behav-

ior that occurs during the retention interval, rather than with rehearsal of the sample. The presentation of auditory stimuli have little effect on matching performance; see Wilkie, Summers, and Spetch (1981); Worsham and D'Amato (1973).

26. Cook (1980); Parker and Glover (1987). Wright, Urcuioli, Sands, and Santiago (1981) found that colors were more disruptive than was white light. This finding suggests that subjects show a decline in delayed matching-to-sample accuracy because they confuse the sample with the intrusive key light.

27. Grant (1988b); Parker and Glover (1987). Cook (1980), however, found the opposite effect—namely, that a reduction in illumination was as disruptive as an increase in illumination. Cook's hypothesis was that an unexpected change in the level of illumination caused surprise and disruption. The onset of a house light interferes not only with memory for a visual sample, but also with the subject's memory of its own behavior. Maki, Moe, and Bierley (1977), for instance, required that the pigeon subjects peck at the sample key either 1 or 20 times. The correct match later depended on which response requirement had been in effect. If the requirement had been 1 peck, then one comparison stimulus was appropriate, but if the requirement had been 20 pecks, then a different stimulus was appropriate. Illumination caused interference with the response memory, as well as the stimulus memory. That is, turning on the lights caused the birds to forget whether they had just pecked 1 or 20 times.

28. Grant (1988b, Experiment 2) showed that the onset of the house light near the end of the retention interval disrupted matching more than did the onset of the light during the earlier portions of the interval (although this outcome was reversed with extended testing). Grant argued that the disrupted-rehearsal hypothesis cannot explain this finding.

29. See also Grant (1975).

30. Grant (1982a) used a more complicated design, in which vertical and horizontal lines also served as sample, comparison, and interfering stimuli.

31. Zentall and Hogan (1977, Experiment 1) showed that proactive interference was not obtained when the initial stimulus was different from the incorrect comparison stimulus. In other words, inferior matching performance was obtained only in subjects for which the interfering stimulus was the incorrect comparison.

32. Additional studies by Grant (1982a) showed that when the interfering stimulus and the incorrect comparison are the same, it makes no difference to the size of the interference effect whether they are drawn from the same dimension as the sample. For instance, horizontal lines proactively interfere with the processing of a color sample when the incorrect comparison stimulus is also the horizontal line. Interestingly, the temporal interval between the interfering stimulus and the sample has little effect on the degree of interference caused in this situation; see Medin (1980).

33. D'Amato (1973); D'Amato and Cox (1976).

34. Worsham (1975).

35. See Honig and Thompson (1982); Roitblat (1982).

36. Research discussed in Chapter 6, on theories of classical conditioning, emphasized the concept of retroactive rehearsal. More specifically, following a CS-US pairing, subjects are claimed to retroactively rehearse the connection, thus strengthening the association between the two stimuli.

37. See also Roitblat and Scopatz (1983).

38. Farthing, Wagner, Gilmour, and Waxman (1977).

39. A fourth source of evidence for prospective encoding comes from a study by Roitblat (1980), Experiment 3; see also Grant (1982b).

40. See Honig and Wasserman (1981).
41. Counterbalancing of stimuli was used throughout.
42. A second series of 25 test sessions was conducted using, in addition, an 8-second retention interval. Results were essentially the same in each test series.
43. See also Edwards, Jagielo, Zentall, and Hogan (1982); Zentall and Sherburne (1994).
44. Stimuli were red and green colors, and vertical or slanted lines. The retention interval varied from 0 to 10 seconds.
45. DeLong and Wasserman (1981) studied separately the matching between color and line, and between line and color.
46. Hoffman, Selekman, and Fleshler (1966); Skinner (1950a).
47. Loftus and Kallman (1979).
48. Current research on memory, in fact, has all but abandoned the idea that short- and long-term memory are distinct memory processes that reside in separate storage sites. Rather, information is said to be in working memory when it is being rehearsed and processed, and permanent, or reference, memory thereafter.
49. The procedure was actually more complicated. Pecking was reinforced following the presentation of an S+ slide on a VI-10 second schedule, but only if the bird responded within 2 seconds of the end of the interval. Furthermore, if no peck was made within 1 minute on S+ trials, food was delivered automatically.
50. See Standing (1973).
.51. Although the first test session showed some forgetting, their mastery of the discrimination, that is, their ability to identify whether the slide was a positive or negative instance, increased thereafter.
52. Schreurs (1993) also tested subjects at 9 months, but their performance was virtually the same as those tested at 6 months and so are not discussed here.
53. See Miller and Matzel (1987).
54. Shurtleff and Ayres (1981); Campeau, Liang, and Davis (1990).
55. Spear, Hamburg, and Bryan (1980).
56. See Spear and Riccio (1994).
57. Other amnesic agents include convulsive drugs such as Metrazol (Palfai and Chillag, 1971), hypothermia (Hinterliter, Webster, and Riccio, 1975), and hyperthermia (Mactutus, Ferek, and Riccio, 1980).
58. See Riccio and Richardson (1984); for an earlier review, see Lewis (1969).
59. The first demonstration of the effect of the learning-electroconvulsive shock interval was by Duncan (1949).
60. See Miller and Springer (1973); Riccio and Richardson (1984).
61. See Spear and Riccio (1994), p. 93; Wright, Urcuioli, and Sands (1986).
62. See also Revusky (1971); Wickens, Tuber, and Wickens (1983).
63. Kraemer (1984) actually had 12 conditions. Half of the subjects were trained on a feature-positive discrimination, the other half on a feature-negative discrimination (see Chapter 13). There were no differences in memory across this factor and so the data are combined for purposes of clarity.
64. See Campbell and Coulter (1976); Campbell and Spear (1972); Rovee-Collier (1984).
65. Although much of this research has focused on memories for aversive events, even memories for appetitive tasks may be lost if they were learned during an early age; see Campbell, Jaynes, and Misanin (1968).
66. See also Campbell and Campbell (1962).

67. Rats are weaned at the age of 21 days and reach sexual maturity by about 35 to 45 days of age.
68. The age-retention phenomenon is not limited to Pavlovian fear training. Escape reactions (N. F. Smith, 1968), active (Feigley and Spear, 1970), and passive (Schulenburg, Riccio, and Stikes, 1971) avoidance reactions, and taste aversions (Steinert, Infurna, and Spear, 1980) are more easily forgotten when trained at a young age.
69. The improvement in memory as a function of age is a gradual process. Mice may remember a response for a few hours when they are 5 to 7 days of age and they are capable of retaining material for 24 hours by 9 days of age. It is not until the age of 21 days that the ability to remember over a longer period of time develops; see Nagy, Misanin, Newman, Olsen, and Hinderliter (1972); Misanin, Nagy, Keiser, and Bowen (1971); Nagy and Mueller (1973).
70. The concept of a limited memory span was discussed in a noted paper by Miller (1956).
71. See Capaldi (1992).
72. Capaldi (1992, 1994); see also Capaldi, Nawrocki, Miller, and Verry (1986); Fountain (1990); Fountain and Rowan (1995).
73. Indeed, in phase 2 of the study, four additional nonreward trials were given following the RNNNN sequence and the same effect was observed, namely, speed remained low throughout indicating that the subjects were remembering the outcome on the first of nine trials.
74. Because the subject has organized the series of trials into a chunk, it is better able to anticipate future outcomes; see Chatlosh and Wasserman (1992); Capaldi (1992). In another example, Capaldi and Miller (1988b) used two kinds of reward/nonreward series (see also Capaldi, Nawrocki, and Verry, 1983). One series involved RNR trials, the other RNN trials. Subjects anticipated reward and thus ran fast on the first trial of both series. Speed on the second trial in each series was much lower, indicating that subjects anticipated receiving no reward. However, the interesting outcome was that subjects ran faster on trial two if they anticipated receiving reward on trial three.
75. See also Capaldi, Nawrocki, and Verry (1983); Haggbloom, Birmingham, and Scranton (1992).
76. See Miller, Kasprow, and Schachtman (1986); Spear (1973, 1978); Spear and Parsons (1976).
77. The reinstatement effects have been concerned primarily with the forgetting of long-term memories, although similar findings have been shown for short-term memories; see, Kasprow (1987).
78. Spear (1973), p. 163. The retrieval theory of memory is really the same as the generalization decrement theory of extinction discussed in Chapter 10. According to the generalization decrement theory, extinction involves a change in the environment due to the elimination of reward, and thus a loss of stimulus control. Forgetting may also be considered to be a result of a change in the environment with the passage of time. New stimuli are added to the stimulus complex, and once-relevant stimuli are lost or omitted during the retention interval. The net effect is an inability for the stimulus complex to elicit the relevant behavior. Such a theory describes why behavior declines during normal extinction, and why subjects forget during a retention interval.
79. See also Lewis, Misanin, and Miller (1968).

80. See also Miller, Ott, Berk, and Springer (1974).
81. Spear (1973, 1978); see Campbell and Jaynes (1966); Spear, Miller, and Jagielo (1990).
82. See also Berk, Vigorito, and Miller (1979) for an alternative theory of infantile amnesia.
83. See also Spear and Parsons (1976).
84. Reinstatement also occurs for appetitive discriminations (Campbell and Randall, 1976) or when animals are merely exposed to the fear cues that comprised original training (Silvestri, Rohrbaugh, and Riccio, 1970).
85. If the animals were placed in a different apparatus and given CS-US pairings, they only took 366.0 seconds.
86. See also Deweer, Sara, and Hars (1980); Feldman and Gordon (1979); Gordon and Feldman (1978); Gordon and Spear (1973); Hickis, Robles, and Thomas (1977); but see Powell (1972).
87. Most of the research on memory reactivation, including the work on reinstatement of memory in infant subjects, has shown that reminders, in and of themselves, do not teach the response; animals given only the reminders are unable to perform the reaction effectively.
88. The sequence of turns was the same as reported in the Deweer and Sara (1984) study, namely LRRLLR or RLLRRL.
89. These subjects were further divided into two conditions. Some were given the stimulation during slow wave sleep whereas other were given the reminder stimulation during paradoxical sleep. Paradoxical sleep occurs when the brain waves become desynchronized. In humans, this stage of sleep is associated with dreaming; see Mendelson (1987), for a general review of sleep research in humans.
90. Experiment 3, however, showed that memory was actually impaired when the reactivation treatment was given during paradoxical sleep. Thus, processing of the memory many take place during certain stages of sleep.
91. See Balsam and Tomie (1985); Spear (1978).
92. Bouton (1994).
93. See Bouton (1993).
94. Spear (1978) p. 106.
95. See also Honey, Willis, and Hall (1990).
96. In this sense, the context functions much like an occasion setter (see Chapter 5).
97. Context and CS conditions were counterbalanced.
98. See also Bouton and Bolles (1979, 1985); Bouton and King (1983); Bouton and Peck (1989).
99. Changes in the context are not limited to external stimuli. Changes in a subject's internal environment are equally important. For example, hormonal changes related to stress, or changes related to alterations in the subject's drug state affect memory retrieval in a similar fashion to changes in the external environment; see Klein (1972); Overton (1985).
100. See Capaldi, Nawrocki, Miller, and Verry (1986), for an interesting demonstration of time as context.
101. Bouton proposed an additional principle, namely that different memories depend differentially on changes in the context. Some memories are more susceptible to changes in the context than others. Excitatory responses, for example, are less easily disrupted by a change in context than inhibitory responses.
102. See Gordon and Klein (1994); Miller and Schachtman (1985b).
103. See Bouton (1993); Spear (1978).

104. See also Olton (1978); Roberts (1984).
105. Mazmanian and Roberts (1983); see also Balda and Kamil (1988); Roberts and van Veldhuizen (1985).
106. Mazmanian and Roberts (1983).
107. Brown (1990); Brown and Lesniak-Karpiak (1993).
108. Roberts, Phelps, and Schacter (1992) argue persuasively that various features of the radial-arm-maze environment (specifically, whether the alleyways are covered, the size of the food reward, and whether the alleyways intersect at the center) elicit a form of central-place foraging.
109. See Gallistel (1990) for a review, and Poucet (1993) for a discussion of the possible neural structure of cognitive maps.
110. The center of the black platform was recessed, such that when a subject stood on it, the platform was submerged in approximately the same depth of water as when a subject stood on the white platform. This precaution was taken so that the reinforcing effect of climbing onto a safe platform would be the same for both the black and the white platforms.
111. See Shettleworth (1990) for a review.
112. This behavior contrasts with the typical strategy of other species, such as the great tit, which do not store food items, but rather eat them at the source.
113. Similar results have been shown for black-capped chickadees (Sherry, 1984) and Clark's nutcrackers (Kamil and Balda, 1985).
114. Subsequent studies confirmed that the birds do not simply visit the same storage sites each time, but rather have a memory for the specific sites used.
115. See also Shettleworth and Krebs (1986).
116. See Gould (1987, 1990).
117. Dyer (1991); see Gallistel (1994) for a review.

CHAPTER 15

Complex Cognitive Functioning

Previous chapters discussed basic learning processes in Pavlovian and instrumental conditioning, as well as many higher-order learning processes, including generalization, discrimination, and memory. This chapter examines the implications or extensions of those conditioning processes to more complex cognitive functioning.

Four major topics are considered. First, stimuli occur in a temporal and sequential context. Thus, an animal's sense of timing and its ability to count are important higher-order functions. Second, animals form complex conceptual categories. Concept acquisition reflects information processing on a higher level than simple generalization. Third, subjects make decisions and solve problems. An understanding of the processes by which animals accomplish this is critical to an understanding of how they cope in their natural environment. Finally, many animals are capable of communicating with others. Often, the communication is by means of visual signals (sexual or aggressive displays) or chemical cues (marking territories). Are animals capable of more complex languagelike processes, however? This chapter discusses this issue in detail.

COUNTING AND TIMING

Time and number are dimensions that characterize all environments. Stimuli are located both spatially and temporally within the environment, and they occur in greater or lesser numbers. Thus, from an ecological point of view, the abilities to estimate time and to count are important. Crickets, for example, implicitly time the rate at which they produce their mating calls; a series of clicks that does not conform to the appropriate temporal pattern is not answered. Birds and humans are sensitive to the diurnal (or circadian) rhythms established by the light–dark cycle; much of what we do, including our sleep pattern, is set by this cycle. Many animals migrate at certain times

520

of the year; failure to do so at precisely the right time jeopardizes survival. Although these examples differ in terms of the time periods involved (fractions of a second, 24 hours, several months), nevertheless, all illustrate the notion that a sense of time is essential in coping with the demands of the environment.

Processing of Temporal Intervals

There is good evidence to suggest that animals process temporal intervals. Several procedures have been used to demonstrate this fact.

Timing Tasks.

A **go/no-go discrimination** procedure was used by Church and Gibbon (1982). Rats were first rewarded for pressing a lever if the house light was turned off for 4 seconds. Then, the same reinforcement contingency was in effect, but the house light was turned off for 0.8, 4, or 7.2 seconds. If the rat pressed after the house light had been off for a time period other than 4 seconds, the lever was withdrawn from the cage, and reward was not presented. Finally, subjects were given nine different durations (0.8, 1.6, 2.4, 3.2, 4.0, 4.8, 5.6, 6.4, and 7.2 seconds). Again, if the house light offset lasted 4 seconds, a response was reinforced, but if the signal lasted for one of the other durations, pressing was not rewarded. This procedure is called a "go/no-go discrimination" because the subjects respond (go) if the signal is an S+ (here, the house light offset lasting 4 seconds), but not respond (that is, no-go) if the signal is an S− (a stimulus of any other duration).

Accuracy of performance is shown in Figure 15-1. Stimulus control based on temporal duration was evident; subjects attended to the temporal length of the house light offset. This was shown by the fact that the peak of responding was to the S+ (4-second offset), whereas probability declined systematically as the duration became more dissimilar to the S+ duration.

A study by Roberts, Cheng, and Cohen (1989) used the **peak procedure** to study the pigeon's ability to time light and tone signals.[1] The peak procedure takes advantage of the fact that rate of response on a fixed interval (FI) schedule of reinforcement accelerates during the interval (see Chapter 9). Specifically, the rate of response is low immediately after receiving reward, but it increases as the interval elapses. In the peak procedure, the FI interval is accompanied by a signal. Occasionally, however, a blank test trial is given, where the signal remains on for double the time of the fixed interval; no rewards are given for responding on these trials. If the subject anticipates receiving a reward precisely at the time the fixed interval expires, then the response rate should be maximum at about that time. Furthermore, as time continues beyond the expected length of the fixed interval, the subject should show a reduction in response rate if its behavior is controlled by the temporal interval itself.

In this study, two FI schedules were used, lasting either 15 or 30 seconds. They were signaled by a red light and 1325-Hz tone. The intervals for one

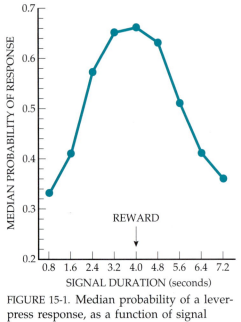

FIGURE 15-1. Median probability of a lever-press response, as a function of signal duration (after Church & Gibbon, 1982).

group were 15-seconds–light and 30-seconds–tone; the intervals for the other group were 30-seconds–light and 15-seconds–tone.

Timing on the test trials was quite accurate, as shown in Figure 15-2. The peak of responding occurred appropriately at 15 and 30 seconds, regardless of which stimulus was used. Thus, the animals demonstrated a good sense of timing. Although the peaks of responding were appropriate for both the tone and the light, the data also reveal that pigeons time lights more easily than they do tones. This conclusion is based on a comparison of the response rates for subjects that received the tone for 15 seconds and those that got the light for 15 seconds. Here, the former animals showed a greater spread of scores than did the latter subjects. Moreover, pigeons were slower to differentiate between short and long tones than between short and long lights. The difficulty that pigeons have in processing the temporal duration of tones relative to lights contrasts with that found for rats. Rats have less difficulty in timing tones than do pigeons.[2]

A third technique for measuring temporal discrimination was used by Dreyfus, Fetterman, Smith, and Stubbs (1988).[3] Here, pigeons were given two stimuli and then required to peck one of two keys, depending on the relationship between the durations of the stimuli. If stimulus A was longer than stimulus B, then pecking one key was reinforced, but pecking the other was not. If A was shorter than B, the reward conditions were reversed. Using this procedure, it is possible to vary both the relative and absolute stimulus durations over a wide range of values, and thus to determine how accurately these

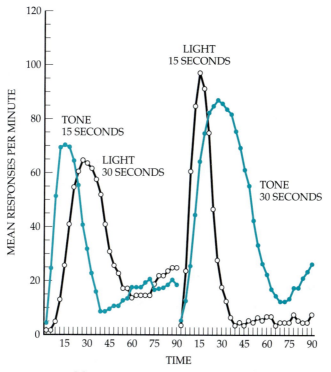

FIGURE 15-2. Mean responses per minute, as a function of time on the test trials, for groups that differed in terms of the duration (seconds) of the light and the tone (after Roberts, Cheng, & Cohen, 1989).

animals sense the difference. For example, if one stimulus lasts considerably longer than the other, then the animal should have little difficulty in choosing the correct response. However, if the two durations are so similar that the subject cannot readily discriminate between them, then choice behavior should be closer to being random. The results showed that subjects could perform this task accurately and that responding was determined by the ratio of the two durations, although accuracy declined as the absolute duration of the two stimuli increased.[4]

Characteristics of Temporal Processing.

The characteristics of the internal timing process appear to be exactly like those of a stopwatch.[5] For example, like a stopwatch, if subjects are given a time-out period during the interval, their subjective timing ceases; the internal clock stops timing. Once the time-out has finished and the stimulus goes back on, subjects begin to time once again.

Second, the internal clock, like a stopwatch, allows an animal to time intervals of different lengths, despite the fact that the events may be from different modalities. A stopwatch, for instance, could verify that a 5-second light lasts the same duration as a 5-second tone. The interval clock may be used in the same fashion.

A third characteristic is that the internal clock times from zero upward, like a stopwatch, rather than from some value to zero, like a kitchen timer. If a rat is trained to press one lever following a short-duration cue, and then is given no stimuli at all (in other words, a stimulus with a duration of zero), it responds to this event as if it were of a short duration.[6] If the internal clock always timed from a preset value to zero, then the animal would not be expected to respond in this fashion.

Fourth, the internal clock is similar to a stopwatch in that both may be reset to zero quite readily. In the case of rats responding on an FI schedule, for example, the internal clock resets after a reinforcement is delivered. Response rate drops to near zero following reward but accelerates thereafter.

An interesting characteristic of the internal clock is that an animal's estimation of the duration of a stimulus decreases with the passage of time itself. Spetch (1987) demonstrated this by showing a choose-short bias among pigeons.[7] Birds were given a delayed matching-to-sample task (see Chapters 13 and 14) involving samples (white key lights) that differed in their duration. Specifically, pigeons were reinforced for pecking a red comparison key following a short-duration sample (2 seconds) and rewarded for pecking a blue comparison key if the prior sample was a long-duration event (8 seconds).[8] When pigeons are allowed to identify the duration of a sample stimulus immediately, they have little trouble in doing so; they peck the appropriate key on about 95% of the trials. If, however, a delay is inserted between the white key-light sample and the two comparison colors, then the pigeons tend to misremember the length of the sample. They identify the longer-duration sample as a short-duration cue. Their subjective memory for the sample duration is altered with time.

Finally, a characteristic of the timing process is that animals time stimuli from different sense modalities, and they do so, simultaneously and independently, by means of two separate internal clocks. This was shown by Meck and Church (1984). Rats were reinforced for responding to a special kind of FI schedule. Specifically, a light stimulus was presented during the entire 50-second fixed interval, but a tone, which was much shorter in duration, was also presented. The tone divided the longer interval into shorter segments. Thus, one fixed interval (tone) was embedded in another (light). Rats showed an accelerating response rate throughout the entire light signal, and, simultaneously and independently, accelerating response patterns during the tone.

Theories of Timing.

Several theories of timing have been proposed. Some focus on the biological determinants of timing, whereas others consider the psychological concepts that underlie timing behavior, such as memory, perception, and attention.[9]

One model is based on the physiological effect of chemical substances in the brain.[10] Research by Meck and associates has confirmed that particular drugs affect timing behavior. In one experiment, Meck (1983) trained rats to press the left lever when a 2-second noise was sounded, but the right lever when an 8-second noise was presented. Once subjects mastered this behavior, they were given the 2- and 8-second noises, plus five noises of intermediate duration (2.6, 3.2, 4.0, 5.0, and 6.4 seconds). Although food reward was withheld if the subjects responded to these intermediate noises, the subjects generalized to these stimuli and pressed the levers nonetheless. The shorter cues were responded to as if they were 2-second durations, whereas the longer noises, on average, were judged more similar to the 8-second noise.

Meck also injected subjects during this period of training with either physiological saline (which is a harmless placebo substance), methamphetamine (which increases dopamine, a brain neurotransmitter), or haloperidol (which blocks dopamine).[11] Two results were noteworthy. First, both drug substances impaired discrimination learning. Identification of the 2-second and the 8-second noises was less accurate for the two drug groups than for the saline control animals. Second, the two drugs affected the animals' sense of time. The methamphetamine subjects responded to shorter periods of time as if they were longer; placebo subjects did not. This result suggests that, like a stopwatch that times faster than normal, the internal timing mechanism runs at a faster pace under such a drug state. Administration of haloperidol, on the other hand, had the opposite effect. Subjects tended to judge intervals as being shorter than they were in reality, suggesting that the internal clock in these subjects was operating at a slower pace. In summary, a rat's internal clock may be selectively manipulated by drugs that affect the dopamine system.[12] Although this study focused on the biochemical substrate of the timing process, other researchers have shown that specific anatomical locations are important to the timing process—for instance, the substantia nigra, the medial septal area, and the nucleus basalis magnocellularis.[13]

An explanation of timing behavior employing psychological mechanisms was proposed by Church (1984).[14] According to this theory, timing is accomplished by means of four mechanisms. They are the internal clock, reference memory, working memory, and a comparator. These mechanisms are diagramed in Figure 15-3. The clock itself has three components. The pacemaker provides a steady stream of pulses, much like the crystal in a quartz watch.[15] These pulses pass through a switch or gate, which is opened whenever a signal is presented, and then the pulses are summated in an accumulator or counter. The reference memory retains a representation of the durations experienced in the past. The comparator receives information from both the accumulator and the reference memory. When the comparator senses that the accumulator's count approximately matches the value contained in the reference memory, then it triggers a decision: either "yes," if these two values are acceptably close, or "no," if they are not. Finally, the working memory stores information from the accumulator and affects the comparator as well. For example, if an animal is given a time-out procedure while it is timing (which effectively stops the clock), the working memory retains the value in the accumulator until a later time, when it is used by the comparator.

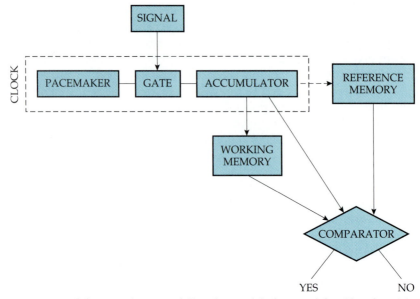

FIGURE 15-3. Schematic diagram of Church's model of timing (after Church, 1984).

The clock controls timing behavior. Imagine that a subject is given a noise and then asked to judge whether it lasted 2 or 8 seconds. The accumulator begins to summate pulses at the onset of the signal. At the offset of the cue, the comparator assesses the value of the accumulator and compares it with a value in reference memory. The subject makes the appropriate response based on this comparison.

Processing of Number

Rats and pigeons can count, as well as time.[16] One example was shown by Fernandes and Church (1982). Rats were trained to press the right lever following two short bursts of noise, but the left lever following a sequence of four bursts. The two-burst pattern actually was given in two forms. In the short form, the interburst interval was 0.8 seconds; in the long form, it was 2.8 seconds. Because the interburst interval was 0.8 seconds for the four-burst sequence, the long version of the two-burst cue lasted the same duration as the four-burst pattern. After training, subjects were tested with sequences containing two or four bursts of noise, but the interburst interval varied from 0.8 to 2.8 seconds. Thus, the test examined whether a subject classified a stimulus on the basis of the number of bursts it contained, or the total duration of the pattern.[17]

As shown in Figure 15-4, the probability of identifying any given four-burst sequence as containing four bursts was high for all of the four-burst sequences. Few of the two-burst sequences were identified in this manner. In other words, subjects identified the stimuli on the basis of the number of bursts, rather than the absolute duration of the stimulus patterns.

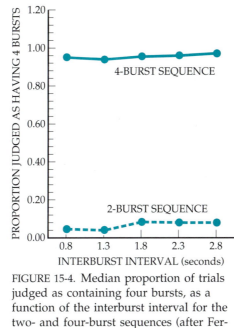

FIGURE 15-4. Median proportion of trials judged as containing four bursts, as a function of the interburst interval for the two- and four-burst sequences (after Fernandes & Church, 1982).

Counting and timing abilities are similar in many respects.[18] Recall that pigeons are able to identify a stimulus by its duration. If, however, a delay is inserted between the sample and comparison stimuli, performance deteriorates; subjects classify the longer-duration sample as if it had a shorter duration. A similar finding occurs for counting. To show this, Roberts, Macuda, and Brodbéck (1995) flashed a red light either two or eight times. If the light flashed eight times, pigeons received food for pecking a red comparison key. If it flashed twice, the animals received a reward for pecking a green comparison key. Performance was over 85% accurate, suggesting that subjects were counting. When a 10-second delay was imposed between the sample and the choice keys, however, accuracy declined. The pigeons adopted a choose-small strategy. They judged the more numerous event (eight flashes) as having a smaller number. The authors speculated that the deterioration in performance occurs because animals forget the number of pulses when that number is in working memory.

Joint Processing of Time and Number

It is not surprising that pigeons and rats perform counting and timing functions simultaneously. For example, Roberts and Mitchell (1994) trained pigeons to discriminate between 2- and 8-second sequences that contained either two or eight separate flashes.[19] Specifically, subjects experienced a flashing red light lasting either 2 or 8 seconds. The duration of each flash, and the interflash interval, were identical in both patterns, and so the 8-second sequence not only was longer than the 2-second pattern, it also contained more flashes. Subjects were reinforced for responding to the right key following an 8-second signal, but to the left key following a 2-second stimulus.

After reaching a criterion of performance, subjects were then tested. Here, either the duration of the pattern or the number of flashes was varied systematically. On the former kind of trial four flashes were given, but the interflash interval was varied so that the total duration varied between 2 and 8 seconds. On the latter trials, the pattern was held constant at 4 seconds, but the number of flashes was 2, 3, 4, 5, 6, 7, or 8.

Figure 15-5 shows the results. Subjects showed a remarkable sensitivity to both the number of flashes and the overall duration. The percentage of stimuli that was identified as being long in duration (or having many flashes) increased as the actual stimulus duration (or number) increased. The slopes of the two functions differed, however. The curve showing performance as a function of duration was steeper than the curve showing performance as a function of number. This means that pigeons were better able to differentiate

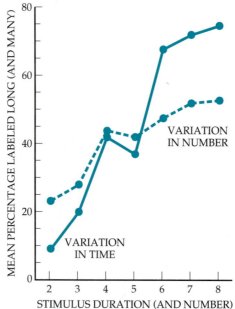

FIGURE 15-5. Mean percentage of trials for which the test pattern was judged to be long (duration) or large (number), as a function of the duration (and number) of the stimulus for the conditions in which the number or duration was varied (after Roberts & Mitchell, 1994).

short- from long-duration sequences than patterns containing few flashes from those containing many flashes. In other words, time estimations were somewhat more accurate than were number estimations, although subjects showed evidence of performing both kinds of judgments.

Church's theory of timing, presented earlier, was modified to accommodate this result.[20] The model is shown in Figure 15-6. Like the model discussed earlier, this version contains a clock, memory processes, and a comparator. Again, the pacemaker emits pulses at a constant rate, which, after passing through the switch or gate, activate the appropriate accumulators. The difference between this model and the one shown in Figure 15-3 is that separate accumulators and working memories are specified here for the timing and counting operations. Thus, the total count in each accumulator is transferred to the appropriate working-memory site. As with the earlier model, a comparison is made between the accumulator values and the values stored in the reference memory. An output rule is then developed in the comparator, based on this comparison.

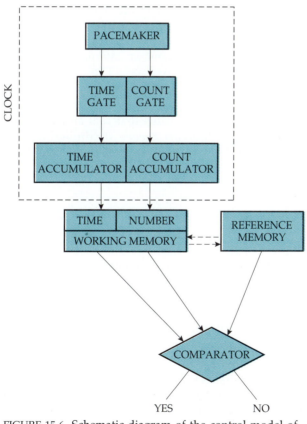

FIGURE 15-6. Schematic diagram of the control model of timing and counting (after Roberts & Mitchell, 1994).

INTERIM SUMMARY

Because time and number are dimensions that characterize all environments, the ability to time and to count are important from an ecological point of view. Using various tasks, such as a go/no-go discrimination, the peak procedure, and a comparison procedure, researchers have shown that rats and pigeons are able to time intervals quite accurately. The peak procedure, for example, shows that rate of response is maximum at the point in an FI schedule where reinforcement is normally available. The internal timing process has the same characteristics as a stopwatch. For instance, (a) during time-out periods, subjective timing ceases momentarily, (b) the internal clock times intervals of different lengths from different sense modalities, (c) it times from zero upward rather than from some value to zero, and (d) the internal clock may be reset to zero readily. An individual's memory for duration decreases with time itself. Animals time stimuli from different sense modalities simultaneously and independently by means of two separate internal clocks. One theory of timing is based on the physiological effects of biochemical substances. For example, the blocking of dopamine (a brain neurotransmitter) slows subjective time, whereas the enhancing dopamine increases the subject's sense of time. According to Church's model, timing is governed by four mechanisms: an internal clock, reference memory, working memory, and a comparator. The clock comprises a pacemaker, which provides a stream of pulses; a switch or gate, which is open whenever the signal is presented; and an accumulator, which counts the pulses. Research confirms that rats and pigeons simultaneously count and time. Church's theory of timing was modified to accommodate this result. Here, separate counting clocks, one for timing and the other for counting, are included.

CONCEPT ACQUISITION

Behaviorists argue that generalization is the essential mechanism of conceptual behavior. Stated differently, a class of stimuli to which a subject reacts in a similar fashion (that is, generalizes) is the behavioral definition of a conceptual category. One implication of this definition is that all subjects that are capable of generalizing across the members of a given class of stimuli are capable of engaging in conceptual behavior, even though, for centuries, humans were the only species thought to have a talent for such behavior.

The problem of deciding whether nonhuman animals engage in conceptual behavior is more complicated than it appears. Many issues are not easily resolved. For example, what exactly constitutes a category of stimuli? Philosophers identify two kinds of categories. One involves well-defined examples, such as the books published by McGraw-Hill, or the models of cars made by General Motors. The members of a **well-defined conceptual category** meet specific and objective criteria for membership. One is able to say unambiguously whether an exemplar is a member by determining whether it meets the stated criteria.

A different kind of category is an **ill-defined, or fuzzy, category.** Here, boundaries are not exact. One cannot say with complete certainty that an exemplar belongs to the category. Consider the category "house." Imagine the many shapes and sizes that are possible, from apartment buildings, mansions, and cottages, to adobe dwellings, tents, igloos, and even cardboard shelters. The category is not well-defined, even though human observers may agree in a very general way about class membership.

One issue in this area of psychology concerns how humans and other creatures learn to identify stimuli that compose a conceptual class. A second issue concerns animal learning research more directly. Are humans, rats, pigeons, and monkeys more or less equivalent in their abstract, conceptual abilities? Do species other than humans develop highly abstract concepts, or is their behavior based merely on sensory experience?

Theories of Classification

The following sections review several theories of categorization.

Rote Learning.

Animals may form conceptual categories by memorizing individual members of the class. Although it is unlikely that such a strategy could serve for many concepts in the natural environment, which are highly complex and extensive, nevertheless rote memory may serve as one means by which subjects categorize stimuli.

The capacity of pigeons to form categories based on rote memory was demonstrated in a study by Vaughan and Greene (1984). In their experiment (which is also discussed in Chapter 14), pigeons were shown photographic slides on a small projection screen located in the test box. Each slide contained either 1 or 2 random squiggles that had been hand-drawn on the photographic negative. In all, 80 pairs of slides were used, one slide in each pair serving as the S+ and the other as the S−. Although it took nearly 1,000 sessions of training, the birds discriminated accurately. That is, they reliably remembered which slide was S+ for each of the 80 pairs.[21] Because both the shape of the squiggles and their designation as S+ or S− events were entirely random, there is no possibility that the sets of images formed a natural category. No criteria whatsoever could be cited as a basis for membership in either the S+ or the S− classes, yet the pigeons actually learned category membership for hundreds of exemplars. The logical conclusion is that they did so on the basis of rote memory alone.

Feature Theory.

Members of conceptual categories, at least in the natural environment, are more likely to share certain defining features. Thus, to identify a given stimulus as a member of a category, subjects must compare the features of the stimulus in question to those that are typical of the category. Some researchers argue that they do this by comparing the stimulus to an average exemplar, termed a **prototype.** For instance, when humans think of the category "bird," they typically visualize a robin. When judging whether, say, a chicken is also a bird, people implicitly compare the image in question to the prototype or average exemplar, the robin. If there is a good fit, then the stimulus is included as a member of the category.

The **feature theory** of categorization suffers from two important problems. First, the defining or relevant features are often unclear, especially in the natural environment, where objects are highly complex. Consider the category mentioned previously—namely, "house." Houses come in so many shapes and sizes that providing a list of critical defining features seems highly unlikely. Second, not all features have equal status as defining properties of the category. Some are more important, or more heavily weighted, than others.

Polymorphous Concepts.

A modification of feature theory claims that conceptual categories are polymorphous, and thus, membership is probabilistic. **Polymorphous concepts** are categories for which the exemplars may take many shapes; no single feature or set of features is essential. Exemplars contain some of the relevant features that define the category, but they do not necessarily share all, or even the same, features. Assume, for instance, that there are seven hypothetical features relating to a category: A, B, C, D, and X, Y, Z. Stimuli that have at least two of the first four (A, B, C, or D) are designated as positive exemplars. Stimuli having two or more negative features (X, Y, or Z) are not part of the category. Thus, valid exemplars of the category would be ABX, ACY, BCZ, and so forth. Examples that would not be valid members of the class would be XYA, XZB, and so forth.

Exemplars of the category, therefore, do not have to possess all of the features, or even particular features, to be valid; they need to contain only two of the positive features. This leads to the interesting situation where two exemplars are positive instances of the same category, yet they are entirely nonoverlapping in their list of features. For example, both ABX and CDY qualify as exemplars because two of their three features are drawn from the set of positive characteristics, yet they do not share any features at all.

Many studies show that animals categorize artificially constructed stimuli on this basis. For example, Jitsumori (1993) examined whether pigeons could learn arrays of symbols on colored backgrounds.[22] The eight stimuli differed along three dimensions. The symbols could be either black or white, the shapes could be either circles or triangles, and the background color could be either green or red.[23] Examples are shown in Figure 15-7.

One value of each feature was arbitrarily designated as positive, the other as negative. Targets that contained any two positive features were designated as S+ cues, whereas targets with two negative features were S− exemplars. For example, if black, circle, and red were designated as positive features, then any of the four combinations that contained two of these would be an S+.[24]

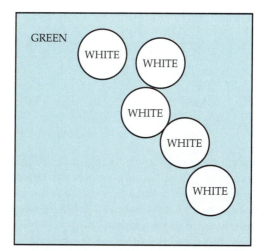

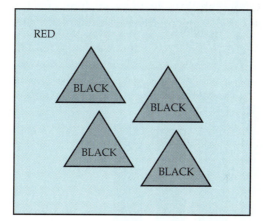

FIGURE 15-7. Representations of two examples of stimuli used to test the acquisition of a polymorphous category (after Jitsumori, 1993).

Subjects were given 60 trials per session, during which each stimulus was presented for about 30 seconds (the order of presentation was random). Pecking during an S+ target was reinforced on a VI schedule; pecking during an S− was not. Training continued until 90% of the responses on 3 consecutive sessions was given to positive stimuli. Results showed that the birds acquired the category within a maximum of 105 sessions.

Once the pigeons had mastered this task, a transfer test was given. Here, subjects were tested for their ability to transfer their knowledge about the category to novel exemplars. These stimuli included the same features as those used during original training, but they differed in other respects (for instance, in terms of the number of symbols and their position on the background). It is important to note that tests of concept acquisition, to be convincing, require the use of novel stimuli. This ensures that the subject's reaction is not based simply on rote memorization of slides seen previously. If subjects respond to *new* stimuli in the same manner as they responded to the training stimuli, performance must be due to the presence of a conceptual category rather than simply good memory for those stimuli already experienced. Although the subjects had never seen these stimuli, identifying them as S+ and S− exemplars should be possible if, indeed, the rules of category membership had been learned earlier.

The results for one bird are shown in Figure 15-8. Both strong responding for positive instances (identified by uppercase letters) and little or no responding for the negative S− values (lowercase letters) were found. Thus, pigeons accurately categorized novel stimuli on the basis of the rules of the polymorphous category learned previously.[25]

Although none of the subjects in this study showed superior responding to the target containing all three features, such an effect has been shown by Aydin and Pearce (1994).[26] Here, the best exemplar, called the "prototype,"

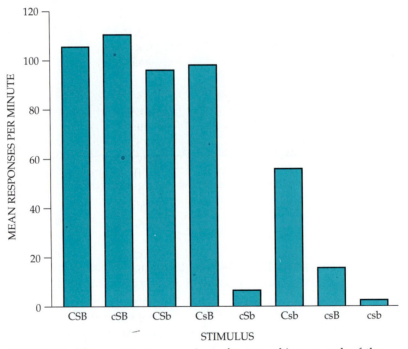

FIGURE 15-8. Mean responses per minute for one subject on each of the eight novel stimulus combinations used in the first transfer test (C = positive symbol color; c = negative symbol color; S = positive symbol shape; s = negative symbol shape; B = positive background color; b = negative background color) (after Jitsumori, 1993).

which contained all possible features, elicited even stronger responding than did targets containing only two features.

Natural Concepts

In contrast to well-defined artificial categories, such as the one just described, **natural categories** are polymorphous categories that appear in the natural environment. Like all polymorphous categories, they often defy clear definition; they have fuzzy boundaries. Consider the concept "furniture." Chairs and tables immediately come to mind, but other items, such as lamps or rugs, are also considered by most people to be items of furniture, even though they bear little resemblance to chairs and tables. Similarly, both a fishing net and a fishing lure are used to catch fish (they both belong to the same conceptual category of "items used to catch fish"), yet there is virtually no similarity between them.

Natural categories may involve different levels of abstraction.[27] These are described in the following sections.

Open-Ended Categories.

Open-ended categories are classes of objects or stimuli that have unlimited membership. One example is the concept "oak leaf." This is an open-ended category, in that the number of exemplars of the category is, for all practical purposes, infinite. Presumably, the mechanism for identifying members of such an open-ended category is based on some kind of feature analysis, such as that described previously.

There are many examples in which pigeons have used open-ended categories. One was from a study by Bhatt, Wasserman, Reynolds, and Knauss (1988).[28] A 7- × 7-centimeter viewing screen was located on the front wall of the test chamber, behind which was a slide projector. Near each corner of the screen was a response key. Eighty colored slides were randomly projected onto the viewing screen, and subjects could earn food if they pecked the correct key. Twenty of the slides depicted cats in various positions; 20 showed flowers; 20 slides portrayed automobiles; and 20 pictured chairs. The slides within each category differed in a variety of ways, including the size, color, orientation, and context of the object. In some cases, the object was even partially obscured.

During the learning phase, 10 slides from each category were presented each day for 60 days. The subjects' task was to identify the category to which the slide belonged by pecking the designated key (one key for each category).[29] In Phase 2, subjects were given a transfer test. Here, the remaining 10 new slides in each category were used, along with the original training slides.

The results are shown in Figure 15-9. The left side of Figure 15-9 shows the development of the open-ended categories during acquisition. Because there were four different classifications (cats, flowers, automobiles, and chairs), the chance performance is 25%. By the end of training, subjects, on the average, were responding at almost 70% correct. The right side of the figure shows the test performance.

Photograph showing the apparatus used by Bhatt, Wasserman, Reynolds, and Knauss (1988) to study concept formation in pigeons.
Courtesy of American Scientist *(May-June 1995 edition, page 248, figure 2).*

Animals were nearly as good at identifying new instances of the categories as old. Performance averaged about 58% correct for the new items, well above the chance level. This study therefore shows that pigeons form natural concepts with little difficulty. Interestingly, no difference was found in the pattern of errors committed for natural (flowers and cats) versus artificial (automobiles and chairs) concepts. For example, when making errors, the pigeons did not respond to the key appropriate to a cat when given a flower stimulus, nor did they tend to identify an automobile by pecking at the key appropriate to chairs.

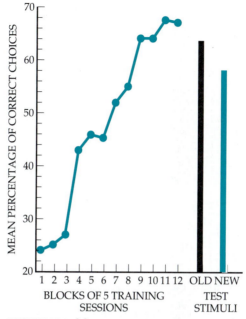

FIGURE 15-9. Mean percentage of correct responses on twelve 5-day blocks of training trials during acquisition (left panel), and mean percentage of correct responses, averaged for two test sessions for the old and the new stimuli (after Bhatt, Wasserman, Reynolds, & Knauss, 1988).

The notion that successful categorization of novel stimuli was accomplished on the basis of a conceptual generalization was further supported by Wasserman, Kiedinger, and Bhatt (1988).[30] Here, half of the pigeons were given the same task as described in the preceding study (the pigeons were reinforced for identifying each slide on the basis of the category to which it belonged). The other half, the pseudocategory subjects, performed a similar task, but their slides were divided into four arbitrary groupings, consisting of equal numbers of cats, automobiles, flowers, and chair slides.

These results are shown in Figure 5-10. Performance differed significantly between groups. The pseudocategory group improved to only about 42% correct by the end of training.[31] Performance by subjects that sorted stimuli according to the natural categories (as identified in human language by the terms "cat," "flower," "chair," and "automobile"), however, was good. In summary, both experiments by Wasserman and colleagues indicate that pigeons are capable of forming complex, open-ended categories. Although it is impossible to say precisely what features were analyzed by the pigeons,

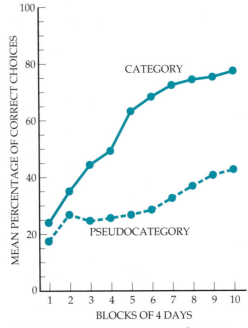

FIGURE 15-10. Mean percentage of correct responses, as a function of ten 4-day blocks of training for the category and the pseudo-category groups (after Wasserman, Kiedinger, & Bhatt, 1988).

presumably, they were the same features that humans detect when looking at these slides.[32]

Rather than discriminating the presence versus absence of an object, some experiments have shown that pigeons learn about the properties of objects. For example, birds are able to master the concept of symmetry.[33] Similarly, Dittrich and Lea (1993) demonstrated that pigeons acquire the concept of motion. Here, videotaped sequences were projected onto a viewing screen. The scenes had been recorded in the bird's aviary, so all subjects were familiar with the background. Forty scenes of pigeons moving across a ledge were randomly mixed with 40 identical scenes containing no motion. The motion and static scenes were identical in every respect except for the fact that the former involved motion cues, whereas the latter did not.

During acquisition, pigeons earned a reward by pecking during the S+; during S− presentations, no reward was ever presented.[34] For some birds, 20 motion scenes served as the S+ condition, whereas for other subjects, 20 static scenes were the S+ cues. In addition, some animals received pseudo-category training, in which 20 randomly chosen scenes from both categories formed an arbitrary class of stimuli. Finally, subjects were given a test using the 20 motion and 20 static scenes not used previously. Correct classification of these novel scenes on the basis of motion constituted evidence of the concept. The measure of performance, called the "discrimination ratio," was the total number of responses executed during the S+, divided by the total S+ and S− responses (thus, a ratio of 0.5 indicates that the subject responded equally to the S+ and S− cues, whereas a ratio greater than 0.5 indicates more responding to the S+ than to the S−).

Test results are shown in Figure 15-11. Although pigeons in the pseudo-category performed only at the chance level, birds in the other two conditions were significantly more accurate; they responded significantly more during the S+ than during the S− presentations. The data therefore suggest that pigeons are capable of discriminating natural scenes on the basis of whether they contain motion cues, and of identifying new instances on these grounds.

Finally, several experiments demonstrated that pigeons conceptualize abstract properties of complex stimuli, correctly generalizing to new examples. In one study by Porter and Neuringer (1984), subjects were reinforced for pecking a key during a 2-minute episode of music composed by Bach. Examples of music composed by Stravinsky, a modern composer, served as the S− cue. Not only were the birds able to learn this discrimination, but they also generalized to music written by other composers of the relevant time period. For example, the birds correctly identified music selections by Scarlatti, another Baroque composer, and distinguished them from episodes of music by Eliot Carter, a composer from the modern era.

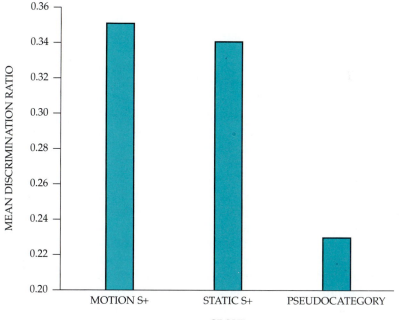

FIGURE 15-11. Mean discrimination ratio for each condition on the concept identification test (after Dittrich & Lea, 1993).

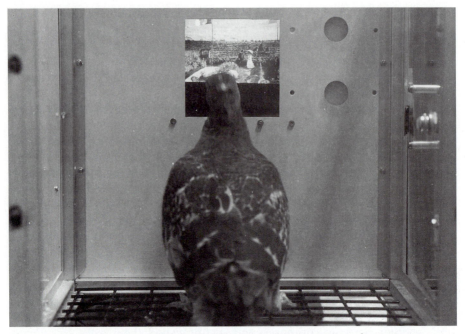

Photograph showing the apparatus used to study discrimination of paintings in pigeons (after Watanabe, Sakamoto, and Wakita, 1995).
Courtesy of Professor S. Watanabe, Department of Psychology, Keio University, Tokyo.

In a similar kind of study, Watanabe, Sakamoto, and Wakita (1995) showed that pigeons are able to categorize paintings. First, pigeons were reinforced for discriminating paintings by Monet, a French Impressionist, from those by Picasso, a more modern artist. During the test, subjects correctly identified other paintings by Monet and Picasso. Furthermore, paintings by Cezanne and Renoir, two other French Impressionist painters, were identified as being similar to those by Monet, whereas pictures by Braque and Matisse, more modern artists, were classified with those by Picasso.

Higher-Level Concepts.

An important paper by Lea (1984) distinguished between open-ended categorization, as described previously, and **higher-level concepts**.[35] According to Lea, acquisition of an open-ended category reflects concept discrimination in which a subject develops its sense of which stimuli belong in the S+ category and which do not, on the basis of the *physical* characteristics of the stimuli (although, as noted previously, the features themselves may not be at all obvious). Lea argues that higher-level concepts, in contrast, are different, in that more than physical feature analysis is used to generate categories.

According to Lea, "to say of a person that he or she has a certain concept is to say that he or she has some unique mental structure which is active when and only when an instance of that concept is presented in the external, physical environment."[36] The identity of this "unique mental structure" is not clear, although it may be a special physiological structure in the brain, or a learned connection (see the following discussion). Either way, Lea argues that to demonstrate that an animal has a higher-level concept, one must show that the animal is not simply processing the physical features of the stimuli, regardless of how subtle those features are to human judges. Rather, an adequate test for higher-level concepts would involve training a subject to acquire a concept in the usual fashion (that is, provide S+ and S− instances), take one (or a small number) of the original S+ and S− cues and establish an entirely new response to them, and then, finally, test the subject's reaction to the remaining exemplars. If the subject developed a higher-level concept—that is, was not simply using feature analysis as a basis for discriminating novel S+ from novel S− cues—then the subject should respond to *all* of the exemplars with the same reaction that it most recently learned to only two of them (because all of the exemplars would be members of the same higher-level category).

Such a test was conducted by Bhatt and Wasserman (1989). The apparatus and procedure were similar to those described previously—namely, a viewing screen with four response keys at each corner, and 20 slides each of cats, flowers, automobiles, and chairs. Twelve slides from each category were used during original acquisition. Reassignment training then began. Here, pigeons were trained to peck a different key from the one that had been correct originally for one stimulus from each of the four categories. This training continued until each subject performed at 70% or better on two consecutive sessions. In Phase 3, birds were tested, using the remaining stimuli not used during the reassignment phase. Performance was consistent with original training, although, for some animals, choices that were not correct were consistent with the response taught during reassignment training. Overall, then, the results did not provide compelling support for Lea's theory because the reassignment training did not cause subjects to respond to all of the exemplars on the basis of reassignment training.

Although this study did not provide the evidence demanded by Lea's theory, other results are more promising. Vaughan (1988), for example, trained pigeons to discriminate 20 S+ slides from 20 S− slides. In Phase 2, the reinforcement contingencies were reversed; S− slides were now the S+ cues; former S+ slides were now S− cues. A second reversal was then made, followed by a third, a fourth, and so on. Although the accuracy of performance was adversely affected on the first reversal, subjects began to respond appropriately later even after only a few slides had been presented. In other words, continuous reversals eventually produced correct performance even when only a few exemplars had been presented. This study, therefore, shows that the pigeons viewed these sets of slides as being equivalent (all of them involving the same reinforcement contingency), rather than just perceptually similar.[37]

Abstract Relations.

There is a conceptual level of organization above even the level of a higher-order concept. Herrnstein (1990) argues that the highest level of conceptualization involves knowledge of the **abstract relations** among objects.[38] Exemplars of a category may be members by virtue of their *relationship* to members of another category. For example, they may be uniformly larger or smaller, brighter or dimmer, heavier or lighter. Are animals able to discriminate objects on the basis of their abstract relationships?[39]

Support for the ability to discriminate on this basis comes from studies using a matching or oddity procedure. In the former case, subjects match a comparison stimulus to a sample. If the subject matches two *novel* stimuli on the basis of a similarity in their relations, despite the fact that the stimuli do not look alike or resemble those used in training, then the animal has categorized on the basis of abstract relations. In the oddity procedure, a subject identifies a new stimulus as being different from those in a set of stimuli, based on that animal's sense of the concept "different." Again, if new stimuli are excluded because they conform to the same abstract rule about membership, then the subject has responded on the basis of an abstract relation.

An interesting demonstration of the pigeons' ability to solve matching and oddity problems was a study by Wright and Delius (1994).[40] The apparatus was a plastic tray divided into three compartments. Each compartment contained a shallow ceramic dish filled with approximately half an inch of gravel. Pigeons were first taught to forage for seeds by scratching and displacing the gravel. This kind of foraging activity is common among birds and was therefore learned quite easily.

During acquisition, the tray was attached to the pigeon's home cage, and the lid that covered the center dish was removed. The pigeon foraged in this sample for three seeds that had been buried. After consuming the second seed, the lids that covered the two comparison dishes (on the left and the right) were removed, and the pigeons then chose one of those dishes in which to forage. The correct dish contained buried seeds; the incorrect dish did not (if the subject chose the incorrect dish, a 30-second time-out period was given, after which the bird could make the correct choice). The sample dish contained one or two types of gravel—namely, a white coarse gravel and a finer, dark-gray gravel. One comparison dish contained the white, coarse gravel, whereas the other contained the fine, dark-gray gravel. One group of birds was reinforced for matching the type of gravel (matching problem), and the other group was rewarded for choosing the kind of gravel that did not match the sample (oddity problem).

In summary, the experiment involved presenting one type of gravel as a sample, and then giving subjects a choice between both types. Accurate matching was demonstrated if the subject chose the comparison having the same type of gravel as the sample. Accurate oddity performance occurred when the subject chose the gravel that did not match the sample.

Following acquisition, all subjects were tested using novel stimuli. Here, various types of gravel were used, including gravel having the same texture but a different color, gravel colored in the same way but with a different texture, and gravel that contained small stones and beads. The results are shown in Figure 15-12. The pigeons performed these tasks quite readily. After about 11 trials, they were accurate more than 75% of the time (well above the 50% chance level).

Thus, the study showed acquisition of the relational concept.[41] Although the pigeons had a sense of the abstract relations "same" and "different," performance did not transfer to the new stimuli. That is, when the subjects were given novel forms of gravel, performance remained at about chance level.[42] In short, this experiment showed that pigeons are capable of learning oddity and identity relationships, but do not show positive transfer to novel stimuli.[43]

A somewhat different strategy for showing discrimination on the basis of abstract relations was used by Neiworth and Wright (1994).[44] Rhesus monkeys were given 12 examples of 18 different categories (apples, bottles, buckets, gloves, and so forth). For each pair, the subject's task was to indicate whether the two members belonged to the same category or to a different category. The monkeys readily learned this task and were able to transfer the concept of same–different to new items, despite the fact that objects physically looked different (for example, were larger or shown in different orientation).

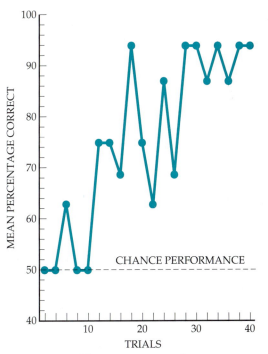

FIGURE 15-12. Mean percentage of correct responses as a function of two-trial blocks for the oddity and the matching subjects combined (after Wright & Delius, 1994).

Given the results described previously for pigeons and rhesus monkeys, it appears that nonhuman primates fare better on oddity and identity problems than do birds. The former are able to transfer the concept of same–different to new exemplars, whereas the latter are not.[45] Recent work, however, shows this to be false. Pigeons are able to solve matching and oddity problems, as shown by Wasserman, Hugart, and Kirkpatrick-Steger (1995).[46] Thirty-two 4 × 4 arrays of visual stimuli were created using computer icons. Examples are shown in Figure 15-13.[47] Half of the stimuli contained arrays of the same item; the other 16 contained arrays of different icons.

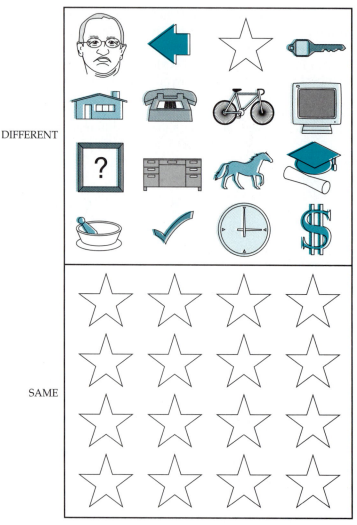

FIGURE 15-13. Sample stimuli of same and different arrays of icons used to test the same/different concept in pigeons (after Wasserman, Hugart, & Kirkpatrick-Steger, 1995).

The pigeon's task was to peck one key when a "same" array was presented, but to peck a different key when an array of "different" icons was given. The transfer test involved new composite stimuli, 16 "same" and 16 "different." Furthermore, the stimuli used on the test were constructed with novel icons; the subjects had never encountered them before. Thus, correctly categorizing the new displays as involving same or different icons must be based on the use of the same–different concept, not on the basis of having seen the icons previously. Results supported the notion that pigeons are able to form the concept of same–different. Correct responding to these new test items occurred on 71% of the presentations. Thus, many nonhuman species, including pigeons, form higher-level conceptual categories based on the abstract relations among objects.

Finally, Herrnstein, Vaughan, Mumford, and Kosslyn (1989) studied whether pigeons can learn a concept involving spatial arrangements—for instance, whether one stimulus is inside or outside another. Subjects were shown patterns containing an enclosed figure and a dot. They had to indicate whether the dot was inside or outside the figure. Good performance was shown, provided that the task was initially made easy.[48]

Mediated Generalization.

If, as Lea (1984) claims, true higher-level concepts, including abstract relations, require something more than simple feature detection based on physical characteristics, then how, in principle, are animals able to acquire concepts? Stated differently, if stimuli are not physically similar in some way, how is it possible to classify them as being members of the same category? One answer is that membership in a category may be based on the notion of **mediated generalization** or **learned stimulus equivalence.**

An experiment by Wasserman, DeVolder, and Coppage (1992) illustrates this concept. The apparatus and initial procedure were similar to those described previously. The apparatus included a viewing screen with four response keys at each corner, referred to as Responses 1, 2, 3, and 4. The general procedure is shown in Figure 15-14.

Original acquisition			Reassignment training			Test	
Concept	RF key	No-RF key	Concept	RF key	No-RF key	Concept	RF key
1	1	2	1	3	4		
2	1	2				2	3 & 4
3	2	1	3	4	3		
4	2	1				4	3 & 4

FIGURE 15-14. Schematic diagram of the procedure used to study mediated generalization (after Wasserman, DeVolder, & Coppage, 1992).

In Phase 1, subjects were trained to identify 12 different exemplars from each of four categories (flowers, people, chairs, and automobiles), with stimuli being combined into larger aggregate groups. For example, the top right key (Response 1) was reinforced when a slide from Category 1 or 2 (say, flowers or people) was given; Response 2 was not rewarded. The reverse was true for the other aggregate category. Pecking the bottom left key (Response 2) was correct when given an example from Category 3 or 4 (automobiles or chairs); pecking or Response 1 gave no food reward. Slides in Categories 1 and 2 were thus functionally equivalent; similarly, stimuli in Categories 3 and 4 were equivalent in terms of the reinforcement contingencies.

In Phase 2, the response requirement for two of the categories was reassigned. Here, pigeons were trained to peck Response 3 when a member of Category 1 was shown (Response 4 was not rewarded), and Response 4 when an exemplar from Category 3 was given (Response 3 was not rewarded). Finally, subjects were tested with examples from the nonreassigned categories. The question was whether subjects would respond to the nonreassigned stimuli (Categories 2 and 4) in the same way that they most recently responded to the reassigned stimuli (Categories 1 and 3), based on the fact that categories in each pair (1 and 2, and 3 and 4) had become functionally equivalent in Phase 1. In other words, would a subject identify an exemplar from Category 2 as being similar to an exemplar from Category 1 because both had been part of a larger unit during Phase 1?

The results showed significant transfer to exemplars in Categories 2 and 4, based on the reassignment training in Phase 2. As shown in Figure 15-15, transfer was significantly above the 50% chance level for all categories. According to the authors, "Merely by being associated with a common response in the first step, classes of perceptually dissimilar stimuli, like cars and chairs, appear to amalgamate into a new category of functionally equivalent stimuli. Thus, requiring a new response to be performed to only one of these two stimulus classes in the second step transfers to the other stimulus class in the third step."[49]

In summary, higher-order concepts may be formed because the members of the conceptual class trigger an equivalent representation. Such functional equivalence does not have to be based on physical similarity. To illustrate the notion of mediated generalization, Wasserman, DeVold, and Coppage (1992) provide a useful analogy. Fishing poles and basketballs do not look alike in any respect, nor do they perform the same function. However, they are members of the same conceptual class (sporting goods) because each is independently associated with sporting-goods stores. The category "sporting goods" is not based on feature analysis, but rather on a higher-order conceptual grouping.

INTERIM SUMMARY

Well-defined categories have specific criteria for membership; ill-defined, or fuzzy, categories do not. One theory of classification is that animals form categories by rote memorizing of individual members. The feature

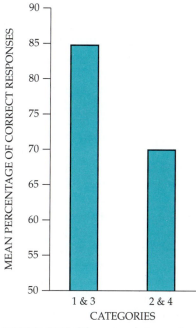

FIGURE 15-15. Mean percentage of correct responses for the reassigned (Categories 1 and 3) and the nonreassigned (Categories 2 and 4) stimuli (after Wasserman, DeVolder, & Coppage, 1992).

theory claims that subjects compare the physical features of the stimulus in question with those that are typical of the category. Often, this is done by comparing the stimulus with an average exemplar, called the "prototype." A polymorphous concept is one for which exemplars may take many shapes; no single feature or set of features is essential. Polymorphous categories may be well-defined, or they may be natural, having fuzzy boundaries. Many studies show that rats and pigeons are able to form polymorphous categories and to judge novel stimuli according to the category. Natural categories involve different levels of abstraction. Open-ended categories include an infinite number of members (examples are "flowers" and "automobiles"). Nonhuman animals have no difficulty learning these classifications. Higher-level concepts are even more abstract, in that membership is not based on a physical characteristic of the stimuli. According to Lea, a test for a higher-level concept involves training with exemplars, establishing a new response to only one or two of the exemplars, and then testing the remaining exemplars. If the subject had developed a higher-level concept, then it should react to all of the stimuli in the same way as it reacted to the one or two that were reassigned. This study has been done, but transfer to new stimuli was not shown. Abstract relations is a conceptual level of organization above that of a higher-order concept. Stimuli are members of a category by virtue of their relationship to other exemplars. These have been shown in pigeons, which solve oddity and matching problems, and in nonhuman primates, which solve same and different categorization problems. Higher-level concepts and abstract relations are formed because of learned stimulus equivalence (mediated generalization). That is, the exemplars are members of the same class because each is independently associated with a common representation.

REASONING AND INFERENCE

Reasoning and inference are closely related to concept formation. Historically, humans have been considered to be superior to other species in having an ability to think and reason. The work on higher-order conceptual behavior suggests that this egocentric point of view is no longer tenable. Evidence for reasoning and inference in animals is common. Indeed, animals show an ability to make inferences even when they perform simple conditioned reactions. For example, a conditioned response triggered by the presence of a discriminative stimulus implies an inferential judgment of the sort, "if the red S+ is on, then peck the key." Similarly, a Pavlovian CR suggests a basic form of reasoning, such as, "if the tone CS is sounded, then the food US will soon follow." Nonhuman species also exercise a higher level of reasoning than is displayed by a simple conditioned reflex, however. This section describes several areas of research that bear on the characteristics of the reasoning process in animals.

Relational Learning

One thing that characterizes the reasoning process is the ability to respond relationally to stimuli.

Analogies.

For example, chimpanzees are able to solve analogies. **Analogical reasoning** takes the following form: A is to A', as B is to B'. An example of an analogy would be "a puppy is to a dog, as a kitten is to a cat." Solving analogies is interesting and important because it reveals something about the thinking process—namely, that the subject is able to transfer knowledge of the *relationship* between two items (such as puppy and dog) to a different set of items that are physically dissimilar (kitten and cat).

Gillan, Premack, and Woodruff (1981) studied a chimpanzee named Sarah. Over a period of 6 weeks, Sarah was given training trials in which a tray containing several plastic items was presented. As shown in Figure 15-16, the items differed in shape, size, color, and the presence of a distinctive dot mark.

Two kinds of problems were used. In the type I problems (top half of Fig-

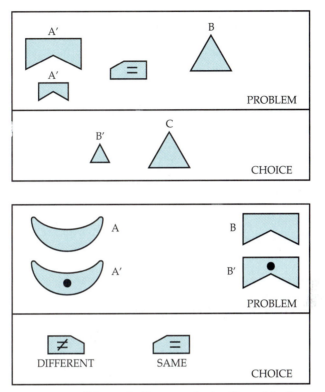

FIGURE 15-16. Schematic diagram of stimuli used in the analogical reasoning task with Sarah (after Gillan, Premack, & Woodruff, 1981).

ure 15-16), Sarah was given the stimuli that corresponded to A, A' and B, and then was asked to indicate which of two stimuli (B' or C) was the correct answer (the symbol placed between the two sets was known by Sarah to mean "equals"). In type II problems (bottom half of figure), Sarah was given A, A', B, and B', and then was given a choice of two symbols, one meaning "equals" and the other meaning "different." Here, Sarah's task was to indicate whether the analogy was correct as stated.

Each trial was administered individually by positioning the symbols on a tray, with the alternative choices placed below the symbols. Once the items were in position, Sarah was summoned, and the experimenter left the room. Thus, Sarah's performance could not have been inadvertently influenced by the experimenter's presence; that is, correct performance would reflect Sarah's ability to reason analogically on her own.

Overall, Sarah was very proficient at this task. On type I problems, 75% of the trials were correct; on type II trials, Sarah chose the correct symbol 72.2% of the time.[50] In both cases, the level of accuracy was well above chance performance. Thus, one form of inductive reasoning—namely, solving analogies—has been demonstrated in chimpanzees. Other forms of logical reasoning, especially in other species, remain unexplored.

Transitivity.

One of the hallmarks of intelligence in the ability to use the rules of logic in solving syllogisms (see Chapter 2). One rule is **transitivity.** When a subject responds transitively to a set of stimuli, the subject infers the relationship between two items, based on the relationship between two different items. More specifically, if a subject is given the sequence A > B and B > C, then transitivity occurs if the subject perceives that A > C. Although the relationship between A and C is never presented directly, it is inferred logically from the relationships between A and B, and between B and C. The two premises, A > B, and B > C, logically imply that the conclusion is true. Failure to respond transitively to this kind of problem indicates that the formal rules of inferential logic have not been followed.

A concrete example of transivity is the following:

1. Jean is shorter than David.
2. Jean is taller than Elizabeth.
3. Who is the tallest—Jean, David, or Elizabeth?

If a subject answers, David, then transitivity is demonstrated. The correct conclusion is reached, even though no direct information about the relationship between David and Elizabeth is given.

Maintaining transivity is characteristic of adult human thinking. For centuries, animals were believed to be incapable of such thought. The noted developmental psychologist Piaget (1928) claimed that even children under the age of 7 years were incapable of using this form of logical reasoning. Not only have preschool children been shown to use transitive reasoning, but also other species have, as well, including chimpanzees, squirrel monkeys, rats, and even pigeons.[51]

For example, a study of pigeons by Steirn, Weaver, & Zentall (1955) used five colored key lights, designated as A (red), B (yellow), C (white), D (blue), E (green). Four pairs of stimuli were given in a random order over the training session ("+" identifies the rewarded stimulus, "−" indicates the nonrewarded stimulus in each pair). The pairs were A+B−, B+C−, C+D−, and D+E−.[52] Training continued until subjects were 90% correct over two consecutive sessions. Animals were then given a single 96-trial test session with the B and the D stimuli.

The issue was whether the pigeons would respond in a transitive fashion by pecking at B rather than D. Responding to B had been reinforced when presented with C, but B and D had never occurred together. The mean percentage of trials on which the birds made the correct choice was 87.5%. Such performance is significantly above the chance level. In other words, even though the subjects had never been taught to choose B relative to D, the birds did so, based on having learned the relationships between B and C, and C and D, and then making the correct inference about B and D.

As Davis (1992a) commented, "It is both comforting and surprising to suppose that different species might approach transitive inference in the same manner. The comfort lies in finding such obvious evidence of a continuum of mental ability. The surprise comes from acknowledging the existence of large neurological differences between humans . . . and chimpanzees, monkeys, rats, and pigeons. It is hard to imagine that such [brain] tissue or organizational differences would not result in cognitive disparities. If different species are truly approaching logical transitivity in the same way then, putting the case crudely, either rats much be stretching their abilities to the breaking point or children must be barely using theirs."[53]

Cognitive Development

Piaget also claimed that humans go through discrete stages of intellectual development.[54] The earliest stage, which he called the "sensorimotor period," extends from birth to about age 2 years. It is divided into six phases. Reflex actions predominate during the first few months of life, followed by visually guided manual activity. Here, a baby shows increasing interest in the external world and in how its behavior affects objects in the environment. By the end of the first year, children develop incipient cognitive skills such as anticipation, goal direction, and imitative and play behaviors. In Phase 5 of the sensorimotor stage, from approximately 1 to 1½ years of age, children show curiosity, and their interaction with the environment is more differentiated. They manipulate objects, such as mobiles or toys. Finally, during Phase 6, from about 18 to 24 months of age, children develop the ability to recognize objects by means of symbols and to act intelligently with respect to these symbols. For instance, children develop the ability to differentiate between a symbol or word and its referent, and are capable of deferred imitation (imitated actions that are not reproduced until a later time). Symbolic play, in which children use imaginary objects in their play, also appears during this critical time.

Object Permanence.

Children also develop their sense of objects, and, in particular, **object permanence** during the sensorimotor stage of development. By the time they have completed Phase 6 of this stage, they are able to infer the location of an object that has been invisibly displaced to a new position. For example, if a child is shown a coin, which is then hidden by the experimenter's hand under a cloth, and the hand is withdrawn without the coin, then the child typically searches under the cloth. The searching behavior suggests that the child knows the coin's location, even though physical evidence for its being placed there is not available. Such object permanence is essential for developing the ability to solve abstract problems.

If object permanence reflects the onset of higher-level cognitive processing, then to what extent do nonhuman species display this talent? Consistent with the work described previously on concept acquisition, many studies have shown that nonhuman primates, dogs and cats, and even birds, show forms of object permanence.[55] One study, by Wood, Moriarty, Gardner, and Gardner (1980), compared object-permanence tasks in children and chimpanzees.[56] These authors used 15 separate tasks that were designed to assess infant development.[57] Two chimpanzees and three human infants (aged 8, 18, and 24 months) were the subjects. A variety of toys were used as objects, including some beads, a whistle, doll, ball, and key. An object was invisibly displaced to a new location in a plastic container. Then it was covered with a washcloth.

Each subject was tested individually on 15 displacement tasks until it completed the appropriate action within 1 minute on three successive sessions. Tasks 1 and 2 involve the ability to visually follow an object; Tasks 3 through 7 involve finding an object that had been hidden; Tasks 8 through 15 are more complex, in that they involve both the displacement and the hiding of objects; Tasks 10 through 13 are similar to Tasks 4–7, except that the displacement of the object is done invisibly (the object is placed in the plastic container so that the subject cannot visibly see it being transported); the last two tasks are the most complex.

The 15 tasks, and the corresponding behaviors that indicate task completion, are as follows:

Task 1 = following a slowly moving object through a 180-degree arc (behavior = follows object smoothly through complete arc)

Task 2 = noticing the disappearance of a slowly moving object (behavior = lingers with glance on point of disappearance, and returns glance to starting point after several presentations)

Task 3 = finding an object that is partially hidden (behavior = obtains the object)

Task 4 = finding an object that is completely covered (behavior = pulls cover off and obtains object)

Task 5 = finding an object completely covered when there are two covers present (behavior = searches for object where it is last hidden)

Task 6 = finding an object completely hidden under two covers alternately (behavior = searches directly under correct screen)

Task 7 = finding a completely covered object when there are three covers present (behavior = searches correctly under each of the covers)

Task 8 = finding an object after three successive visible displacements (behavior = searches directly under the last screen in path)

Task 9 = finding an object that is wrapped in one cover and then covered by a second and a third cover (behavior = removes all screens and obtains object)

Task 10 = finding an object following one invisible displacement (behavior = checks the box and searches under the screen, and searches under the cover directly)

Task 11 = finding an object following one invisible displacement with two covers (searches directly under correct cover)

Task 12 = finding an object following one invisible displacement with two covers alternated (behavior = searches directly under correct cover)

Task 13 = finding an object following invisible displacement using three covers (behavior = searches directly under correct cover)

Task 14 = finding an object following a series of three invisible displacements (behavior = searches under all screens in the path in the order of hiding, and searches directly under the last screen in the path)

Task 15 = finding an object that the experimenter had invisible displaced under a cover, although the experimenter had continued to move the hands to the other covers as if concealing the object under one of them (behavior = searches systematically from the last screen back to the first)

The visual-pursuit behaviors in Tasks 1 and 2 were highly inconsistent, so the data were not scored. For the remaining tasks, however, there was a remarkable similarity and consistency between the chimps and the children. All subjects completed Tasks 3–7 within 3 sessions. The infants completed Tasks 8 and 9 within 3.7 sessions, on average, compared to 3 sessions for the chimpanzees. Search behavior following an invisible displacement—tasks 10 through 13—were accomplished within 4.3 sessions by the humans, and 4.0 sessions by the chimps. Tasks 14 and 15, however, were more difficult for all subjects. One child accomplished them in 3 sessions, and one chimp in 5.5 sessions, but the other subjects took more than 6. According to the authors, "The results showed similarities in the number of steps achieved, in the order and rate of achieving steps, and in detailed characteristics of searching behavior. The differences that appeared—in response latency and in the greater number of sessions that the oldest chimpanzee required to achieve criterion on the most advanced tasks—did not seem major."[58] In short, the course of cognitive development, as outlined by Piaget, appears to hold for humans and chimpanzees alike.

Although many people argue that mammals are the most intelligent forms of life, with primates and especially humans at the top of the intelligence hierarchy, this is not defensible in terms of the ability to maintain object permanence. Pepperberg and Funk (1990), for example, showed that various species of birds perform object permanence tasks nearly as easily as humans.[59] Here, the species were an African Grey parrot, an Illiger macaw, a parakeet, and a cockatiel. Various items were used, including seeds, grapes, peanuts, jelly beans, cherries, and slices of banana.[60] The items were hidden under crumpled newspaper, paper plates, bags, and measuring cups. All 15 tasks described previously were used in this study. They were administered by two experimenters—the owner and another person—to ensure that inadvertent visual prompts, such as staring at the location of a hidden object, would not be provided. The criterion of performance was also the same. All four birds performed these object-permanence tasks. Indeed, the number of sessions required to master these tasks was comparable to that shown by primates.

Conservation.

During what Piaget called the "preoperational period," which extends from ages 2 to 7 years, a child further develops the mental representations of objects and, importantly, develops language. However, children in this stage still have limitations. For example, they are unable to see processes as being reversible. It is not until the next period of development—namely, the period of concrete operations (ages 7 to 11)—that children begin fully to understand the manner in which operations are reversible.

One of the tests that illustrates a child's understanding of reversibility is the **conservation** test (see Figure 15–17). Imagine that a child sees two identical glasses containing the same amount of water (top portion of figure). Then, while the child is looking, the water from Glass 2 is poured into a tall, thin beaker (bottom). Finally, the child is asked whether the two amounts are the same, or whether Glass 1 contains more water or less water than the beaker. A child younger than about 7 years of age typically says that the thin beaker contains more water than the glass. The reason is that the height of the surface of the water suggests that it contains a larger quantity. What the child fails to understand is that the shape of an object may change without its volume changing simultaneously.

An ability to recognize conservation of volume has been shown in species other than humans—namely, rhesus monkeys—by Pasnak (1979). The animals were trained in an apparatus identical to that used to study learning sets (see Chapter 13). Briefly, it contained a sliding tray mounted to the front of the monkey's cage. When the screen was raised, the tray was moved toward the cage, and the animal chose one of the two items. A correct choice resulted in the presentation of a small food reward. In Pasnak's experiment, many of

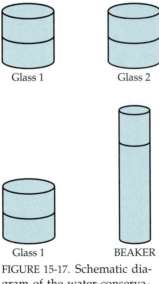

Glass 1   Glass 2

Glass 1   BEAKER

FIGURE 15-17. Schematic diagram of the water-conservation problem.

Photograph of flasks of colored fluid used to test children on the conservation problem.
Runk/Schoenberger/Grant Heilman Photography, Inc.

the stimuli were constructed out of playdough shaped as oblongs or as balls. Others were soda straws (which could be placed in a long single row), stacks of plastic spoons (which could be fanned out), blocks of wood (which could be rearranged into different configurations), stacks of sponge cubes (which could be rearranged to make a tower), and rubber bands (which could be made into a ring).

The subject was first shown two identical objects that were placed on the tray beyond reach. The experimenter than handled both objects in an identical fashion. On some trials, the experimenter added or removed a small amount of playdough. On other trials, the experimenter handled the objects and changed the shape of one (or both), without adding to or subtracting from them. For instance, the experimenter rolled a ball of playdough into the shape of a cylinder. To test the animal's response, the tray was positioned so that the objects were within reach, and the animal was allowed to pick one of the items. For one monkey, picking the changed object resulted in reward; the other subject was reinforced for picking the item that remained the same. After discrimination training of this sort, the subjects' ability to generalize to new problems was determined.

The monkeys were relatively good at discriminating objects that had been added to or subtracted from, especially when the problem involved stacks of discrete objects, such as wooden blocks. When playdough oblongs were flattened or rolled into a ball, performance was also quite accurate.[61] After about 13 to 15 training sessions, for example, the monkeys scored between 80% and 90% correct on these conservation problems. Thus, rhesus monkeys have the ability to recognize objects for which their shape or size has been changed.

INTERIM SUMMARY

Contemporary research shows that nonhuman animals have an ability to reason and to make inferences. One example is their ability to solve analogies, such as A is to A' as B is to B'. Another is that they follow the rule of logic called "transitivity." For example, if a subject is given A > B and B > C, then transitivity occurs when the subject perceives that A > C. Object permanence appears toward the end of the sensorimotor stage of development in humans. Nonhuman animals, including chimpanzees and birds, also show object permanence on a variety of tasks. Finally, conservation, which develops during the preoperational stage in humans, is also shown by nonhuman animals.

ANIMAL LANGUAGE

The work described up to this point documents the impressive ability by many species to form conceptual categories and to reason. Another important and salient cognitive system is language. Language is one of the distinctive features of human existence. Many consider it to be a species-typical potential, arguing that humans are the only kind of animal that possesses a complicated and flexible language.[62] From an ecological viewpoint, it is difficult to exaggerate its importance to our species as a means of coping with environmental demands.

Many species of animal have an elaborate system of communication. Honeybees communicate the location of food sources by performing a complicated dance.[63] Birds acquire songs that communicate a variety of messages (see Chapter 12). Other forms of communication include odor markings, behavioral displays related to mating or aggression, and utterances that attract mates or repel enemies. The major question, therefore, is not whether animals communicate with each other, but whether animals are capable of anything that approaches human language.[64]

What Is Language?

Human language is characterized by a number of qualities. Although a complete account of language is beyond the scope of this text, several of these qualities are mentioned. First, language has **semanticity**—the ability for words or symbols to have meaning. When a person says "here is a book," the term *book* is an arbitrary symbol that represents an object in the real world. Semanticity is not unique to human language. Much of the research described in previous chapters suggests that many species, including rats and pigeons, use symbols that evoke a representation of an object. In Pavlovian conditioning, CSs and USs evoke representations of stimuli in the real world. The representations or memories, not the actual sensory events produced by the stimuli, become associated (see Chapters 5 and 6). Similarly, various forms of animal communication show semanticity. For example, elements of the dance of the honeybee (direction of dance, number of vibrations per second) are symbolically linked to objects in the real world—namely, food sources.

A second characteristic of human language is **displacement.** This means that an individual is able to describe events or objects that are remote in time and place. Humans cannot point directly to, or experience, "my headache last Thursday," but they are able to refer to that event indirectly via language.

A third feature is **productivity.** Human language users are able to create an infinite number of sentences and thoughts, given a finite set of words, and to describe things yet unseen. This quality may be the most difficult to show in nonhuman animals. Consider the sentence "the green Martians had large antennae." This fanciful thought refers to objects never seen, and thus attests to the sense in which language allows humans to be infinitely productive in creating ideas. Although generating such sentences is routine for humans, getting other species to do the same is a daunting prospect.

Finally, language has **syntax.** This refers to the rules by which words combine into phrases, and phrases into sentences. A sentence must obey these rules to have meaning. Nonhuman animals must also display rules of syntax in their communications if they are to be judged as having humanlike language skills.

In deciding whether nonhuman species can learn a humanlike language, performance must be judged according to all of these characteristics. That is, animals must perform with respect to the meaning of symbols, not just react to symbols as discriminative stimuli the way a pigeon pecks a lighted S+ key. Similarly, animals must show correct syntax; otherwise the message conveyed by the symbols is meaningless. Finally, animals must shown flexibility and productivity; they must arrange symbols in appropriate and novel ways to convey new messages. If they do not, their communications show little beyond repetition of sentences learned by rote.

Language in Nonhuman Primates

Hayes (1951) reported the first major effort to teach language to a chimpanzee. Despite extensive speech training, the animal could utter no more than "mamma" and "cup." One of the reasons for this poor performance was the fact that chimpanzees do not have the vocal capacity to produce speech. Although humans have a species-specific mechanism that allows for speech production, nonhuman primates do not.[65]

Sign-Language Studies.

An entirely different approach used sign language. Some researchers speculated that chimpanzees could learn sign language because they are facile with their hands, and they were known to gesture to one another in the wild. Fortunately, hearing-impaired people had developed an elaborate system of sign language, called American Sign Language (Ameslan), and thus a well-developed set of hand symbols could be used in training the animals.

The first animal chosen for language training was Washoe, a young female chimpanzee.[66] For 4 years, Washoe spent all of her waking hours with a team of trainers, all of whom signed in Ameslan. They taught her symbols by reinforcing her with bits of food for making the correct gestures and by molding her hands into the appropriate sign. Some symbols were learned through observation. For example, Washoe learned to sign the symbol for "sweet" (which is simply touching the tip of the tongue and lower lip with the index and second finger extended from the hand) by observing the trainer perform it. In 4 years, Washoe learned about 130 symbols, considerably below the average human child's vocabulary but still fairly impressive for a chimp.

On several occasions, Washoe combined words using appropriate syntax. For example, she said "gimme sweet" and "come open" when she wanted to convey those particular messages. Lucy, another chimpanzee in the same training program, created several even more elaborate combinations. For example, Lucy's trainer consistently used two symbols, "water" and "melon," to refer to a "watermelon." Lucy devised her own set of signs, specifically the signs meaning "drink fruit" and, later, "candy fruit." On a different occasion, after eating a radish for the first time, Lucy signaled "cry hurt food." These novel combinations suggested that Lucy possessed the underlying cognitive components typically associated with human language (but see the following discussion of criticisms).

Synthetic-Language Studies.

Other projects on chimpanzee language took a different approach—namely, using concrete symbols, rather than gestures, to represent objects or actions. One chimp, Lana, for example, was taught by Rumbaugh (1977) to respond to symbols that were affixed to a computer keyboard.[67] By pressing the appropriate keys in the right sequence, Lana could convey various messages, which, in turn, caused the trainer to deliver rewards, praise, or attention. For example, pressing the symbols that stood for "please machine give juice" resulted in being given that reward.

Lana mastered numerous symbols for objects, colors, and actions. She was able to complete sentences based on their meaning and could reject incomplete sentences that were grammatically incorrect. Moreover, Lana created new names. For examples, her name for the fruit orange was expressed by pressing three computer keys; the symbol for "apple," the symbol for "which is," and the key that signified the color orange. In another instance, Lana called a cucumber "banana which is [the color] green." Lana even learned to identify objects by touch; that is, after the computer named the object, Lana would reach inside a box and retrieve the unseen object, recognizing it only by its feel.[68]

In another research program, led by Premack (1976), language was taught to a chimpanzee named Sarah by using small plastic chips to signify objects such as food rewards.[69] Sarah could convey her message by arranging the chips on a magnetic board.[70] On some occasions, the trainer placed various chips on the table, and Sarah was able to construct an appropriate message, such as "Mary give apple." On others, Sarah responded to an ordered set of chips by performing the correct task. Sarah mastered various concepts, such as "same" versus "different," and she learned the meaning of the word "on."[71] For example, she would place one color on top of another when told to do so, and she could arrange plastic symbols in the appropriate order when the trainer placed one color on another.

Do Apes Have Language?

Many psychologists strongly believe that chimpanzees possess at least some capacity for language, although admittedly not to the same extent as humans.[72] Others argue that the existing studies have failed to demonstrate in a convincing fashion a true facility for language among apes.[73] The issues are by no means clear; impressive evidence for language has been shown, but many researchers retain serious doubt.

One essential feature of language concerns the use of symbols or labels. Chimpanzees use arbitrary symbols similar to the way human language users employ words. The problem, however, is that we cannot determine unequivocally that these symbols have the same status in the chimp's cognitive system that words have in human language.[74] Simply showing an appreciation of the symbol's referent is insufficient. Even pigeons are able to associate a red light with food, but their pecking behavior surely does not mean that they use the red light symbolically in the same way that a human uses the word "food."

The work on category acquisition described previously supports the idea that chimpanzees use labels appropriately. For example, Sarah was trained with the sentence "brown color of chocolate" but she was never given these words in the presence of chocolate itself. During a test, Sarah was given four colored disks and asked to "take brown." Her performance was accurate, suggesting that she had understood the idea of the color brown from the reference to chocolate. Similarly, Savage-Rumbaugh, Rumbaugh, Smith, and Lawson (1980) trained two chimpanzees named Austin and Sherman to sort objects into two categories: food and tools. Later, these apes classified novel objects as being instances of the food and the tool categories.[75]

When a chimp places plastic or computer symbols in the correct sequence, its behavior implies that it understands the meaning of the sentence. This conclusion has been challenged, however, on the grounds that the behavior could be little more than a chain of conditioned reactions.[76] Pigeons, for example, can learn to peck a series of colored keys, despite the fact that the spatial location of the

Photograph of the chimp Lana responding to a specialized computer keyboard. The symbols on the keyboard represented various objects and commands.
UPI/Bettmann Newsphotos/Corbis

colors changes randomly.[77] Does this mean that the pigeons understand anything beyond the order in which the colors should be pecked? Does the syntactical order itself have any higher meaning, as would a sentence? Many doubt that it does. This point is important because, in language, the order of words is critical. The meaning of "the boy hit the ball" is entirely different from "the ball hit the boy."

Further criticism of the chimpanzee's ability to understand syntax came from work by Terrace (1979) with a chimp named Nim. Nim had been taught sign language but showed little facility for syntax. For example, when asking for a piece of orange, Nim signed, "give orange me give eat orange me eat orange give me eat orange give me you."[78] The authors concluded that although Nim signed many messages, it was difficult to verify that the sentences followed the rules of syntax.

Finally, the same criticism has been leveled in terms of the production of novel messages, which many believe provide strong support for language competency in chimps. Critics argue that even novel sentences do not unequivocally indicate higher-level symbolic functioning. For example, Washoe, upon seeing a swan, signed "water bird."[79] Washoe's trainer argued that the chimp was using "water" as an adjective, much in the way a human would use the word. However, the animal could simply have combined two symbols, "bird" and "water," that were associated with each other.[80] In other words, rather than describing the bird in a particular way (as being a "water bird"), Washoe may have simply used two well-known signs ("water" and "bird") at the same moment because both referents (the water and a bird) were present.

Are chimpanzees capable of learning language? The case is far from proven, although some research, especially that by Rumbaugh and Savage-Rumbaugh (1994) with Austin and Sherman, and with a bonobo chimpanzee named Kanzi, provides many provocative examples of language skills. Perhaps the best conclusion is "Though none will argue that any animal has the full capacity of humans for language, none should deny that at least some animals have quite impressive competencies for language skills."[81]

INTERIM SUMMARY

An important cognitive system is language, a distinctive ability shown by humans. Human language is characterized by semanticity (ability for symbols to stand for referents), displacement (ability to describe objects remote in time and place), productivity (ability to create an infinite number of messages, given a finite set of symbols), and syntax (rules for combining symbols). Language performance in nonhuman animals must be judged according to all of these characteristics. The first research to show progress in this area studied sign-language use in chimpanzees. On several occasions, subjects showed correct syntax, semanticity, and productivity. Synthetic-language studies allowed chimps to communicate via symbols on a computer keyboard or plastic chips. Impressive results in both cases were shown. Many doubt, however, that the results provide compelling evidence for use of humanlike language. For instance, it is not clear that the symbols have a status in the chimp's cognitive system comparable to the status that words have in human language. Use of correct syntax by chimps has been questioned, as have many examples of productivity.

ENDNOTES

1. See also Roberts and Church (1978).
2. Meck and Church (1982); Roberts (1982).
3. There are other kinds of relational techniques. Church and Deluty (1977), for instance, had subjects respond to one of two levers, based on the remembered duration of two stimuli. Similarly, Gibbon and Church (1981) used a time-left procedure in which the animals respond based on the difference between a remembered stimulus duration and a stimulus duration that is currently elapsing.

4. It is relatively easy for a pigeon to differentiate between stimuli that last, say, 1 versus 4 seconds, but much more difficult to distinguish between stimuli that last 31 and 34 seconds, even though the absolute difference is the same in each case; see Tarpy (1969). For a theory of relative timing, see Killeen and Weiss (1987).

5. See Church (1978); Roberts (1983); Roberts and Church (1978).

6. Church (1980).

7. See also Spetch and Wilkie (1983).

8. Color and duration were counterbalanced. Some animals pecked red after the long-duration stimulus (and blue after the shorter-duration cue), whereas the other subjects got the reverse training.

9. Church (1989) provides an excellent summary of timing theories. One category of theory includes behavioral explanations, which, according to Church, are atheoretical approaches to timing. These focus primarily on the psychophysical relationship between the conditions or treatments that affect timing and a subject's performance. Although Killeen and Fetterman (1988) refer to their theory of timing as a behavioral theory, it is unclear that it is behavioral in the sense that Church uses the term. Killen and Fetterman hypothesize that the timing clock moves subjects from one state to the next, causing various adjunctive (or mediating) behaviors, appropriate to the state, to be performed. These adjunctive behaviors, in turn, mediate temporal control; see also Fetterman and Killeen (1991, 1995); Killeen and Weiss (1987).

10. See Meck and Church (1987).

11. On the last few sessions, the subjects' drug state was reversed. Former placebo subjects now received either methamphetamine or haloperidol, whereas subjects that had received those drugs during original training got saline.

12. Drugs that affect other neurotransmitter systems are effective, too.

13. See Meck, Church, and Olton (1984).

14. The quantitative counterpart to Church's model is scalar-expectancy theory, developed by Gibbon (1977); see also Gibbon and Church (1984). Network models of timing have been proposed by Church and Broadbent (1992) and by Weardon and Doherty (1995).

15. Many of the biological agents that affect timing are thought to do so by means of altering the rate at which the pacemaker emits pulses. For a quantitative account of the pacemaker rate, see Bizo and White (1994).

16. Davis and Memmott (1982) reviewed this area of research and concluded that counting occurs only under a restricted set of conditions; it is a last-resort strategy; see Davis and Perusse (1988b). Other evidence, however, shows that rats readily count events (Capaldi & Miller, 1988a) and that the number of events composing a stimulus better predicts the subject's choice behavior than does the elapsed time of the stimulus; see Fetterman, Dreyfus, and Stubbs (1985).

17. Extinction was used during the first five test sessions. The procedure, however, was continued for an additional 10 days, during which reward was provided. Finally, after a 70-day interval, subjects were once again tested with all 10 sequences. The results described here are from the final test period.

18. See Fetterman (1993).

19. This study was based on an experiment by Meck and Church (1983); see also Meck, Church, and Gibbon (1985).

20. Roberts and Mitchell (1994). The mode-control model is a modification of an earlier model; see Meck, Church, and Gibbon (1985).

21. Other experiments in this paper used as many as 320 photographic images of outdoor scenes and found essentially the same level of accuracy.

22. See also Huber and Lenz (1993); Lea and Harrison (1978); von Feresen and Lea (1990); but see Lea, Lohmann, and Ryan (1993); Lea and Ryan (1990).

23. The specific symbols were black/circle/green, white/circle/green, black/triangle/green, white/triangle/green, black/circle/red, white/circle/red, black triangle/red, and white/triangle/red.

24. These included black/circle/red, black/circle/green, black/triangle/red, and white/circle/red.

25. Pigeons showed positive transfer even when the new stimulus contained only one positive feature, provided that one other positive feature had been replaced with a novel feature.

26. The notion of a prototype has often been used to explain how humans classify stimuli; see, for example, Reed (1972). Targets that come close to this average, or prototypical, stimulus are seen as instances of the category; but see Watanabe (1988) for conflicting findings.

27. Herrnstein (1990).

28. See Wasserman (1993); Wasserman and Bhatt (1992) for reviews.

29. The order of slides varied from day to day, and the correct key for each category varied across subjects.

30. See also Edwards and Honig (1987).

31. That these subjects improved at all indicates some ability to categorize by means of rote memorization.

32. Herrnstein and Loveland (1964) pioneered the technique of presenting human versus nonhuman slides to pigeons as a means of studying their concept acquisition; see also Herrnstein, Loveland, and Cable (1976). Schrier, Angarella, and Povar (1984), and Schrier and Brady (1987) demonstrated a comparable effect using stumptailed and rhesus monkeys (respectively) as subjects, but see D'Amato and van Sant (1988).

33. Delius and Habers (1978).

34. An autoshaping procedure was used; if pecking failed to occur, reward was automatically delivered after 6 seconds.

35. A similar point, based on Lea's argument, was made by Herrnstein (1990).

36. Lea (1984, p. 270).

37. See Herrnstein (1979) for an alternative approach to this issue.

38. Herrnstein (1990).

39. See Wasserman (1993); Wright (1992); Zentall (1993) for reviews.

40. Zentall, Edwards, Moore and Hogan (1981) suggested that pigeons solve the oddity problem not by choosing the nonmatching comparison stimulus, but rather by avoiding the comparison stimulus that matches the sample; see also Zentall, Hogan, and Edwards (1980).

41. See Wright, Cook, Rivera, Sands, and Delius (1988).

42. Thomas and Noble (1988) failed to show transfer to novel oddity problems in rats.

43. However, see Lombardi, Fachinelli, and Delius (1984); Santiago and Wright (1984). One problem is that the kind of stimulus used in the matching task may be important. Macphail, Good, Honey, and Willis (1995), for instance, were unsuccessful in showing transfer when using two pictorial stimuli that were projected onto different keys.

44. However, see D'Amato, Salmon, and Colombo (1985); Sands, Lincoln, and Wright (1982).
45. See D'Amato, and Salmon (1984); Premack (1983).
46. See also Cook, Cavoto, and Cavoto (1995).
47. The images shown in the figure are not the actual icons used by the authors, but rather were chosen merely to show the general kind of stimuli (same or different) that was used in the study.
48. When the interior portion of the figure was colored red, the task was relatively easy. The red color was then faded out to the point that the color was eliminated entirely; pigeons maintained good performance.
49. Wasserman, DeVolder, and Coppage (1992, p. 378).
50. Additional studies in this series showed that Sarah could complete the analogies when using common items that were familiar, such as a lock and key, a paintbrush, and a can opener.
51. Bryant and Trabasso (1971) (children); Boysen, Berntson, Shreyer, and Quigley (1993) (chimpanzees); McGonigle and Chalmers (1992) (squirrel monkeys); Davis (1992b) (rats); von Fersen, Wynne, Delius and Staddon (1991); Steirn, Weaver, and Zentall (1995) (pigeons); see Davis (1992a) for a review and Wynne (1995) for a model of transitivity.
52. Half of the subjects had the reverse designation—that is, A−B+, B−C+, C−D+, and D−E+.
53. Davis (1992a, pp. 422–423). Davis further argues that humans may not use formal logical syllogisms in their reasoning. Furthermore, until psychology has a better theory about how the mind reasons, it may be unwise to conclude that reasoning must be accomplished by the use of formal logical syllogisms. Tests of the sort described here may show an ability by both human and nonhuman species to maintain transitivity, but they do not necessarily prove that differences in reasoning between species do not exist.
54. See Flavell (1985) for a complete account of Piaget's theory.
55. See Doré and Dumas (1987) for a review.
56. See also Natale, Antinucci, Spinozzi, and Poti (1986). Gagnon and Doré (1993) and Triana and Pasnak (1981) have shown analogous effects in dogs and cats.
57. The tasks were developed by Uzgiris and Hunt (1975).
58. Wood, Moriarty, Gardner, and Gardner (1980, p. 7).
59. See also Pepperberg and Kozak (1986).
60. One of the animals was also tested with rings, clips, and a keychain.
61. An initial training period was required before the accuracy was high, however.
62. Chomsky (1959) is credited with articulating the nativist side of this argument, although others have made a similar point; see Lenneberg (2967); McNeill (1970). According to McNeill, humans evolved language because, unlike other animals (including other primates), they had a particular need for language. According to this argument, the human skull increased in size during evolution to accommodate the development of an ever-larger brain. The enlarged brain was beneficial because it permitted humans to be more adaptive in their environment and to cope with changing conditions. At the same time, human beings evolved an upright position. Walking on two legs gave them added mobility and thus was also an adaptive trait. These two developmental changes were in conflict, however, because the upright position meant that the birth canal could not enlarge sufficiently to accommodate the larger skull. According to McNeill, infants were therefore born at an earlier time (relative to their nonhuman primate relatives), when

their skulls were still sufficiently small. Although this evolutionary strategy eliminated one problem, stemming from the limitations of the birth canal, a second
problem was created. The brains housed in these skulls were relatively undevel-
oped, and thus the infants were practically helpless at birth. This new problem was
solved, according to this theory, by the evolution of language. Whether this particular anthropological theory is correct, it still highlights the important fact that
human beings have a far greater capacity for language than any other animal.

63. See Winston (1987) for a general review.
64. Most of the research has been done with nonhuman primates. Languagelike behavior, however, has also been studied in an African Grey parrot (Pepperberg, 1983),
in dolphins (Herman, Richards, and Wolz, 1984), and in sea lions (Schusterman,
Gisiner, Grimm, and Hanggi, (1993).
65. See Lieberman, Klatt, and Wilson (1969).
66. See Fouts and Rigby (1977); Gardner, Gardner, and Van Cantfort (1989) for reviews.
67. See also Rumbaugh and Gill (1976).
68. Rumbaugh, Savage-Rumbaugh, and Scanlon (1982). Two other chimps, Austin and
Sherman, showed an even greater ability to do this; see Savage-Rumbaugh, Sevcik, and Hopkins (1988).
69. See also Premack and Premack (1983).
70. Sarah learned approximately 130 symbols, although the primary focus of the
research was to evaluate word use, rather than merely the number of symbols mastered.
71. See Oden, Thompson, and Premack (1990).
72. See Rumbaugh, Hopkins, Washburn, and Savage-Rumbaugh (1991); Rumbaugh
and Savage-Rumbaugh (1994); Savage-Rumbaugh and Lewin (1994); Savage-Rumbaugh, Murphy, Sevcik, Brakke, Williams, and Rumbaugh (1993) for reviews.
73. See Ristau and Robbins (1982); Terrace (1979); Terrace, Petitto, Sanders, and Bever
(1979); Umiker-Sebeok and Sebeok (1981).
74. See Savage-Rumbaugh, Pate, Lawson, Smith, and Rosenbaum (1983).
75. According to Rumbaugh and Savage-Rumbaugh (1994) Lana could not perform
this task. Lana had many hours of ambiguous training, during which symbols were
inconsistently paired with food objects. For instance, the reward for naming the
symbol for, say, banana was a piece of banana or apple. Training for Austin and
Sherman, on the other hand, was consistent in always pairing the symbol for a
reward with the reward itself. For this reason, Austin and Sherman were better
users of these symbols than was Lana.
76. Ristau and Robbins (1982).
77. Straub, Seidenberg, Bever, and Terrace (1979).
78. Terrace, Petitto, Sanders, and Bever (1979).
79. See Fouts and Rigby (1977).
80. Terrace, Petitto, Sanders, and Bever (1979).
81. Rumbaugh and Savage-Rumbaugh (1994, p. 328).

Glossary

abstract relations: class of objects, the membership of which is based on the relationship of members to one another. [15]

acquired taste aversion: a Pavlovian response resulting from a flavor becoming associated with an illness-inducing outcome. [7]

acquisition: the stage of learning during which the subject acquires an association or a response. [3]

action pattern: specific movements and motor reactions that are executed in a stereotyped fashion. [12]

age-retention effect: the finding that memories learned early in life are forgotten more easily than memories formed during adulthood. [14]

analogical reasoning: reasoning that takes the form: A is to A', as B is to B'. [15]

analyzer: hypothetical mechanism that determines attention. [13]

anxiety hypothesis: the theory of learned helplessness claiming that animals that receive inescapable shock become chronically anxious, and that such a stressful experience causes them to learn poorly later on. [10]

attention theory of discrimination: theory of discrimination claiming that learning involves both an attention reaction and an instrumental response based on the attention. [13]

autoshaping: a form of Pavlovian conditioning, usually used with birds, in which a lighted key followed by food results in key pecking behavior. [3]

avoidance: a form of instrumental conditioning in which a response, usually made to a discriminative stimulus, causes the aversive US to be omitted on that trial. [8]

backward conditioning: a conditioning procedure in which the US precedes the CS; leads to the development of conditioned inhibition. [3, 4]

behavior-analysis approach: theories claiming that behavior is selected and strengthened by the environmental consequences of an action. [2]

behavior modification (also termed **behavior therapy**): a general theory of treatment and a set of specific techniques that are designed to help alter the frequency of maladaptive behavior. [1, 8]

behavior systems approach: a theoretical approach claiming that a subject's behavior, and its perceptual reactions to stimuli, are preorganized into functional units—the subject therefore reacts to the stimulus according to an existing, preorganized framework or set of perceptual reactions. [12]

bias: a special affinity or preference for one of the choices in a matching experiment. [10]

biofeedback: an instrumental learning situation in which a subject receives reward or is provided with some sort of feedback, contingent on making a biological response. [8]

bliss point: the combination of two activities that a subject prefers. [11]

blocking: the finding that conditioning to a CS may fail to occur if that CS is presented simultaneously with another CS that is already powerful. [5]

Blough's model of generalization: a model of generalization claiming that the presentation of a reinforcer modifies the probability of a response to the training CS, and to other generalized CSs that share elements or characteristics with the training CS. [13]

budget line: a function relating goods purchased as a function of income. [11]

cell assemblies: clusters of neurons that form larger functional units. [11]

central tendency effect: the finding that the peak of a generalization gradient may shift away from the CS in a direction toward previously encountered test stimuli. [13]

CER (conditional emotional response) ratio: a measure of disruption of responding in a CER experiment, which equals the number of lever presses executed during the CS, divided by the total number of lever presses executed both during the CS and during a period of equal duration just prior to the CS onset. [3]

chain schedule: an intermittent schedule of reinforcement under which the subject must complete the requirements of two or more individual schedules in succession (both of which are signaled by a separate discriminative cue) before reinforcement is delivered. [9]

chaining technique: a technique for demonstrating secondary reinforcement, in which responding during S_2 is not followed by primary reinforcement but by the presentation of S_1, a conditioned reinforcer. [10]

closed-economy experiment: a procedure in which the subjects are required to earn all of their daily food in the experimental chamber. [9]

cognitive map: mental representation of the environment. [11, 14]

cognitive processing theory of learned helplessness: the theory of learned helplessness claiming that animals show retarded learning because they process information inappropriately—for instance, their performance is adversely affected by irrelevant cues. [10]

cognitive theory: teleological theory that makes reference to, defines, and describes the purpose or goal toward which behavior is directed, rather than the causes of behavior. [2]

collateral behavior: incidental behaviors executed during a DRL schedule, which inhibit the instrumental target response. [9]

comparator hypothesis: a theory of conditioning claiming that a subject unconsciously compares the excitatory strength of the explicit CS to the excitatory strength of other cues in the situation, such as apparatus cues. [3]

compensatory CR: a CR that is opposite to the UR. [7]

compound schedule: an intermittent schedule of reinforcement under which a reward is contingent on the completion of two distinct schedules. [9]

conditional discrimination: a situation in which a subject performs R_1 in the presence of S_1, but R_2 in the presence of S_2. [13]

conditional technique: a technique for creating conditioned inhibition in which a CS_E is paired with a US on excitatory trials, and the CS_E is given simultaneously with CS_I on trials not involving the US. [3]

conditioned attention theory: a theory claiming that the strength of an attention response to a CS increases when the stimulus predicts an important consequence but declines when it predicts no important consequence. [5]

conditioned emotional response (CER) technique: an indirect way of assessing the presence of an association by measuring the degree to which an aversive CS disrupts an ongoing behavior, such as lever pressing. [3]

conditioned excitation: a form of Pavlovian conditioning in which the CS presentation is followed by the US presentation. [3]

conditioned inhibition: a form of Pavlovian conditioning in which the CS is paired with "no US" in the course of normal excitatory conditioning; such a stimulus acquires properties that are antagonistic to a conditioned excitor. [3]

conditioned response (CR): the response elicited by the CS, which represents the learned behavior. [3]

conditioned (secondary) reinforcement: an innocuous stimulus that acquires the properties of a primary reinforcer through consistent pairings with the primary reinforcement. [10]

conditioned stimulus (CS): an innocuous or biologically weak stimulus. [3]

conditioned taste preference: a preference for a substance, such as a flavor, as a result of having that substance paired with a beneficial outcome. [7]

conditioning theory of imprinting: theory claiming that precocial birds are innately disposed to respond to moving objects, and that, through Pavlovian conditioning, the visual appearance (and perhaps sound) of the imprinting object acquires the capacity to elicit the filial behavior, as well. [12]

conservation: the ability to perceive that an object may take many forms and shapes. [15]

consolidation theory of memory: a theory claiming that memories must undergo a period of consolidation if they are to endure. [14]

consummatory response theory of reinforcement: a theory of reinforcement claiming that reinforcement is the facilitation of activity in neurons that underlie the expression of behaviors that are important for the survival of the organism. [11]

contingency space: a graphic representation in which the vertical axis plots the probability that the US is signaled by the CS, whereas the horizontal axis shows the probability that the US is not signaled by a prior CS. [3]

contingency theory of Pavlovian conditioning: the theory of Pavlovian conditioning claiming that a CS develops associative strength only when it differentially conveys information about the US occurrence. [3]

counterconditioning: a form of omission training in which reinforcement is presented following a specific alternative response rather than merely following no response. [8]

CR renewal: a recovery of the CR when extinction of the CS takes place in an environment that is different from the one used in acquisition. [3]

critical period: the sensitive or critical time period during which phase-specific learning may take place. [12]

defensive burying: a defensive reaction of burying an aversive object. [12]

delayed conditioning: a forward-conditioning procedure in which the CS continues at least until the US is presented. [4]

delayed matching-to-sample: a procedure involving the presentation of a sample stimulus and then, after a short retention interval, two comparison stimuli; the subject's task is to pick the comparison stimulus that matches the sample. [14]

demand function: an individual's demand for a good. [11]

dependent variable: the condition or variable that depends on, or is influenced by, the independent variable. [2]

differential outcome effect: the finding that responding differentially to S_1 and S_2 (by performing R_1 and R_2, respectively) occurs more readily when R_1 leads to O_1 (one outcome), but R_2 results in O_2 (a different outcome). [13]

differential reinforcement of low rates of responding (DRL) schedule: an intermittent schedule of reinforcement, under which a subject must withhold its response until a certain period of time has elapsed. [9]

differential technique: a technique for creating conditioned inhibition, in which the CS_E is followed by the US, and the CS_I is followed by no US. [3]

discrimination: responding differently to two stimuli on the basis of their apparent differences. [13]

discriminative stimulus (S_d): a neutral stimulus that signals that a response will or will not lead to a given outcome. [8]

disinhibition: a procedure in which a novel stimulus is given during extinction, causing the subject to execute the CR immediately. [3]

displacement: the ability to describe events or objects that are remote in time and place, using language. [15]

drive: a psychological state corresponding to, and covarying with, the biological imbalance. [11]

drug tolerance: a decline in the effectiveness of a drug as a result of the development of a conditioned compensatory reaction, which neutralizes or counteracts the unconditioned effects of the drug. [7]

dualism: Descartes's theory that mind and body are separate realities. [1]

easy-to-hard effect: the finding that prior experience with an easy discrimination problem improves discrimination learning of a second more difficult problem. [13]

elasticity of demand: the extent to which the demand for a good changes as a function of the price of the good. [11]

electroconvulsive shock: a traumatic shock used to treat depression in humans, which cause seizures and amnesia. [14]

empiricism: the claim that all knowledge, with the possible exceptions of logic and mathematics, is derived from experience. [1]

equipotentiality: the claim that other areas of the brain take over the functions of a damaged area. [11]

escape: a form of instrumental conditioning in which a response terminates an aversive US. [8]

excitatory–appetitive conditioning: a form of excitatory Pavlovian conditioning in which a CS is followed by an appetitive US, such as food or water. [3]

excitatory–aversive conditioning: a form of excitatory Pavlovian conditioning in which a CS is followed by an aversive US, such as shock. [3]

explicit unpaired presentations: a technique for creating conditioned inhibition, in which the CS_I and the US are explicitly unpaired. [3]

extinction: the stage of learning during which the US (or reward) is not presented following the CS (or response). [3]

extradimensional shift: a procedure in which a correct choice response is shifted and the stimulus dimension on which the choices differ is shifted as well. [13]

feature-positive effect: the finding that discrimination learning is facilitated when the single predictive feature that distinguishes the S+ from the S− is physically part of the S+ display. [13]

feature theory: theory of categorization claiming that to identify a given stimulus as a member of a category, a subject must compare the features of the stimulus in question to those that are typical of the category. [15]

fixed-interval (FI) schedule: an intermittent reinforcement schedule under which the subject receives reward for responding after a fixed period of time has elapsed. [9]

fixed-ratio (FR) schedule: an intermittent reinforcement schedule under which the subject receives reward for executing a fixed number of responses. [9]

forward-conditioning techniques: Pavlovian conditioning procedures that involve presenting the CS prior to the US. [4]

frustration theory: a theory of extinction and of the partial-reinforcement effect, claiming that subjects experience frustration during extinction, thus causing either increased or decreased persistence, depending on the kind of reinforcement schedule used during acquisition. [10]

generalization: responding to novel stimuli that are similar to an original CS. [13]

generalization gradient: the orderly relationship between the strength of the response to the generalized stimuli and the similarity of those stimuli to the original CS or S_d. [13]

go/no-go discrimination: discrimination procedure in which reward occurs for responding in the presence of the S_d but not in its absence. [15]

goals of science: description, explanation, prediction, and control. [2]

good theory: theory that is testable, simple, general, and fruitful, and that agrees with the data. [2]

habituation: a waning of the orienting response (OR) with repeated presentations of a CS. [5]

hierarchical association: an association between a stimulus and a particular response–outcome relationship. [11]

higher-level concept: class of objects, the membership of which is not based on the similarity of physical features. [15]

hippocampus: a brain structure that is implicated in the processing of memories. [11]

Hullian conditioned inhibition ($_sI_R$):   according to Hull, a conditioned form of non-responding that develops when reactive inhibition is followed by a rest interval. [11]

Hullian excitatory potential ($_sE_R$):   a subject's performance, which is a function of both drive and habit. [11]

Hullian habit strength ($_sHs_R$):   the tendency to perform a given reaction in the presence of a particular stimulus. [11]

Hullian reactive inhibition (I_R):   fatigue that builds up as a result of responding. [11]

Hull–Spence theory of discrimination: theory of generalization and discrimination claiming that reinforcement leads to conditioned excitation to the S+, nonreinforcement leads to conditioned inhibition to the S−, and that excitation and inhibition algebraically summate for any given stimulus. [13]

hypothesis: a theoretical argument or unproved theory designed to explain certain facts or phenomena in question. [2]

ill-defined (fuzzy) category: a class of stimuli for which the criteria for membership is not exact. [15]

immunization: the finding that learned helplessness may be avoided if subjects are given escapable shocks prior to the uncontrollable-shock session. [10]

imprinting: the learning process by which many species, especially birds, develop filial attachments and learn species identification. [12]

incentive contrast: a marked overshooting in responding following a shift in the parameters of reward. [9]

independent variable: the treatment or condition that, according to the hypothesis, affects the behavior being studied. [2]

indifference curve: a series of points, each of which represents an equally valuable combination of products. [11]

innate behavior: unlearned behavior. [1]

instrumental (response) conditioning: a form of learning in which a stimulus (or an outcome) is dependent—or contingent—on the subject's behavior. [8]

interresponse time (IRT):   the pause between each response. [9]

intradimensional shift: a procedure in which a correct choice response is shifted, but the stimulus dimension on which the choices differ is not shifted. [13]

inverse hypothesis: the claim that generalization is a failure to discriminate. [13]

isolation effect: a finding that conditioning is stronger when the CS–US episode is relatively isolated in time. [4]

Lashley–Wade theory: a theory of generalization claiming that subjects are confused during the generalization test, and that a subject learns about the dimension along which generalization takes place. [13]

latent inhibition (CS preexposure effect):   a procedure in which a CS is given by itself prior to conditioning. [5]

latent learning: learning that takes place despite the fact that the subject receives no reward for responding. [11]

law of cause and effect: a law of association, according to which the first of two contiguous events will lead to the belief that the first event is the cause of the second event. [1]

law of contiguity: a law of association, according to which one idea triggers the memory of another idea if the impressions on which the ideas are based had been experienced continguously. [1]

law of resemblance: a law of association, according to which an impression triggers an idea because the two are similar. [1]

laws of association: laws derived by the British Empiricists, which describe the way in which mental contents are created or combined. [1]

learned helplessness: the finding that future learning is retarded if an animal is given uncontrollable reinforcers prior to the learning task; also refers to a theory of the deficit in future learning, based on the transfer of a belief that behavior is ineffective. [10]

learned irrelevance: a theory claiming that animals come to regard a CS as being irrelevant, and thus show retardation of learning if that CS is used in a conditioning experiment, if the CS fails to predict an important consequence. [7]

learned laziness: the finding that future autoshaping is retarded if an animal is given uncontrollable food presentations prior to the learning task. [10]

learned mastery: the finding that subjects may be unusually persistent in the face of uncontrollable shock if they received controllable shock previously. [10]

learned-safety theory: a theory of long-delay learning, claiming that during the CS–US interval, animals learn that a given flavor is safe. [7]

learning: an inferred change in the organism's mental state, which results from experience, and which influences in a relatively permanent fashion the organism's potential for subsequent adaptive behavior. [1]

learning set: the finding that discrimination between novel objects is improved if prior discrimination training, using other stimuli, is given beforehand. [13]

learning versus performance distinction: the recognition that learning is not directly observable but must be inferred from the overt performance (behavior) of the animal. [2]

list chunk: a hierarchy of several series chunks. [14]

long-delay learning: the finding that a taste aversion CR will develop even when the CS and the US are separated by a considerable period of time. [7]

long-term memory: information that is said to last indefinitely in the memory system. [14]

long-term potentiation: an enduring increase in postsynaptic responsivity following a period of stimulation. [11]

marking hypothesis: a theory of the facilitation of learning, which claims that the presentation of a cue following a choice response marks the choice response in the animal's memory, so that it is more likely to recall this response when later tested. [9]

mass action: the claim that cortical areas of the brain are not specialized. [11]

matching law: a mathematical statement describing the relationship between rate of responding and rate of reward. [10]

maximization theory of matching: a theory of matching claiming that matching behavior yields the greatest possible rate of reinforcement. [10]

mechanistic theory: any theory that explains behavior in terms of the mechanisms that underlie the process. [2]

medial forebrain bundle: the predominant area that constitutes the pleasure center in the brain. [11]

mediated generalization (learned stimulus equivalence): generalization based on the fact that the stimuli are functionally equivalent to one another. [15]

melioration: a theory of matching claiming that matching behavior occurs because the subject is continuously choosing the more promising option—namely, the schedule with the momentarily higher rate of reinforcement. [10]

misbehavior: behaviors innately evoked by reward. [9, 12]

mixed schedule: an intermittent schedule of reinforcement, under which the subject may obtain reinforcement during each of several individual component schedules, but the various schedules are presented in a random order. [9]

mode: a motivational substrate related to the sequential and temporal organization of action patterns with respect to terminal stimuli in the system. [12]

modified trace theory: a theory of delayed-matching-to-sample, claiming that presentation of the sample creates a neural trace that fades over time; matching accuracy is related to the strength of the trace. [14]

module: a predisposition to respond to particular stimuli with particular response components. [12]

multiple schedule: an intermittent schedule of reinforcement, under which the subject may obtain reinforcement during each of several individual component schedules (both of which are signaled by a discriminative cue). [9]

natural category: polymorphous category that appears in the natural environment. [15]

negative contrast: a decline in responding following a decrease in the parameters of reward to a level below that shown by an unshifted group. [9]

negative reinforcement: a form of reinforcement in which the escape from, or an avoidance of, an aversive event produces an increase in the probability of the behavior. [8]

neophobia: a fear of new objects, environments, and especially, novel flavors. [7]

nonequivalence of associability: the finding that not all CSs are equally associable with all USs. [7]

object permanence: the ability to perceive that an object continues to exist even when physical evidence is lacking. [15]

occasion setter (facilitator): a stimulus that sets the occasion for, or facilitates, the conditioning of another stimulus. [5]

omission training: a form of instrumental conditioning in which the outcome following a response is the absence of an appetitive US. [8]

open-ended category: class of objects or stimuli that has unlimited membership. [15]

optimality theory: a theoretical approach to behavior, claiming that various behavior plans reflect an unconscious decision to maximize the benefit relative to the costs. [11]

overlearning reversal effect: the finding that overtraining an original choice makes it easier to reverse the subject's choice in the future. [13]

overmatching: a higher rate of response for the better of two schedules than what the matching formula predicts. [10]

overshadowing: a phenomenon in which one stimulus interferes with the conditioning of another with which it is compounded. [5]

partial reinforcement effect: the finding that continuously reinforced animals persist less during extinction than partially reinforced animals do. [10]

passive avoidance: a form of avoidance in which a subject avoids an aversive US by remaining passively away from the location of the US. [8]

Pavlovian (stimulus) conditioning: a form of learning in which two stimuli are presented independent of the subject's behavior. [3]

peak procedure: procedure used to study an animal's ability to time the duration of a stimulus. [15]

peak shift: a displacement of the peak of the excitatory generalization gradient away from the original S+, in the direction opposite to that of the S−. [13]

Pearce–Hall model: a theory of Pavlovian conditioning claiming that when a subject is surprised, both attention to and processing of a CS occur, thus increasing the associative strength of that CS. [6]

Pearce's model of generalization: a model of generalization claiming that animals have a memory buffer containing the pattern of stimulation currently being experienced by the subject; during learning, the CS representations in memory, in their entirety, gain associative strength. [13]

periventricular tract: the predominent area that constitutes the punishment center in the brain. [11]

phase sequence: collection of cell assemblies into larger units of neural material. [11]

phase-specific learning: learning that occurs only, or at least most strongly, during a certain period of time in an animal's life. [12]

phobia: maladaptive, irrational fear. [1]

pleasure center: an anatomical site that supports self-stimulation. [11]

polymorphous concept: conceptual categories for which the exemplars may take many shapes. [15]

positive contrast: an increase in responding, following an increase in the parameters of reward, to a level above that shown by an unshifted group. [9]

postreinforcement pause: the time following reward delivery during which a subject ceases to respond; occurs most notably on fixed-ratio schedules. [9]

potentiation: an increase in conditioning of a weak CS that occurs when a taste is compounded with that CS. [7]

Premack's principle: a theory claiming that a reinforcement relationship occurs when a less probable activity is made contingent on a more probable activity. [8]

proactive interference: existing memories or information that cause an individual to forget a new memory. [14]

productivity: the ability to create an infinite number of sentences and thoughts, given a finite set of words, and to describe things yet unseen, using language. [15]

programmed instruction: a technique that tries to optimize the underlying elements of instruction (for example, the specific behaviors that students make, the clarity with which questions are posed, and the immediacy with which feedback is given). [1]

prospective encoding: the tendency on a delayed-matching-to-sample task to think ahead to the to-be-presented comparison stimuli, and to develop a set of instructions about future responding. [14]

prototype: average exemplar of a class. [15]

pseudoconditioned reaction: response that occurs as a result of processes other than conditioning. [4]

punishment: a form of instrumental conditioning in which a response is followed by an aversive outcome, often shock or loud noise. [8]

reflex arc: a simple kind of information-processing system, which includes (a) an input (nerve to the brain), (b) a point in the spinal cord or brain where the incoming impulse is processed and transferred to an outgoing pulse and (c) the output. [1]

reinforcement contingency: the dependency of reward delivery on the prior execution of the instrumental response. [8]

reinforcer: an event that increases the probability of the contingent behavior. [8]

reinforcer contiguity: the immediacy of the presentation of the reinforcer. [8]

reminder treatment: procedure involving the presentation of partial reminders that increase the retrieval of a memory. [14]

Rescorla–Wagner model: a theory of Pavlovian conditioning claiming that the amount of conditioning to a CS depends on the degree to which the US is processed. [6]

response–deprivation hypothesis: a theory of behavioral regulation, according to which the predictable change in the rate of an instrumental behavior results because the subject is deprived of the activity on which the instrumental behavior is contingent. [11]

response–outcome associations: an association between an animal's own behavior and an outcome such as food. [11]

response shaping: a method of strengthening an instrumental behavior, whereby successive approximations to the final target response are reinforced. [8]

retardation of learning technique: a test of inhibition in which a putative CS− is paired with a US; inhibition is revealed by a reduction in the rate of excitatory learning. [3]

retrieval-failure hypothesis: a theory claiming that learning occurs but that animals may fail to retrieve the memory, and thus fail to demonstrate the learning, during a test. [5]

retrieval theory of memory: theory claiming that a response is elicited by a network or complex of stimuli, and that any manipulation that changes the network alters the degree to which the network evokes the memory. [14]

retroactive interference: new memories or information that cause an individual to forget an older memory. [14]

retrospective coding: the tendency on a delayed-matching-to-sample task to reflect back on, and rehearse, the characteristics of the sample and code them into memory. [14]

reversibility: the finding that learned helplessness may be reversed by forcing the subject to respond during the learning session. [10]

reward training: a form of instrumental conditioning in which a response produces, or leads to, a desirable outcome, usually food. [8]

schedules of intermittent reinforcement: designated plans for providing reinforcement only occasionally for a response. [9]

search image: a perceptual reaction involving selective attention to the characteristics of a prey item. [7]

second-order conditioning (higher-order conditioning): a procedure in which CS_2 is paired with an already powerful CS_1. [5]

self-control: a condition describing the situation in which a subject chooses the more delayed but larger of two reward options. [10]

semanticity: the ability for words or symbols to have meaning. [15]

sensory channeling theory: an explanation for potentiation claiming that because taste belongs to a rat's feeding system, it channels other cues with which it is combined into this feeding system, thus potentiating conditioning. [7]

sensory preconditioning: a procedure in which two CSs are paired before one of the two is paired with a US. [5]

sensory reinforcement: an increase in the probability of a response when made contingent on the presentation of a sensory event. [9]

sequential (aftereffects) hypothesis: a theory of extinction and the partial reinforcement effect, claiming that subjects remember the aftereffects from previous trials, thus causing either increased or decreased persistence. [10]

series chunk: an aggregate of several trial chunks. [14]

short-term memory: information that is said to last only 15 to 20 seconds. [14]

Sidman avoidance: a form of avoidance in which a subject postpones an aversive US. [8]

sign tracking: approaching and contacting of a CS, usually by birds. [3]

simultaneous conditioning: a conditioning procedure in which the CS onset occurs simultaneously with the US onset. [4]

SOP (sometimes opponent process) model: a theory of Pavlovian conditioning, claiming that conditioning occurs as a result of the interaction among memory states. [6]

spatial memory: memory for direction and places in the environment. [14]

species-specific defense reaction (SSDR): innate defensive reactions that are specific to a given species. [12]

spontaneous recovery: the finding that CR strength recovers, spontaneousy, if a rest interval follows the extinction period. [3]

stimulus control: the extent to which a given stimulus evokes a response. [13]

stimulus–response (S–R) learning: the theory that the associative bond is between a CS and the response. [5, 6]

stimulus–stimulus (S–S) learning: the theory that the associative bond is between a CS and another stimulus, usually the US. [5, 6]

substitutability: the extent to which a subject will substitute one commodity for another when the price increases. [11]

subsystem: coherent global strategies that serve the general function of a behavior system. [12]

summation test: a test of inhibition in which a CS+ and a CS− are given simultaneously; inhibition is revealed by a reduction in the level of excitation given to the CS+ alone. [3]

superconditioning: a phenomenon in which the conditioning of a CS is inflated when that CS is presented simultaneously with a CS−. [5]

syntax: the rules by which words combine into phrases, and phrases into sentences. [15]

system level: the general function that a behavior system serves. [12]

tandem schedule: an intermittent schedule of reinforcement under which the subject must complete the requirements of two or more individual schedules in succession before reinforcement is delivered. [9]

template theory: a theory claiming that birds are born with a pattern, or template, that is responsible for shaping the details of their song. [12]

temporal-discrimination hypothesis: a theory of delayed-matching-to-sample, claiming that the decline in performance as a function of the retention interval reflects a kind of confusion. [14]

Thomas's adaptation-level effect model: a model of generalization claiming that subjects judge generalized stimuli relative to subjective representation of the average value they have encountered. [13]

time horizon: the time period over which a subject assesses rate of intake prior to leaving a patch. [11]

trace conditioning: a forward-conditioning procedure in which the CS offset occurs before the US onset; conditioned inhibition occurs if the CS is given well in advance of the US onset. [3, 4]

transitivity: responding that maintains a relationship between two items, based on the inferred relationship between two other different items. [15]

trial chunk: an aggregate of individual responses that is organized in a meaningful way. [14]

truly random control: a procedure in which the probability of receiving a US during a CS is equal to the probability of receiving no US. [3]

unblocking: the finding that blocking no longer occurs when the animal is surprised in Phase 2 of a blocking experiment. [5]

unconditioned response (UR): an unlearned response that is triggered by the US. [3]

unconditioned stimulus (US): a biologically potent stimulus, which reliably evokes an unlearned (reflexive) reaction. [3]

undermatching: a lower rate of response for the better of two schedules than what the matching formula predicts. [10]

US preexposure effect: a phenomenon in which subjects, after being given exposure to unsignaled USs, show retarded excitatory learning. [3]

variable interval (VI) schedule: an intermittent reinforcement schedule under which the subject receives reward for responding after a predetermined period of time has elapsed, except that the precise length of time varies from one reward to the next. [9]

variable ratio (VR) schedule: an intermittent reinforcement schedule under which the subject receives reward for executing a predetermined number of responses, except that the specific number varies from one reward to the next. [9]

warm-up decrement: typically poor performance at the beginning of a session, but improvement thereafter. [14]

well-defined conceptual category: a class of stimuli in which exemplars meet specific and objective criteria for membership. [15]

References

Adamec, R., & Melzack, R. (1970). The role of motivation and orientation in sensory preconditioning. *Canadian Journal of Psychology, 24,* 230–239. [5]

Adams, C. D. (1982). Variations in the sensitivity of instrumental responding to reinforcer devaluation. *The Quarterly Journal of Experimental Psychology, 34B,* 77–98. [11]

Adams, C. D., & Dickinson, A. (1981). Instrumental responding following reinforcer devaluation. *The Quarterly Journal of Experimental Psychology, 33B,* 109–121. [11]

Adkins, C. K., Domjan, M., & Gutierrez, G. (1994). Topography of sexually conditioned behavior in male Japanese quail (*Coturnix japonica*) depends on the CS–US interval. *Journal of Experimental Psychology: Animal Behavior Processes, 20,* 199–209. [7]

Aguado, L., Symonds, M., & Hall, G. (1994). Interval between preexposure and test determines the magnitude of latent inhibition: Implications for an interference account. *Animal Learning and Behavior, 22,* 188–194. [5]

Ahlers, R. H., & Best, P. J. (1971). Novelty vs. temporal contiguity in learned taste aversions. *Psychonomic Science, 25,* 34–36. [7]

Ainslie, G. W. (1974). Impulse control in pigeons. *Journal of the Experimental Analysis of Behavior, 21,* 485–489. [10]

Ainslie, G. W. (1975). Specious reward: A behavioral theory of impulsiveness and impulse control. *Psychological Bulletin, 82,* 463–496. [10]

Albert, M., & Ayres, J. J. B. (1989). With number of preexposures constant latent inhibition increases with preexposure CS duration or total CS exposure. *Learning and Motivation, 20,* 278–294. [5]

Alberts, J. R. (1978). Huddling by rat pups: Multisensory control of contact. *Journal of Comparative and Physiological Psychology, 92,* 220–230. [4, 6]

Allison, J. (1983). *Behavioral economics.* New York: Praeger. [11]

Allison, J. (1989). The nature of reinforcement. In S. B. Klein & R. R. Mowrer (Eds.), *Contemporary learning theories: Instrumental conditioning theory and the impact of biological constraints on learning* (pp. 13–39). Hillsdale, NJ: Erlbaum. [11]

Allison, J. (1993). Response deprivation, reinforcement, and economics. *Journal of the Experimental Analysis of Behavior, 60,* 129–140. [11]

Allison, J., Buxton, A., & Moore, K. E. (1987). Bliss points, stop lines, and performance under schedule constraint. *Journal of Experimental Psychology: Animal Behavior Processes, 13,* 331–340. [11]

Allison, J., Larson, D., & Jensen, D. D. (1967). Acquired fear, brightness preference, and one-way shuttle box performance. *Psychonomic Science, 8,* 269–270. [4]

Allison, J., & Timberlake, W. (1974). Instrumental and contingent saccharin-licking in rats: Response deprivation and reinforcement. *Learning and Motivation, 5,* 231–247. [11]

Allison, J., & Timberlake, W. (1975). Response deprivation and instrumental performance in the controlled-amount paradigm. *Learning and Motivation, 6,* 122–142. [11]

Altenor, A., Kay, E., & Richter, M. (1977). The generality of learned helplessness in the rat. *Learning and Motivation, 8,* 54–62. [10]

Amiro, T. W., & Bitterman, M. E. (1980). Second-order appetitive conditioning in goldfish. *Journal of Experimental Psychology: Animal Behavior Processes, 6,* 41–48. [5]

Amsel, A. (1958). The role of frustrative nonreward in noncontinuous reward situations. *Psychological Bulletin, 55,* 102–119. [10]

Amsel, A. (1962). Frustrative nonreward in partial reinforcement and discrimination learning: Some recent history and a theoretical extension. *Psychological Review, 69,* 306–328. [10]

Amsel, A. (1972). Behavioral habituation, counterconditioning, and a general theory of persistence. In A. H. Black & W. F. Prokasy (Eds.), *Classical conditioning II: Current research and theory* (pp. 409–426). New York: Appleton-Century-Crofts. [10]

Amsel, A. (1992). *Frustration theory: An analysis of dispositional learning and memory.* New York: Cambridge University Press. [2, 10, 11]

Amsel, A., & Roussel, J. (1952). Motivational properties of frustration: I. Effect on a running response of the addition of frustration to the motivational complex. *Journal of Experimental Psychology, 43,* 363–368. [10]

Anderson, N. H. (1963). Comparison of different populations: Resistance to extinction and transfer. *Psychological Review, 70,* 162–179. [10]

Andrews, E. A., & Braveman, N. S. (1975). The combined effects of dosage level and interstimulus interval on the formation of one-trial poison-based aversions in rats. *Animal Learning and Behavior, 3,* 287–289. [4, 7]

Anisman, H., DeCatanzaro, D., & Remington, G. (1978). Escape performance following exposure to inescapable shock: Deficits in motor response maintenance. *Journal of Experimental Psychology: Animal Behavior Processes, 4,* 197–218. [10]

Annau, Z., & Kamin, L. J. (1961). The conditioned emotional response as a function of intensity of the US. *Journal of Comparative and Physiological Psychology, 54,* 428–432. [4]

Arbuckle, J. L., & Lattal, K. A. (1988). Changes in functional response units with briefly delayed reinforcement. *Journal of the Experimental Analysis of Behavior, 49,* 249–263. [9]

Aristotle (1952). (W. D. Ross, trans.). *Metaphysics.* In R. M. Hutchens (Eds.), *Great books of the western world, vol. 8* (pp. 499–626). Chicago, Il: Encyclopedia Britania. [1]

Arnaut, L., & Shettleworth, S. J. (1981). The role of spatial and temporal contiguity in defensive burying in rats. *Animal Learning and Behavior, 9,* 275–280. [12]

Auge, R. J. (1977). Stimulus functions within a fixed-interval clock schedule: Reinforcement, punishment, and discriminative stimulus control. *Animal Learning and Behavior, 5,* 117–123. [9]

Aydin, A., & Pearce, J. M. (1994). Prototype effects in categorization by pigeons. *Journal of Experimental Psychology: Animal Behavior Processes, 20,* 264–277. [15]

Ayllon, T., & Houghton, E. (1962). Control of the behavior of schizophrenics by food. *Journal of the Experimental Analysis of Behavior, 5,* 343–352. [8]

Ayres, J. J. B., Axelrod, H., Mercker, E., Mucknik, F., & Vigorito, M. (1985). Concurrent observations of bar-press suppression and freezing: Effects of CS modality and on-line vs. off-line training upon posttrial behavior. *Animal Learning and Behavior, 13,* 44–50. [4]

Ayres, J. J. B., & Bombace, J. C. (1982). A surprising extension of the preconditioned stimulus beyond the cotermination of the US and the added element does not alleviate blocking to the added element. *Animal Learning and Behavior, 10,* 263–268. [6]

Ayres, J. J. B., Haddad, C., & Albert, M. (1987). One-trial excitatory backward conditioning as assessed by conditioned suppression of licking in rats: Concurrent observations of lick suppression and defensive behaviors. *Animal Learning and Behavior, 15,* 212–217. [4]

Ayres, J. J. B., Philbin, D., Cassidy, S., Bellino, L., & Redlinger, E. (1992). Some parameters of latent inhibition. *Learning and Motivation, 23,* 269–287. [5]

Azorlosa, J. L., & Cicala, G. A. (1986). Blocking of conditioned suppression with 1 or 10 compound trials. *Animal Learning and Behavior, 14,* 163–167. [6]

Bacon, W. E. (1962). Partial-reinforcement extinction effect following different amounts of training. *Journal of Comparative and Physiological Psychology, 55,* 998–1003. [10]

Badia, P., & Defran, R. H. (1970). Orienting responses and GSR conditioning: A dilemma. *Psychological Review, 77,* 171–181. [4]

Baker, A. G. (1976). Learned irrelevance and learned helplessness: Rats learn that stimuli, reinforcers and responses are uncorrelated. *Journal of Experimental Psychology: Animal Behavior Processes, 2,* 130–141. [10]

Baker, A. G., & Mackintosh, N. J. (1979). Preexposure to the CS alone, US alone, or CS and US uncorrelated: Latent inhibition, blocking by context, or learned irrelevance? *Learning and Motivation, 10,* 278–294. [3, 6, 7, 10]

Baker, A. G., Mercier, P., Gabel, J., & Baker, P. A. (1981). Contextual conditioning and the US preexposure effect in conditioned fear. *Journal of Experimental Psychology: Animal Behavior Processes, 7,* 109–128. [6]

Baker, A. G., Singh, M., & Bindra, D. (1985). Some effects of contextual conditioning and US predictability on Pavlovian conditioning. In P. D. Balsam & A. Tomie (Eds.), *Context and learning* (pp. 73–103). Hillsdale, NJ: Erlbaum. [6]

Baker, A. G., Woods, W., Tait, R., & Gardiner, K. (1986). Punishment suppression: Some effects on alternative behaviour. *The Quarterly Journal of Experimental Psychology, 38B,* 191–215. [8]

Baker, T. B., & Tiffany, S. T. (1985). Morphine tolerance as habituation. *Psychological Review, 92,* 78–108. [7]

Balaz, M. A., Capra, S., Kasprow, W. J., & Miller, R. R. (1982). Latent inhibition of the conditioning context: Further evidence of contextual potentiation of retrieval in the absence of appreciable context–US associations. *Animal Learning and Behavior, 10,* 242–248. [5]

Balaz, M. A., Gutsin, P., Cachiero, H., & Miller, R. R., (1982). Blocking as a retrieval failure: Reactivation of associations to a blocked stimulus. *The Quarterly Journal of Experimental Psychology, 34B,* 99–113. [5]

Balaz, M. A., Kasprow, W. J., & Miller, R. R. (1982). Blocking with a single compound trial. *Animal Learning and Behavior, 10,* 271–276. [6]

Balda, R. P., & Kamil, A. C. (1988). The spatial memory of Clark's nutcrackers (*Nucifraga columbiana*) in an analogue of the radial arm maze. *Animal Learning and Behavior, 16,* 116–122. [14]

Balleine, B., & Soames Job, R. F. (1991). Reconsideration of the role of competing responses in demonstrations of the interference effect (learned helplessness). *Journal of Experimental Psychology: Animal Behavior Processes, 17,* 270–280. [10]

Balsam, P. D. (1984). Relative time in trace conditioning. In J. Gibbon & L. Allan (Eds.), *Annals of the New York Academy of Sciences: Timing and Time Perception* (Vol. 423, pp. 211–227). New York: New York Academy of Sciences. [4]

Balsam, P. D., & Payne, D. (1979). Intertrial interval and unconditioned stimulus durations in autoshaping. *Animal Learning and Behavior, 7,* 477–482. [4]

Balsam, P. D., & Tomie, A. (1985). *Context and learning.* Hillsdale, NJ: Erlbaum. [14]

Bandura, A. (1977). *Social learning theory.* Englewood Cliffs, NJ: Prentice-Hall. [1]

Baptista, L. F., & Petrinovich, L. (1984). Social interaction, sensitive phases and the song template hypothesis in the white-crowned sparrow. *Animal Behaviour, 32,* 172–181. [12]

Barber, J. G., & Winefield, A. H. (1986). Learned helplessness as conditioned inattention to the target stimulus. *Journal of Experimental Psychology: General, 115,* 236–246. [10]

Barker, L. M. (1976). CS duration, amount, and concentration effects in conditioned taste aversions. *Learning and Motivation, 7,* 265–273. [4, 7]

Barker, L. M., Best, M. R., & Domjan, M. (Eds.). (1977). *Learning mechanisms in food selection.* Waco, TX: Baylor University Press. [3, 7]

Barker, L. M., & Weaver, C. A. (1991). Conditioning flavor preferences in rats: Dissecting the "medicine effect." *Learning and Motivation, 22,* 311–328. [7]

Barnet, R. C., Arnold, H. M., & Miller, R. R. (1991). Simultaneous conditioning demonstrated in second-order conditioning: Evidence for similar associative structure in forward and simultaneous conditioning. *Learning and Motivation, 22,* 253–268. [5]

Barnet, R. C., Grahame, N. J., & Miller, R. R. (1993a). Local context and the comparator hypothesis. *Animal Learning and Behavior, 21,* 1–13. [3]

Barnet, R. C., Grahame, N. J., & Miller, R. R. (1993b). Local time horizons in Pavlovian learning. *Journal of Experimental Psychology: Animal Behavior Processes, 19,* 215–230. [3]

Barnet, R. C., Grahame, N. J., & Miller, R. R. (1993c). Temporal encoding as a determinant of blocking. *Journal of Experimental Psychology: Animal Behavior Processes, 19,* 327–341. [6]

Baron, A. (1965). Delayed punishment of a runway response. *Journal of Comparative and Physiological Psychology, 60,* 131–134. [9]

Baron, A., Kaufman, A., & Fazzini, D. (1969). Density and delay of punishment of free-operant avoidance. *Journal of the Experimental Analysis of Behavior, 12,* 1029–1037. [9]

Barr, W. B., Goldberg, E., Wasserstein, S., & Novelly, R. A. (1990). Retrograde amnesia following unilateral temporal lobectomy. *Neuropsychologia, 28,* 243–255. [11]

Bateson, P. P. G. (1966). The characteristics and context of imprinting. *Biological Reviews, 41,* 177–220. [12]

Bateson, P. P. G., & Reese, E. P. (1969). The reinforcing properties of conspicuous stimuli in the imprinting situation. *Animal Behaviour, 17,* 692–699. [12]

Bauer, R. H. (1972). The effects of CS and US intensity on shuttlebox avoidance. *Psychonomic Science, 27,* 266–268. [9]

Baum, W. M. (1973). Time allocation and negative reinforcement. *Journal of the Experimental Analysis of Behavior, 20,* 313–322. [10]

Baum, W. M. (1974). On two types of deviation from the matching law: Bias and undermatching. *Journal of the Experimental Analysis of Behavior, 22,* 231–242. [10]

Baum, W. M. (1979). Matching, undermatching, and overmatching in studies of choice. *Journal of the Experimental Analysis of Behavior, 32,* 269–281. [10]

Baum, W. M. (1981). Optimization and the matching law as accounts of instrumental behavior. *Journal of the Experimental Analysis of Behavior, 36,* 387–403. [10]

Bechtel, W. (1988). *Philosophy of science: An overview for cognitive science.* Hillsdale, NJ: Erlbaum. [2]

Behar, I., & LeBedda, J. M. (1974). Effects of differential pretraining on learning-set formation in rhesus monkeys. *Journal of Comparative and Physiological Psychology, 87,* 277–283. [13]

Bekhterev, V. M. (1913). *La psychologie objective.* Paris: Alcan. [3]

Bellack, A. S., Hersen, M., & Kazdin, A. E. (1985). *International handbook of behavior modification and therapy.* New York: Plenum. [1]

Benedict, J. O., & Ayres, J. J. B. (1972). Factors affecting conditioning in the truly random control procedure in the rat. *Journal of Comparative and Physiological Psychology, 78,* 323–330. [3]

Benson, H., Shapiro, D., Tursky, B., & Schwartz, G. F. (1971). Decreased systolic blood pressure through operant conditioning techniques in patients with essential hypertension. *Science, 173,* 740–742. [8]

Berk, A. M., Vigorito, M., & Miller, R. R. (1979). Retroactive stimulus interference with conditioned emotional response retention in infant and adult rats: Implications for infantile amnesia. *Journal of Experimental Psychology: Animal Behavior Processes, 5,* 284–299. [14]

Bernstein, I. L. (1978). Learned taste aversions in children receiving chemotherapy. *Science, 200,* 1302–1303. [7]

Bernstein, I. L. & Borson, S. (1986). Learned food aversion: A component of anorexia syndromes. *Psychological Review, 93,* 462–372. [7]

Bersh, P. J. (1951). The influence of two variables upon the establishment of a secondary reinforcer for operant responses. *Journal of Experimental Psychology, 41,* 62–73. [10]

Bertsch, G. J., & Leitenberg, H. A. (1970). "Frustration Effect" following electric shock. *Learning and Motivation, 1,* 150–156. [10]

Best, M. R. (1975). Conditioned and latent inhibition in taste-aversion learning: Clarifying the role of learned safety. *Journal of Experimental Psychology: Animal Behavior Processes, 1,* 97–113. [5, 7]

Best, M. R., Batson, J. D., Meachum, C. L., Brown, E. R., & Ringer, M. (1985). Characteristics of taste-mediated environmental potentiation in rats. *Learning and Motivation, 16,* 190–209. [7]

Best, M. R., Brown, E. R., & Sowell, M. K. (1984). Taste-mediated potentiation of noningestional stimuli in rats. *Learning and Motivation, 15,* 244–258. [7]

Best, M. R., & Gemberling, G. A. (1977). Role of short-term processes in the conditioned stimulus preexposure effect and the delay of reinforcement gradient in long-delay taste-aversion learning. *Journal of Experimental Psychology: Animal Behavior Processes, 3,* 253–263. [7]

Best, M. R., Gemberling, G. A., & Johnson, P. E. (1979). Disrupting the conditioned stimulus preexposure effect in flavor-aversion learning: Effects of interoceptive distractor manipulations. *Journal of Experimental Psychology: Animal Behavior Processes, 5,* 321–334. [5]

Best, P. J., Best, M. R., & Mickley, G. A. (1973). Conditioned aversion to distinct environmental stimuli resulting from gastrointestinal distress. *Journal of Comparative and Physiological Psychology, 85,* 250–257. [7]

Bhatt, R. S., & Wasserman, E. A. (1989). Secondary generalization and categorization in pigeons. *Journal of the Experimental Analysis of Behavior, 52,* 213–224. [15]

Bhatt, R. S., Wasserman, E. A., Reynolds, W. F., & Knauss, K. S. (1988). Conceptual behavior in pigeons: Categorization of both familiar and novel examples from four classes of natural and artificial stimuli. *Journal of Experimental Psychology: Animal Behavior Processes, 14,* 219–234. [15]

Bickel, W. K., & Etzel, B. C. (1985). The quantal nature of controlling stimulus–response relations as measured in tests of stimulus generalization. *Journal of the Experimental Analysis of Behavior, 44,* 245–270. [13]

Bitterman, M. E., Tyler, D. W., & Elam, C. B. (1955). Simultaneous and successive discrimination under identical stimulating conditions. *American Journal of Psychology, 68,* 237–248. [13]

Bizo, L. A., & White, K. G. (1994). Pacemaker rate in the behavioral theory of timing. *Journal of Experimental Psychology: Animal Behavior Processes, 20,* 308–321. [15]

Black, A. H., Carlson, N. J., & Solomon, R. L. (1962). Exploratory studies of the conditioning of autonomic responses in curarized dogs. *Psychological Monographs, 76,* (Whole No. 548). [4]

Blackman, D. E. (1983). On cognitive theories of animal learning: Extrapolation from humans to animals? In G. C. L. Davey (Ed.), *Animal models of human behavior: conceptual, evolutionary, and neurobiological perspectives* (pp. 37–50). New York: Wiley. [2]

Blanchard, R. J., & Blanchard, D. C. (1969a). Crouching as an index of fear. *Journal of Comparative and Physiological Psychology, 67,* 370–375. [6, 7, 9]

Blanchard, R. J., & Blanchard, D. C. (1969b). Passive and active reactions to fear-eliciting stimuli. *Journal of Comparative and Physiological Psychology, 68,* 129–135. [9]

Blanchard, R. J., & Blanchard, D. C. (1971). Defensive reactions in the albino rat. *Learning and Motivation, 2,* 351–362. [12]

Blanchard, R. J., & Blanchard, D. C. (1989). Antipredator defensive behaviors in a visible burrow system. *Journal of Comparative Psychology, 103,* 70–82. [7]

Blanchard, R. J., Blanchard, D. C., Takahashi, T., & Kelley, M. J. (1977). Attack and defensive behaviour in the albino rat. *Animal Behaviour, 25,* 622–634. [12]

Blanchard, R. J., Flannelly, K. J., & Blanchard, D. C. (1986). Defensive behaviors of laboratory and wild *Rattus norvegicus. Journal of Comparative Psychology, 100,* 101–107. [7, 12]

Blanchard, R. J., Kleinschmidt, C. F., Fukunaga-Stinson, C., & Blanchard, D. C. (1980). Defensive attack behavior in male and female rats. *Animal Learning and Behavior, 8,* 177–183. [12]

Blough, D. S. (1969a). Attention shifts in a maintained discrimination. *Science, 166,* 125–126. [13]

Blough, D. S. (1969b). Generalization gradient shape and summation in steady-state tests. *Journal of the Experimental Analysis of Behavior, 12,* 91–104. [13]

Blough, D. S. (1973). Two-way generalization peak shift after two-key training in the pigeon. *Animal Learning and Behavior, 1,* 171–174. [13]

Blough, D. S. (1975). Steady-state data and a quantitative model of operant generalization. *Journal of Experimental Psychology: Animal Behavior Processes, 1,* 3–21. [13]

Blough, D. S. (1993). Effects on search speed of the probability of target–distractor combinations. *Journal of Experimental Psychology: Animal Behavior Processes, 19,* 231–243. [7]

Blough, P. M. (1972). Wavelength generalization and discrimination in the pigeon. *Perception and Psychophysics, 12,* 342–348. [13]

Blough, P. M. (1991). Selective attention and search images in pigeons. *Journal of Experimental Psychology: Animal Behavior Processes, 17,* 292–298. [7]

Boakes, R. A., Poli, M., Lockwood, M. J., & Goodall, G. (1978). A study of misbehavior: Token reinforcement in the rat. *Journal of the Experimental Analysis of Behavior, 29,* 115–134. [12]

Bolhuis, J. J., de Vos, G. J., & Kruijt, J. P. (1990). Filial imprinting and associative learning. *The Quarterly Journal of Experimental Psychology, 42B,* 313–329. [12]

Bolhuis, J. J., & Honey, R. C. (1994). Within-event learning during filial imprinting. *Journal of Experimental Psychology: Animal Behavior Processes, 20, 240–248. [12]*

Bolles, R. C. (1970). Species-specific defense reactions and avoidance learning. *Psychological Review, 77,* 32–48. [7, 12]

Bolles, R. C. (1972). Reinforcement, expectancy, and learning. *Psychological Review, 79,* 394–409. [11]

Bolles, R. C. (1975). *Theory of motivation* (2nd ed.). New York: Harper & Row. [11]

Bolles, R. C., & Collier, A. C. (1976). The effect of predictive cues on freezing in rats. *Animal Learning and Behavior, 4,* 6–8. [6, 9]

Bolles, R. C., & Fanselow, M. S. (1980). A perceptual-defense–recuperative model of fear and pain. *Behavioral and Brain Sciences, 3,* 291–301. [7]

Bolles, R. C., & Fanselow, M. S. (1982). Endorphins and behavior. *Annual Review of Psychology, 33,* 87–101. [7]

Bolles, R. C., & Hayward, L., & Crandall, C. (1981). Conditioned taste preferences based on caloric density. *Journal of Experimental Psychology: Animal Behavior Processes, 7,* 59–69. [7]

Bolles, R. C., Holtz, R., Dunn, T., & Hill, W. (1980). Comparisons of stimulus learning and response learning in a punishment situation. *Learning and Motivation, 11,* 78–96. [11]

Bolles, R. C., & Riley, A. L. (1973). Freezing as an avoidance response: Another look at the operant–respondent distinction. *Learning and Motivation, 4,* 268–275. [6]

Bolles, R. C., & Seelbach, S. E. (1964). Punishing and reinforcing effects of noise onset and termination for different responses. *Journal of Comparative and Physiological Psychology, 58,* 127–131. [9]

Bond, A. B. (1983). Visual search and selection of natural stimuli in the pigeon: The attention threshold hypothesis. *Journal of Experimental Psychology: Animal Behavior Processes, 9,* 292–306. [7]

Bond, N., & Harland, W. (1975). Higher order conditioning of a taste aversion. *Animal Learning and Behavior, 3,* 295–296. [7]

Bond, N. W. (1983). Reciprocal overshadowing in flavour-aversion learning. *The Quarterly Journal of Experimental Psychology, 35B,* 265–274. [4]

Bond, N. W. (1984a). Avoidance, classical, and pseudoconditioning as a function of species-specific defense reactions in high- and low-avoider rat strains. *Animal Learning and Behavior, 12,* 323–331. [12]

Bond, N. W. (1984b). The poisoned partner effect in rats: Some parametric considerations. *Animal Learning and Behavior, 12,* 89–96. [7]

Bonem, M., & Crossman, E. K. (1988). Elucidating the effects of reinforcement magnitude. *Psychological Bulletin, 104,* 348–362. [9]

Boren, J. J., Sidman, M., & Herrnstein, R. J. (1959). Avoidance, escape, and extinction as functions of shock intensity. *Journal of Comparative and Physiological Psychology, 52,* 420–425. [9]

Bouton, M. E. (1991). Context and retrieval in extinction and in other examples of interference in simple associative learning. In L. W. Dachowski, & C. F. Flaherty (Eds.), *Current topics in animal learning: Brain, emotion, and cognition* (pp. 25–53). Hillsdale, NJ: Erlbaum. [3]

Bouton, M. E. (1993). Context, time, and memory retrieval in the interference paradigms of Pavlovian learning. *Psychological Bulletin, 114,* 80–99. [14]

Bouton, M. E. (1994). Conditioning, remembering, and forgetting. *Journal of Experimental Psychology: Animal Behavior Processes, 20,* 219–231. [14]

Bouton, M. E., & Bolles, R. C. (1979). Contextual control of the extinction of conditioned fear. *Learning and Motivation, 10,* 445–466. [3]

Bouton, M. E., & Bolles, R. C. (1985). Context, event-memories, and extinction. In P. D. Balsam & A. Tomie (Eds.), *Context and learning* (pp. 133–166). Hillsdale, NJ: Erlbaum. [14]

Bouton, M. E., Dunlap, C. M., & Swartzentruber, D. (1987). Potentiation of taste by another taste during compound aversion learning. *Animal Learning and Behavior, 15,* 433–438. [7]

Bouton, M. E., Jones, D. L., McPhillips, S. A., & Swartzentruber, D. (1986). Potentiation and overshadowing in odor-aversion learning: Role of method of odor presentation, the distal–proximal cue distinction, and the conditionability of odor. *Learning and Motivation, 17,* 115–138. [6, 7]

Bouton, M. E., & King, D. A. (1983). Contextual control of the extinction of conditioned fear: Tests for the associative value of the context. *Journal of Experimental Psychology: Animal Behavior Processes, 9,* 248–265. [3, 14]

Bouton, M. E., & Peck, C. A. (1989). Context effects on conditioning, extinction, and reinstatement in an appetitive conditioning preparation. *Animal Learning and Behavior, 17,* 188–198. [14]

Bouton, M. E., & Swartzentruber, D. (1991). Sources of relapse after extinction in Pavlovian and instrumental learning. *Clinical Psychology Review, 11,* 123–140. [3]

Bowe, C. A., Green, L., & Miller, J. D. (1987). Differential acquisition of discriminated autoshaping as a function of stimulus qualities and locations. *Animal Learning and Behavior, 15,* 285–292. [4]

Bower, G. H. (1962). The influence of graded reductions in reward and prior frustration events upon the magnitude of the frustration effect. *Journal of Comparative and Physiological Psychology, 55,* 582–587. [10]

Bowers, R. L., & Richards, R. W. (1990). Pigeons' short-term memory for temporal and visual stimuli in delayed matching-to-sample. *Animal Learning and Behavior, 18,* 23–28. [14]

Bowlby, J. (1969). *Attachment and loss: Vol. 1. Attachment.* New York: Basic Books. [12]

Boysen, S. T., Berntson, G. G., Shreyer, T. A., & Quigley, K. S. (1993). Processing of ordinality and transitivity by champanzees (*Pan troglodytes*). *Journal of Comparative Psychology, 107,* 1–8. [15]

Bradshaw, C. M., Ruddle, H. V., & Szabadi, E. (1981). Relationship between response rate and reinforcement frequency in variable-interval schedules: II. Effect of the value of sucrose reinforcement. *Journal of Experimental Analysis of Behavior, 35,* 263–269. [9]

Bradshaw, C. M., Szabadi, E., & Bevan, P. (1978). Relationship between response rate and reinforcement frequency in variable-interval schedules: The effect of the concentration of sucrose reinforcement. *Journal of the Experimental Analysis of Behavior, 29,* 447–452. [9]

Brandon, S. E., & Paul, H. (1987). The effects of activity conditioned in random CS/US training on performance in autoshaping. *Animal Learning and Behavior, 15,* 263–284. [3]

Breger, L., & McGaugh, J. L. (1965). Critique and reformulation of "learning theory" approaches to psychotherapy and neurosis. *Psychological Bulletin, 63,* 338–358. [1]

Breland, K., & Breland, M. (1961). The misbehavior of organisms. *American Psychologist, 16,* 681–684. [9, 12]

Brinton, R. E. (1991). Biochemical correlates of learning and memory. In J. L. Martinez & R. P. Kesner (Eds.), *Learning and memory: A biological view* (pp. 199–257). San Diego, CA: Academic Press. [11]

Brodbeck, D. R. (1994). Memory for spatial and local cues: A comparison of a storing and a nonstoring species. *Animal Learning and Behavior, 22,* 119–133. [14]

Brodigan, D. L., & Peterson, G. B. (1976). Two-choice discrimination performance of pigeons as a function of reward expectancy, prechoice delay, and domesticity. *Animal Learning and Behavior, 4,* 121–124. [13]

Brogden, W. J., Lipman, E. A., & Culler, E. (1938). The role of incentive in conditioning and extinction. *American Journal of Psychology, 51,* 100–117. [12]

Brooks, C. I. (1975). Primary frustration differences following brief partial reinforcement acquisition under varying magnitudes of reward. *Animal Learning and Behavior, 3,* 67–72. [10]

Brooks, D. C., & Bouton, M. E. (1994). A retrieval cue for extinction attenuates response recovery (renewal) caused by a return to the conditioning context. *Journal of Experimental Psychology: Animal Behavior Processes, 20,* 366–379. [14]

Brower, L. P. (1969). Ecological chemistry. *Scientific American, 220,* 22–29. [7]

Brower, L. P., Ryerson, W. N., Coppinger, L. L., & Glazier, S. C. (1968). Ecological chemistry and the palatability spectrum. *Science, 161,* 1349–1351. [7]

Brown, B. L. (1970). Stimulus generalization in salivary conditioning. *Journal of Comparative and Physiological Psychology, 71,* 467–477. [13]

Brown, M. F. (1990). The effects of maze-arm length on performance in the radial-arm maze. *Animal Learning and Behavior, 18,* 13–22. [14]

Brown, M. F., & Lesniak-Karpiak, K. B. (1993). Choice criterion effects in the radial-arm maze: Maze-arm incline and brightness. *Learning and Motivation, 24,* 23–39. [14]

Brown, P. L., & Jenkins, H. M. (1968). Auto-shaping the pigeon's key peck. *Journal of the Experimental Analysis of Behavior, 11,* 1–8. [3]

Brown, R. G. B. (1965). Courtship behavior in the *Drosophila obscura* group II. *Behaviour, 25,* 281–323. [1]

Brownstein, A. J. (1971). Concurrent schedules of response-independent reinforcement: Duration of a reinforcing stimulus. *Journal of the Experimental Analysis of Behavior, 15,* 211–214. [10]

Brush, F. R., Froehlich, J. C., & Sakellaris, P. C. (1979). Genetic selection for avoidance behavior in the rat. *Behavior Genetics, 9,* 309–316. [12]

Bryant, P. E., & Trabasso, T. (1971). Transitive inferences and memory in young children. *Nature, 232,* 456–458. [15]

Burdick, C. K., & James, J. P. (1970). Spontaneous recovery of conditioned suppression of licking by rats. *Journal of Comparative and Physiological Psychology, 72,* 467–470. [3]

Burkhardt, P. E., & Ayres, J. J. B. (1978). CS and US duration effects in one-trial simultaneous fear conditioning as assessed by conditioned suppression of licking in rats. *Animal Learning and Behavior, 6,* 225–230. [4]

Burns, J. D., & Malone, J. C. (1992). The influence of "preparedness" on autoshaping, schedule performance, and choice. *Journal of the Experimental Analysis of Behavior, 58,* 399–413. [12]

Burr, D. E. S., & Thomas, D. R. (1972). Effect of proactive inhibition upon the post-discrimination generalization gradient. *Journal of Comparative and Physiological Psychology, 81,* 441–448. [13]

Butler, R. A. (1953). Discrimination learning by rhesus monkeys to visual exploration motivation. *Journal of Comparative and Physiological Psychology, 46,* 95–98. [11]

Butter, C. M., & Thomas, D. R. (1958). Secondary reinforcement as a function of the amount of primary reinforcement. *Journal of Comparative and Physiological Psychology, 51,* 346–348. [10]

Camp, D. S., Raymond, G. A., & Church, R. M. (1967). Temporal relationship between response and punishment. *Journal of Experimental Psychology, 74,* 114–123. [9]

Campbell, B. A., & Campbell, E. H. (1962). Retention and extinction of learned fear in infant and adult rats. *Journal of Comparative and Physiological Psychology, 55,* 1–8. [14]

Campbell, B. A., & Coulter, X. (1976). The ontogeny of learning and memory. In M. R. Rosenzweig & L. Bennett (Eds.), *Neural mechanisms of learning and memory* (pp. 209–235). Cambridge, MA: Massachusetts Institute of Technology Press. [14]

Campbell, B. A., & Jaynes, J. (1966). Reinstatement. *Psychological Review, 73,* 478–480. [14]

Campbell, B. A., Jaynes, J., & Misanin, J. R. (1968). Retention of a light–dark discrimination in rats of different ages. *Journal of Comparative and Physiological Psychology, 66,* 467–472. [14]

Campbell, B. A., & Randall, P. (1976). The effect of reinstatement stimulus conditions on the maintenance of long-term memory. *Developmental Psychobiology, 9,* 325–333. [14]

Campbell, B. A., Smith, N. F., & Misanin, J. R. (1966). Effects of punishment on extinction of avoidance behavior: Avoidance–avoidance conflict or vicious circle behavior. *Journal of Comparative and Physiological Psychology, 62,* 495–498. [9]

Campbell, B. A., & Spear, N. E. (1972). Ontogeny of memory. *Psychological Review, 79,* 215–236. [14]

Campeau, S., Liang, K. C., & Davis, M. (1990). Long-term retention of fear potentiated startle following a short training session. *Animal Learning and Behavior, 18,* 462–468. [14]

Candland, D. K. (1993). *Feral children and clever animals: Reflections on human nature.* New York: Oxford University Press. [8]

Candland, D., Horowitz, S., & Culbertson, J. (1962). Acquisition and retention of acquired avoidance with gentling as reinforcement. *Journal of Comparative and Physiological Psychology, 55,* 1062–1064. [9]

Capaldi, E. D., & Sheffer, J. D. (1992). Contrast and reinforcement in consumption. *Learning and Motivation, 23,* 63–79. [9]

Capaldi, E. D., Sheffer, J., & Owens, J. (1991). Food deprivation and conditioned flavor preferences based on sweetened and unsweetened foods. *Animal Learning and Behavior, 19,* 361–368. [7]

Capaldi, E. J. (1958). The effect of different amounts of training on the resistance to extinction of different patterns of partially reinforced responses. *Journal of Comparative and Physiological Psychology, 51,* 367–371. [10]

Capaldi, E. J. (1964). Effect on N-length, number of different N-lengths, and number of reinforcements on resistance to extinction. *Journal of Experimental Psychology, 68,* 230–239. [10]

Capaldi, E. J. (1966). Partial reinforcement: A hypothesis of sequential effects. *Psychological Review, 73,* 459–477. [10]

Capaldi, E. J. (1967). A sequential hypothesis of instrumental learning. In K. W. Spence & J. T. Spence (Eds.), *The psychology of learning and motivation* (Vol. 1, pp. 67–156). New York: Academic Press. [10]

Capaldi, E. J. (1992). Levels of organized behavior in rats. In W. K. Honig & G. Fetterman (Eds.), *Cognitive aspects of stimulus control* (pp. 385–404). Hillsdale, NJ: Erlbaum. [10, 14]

Capaldi, E. J. (1994). The sequential view: From rapidly fading stimulus traces to the organization of memory and the abstract concept of number. *Psychonomic Bulletin and Review, 1,* 156–181. [10, 14]

Capaldi, E. J., & Capaldi, E. D. (1970). Magnitude of partial reward, irregular reward schedules, and a 24-hour ITI: A test of several hypotheses. *Journal of Comparative and Physiological Psychology, 72,* 203–209. [10]

Capaldi, E. J., & Deutsch, E. A. (1967). Effects of severely limited acquisition training and pretraining on the partial reinforcement effect. *Psychonomic Science, 9,* 171–172. [10]

Capaldi, E. J., & Hart, D. (1962). Influence of a small number of partial reinforcement training trials on resistance to extinction. *Journal of Experimental Psychology, 64,* 166–171. [10]

Capaldi, E. J., & Hart, D., & Stanley, L. R. (1963). Effect of intertrial reinforcement on the aftereffect of non-reinforcement and resistance to extinction. *Journal of Experimental Psychology, 65,* 70–74. [10]

Capaldi, E. J., Lanier, A. T., & Godbout, R. C. (1968). Reward schedule effects following severely limited acquisition training. *Journal of Experimental Psychology, 78,* 521–524. [10]

Capaldi, E. J., & Miller, D. J. (1988a). Counting in rats: Its functional significance and the independent cognitive processes that constitute it. *Journal of Experimental Psychology: Animal Behavior Processes, 14,* 3–17. [15]

Capaldi, E. J., & Miller, D. J. (1988b). The rat's simultaneous anticipation of remote events and current events can be sustained by event memories alone. *Animal Learning and Behavior, 16,* 1–7. [10, 14]

Capaldi, E. J., Miller, D. J., Alptekin, S., & Barry, K. (1990). Organized responding in instrumental learning: Chunks and superchunks. *Learning and Motivation, 21,* 415–433. [10, 14]

Capaldi, E. J., Nawrocki, T. M., Miller, D. J., & Verry, D. R. (1986). Time between events as a retrieval cue: Recall and the temporal similarity between the storage and retrieval intervals. *Journal of Experimental Psychology: Animal Behavior Processes, 12,* 258–269. [14]

Capaldi, E. J., Nawrocki, T. M., & Verry, D. R. (1983). The nature of anticipation: An inter- and intraevent process. *Animal Learning and Behavior, 11,* 193–198. [10, 14]

Capaldi, E. J., & Spivey, J. E. (1963). Effect of goal box similarity on the aftereffect of nonreinforcement and resistance to extinction. *Journal of Experimental Psychology, 66,* 461–465. [10]

Capaldi, E. J., & Spivey, J. E. (1964). Intertrial reinforcement and aftereffects at 24-hour intervals. *Psychonomic Science, 1,* 181–182. [10]

Capaldi, E. J., & Verry, D. R. (1981). Serial order anticipation learning in rats: Memory for multiple hedonic events and their order. *Animal Learning and Behavior, 9,* 441–453. [14]

Capaldi, E. J., Verry, D. R., & Davidson, T. L. (1980). Memory, serial anticipation pattern learning, and transfer in rats. *Animal Learning and Behavior, 8,* 575–585. [9]

Capaldi, E. J., Verry, D. R., & Nawrocki, T. M. (1982). Multiple hedonic memory: Memory for more than one hedonic event in rats. *Animal Learning and Behavior, 10,* 351–357. [9]

Capehart, G. W., Eckerman, D. A., Guilkey, M., & Shull, R. L. (1980). A comparison of ratio and interval reinforcement schedules with comparable interreinforcement times. *Journal of the Experimental Analysis of Behavior, 34,* 61–76. [9]

Capehart, J., Tempone, V. J., & Hébert, J. A. (1969). A theory of stimulus equivalence. *Psychological Review, 76,* 405–418. [13]

Caplan, H. J., Karpicke, J., & Rilling, M. (1973). Effects of extended fixed-interval training on reversed scallops. *Animal Learning and Behavior, 1,* 293–296. [9]

Carey, M. P., & Burish, T. G. (1988). Etiology and treatment of the psychological side effects associated with cancer chemotherapy: A critical review and discussion. *Psychological Bulletin, 104,* 307–325. [6]

Carlson, J. G., & Wielkiewicz, R. M. (1972). Delay of reinforcement in instrumental discrimination learning in rats. *Journal of Comparative and Experimental Psychology, 81,* 365–370. [13]

Carlson, J. G., & Wielkiewicz, R. M. (1976). Mediators of the effects of magnitude of reinforcement. *Learning and Motivation, 7,* 184–196. [13]

Carr, G. D., & White, N. (1984). The relationship between stereotypy and memory improvement produced by amphetamine. *Psychopharmacology, 82,* 203–209. [11]

Caspy, T., & Lubow, R. E. (1981). Generality of US preexposure effects: Transfer from food to stock or shock to food with and without the same response requirements. *Animal Learning and Behavior, 9,* 524–532. [10]

Catania, A. C. (1981). The flight from experimental analysis. In C. M. Bradshaw, E. Szabadi, & C. F. Lowe (Eds.), *Quantification of steady-state operant behaviour* (pp. 49–64). Amsterdam: Elsevier/North Holland Biomedical Press. [9]

Catania, A. C., & Reynolds, G. S. (1968). A quantitative analysis of the responding maintained by interval schedules of reinforcement. *Journal of the Experimental Analysis of Behavior, 11,* 327–383. [9]

Chaplin, J. P., & Krawiec, T. S. (1974). *Systems and theories of psychology* (3rd ed.). New York: Holt, Rinehart and Winston. [2]

Charlton, S. G. (1983). Differential conditionability: Reinforcing grooming in golden hamsters. *Animal Learning and Behavior, 11,* 27–34. [9]

Charnov, E. L. (1976). Optimal foraging: The marginal value theorem. *Theoretical Population Biology, 9,* 129–136. [11]

Chatlosh, D. L., & Wasserman, E. A. (1992). Memory and expectancy in delayed discrimination procedures. In I. Gormezano & E. A. Wasserman (Eds.), *Learning and memory: The behavioral and biological substrates* (pp. 61–79). Hillsdale, NJ: Erlbaum. [14]

Chatlosh, D. L., Neunaber, D. J., & Wasserman, E. A. (1985). Response–outcome contingency: Behavioral and judgmental effects of appetitive and aversive outcomes with college students. *Learning and Motivation, 16,* 1–34. [8]

Chomsky, N. A. (1959). Review of *Verbal behavior*, by B. F. Skinner. *Language, 35,* 26–58. [15]

Chung, S., & Herrnstein, R. J. (1967). Choice and delay of reinforcement. *Journal of the Experimental Analysis of Behavior, 10,* 67–74. [10]

Church, R. M. (1978). The internal clock. In S. H. Hulse, H. Fowler, & W. K. Honig (Eds.), *Cognitive processes in animal behavior* (pp. 277–310). Hillsdale, NJ: Erlbaum. [15]

Church, R. M. (1980). Short-term memory for time intervals. *Learning and Motivation, 11,* 208–219. [15]

Church, R. M. (1984). Properties of the internal clock. In J. Gibbon & L. G. Allan (Eds.), *Annals of the New York Academy of Sciences: Vol 423. Timing and time perception* (pp. 566–582). New York: New York Academy of Sciences. [15]

Church, R. M. (1989). Theories of timing behavior. In S. B. Klein & R. R. Mowrer (Eds.), *Contemporary learning theories: Instrumental conditioning theory and the impact of biological constraints on learning* (pp. 41–71). Hillsdale, NJ: Erlbaum. [15]

Church, R. M., & Broadbent, H. (1992). A connectionist model of timing. In M. L. Commons, S. Grossberg, & J. E. R. Staddon (Eds.), *Neural network models of conditioning and action* (pp. 225–240). Hillsdale, NJ: Erlbaum. [15]

Church, R. M., & Deluty, M. Z. (1977). Bisection of temporal intervals. *Journal of Experimental Psychology: Animal Behavior Processes, 3,* 216–228. [15]

Church, R. M., & Gibbon, J. (1982). Temporal generalization. *Journal of Experimental Psychology: Animal Behavior Processes, 8,* 165–186. [15]

Church, R. M., Raymond, G. A., & Beauchamp, R. D. (1967). Response suppression as a function of intensity and duration of a punishment. *Journal of Comparative and Physiological Psychology, 63,* 39–44. [9]

Church, R. M., Wooten, C. L., & Matthews, T. J. (1970). Discriminative punishment and the conditioned emotional response. *Learning and Motivation, 1,* 1–17. [8]

Clayton, N. S. (1987). Song learning in cross-fostered zebra finches: A re-examination of the sensitive phase. *Behaviour, 102,* 67–81. [12]

Coleman, S. R., & Gormezano, I. (1971). Classical conditioning of the rabbit's (*Oryctolagus cuniculus*) nictitating membrane response under symmetrical CS–US interval shifts. *Journal of Comparative and Physiological Psychology, 77,* 447–455. [4]

Collier, G. H., Johnson, D. F., Hill, W. L., & Kaufman, L. W. (1986). The economics of the law of effect. *Journal of the Experimental Analysis of Behavior, 46,* 113–136. [9]

Colwill, R. M., & Rescorla, R. A. (1985a). Postconditioning devaluation of a reinforcer affects instrumental responding. *Journal of Experimental Psychology: Animal Behavior Processes, 11,* 120–132. [11]

Colwill, R. M., & Rescorla, R. A. (1985b). Extensive training, partial reinforcement, and temporal gaps do not affect S–S learning in second-order autoshaping. *Animal Learning and Behavior, 13,* 165–170. [5]

Colwill, R. M., & Rescorla, R. A. (1988a). Associations between the discriminative stimulus and the reinforcer in instrumental learning. *Journal of Experimental Psychology: Animal Behavior Processes, 14,* 155–164. [11]

Colwill, R. M., & Rescorla, R. A. (1988b). The role of response–reinforcer associations increases throughout extended instrumental training. *Animal Learning and Behavior, 16,* 105–111. [11]

Colwill, R. M., & Rescorla, R. A. (1990). Evidence for the hierarchical structure of instrumental learning. *Animal Learning and Behavior, 18,* 71–82. [11]

Cook, R. G. (1980). Retroactive interference in pigeon short-term memory by a reduction in ambient illumination. *Journal of Experimental Psychology: Animal Behavior Processes, 6,* 326–338. [14]

Cook, R. G., Brown, M. F., & Riley, D. A. (1985). Flexible memory processing by rats: Use of prospective and retrospective information in the radial maze. *Journal of Experimental Psychology: Animal Behavior Processes, 11,* 453–469. [14]

Cook, R. G., Cavoto, K. K., & Cavoto, B. R. (1995). Same–different texture discrimination and concept learning by pigeons. *Journal of Experimental Psychology: Animal Behavior Processes, 21,* 253–260. [15]

Coombes, S., Revusky, S., & Lett, B. T. (1980). Long-delay taste aversion learning in an unpoisoned rat: Exposure to a poisoned rat as the unconditioned stimulus. *Learning and Motivation, 11,* 256–266. [7]

Cooper, L. D. (1991). Temporal factors in classical conditioning. *Learning and Motivation, 22,* 129–152. [4]

Coulter, X., Collier, A. C., & Campbell, B. A. (1976). Long-term retention of early Pavlovian fear conditioning in infant rats. *Journal of Experimental Psychology: Animal Behavior Processes, 2,* 48–56. [14]

Couvillon, P. A., Brandon, S. E., Woodard, W. T., & Bitterman, M. E. (1980). Performance of pigeons in patterned sequences of rewarded and nonrewarded trials. *Journal of Experimental Psychology: Animal Behavior Processes, 6,* 137–154. [9]

Cowie, R. J. (1977). Optimal foraging in great tits *Parus major. Nature, 268,* 137–139. [11]

Cox, J. K., & D'Amato, M. R. (1982). Matching to compound samples by monkeys (*Cebus appela*): Shared attention or generalization decrement? *Journal of Experimental Psychology: Animal Behavior Processes, 8,* 209–225. [14]

Crawford, M., & Masterson, F. (1978). Components of the flight response can reinforce bar-press avoidance learning. *Journal of Experimental Psychology: Animal Behavior Processes, 4,* 144–151. [12]

Crawford, M., & Masterson, F. A. (1982). Species-specific defense reactions and avoidance learning. *The Pavlovian Journal of Biological Science, 17*, 204–214. [12]

Crawford, M., Masterson, F., & Wilson, D. (1977). Species-specific defense reactions in escape-from-fear situations. *Animal Learning and Behavior, 5*, 63–72. [12]

Crespi, L. P. (1942). Quantitative variation in incentive and performance in the white rat. *American Journal of Psychology, 55*, 467–517. [9]

Crossman, E. K., Bonem, E. J., & Phelps, B. J. (1987). A comparison of response patterns on fixed-, variable-, and random-ratio schedules. *Journal of the Experimental Analysis of Behavior, 48*, 395–406. [9]

Crowell, C. R., & Anderson, D. C. (1972). Variations in intensity, interstimulus interval, and interval between preconditioning CS exposures and conditioning with rats. *Journal of Comparative and Physiological Psychology, 79*, 291–298. [5]

Crowell, C. R., & Bernhardt, T. P. (1979). The feature-positive effect and sign-tracking behavior during the discrimination learning in the rat. *Animal Learning and Behavior, 7*, 313–317. [13]

Crowell, C. R., Hinson, R. E., & Siegel, S. (1981). The role of conditional drug responses in tolerance to the hypothermic effects of ethanol. *Psychopharmacology, 73*, 51–54. [7]

Curio, E. (1993). Proximate and developmental aspects of antipredator behavior. In P. J. B. Slater, J. S. Rosenblatt, C. T. Snowdon, & M. Milinski (Eds.), *Advances in the study of behavior* (Vol. 22, pp. 135–238). San Diego, California: Academic Press. [1]

Dafters, R., Hetherington, M., & McCartney, H. (1983). Blocking and sensory preconditioning effects in morphine analgesic tolerance: Support for a Pavlovian conditioning model of drug tolerance. *The Quarterly Journal of Experimental Psychology, 35B*, 1–11. [7]

Daly, H. B. (1968). Excitatory and inhibitory effects of complete and incomplete reward reduction in the double runway. *Journal of Experimental Psychology, 76*, 430–438. [10]

Daly, H. B. (1969). Learning of a hurdle-jump response to escape cues paired with reduced reward or frustrative nonreward. *Journal of Experimental Psychology, 79*, 146–157. [2]

Daly, H. B. (1970). Combined effects of fear and frustration on acquisition of a hurdle-jump response. *Journal of Experimental Psychology, 83*, 89–93. [2, 10]

Daly, H. B. (1991). Changes in learning about aversive nonreward accounts for ontogeny of paradoxical appetitive reward effects in the rat pup: A mathematical model (DMOD) integrates results. *Psychological Bulletin, 109*, 325–339. [10]

Daly, H. B., & Daly, J. T. (1982). A mathematical model of reward and aversive nonreward: Its application in over 30 appetitive learning situations. *Journal of Experimental Psychology: General, 111*, 441–480. [10]

D'Amato, M. R. (1973). Delayed matching and short-term memory in monkeys. In G. H. Bower (Ed.), *The psychology of learning and motivation: Vol. 7. Advances in research and theory* (pp. 227–269). New York: Academic Press. [14]

D'Amato, M. R., & Buckiewicz, J. (1980). Long-delay, one-trial conditioned preference and retention in monkeys (*Cebus apella*). *Animal Learning and Behavior, 8*, 359–362. [9]

D'Amato, M. R., & Cox, J. K. (1976). Delay of consequences and short-term memory in monkeys. In D. L. Medin, W. A. Roberts, & R. T. Davis (Eds.), *Processes of animal memory* (pp. 49–78). Hillsdale, NJ: Erlbaum. [14]

D'Amato, M. R., & O'Neill, W. (1971). Effect of delay-interval illumination on matching behavior in the capuchin monkey. *Journal of Experimental Psychology, 15*, 327–333. [14]

D'Amato, M. R., & Salmon, D. P. (1984). Cognitive processes in cebus monkeys. In H. L. Roitblat, T. G. Bever, & H. S. Terrace (Eds.), *Animal cognition* (pp. 149–168). Hillsdale, NJ: Erlbaum. [15]

D'Amato, M. R., Salmon, D. P., & Colombo, M. (1985). Extent and limits of the matching concept in monkeys (*Cebus apella*). *Journal of Experimental Psychology: Animal Behavior Processes, 11*, 35–51. [15]

D'Amato, M. R., & Schiff, D. (1964). Long-term discriminated avoidance performance in the rat. *Journal of Comparative and Physiological Psychology, 57*, 123–126. [12]

D'Amato, M. R., & van Sant, P. (1988). The person concept in monkeys (*Cebus apella*). *Journal of Experimental Psychology: Animal Behavior Processes, 14*, 43–55. [15]

Dantzer, R. (1977). Behavioral effects of benzodiazepines: A review. *Biobehavioral Reviews, 1*, 71–86. [10]

Davey, G. (1989). *Ecological learning theory.* New York: Routledge. [1, 4, 7]

Davey, G. C. L., & Cleland, G. G. (1982). Topography of signal-centered behavior in the rat: Effects of deprivation state and reinforcer type. *Journal of the Experimental Analysis of Behavior, 38*, 291–304. [6]

Davey, G. C. L., & McKenna, I. (1983). The effects of postconditioning revaluation of CS₁ and UCS following Pavlovian second-order electrodermal conditioning in humans. *The Quarterly Journal of Experimental Psychology, 35B*, 125–133. [5]

Davey, G. C. L., Phillips, J. H., & Witty, S. (1989). Signal-directed behavior in the rat: Interactions between the nature of the CS and the nature of the UCS. *Animal Learning and Behavior, 17*, 447–456. [4, 6]

Davidson, M., & McCarthy, D. (1987). *The matching law: A research review.* Hillsdale, NJ: Erlbaum. [10]

Davidson, T. L., & Rescorla, R. A. (1986). Transfer of facilitation in the rat. *Animal Learning and Behavior, 14,* 380–386. [5]

Davis, E. R., & Platt, J. R. (1983). Contiguity and contingency in the acquisition and maintenance of an operant. *Learning and Motivation, 14,* 487–512. [8]

Davis, H. (1992a). Logical transitivity in animals. In W. K. Honig & J. G. Fetterman (Eds.), *Cognitive aspects of stimulus control* (pp. 405–429). Hillsdale, NJ: Erlbaum. [15]

Davis, H. (1992b). Transitive inference in rats (*Rattus norvegicus*). *Journal of Comparative Psychology, 106,* 342–349. [15]

Davis, H., & Memmott, J. (1982). Counting behavior in animals: A critical evaluation. *Psychological Bulletin, 92,* 547–571. [15]

Davis, H., & Perusse, R. (1988a). Human-based social interaction can reward a rat's behavior. *Animal Learning and Behavior, 16,* 89–92. [9]

Davis, H., & Perusse, R. (1988b). Numerical competence in animals: Definitional issues, current evidence, and a new research agenda. *Behavioral and Brain Sciences, 11,* 561–615. [15]

Davis, H. P., & Squire, L. R. (1984). Protein synthesis and memory: A review. *Psychological Bulletin, 96,* 518–559. [11]

Davis, S. F., Moore, S. A., Cowen, C. L., Thurston, D., & Maggio, J. C. (1982). Defensive burying in the Mongolian gerbil (*Meriones unguiculatus*) as a function of size and shape of the test chamber. *Animal Learning and Behavior, 10,* 516–520. [12]

Dawkins, M. (1971). Shifts of 'attention' in chicks during feeding. *Animal Behaviour, 19,* 575–582. [7]

Dawson, G. R., & Dickinson, A. (1990). Performance on ratio and interval schedules with matched reinforcement rates. *The Quarterly Journal of Experimental Psychology, 42B,* 225–239. [9]

Deane, G. E. (1965). Cardiac conditioning in the albino rabbit using three CS–UCS intervals. *Psychonomic Science, 3,* 119–120. [4]

DeCola, J. P., Rosellini, R. A., & Warren, D. A. (1988). A dissociation of the effects of control and prediction. *Learning and Motivation, 19,* 269–282. [10]

Deese, J. (1972). *Psychology as science and art.* New York: Harcourt Brace Jovanovich. [2]

Delgado, J. M. R., Roberts, W. W., & Miller, N. E. (1954). Learning motivated by electrical stimulation of the brain. *American Journal of Physiology, 179,* 587–593. [11]

Delius, J. D., & Habers, G. (1978). Symmetry: Can pigeons conceptualize it? *Behavioral Biology, 22,* 336–342. [15]

DeLong, R. E., & Wasserman, E. A. (1981). Effects of differential reinforcement expectancies on successive matching-to-sample performance in pigeons. *Journal of Experimental Psychology: Animal Behavior Processes, 7,* 394–412. [14]

Delprato, D. J., & Holmes, P. A. (1977). Facilitation of discriminated lever-press avoidance by noncontingent shocks. *Learning and Motivation, 8,* 238–246. [12]

Denny, M. R. (1970). Elicitation theory applied to an analysis of the overlearning reversal effect. In J. H. Reynierse (Ed.), *Current issues in animal learning: A colloquium* (pp. 175–194). Lincoln: University of Nebraska Press. [13]

Denny, M. R. (1991). *Fear, avoidance, and phobias: A fundamental analysis.* Hillsdale, NJ: Erlbaum. [1]

Desiderato, O., Butler, B., & Meyer, C. (1966). Changes in fear generalization gradients as a function of delayed testing. *Journal of Experimental Psychology, 72,* 678–682. [13]

Dess, N. K., Linwick, D., Patterson, J. Overmier, J. B., & Levine, S. (1983). Immediate and proactive effects of controllability and predictability on plasma cortisol responses to shock in dogs. *Behavioral Neuroscience, 97,* 1005–1016. [10]

Dess, N. K., Raizer, J., Chapman, C. D., & Garcia, J. (1988). Stressors in the learned helplessness paradigm: Effects on body weight and conditioned taste aversions in rats. *Physiology and Behavior, 44,* 483–490. [10]

Detke, M. J. (1991). Extinction of sequential conditioned inhibition. *Animal Learning and Behavior, 19,* 345–354. [3]

Deutsch, R. (1978). Effects of CS amount on conditioned taste aversion at different CS–US intervals. *Animal Learning and Behavior, 6,* 258–260. [4, 7]

DeVietti, T. L., Bauste, R. L., Nutt, G., Barrett, O. V., Daly, K., & Petree, A. D. (1987). Latent inhibition: A trace conditioning phenomenon? *Learning and Motivation, 18,* 185–201. [5]

de Villiers, P. A. (1974). The law of effect and avoidance: A quantitative relationship between response rate and shock-frequency reduction. *Journal of the Experimental Analysis of Behavior, 21,* 223–235. [10]

de Villiers, P. A. (1980). Toward a quantitative theory of punishment. *Journal of the Experimental Analysis of Behavior, 33,* 15–25. [10]

de Villiers, P. A., & Herrnstein, R. J. (1976). Toward a law of response strength. *Psychological Bulletin, 83,* 1131–1153. [10]

Devine, J. V. (1970). Stimulus attributes and training procedures in learning-set formation of rhesus and cebus monkeys. *Journal of Comparative and Physiological Psychology, 73,* 62–67. [13]

Devine, J. V., Jones, L. C., Neville, J. W., & Sakai, D. J. (1977). Sample duration and type of stimuli in delayed matching-to-sample in rhesus monkeys. *Animal Learning and Behavior, 5,* 57–62. [14]

DeVito, P. L., & Fowler, H. (1986). Effects of contingency violations on the extinction of a conditioned fear inhibitor and a conditioned fear excitor. *Journal of Experimental Psychology: Animal Behavior Processes, 12*, 99–115. [3]

DeVito, P. L., & Fowler, H. (1987). Enhancement of conditioned inhibition via an extinction treatment. *Animal Learning and Behavior, 15*, 448–454. [3]

de Vos, G. J., & Bolhuis, J. J. (1990). An investigation into blocking of filial imprinting in the chick during exposure to a compound stimulus. *The Quarterly Journal of Experimental Psychology, 42B*, 289–312. [12]

Deweer, B., & Sara, S. J. (1984). Background stimuli as a reminder after spontaneous forgetting: Role of duration of cuing and cuing-test interval. *Animal Learning and Behavior, 12*, 238–247. [14]

Deweer, B., Sara, S. J., & Hars, B. (1980). Contextual cues and memory retrieval in rats: Elimination of forgetting by a pretest exposure to background stimuli. *Animal Learning and Behavior, 8*, 265–272. [14]

Dews, P. B. (1969). Studies on responding under fixed-interval schedules of reinforcement: The effects on the pattern of responding of changes in requirement at reinforcement. *Journal of the Experimental Analysis of Behavior, 12*, 191–199. [9]

Dickinson, A., Hall, G., & Mackintosh, N. J. (1976). Surprise and the attenuation of blocking. *Journal of Experimental Psychology: Animal Behavior Processes, 2*, 313–322. [5, 6]

Dickinson, A., & Mackintosh, N. J. (1979). Reinforcer specificity in the enhancement of conditioning by post-trial surprise. *Journal of Experimental Psychology: Animal Behavior Processes, 5*, 162–177. [5]

Dickinson, A., Watt, A., & Griffiths, W. J. H. (1992). Free-operant acquisition with delayed reinforcement. *The Quarterly Journal of Experimental Psychology, 45B*, 241–258. [9]

Dinsmoor, J. A. (1950). A quantitative comparison of the discriminative and reinforcing functions of a stimulus. *Journal of Experimental Psychology, 40*, 458–472. [10]

Dinsmoor, J. A., & Clayton, M. H. (1963). Chaining and secondary reinforcement based on escape from shock. *Journal of the Experimental Analysis of Behavior, 6*, 75–80. [10]

Dittrich, W. H., & Lea, S. E. G. (1993). Motion as a natural category for pigeons: Generalization and a feature-positive effect. *Journal of the Experimental Analysis of Behavior, 59*, 115–129. [15]

Domjan, M. (1972). CS preexposure in taste aversion learning: Effects of deprivation and preexposure duration. *Learning and Motivation, 3*, 389–402. [5, 7]

Domjan, M. (1977). Selective suppression of drinking during a limited period following aversive drug treatment in rats. *Journal of Experimental Psychology: Animal Behavior Processes, 3*, 66–76. [4]

Domjan, M. (1980). Ingestional aversion learning: Unique and general processes. In J. S. Rosenblatt, R. A. Hinde, C. Beer, & M.-C. Busnel (Eds.), *Advances in the study of behavior* (Vol 11, pp. 275–336). New York: Academic Press. [7]

Domjan, M. (1983). Biological constraints on instrumental and classical conditioning: Implications for general process theory. In G. Bower (Ed.), *The psychology of learning and motivation* (Vol 17, pp. 215–277). New York: Academic Press. [7]

Domjan, M., Greene, P., & North, N. C. (1989). Contextual conditioning and the control of copulatory behavior by species specific signal stimuli in male Japanese quail. *Journal of Experimental Psychology: Animal Behavior Processes, 15*, 147–153. [7]

Domjan, M., & Hanlon, M. J. (1982). Poison-avoidance learning to food-related tactile stimuli: Avoidance of texture cues by rats. *Animal Learning and Behavior, 10*, 293–300. [7]

Domjan, M., Huber-McDonald, M., & Holloway, K. S. (1992). Conditioning copulatory behavior to an artifical object: Efficacy of stimulus fading. *Animal Learning and Behavior, 20*, 350–362. [7]

Domjan, M., O'Vary, D., & Greene, P. (1988). Conditioning of appetitive and consummatory sexual behavior in male Japanese quail. *Journal of the Experimental Analysis of Behavior, 50*, 505–519. [7]

Domjan, M., & Siegel, S. (1971). Conditioned suppression following CS preexposure. *Psychonomic Science, 25*, 11–12. [5]

Domjan, M., & Wilson, N. E. (1972). Contribution of ingestive behaviors to taste-aversion learning in the rat. *Journal of Comparative and Physiological Psychology, 80*, 403–412. [7]

Donahoe, J. W., & Palmer, D. C. (1988). Inhibition: A cautionary tale. *Journal of the Experimental Analysis of Behavior, 50*, 333–341. [3]

Donegan, N. H., & Thompson, R. F. (1991). The search for the engram. In J. L. Martinez & R. P. Kesner (Eds.), *Learning and memory: A biological view* (pp. 3–58). San Diego, CA: Academic Press. [11]

Doré, F. Y., & Dumas, C. (1987). Psychology of animal cognition: Piagetian studies. *Psychological Bulletin, 102*, 219–233. [15]

Dougan, J. D., Farmer-Dougan, V. A., & McSweeney, F. K. (1989). Behavioral contrast in pigeons and rats: A comparative analysis. *Animal Learning and Behavior, 17*, 247–255. [9]

Dreyfus, L. R., Fetterman, J. G., Smith, L. D., & Stubbs, D. A. (1988). Discrimination of temporal relations by pigeons. *Journal of Experimental Psychology: Animal Behavior Processes, 14*, 349–367. [15]

Droungas, A., & LoLordo, V. M. (1991). Taste-mediated potentiation of odor aversion induced by lithium chloride: Effects of preconditioning exposure to the conditioned stimulus and postconditioning extinction of the taste aversion. *Learning and Motivation, 22*, 291–310. [7]

Drugan, R. C., & Maier, S. F. (1982). The nature of the activity deficit produced by inescapable shock. *Animal Learning and Behavior, 10,* 401–406. [10]

Duncan, C. P. (1949). The retroactive effect of electroshock on learning. *Journal of Comparative and Physiological Psychology, 42,* 32–44. [14]

Dunham, P. J. (1971). Punishment: Method and theory. *Psychological Review, 78,* 58–70. [8]

Dunham, P. J. (1978). Changes in unpunished responding during response-contingent punishment. *Animal Learning and Behavior, 6,* 174–180. [8]

Dunham, P. J., & Grantmyre, J. (1982). Changes in a multi-response repertoire during response-contingent punishment and response restriction: Sequential relationships. *Journal of the Experimental Analysis of Behavior, 37,* 123–133. [8]

Dunn, A. J. (1980). Neurochemistry of learning and memory: An evaluation of recent data. *Annual Review of Psychology, 31,* 343–390. [11]

Durlach, P. J., & Rescorla, R. A. (1980). Potentiation rather than overshadowing in flavor-aversion learning: An analysis in terms of within-compound associations. *Journal of Experimental Psychology: Animal Behavior Processes, 6,* 175–187. [7]

Dyal, J. A., & Sytsma, D. (1976). Relative persistence as a function of order of reinforcement schedules. *Journal of Experimental Psychology: Animal Behavior Processes, 2,* 370–375. [10]

Dyer, F. C. (1991). Bees acquire route-based memories but not cognitive maps in a familiar landscape. *Animal Behaviour, 41,* 239–246. [14]

Eales, L. A. (1985). Song learning in zebra finches: Some effects of song model availability on what is learnt and when. *Animal Behaviour, 33,* 1293–1300. [12]

Eales, L. A. (1987a). Do zebra finch males that have been raised by another species still tend to select a conspecific song tutor? *Animal Behaviour, 35,* 1347–1355. [12]

Eales, L. A. (1987b). Song learning in female-raised zebra finches: Another look at the sensitive phase. *Animal Behaviour, 35,* 1356–1365. [12]

Ebbinghaus, H. (1885). *Uber das Gedachtnis.* Leipzig: Duncker & Humbolt (H. A. Ruger & C. E. Bussenius, Trans.) (Reprinted as *Memory,* 1913, New York: Teachers College; 1964, New York: Dover) [1]

Edwards, C. A., & Honig, W. K. (1987). Memorization and "feature selection" in the acquisition of natural concepts in pigeons. *Learning and Motivation, 18,* 235–260. [15]

Edwards, C. A., Jagielo, J. A., Zentall, T. R., & Hogan, D. E. (1982). Acquired equivalence and distinctiveness in matching to sample by pigeons: Mediation by reinforcer-specific expectancies. *Journal of Experimental Psychology: Animal Behavior Processes, 8,* 244–259. [14]

Egger, M. D., & Miller, N. E. (1962). Secondary reinforcement in rats as a function of information value and reliability of the stimulus. *Journal of Experimental Psychology, 64,* 97–104. [4]

Eikelboom, R., & Stewart, J. (1982). Conditioning of drug-induced physiological responses. *Psychological Review, 89,* 507–528. [7]

Eisenberger, R. (1972). Explanation of rewards that do not reduce tissue needs. *Psychological Bulletin, 77,* 319–339. [9]

Eisenberger, R., Weier, F., Masterson, F. A., & Theis, L. Y. (1989). Fixed-ratio schedules increase generalized self-control: Preference for large rewards despite high effort or punishment. *Journal of Experimental Psychology: Animal Behavior Processes, 15,* 383–392. [10]

Eiserer, L. A. (1978). The effects of tactile stimulation on imprinting in ducklings after the sensitive period. *Animal Learning and Behavior, 6,* 27–29. [12]

Eiserer, L. A. (1980). Long-term potential for imprinting in ducks and chickens. *Journal of the Experimental Analysis of Behavior, 33,* 383–395. [12]

Eiserer, L. A., & Hoffman, H. S. (1974). Imprinting of ducklings to a second stimulus when a previously imprinted stimulus is occasionally presented. *Animal Learning and Behavior, 2,* 123–125. [12]

Eiserer, L. A., Hoffman, H. S., & Klein, S. H. (1975). Persistence of acquired behavioral control in the context of imprinting. *Journal of the Experimental Analysis of Behavior, 24,* 255–266. [12]

Eiserer, L. A., & Swope, R. L. (1980). Acquisition of behavioral control by static visual features of an imprinting object: Species generality. *Animal Learning and Behavior, 8,* 481–484. [12]

Ellins, S. R., Thompson, L., & Swanson, W. E. (1983). Effects of novelty and familiarity on illness-induced aversion to food and place cues in coyotes (*Canis latrans*). *Journal of Comparative Psychology, 97,* 302–309. [7]

Ellis, W. R. (1970). Role of stimulus sequences in stimulus discrimination and stimulus generalization. *Journal of Experimental Psychology, 83,* 155–163. [13]

Ellison, G. D. (1964). Differential salivary conditioning to traces. *Journal of Comparative and Physiological Psychology, 57,* 373–380. [4]

Emmelkamp, P. M. G. (1985). Anxiety and fear. In A. S. Bellack, M. Hersen, & A. E. Kazdin (Eds.), *International handbook of behavior modification and therapy* (pp. 125–171). New York: Plenum Press. [1]

Erichsen, J. T., Krebs, J. R., & Houston, A. I. (1980). Optimal foraging and cryptic prey. *Journal of Animal Ecology, 49,* 271–276. [11]

Ettenberg, A. (1989). Dopamine, neuroleptics and reinforced behavior. *Neuroscience and Biobehavioral Reviews, 13*, 105–111. [11]

Eysenck, H. J. (1952). The effects of psychotherapy: An evaluation. *Journal of Consulting Psychology, 16*, 319–324. [1]

Fagan, A. M., & Olton, D. S. (1987). Spatial learning set acquisition in rats. *The Quarterly Journal of Experimental Psychology, 39*, 65–75. [13]

Fallon, D. (1971). Increased resistance to extinction following punishment and reward: High frustration tolerance or low frustration magnitude? *Journal of Comparative and Physiological Psychology, 77*, 245–255. [10]

Fanselow, M. S. (1986). Associative vs. topographical accounts of the immediate shock-freezing deficit in rats: Implications for the response selection rules governing species-specific defensive reactions. *Learning and Motivation, 17*, 16–39. [7, 12]

Fanselow, M. S. (1994). Neural organization of the defensive behavior system responsible for fear. *Psychonomic Bulletin and Review, 1*, 429–438. [12]

Fanselow, M. S., DeCola, J. P., & Young, S. L. (1993). Mechanisms responsible for reduced contextual conditioning with massed unsignaled unconditional stimuli. *Journal of Experimental Psychology: Animal Behavior Processes, 19*, 121–137. [12]

Fanselow, M. S., & Lester, L. S. (1988). A functional behavioristic approach to aversively motivate behavior: Predatory imminence as a determinant of the topography of defensive behavior. In R. C. Bolles & M. D. Beecher (Eds.), *Evolution and learning* (pp. 185–211). Hillsdale, NJ: Erlbaum. [12]

Fanselow, M. S., Lester, L. S., & Helmstetter, F. J. (1988). Changes in feeding and foraging as an antipredator defensive strategy: A laboratory simulation using aversive stimulation in a closed economy. *Journal of the Experimental Analysis of Behavior, 50*, 361–374. [11]

Fanselow, M. S., & Sigmundi, R. A. (1986). Species-specific danger signals, endogenous opioid analgesia, and defensive behavior. *Journal of Experimental Psychology: Animal Behavior Processes, 12*, 301–309. [7]

Farley, J. (1980). Reinforcement and punishment effects in concurrent schedules: A test of two models. *Journal of the Experimental Analysis of Behavior, 33*, 311–326. [10]

Farthing, G. S., Wagner, J. M., Gilmour, S., & Waxman, H. M. (1977). Short-term memory and information processing in pigeons. *Learning and Motivation, 8*, 520–532. [14]

Fedorchak, P. M., & Bolles, R. C. (1986). Differential outcome effect using a biologically neutral outcome difference. *Journal of Experimental Psychology: Animal Behavior Processes, 12*, 125–130 [13]

Fedorchak, P. M., & Bolles, R. C. (1987). Hunger enhances the expression of calorie- but not taste-mediated conditioned flavor preferences. *Journal of Experimental Psychology: Animal Behavior Processes, 13*, 73–79. [7]

Feigley, D. A., & Spear, N. E. (1970). Effect of age and punishment condition on long-term retention by the rat of active- and passive-avoidance learning. *Journal of Comparative and Physiological Psychology, 73*, 515–526. [14]

Feldman, D. T., & Gordon, W. C. (1979). The alleviation of short-term retention decrements with reactivation. *Learning and Motivation, 10*, 198–210. [14]

Felton, M., & Lyon, D. O. (1966). The post-reinforcement pause. *Journal of the Experimental Analysis of Behavior, 9*, 131–134. [9]

Fernald, D. (1979). *The Hans legacy: A story of science.* Hillsdale, NJ: Erlbaum. [2]

Fernandes, D. M., & Church, R. M. (1982). Discrimination of the number of sequential events by rats. *Animal Learning and Behavior, 10*, 171–176. [15]

Ferrandiz, P., & Pardo, A. (1990). Immunization to learned helplessness in appetitive noncontingent contexts. *Animal Learning and Behavior, 18*, 252–256. [10]

Ferster, C. B. (1953). Sustained behavior under delayed reinforcement. *Journal of Experimental Psychology, 45*, 218–224. [10]

Ferster, C. B., & Skinner, B. F. (1957). *Schedules of reinforcement.* New York: Appleton-Century-Crofts. [9]

Fetterman, J. G. (1993). Numerosity discrimination: Both time and number matter. *Journal of Experimental Psychology: Animal Behavior Processes, 19*, 149–164. [15]

Fetterman, J. G., Dreyfus, L. R., & Stubbs, D. A. (1985). Scaling of response-based events. *Journal of Experimental Psychology: Animal Behavior Processes, 11*, 388–404. [15]

Fetterman, J. G., & Killeen, P. R. (1991). Adjusting the pacemaker. *Learning and Motivation, 22*, 226–252. [15]

Fetterman, J. G., & Killeen, P. R. (1995). Categorical scaling of time: Implications for clock–counter models. *Journal of Experimental Psychology: Animal Behavior Processes, 21*, 43–63. [15]

Fitzgerald, R. D., & Martin, G. K. (1971). Heart-rate conditioning in rats as a function of inter-stimulus interval. *Psychological Reports, 29*, 1103–1110. [4]

Fitzgerald, R. D., & Teyler, T. J. (1970). Trace and delayed heart-rate conditioning in rats as a function of US intensity. *Journal of Comparative and Physiological Psychology, 70*, 242–253. [4]

Flaherty, C. F. (1982). Incentive contrast: A review of behavioral changes following shifts in reward. *Animal Learning and Behavior, 10*, 409–440. [9]

Flaherty, C. F., Grigson, P. S., & Brady, A. (1987). Relative novelty of conditioning context influences directionality of glycemic conditioning. *Journal of Experimental Psychology: Animal Behavior Processes, 13,* 144–149. [7]

Flaherty, C. F., & Rowan, G. A. (1985). Anticipatory contrast: Within-subjects analysis. *Animal Learning and Behavior, 13,* 2–5. [9]

Flaherty, C. F., & Rowan, G. A. (1986). Successive, simultaneous and anticipatory contrast in the consumption of saccharin solutions. *Journal of Experimental Psychology: Animal Behavior Processes, 12,* 381–393. [9]

Flaherty, C. F., Uzwiak, A. J., Levine, J., Smith, M., Hall, P., & Schuler, R. (1980). Apparent hyperglycemic and hypoglycemic conditioned responses with exogenous insulin as the unconditioned stimulus. *Animal Learning and Behavior, 8,* 382–386. [7]

Flavell, J. H. (1985). *Cognitive development* (2nd ed.). Englewood Cliffs, NJ: Prentice-Hall. [15]

Fountain, S. B. (1990). Rule abstraction, item memory, and chunking in rat serial-pattern tracking. *Journal of Experimental Psychology: Animal Behavior Processes, 16,* 96–105. [14]

Fountain, S. B., & Hulse, S. H. (1981). Extrapolation of serial stimulus patterns by rats. *Animal Learning and Behavior, 9,* 381–384. [9]

Fountain, S. B., & Rowan, J. D. (1995). Sensitivity to violations of "run" and "trill" structures in rat serial-pattern learning. *Journal of Experimental Psychology: Animal Behavior Processes, 21,* 78–81. [00]

Fouts, R. S., & Rigby, R. L. (1977). Man–chimpanzee communication. In T. A. Sebeok (Ed.), *How animals communicate* (pp. 1034–1054). Bloomington, IN: Indiana University Press. [15]

Fowler, H. (1967). Satiation and curiosity. In K. W. Spence & J. T. Spence (Eds.), *The psychology of learning and motivation* (Vol. 1, pp. 158–227). New York: Academic Press. [9]

Fowler, H., Lysle, D. T., & DeVitto, P. L. (1991). Conditioned excitation and conditioned inhibition of fear: Asymmetrical processes as evident in extinction. In M. R. Denny (Ed.), *Fear, avoidance, and phobias* (pp. 317–362). Hillsdale, NJ: Erlbaum. [3]

Fowler, H., & Trapold, M. A. (1962). Escape performance as a function of delay of reinforcement. *Journal of Experimental Psychology, 63,* 464–467. [9]

Franchina, J. J. (1969). Escape behavior and shock intensity: Within-subject versus between-groups comparisons. *Journal of Comparative and Physiological Psychology, 69,* 241–245. [9]

Freedman, P. E., Hennessy, F. W., & Groner, D. (1974). Effects of varying active/passive shock levels in shuttle box avoidance in rats. *Journal of Comparative and Physiological Psychology, 86,* 79–84. [9]

Frey, P. W., Maisiak, R., & Duque, G. (1976). Unconditioned stimulus characteristics in rabbit eyelid conditioning. *Journal of Experimental Psychology: Animal Behavior Processes, 2,* 175–190. [4]

Friedman, H., & Guttman, N. (1965). Further analysis of the various effects of discrimination training upon stimulus generalization gradients. In D. J. Mostofsky (Ed.), *Stimulus generalization* (pp. 255–267). Stanford, CA: Stanford University Press. [13]

Fudim, D. K. (1978). Sensory preconditioning of flavors with a formalin-produced sodium need. *Journal of Experimental Psychology: Animal Behavior Processes, 4,* 276–285. [5]

Fuller, G. D. (1978). Current status of biofeedback in clinical practice. *American Psychologist, 33,* 39–48. [8]

Gaffan, D., & Gowling, E. A. (1984). Recall of the goal box in latent learning and latent discrimination. *The Quarterly Journal of Experimental Psychology, 36B,* 39–51. [11]

Gaffan, E. A., & Hart, M. M. (1981). Pigeons' withdrawal from an appetitive conditioned inhibitor under two training procedures. *The Quarterly Journal of Experimental Psychology, 33B,* 77–94. [3]

Gaffan, E. A., & Keeble, S. (1976). The effect of frustrative nonreward on the attractiveness of the omitted reward. *Learning and Motivation, 7,* 50–65. [2]

Gage, F. H., Evans, S. H., & Olton, D. S. (1979). Multivariate analyses of performance in a DRL paradigm. *Animal Learning and Behavior, 7,* 323–327. [9]

Gagnon, S., & Doré, F. Y. (1993). Search behavior of dogs (*Canis familiaris*) in invisible displacement problems. *Animal Learning and Behavior, 21,* 246–254. [15]

Gaioni, S. J., Hoffman, H. S., DePaulo, P., & Stratton, V. N. (1978). Imprinting in older ducklings: Some tests of a reinforcement model. *Animal Learning and Behavior, 6,* 19–26. [12]

Gaioni, S. J., & Ross, L. E. (1982). Distress calling induced by reductions in group size in ducklings reared with conspecifics or imprinting stimuli. *Animal Learning and Behavior, 10,* 521–529. [12]

Galbicka, G. (1988). Differentiating the behavior of organisms. *Journal of the Experimental Analysis of Behavior, 50,* 343–354. [8]

Galbicka, G., & Platt, J. R. (1986). Parametric manipulation of interresponse-time contingency independent of reinforcement rate. *Journal of Experimental Psychology: Animal Behavior Processes, 12,* 371–380. [9]

Galef, B. G. (1986). Social identification of toxic diets by Norway rats (*Rattus norvegicus*). *Journal of Comparative Psychology, 100,* 331–334. [7]

Galef, B. G., McQuoid, L. M., & Whiskin, E. E. (1990). Further evidence that Norway rats do not socially transmit learned aversions to toxic baits. *Animal Learning and Behavior, 18,* 199–205. [7]

Gallistel, C. R. (1990). *The organization of learning.* Cambridge, MA: Bradford Books/MIT Press. [14]

Gallistel, C. R. (1994). Space and time. In N. J. Mackintosh (Ed.), *Animal learning and cognition* (pp. 221–253). New York: Academic Press. [14]

Ganesan, R., & Pearce, J. M. (1988). Effect of changing the unconditioned stimulus on appetitive blocking. *Journal of Experimental Psychology: Animal Behavior Processes, 14,* 280–291. [5]

Garcia, J. (1989). Food for Tolman: Cognition and cathexis in concert. In T. Archer & L.-G. Nilsson (Eds.), *Aversion, avoidance, and anxiety: Perspectives on aversively motivated behavior* (pp. 45–85). Hillsdale, NJ: Erlbaum. [7]

Garcia, J., Ervin, F. R., & Koelling, R. A. (1966). Learning with prolonged delay of reinforcement. *Psychonomic Science, 5,* 121–122. [4, 7]

Garcia, J., Forthman Quick, D., & White, B. (1984). Conditioned disgust and fear from mollusk to monkey. In D. L. Alkon & J. Farley (Eds.), *Primary neural substrates of learning and behavior change* (pp. 47–61). Cambridge: Cambridge University Press. [7]

Garcia, J., & Koelling, R. A. (1966). Relation of cue to consequence in avoidance learning. *Psychonomic Science, 4,* 123–124. [7]

Gardner, R. G., Gardner, B. T., & Van Cantfort, T. E. (1989). *Teaching sign language to chimpanzees.* New York: State University of New York Press. [15]

Gentry, G. D., Weiss, B., & Laties, V. G. (1983). The microanalysis of fixed-interval responding. *Journal of the Experimental Analysis of Behavior, 39,* 327–343. [9]

Gibbon, J. (1977). Scalar expectancy theory and Weber's law in animal timing. *Psychological Review, 84,* 279–325. [15]

Gibbon, J., Baldock, M. D., Locurto, C., Gold, L., & Terrace, H. S. (1977). Trial and intertrial durations in autoshaping. *Journal of Experimental Psychology: Animal Behavior Processes, 3,* 264–284. [4]

Gibbon, J., & Church, R. M. (1981). Time left: Linear versus logarithmic subjective time. *Journal of Experimental Psychology: Animal Behavior Processes, 7,* 87–107. [15]

Gibbon, J., & Church, R. M. (1984). Sources of variance in an information processing theory of timing. In H. L. Roitblat, T. G. Bever, & H. S. Terrace (Eds.), *Animal cognition* (pp. 465–488). Hillsdale, NJ: Erlbaum. [15]

Gibbon, J., Locurto, C., & Terrace, H. S. (1975). Signal–food contingency and signal frequency in a continuous trials autoshaping paradigm. *Animal Learning and Behavior, 3,* 317–324. [3]

Gibbs, C. M., Kehoe, E. J., & Gormezano, I. (1991). Conditioning of the rabbit's nictitating membrane response to a CSA–CSB–US serial compound: Manipulations of CSB's associative character. *Journal of Experimental Psychology: Animal Behavior Processes, 17,* 423–432. [4]

Gibson, W. E., Reid, L. D., Sakai, M., & Porter, P. B. (1965). Intracranial reinforcement compared with sugar-water reinforcement. *Science, 148,* 1357–1359. [11]

Gillan, D. J. (1979). Learned suppression of ingestion: Role of discriminative stimuli, ingestive responses, and aversive tastes. *Journal of Experimental Psychology: Animal Behavior Processes, 5,* 258–272. [7]

Gillan, D. J., Premack, D., & Woodruff, G. (1981). Reasoning in the chimpanzee: I. Analogical reasoning. *Journal of Experimental Psychology: Animal Behavior Processes, 7,* 1–17. [15]

Gillette, K., Martin, G. M., & Bellingham, W. P. (1980). Differential use of food and water cues in the formation of conditioned aversions by domestic chicks (*Gallus gallus*). *Journal of Experimental Psychology: Animal Behavior Processes, 6,* 99–111. [7]

Ginn, S. R., Valentine, J. D., & Powell, D. A. (1983). Concomitant Pavlovian conditioning of heart rate and leg flexion responses in the rat. *Pavlovian Journal of Biological Science, 18,* 154–160. [4]

Gisquet-Verrier, P., & Alexinsky, T. (1986). Does contextual change determine long-term forgetting? *Animal Learning and Behavior, 14,* 349–358. [13]

Giulian, D., & Schmaltz, L. W. (1973). Enhanced discriminated bar-press avoidance in the rat through appetitive preconditioning. *Journal of Comparative and Physiological Psychology, 83,* 106–112. [12]

Glickman, S. E., & Schiff, B. B. (1967). A biological theory of reinforcement. *Psychological Review, 74,* 81–109. [11]

Glow, P. H., & Winefield, A. H. (1978). Response-contingent sensory change in a causally structured environment. *Animal Learning and Behavior, 6,* 1–18. [9]

Gonzalez, R. C., Gentry, B. V., & Bitterman, M. E. (1954). Relational discrimination of intermediate size in the chimpanzee. *Journal of Comparative and Physiological Psychology, 47,* 385–388. [13]

Goodall, G. (1984). Learning due to the response–shock contingency in signalled punishment. *The Quarterly Journal of Experimental Psychology, 36B,* 259–279. [8]

Goodkin, F. (1976). Rats learn the relationship between responding and environmental events: An expansion of the learned helplessness hypothesis. *Learning and Motivation, 7,* 382–394. [10]

Gordon, W. C., & Feldman, D. T. (1978). Reactivation-induced interference in a short-term retention paradigm. *Learning and Motivation, 9,* 164–178. [14]

Gordon, W. C., & Klein, R. L. (1994). Animal memory: The effects of context change on retention performance. In N. J. Mackintosh (Ed.), *Animal learning and cognition* (pp. 255–279). New York: Academic Press. [14]

Gordon, W. C., & Mowrer, R. R. (1980). An extinction trial as a reminder treatment following electrocon-vulsive shock. *Animal Learning and Behavior, 8,* 363–367. [14]

Gordon, W. C., & Spear, N. E. (1973). The effect of reactivation of a previously acquired memory on the interaction between memories in the rat. *Journal of Experimental Psychology, 99,* 349–355. [14]

Gormezano, I. (1972). Investigations of defense and reward conditioning in the rabbit. In A. H. Black & W. F. Prokasy (Eds.), *Classical conditioning II: Current theory and research* (pp. 151–181). New York: Appleton-Century-Crofts. [4]

Gormezano, I., Kehoe, E. J., & Marshall, B. S. (1983). Twenty years of classical conditioning research with the rabbit. In J. M. Prague & A. N. Epstein (Eds.), *Progress in psychobiology and physiological psychology* (pp. 197–275). New York: Academic Press. [3]

Gormezano, I., & Moore, J. W. (1969). Classical conditioning. In M. H. Marx (Ed.), *Learning processes.* New York: Macmillan. [4]

Goss-Custard, J. D. (1981). Feeding behavior of redshank, *Tringa totanus,* and optimal foraging theory. In A. C. Kamil & T. D. Sargent (Eds.), *Foraging behavior: Ecological, ethological and psychological approaches* (pp. 115–134). New York: Garland. [11]

Gottlieb, G. (1979). Development of species identification in ducklings: V. Perceptual differentiation in the embryo. *Journal of Comparative and Physiological Psychology, 93,* 831–854. [12]

Gottlieb, G. (1980a). Development of species identification in ducklings: VII. Highly specific early experi-ence fosters species-specific perception in wood ducklings. *Journal of Comparative and Physiological Psy-chology, 94,* 1019–1027. [12]

Gottlieb, G. (1980b). Development of species identification in ducklings: VI. Specific embryonic experience required to maintain species-typical perception in Peking ducklings. *Journal of Comparative and Physi-ological Psychology, 94,* 579–587. [12]

Gould, J. L. (1986). The locale map of honey bees: Do insects have cognitive maps? *Science, 232,* 861–863. [14]

Gould, J. L. (1987). Landmark learning by honey bees. *Animal Behaviour, 35,* 26–34. [14]

Gould, J. L. (1990). Honey bee cognition. *Cognition, 37,* 83–103. [14]

Graft, D. A., Lea, S. E. G., & Whitworth, T. L. (1977). The matching law in and within groups of rats. *Jour-nal of the Experimental Analysis of Behavior, 27,* 183–194. [10]

Grant, D. S. (1975). Proactive interference in pigeon short-term memory. *Journal of Experimental Psychology: Animal Behavior Processes, 1,* 207–220. [14]

Grant, D. S. (1981). Stimulus control of information processing in pigeon short-term memory. *Learning and Motivation, 12,* 19–39. [14]

Grant, D. S. (1982a). Intratrial proactive interference in pigeon short-term memory: Manipulation of stimu-lus dimension and dimensional similarity. *Learning and Motivation, 13,* 417–433. [14]

Grant, D. S. (1982b). Prospective versus retrospective coding of samples of stimuli, responses, and rein-forcers in delayed matching with pigeons. *Learning and Motivation, 13,* 265–280. [14]

Grant, D. S. (1982c). Stimulus control of information processing in rat short-term memory. *Journal of Exper-imental Psychology: Animal Behavior Processes, 8,* 154–164. [14]

Grant, D. S. (1988a). Directed forgetting in pigeons: Tests of transfer of cue effectiveness across samples from different dimensions. *Learning and Motivation, 19,* 122–141. [14]

Grant, D. S. (1988b). Sources of visual interference in delayed matching-to-sample with pigeons. *Journal of Experimental Psychology: Animal Behavior Processes, 14,* 368–375. [14]

Grant, D. S., & MacDonald, S. E. (1986). Matching to element and compound samples in pigeons: The role of sample coding. *Journal of Experimental Psychology: Animal Behavior Processes, 12,* 160–171. [14]

Grant, D. S., & Roberts, W. A. (1976). Sources of retroactive inhibition in pigeon short-term memory. *Jour-nal of Experimental Psychology: Animal Behavior Processes, 2,* 1–16. [14]

Gray, J. A. (1965). Stimulus intensity dynamism. *Psychological Bulletin, 63,* 180–196. [4]

Gray, J. A. (1985). Issues in neuropsychology of anxiety. In A. J. Tuma & J. Masur (Eds.), *Anxiety and the anxiety disorders* (pp. 5–25). Hillsdale, NJ: Erlbaum. [11]

Green, K. F., & Garcia, J. (1971). Recuperation from illness: Flavor enhancement for rats. *Science, 173,* 749–751. [7]

Green, L., & Kagel, J. H. (Eds.). (1987). *Behavioral economics.* Norwood, NJ: Ablex. [11]

Green, L., & Rachlin, H. (1976). Learned taste aversions in rats as a function of delay, speed, and duration of rotation. *Learning and Motivation, 7,* 283–289. [7]

Green, L., & Rachlin, H. (1991). Economic substitutability of electrical brain stimulation, food, and water. *Journal of the Experimental Analysis of Behavior, 55,* 133–143. [11]

Greenspoon, J. (1955). The reinforcing effect of two spoken sounds on the frequency of two responses. *Amer-ican Journal of Psychology, 68,* 409–416. [8]

Grice, G. R. (1948). The relation of secondary reinforcement to delayed reward in visual discrimination learning. *Journal of Experimental Psychology, 38,* 1–16. [9]

Grice, G. R. (1968). Stimulus intensity and response evocation. *Psychological Review, 75,* 359–373. [4]

Grosch, J., & Neuringer, A. (1981). Self-control in pigeons under the Mischel paradigm. *Journal of the Experimental Analysis of Behavior, 35,* 3–21. [10]

Grossen, N. E., & Kelley, M. J. (1972). Species-specific behavior and acquisition of avoidance behavior in rats. *Journal of Comparative and Physiological Psychology, 81,* 307–310. [12]

Guilford, T., & Dawkins, M. S. (1987). Search images not proven: A reappraisal of recent evidence. *Animal Behavior, 35,* 1838–1845. [7]

Gustavson, C. R., Garcia, J., Hankins, W. G., & Rusiniak, K. W. (1974). Coyote predation control by aversive conditioning. *Science, 184,* 581–583. [6, 7]

Gustavson, C. R., Jowsey, J. R., & Milligan, D. N. (1982). A 3-year evaluation of taste aversion coyote control in Saskatchewan. *Journal of Range Management, 35,* 57–59. [7]

Gustavson, C. R., Kelly, D. J., Sweeney, M., & Garcia, J. (1976). Prey–lithium aversion: I. Coyotes and wolves. *Behavioral Biology, 17,* 61–72. [7]

Guttman, N., & Kalish, H. I. (1956). Discriminability and stimulus generalization. *Journal of Experimental Psychology, 51,* 79–88. [13]

Haberlandt, K. (1971). Transfer along a continuum in classical conditioning. *Learning and Motivation, 2,* 164–172. [13]

Haggbloom, S. J., Birmingham, K. M., & Scranton, D. L. (1992). Hierarchical organization of series information by rats: Series chunks and list chunks. *Learning and Motivation, 23,* 183–199. [14]

Halgren, C. R. (1974). Latent inhibition in rats: Associative or nonassociative. *Journal of Comparative and Physiological Psychology, 86,* 74–78. [5]

Halgren, E., Walter, R. D., Cherlow, A. G., & Crandall, P. H. (1978). Mental phenomena evoked by electrical stimulation of the human hippocampal formation and amygdala. *Brain, 101,* 83–117. [11]

Hall, G. (1973a). Overtraining and reversal learning in the rat: Effects of stimulus salience and response strategies. *Journal of Comparative and Physiological Psychology, 84,* 169–175. [13]

Hall, G. (1973b). Response strategies after overtraining in the jumping stand. *Animal Learning and Behavior, 1,* 157–160. [13]

Hall, G. (1974). Transfer effects produced by overtraining in the rat. *Journal of Comparative and Physiological Psychology, 87,* 938–944. [13]

Hall, G. (1975). An analysis of positive general transfer in discrimination learning in the rat. *Animal Learning and Behavior, 3,* 212–216. [13]

Hall, G. (1991). *Perceptual and associative learning.* Oxford, England: Clarendon. [5]

Hall, G., & Channell, S. (1985). Differential effects of contextual change on latent inhibition and on the habituation of an orienting response. *Journal of Experimental Psychology: Animal Behavior Processes, 11,* 470–481. [5]

Hall, G., & Honey, R. C. (1990). Context-specific conditioning in the conditioned-emotional response procedure. *Journal of Experimental Psychology: Animal Behavior Processes, 16,* 271–278. [14]

Hall, G., & Minor, H. (1984). A search for context–stimulus associations in latent inhibition. *The Quarterly Journal of Experimental Psychology, 36B,* 145–169. [5]

Hall, G., & Pearce, J. M. (1979). Latent inhibition of a CS during CS–US pairings. *Journal of Experimental Psychology: Animal Behavior Processes, 5,* 31–42. [6]

Hall, G., & Pearce, J. M. (1982a). Changes in stimulus associability during conditioning: Implications for theories of acquisition. In M. L. Commons, R. J. Herrnstein, & A. R. Wagner (Eds.), *Quantitative analyses of behavior: Vol 3. Acquisition* (pp. 221–239). Cambridge, MA: Ballinger. [6]

Hall, G., & Pearce, J. M. (1982b). Restoring the associability of a preexposed CS by a surprising event. *The Quarterly Journal of Experimental Psychology, 34B,* 127–140. [6]

Hall, G., & Schachtman, T. R. (1987). Differential effects of a retention interval on latent inhibition and the habituation of an orienting response. *Animal Learning and Behavior, 15,* 76–82. [5]

Hall, J. F. (1984). Backward conditioning in Pavlovian type studies: Reevaluation and present status. *Pavlovian Journal of Biological Sciences, 19,* 163–168. [4]

Hallam, S. C., Grahame, N. J., & Miller, R. R. (1992). Exploring the edges of Pavlovian contingency space: An assessment of contingency theory and its various metrics. *Learning and Motivation, 23,* 225–249. [3]

Hamilton, W. F., & Coleman, T. B. (1933). Trichromatic vision in the pigeon as illustrated by the spectral hue discrimination curve. *Journal of Comparative Psychology, 15,* 183–191. [13]

Hammond, L. J. (1967). A traditional demonstration of the active properties of Pavlovian inhibition using differential CER. *Psychonomic Science, 9,* 65–66. [3]

Hammond, L. J. (1980). The effect of contingency upon the appetitive conditioning of free operant behavior. *Journal of the Experimental Analysis of Behavior, 34,* 297–304. [8]

Hanson, H. M. (1959). Effects of discrimination training on stimulus generalization. *Journal of Experimental Psychology, 58,* 321–334. [13]

Hanson, H. M. (1961). Stimulus generalization following three-stimulus discrimination training. *Journal of Comparative and Physiological Psychology, 54,* 181–185. [13]

Hanson, S. J., & Killeen, P. R. (1981). Measurement and modeling of behavior under fixed-interval schedules of reinforcement. *Journal of Experimental Psychology: Animal Behavior Processes, 7,* 129–139. [9]

Hanson, S. J., & Timberlake, W. (1983). Regulation during challenge: A general model of learned performance under schedule constraint. *Psychological Review, 90,* 262–282. [11]

Harlow, H. F. (1949). The formation of learning sets. *Psychological Review, 56,* 51–65. [13]

Harlow, H. F. (1953). Mice, monkeys, men, and motives. *Psychological Review, 60,* 23–32. [11]

Harlow, H. F. (1959). Learning sets and error-factor theory. In S. Koch (Ed.), *Psychology: A study of a science* (Vol. 2, pp. 492–537). New York: McGraw-Hill. [8, 13]

Hars, B., & Hennevin, E. (1990). Reactivation of an old memory during sleep and wakefulness. *Animal Learning and Behavior, 18,* 363–376. [14]

Harzem, P., Lowe, C. F., & Priddle-Higson, P. J. (1978). Inhibiting function of reinforcement: Magnitude effects on variable-interval schedules. *Journal of the Experimental Analysis of Behavior, 30,* 1–10. [9]

Hastings, S. E., & Obrist, P. A. (1967). Heart rate during conditioning in humans: Effect of varying interstimulus (CS–UCS) interval. *Journal of Experimental Psychology, 74,* 431–442. [4]

Hayes, C. (1951). *The ape in our house.* New York: Harper and Row. [15]

Hearst, E. (1971). Differential transfer of excitatory versus inhibitory pretraining to intradimensional discrimination learning in pigeons. *Journal of Comparative and Physiological Psychology, 75,* 206–215. [13]

Hearst, E. (1978). Stimulus relationships and feature selection in learning and behavior. In S. H. Hulse, H. Fowler, & W. K. Honig (Eds.), *Cognitive processes in animal behavior* (pp. 51–88). Hillsdale, NJ: Erlbaum. [13]

Hearst, E. (1987). Extinction reveals stimulus control: Latent learning of feature-negative discrimination in pigeons. *Journal of Experimental Psychology: Animal Behavior Processes, 13,* 52–64. [13]

Hearst, E. (1989). Backward associations: Differential learning about stimuli that follow the pressure versus the absence of food in pigeons. *Animal Learning and Behavior, 17,* 280–290. [4]

Hearst, E., Besley, S., & Farthing, G. W. (1970). Inhibition and the stimulus control of operant behavior. *Journal of the Experimental Analysis of Behavior, 14,* 373–409. [13]

Hearst, E., & Franklin, S. R. (1977). Positive and negative relations between a signal and food: Approach–withdrawal behavior to the signal. *Journal of Experimental Psychology: Animal Behavior Processes, 3,* 37–52. [3]

Hearst, E., & Jenkins, H. M. (1974). *Sign-tracking: The stimulus–reinforcer relation and directed action.* Austin, TX: Psychonomic Press. [3, 13]

Hearst, E., & Koresko, M. B. (1968). Stimulus generalization and amount of prior training on variable-interval reinforcement. *Journal of Comparative and Physiological Psychology, 66,* 133–138. [13]

Hearst, E., & Wolff, W. T. (1989). Addition versus deletion as a signal. *Animal Learning and Behavior, 17,* 120–133. [13]

Heath, R. G. (1963). Electrical self-stimulation of the brain in man. *American Journal of Psychiatry, 120,* 571–577. [11]

Hebb, D. O. (1949). *The organization of behavior: A neuropsychological theory.* New York: Wiley. [11]

Helmstetter, F. J., & Fanselow, M. S. (1989). Differential second-order aversive conditioning using contextual stimuli. *Animal Learning and Behavior, 17,* 205–212. [5]

Helmstetter, F. J., & Fanselow, M. S. (1993). Aversively motivated changes in meal patterns of rats in a closed economy: The effects of shock density. *Animal Learning and Behavior, 21,* 168–175. [11, 12]

Helson, H. (1964). *Adaptation-level theory.* New York: Harper & Row. [13]

Hemmes, N. S., Eckerman, D. A., & Rubinsky, H. J. (1979). A functional analysis of collateral behavior under differential-reinforcement-of-low-rate schedules. *Animal Learning and Behavior, 7,* 328–332. [9]

Hempel, C. G. (1966). *Philosophy of natural science.* Englewood Cliffs, NJ: Prentice-Hall. [2]

Hendry, D. P. (1969). *Conditioned reinforcement.* Homewood, IL: Dorsey Press. [10]

Herman, L. M., Richards, D. G., & Wolz, J. P. (1984). Comprehension of sentences by bottlenosed dolphins. *Cognition, 16,* 129–219. [15]

Hernandez, L. L., Buchanan, S. L., & Powell, D. A. (1981). CS preexposure: Latent inhibition and Pavlovian conditioning of heart rate and eyeblink responses as a function of sex and CS intensity in rabbits. *Animal Learning and Behavior, 9,* 513–518. [5]

Herrnstein, R. J. (1961). Relative and absolute strength of response as a function of frequency of reinforcement. *Journal of the Experimental Analysis of Behavior, 4,* 267–274. [10]

Herrnstein, R. J. (1970). On the law of effect. *Journal of the Experimental Analysis of Behavior, 13,* 243–266. [10]

Herrnstein, R. J. (1974). Formal properties of the matching law. *Journal of the Experimental Analysis of Behavior, 21,* 159–164. [10]

Herrnstein, R. J. (1979). Acquisition, generalization, and discrimination reversal of a natural concept. *Journal of Experimental Psychology: Animal Behavior Processes, 5,* 118–129. [15]

Herrnstein, R. J. (1990). Levels of stimulus control: A functional approach. *Cognition, 37,* 133–166. [15]

Herrnstein, R. J., & Loveland, D. H. (1964). Complex visual concept in the pigeon. *Science, 146,* 549–551. [15]

Herrnstein, R. J., & Loveland, D. H., & Cable, C. (1976). Natural concepts in pigeons. *Journal of Experimental Psychology: Animal Behavior Processes, 2*, 285–311. [15]

Herrnstein, R. J., & Vaughan, W. (1980). Melioration and behavioral allocation. In J. E. R. Staddon (Ed.), *Limits to action* (pp. 143–176). New York: Academic Press. [10]

Herrnstein, R. J., Vaughan, W., Mumford, D. B., & Kosslyn, S. M. (1989). Teaching pigeons an abstract relational rule: Insideness. *Perception and Psychophysics, 46*, 56–64. [15]

Herzog, H. L., Grant, D. S., & Roberts, W. A. (1977). Effects of sample duration and spaced repetition upon delayed matching-to-sample in monkeys (*Macaca arctoides and Saimiri sciureus*). *Animal Learning and Behavior, 5*, 347–354. [14]

Hess, E. H. (1959a). The relationship between imprinting and motivation. In M. R. Jones (Ed.), *Nebraska symposium on motivation* (Vol. 7, pp. 44–77). Lincoln: University of Nebraska Press. [12]

Hess, E. H. (1959b). Imprinting. *Science, 130*, 133–141. [12]

Heth, C. D. (1976). Simultaneous and backward fear conditioning as a function of number of CS–UCS pairings. *Journal of Experimental Psychology: Animal Behavior Processes, 2*, 117–129. [4]

Heth, C. D., & Rescorla, R. A. (1973). Simultaneous and backward fear conditioning in the rat. *Journal of Comparative and Physiological Psychology, 82*, 434–443. [4]

Heyman, G. M., & Herrnstein, R. J. (1986). More on concurrent interval–ratio schedules: A replication and review. *Journal of the Experimental Analysis of Behavior, 46*, 331–351. [10]

Hickis, C. F., Robles, L., & Thomas, D. R. (1977). Contextual stimuli and memory retrieval in pigeons. *Animal Learning and Behavior, 5*, 161–168. [14]

Hill, W. F., & Spear, N. E. (1963). Extinction in a runway as a function of acquisition level and reinforcement percentage. *Journal of Experimental Psychology, 65*, 495–500. [10]

Hinde, R. A., & Stevenson-Hinde, J. (1973). *Constraints on learning: Limitations and predispositions.* New York: Academic Press. [9]

Hinson, R. (1982). Effects of UCS preexposure on excitatory and inhibitory rabbit eyelid conditioning: An associative effect of conditioned contextual stimuli. *Journal of Experimental Psychology: Animal Behavior Process, 8*, 49–61. [6]

Hinson, R. E., & Siegel, S. (1986). Pavlovian inhibitory conditioning and tolerance to pentobarbital-induced hypothermia in rats. *Journal of Experimental Psychology: Animal Behavior Processes, 12*, 363–370. [7]

Hinterliter, C. F., Webster, T., & Riccio, D. C. (1975). Amnesia induced by hypothermia as a function of treatment–test interval and recooling in rats. *Animal Learning and Behavior, 3*, 257–263. [14]

Hiroto, D. S., & Seligman, M. E. P. (1975). Generality of learned helplessness in man. *Journal of Personality and Social Psychology, 31*, 311–327. [10]

Hiss, R. H., & Thomas, D. R. (1963). Stimulus generalization as a function of testing procedure and response measure. *Journal of Experimental Psychology, 65*, 587–592. [13]

Hoebel, B. G. (1988). Neuroscience and motivation: Pathways and peptides that define motivational systems. In R. C. Atkinson, R. J. Herrnstein, G. Lindzey, & R. D. Luce (Eds)., *Steven's handbook of experimental psychology: Vol. 1. Perception and motivation* (pp. 547–625). New York: Wiley. [2]

Hoffman, H. S. (1978). Experimental analysis of imprinting and its behavioral effects. In G. Bower (Ed.), *The psychology of learning and motivation* (Vol. 12, pp. 1–37). New York: Academic Press. [12]

Hoffman, H. S., Eiserer, L. A., & Singer, D. (1972). Acquisition of behavioral control by a stationary imprinting stimulus. *Psychonomic Science, 26*, 146–148. [12]

Hoffman, H. S., & Ratner, A. M. (1973). A reinforcement model of imprinting: Implications for socialization in monkeys and men. *Psychological Review, 80*, 527–544. [12]

Hoffman, H. S., & Ratner, A. M., & Eiserer, L. A. (1972). Role of visual imprinting in the emergence of specific filial attachments in ducklings. *Journal of Comparative and Physiological Psychology, 81*, 399–409. [12]

Hoffman, H. S., Selekman, W., & Fleshler, M. (1966). Stimulus aspects of aversive control: Long term effects of suppression procedures. *Journal of the Experimental Analysis of Behavior, 9*, 659–662. [14]

Hoffman, H. S., Stratton, J. W., & Newby, V. (1969). Punishment by response-contingent withdrawal of an imprinting stimulus. *Science, 163*, 702–704. [12]

Holder, M. D., & Burstein, K. R. (1981). Spontaneous recovery evoked by a nonreinforced stimulus. *Animal Learning and Behavior, 9*, 483–486. [8]

Holland, P. C. (1977). Conditioned stimulus as a determinant of the form of the Pavlovian conditioned response. *Journal of Experimental Psychology: Animal Behavior Processes, 3*, 77–104. [4]

Holland, P. C. (1979). The effects of qualitative and quantitative variation in the US on individual components of Pavlovian appetitive conditioned behavior in rats. *Animal Learning and Behavior, 7*, 424–432. [4]

Holland, P. C. (1980a). CS–US interval as a determinant of the form of Pavlovian appetitive conditioned responses. *Journal of Experimental Psychology: Animal Behavior Processes, 6*, 155–174. [4]

Holland, P. C. (1980b). Influence of visual conditioned stimulus characteristics on the form of Pavlovian appetitive conditioned responding in rats. *Journal of Experimental Psychology: Animal Behavior Processes, 6*, 81–97. [4]

Holland, P. C. (1981). Acquisition of representation-mediated conditioned food aversions. *Learning and Motivation, 12,* 1–18. [6]

Holland, P. C. (1983a). Occasion-setting in Pavlovian feature positive discrimination. In M. L. Commons, R. J. Herrnstein, & A. R. Wagner (Eds.), *Quantitative analyses of behavior: Discrimination processes* (Vol. 4, pp. 183–206). New York: Ballinger. [5]

Holland, P. C. (1983b). Representation-mediated overshadowing and potentiation of conditioned aversions. *Journal of Experimental Psychology: Animal Behavior Processes, 9,* 1–13. [6]

Holland, P. C. (1984). Unblocking in Pavlovian appetitive conditioning. *Journal of Experimental Psychology: Animal Behavior Processes, 10,* 476–497. [5]

Holland, P. C. (1985). The nature of conditioned inhibition in serial and simultaneous feature negative discriminations. In R. R. Miller & N. E. Spear (Eds.), *Information processing in animals: Conditioned inhibition* (pp. 267–297). Hillsdale, NJ: Erlbaum. [5]

Holland, P. C. (1986a). Temporal determinants of occasion setting in feature-positive discriminations. *Animal Learning and Behavior, 14,* 111–120. [5, 13]

Holland, P. C. (1986b). Transfer after serial feature positive discrimination training. *Learning and Motivation, 17,* 243–268. [13]

Holland, P. C. (1988). Excitation and inhibition in unblocking. *Journal of Experimental Psychology: Animal Behavior Processes, 14,* 261–279. [5]

Holland, P. C. (1989a). Acquisition and transfer of conditional discrimination performance. *Journal of Experimental Psychology: Animal Behavior Processes, 15,* 154–165. [13]

Holland, P. C. (1989b). Feature extinction enhances transfer of occasion setting. *Animal Learning and Behavior, 17,* 269–279. [5, 13]

Holland, P. C. (1989c). Occasion setting with simultaneous compounds in rats. *Journal of Experimental Psychology: Animal Behavior Processes, 15,* 183–193(b). [5]

Holland, P. C. (1990). Event representation in Pavlovian conditioning: Image and action. *Cognition, 37,* 105–131. [6]

Holland, P. C., & Coldwell, S. E. (1993). Transfer of inhibitory stimulus control in operant feature-negative discriminations. *Learning and Motivation, 24,* 345–375. [13]

Holland, P. C., & Forbes, D. T. (1982). Control of conditional discrimination performance by CS-evoked event representations. *Animal Learning and Behavior, 10,* 249–256. [6]

Holland, P. C., & Gory, J. (1986). Extinction of inhibition after serial and simultaneous feature negative discrimination training. *The Quarterly Journal of Experimental Psychology, 38B,* 245–265. [3]

Holland, P. C., & Rescorla, R. A. (1975a). Second-order conditioning with food unconditioned stimulus. *Journal of Comparative and Physiological Psychology, 88,* 459–467. [5]

Holland, P. C., & Rescorla, R. A. (1975b). The effect of two ways of devaluing the unconditioned stimulus after first- and second-order appetitive conditioning. *Journal of Experimental Psychology: Animal Behavior Processes, 1,* 355–363. [6]

Holland, P. C., & Ross, R. T. (1983). Savings test for associations between neutral stimuli. *Animal Learning and Behavior, 11,* 83–90. [5]

Holland, P. C., & Straub, J. J. (1979). Differential effects of two ways of devaluing the unconditioned stimulus after Pavlovian appetitive conditioning. *Journal of Experimental Psychology: Animal Behavior Processes, 5,* 65–78. [6]

Holland, V., & Davison, M. C. (1971). Preference for qualitatively different reinforcers. *Journal of the Experimental Analysis of Behavior, 16,* 375–380. [10]

Hollis, K. L. (1982). Pavlovian conditioning of signal-centered action patterns and autonomic behavior: A biological analysis of function. In J. S. Rosenblatt, R. A. Hinde, C. Beer, & M.-C. Busnel (Eds.), *Advances in the study of behavior* (Vol. 12, pp. 1–64). New York: Academic Press. [7]

Hollis, K. L. (1984). The biological function of Pavlovian conditioning: The best defense is a good offense. *Journal of Experimental Psychology: Animal Behavior Processes, 10,* 413–425. [7, 12]

Hollis, K. L., Cadieux, E. L., & Colbert, M. M. (1989). The biological function of Pavlovian conditioning: A mechanism for mating success in the blue gourami (*Trichogaster trichopterus*). *Journal of Comparative Psychology, 103,* 115–121. [7]

Hollis, K. L., Martin, K. A., Cadieux, E. L., & Colbert, M. M. (1984). The biological function of Pavlovian conditioning: Learned inhibition of aggressive behavior in territorial fish. *Learning and Motivation, 15,* 459–478. [7]

Holloway, K. S., & Domjan, M. (1993). Sexual approach conditioning: Unconditioned stimulus factors. *Journal of Experimental Psychology: Animal Behavior Processes, 19,* 38–46. [7]

Holman, J. G., & Mackintosh, N. J. (1981). The control of appetitive instrumental responding does not depend on classical conditioning to the discriminative stimulus. *The Quarterly Journal of Experimental Psychology, 33B,* 21–31. [11]

Holz, W. C., & Azrin, N. H. (1966). Conditioning human verbal behavior. In W. K. Honig (Ed.), *Operant behavior: Areas of research and application* (pp. 790–826). New York: Appleton-Century-Crofts. [8]

Homzie, M. J. (1974). Nonreward anticipated: Effects on extinction runway performance in the rat. *Animal Learning and Behavior, 2,* 77–79. [10]

Honey, R. C., & Hall, G. (1991). Acquired equivalence and distinctiveness of cues using a sensory-preconditioning procedure. *The Quarterly Journal of Experimental Psychology, 43B,* 121–135. [5]

Honey, R. C., Willis, A., & Hall, G. (1990). Context specificity in pigeon autoshaping. *Learning and Motivation, 21,* 125–136. [14]

Honig, W. K. (1974). Effects of extradimensional discrimination training upon previously acquired stimulus control. *Learning and Motivation, 5,* 1–15. [13]

Honig, W. K., & Stewart, K. E. (1993). Relative numerosity as a dimension of stimulus control: The peak shift. *Animal Learning and Behavior, 21,* 346–354. [13]

Honig, W. K., Thomas, D. R., & Guttman, N. (1959). Differential effects of continuous extinction and discrimination training on the generalization gradient. *Journal of Experimental Psychology, 58,* 145–152. [13]

Honig, W. K., & Thompson, R. K. R. (1982). Retrospective and prospective processing in animal working memory. In G. H. Bower (Ed.), *The psychology of learning and motivation: Advances in research and theory* (Vol. 16, pp. 239–283). New York: Academic Press. [14]

Honig, W. K., & Urcuioli, P. J. (1981). The legacy of Guttman and Kalish (1956): 25 years of research on stimulus generalization. *Journal of the Experimental Analysis of Behavior, 36,* 405–445. [13]

Honig, W. K., & Wasserman, E. A. (1981). Performance of pigeons on delayed simple and conditional discriminations under equivalent training procedures. *Learning and Motivation, 12,* 149–170. [14]

Hooper, R. (1967). Variables controlling the overlearning reversal effect (ORE). *Journal of Experimental Psychology, 73,* 612–619. [13]

Houston, A. (1986). The matching law applies to wagtails foraging in the wild. *Journal of the Experimental Analysis of Behavior, 45,* 15–18. [10]

Hovland, C. I. (1937). The generalization of conditioned responses: I. The sensory generalization of conditioned responses with varying frequencies of tone. *Journal of General Psychology, 17,* 125–148. [13]

Hubel, D. H., & Wiesel, T. N. (1979). Brain mechanisms in vision. *Scientific American, 241,* 150–162. [13]

Huber, L., & Lenz, R. (1993). A test of the linear feature model of polymorphous concept discrimination with pigeons. *The Quarterly Journal of Experimental Psychology, 46B,* 1–18. [15]

Hughes, L. F., & Dachowski, L. (1973). The role of reinforcement and nonreinforcement in an operant frustration effect. *Animal Learning and Behavior, 1,* 68–72. [10]

Hull, C. L. (1943). *Principles of behavior.* New York: Appleton-Century-Crofts. [2, 11, 13]

Hull, C. L. (1952). *A behavior system.* New Haven, CT: Yale University Press. [11]

Hulse, S. H., & Dorsky, N. P. (1977). Structural complexity as a determinant of serial pattern learning. *Learning and Motivation, 8,* 488–506. [9]

Hume, D. (1952). *An enquiry concerning human understanding.* In R. M. Hutchens (Ed.), *Great books of the western world, vol. 35* (pp. 451–509). Chicago, Il: Encyclopedia Britania [original work published 1739]. [1]

Hunt, T., & Amit, Z. (1987). Conditioned taste aversion induced by self-administered drugs: Paradox revisited. *Neuroscience and Biobehavioral Reviews, 11,* 107–130. [7]

Hursh, S. R. (1984). Behavioral economics. *Journal of the Experimental Analysis of Behavior, 42,* 435–452. [11]

Hursh, S. R., & Natelson, B. H. (1981). Electrical brain stimulation and food reinforcement dissociated by demand elasticity. *Physiology and Behavior, 26,* 509–515. [11]

Hyde, T. S. (1976). The effect of Pavlovian stimuli on the acquisition of a new response. *Learning and Motivation, 7,* 223–239. [10]

Imada, H., Yamazaki, A., & Morishita, M. (1981). The effects of signal intensity upon conditioned suppression: Effects upon responding during signals and intersignal intervals. *Animal Learning and Behavior, 9,* 269–274. [4]

Immelmann, K. (1969). Song development in the zebra finch and other estrildid finches. In R. A. Hinde (Ed.), *Bird vocalizations* (pp. 61–74). Cambridge; England: Cambridge University Press. [12]

Immelmann, K., & Suomi, S. J. (1981). Sensitive phases in development. In K. Immelmann, G. W. Barlow, L. Petrinovick, & M. Main (Eds.), *Behavioural development* (pp. 395–431). London: Cambridge, University Press. [12]

Iwasa, Y., Higashi, M., & Yamamura, N. (1981). Prey distribution as a factor determining the choice of optimal foraging strategy. *American Naturalist, 117,* 710–723. [11]

Jackson, R. L., Alexander, J. H., & Maier, S. F. (1980). Learned helplessness, inactivity, and associative deficits: Effects of inescapable shock on response choice escape learning. *Journal of Experimental Psychology: Animal Behavior Processes, 6,* 1–20. [10]

Jackson, R. L., & Fritsche, M. B. (1989). Potentiation and overshadowing in pigeons. *Learning and Motivation, 20,* 15–35. [6]

Jackson, R. L., Garbin, C. P., & Hollingsworth, E. M. (1984). Defensive burying of aversive fluids in rats: The possible role of odor. *Learning and Motivation, 15*, 85–105. [12]

Jackson, R. L., & Minor, T. R. (1988). Effects of signaling inescapable shock on subsequent escape learning: Implications for theories of coping and "learned helplessness." *Journal of Experimental Psychology: Animal Behavior Processes, 14*, 390–400. [10]

Jacobs, W. J., & LoLordo, V. M. (1977). The sensory basis of avoidance responding in the rat. *Learning and Motivation, 8*, 448–466. [4]

Jacobs, W. J., & LoLordo, V. M. (1980). Constraints on Pavlovian aversive conditioning: Implications for avoidance learning in the rat. *Learning and Motivation, 11*, 427–455. [4]

Jacobs, W. J., & Nadel, L. (1985). Stress-induced recovery of fears and phobias. *Psychological Review, 92*, 512–531. [1]

Jaynes, J. (1966). The routes of science. *American Scientist, 54*, 94–102. [2]

Jenkins, H. M. (1985). Conditioned inhibition of keypecking in the pigeon. In R. R. Miller & N. E. Spear (Eds.), *Information processing in animals: Conditioned inhibition* (pp. 327–353). Hillsdale, NJ: Erlbaum. [3]

Jenkins, H. M., Barnes, R. A., & Barrera, F. J. (1981). Why autoshaping depends on trial spacing. In C. M. Locurto, H. S. Terrace, & J. Gibbon (Eds.), *Autoshaping and conditioning theory* (pp. 255–284). New York: Academic Press. [3]

Jenkins, H. M., Barrera, F. J., Ireland, C., & Woodside, B. (1978). Signal-centered action patterns in dogs in appetitive classical conditioning: *Learning and Motivation, 9*, 272, 296. [4, 6]

Jenkins, H. M., & Harrison, R. H. (1960). Effect of discrimination training on auditory generalization. *Journal of Experimental Psychology, 59*, 246–253. [13]

Jenkins, H. M., & Harrison, R. H. (1962). Generalization gradients of inhibition following auditory discrimination learning. *Journal of the Experimental Analysis of Behavior, 5*, 435–441. [13]

Jenkins, H. M., & Moore, B. A. (1973). The form of the auto-shaped response with food or water reinforcers. *Journal of the Experimental Analysis of Behavior, 20*, 163–181. [4, 6]

Jenkins, H. M., & Sainsbury, R. S. (1970). Discrimination learning with the distinctive feature on positive or negative trials. In D. I. Mostofsky (Ed.), *Attention: Contemporary theory and analysis* (pp. 239–273). New York: Appleton-Century-Crofts. [13]

Jitsumori, M. (1978). Wavelength discrimination function derived from post-discrimination gradients in the pigeon. *Japanese Psychological Research, 20*, 18–28. [13]

Jitsumori, M. (1993). Category discrimination of artificial polymorphous stimuli based on feature learning. *Journal of Experimental Psychology: Animal Behavior Processes, 19*, 244–254. [15]

Job, R. F. S. (1987). Learned helpnessness in an appetitive discrete-trial T-maze discrimination test. *Animal Learning and Behavior, 15*, 342–346. [10]

Job, R. F. S. (1988). Interference and facilitation produced by noncontingent reinforcement in the appetitive situation. *Animal Learning and Behavior, 16*, 451–460. [10]

Johnston, T. D. (1981). Selective costs and benefits in the evolution of learning. In J. S. Rosenblatt, R. A. Hinde, C. Beer, & M.-C. Busnel (Eds.), *Advances in the study of behavior* (Vol. 12, pp. 65–106). New York: Academic Press. [1]

Johnston, T. D., & Gottlieb, G. (1981). Visual preferences of imprinted ducklings are altered by the maternal call. *Journal of Comparative and Physiological Psychology, 95*, 663–675. [12]

Jones, R. B., & Nowell, N. W. (1974). A comparison of the aversive and female attractant properties of urine from dominant and subordinate male mice. *Animal Learning and Behavior, 2*, 141–144. [9]

Kalat, J. W. (1977). Status of "learned safety" or "learned noncorrelation" as a mechanism in taste-aversion learning. In L. M. Barker, M. R. Best, & M. Domjan (Eds.), *Learning mechanisms in food selection* (pp. 273–293). Waco, TX: Baylor University Press. [7]

Kalat, J. W. (1985). Taste-aversion learning in ecological perspective. In T. D. Johnston & A. T. Pietrewicz (Eds.), *Issues on the ecological study of learning* (pp. 119–141). Hillsdale, NJ: Erlbaum. [7]

Kalat, J. W., & Rozin, P. (1971). Role of interference in taste-aversion learning. *Journal of Comparative and Physiological Psychology, 77*, 53–58. [4, 7]

Kalat, J. W., & Rozin, P. (1973). "Learned safety" as a mechanism in long-delay taste-aversion learning in rats. *Journal of Comparative and Physiological Psychology, 83*, 198–207. [5, 7]

Kalish, H. I. (1958). The relationship between discriminability and generalization: A re-evaluation. *Journal of Experimental Psychology, 55*, 637–644. [13]

Kalish, H. I. (1969). Stimulus generalization. In M. H. Marx (Ed.), *Learning: Processes* (pp. 207–297). New York: Macmillan. [13]

Kalish, H. I., & Haber, A. (1963). Generalization: I. Generalization gradients from single and multiple stimulus points. II. Generalization of inhibition. *Journal of Experimental Psychology, 65*, 176–181. [13]

Kalish, H. I., & Haber, A. (1965). Prediction of discrimination from generalization following variations in deprivation level. *Journal of Comparative and Physiological Psychology, 60*, 125–128. [13]

Kamil, A. C., & Balda, R. P. (1985). Cache recovery and spatial memory in Clark's nutcrackers. *Journal of Experimental Psychology: Animal Behavior Processes, 11,* 95–111. [14]

Kamil, A. C., Krebs, J. R., & Pulliam, H. R. (Eds.). (1987). *Foraging behavior.* New York: Plenum. [11]

Kamil, A. C., Lougee, M., & Shulman, R. I. (1973). Learning-set behavior in the learning-set experienced blue jays (*Cyanocitta cristata*). *Journal of Comparative and Physiological Psychology, 82,* 394–405. [13]

Kamil, A. C., & Roitblat, H. L. (1985). The ecology of foraging behavior: Implications for animal learning and memory. *Annual Review of Psychology, 36,* 141–169. [11]

Kamil, A. C., & Sargent, T. D. (Eds.). (1981). *Foraging behavior: Ecological, ethological, and psychological approaches.* New York: Garland. [11]

Kamin, L. J. (1965). Temporal and intensity characteristics of the conditioned stimulus. In W. F. Prokasy (Ed.), *Classical conditioning: A symposium* (pp. 118–147). New York: Appleton-Century-Crofts. [4]

Kamin, L. J. (1969). Predictability, surprise, attention, and conditioning. In B. A. Campbell & R. M. Church (Eds.), *Punishment and aversive behavior* (pp. 279–296). New York: Appleton-Century-Crofts. [5]

Kamin, L. J., & Schaub, R. E. (1963). Effects of conditioned stimulus intensity on the conditioned emotional response. *Journal of Comparative and Physiological Psychology, 56,* 502–507. [4]

Kaplan, M., Jackson, B., & Sparer, R. (1965). Escape behavior under continuous reinforcement as a function of aversive light intensity. *Journal of the Experimental Analysis of Behavior, 8,* 321–323. [9]

Kaplan, P. S. (1984). Importance of relative temporal parameters in trace autoshaping: From extinction to inhibition. *Journal of Experimental Psychology: Animal Behavior Processes, 10,* 113–126. [3, 4]

Karpicke, J., Christoph, G., Peterson, G., & Hearst, E. (1977). Signal location and positive versus negative conditioned suppression in the rat. *Journal of Experimental Psychology: Animal Behavior Processes, 3,* 105–118. [3]

Kasprow, W. J. (1987). Enhancement of short-term retention by appetitive-reinforcer reminder treatment. *Animal Learning and Behavior, 15,* 412–416. [14]

Kasprow, W. J., Cachiero, H., Balaz, M. A., & Miller, R. R. (1982). Reminder-induced recovery of associations to an overshadowed stimulus. *Learning and Motivation, 13,* 155–166. [5]

Kasprow, W. J., Catterson, D., Schachtman, T. R., & Miller, R. R. (1984). Attenuation of latent inhibition by postacquisition reminder. *The Quarterly Journal of Experimental Psychology, 36B,* 53–63. [5]

Kasprow, W. J., Schachtman, T. R., & Miller, R. R. (1985). Associability of a previously conditioned stimulus as a function of qualitative changes in the US. *The Quarterly Journal of Experimental Psychology, 37B,* 33–48. [6]

Kasprow, W. J., Schachtman, T. R., & Miller, R. R. (1987). The comparator hypothesis of unconditioned response generation: Manifest conditioned excitation and inhibition as a function of relative excitatory associative strengths of CS and conditioning context at the time of testing. *Journal of Experimental Psychology: Animal Behavior Processes, 13,* 395–406. [3]

Kaufman, A., & Baron, A. (1969). Conditioned reinforcing and aversive aspects of the stimuli defining the components of a two-component chain. *Genetic Psychology Monographs, 80,* 151–201. [10]

Kaye, H., & Pearce, J. M. (1984a). The strength of the orienting response during blocking. *The Quarterly Journal of Experimental Psychology, 36B,* 131–144. [6]

Kaye, H., & Pearce, J. M. (1984b). The strength of the orienting response during Pavlovian conditioning. *Journal of Experimental Psychology: Animal Behavior Processes, 10,* 90–109. [6]

Keat, R. (1972). A critical examination of B. F. Skinner's objections to mentalism. *Behaviorism, 1,* 53–70. [2]

Kehoe, E. J. (1982). Overshadowing and summation in compound stimulus conditioning of the rabbit's nictitating membrane response. *Journal of Experimental Psychology: Animal Behavior Processes, 8,* 313–328. [4, 5]

Kehoe, E. J. (1983). CS–US contiguity and CS intensity in conditioning of the rabbit's nictitating membrane response to serial compound stimuli. *Journal of Experimental Psychology: Animal Behavior Processes, 9,* 307–319. [4]

Kehoe, E. J., Feyer, A.-M., & Moses, J. L. (1981). Second-order conditioning of the rabbit's nictitating membrane response as a function of the CS2–CS1 and CS1–US intervals. *Animal Learning and Behavior, 9,* 304–315. [5]

Kehoe, E. J., Gibbs, C. M., Garcia, E., & Gormezano, I. (1979). Associative transfer and stimulus selection in classical conditioning of the rabbit's nictitating membrane response to serial compound CSs. *Journal of Experimental Psychology: Animal Behavior Processes, 5,* 1–18. [4]

Kehoe, E. J., & Morrow, L. D. (1984). Dynamics of the rabbit's nictitating membrane response in serial compound conditioned stimuli. *Journal of Experimental Psychology: Animal Behavior Processes, 10,* 205–220. [4]

Keifer, S. W., Cabral, R. J., Rusiniak, K. W., & Garcia, J. (1980). Ethanol-induced flavor aversions in rats with subdiaphragmatic vagotomies. *Behavioral and Neural Biology, 29,* 246–254. [7]

Keith-Lucas, T., & Guttman, N. (1975). Robust single trial delayed backward conditioning. *Journal of Comparative and Physiological Psychology, 88,* 468–476. [4]

Kelleher, R. T., & Fry, W. T. (1962). Stimulus functions in chained fixed-interval schedules. *Journal of the Experimental Analysis of Behavior, 5,* 167–173. [10]

Keller, F. S. (1968). "Goodbye, teacher . . . ." *Journal of Applied Behavior Analysis, 1,* 79–89. [1]

Keller, R. J., Ayres, J. J. B., & Mahoney, W. J. (1977). Brief versus extended exposure to truly random control procedures. *Journal of Experimental Psychology: Animal Behavior Processes, 3,* 53–65. [3]

Kello, J. E. (1972). The reinforcement-omission effect on fixed-interval schedules: Frustration or inhibition? *Learning and Motivation, 3,* 138–147. [9]

Kendall, S. B. (1972). Some effects of response-dependent clock stimuli in a fixed-interval schedule. *Journal of the Experimental Analysis of Behavior, 17,* 161–168. [9]

Kendrick, D. F., & Rilling, M. (1984). The role of interpolated stimuli in the retroactive interference of pigeon short-term memory. *Animal Learning and Behavior, 12,* 391–401. [14]

Kendrick, D. F., Rilling, M. E., & Denny, M. R. (1986). *Theories of animal memory.* Hillsdale, NJ: Erlbaum. [14]

Kertzman, C., & Demarest, J. (1982). Irreversibility of imprinting after active versus passive exposure to the object. *Journal of Comparative and Physiological Psychology, 96,* 130–142. [12]

Killeen, P. (1969). Reinforcement frequency and contingency as factors in fixed-ratio behavior. *Journal of the Experimental Analysis of Behavior, 12,* 391–395. [9]

Killeen, P. R. (1985). Incentive theory: IV. Magnitude of reward. *Journal of the Experimental Analysis of Behavior, 43,* 407–417. [9]

Killeen, P. R. (1987). Emergent behaviorism. In S. Modgil & C. Modgil (Eds.), *B. F. Skinner: Consensus and controversy* (pp. 219–234). Philadelphia: Falmer Press. [2]

Killeen, P. R., Cate, H., & Tran, T. (1993). Scaling pigeon's choice of feeds: Bigger is better. *Journal of the Experimental Analysis of Behavior, 60,* 203–217. [9]

Killeen, P. R., & Fetterman, J. C. (1988). A behavioral theory of timing. *Psychological Review, 95,* 274–295. [15]

Killeen, P. R., Smith, J. P., & Hanson, S. J. (1981). Central place foraging in *Rattus norvegicus. Animal Behavior, 29,* 64–70. [11]

Killeen, P. R., & Weiss, N. A. (1987). Optimal timing and the Weber function. *Psychological Review, 94,* 455–468. [15]

Kimble, G. A. (1993). A modest proposal for a minor revolution in the language of psychology. *Psychological Science, 4,* 253–255. [8]

Kimmel, H. D., Brennan, A. F., McLeod, D. C., Raich, M. S., & Schonfeld, L. I. (1979). Instrumental electrodermal conditioning in the monkey (*Cebus albifrons*): Acquisition and long-term retention. *Animal Learning and Behavior, 7,* 447–451. [8]

Kinsman, R. A., & Bixenstine, V. E. (1968). Secondary reinforcement and shock termination. *Journal of Experimental Psychology, 76,* 62–68. [10]

Kish, G. B. (1966). Studies of sensory reinforcement. In W. K. Honig (Ed.), *Operant behavior: Areas of research and application* (pp. 109–159). New York: Appleton-Century-Crofts. [9]

Klein, S. B. (1972). Adrenal–pituitary influence in reactivation of avoidance-memory in the rat after intermediate intervals. *Journal of Comparative and Physiological Psychology, 79,* 341–359. [14]

Klopfer, P. H. (1971). Imprinting: Determining its perceptual basis in ducklings. *Journal of Comparative and Physiological Psychology, 54,* 560–565. [9]

Kraemer, P. J. (1984). Forgetting of visual discriminations by pigeons. *Journal of Experimental Psychology: Animal Behavior Processes, 10,* 530–542. [13, 14]

Kraemer, P. J., & Roberts, W. A. (1984). Short-term memory for visual and auditory stimuli in pigeons. *Animal Learning and Behavior, 12,* 275–284. [14]

Kramer, T. J., & Rilling, M. (1970). Differential reinforcement of low rates: A selective critique. *Psychological Review, 74,* 225–254. [9]

Krane, R. V., & Wagner, A. R. (1975). Taste aversion learning with a delayed shock US: Implications for the "generality of the laws of learning." *Journal of Comparative and Physiological Psychology, 88,* 882–889. [7]

Krebs, J. R., Erichsen, J. T., Webber, J. I., & Charnov, E. L. (1977). Optimal prey selection in the great tit (*Parus major*). *Animal Behavior, 25,* 30–38. [11]

Krebs, J. R., Kacelnik, A., & Taylor, P. (1978). Test of optimal sampling by foraging great tits. *Nature, 275,* 27–31. [11]

Krebs, J. R., Ryan, J. C., & Charnov, E. L. (1974). Hunting by expectation or optimal foraging? A study of patch use by chickadees. *Animal Behavior, 22,* 953–964. [11]

Krechevsky, I. (1938). Hypotheses in rats. *Psychological Review, 39,* 516–532. [13]

Kremer, E. F. (1971). Truly random and traditional control procedures in CER conditioning in the rat. *Journal of Comparative and Physiological Psychology, 76,* 441–448. [3]

Kremer, E. F. (1974). The truly random control procedure: Conditioning to static cues. *Journal of Comparative and Physiological Psychology, 86,* 700–707. [3]

Kremer, E. F., & Kamin, L. J. (1971). The truly random procedure: Associative or nonassociative effects in rats. *Journal of Comparative and Physiological Psychology, 74,* 203–210. [3]

Kroodsma, D. E. (1978). Aspects of learning in the ontogeny of bird song: Where, from whom, when, how many, which and how accurately. In G. M. Burghardt & M. Bekoff (Eds.), *The development of behavior: Comparative and evolutionary aspects* (pp. 215–230). New York: Garland. [12]

Kroodsma, D. E. (1984). Songs of the alder flycatcher (*Empidonax alnorium*) and willow flycatcher (*Empidonax traillii*) are innate. *Auk, 101*, 13–24. [12]

Kuhn, T. S. (1962). *The structure of scientific revolutions.* Chicago: University of Chicago Press. [2]

Lacey, J. I., Smith, R. L., & Green, A. (1955). Use of conditioned autonomic responses in the study of anxiety. *Psychosomatic Medicine, 17*, 208–217. [13]

Lamarre, J., & Holland, P. C. (1987). Transfer of inhibition after serial feature negative discrimination training. *Learning and Motivation, 18*, 319–342. [13]

Lamb, M. R. (1988). Selective attention: Effects of cuing on the processing of different types of compound stimuli. *Journal of Experimental Psychology: Animal Behavior Processes, 14*, 96–104. [13]

Lamb, M. R., & Riley, D. A. (1981). Effects of element arrangement on the processing of compound stimuli in pigeons (*Columba livia*). *Journal of Experimental Psychology: Animal Behavior Processes, 7*, 45–58. [13]

Lane, H. L. (1960). Temporal and intensive properties of human vocal responding under a schedule of reinforcement. *Journal of the Experimental Analysis of Behavior, 6*, 179–188. [8]

Lashley, K. S. (1929). *Brain mechanisms and intelligence.* Chicago: University of Chicago Press. [11]

Lashley, K. S., & Wade, M. (1946). The Pavlovian theory of generalization. *Psychological Review, 53*, 72–87. [13]

Laties, V. C., Weiss, B., Clark, R. L., & Reynolds, M. D. (1965). Overt "mediating" behavior during temporally spaced responding. *Journal of the Experimental Analysis of Behavior, 8*, 107–116. [9]

Laties, V. C., Weiss, B., & Weiss, A. B. (1969). Further observations on overt "mediating" behavior and the discrimination of time. *Journal of the Experimental Analysis of Behavior, 12*, 43–57. [9]

Lattal, K. A., & Gleeson, S. (1990). Response acquisition with delayed reinforcement. *Journal of Experimental Psychology: Animal Behavior Processes, 16*, 27–39. [9]

Lavin, M. J. (1976). The establishment of flavor–flavor associations using a sensory preconditioning training procedure. *Learning and Motivation, 7*, 173–183. [5, 7]

Lavin, M. J., Freise, B., & Coombes, S. (1980). Transferred flavor aversions in adult rats. *Behavioral and Neural Biology, 28*, 15–33. [7]

Lawrence, D. H. (1952). The transfer of a discrimination along a continuum. *Journal of Comparative and Physiological Psychology, 45*, 511–516. [13]

Lawrence, D. H., & DeRivera, J. (1954). Evidence for relational discrimination. *Journal of Comparative and Physiological Psychology, 47*, 465–471. [13]

Lea, S. E. G. (1978). The psychology and economics of demand. *Psychological Bulletin, 85*, 441–466. [11]

Lea, S. E. G. (1981). Correlation and contiguity in foraging behaviour. In P. Harzem & M. D. Zeiler (Eds.), *Predictability, correlation, and contiguity* (pp. 355–406). New York: Wiley. [11]

Lea, S. E. G. (1984). In what sense do pigeons learn concepts? In H. L. Roitblat, T. G. Bever, & H. S. Terrace (Eds.), *Animal cognition* (pp. 263–276). Hillsdale, NJ: Erlbaum. [15]

Lea, S. E. G., & Harrison, S. M. (1978). Discrimination of polymorphous stimulus sets by pigeons. *The Quarterly Journal of Experimental Psychology, 30*, 521–537. [15]

Lea, S. E. G., Lohmann, A., & Ryan, C. M. E. (1993). Discrimination of five-dimensional stimuli by pigeons: Limitations of feature analysis. *The Quarterly Journal of Experimental Psychology, 46B*, 19–42. [15]

Lea, S. E. G., & Roper, R. J. (1977). Demand for food on fixed-ratio schedules as a function of the quality of concurrently available reinforcement. *Journal of the Experimental Analysis of Behavior, 27*, 371–380. [11]

Lea, S. E. G., & Ryan, C. M. E. (1990). Unnatural concepts and the theory of concept discrimination in birds. In M. L. Commons, R. J. Herrnstein, S. Kosslyn, & D. Mumford (Eds.), *Quantitative analysis of behavior: Vol. VIII. Behavioral approaches to pattern recognition and concept formation* (pp. 165–185). Hillsdale, NJ: Erlbaum. [15]

Lea, S. E. G., Tarpy, R. M., & Webley, P. (1987). *The individual in the economy: A survey of economic psychology.* New York: Cambridge University Press. [11]

Leitenberg, H., Rawson, R. A., & Mulick, J. A. (1975). Extinction and reinforcement of alternative behavior. *Journal of Comparative and Physiological Psychology, 88*, 640–652. [8]

Leith, C. R., & Maki, W. S. (1975). Attention shifts during matching-to-sample performance in pigeons. *Animal Learning and Behavior, 3*, 85–89. [13]

Leith, C. R., & Maki, W. S. (1977). Effects of compound configuration on stimulus selection in the pigeon. *Journal of Experimental Psychology: Animal Behavior Processes, 3*, 229–239. [13]

Lejeune, H., & Jasselette, P. (1986). Accurate DRL performance in the pigeon: Comparison between perching and treadle pressing. *Animal Learning and Behavior, 14*, 205–211. [9]

Lenneberg, E. H. (1967). *Biological foundations of language.* New York: Wiley. [15]

Lenzer, I. I. (1972). Differences between behavior reinforced by electrical stimulation of the brain and conventionally reinforced behavior: An associative analysis. *Psychological Bulletin, 78*, 103–118. [11]

Leonard, D. W. (1969). Amount and sequence of reward in partial and continuous reinforcement. *Journal of Comparative and Physiological Psychology, 67*, 204–211. [10]

Leslie, J. C. (1981). Effects of variations in local reinforcement rate on local response rate in variable interval schedules. *Journal of the Experimental Analysis of Behavior, 35*, 45–53. [9]

Lett, B. T. (1973). Delayed reward learning: Disproof of the traditional theory. *Learning and Motivation, 4*, 237–246. [8, 9]

Lett, B. T. (1974). Visual discrimination learning with a 1-min delay of reward. *Learning and Motivation, 5*, 174–181. [9]

Lett, B. T. (1975). Long delay learning in the T-maze. *Learning and Motivation, 6*, 80–90. [8, 9]

Lett, B. T. (1984). Extinction of taste aversion does not eliminate taste potentiation of odor aversion in rats or color aversion in pigeons. *Animal Learning and Behavior, 12*, 414–420. [7]

Levine, M. (1959). A model of hypothesis behavior in discrimination learning set. *Psychological Review, 66*, 353–366. [13]

Levine, M. (1975). *A cognitive theory of learning: Research hypothesis testing.* Hillsdale, NJ: Erlbaum. [13]

Levine, S. (1966). UCS intensity and avoidance learning. *Journal of Experimental Psychology, 71*, 163–164. [9]

Lewis, D. J. (1969). Sources of experimental amnesia. *Psychological Review, 76*, 461–472. [14]

Lewis, D. J., Misanian, J. R., & Miller, R. R. (1968). Recovery of memory following amnesia. *Nature, 220*, 704–705. [14]

Liddell, A., & Lyons, M. (1978). Thunderstorm phobias. *Behaviour Research and Therapy, 16*, 306–308. [1]

Lieberman, D. A., Davidson, F. H., & Thomas, G. V. (1985). Marking in pigeons: The role of memory in delayed reinforcement. *Journal of Experimental Psychology: Animal Behavior Processes, 11*, 611–624. [8, 9]

Lieberman, D. A., McIntosh, D. C., & Thomas, G. V. (1979). Learning when reward is delayed: A marking hypothesis. *Journal of Experimental Psychology: Animal Behavior Processes, 5*, 224–242. [9]

Lieberman, P. H., Klatt, D. H., & Wilson, W. H. (1969). Vocal tract limitations on the vowel repertoires of rhesus monkeys and other nonhuman primates. *Science, 164*, 1185–1187. [15]

Linden, D. R., & Hallgren, S. O. (1973). Transfer of approach responding between punishment and frustrative nonreward sustained through continuous reinforcement. *Learning and Motivation, 4*, 207–217. [10]

Lipp, O. V., Siddle, D. A., & Vaitl, D. (1992). Latent inhibition in humans: Single-cue conditioning revisited. *Journal of Experimental Psychology: Animal Behavior Processes, 18*, 115–125. [5]

Locurto, C. M., Terrace, H. S., & Gibbon, J. (Eds.). (1981). *Autoshaping and conditioning theory.* New York: Academic Press. [3]

Loftus, E. F., & Loftus, G. R. (1980). On the permanence of stored information in the human brain. *American Psychologist, 35*, 49–72. [11]

Loftus, G. R., & Kallman, H. J. (1979). Encoding and use of detail information in picture recognition. *Journal of Experimental Psychology: Human Learning and Memory, 5*, 197–211. [14]

Logue, A. W. (1979). Taste aversion and the generality of the laws of learning. *Psychological Bulletin, 86*, 276–296. [7]

Logue, A. W. (1988). Research on self-control: An integrating framework. *Behavioral and Brain Sciences, 11*, 665–709. [10]

Logue, A. W., & Chavarro, A. (1987). Effect on choice of absolute and relative values of reinforcer delay, amount, and frequency. *Journal of Experimental Psychology: Animal Behavior Processes, 13*, 280–291. [10]

Logue, A. W., Forzano, L. B., & Tobin, H. (1992). Independence of reinforcer amount and delay: The generalized matching law and self-control in humans. *Learning and Motivation, 23*, 326–342. [10]

Logue, A. W., & Pena-Correal, T. E. (1984). Responding during reinforcement delay in a self-control paradigm. *Journal of the Experimental Analysis of Behavior, 41*, 267–277. [10]

LoLordo, V. M., & Fairless, J. L. (1985). Pavlovian conditioned inhibition: The literature since 1969. In R. R. Miller & N. E. Spear (Eds.), *Information processing in animals: Conditioned inhibition* (pp. 1–49). Hillsdale, NJ: Erlbaum. [3]

Lombardi, C. M., Fachinelli, C. C., & Delius, J. D. (1984). Oddity of visual patterns conceptualized by pigeons. *Animal Learning and Behavior, 12*, 2–6. [15]

Looney, T. A., & Griffin, R. W. (1978). A sequential feature-positive effect using tone as the distinguishing feature in an auto-shaping procedure. *Animal Learning and Behavior, 6*, 401–405. [13]

Lorenz, K. Z. (1937). The companion in the bird's world. *Auk, 54*, 245–273. [12]

Lovejoy. E. (1966). Analysis of the overlearning reversal effect. *Psychological Review, 78*, 87–103. [13]

Lovibond, P. F., Preston, G. C., & Mackintosh, N. J. (1984). Context specificity of conditioning, extinction, and latent inhibition. *Journal of Experimental Psychology: Animal Behavior Processes, 10*, 360–375. [5]

Lowe, C. F. (1979). Determinants of human operant behaviour. In M. D. Zeiler & P. Harzem (Eds.), *Advances in the analysis of behavior: Vol. 1: Reinforcement and the organization of behavior* (pp. 159–192). New York: Wiley. [9]

Lowe, C. F. (1983). Radical behaviorism and human psychology. In G. C. L. Davey (Ed.), *Animal models of human behavior: Conceptual, evolutionary, and neurobiological perspectives* (pp. 71–93). Chichester, England: Wiley. [9]

Lowe, C. F., & Weardon, J. H. (1981). A quantitative model of temporal control on fixed-interval schedules: Dynamic properties of behaviour. In C. M. Bradshaw, E. Szabadi, & C. F. Lowe (Eds.), *Quantification of steady-state operant behaviour* (pp. 177–188). Amsterdam: Elsevier/North Holland Biomedical Press. [9]

Lubow, R. E. (1973). Latent inhibition. *Psychological Bulletin, 79,* 398–407. [5]

Lubow, R. E. (1989). *Latent inhibition and conditioned attention theory.* New York: Cambridge University Press. [5]

Lubow, R. E., Markman, R. E., & Allen, J. (1968). Latent inhibition and classical conditioning of the rabbit pinna response. *Journal of Comparative and Physiological Psychology, 66,* 688–694. [5]

Lubow, R. E., Rifkin, B., & Alek, M. (1976). The context effect: The relationship between stimulus preexposure and environmental preexposure determines subsequent learning. *Journal of Experimental Psychology: Animal Behavior Processes, 2,* 38–47. [6]

Lubow, R. E., Schnur, P., & Rifkin, B. (1976). Latent inhibition and conditioned attention theory. *Journal of Experimental Psychology: Animal Behavior Processes, 2,* 163–174. [5]

Lubow, R. E., Wagner, M., & Weiner, I. (1982). The effects of compound stimulus preexposure of two elements differing in salience on the acquisition of conditioned suppression. *Animal Learning and Behavior, 10,* 483–489. [5]

Lubow, R. E., Weiner, I., & Schnur, P. (1981). Conditioned attention theory. In G. H. Bower (Ed.), *The psychology of learning and motivation* (Vol. 15, pp. 1–49). New York: Academic Press. [5]

Lucas, G. A., Deich, J. D., & Wasserman, E. A. (1981). Trace autoshaping: Acquisition, maintenance, and path dependence at long trace intervals. *Journal of the Experimental Analysis of Behavior, 36,* 61–74. [4]

Lucas, G. A., & Wasserman, E. A. (1982). US duration and local trial spacing affect autoshaped responding. *Animal Learning and Behavior, 10,* 490–498. [4]

Lyness, W. G., Friedle, N. M., & Moore, K. E. (1979). Destruction of dopaminergic nerve terminals in nucleus accumbens: Effect on d-amphetamine self-administration. *Pharmacology, Biochemistry, and Behavior, 11,* 553–556. [11]

Lyons, J., Klipec, W. D., & Steinsultz, G. (1973). The effect of chlorpromazine on discrimination performance and the peak shift. *Physiological Psychology, 1,* 121–124. [13]

MacArthur, R. H., & Pianka, E. R. (1966). On optimal use of a patchy environment. *The American Naturalist, 100,* 603–609. [11]

MacDonald, S. E., & Grant, D. S. (1987). Effects of signaling retention interval length on delayed matching-to-sample in pigeons. *Journal of Experimental Psychology: Animal Behavior Processes, 13,* 116–125. [14]

Mackintosh, N. J. (1963). The effect of irrelevant cues on reversal learning in the rat. *British Journal of Psychology, 54,* 127–134. [13]

Mackintosh, N. J. (1964). Overtraining and transfer within and between dimensions in the rat. *The Quarterly Journal of Experimental Psychology, 16,* 250–256. [13]

Mackintosh, N. J. (1965a). Overtraining, reversal, and extinction in rats and chicks. *Journal of Comparative and Physiological Psychology, 59,* 31–36. [13]

Mackintosh, N. J. (1965b). Overtraining, transfer to proprioceptive control, and position reversal. *The Quarterly Journal of Experimental Psychology, 17,* 26–36. [13]

Mackintosh, N. J. (1969). Further analysis of the overtraining reversal effect. *Journal of Comparative and Physiological Psychology Monograph Supplement, 67* (Pt. 2), 1–18. [13]

Mackintosh, N. J. (1975a). A theory of attention: Variation of the associability of stimuli with reinforcement. *Psychological Review, 82,* 276–298. [5, 13]

Mackintosh, N. J. (1975b). Blocking of conditioned suppression: Role of the first compound trial. *Journal of Experimental Psychology: Animal Behavior Processes, 1,* 335–345. [6]

Mackintosh, N. J. (1976). Overshadowing and stimulus intensity. *Animal Learning and Behavior, 4,* 186–192. [5]

Mackintosh, N. J. (1977). Stimulus control: Attentional factors. In W. K. Honig & J. E. R. Staddon (Eds.), *Handbook of operant behavior* (pp. 481–513). Englewood Cliffs, NJ: Prentice-Hall. [13]

Mackintosh, N. J. (1983). *Conditioning and associative learning.* New York: Oxford University Press. [11]

Mackintosh, N. J., Bygrave, D. J., & Picton, B. M. B. (1977). Locus of the effect of a surprising reinforcer in the attenuation of blocking. *The Quarterly Journal of Experimental Psychology, 29,* 327–336. [6]

Mackintosh, N. J., & Honig, W. K. (1970). Blocking and attentional enhancement in pigeons. *Journal of Comparative and Physiological Psychology, 73,* 78–85. [13]

Mackintosh, N. J., & Little, L. (1969). Intradimensional and extradimensional shift learning by pigeons. *Psychonomic Science, 14,* 5–6. [13]

Mackintosh, N. J., & Little, L. (1970). An analysis of transfer along a continuum. *Canadian Journal of Psychology, 24,* 362–369. [13]

Macphail, E. M., Good, M., Honey, R. C., & Willis, A. (1995). Relational learning in pigeons: The role of perceptual processes in between-key recognition of complex stimuli. *Animal Learning and Behavior, 23,* 83–92. [15]

Mactutus, C. F., Ferek, J. M., & Riccio, D. C. (1980). Amnesia induced by hyperthermia: An unusually profound, yet reversible, memory loss. *Behavioral and Neural Biology, 30,* 260–277. [14]

Mahoney, W. J., & Ayres, J. J. B. (1976). One-trial simultaneous and backward fear conditioning as reflected in conditioned suppression of licking in rats. *Animal Learning and Behavior, 4*, 357–362. [4]

Maier, S. F. (1989). Learned helplessness: Event covariation and cognitive changes. In S. B. Klein & R. R. Mowrer (Eds.), *Contemporary learning theories: Instrumental conditioning theory and the impact of biological constraints on learning* (pp. 73–110). Hillsdale, NJ: Erlbaum. [10]

Maier, S. F. (1990). Role of fear in mediating shuttle escape learning deficit produced by inescapable shock. *Journal of Experimental Psychology: Animal Behavior Processes, 16*, 137–149. [10]

Maier, S. F., & Jackson, R. L. (1979). Learned helplessness: All of us were right (and wrong): Inescapable shock has multiple effects. In G. H. Bower (Ed.), *The psychology of learning and motivation* (Vol. 13, pp. 155–218). New York: Academic Press. [10]

Maier, S. F., Jackson, R. L., & Tomie, A. (1987). Potentiation, overshadowing, and prior exposure to inescapable shock. *Journal of Experimental Psychology: Animal Behavior Processes, 13*, 260–270. [10]

Maier, S. F., & Seligman, M. E. P. (1976). Learned helplessness: Theory and evidence. *Journal of Experimental Psychology: General, 105*, 3–46. [10]

Maier, S. F., Seligman, M. E. P., & Solomon, R. L. (1969). Pavlovian fear conditioning and learned helplessness: Effects on escape and avoidance behavior of (a) the CS–US contingency and (b) the independence of the US and voluntary responding. In B. A. Campbell & R. M. Church (Eds.), *Punishment and aversive behavior* (pp. 299–342). New York: Appleton-Century-Crofts. [10]

Maki, W. S., & Leith, C. R. (1973). Shared attention in pigeons. *Journal of the Experimental Analysis of Behavior, 19*, 345–349. [14]

Maki, W. S., Moe, J. C., & Bierley, C. M. (1977). Short-term memory for stimuli, responses, and reinforcers. *Journal of Experimental Psychology: Animal Behavior Processes, 3*, 156–177. [14]

Maki, W. S., Olson, D., & Rego, S. (1981). Directed forgetting in pigeons: Analysis of cue functions. *Animal Learning and Behavior, 9*, 189–195. [14]

Maki, W. S., Riley, D. A., & Leith, C. R. (1976). The role of test stimuli in matching to compound samples by pigeons. *Animal Learning and Behavior, 4*, 13–21. [14]

Malone, J. C. (1991). *Theories of learning: A historical approach.* Belmont, CA: Wadsworth. [11]

Manning, A. A., Schneiderman, N., & Lordahl, D. S. (1969). Delay vs. trace heart rate classical discrimination conditioning in rabbits as a function of ISI. *Journal of Experimental Psychology, 80*, 225–230. [4]

Mansfield, J. G., & Cunningham, C. L. (1980). Conditioning and extinction of tolerance to the hypothermic effect of ethanol in rats. *Journal of Comparative and Physiological Psychology, 94*, 962–969. [7]

Marler, P. (1970). A comparative approach to vocal learning: Song development in white-crowned sparrows. *Journal of Comparative and Physiological Psychology, Monograph 71*(2), 1–25. [12]

Marler, P. (1976). Sensory templates in species-specific behavior. In J. C. Fentress (Ed.), *Simpler networks and behavior* (pp. 314–329). Sunderland, MA: Sinauer. [12]

Marler, P. (1984). Song learning: Innate species differences in the learning process. In P. Marler & H. S. Terrace (Eds.), *The biology of learning* (pp. 289–309). New York: Springer-Verlag. [12]

Marler, P., & Peters, S. (1977). Selective vocal learning in a sparrow. *Science, 198*, 519–521. [12]

Marlin, N. A. (1981). Contextual associations in trace conditioning. *Animal Learning and Behavior, 9*, 519–523. [4]

Marlin, N. A. (1983). Second-order conditioning using a contextual stimulus as S1. *Animal Learning and Behavior, 11*, 290–294. [3, 5]

Marsh, G. (1969). An evaluation of three explanations for the transfer of discrimination effect. *Journal of Comparative and Physiological Psychology, 68*, 268–275. [13]

Marsh, G. (1972). Prediction of the peak shift in pigeons from gradients of excitation and inhibition. *Journal of Comparative and Physiological Psychology, 81*, 262–266. [13]

Martinez, J. E., Schulteis, G., & Weinberger, S. B. (1991). How to increase and decrease the strength of memory traces: The effects of drugs and hormones. In J. L. Martinez & R. P. Kesner (Eds.), *Learning and memory: A biological view* (pp. 149–198). San Diego, CA: Academic Press. [11]

Mason, W. A. (1970). Motivation factors in psychosocial development. In W. J. Arnold & M. M. Page (Eds.), *Nebraska symposium on motivation* (Vol. 18, pp. 35–67). Lincoln: University of Nebraska Press. [12]

Masters, J. C., Burish, T. G., Hollon, S. D., & Rimm, D. C. (1987). *Behavior therapy: Techniques and empirical findings* (3rd ed.). New York: Harcourt Brace Jovanovich. [1, 8]

Masterson, F. A., & Crawford, M. (1982). The defense motivation system: A theory of avoidance behavior. *The Behavioral and Brain Sciences, 5*, 661–696. [12]

Masterson, F. A., Crawford, M., & Bartter, W. D. (1978). Brief escape from a dangerous place: The role of reinforcement in the rat's one-way avoidance acquisition. *Learning and Motivation, 9*, 141–163. [9]

Matzel, L. D. (1985). Signal properties of reinforcement and reinforcement omission on a multiple fixed-ratio schedule. *Animal Learning and Behavior, 13*, 187–193. [2, 10]

Matzel, L. D., Brown, A. M., & Miller, R. R. (1987). Associative effects of US preexposure: Retarded conditioned responding mediated by an excitatory training context. *Journal of Experimental Psychology: Animal Behavior Processes, 13*, 65–72. [6]

Matzel, L. D., Gladstein, L., & Miller, R. R. (1988). Conditioned excitation and conditioned inhibition are not mutually exclusive. *Learning and Motivation, 19,* 99–121. [3]

Matzel, L. D., Held, F. P., & Miller, R. R. (1988). Information and expression of simultaneous and backward associations: Implications for contiguity theory. *Learning and Motivation, 19,* 317–344. [4, 5]

Matzel, L. D., Schachtman, T. R., & Miller, R. R. (1988). Learned irrelevance exceeds the sum of CS-preexposure and US-preexposure deficits. *Journal of Experimental Psychology: Animal Behavior Processes, 14,* 311–319. [3]

Mayr, E. (1974). Behavior programs and evolutionary strategies. *American Scientist, 62,* 650–659. [1]

Mazmanian, D. S., & Roberts, W. A. (1983). Spatial memory in rats under restricted viewing conditions. *Learning and Motivation, 14,* 123–139. [14]

Mazur, J. E., & Logue A. W. (1978). Choice in a "self-control" paradigm: Effects of a fading procedure. *Journal of the Experimental Analysis of Behavior, 30,* 11–17. [10]

Mazur, J. E., & Wagner, A. R. (1982). An episodic model of associative learning. In M. L. Commons, R. J. Herrnstein, & A. R. Wagner (Eds.), *Quantitative analyses of behavior: Vol. 3. Acquisition* (pp. 3–39). Cambridge, MA: Ballinger. [6]

McAllister, D. E., McAllister, W. R., & Dieter, S. E. (1976). Reward magnitude and shock variables (continuity and intensity) in shuttle-box avoidance learning. *Animal Learning and Behavior, 4,* 204–209. [9]

McAllister, W. R., McAllister, D. E., & Douglass, W. K. (1971). The inverse relationship between shock intensity and shuttle-box avoidance learning in rats: A reinforcement explanation. *Journal of Comparative and Physiological Psychology, 74,* 426–433. [9]

McCoy, D. F., & Yanko, D. M. (1983). Feature-positive and feature-negative discrimination learning maintained by negative reinforcement in rhesus monkeys. *Animal Learning and Behavior, 11,* 460–464. [13]

McCain, G., & Segal, E. M. (1977). *The game of science* (3rd ed.). Monterey, CA: Brooks/Cole. [2]

McGaugh, J. L. (1966). Time-dependent processes in memory storage, *Science, 153,* 1351–1358. [14]

McGaugh, J. L. (1983). Hormonal influences on memory. *Annual Review of Psychology, 34,* 297–323. [11]

McGonigle, B., & Chalmers, M. (1992). Monkeys are rational! *The Quarterly Journal of Experimental Psychology, 45B,* 189–228. [15]

McGregor, P. K., & Avery, M. I. (1986). The unsung songs of great tits (*Parus major*): Learning neighbours' songs for discrimination. *Behavioral Ecology and Sociobiology, 18,* 311–316. [12]

McMichael, J. S., & Corey, J. R. (1969). Contingency management in an introductory psychology course produces better learning. *Journal of Applied Behavior Analysis, 2,* 79–83. [1]

McNamara, J. (1982). Optimal patch use in a stochastic environment. *Theoretical Population Biology, 21,* 269–288. [11]

McNeill, D. (1970). *The acquisition of language.* New York: Harper & Row. [15]

McSweeney, F. K., Melville, C. L., & Whipple, J. E. (1983). Herrnstein's equation for the rates of responding during concurrent schedules. *Animal Learning and Behavior, 11,* 275–289. [10]

Meachum, C. L., & Bernstein, I. L. (1990). Conditioned responses to a taste conditioned stimulus paired with lithium chloride administration. *Behavioral Neuroscience, 104,* 711–715. [6, 7]

Meck, W. H. (1983). Selective adjustments of the speed of internal clock and memory processes. *Journal of Experimental Psychology: Animal Behavior Processes, 9,* 171–201. [15]

Meck, W. H., & Church, R. M. (1982). Abstraction of temporal attributes. *Journal of Experimental Psychology: Animal Behavior Processes, 8,* 226–243. [15]

Meck, W. H., & Church, R. M. (1983). A mode control model of counting and timing processes. *Journal of Experimental Psychology: Animal Behavior Processes, 9,* 320–334. [15]

Meck, W. H., & Church, R. M. (1984). Simultaneous temporal processing. *Journal of Experimental Psychology: Animal Behavior Processes, 10,* 1–29. [15]

Meck, W. H., & Church, R. M. (1987). Cholinergic modulation of the content of temporal memory. *Behavioral Neuroscience, 101,* 457–464. [15]

Meck, W. H., Church, R. M., & Gibbon, J. (1985). Temporal integration in duration and number discrimination. *Journal of Experimental Psychology: Animal Behavior Processes, 11,* 591–597. [15]

Meck, W. H., Church, R. M., & Olton, D. S. (1984). Hippocampus, time, and memory. *Behavioral Neuroscience, 98,* 3–22. [15]

Medin, D. L. (1972). Role of reinforcement in discrimination learning set in monkeys. *Psychological Bulletin, 77,* 305–318. [13]

Medin, D. L. (1980). Proactive interference in monkeys: Delay and intersample interval effects are noncomparable. *Animal Learning and Behavior, 8,* 553–560. [14]

Mehiel, R., & Bolles, R. C. (1984). Learned flavor preferences based on caloric outcome. *Animal Learning and Behavior, 12,* 421–427. [7]

Mehiel, R., & Bolles, R. C. (1988). Learned flavor preferences based on calories are independent of initial hedonic value. *Animal Learning and Behavior, 16,* 383–387. [7]

Mellgren, R. L., Fouts, R. S., & Martin, J. W. (1973). Approach and escape to conspecific odors of reward and nonreward in rats. *Animal Learning and Behavior, 1,* 129–132. [9]

Mellgren, R. L., Seybert, J. A., & Dyck, D. G. (1978). The order of continuous, partial and nonreward trials and resistance to extinction. *Learning and Motivation, 9,* 359–371. [10]

Mendelson, W. B. (1987). *Human sleep: Research and clinical care.* New York: Plenum. [14]

Mercier, P., & Baker, A. G. (1985). Latent inhibition, habituation, and sensory preconditioning: A test of priming in short-term memory. *Journal of Experimental Psychology: Animal Behavior Processes, 11,* 485–501. [5]

Midgley, M., Lea, S. E. G., & Kriby, R. M. (1989). Algorithmic shaping and misbehavior in the acquisition of token deposit by rats. *Journal of the Experimental Analysis of Behavior, 52,* 27–40. [8]

Miles, R. C. (1956). The relative effectiveness of secondary reinforcers throughout deprivation and habit-strength parameters. *Journal of Comparative and Physiological Psychology, 49,* 126–130. [10]

Milgram, N. W., Krames, L., & Alloway, T. M. (1977). *Food aversion learning.* New York: Plenum. [7]

Milinski, M., & Heller, R. (1978). Influence of a predator on the optimal foraging behavior of sticklebacks (*Gasterosteus oculeatus*). *Nature, 275,* 642–644. [11]

Millenson, J. R., Kehoe, E. J., & Gormezano, I. (1977). Classical conditioning of the rabbit's nictitating membrane response under fixed and mixed CS–US intervals. *Learning and Motivation, 8,* 351–366. [4]

Miller, G. A. (1956). The magical number seven, plus or minus two: Some limits on our capacity for processing information. *Psychological Review, 63,* 81–97. [14]

Miller, H. L. (1976). Matching-based hedonic scaling in the pigeon. *Journal of the Experimental Analysis of Behavior, 26,* 335–347. [10]

Miller, J. S., Jagielo, J. A., & Spear, N. E. (1990). Changes in the retrievability of associations to elements of the compound CS determine the expression of overshadowing. *Animal Learning and Behavior, 18,* 157–161. [5]

Miller, J. S., McCoy, D. F., Kelly, K. S., & Bardo, M. T. (1986). A within-event analysis of taste-potentiated odor and contextual aversions. *Animal Learning and Behavior, 14,* 15–21. [7]

Miller, N. E. (1978). Biofeedback and visceral learning. *Annual Review of Psychology, 29,* 373–404. [8]

Miller, R. R., Barnet, R. C., & Grahame, N. J. (1995). Assessment of the Rescorla–Wagner model. *Psychological Bulletin, 117,* 363–387. [6]

Miller, R. R., Hallam, S. C., Hong, J. Y., & Dufore, D. S. (1991). Associative structure of differential inhibition: Implications for models of conditioned inhibition. *Journal of Experimental Psychology: Animal Behavior Processes, 17,* 141–150. [3]

Miller, R. R., Kasprow, W. J., & Schachtman, T. R. (1986). Retrieval variability: Sources and consequences. *American Journal of Psychology, 99,* 145–218. [14]

Miller, R. R., & Matzel, L. D. (1987). Memory for associative history of a conditioned stimulus. *Learning and Motivation, 18,* 118–130. [14]

Miller, R. R., & Matzel, L. D. (1989). Contingency and relative associative strength. In S. B. Klein & R. R. Mowrer (Eds.), *Contemporary learning theories: Pavlovian conditioning and the status of traditional learning theory* (pp. 61–84). Hillsdale, NJ: Erlbaum. [13]

Miller, R. R., Ott, C. A., Berk, A. M., & Springer, A. D. (1974). Appetitive memory restoration after electroconvulsive shock in the rat. *Journal of Comparative and Physiological Psychology, 87,* 717–723. [14]

Miller, R. R., & Schachtman, T. R. (1985a). Conditioning context as an associative baseline: Implications for response generation and the nature of conditioned inhibition. In R. R. Miller & N. E. Spear (Eds.), *Information processing in animals: Conditioned inhibition* (pp. 51–88). Hillsdale, NJ: Erlbaum. [3]

Miller, R. R., & Schachtman, T. R. (1985b). The several roles of context at the time of retrieval. In P. D. Balsam & A. Tomie (Eds.), *Context and learning* (pp. 167–194). Hillsdale, NJ: Erlbaum. [3, 14]

Miller, R. R., & Spear, N. E. (1985). *Information processing in animals: Conditioned inhibition.* Hillsdale, NJ: Erlbaum. [3]

Miller, R. R., & Springer, A. D. (1973). Amnesia, consolidation and retrieval. *Psychological Review, 80,* 69–79. [14]

Miller, V. (1984). Selective association learning in the rat: Generality of response system. *Learning and Motivation, 15,* 58–84. [7]

Miller, V., & Domjan, M. (1981). Specificity of cue to consequence in aversion learning in the rat: Control for US-induced differential orientations. *Animal Learning and Behavior, 9,* 339–345. [7]

Milner, B., Corkin, S., & Teuber, H. L. (1968). Further analysis of the hippocampal amnesic syndrome: Fourteen-year follow-up study of H. M. *Neuropsychologia, 6,* 215–234. [11]

Milner, P. M. (1989). The discovery of self-stimulation and other stories. *Neuroscience and Biobehavioral Reviews, 13,* 61–67. [11]

Mineka, S. (1985a). Animal models of anxiety based disorders: Their usefulness and limitations. In J. Maser & A. H. Tuma (Eds.), *Anxiety and anxiety disorders* (pp. 199–244). Hillsdale, NJ: Erlbaum. [2]

Mineka, S. (1985b). The frightful complexity of the origins of fears. In F. R. Brush & J. B. Overmier (Eds.), *Affect, conditioning, and cognition: Essays on the determinants of behavior* (pp. 55–73). Hillsdale, NJ: Erlbaum. [1]

Mineka, S., Cook, M., & Miller, S. (1984). Fear conditioned with escapable and inescapable shock: Effects of a feedback stimulus. *Journal of Experimental Psychology: Animal Behavior Processes, 10,* 307–323. [10]

Minor, T. R., Dess, N. K., & Overmier, J. B. (1991). Inverting the traditional view of "learned helplessness." In M. R. Denny (Ed.), *Fear, avoidance, and phobias* (pp. 87–133). Hillsdale, NJ: Erlbaum. [10]

Minor, T. R., Jackson, R. L., & Maier, S. F. (1984). Effects of task-irrelevant cues and reinforcement delay on choice-escape learning following inescapable shock: Evidence for a deficit in selective attention. *Journal of Experimental Psychology: Animal Behavior Processes, 10,* 543–556. [10]

Minor, T. R., & LoLordo, V. M. (1984). Escape deficits following inescapable shock: The role of contextual odor. *Journal of Experimental Psychology: Animal Behavior Processes, 10,* 168–181. [10]

Minor, T. R., Trauner, M. A., Lee, C.-Y., & Dess, N. K. (1990). Modeling signal features of escape response: Effects of cessation conditioning in "learned helplessness" paradigm. *Journal of Experimental Psychology: Animal Behavior Processes, 16,* 123–136. [10]

Misanin, J. R., Nagy, Z. M., Keiser, E. F., & Bowen, W. (1971). Emergence of long-term memory in the neonatal rat. *Journal of Comparative and Physiological Psychology, 77,* 188–199. [14]

Mitchell, D., Kirschbaum, E. H., & Perry, R. L. (1975). Effects of neophobia and habituation on the poison-induced avoidance of exteroceptive stimuli in the rat. *Journal of Experimental Psychology: Animal Behavior Processes, 1,* 47–55. [7]

Modaresi, H. A. (1978). Facilitating effects of a safe platform on two-way avoidance learning. *Journal of Experimental Psychology: Animal Behavior Processes, 4,* 83–94. [9]

Modaresi, H. A. (1982). Defensive behavior of the rat in a shock-prod situation: Effects of the subject's location preference. *Animal Learning and Behavior, 10,* 97–102. [12]

Modaresi, H. A. (1989). Reinforcement versus species-specific defense reactions as determinants of avoidance barpressing. *Journal of Experimental Psychology: Animal Behavior Processes, 15,* 65–74. [12]

Modaresi, H. A. (1990). The avoidance barpress problem: Effects of enhanced reinforcement and an SSDR-congruent lever. *Learning and Motivation, 21,* 199–220. [12]

Modgil, S., & Modgil, C. (1987). *B. F. Skinner: Consensus and controversy.* Philadelphia: Falmer Press. [2, 11]

Molliver, M. E. (1963). Operant control of vocal behavior in the cat. *Journal of the Experimental Analysis of Behavior, 6,* 197–202. [8]

Moltz, H., & Stettner, L. J. (1961). The influence of patterned-light deprivation on the critical period for imprinting. *Journal of Comparative and Physiological Psychology, 54,* 279–283. [12]

Mondadori, C., Ornstein, K., Waser, P. G., & Houston, J. P. (1976). Post-trial reinforcing hypothalamic stimulation can facilitate avoidance learning. *Neuroscience Letters, 2,* 183–187. [11]

Morgan, M. J., & Nicholas, D. J. (1979). Discrimination between reinforced action patterns in the rat. *Learning and Motivation, 10,* 1–22. [9]

Morris, R. G. M. (1981). Spatial localization does not require the presence of local cue. *Learning and Motivation, 12,* 239–260. [14]

Morris, R. G. M. (1994). The neural basis of learning with particular reference to the role of synaptic plasticity: Where are we a century after Cajal's speculations? In N. J. Mackintosh (Ed.), *Animal learning and cognition* (pp. 135–183). New York: Academic Press. [11]

Moser, C. G., & Tait, R. W. (1983). Environmental control of multiple defensive responses in a conditioned burying paradigm. *Journal of Comparative Psychology, 97,* 338–352. [12]

Mowrer, O. H. (1950). *Learning theory and personality dynamics.* New York: Arnold Press. [1]

Moyer, K. E., & Korn, J. H. (1964). Effect of UCS intensity on the acquisition and extinction of an avoidance response. *Journal of Experimental Psychology, 67,* 352–359. [9]

Murray, A. K., & Strandberg, J. M. (1965). Development of a conditioned positive reinforcer through removal of an aversive stimulus. *Journal of Comparative and Physiological Psychology, 60,* 281–283. [10]

Murray, E. J., & Foote, F. (1979). The origins of fear of snakes. *Behaviour Research and Therapy, 17,* 489–493. [1]

Myers, A. K. (1977). Shock intensity and warning signal effects on several measures of operant avoidance acquisition. *Animal Learning and Behavior, 5,* 51–56. [9]

Nachman, M., & Ashe, J. H. (1973). Learned taste aversions in rats as a function of administration of LiCl. *Physiology and Behavior, 10,* 73–78. [4, 7]

Nachman, M., & Hartley, P. L. (1975). Role of illness in producing learned taste aversions in rats: A comparison of several rodenticides. *Journal of Comparative and Physiological Psychology, 89,* 1010–1018. [7]

Nachman, M., & Jones, D. R. (1974). Learned taste aversions over long delays in rats: The role of learned safety. *Journal of Comparative and Physiological Psychology, 86,* 949–956. [7]

Nagy, Z. M., Misanin, J. R., Newman, J. A., Olsen, P. L., & Hinderliter, C. F. (1972). Ontogeny of memory in the neonatal mouse. *Journal of Comparative and Physiological Psychology, 81,* 380–393. [14]

Nagy, Z. M., & Mueller, P. W. (1973). Effect of amount of original training upon onset of a 24-hour memory capacity in neonatal mice. *Journal of Comparative and Physiological Psychology, 85,* 151–159. [14]

Nairne, J. S., & Rescorla, R. A. (1981). Second-order conditioning with diffuse auditory reinforcers in the pigeon. *Learning and Motivation, 12,* 65–91. [5]

Nakagawa, E. (1992). Effects of overtraining on reversal learning by rats in concurrent and single discriminations. *The Quarterly Journal of Experimental Psychology, 44B,* 37–56. [13]

Nakajima, S. (1989). Subtypes of dopamine receptors involved in the mechanism of reinforcement. *Neuroscience and Biobehavioral Reviews, 13*, 123–128. [11]

Nakajima, S. (1993). Asymmetrical effect of a temporal gap between feature and target stimuli on Pavlovian serial feature-positive and feature-negative discriminations. *Learning and Motivation, 24*, 255–265. [13]

Nash, A. N., Muczyk, J. P., & Vettori, F. L. (1971). The relative practical effectiveness of programmed instruction. *Personnel Psychology, 24*, 397–418. [1]

Natale, F., Antinucci, F., Spinozzi, G., & Poti, P. (1986). Stage 6 object concept in nonhuman primate cognition: A comparison between gorilla (*Gorilla gorilla gorilla*) and Japanese macaque (*Macaca fuscata*). *Journal of Comparative Psychology, 100*, 335–339. [15]

Navarro, J. I., Hallam, S. C., Matzel, L. D., & Miller, R. R. (1989). Superconditioning and overshadowing. *Learning and Motivation, 20*, 130–152. [5]

Neiworth, J. J., & Wright, A. A. (1994). Monkeys (*Macaca mulatta*) learn category matching in a nonidentical same–different task. *Journal of Experimental Psychology: Animal Behavior Processes, 20*, 429–435. [15]

Nelson, K. R., & Wasserman, E. A. (1978). Temporal factors influencing the pigeon's successive matching to sample performance: Sample duration, intertrial interval, and retention interval. *Journal of the Experimental Analysis of Behavior, 30*, 153–162. [14]

Neuringer, A. (1991). Operant variability and repetition as functions of interresponse time. *Journal of Experimental Psychology: Animal Behavior Processes, 17*, 3–12. [8]

Neuringer, A. (1993). Reinforced variation and selection. *Animal Learning and Behavior, 21*, 83–91. [8]

Neuringer, A. J., & Schneider, B. A. (1968). Separating the effects of interreinforcement time and number of interreinforcement responses. *Journal of the Experimental Analysis of Behavior, 11*, 661–667. [9]

Newlin, R. J., & LoLordo, V. M. (1976). A comparison of pecking generated by serial, delay, and trace autoshaping procedures. *Journal of the Experimental Analysis of Behavior, 25*, 277–241. [4]

Newman, F. L., & Baron, M. R. (1965). Stimulus generalization along the dimension of angularity. *Journal of Comparative and Physiological Psychology, 60*, 59–63. [13]

O'Connell, J. M., & Rashotte, M. E. (1982). Reinforcement magnitude effects in first- and second-order conditioning of directed action. *Learning and Motivation, 13*, 1–25. [5]

Oden, D. L., Thompson, R. K., & Premack, D. (1990). Infant chimpanzees spontaneously perceive both concrete and abstract same/different relations. *Child Development, 61*, 621–631. [15]

Olds, J., & Milner, P. (1954). Positive reinforcement produced by electrical stimulation of the septal area and other regions of the rat brain. *Journal of Comparative and Physiological Psychology, 47*, 419–427. [11]

Olton, D. S. (1978). Characteristics of spatial memory. In S. H. Hulse, H. Fowler, & W. K. Honig (Eds.), *Cognitive processes in animal behavior* (pp. 341–373). Hillsdale, NJ: Erlbaum. [14]

Olton, D. S., & Samuelson, R. J. (1976). Remembrance of places passed: Spatial memory in rats. *Journal of Experimental Psychology: Animal Behavior Processes, 2*, 97–116. [14]

Osborne, S. R. (1978). A quantitative analysis of the effects of amount of reinforcement on two response classes. *Journal of Experimental Psychology: Animal Behavior Processes, 4*, 297–317. [9]

Overmier, J. B. (1985). Toward a reanalysis of the causal structure of the learned helplessness syndrome. In F. R. Brush & J. B. Overmier (Eds.), *Affect, conditioning, and cognition: Essays on the determinants of behavior* (pp. 211–227). Hillsdale, NJ: Erlbaum. [10]

Overmier, J. B., & Wielkiewicz, R. M. (1983). On unpredictability as a causal factor in "learned helplessness." *Learning and Motivation, 14*, 324–337. [10]

Overton, D. A. (1985). Contextual stimulus effects of drugs and internal states. In P. D. Balsam & A. Tomie (Eds.), *Context and learning* (pp. 357–384). Hillsdale, NJ: Erlbaum. [14]

The Oxford Encyclopedic English Dictionary (1991). Oxford, England: Oxford University Press. [1]

Pacitti, W. A., & Smith, N. F. (1977). A direct comparison of four methods for eliminating a response. *Learning and Motivation, 8*, 229–237. [8]

Page, S., & Neuringer, A. (1985). Variability is an operant. *Journal of Experimental Psychology: Animal Behavior Processes, 11*, 429–452. [8]

Paletta, M. S., & Wagner, A. R. (1986). Development of context-specific tolerance to morphine: Support for a dual-process interpretation. *Behavioral Neuroscience, 100*, 61–623. [7]

Palfai, T., & Chillag, D. (1971). Time-dependent memory deficits produced by pentylenetetrazol (Metrazol): The effects of reinforcer magnitude. *Physiology and Behavior, 7*, 439–442. [14]

Panksepp, J. (1982). Toward a general psychobiological theory of emotions [with commentaries]. *The Behavioral and Brain Sciences, 5*, 407–467. [11]

Panksepp, J. (1986). The neurochemistry of behavior. *Annual Review of Psychology, 37*, 77–107. [11]

Panlilio, L. V., & Weiss, S. J. (1993). Reversibility of single-incentive selective associations. *Journal of the Experimental Analysis of Behavior, 60*, 85–104. [4]

Papini, M. R., & Bitterman, M. E. (1990). The role of contingency in classical conditioning. *Psychological Review, 97*, 396–403. [3]

Papini, M. R., & Bitterman, M. E. (1993). The two-test strategy in the study of inhibitory conditioning. *Journal of Experimental Psychology: Animal Behavior Processes, 19*, 342–352. [3]

Parker, B. K., & Glover, R. L. (1987). Event duration memory: The effects of delay-interval illumination and instructional cuing. *Animal Learning and Behavior, 15*, 241–248. [14]

Parker, H. B., & Smith, R. F. (1981). Flavor- vs. tone-cued shock avoidance. *Animal Learning and Behavior, 9*, 335–338. [7]

Parker, L. A. (1982). Nonconsummatory and consummatory behavioral CRs elicited by lithium- and amphetamine-paired flavors. *Learning and Motivation, 13*, 281–303. [6]

Parker, L. A. (1988). Positively reinforcing drugs may produce a different kind of CTA than drugs which are not positively reinforcing. *Learning and Motivation, 19*, 207–220. [7]

Parker, L. A., Hills, K., & Jensen, K. (1984). Behavioral CRs elicited by a lithium- or an amphetamine-paired contextual test chamber. *Animal Learning and Behavior, 12*, 307–315. [6]

Parsons, P. J., & Spear, N. E. (1972). Long-term retention of avoidance learning by immature and adult rats as a function of environmental enrichment. *Journal of Comparative and Physiological Psychology, 80*, 297–303. [14]

Pasnak, R. (1979). Acquisition of prerequisites to conservation by macaques. *Journal of Experimental Psychology: Animal Behavior Processes, 5*, 194–210. [15]

Patterson, M. M., & Romano, A. G. (1987). The rabbit in Pavlovian conditioning. In I. Gormezano, W. F. Prokasy, & R. F. Thompson (Eds.), *Classical conditioning* (3rd ed., pp. 1–36). Hillsdale, NJ: Erlbaum. [3]

Pavlov, I. P. (1927). *Conditioned reflexes* (G. V. Anrep, Trans.). London: Oxford University Press. [1, 3, 13]

Pavlov, I. P. (1928). *Lectures on conditioned reflexes* (W. H. Gantt, Trans.). New York: Liveright. [3]

Payne, R. B., & Payne, L. L. (1993). Song copying and cultural transmission in indigo buntings. *Animal Behaviour, 46*, 1045–1065. [12]

Peacock, E. J., & Wong, P. T. P. (1982). Defensive burying in the rat: A behavioral field analysis. *Animal Learning and Behavior, 10*, 103–107. [12]

Pear, J. J., & Legris, J. A. (1987). Shaping by automated tracking of an arbitrary operant response. *Journal of the Experimental Analysis of Behavior, 47*, 241–247. [8]

Pearce, J. M. (1978). The relationship between shock magnitude and passive avoidance learning. *Animal Learning and Behavior, 6*, 341–345. [9, 12]

Pearce, J. M. (1987). A model for stimulus generalization in Pavlovian conditioning. *Psychological Review, 94*, 61–73. [13]

Pearce, J. M., Colwill, R. M., & Hall, G. (1978). Instrumental conditioning of scratching in the laboratory rat. *Learning and Motivation, 9*, 255–271. [9]

Pearce, J. M., & Hall, G. (1980). A model of Pavlovian learning: Variations in the effectiveness of conditioned but not of unconditioned stimuli. *Psychological Review, 87*, 532–552. [5, 6]

Pearce, J. M., & Kaye, H. (1985). Strength of the orienting response during inhibitory conditioning. *Journal of Experimental Psychology: Animal Behavior Processes, 11*, 405–420. [6]

Pearce, J. M., Kaye, H., & Hall, G. (1982). Predictive accuracy and stimulus associability: Development of a model for Pavlovian learning. In M. L. Commons, R. J. Herrnstein, & A. R. Wagner (Eds.), *Quantitative analyses of behavior: Vol. 3. Acquisition* (pp. 241–255). Cambridge, MA: Ballinger. [6]

Peck, C. A., & Bouton, M. E. (1990). Context and performance in aversive-to-appetitive and appetitive-to-aversive transfer. *Learning and Motivation, 21*, 1–31. [14]

Peckham, R. H., & Amsel, A. (1967). The within-S demonstration of a relationship between frustration and magnitude of reward in a differential magnitude of reward discrimination. *Journal of Experimental Psychology, 73*, 187–195. [10]

Peele, D. B., Casey, J., & Silberberg, A. (1984). Primacy of interresponse-time reinforcement in accounting for rate differences under variable-ratio and variable-interval schedules. *Journal of Experimental Psychology: Animal Behavior Processes, 10*, 149–167. [9]

Peele, D. B., & Ferster, C. B. (1982). Autoshaped key pecking maintained by access to a social space. *Journal of the Experimental Analysis of Behavior, 38*, 181–189. [6]

Pelchat, M. L., Grill, H. J., Rozin, P., & Jacobs, J. (1983). Quality of acquired responses to tastes by *Rattus norvegicus* depends on type of associated discomfort. *Journal of Comparative Psychology, 97*, 140–153. [7]

Penfield, W., & Jasper, H. (1954). *Epilepsy and the functional anatomy of the human brain*. Boston: Little, Brown. [11]

Penfield, W., & Perot, P. (1963). The brain's record of auditory and visual experience. *Brain, 86*, 595–696. [11]

Pepperberg, I. M. (1983). Cognition in the African Grey parrot: Preliminary evidence for auditory/vocal comprenhension of a class concept. *Animal Learning and Behavior, 11*, 179–185. [15]

Pepperberg, I. M., & Funk, M. S. (1990). Object permanence in four species of psittacine birds: An African Grey parrot (*Psittacus erithacus*), an Illiger mini macaw (*Ara maracana*), a parakeet (*Melopsittacus undulatus*), and a cockatiel, (*Nymphicus hollandicus*). *Animal Learning and Behavior, 18*, 97–108. [15]

Pepperberg, I. M., & Kozak, F. A. (1986). Object permanence in the African Grey parrot. *Animal Learning and Behavior, 14*, 322–330. [15]

Perin, C. T. (1942). Behavior potentiality as a joint function of the amount of training and degree of hunger at the time of extinction. *Journal of Experimental Psychology, 30*, 93–113. [11]

Perkins, C. C., & Weyant, R. G. (1958). The interval between training and test trial as determiner of the slope of generalization gradients. *Journal of Comparative and Physiological Psychology, 51,* 596–600. [13]

Perone, M., & Courtney, K. (1992). Fixed-ratio pausing: Joint effects of past reinforcer magnitude and stimuli correlated with upcoming magnitude. *Journal of the Experimental Analysis of Behavior, 57,* 33–46. [9]

Peterson, C., & Seligman, M. E. P. (1984). Causal explanations as a risk factor for depression: Theory and evidence. *Psychological Review, 91,* 347–374. [10]

Peterson, G. B., Wheeler, R. L., & Armstrong G. D. (1978). Expectancies as mediators in the differential-reward conditioned discrimination performance of pigeons. *Animal Learning and Behavior, 6,* 279–285. [13]

Petri, H. L., & Mishkin, M. (1994). Behaviorism, cognitivism and the neuropsychology of memory. *American Scientist, 82,* 30–37. [11]

Petrinovich, L. (1985). Factors influencing song development in the white-crowned sparrow (*Zonotrichia leucophrys*). *Journal of Comparative Psychology, 99,* 15–29. [12]

Pfautz, P. L., Donegan, N. H., & Wagner, A. R. (1978). Sensory preconditioning versus protection from habituation. *Journal of Experimental Psychology: Animal Behavior Processes, 4,* 286–295. [5]

Piaget, J. (1928). *Judgment and reasoning in the child.* London: Kegan Paul, Trench, & Trubner. [15]

Pietrewicz, A. T., & Kamil, A. C. (1979). Search image formation in the blue jay (*Cyanocitta cristata*). *Science, 204,* 1332–1333. [7]

Pietrewicz, A. T., & Kamil, A. C. (1981). Search images and the detection of cryptic prey: An operant approach. In A. C. Kamil & T. D. Sargent (Eds.), *Foraging behavior: Ecological, ethological and psychological approaches* (pp. 311–331). New York: Garland Press. [7]

Pinel, J. P. J., Petrovic, D. M., & Hilton Jones, C. (1990). Defensive burying, nest relocation, and pup transport in lactating female rats. *The Quarterly Journal of Experimental Psychology, 42B,* 401–411. [12]

Pinel, J. P. J., & Treit, D. (1978). Burying as a defensive response in rats. *Journal of Comparative and Physiological Psychology, 92,* 708–712. [12]

Plato (1952). *Meno.* In R. M. Hutchens (Ed.), *Great books of the western world, vol. 7* (pp. 174–190). Chicago, Il: Encyclopedia Britania. [1]

Plotkin, H. C. (1983). The functions of learning and cross-species comparison. In G. C. L. Davey (Ed.), *Animal models of human behavior* (pp. 117–134). Chichester, England: Wiley. [1]

Plotkin, H. C., & Oakley, D. A. (1975). Backward conditioning in the rabbit (*Oryctologus cuniculus*). *Journal of Comparative and Physiological Psychology, 88,* 586–590. [4]

Plotkin, H. C., & Odling-Smee, F. J. (1979). Learning, change, and evolution: An enquiry into the teleonomy of learning. In J. S. Rosenblatt, R. A. Hinde, C. Beer, & M.-C. Busnel (Eds.), *Advances in the study of behavior* (Vol. 10, pp. 1–41). New York: Academic Press. [1]

Polenchar, B. E., Romano, A. G., Steinmetz, J. E., & Patterson, M. M. (1984). Effects of US parameters on classical conditioning of cat hindlimb flexion. *Animal Learning and Behavior, 12,* 69–72. [4]

Popper, K. R. (1959). *The logic of scientific discovery.* New York: Basic Books. [2]

Porter, D., & Neuringer, A. (1984). Music discriminations by pigeons. *Journal of Experimental Psychology: Animal Behavior Processes, 10,* 138–148. [15]

Porterfield, J. K., Herbert-Jackson, E., & Risley, T. R. (1976). Contingent observation: An effective and acceptable procedure for reducing disruptive behavior of young children in a group setting. *Journal of Applied Behavior Analysis, 9,* 55–64. [1]

Poucet, B. (1993). Spatial cognitive maps in animals: New hypotheses on their structure and neural mechanisms. *Psychological Review, 100,* 163–182. [14]

Poulos, C. X., & Cappell, H. (1991). Homeostatic theory of drug tolerance: A general model of physiological adaptation. *Psychological Review, 98,* 390–408. [7]

Poulos, C. X., Wilkinson, D. A., & Cappell, H. (1981). Homeostatic regulation and Pavlovian conditioning in tolerance to amphetamine-induced anorexia. *Journal of Comparative and Physiological Psychology, 95,* 735–746. [7]

Powell, R. W. (1970). The effect of punishment shock intensity upon responding under multiple schedules. *Journal of the Experimental Analysis of Behavior, 14,* 201–211. [9]

Powell, R. W. (1972). Analysis of warm-up effects during avoidance in wild and domesticated rodents. *Journal of Comparative and Physiological Psychology, 78,* 311–316. [14]

Premack, D. (1959). Toward empirical behavior laws: I. Positive reinforcement. *Psychological Review, 66,* 219–233. [8]

Premack, D. (1963). Predictions of the comparative reinforcement values of running and drinking. *Science, 139,* 1062–1063. [8]

Premack, D. (1965). Reinforcement theory. In D. Levine (Ed.), *Nebraska symposium on motivation* (Vol. XIII, pp. 123–180). Lincoln: University of Nebraska Press. [8]

Premack, D. (1976). *Intelligence in ape and man.* Hillsdale, NJ: Erlbaum. [15]

Premack, D. (1983). The codes of beast and man. *Behavioral and Brain Sciences, 6,* 125–167. [15]

Premack, D., & Premack, A. J. (1983). *The mind of an ape*. New York: Norton. [15]

Prewitt, E. P. (1967). Number of preconditioning trials in sensory preconditioning using CER training. *Journal of Comparative and Physiological Psychology, 64*, 360–362. [5]

Prokasy, W. F., Hall, J. F., & Fawcett, J. T. (1962). Adaptation sensitization, forward and backward conditioning and pseudoconditioning of the GSR. *Psychological Reports, 10*, 103–106. [4]

Prokasy, W. F., & Whaley, F. L. (1963). Intertrial interval range shift in classical eyelid conditioning. *Psychological Reports, 12*, 55–58. [4]

Purdy, J. E., & Cross, H. A. (1979). The role of R–S* expectancy in discrimination and discrimination reversal learning. *Learning and Motivation, 10*, 211–227. [13]

Purtle, R. B. (1973). Peak shift: A review. *Psychological Bulletin, 80*, 408-421. [13]

Pyke, G. H., Pulliam, H. R., & Charnov, E. L. (1977). Optimal foraging: A selective review of theory and tests. *The Quarterly Review of Biology, 52*, 137–154. [11]

Quartermain, D., Paolino, R. M., & Miller, N. E. (1965). A brief temporal gradient of retrograde amnesia independent of situational change. *Science, 149*, 1116–1118. [14]

Rabin, B. M., & Rabin, J. S. (1984). Acquisition of radiation and lithium chloride-induced conditioned taste aversions in anesthetized rats. *Animal Learning and Behavior, 12*, 439–441. [7]

Rachlin, H. (1969). Autoshaping of key pecking in pigeons with negative reinforcement. *Journal of the Experimental Analysis of Behavior, 12*, 521–531. [12]

Rachlin, H. (1987). The explanatory power of Skinner's radical behaviorism. In S. Modgil & C. Modgil (Eds.), *B. F. Skinner: Consensus and controversy* (pp. 155–164). Philadelphia: Falmer Press. [2]

Rachlin, H., Battalio, R. C., Kagel, J. H., & Green, L. (1981). Maximization theory in behavioral psychology. *The Behavioral and Brain Sciences, 4*, 371–388. [10]

Rachlin, H., & Burkhard, B. (1978). The temporal triangle: Response substitution in instrumental conditioning. *Psychological Review, 85*, 22–47. [11]

Rachlin, H., & Green, L. (1972). Commitment, choice and self-control. *Journal of the Experimental Analysis of Behavior, 17*, 15–22. [10]

Rachlin, H., Green, L., Kagel, J. H., & Battalio, R. C. (1976). Economic demand theory and psychological studies of choice. In G. H. Bower (Ed.), *The psychology of learning and motivation* (Vol. 10, pp. 129–154). New York: Academic Press. [10, 11]

Rachlin, H., Green, L., & Tormey, B. (1988). Is there a decisive test between matching and maximizing? *Journal of the Experimental Analysis of Behavior, 50*, 113–123. [10]

Rachlin, H., Kagel, J. H., & Battalio, R. C. (1980). Substitutability in time allocation. *Psychological Review, 87*, 355–374. [11]

Rachlin, H., Logue, A. W., Gibbon, J., & Frankel, M. (1986). Cognition and behavior in studies of choice. *Psychological Review, 93*, 33–45. [10]

Rachman, S. (1963). *Critical essays on psychoanalysis*. New York: Macmillan. [1]

Rachman, S., Eysenck, H. J. (1966). Reply to a "critique and reformulation" of behavior therapy. *Psychological Bulletin, 65*, 165–169. [1]

Rajecki, D. W. (1973). Imprinting in precocial birds: Interpretation, evidence, and evaluation. *Psychological Bulletin, 79*, 48–58. [12]

Randall, P. K., & Riccio, D. C. (1969). Fear and punishment as determinants of passive–avoidance responding. *Journal of Comparative and Physiological Psychology, 69*, 550–553. [9]

Randich, A., & LoLordo, V. M. (1979a). Associative and nonassociative theories of the UCS preexposure phenomenon: Implications for Pavlovian conditioning. *Psychological Bulletin, 86*, 523–548. [3]

Randich, A., & LoLordo, V. M. (1979b). Preconditioning exposure to the unconditioned stimulus affects the acquisition of a conditioned emotional response. *Learning and Motivation, 10*, 245–277. [3]

Rashotte, M. E., Griffin, R. W., & Sisk, C. L. (1977). Second-order conditioning of the pigeon's keypeck. *Animal Learning and Behavior, 5*, 25–38. [5]

Ratliff, R. G., & Ratliff, A. R. (1971). Runway acquisition and extinction as a joint function of magnitude of reward and percentage of rewarded acquisition trials. *Learning and Motivation, 2*, 289–295. [9, 10]

Ratner, S. C. (1956). Reinforcing and discriminative properties of the click in a Skinner box. *Psychological Reports, 2*, 232. [10]

Rawson, R. A., & Leitenberg, H. (1973). Reinforced alternative behavior during punishment and extinction with rats. *Journal of Comparative and Physiological Psychology, 85*, 593–600. [8]

Rawson, R. A., Leitenberg, H., Mulick, J. A., & Lefebvre, M. F. (1977). Recovery of extinction responding in rats following discontinuation of reinforcement of alternative behavior: A test of two explanations. *Animal Learning and Behavior, 5*, 415–420. [8]

Reed, P. (1991). Multiple determinants of the effects of reinforcement magnitude on free operant response rates. *Journal of the Experimental Analysis of Behavior, 55*, 109–123. [9]

Reed, P. (1993). Differential outcome effect does not control performance in a two-choice discrimination task with visual stimuli. *Learning and Motivation, 24*, 101–118. [13]

Reed, P., & Reilly, S. (1990). Context extinction following conditioning with delayed reward enhances subsequent instrumental responding. *Journal of Experimental Psychology: Animal Behavior Processes, 16,* 48–55. [9]

Reed, P., & Wright, J. E. (1988). Effects of magnitude of food reinforcement on free-operant response rates. *Journal of the Experimental Analysis of Behavior, 49,* 75–85. [9]

Reed, S. K. (1972). Pattern recognition and categorization. *Cognitive Psychology, 3,* 382–407. [15]

Reese, H. W. (1964). Discrimination learning set in rhesus monkeys. *Psychological Bulletin, 61,* 321–340. [13]

Reid, P. J., & Shettleworth, S. J. (1992). Detection of cryptic prey: Search image or search rate? *Journal of Experimental Psychology: Animal Behavior Processes, 18,* 273–286. [7]

Reilly, S., & Schachtman, T. R. (1987). The effects of ITI fillers in autoshaping. *Learning and Motivation, 18,* 202–219. [3]

Reiss, S., & Wagner, A. R. (1972). CS habituation produces a "latent inhibition effect" but no active "conditioned inhibition." *Learning and Motivation, 3,* 237–245. [5]

Rescorla, R. A. (1967). Pavlovian conditioning and its proper control procedures. *Psychological Review, 74,* 71–80. (b) [3]

Rescorla, R. A. (1968). Probability of shock in the presence and absence of CS in fear conditioning. *Journal of Comparative and Physiological Psychology, 66,* 1–5. [3]

Rescorla, R. A. (1969). Pavlovian conditioned inhibition. *Psychological Bulletin, 72,* 77–94. [3]

Rescorla, R. A. (1971a). Summation and retardation tests of latent inhibition. *Journal of Comparative and Physiological Psychology, 75,* 77–81. [5]

Rescorla, R. A. (1971b). Variation in the effectiveness of reinforcement and nonreinforcement following prior inhibitory conditioning. *Learning and Motivation, 2,* 113–123. [5]

Rescorla, R. A. (1972). Informational variables in Pavlovian conditioning. In G. H. Bower (Ed.), *The psychology of learning and motivation* (pp. 1–46). New York: Academic Press. [3]

Rescorla, R. A. (1973). Effect of US habituation following conditioning. *Journal of Comparative and Physiological Psychology, 82,* 137–143. [6]

Rescorla, R. A. (1974). Effect of inflation of the unconditioned stimulus value following conditioning. *Journal of Comparative and Physiological Psychology, 86,* 101–106. [6]

Rescorla, R. A. (1976a). Second-order conditioning of Pavlovian conditioned inhibition. *Learning and Motivation, 7,* 161–172. [5]

Rescorla, R. A. (1976b). Stimulus generalization: Some predictions from a model of Pavlovian conditioning. *Journal of Experimental Psychology: Animal Behavior Processes, 2,* 88–96. [13]

Rescorla, R. A. (1979). Aspects of the reinforcer learned in second-order Pavlovian conditioning. *Journal of Experimental Psychology: Animal Behavior Processes, 5,* 79–95. [5, 6]

Rescorla, R. A. (1980a). *Pavlovian second-order conditioning: Studies in associative learning.* Hillsdale, NJ: Erlbaum. [5]

Rescorla, R. A. (1980b). Simultaneous and successive associations in sensory preconditioning. *Journal of Experimental Psychology: Animal Behavior Processes, 6,* 207–216. [5]

Rescorla, R. A. (1982a). Effect of a stimulus intervening between CS and US in autoshaping. *Journal of Experimental Psychology: Animal Behavior Processes, 1982,* 8–131. [4]

Rescorla, R. A. (1982b). Simultaneous second-order conditioning produces S–S learning in conditioned suppression. *Journal of Experimental Psychology: Animal Behavior Processes, 8,* 23–32. [5]

Rescorla, R. A. (1985). Conditioned inhibition and facilitation. In R. R. Miller & N. E. Spear (Eds.), *Information processing in animals: Conditioned inhibition* (pp. 229–326). Hillsdale, NJ: Erlbaum. [5]

Rescorla, R. A. (1986). Facilitation and excitation. *Journal of Experimental Psychology: Animal Behavior Processes, 12,* 325–332. [5]

Rescorla, R. A. (1988). Facilitation based on inhibition. *Animal Learning and Behavior, 16,* 169–176. [5]

Rescorla, R. A. (1990a). Evidence for an association between the discriminative stimulus and the response–outcome association in instrumental learning. *Journal of Experimental Psychology: Animal Behavior Processes, 16,* 326–334. [11]

Rescorla, R. A. (1990b). Instrumental responses become associated with reinforcers that differ in one feature. *Animal Learning and Behavior, 18,* 206–211. [11]

Rescorla, R. A. (1991a). Associations of multiple outcomes with an instrumental response. *Journal of Experimental Psychology: Animal Behavior Processes, 17,* 465–474. [11]

Rescorla, R. A. (1991b). Associative relations in instrumental learning: The eighteenth Bartlett Memorial lecture. *The Quarterly Journal of Experimental Psychology, 43B,* 1–23. [11]

Rescorla, R. A. (1991c). Separate reinforcement can enhance the effectiveness of modulators. *Journal of Experimental Psychology: Animal Behavior Processes, 17,* 259–269. [5]

Rescorla, R. A. (1992). Response–outcome versus outcome–response associations in instrumental learning. *Animal Learning and Behavior, 20,* 223–232. [11]

Rescorla, R. A. (1993a). Inhibitory associations between S and R extinction. *Animal Learning and Behavior, 21,* 327–336. [11]

Rescorla, R. A. (1993b). Preservation of response–outcome associations through extinction. *Animal Learning and Behavior, 21,* 238–245. [11]

Rescorla, R. A. (1994). Control of instrumental performance by Pavlovian and instrumental stimuli. *Journal of Experimental Psychology: Animal Behavior Processes, 20,* 44–50. [8, 11]

Rescorla, R. A., & Colwill, R. M. (1989). Associations with anticipated and obtained outcomes in instrumental learning. *Animal Learning and Behavior, 17,* 291–303. [11]

Rescorla, R. A., & Cunningham, C. L. (1979). Spatial contiguity facilitates Pavlovian second-order conditioning. *Journal of Experimental Psychology: Animal Behavior Processes, 5,* 152–161. [5]

Rescorla, R. A., & Furrow, D. R. (1977). Stimulus similarity as a determinant of Pavlovian conditioning. *Journal of Experimental Psychology: Animal Behavior Processes, 3,* 203–215. [5]

Rescorla, R. A., & Gillam, D. J. (1980). An analysis of the facilitative effect of similarity on second-order conditioning. *Journal of Experimental Psychology: Animal Behavior Processes, 6,* 339–351. [5]

Rescorla, R. A., & Solomon, R. L. (1967). Two-process learning theory: Relationships between Pavlovian conditioning and instrumental learning. *Psychological Review, 74,* 151–182. [3]

Rescorla, R. A., & Wagner, A. R. (1972). A theory of Pavlovian conditioning: Variations in the effectiveness of reinforcement and nonreinforcement. In A. H. Black & W. F. Prokasy (Eds.), *Classical conditioning II: Current research and theory* (pp. 64–99). New York: Appleton-Century-Crofts. [6, 13]

Revusky, S. (1971). The role of interference in association over a delay. In W. K. Honig, & P. H. R. James (Eds.), *Animal memory* (pp. 155–213). New York: Academic Press. [14]

Revusky, S. (1977). Learning as a general process with an emphasis on data from feeding experiments. In N. W. Milgram, L. Krames, & T. M. Alloway (Eds.), *Food aversion learning* (pp. 1–51). New York: Plenum. [4]

Revusky, S. H., & Bedarf, E. W. (1967). Association of illness with prior ingestion of novel foods. *Science, 155,* 219–220. [7]

Revusky, S., & Parker, L. H. (1976). Aversions to unflavored water and cup drinking produced by delayed sickness. *Journal of Experimental Psychology: Animal Behavior Processes, 2,* 342–253. [7]

Reynolds, T. J., & Medin, D. L. (1979). Strength vs. temporal-order information in delayed-matching-to-sample performance by monkeys. *Animal Learning and Behavior, 7,* 294–300. [14]

Ricciardi, A. M., & Treichler, F. R. (1970). Prior training influences on transfer to learning set by squirrel monkeys. *Journal of Comparative and Physiological Psychology, 73,* 314–319. [13]

Riccio, D. C., Ackil, J., & Burch-Vernon, A. (1992). Forgetting of stimulus attributes: Methodological implications for assessing associative phenomena. *Psychological Bulletin, 112,* 433–445. [13]

Riccio, D. C., & Richardson, R. (1984). The status of memory following experimentally induced amnesias: Gone, but not forgotten. *Physiological Psychology, 12,* 59–72. [14]

Riccio, D. C., Richardson, R., & Ebber, D. L. (1984). Memory retrieval deficits based upon altered contextual cues: A paradox. *Psychological Bulletin, 96,* 152–165. [13]

Richman, C. L., & Coussens, W. (1970). Undertraining reversal effect in rats. *Journal of Experimental Psychology, 86,* 340–342. [13]

Richman, C. L., Knoblock, K., & Coussens, W. (1972). The overtraining reversal effect in rats: A function of task difficulty. *The Quarterly Journal of Experimental Psychology, 24,* 291–298. [13]

Riess, D. (1970). Sidman avoidance of rats as a function of shock intensity and duration. *Journal of Comparative and Physiological Psychology, 73,* 481–485. [9]

Riess, D., & Farrar, C. H. (1972). Shock intensity, shock duration, Sidman avoidance acquisition, and the "all or nothing" principle in rats. *Journal of Comparative and Physiological Psychology, 81,* 347–355. [9]

Riess, D., & Farrar, C. H. (1973). UCS duration and conditioned suppression: Acquisition and extinction between-groups and terminal performance within-subjects. *Learning and Motivation, 4,* 366–373. [4]

Riley, A. L., Jacobs, W. J., & LoLordo, V. M. (1976). Drug exposure and the acquisition and retention of a conditioned taste aversion. *Journal of Comparative and Physiological Psychology, 90,* 799–807. [7]

Riley, D. A. (1968). *Discrimination learning.* Boston, MA: Allyn and Bacon. [13]

Riley, D. A. (1984). Do pigeons decompose stimulus compounds? In H. L. Roitblat, T. G. Bever, & H. S. Terrace (Eds.), *Animal cognition* (pp. 333–350). Hillsdale, NJ: Erlbaum. [14]

Rilling, M. (1977). Stimulus control and inhibitory processes. In W. K. Honig & J. E. R. Staddon (Eds.), *Handbook of operant behavior* (pp. 432–480). Englewood Cliffs, NJ: Prentice-Hall. [13]

Ringen, J. D. (1993). Adaptation, teleology, and selection by consequences. *Journal of the Experimental Analysis of Behavior, 60,* 3–15. [11]

Riordan, M. M., Iwata, B. A., Finney, J. W., Wohl, M. K., & Stanley, A. E. (1984). Behavioral assessment and treatment of chronic food refusal in handicapped children. *Journal of Applied Behavior Analysis, 17,* 327–342. [1]

Ristau, C. A., & Robbins, D. (1982). Language in the great apes: A critical review. *Advances in the Study of Behavior, 12,* 141–255. [15]

Rizley, R. C., & Rescorla, R. A. (1972). Associations in second-order conditioning and sensory preconditioning. *Journal of Comparative and Physiological Psychology, 81,* 1–11. [5]

Robbins, D. (1971). Partial reinforcement: A selective review of the alleyway literature since 1960. *Psychological Bulletin, 76*, 415–431. [10]

Robbins, S. J. (1990). Mechanisms underlying spontaneous recovery in autoshaping. *Journal of Experimental Psychology: Animal Behavior Processes, 16*, 235–249. [3]

Roberts, A. C., Robbins, T. W., & Everitt, B. J. (1988). The effects of intradimensional and extradimensional shifts on visual discrimination learning in humans and non-human primates. *The Quarterly Journal of Experimental Psychology, 40B*, 321–341. [13]

Roberts, S. (1982). Cross-modal use of an internal clock. *Journal of Experimental Psychology: Animal Behavior Processes, 8*, 2–22. [15]

Roberts, S. (1983). Properties and function of an internal clock. In R. L. Mellgren (Ed.), *Animal cognition and behavior* (pp. 345–397). New York: North-Holland. [15]

Roberts, S., & Church, R. M. (1978). Control of an internal clock. *Journal of Experimental Psychology: Animal Behavior Processes, 4*, 318–337. [15]

Roberts, W. A. (1969). Resistance to extinction following partial and consistent reinforcement with varying magnitudes of reward. *Journal of Comparative and Physiological Psychology, 67*, 395–400. [9]

Roberts, W. A. (1976). Failure to replicate visual discrimination learning with a 1-min delay of reward. *Learning and Motivation, 7*, 313–325. [9]

Roberts, W. A. (1984). Some issues in animal spatial memory. In H. L. Roitblat, T. G. Bever, & H. S. Terrace (Eds.), *Animal cognition* (pp. 425–443). Hillsdale, NJ: Erlbaum. [14]

Roberts, W. A., Cheng, K., & Cohen, J. S. (1989). Timing light and tone signals in pigeons. *Journal of Experimental Psychology: Animal Behavior Processes, 15*, 23–35. [15]

Roberts, W. A., & Grant, D. S. (1974). Short-term memory in the pigeon with presentation time precisely controlled. *Learning and Motivation, 5*, 393–408. [14]

Roberts, W. A., & Grant, D. S. (1976). Studies of short-term memory in the pigeon using the delayed matching to sample procedure. In D. L. Medin, W. A. Roberts, & R. T. Davis (Eds.), *Processes of animal memory* (pp. 79–112). Hillsdale, NJ: Erlbaum. [14]

Roberts, W. A., & Grant, D. S. (1978a). An analysis of light-induced retroactive inhibition in pigeon short-term memory. *Journal of Experimental Psychology: Animal Behavior Processes, 4*, 219–236. [14]

Roberts, W. A., & Grant, D. S. (1978b). Interaction of sample and comparison stimuli in delayed matching-to-sample with the pigeon. *Journal of Experimental Psychology: Animal Behavior Processes, 4*, 68–82. [14]

Roberts, W. A., Macuda, T., & Brodbeck D. R. (1995). Memory for number of light flashes in the pigeon. *Animal Learning and Behavior, 23*, 182–188. [15]

Roberts, W. A., Mazmanian, D. S., & Kraemer, P. J. (1984). Directed forgetting in monkeys. *Animal Learning and Behavior, 12*, 29–40. [14]

Roberts, W. A., & Mitchell, S. (1994). Can a pigeon simultaneously process temporal and numerical information? *Journal of Experimental Psychology: Animal Behavior Processes, 20*, 66–78. [15]

Roberts, W. A., Phelps, M. T., & Schacter, G. B. (1992). Stimulus control of central place foraging on the radial maze. In W. K. Honig & J. G. Fetterman (Eds.), *Cognitive aspects of stimulus control* (pp. 135–153). Hillsdale, NJ: Erlbaum. [14]

Roberts, W. A., & van Veldhuizen, N. (1985). Spatial memory in pigeons on the radial maze. *Journal of Experimental Psychology: Animal Behavior Processes, 11*, 241–260. [14]

Robertson, D., Krane, R. V., & Garrud, P. (1984). Second-order conditioned taste aversion in rats: Shared modality is not sufficient to promote an association between S2 and S1. *Animal Learning and Behavior, 12*, 316–322. [5]

Robinson, D. N. (1979). *Systems of modern psychology: A critical sketch*. New York: Columbia University Press. [2]

Rodgers, J. P., & Thomas, D. R. (1982). Task specificity in nonspecific transfer and in extradimensional stimulus generalization in pigeons. *Journal of Experimental Psychology: Animal Behavior Processes, 8*, 301–312. [13]

Roitblat, H. L. (1980). Codes and coding processes in pigeons' short-term memory. *Animal Learning and Behavior, 8*, 341–351. [14]

Roitblat, H. L. (1982). The meaning of representation in animal memory. *The Behavioral and Brain Sciences, 5*, 353–406. [14]

Roitblat, H. L. (1984a). Pigeon working memory: Models for delayed matching-to-sample performance. In M. L. Commons, A. R. Wagner, & R. J. Herrnstein (Eds.), *Quantitative analyses of behavior: Discrimination processes* (Vol. 4, pp. 161–181). Cambridge, MA: Ballinger. [14]

Roitblat, H. L. (1984b). Representations in pigeon working memory. In H. L. Roitblat, T. G. Bever, & H. S. Terrace (Eds.), *Animal cognition* (pp. 79–97). Hillsdale, NJ: Erlbaum. [14]

Roitblat, H. L., & Harley, H. E. (1988). Spatial delayed matching-to-sample performance by rats: Learning, memory, and proactive interference. *Journal of Experimental Psychology: Animal Behavior Processes, 14*, 71–82. [14]

Roitblat, H. L., & Scopatz, R. A. (1983). Sequential effects in pigeon delayed matching-to-sample performance. *Journal of Experimental Psychology: Animal Behavior Processes, 9*, 202–221. [14]

Rosellini, R. A. (1978). Inescapable shock interferes with the acquisition of an appetitive operant. *Animal Learning and Behavior, 6,* 155–159. [10]

Rosellini, R. A., & DeCola, J. P. (1981). Inescapable shock interferes with the acquisition of a low-activity response in an appetitive context. *Animal Learning and Behavior, 9,* 487–490. [10]

Rosellini, R. A., & DeCola, J. P., Plonsky, M., Warren, D. A., & Stilman, A. J. (1984). Uncontrollable shock proactively increases sensitivity to response–reinforcer independence in rats. *Journal of Experimental Psychology: Animal Behavior Processes, 10,* 346–359. [10]

Rosellini, R. A., DeCola, J. P., & Shapiro, N. R. (1982). Cross-motivational effects of inescapable shock are associative in nature. *Journal of Experimental Psychology: Animal Behavior Processes, 8,* 376–388. [10]

Rosellini, R. A., DeCola, J. P., & Warren, D. A. (1986). The effect of feedback stimuli on contextual fear depends upon the length of the minimum intertrial interval. *Learning and Motivation, 17,* 229–242. [10]

Ross, R. T. (1985). Blocking and unblocking of conditioned analgesia. *Learning and Motivation, 16,* 173–189. [7]

Ross, R. T. (1986). Pavlovian second-order conditioned analgesia. *Journal of Experimental Psychology: Animal Behavior Processes, 12,* 32–39. [5, 7]

Ross, R. T., & Holland, P. C. (1981). Conditioning of simultaneous and serial feature-positive discriminations. *Animal Learning and Behavior, 9,* 293–303. [5, 13]

Ross, S. M., & Ross, L. E. (1971). Comparison of trace and delay classical eyelid conditioning as a function of interstimulus interval. *Journal of Experimental Psychology, 91,* 165–167. [4]

Routtenberg, A. (1978). The reward system of the brain. *Scientific American, 239,* 154–164. [11]

Routtenberg, A., & Lindy, J. (1965). Effects of the availability of rewarding septal and hypothalamic stimulation on bar pressing for food under conditions of deprivation. *Journal of Comparative and Physiological Psychology, 60,* 158–161. [11]

Rovee-Collier, C. (1984). The ontogeny of learning and memory in human infancy. In R. Kail & N. E. Spear (Eds.), *Comparative perspectives on the development of memory* (pp. 103–134). Hillsdale, NJ: Erlbaum. [14]

Rozin, P. (1968). Specific aversions and neophobia resulting from vitamin deficiency or poisoning in half-wild and domestic rats. *Journal of Comparative and Physiological Psychology, 66,* 82–88. [7]

Rozin, P., & Kalat, J. W. (1971). Specific hungers and poison avoidance as adaptive specializations of learning. *Psychological Review, 78,* 459–486. [7]

Rozin, P., & Ree, P. (1972). Long extension of effective CS–US interval by anesthesia between CS and US. *Journal of Comparative and Physiological Psychology, 80,* 43–48. [7]

Rudy, J. W. (1971). Sequential variables as determiners of the rat's discrimination of reinforcement events: Effects on extinction performance. *Journal of Comparative and Physiological Psychology, 77,* 476–481. [10]

Rumbaugh, D. M. (1977). *Language learning by a chimpanzee.* New York: Academic Press. [15]

Rumbaugh, D. M., & Gill, T. V. (1976). The mastery of language-type skills by the chimpanzee *(Pan). Annals of the New York Academy of Sciences, 280,* 562–578. [15]

Rumbaugh, D. M., Hopkins, W. D., Washburn, D. A., & Savage-Rumbaugh, E. S. (1991). Comparative perspectives of brain, cognition, and language. In N. A. Krasnegor, D. M. Rumbaugh, R. L. Schiefelbusch, & M. Studdert-Kennedy (Eds.), *Biological and behavioral determinants of language development* (pp. 145–164). Hillsdale, NJ: Erlbaum. [15]

Rumbaugh, D. M., & Savage-Rumbaugh, E. S. (1994). Language in comparative perspective. In N. J. Mackintosh (Ed.), *Animal learning and cognition* (pp. 307–333). New York: Academic Press. [15]

Rumbaugh, D. M., Savage-Rumbaugh, E. S., & Scanlon, J. L. (1982). The relationship between language in apes and human beings. In L. Rosenblum (Ed.), *Primate behavior* (pp. 361–384). New York: Academic Press. [15]

Rusiniak, K. W., Hankins, W. G., Garcia, J., & Brett, L. P. (1979). Flavor–illness aversions: Potentiation of odor by taste in rats. *Behavioral and Neural Biology, 25,* 1–17. [7]

Rusiniak, K. W., Palmerino, C. C., Rice, A. G., Forthman, D. L., & Garcia, J. (1982). Flavor–illness aversions: Potentiation of odor by taste with toxin but not shock in rats. *Journal of Comparative and Physiological Psychology, 96,* 527–539. [7]

Russell, A., & Glow, P. H. (1974). Some effects of short-term immediate prior exposure to light change on responding for light change. *Animal Learning and Behavior, 2,* 262–266. [9]

Russell, A., & Glow, P. H. (1976). Exposure to non-contingent light change in separate sessions prior to light-contingent bar pressing. *The Quarterly Journal of Experimental Psychology, 28,* 403–408. [9]

Sainsbury, R. S. (1971). Effect of proximity of elements on the feature-positive effect. *Journal of the Experimental Analysis of Behavior, 16,* 315–325. [13]

Salafia, W. R., Lambert, R. W., Host, K. C., Chiaia, N. L., & Ramirez, J. J. (1980). Rabbit nictitating membrane conditioning: Lower limit of the effective interstimulus interval. *Animal Learning and Behavior, 8,* 85–91. [4]

Salafia, W. R., Mis, F. W., Terry, W. S., Bartosiak, R. S., & Daston, A. P. (1973). Conditioning of the nictitating membrane response of the rabbit *(Oryctolagus cuniculus)* as a function of the length and degree of variation of the intertrial interval. *Animal Learning and Behavior, 1,* 109–115. [4]

Sands, S. F., Lincoln, C. E., & Wright, A. A. (1982). Pictorial similarity judgments and the organization of visual memory in the rhesus monkey. *Journal of Experimental Psychology: General, 111,* 369–389. [15]

Santi, A. (1989). Differential outcome expectancies and directed forgetting effects in pigeons. *Animal Learning and Behavior, 17,* 349–354. [14]

Santiago, H. C., & Wright, A. A. (1984). Pigeon memory: *Same/different* concept learning, serial probe recognition acquisition, and probe delay effects on the serial-position function. *Journal of Experimental Psychology: Animal Behavior Processes, 10,* 498–512. [15]

Savage-Rumbaugh, E. S., & Lewin, R. (1994). *Kanzi: At the brink of the human mind.* New York: Wiley. [15]

Savage-Rumbaugh, E. S., Murphy, J., Sevcik, R. A., Brakke, K., Williams, S., & Rumbaugh, D. M. (1993). Language comprehension in ape and child. *Monographs of the Society for Research in Child Development, 58* (Nos. 3 & 4, pp. 1–221). [15]

Savage-Rumbaugh, E. S., Pate, J. L., Lawson, J., Smith, S. T., & Rosenbaum, S. (1983). Can a chimpanzee make a statement? *Journal of Experimental Psychology: General, 112,* 457–492. [15]

Savage-Rumbaugh, E. S., Rumbaugh, D. M., Smith, S. T., & Lawson, J. (1980). Reference: The linguistic essential. *Science, 210,* 922–924. [15]

Savage-Rumbaugh, E. S., Sevcik, R. A., & Hopkins, W. D. (1988). Symbolic cross-modal transfer in two species of chimpanzees. *Child Development, 59,* 617–625. [15]

Schaal, D. W., & Branch, M. N. (1988). Responding of pigeons under variable-interval schedules of unsignaled, briefly signaled, and completely signaled delays to reinforcement. *Journal of the Experimental Analysis of Behavior, 50,* 33–54. [9, 10]

Schaal, D. W., & Branch, M. N. (1990). Responding of pigeons under variable-interval schedules of signaled–delayed reinforcement: Effects of delay–signal duration. *Journal of the Experimental Analysis of Behavior, 53,* 103–121. [9]

Schachtman, T. R., Brown, A. M., Gordon, E., Catterson, D., & Miller, R. R. (1987). Mechanisms underlying retarded emergence of conditioned responding following inhibitory training: Evidence for the comparator hypothesis. *Journal of Experimental Psychology: Animal Behavior Processes, 13,* 310–322. [3]

Schachtman, T. R., Gee, J.-L., Kasprow, W. J., & Miller, R. R. (1983). Reminder-induced recovery from blocking as a function of the number of compound trials. *Learning and Motivation, 14,* 154–164. [5]

Schachtman, T. R., & Reilly, S. (1987). The role of local context in autoshaping. *Learning and Motivation, 18,* 343–355. [3]

Schneider, B. A. (1969). A two-state analysis of fixed-interval responding in the pigeon. *Journal of the Experimental Analysis of Behavior, 12,* 677–687. [9]

Schneiderman, N. (1966). Interstimulus interval function of the nictitating membrane response of the rabbit under delay versus trace conditioning. *Journal of Comparative and Physiological Psychology, 62,* 397–402. [4]

Schneiderman, N. (1972). Response system divergences in aversive classical conditioning. In A. H. Black & W. F. Prokasy (Eds.), *Classical conditioning: Vol. II. Current research and theory* (pp. 341–376). New York: Appleton-Century-Crofts. [6]

Schnur, P., & Martinez, R. A. (1989). Environmental control of morphine tolerance in the hamster. *Animal Learning and Behavior, 17,* 322–327. [7]

Schoenfeld, W. N. (1970). *Theory of reinforcement schedules.* New York: Appleton-Century-Crofts. [9]

Schreurs, B. G. (1993). Long-term memory and extinction of the classically conditioned rabbit nictitating membrane response. *Learning and Motivation, 24,* 293–302. [14]

Schreurs, B. G., & Westbrook, R. F. (1982). The effects of changes in the CS–US interval during compound conditioning upon an otherwise blocked element. *The Quarterly Journal of Experimental Psychology, 34B,* 19–30. [6]

Schrier, A. M. (1974). Transfer between the repeated reversal and learning set tasks: A reexamination. *Journal of Comparative and Physiological Psychology, 87,* 1004–1010. [13]

Schrier, A. M., Angarella, R., & Povar, M. L. (1984). Studies of concept formation by stumptailed monkeys: Concepts humans, monkeys, and letter A. *Journal of Experimental Psychology: Animal Behavior Processes, 10,* 564–584. [15]

Schrier, A. M., & Brady, P. M. (1987). Categorization of natural stimuli by monkeys (*Macaca mulatta*): Effects of stimulus set size and modification of exemplars. *Journal of Experimental Psychology: Animal Behavior Processes, 13,* 136–143. [15]

Schulenburg, C. J., Riccio, D. C., & Stikes, E. R. (1971). Acquisition and retention of a passive-avoidance response as a function of age in rats. *Journal of Comparative and Physiological Psychology, 74,* 75–83. [14]

Schuster, R. H. (1969). A functional analysis of conditioned reinforcement. In D. P. Hendry (Ed.), *Conditioned reinforcement* (pp. 192–234). Homewood, IL: Dorsey Press. [10]

Schusterman, R. J. (1964). Successive discrimination-reversal training and multiple discrimination training in one-trial learning by chimpanzees. *Journal of Comparative and Physiological Psychology, 58,* 153–156. [13]

Schusterman, R. J., Gisiner, R., Grimm, B. K., & Hanggi, E. B. (1993). Behavior control by exclusion and attempts at establishing semanticity in marine mammals using matching-to-sample paradigms. In H. L. Roitblat, L. M. Herman, & P. E. Nachtigall (Eds.), *Language and communication: Comparative perspectives* (pp. 249–274). Hillsdale, NJ: Erlbaum. [15]

Schusterman, R. J., Hanggi, E. B., & Gisiner, R. (1992). Imprinting and other aspects of pinniped–human interactions. In H. Davis & D. Balfour (Eds.), *The inevitable bond: Examining scientist–animal interactions* (pp. 334–356). New York: Cambridge University Press. [12]

Schwartz, B. (1980). Development of complex, stereotyped behavior in pigeons. *Journal of the Experimental Analysis of Behavior, 33,* 153–166. [8]

Schwartz, B. (1985). On the organization of stereotyped response sequences. *Animal Learning and Behavior, 13,* 261–268. [8]

Schwartz, B., & Reilly, M. (1983). Response stereotypy without automaticity in pigeons. *Learning and Motivation, 14,* 253–270. [8]

Schwartz, B., & Williams, D. R. (1971). Discrete-trials spaced responding in the pigeon: The dependence of efficient performance on the availability of a stimulus for collateral pecking. *Journal of the Experimental Analysis of Behavior, 16,* 155–160. [9]

Schwartz, G. E. (1972). Voluntary control of human cardiovascular integration and differentiation through feedback and reward. *Science, 175,* 90–93. [8]

Schwartz, G. E. (1973). Biofeedback as therapy: Some theoretical and practical issues. *American Psychologist, 28,* 666–673. [8]

Schwartz, G. E. (1975). Biofeedback, self-regulation, and the patterning of physiological processes. *American Scientist, 63,* 314–324. [8]

Schwartz, G. E., & Beatty, J. (Eds.), (1977). *Biofeedback theory and research.* New York: Academic Press. [8]

Scott, G. K., & Platt, J. R. (1985). Model of response–reinforcer contingency. *Journal of Experimental Psychology: Animal Behavior Processes, 11,* 152–171. [8]

Scull, J. (1973). The Amsel frustration effect: Interpretations and research. *Psychological Bulletin, 79,* 352–361. [10]

Seligman, M. E. P. (1970). On the generality of the laws of learning. *Psychological Review, 77,* 406–418. [7, 9, 12]

Seligman, M. E. P., & Maier, S. F. (1967). Failure to escape traumatic shock. *Journal of Experimental Psychology, 74,* 1–9. [10]

Seligman, M. E. P., Maier, S. F., & Solomon, R. L. (1971). Unpredictable and uncontrollable aversive events. In F. R. Brush (Ed.), *Aversive conditioning and learning* (pp. 347–400). New York: Academic Press. [10]

Seligman, M. E. P., Rosellini, R. A., & Kozak, M. J. (1975). Learned helplessness in the rat: Time course, immunization, and reversibility. *Journal of Comparative and Physiological Psychology, 88,* 542–547. [10]

Senkowsi, P. C. (1978). Variables affecting the overtraining extinction effect in discrete-trial lever pressing. *Journal of Experimental Psychology: Animal Behavior Processes, 4,* 131–143. [13]

Senkowski, P. C., & Vogel, V. A. (1976). Effects of number of CS–US pairings on the strength of conditioned frustration in rats. *Animal Learning and Behavior, 4,* 421–426. [10]

Seraganian, P. (1979). Extra dimensional transfer in the easy-to-hard effect. *Learning and Motivation, 10,* 39–57. [13]

Sgro, J. A. (1969). Complete removal and delay of sucrose reward in the double alleyway. *Journal of Comparative and Physiological Psychology, 69,* 442–447. [2, 10]

Sgro, J. A., Glotfelty, R. A., & Moore, B. D. (1970). Delay of reward in the double alleyway: A within-subjects versus between-groups comparison. *Journal of Experimental Psychology, 84,* 82–87. [10]

Shapiro, K. L., Jacobs, W. J., & LoLordo, V. M. (1980). Stimulus–reinforcer interactions in Pavlovian conditioning of pigeons: Implications for selective associations. *Animal Learning and Behavior, 8,* 586–594. [4]

Shapiro, K. L., & LoLordo, V. M. (1982). Constraints on Pavlovian conditioning of the pigeon: Relative conditioned reinforcing effects of red-light and tone CSs paired with food. *Learning and Motivation, 13,* 68–80. [4]

Sheafor, P. J., & Gormezano, I. (1972). Conditioning the rabbit's (*Orydtolagus cuniculus*) jaw-movement response: US magnitude effects on URs, CRs, and pseudo-CRs. *Journal of Comparative and Physiological Psychology, 81,* 449–456. [4]

Sheffield, F. D. (1965). Relation between classical conditioning and instrumental learning. In W. F. Prokasy (Ed.), *Classical conditioning: A symposium* (pp. 302–322). New York: Appleton-Century-Crofts. [8]

Sheffield, V. F. (1949). Extinction as a function of partial reinforcement and distribution of practice. *Journal of Experimental Psychology, 39,* 511–526. [10]

Shepp, B. E., & Eimas, P. D. (1964). Intradimensional and extradimensional shifts in the rat. *Journal of Comparative and Physiological Psychology, 57,* 357–361. [13]

Shepp, B. E., & Schrier, A. M. (1969). Consecutive intradimensional shifts in monkeys. *Journal of Comparative and Physiological Psychology, 67,* 199–203. [13]

Sherman, J. E. (1978). US inflation with trace and simultaneous fear conditioning. *Animal Learning and Behavior, 6,* 463–468. [4]

Sherman, J. E., & Maier, S. F. (1978). The decrement in conditioned fear with increased trials of simultaneous conditioning is not specific to the simultaneous procedure. *Learning and Motivation, 9,* 31–53. [4]

Sherry, D. F. (1984). Food storage by black-capped chickadees: Memory for the location and context to caches. *Animal Behaviour, 32,* 451–464. [14]

Sherry, D. F. (1992). Landmarks, the hippocampus, and spatial search in food-storing birds. In W. K. Honig & J. G. Fetterman (Eds.), *Cognitive aspects of stimulus control* (pp. 185–201). Hillsdale, NJ: Erlbaum. [14]

Sherry, D. F., & Schacter, D. L. (1987). The evolution of multiple memory systems. *Psychological Review, 94,* 439–454. [14]

Shettleworth, S. J. (1972). Constraints on learning. In D. S. Lehrman, R. A. Hinde, & E. Shaw (Eds.), *Advances in the study of behavior* (Vol. 4, pp. 1–68). New York: Academic Press. [9]

Shettleworth, S. J. (1975). Reinforcement and the organization of behavior in golden hamsters: Hunger, environment, and food reinforcement. *Journal of Experimental Psychology: Animal Behavior Processes, 1,* 56–87. [9]

Shettleworth, S. J. (1978). Reinforcement and the organization of behavior in golden hamsters: Punishment of three action patterns. *Learning and Motivation, 9,* 99–123. [9]

Shettleworth, S. J. (1990). Spatial memory in food-storing birds. *Philosophical Transactions of the Royal Society, Series B, 329,* 143–151. [14]

Shettleworth, S. J. (1994). Commentary: What are behavior systems and what use are they? *Psychonomic Bulletin and Review, 1,* 451–456. [12]

Shettleworth, S. J., & Krebs, J. R. (1982). How marsh tits find their hoards: The roles of site preference and spatial memory. *Journal of Experimental Psychology: Animal Behavior Processes, 8,* 354–375. [14]

Shettleworth, S. J., & Krebs, J. R. (1986). Stored and encountered seeds: A comparison of two spatial memory tasks in marsh tits and chickadees. *Journal of Experimental Psychology: Animal Behavior Processes, 12,* 248–257. [14]

Shimoff, E., Catania, A. C., & Matthews, B. A. (1981). Uninstructed human responding: Sensitivity of low-rate performance to schedule contingencies. *Journal of the Experimental Analysis of Behavior, 36,* 207–220. [9]

Shimp, C. P. (1967). The reinforcement of short interresponse times. *Journal of the Experimental Analysis of Behavior, 10,* 425–434. [8, 9]

Shimp C. P. (1969). The concurrent reinforcement of two interresponse times: The relative frequency of an interresponse time equals its relative harmonic length. *Journal of the Experimental Analysis of Behavior, 12,* 403–411. [8]

Shurtleff, D., & Ayres, J. J. B. (1981). One-trial backward excitatory fear conditioning in rats: Acquisition, retention, extinction, and spontaneous recovery. *Animal Learning and Behavior, 9,* 65–74. [14]

Siegel, S. (1972). Conditioning of insulin-induced glycemia. *Journal of Comparative and Physiological Psychology, 78,* 233–241. [7]

Siegel, S. (1974). Flavor preexposure and "learned safety." *Journal of Comparative and Physiological Psychology, 87,* 1073–1082. [5, 7]

Siegel, S. (1975a). Conditioning insulin effects. *Journal of Comparative and Physiological Psychology, 89,* 189–199. [7]

Siegel, S. (1975b). Evidence from rats that morphine tolerance is a learned response. *Journal of Comparative and Physiological Psychology, 89,* 498–506. [7]

Siegel, S. (1976). Morphine analgesic tolerance: Its situation specificity supports a Pavlovian conditioning model. *Science, 193,* 323–325. [7]

Siegel, S. (1977). Morphine tolerance acquisition as an associative process. *Journal of Experimental Psychology: Animal Behavior Processes, 3,* 1–13. [7]

Siegel, S. (1978). Tolerance to the hyperthermic effect of morphine in the rat is a learned response. *Journal of Comparative and Physiological Psychology, 92,* 1137–1149. [7]

Siegel, S. (1983). Classical conditioning, drug tolerance, and drug dependence. In Y. Israel, F. B. Sloser, H. Kalant, R. E. Popham, W. Schmidt, & R. G. Smart (Eds.), *Research advances in alcohol and drug abuse* (Vol. 7, pp. 207–246). New York: Plenum. [7]

Siegel, S. (1984). Pavlovian conditioning and heroin overdose: Reports by overdose victims. *Bulletin of the Psychonomic Society, 22,* 428–430. [7]

Siegel, S. (1989). Pharmacological conditioning and drug effects. In A. J. Goudie & M. W. Emmett-Oglesby (Eds.), *Psychoactive drugs: Tolerance and sensitization* (pp. 115–180). Clifton, NJ: Humana Press. [7]

Siegel, S., Hinson, R. E., & Krank, M. D. (1978). The role of predrug signals in morphine analgesic tolerance: Support for a Pavlovian conditioning model of tolerance. *Journal of Experimental Psychology: Animal Behavior Processes, 4,* 188–196. [7]

Siegel, S., Hinson, R. E., & Krank, M. D. (1981). Morphine-induced attenuation of morphine tolerance. *Science, 212,* 1533–1534. [7]

Siegel, S., Hinson, R. E., Krank, M. D., & McCully, J. (1982). Heroin "overdose" death: The contribution of drug-associated environmental cues. *Science, 216,* 436–437. [7]

Siegel, S., Sherman, J. E., & Mitchell, D. (1980). Extinction of morphine analgesic tolerance. *Learning and Motivation, 11,* 289–301. [7]

Sigmundi, R. A., & Bolles, R. C. (1983). CS modality, context conditioning, and conditioned freezing. *Animal Learning and Behavior, 11,* 205–212. [4]

Silvestri, R., Rohrbaugh, M. J., & Riccio, D. C. (1970). Conditions influencing the retention of learned fear in young rats. *Developmental Psychology, 2,* 389–395. [14]

Singer, B. F. (1969). Role of delay in magnitude of reward effects in discrimination learning in the rat. *Journal of Comparative and Physiological Psychology, 69,* 692–698. [2]

Singh, D., & Wickens, D. D. (1968). Disinhibition in instrumental conditioning. *Journal of Comparative and Physiological Psychology, 66,* 557–559. [9]

Sizemore, O. J., & Maxwell, F. R. (1983). Differential punishment of other behavior: Effects of pause-dependent shock on variable-interval performance. *Animal Learning and Behavior, 11,* 266–274. [8]

Sizemore, O. J., & Maxwell, F. R. (1985). Selective punishment of interresponse times: The roles of shock intensity and scheduling. *Journal of the Experimental Analysis of Behavior, 44,* 355–366. [9]

Skinner, B. F. (1948). 'Superstition' in the pigeon. *Journal of Experimental Psychology, 38,* 168–172. [8]

Skinner, B. F. (1950a). Are theories of learning necessary? *Psychological Review, 57,* 193–216. [11, 14]

Skinner, B. F. (1950b). Teaching machines. *Science, 128,* 969–977. [1]

Skinner, B. F. (1953). *Science and human behavior.* New York: Free Press. [2]

Skinner, B. F. (1962). Two "synthetic social relations." *Journal of the Experimental Analysis of Behavior, 5,* 531–533. [8]

Skinner, B. F. (1963). Behaviorism at fifty. *Science, 140,* 951–958. [2]

Skjoldager, P., Pierre, P. J., & Mittleman, G. (1993). Reinforcer magnitude and progressive ratio responding in the rat: Effects of increased effort, prefeeding, and extinction. *Learning and Motivation, 24,* 303–343. [9]

Slater, P. J. B. (1981). Chaffinch song repertoires: Observations, experiments and a discussion of their significance. *Zeitschrift für Tierpsychologie, 56,* 1–24. [12]

Slater, P. J. B., Eales, L. A., & Clayton, N. S. (1988). Song learning in zebra finches (*Taeniopygia guttata*): Progress and prospects. In J. S. Rosenblatt, C. Beer, M.-C. Busnel, & P. J. B. Slater (Eds.), *Advances in the study of behavior* (Vol. 18, pp. 1–34). New York: Academic Press. [12]

Slotnick, B. M., & Katz, H. M. (1974). Olfactory learning-set formation in rats. *Science, 185,* 796–798. [13]

Smith, M. C. (1968). CS–US interval and US intensity in classical conditioning of the rabbit's nictitating membrane responses. *Journal of Comparative and Physiological Psychology, 66,* 679–687. [4]

Smith, M. C., Coleman, S. R., & Gormezano, I. (1969). Classical conditioning of the rabbit's nictitating membrane response at backward, simultaneous, and forward CS–US intervals. *Journal of Comparative and Physiological Psychology, 69,* 226–231. [4]

Smith, M. C., DiLollo, V., & Gormezano, I. (1966). Conditioned jaw movement in the rabbit. *Journal of Comparative and Physiological Psychology, 62,* 479–483. [3]

Smith, N. F. (1968). Effects of interpolated learning on the retention of an escape response in rats as a function of age. *Journal of Comparative and Physiological Psychology, 65,* 422–426. [14]

Smith, N. F., Misanin, J. R., & Campbell, B. A. (1966). Effect of punishment on extinction of an avoidance response: Facilitation or inhibition? *Psychonomic Science, 4,* 271–272. [9]

Snyderman, M. (1983). Delay and amount of reward in a concurrent chain. *Journal of the Experimental Analysis of Behavior, 39,* 437–447. [10]

Sonoda, A., & Hirai, H. (1993). The differential effect of control vs. loss of control over food acquisition on disk-pull responses elicited by inescapable shocks. *Learning and Motivation, 24,* 40–54. [10]

Sonoda, A., Okayasu, T., & Hirai, H. (1991). Loss of controllability in appetitive situations interferes with subsequent learning in aversive situations. *Animal Learning and Behavior, 19,* 270–275. [10]

Sonuga-Barke, E. J. S., Lea, S. E. G., & Webley, P. (1989). An account of human "impulsivity" on self-control tasks. *The Quarterly Journal of Experimental Psychology, 41B,* 161–179. [10]

Souza, D. G., Moraes, A. B. A., & Todorov, J. C. (1984). Shock intensity and signaled avoidance responding. *Journal of the Experimental Analysis of Behavior, 42,* 67–74. [9]

Spear, N. E. (1973). Retrieval of memory in animals. *Psychological Review, 80,* 163–194. [14]

Spear, N. E. (1978). *The processing of memories: Forgetting and retention.* Hillsdale, NJ: Erlbaum. [14]

Spear, N. E., Gordon, W. C., & Martin, P. A. (1973). Warm-up decrement as failure in memory retrieval in the rat. *Journal of Comparative and Physiological Psychology, 85,* 601–614. [14]

Spear, N. E., Hamberg, J. M., & Bryan, R. (1980). Forgetting of recently acquired or recently reactivated memories. *Learning and Motivation, 11,* 456–475. [14]

Spear, N. E., Miller, J. S., & Jagielo, J. A. (1990). Animal memory and learning. *Annual Review of Psychology, 41,* 169–211. [14]

Spear, N. E., & Parsons, P. J. (1976). Alleviation of forgetting by reactivation treatment: A preliminary analysis of the ontogeny of memory processing. In D. L. Medin, W. A. Roberts, & R. T. Davis (Eds.), *Processes of animal memory* (pp. 135–166). Hillsdale, NJ: Erlbaum. [14]

Spear, N. E., & Riccio, D. C. (1994). *Memory: Phenomena and principles.* Boston, MA: Allyn and Bacon. [14]

Spence, K. W. (1936). The nature of discrimination learning in animals. *Psychological Review, 43,* 427–449. [13]

Spence, K. W. (1937). The differential response of animals to stimuli differing within a single dimension. *Psychological Review, 44,* 430–444. [13]

Spence, K. W. (1947). The role of secondary reinforcement in delayed reward learning. *Psychological Review, 47,* 1–8. [9]

Spence, K. W. (1952). Clark Leonard Hull: 1884–1952. *American Journal of Psychology, 65,* 639–646. [11]

Spence, K. W., & Norris, E. B. (1950). Eyelid conditioning as a function of the intertrial interval. *Journal of Experimental Psychology, 40,* 716–720. [4]

Sperling, S. E. (1965a). Reversal learning and resistance to extinction: A review of the rat literature. *Psychological Bulletin, 63,* 281–297. [13]

Sperling, S. E. (1965b). Reversal learning and resistance to extinction: A supplementary report. *Psychological Bulletin, 64,* 310–312. [13]

Spetch, M. L. (1987). Systematic errors in pigeons' memory for event duration: Interaction between training and test delay. *Animal Learning and Behavior, 15,* 1–5. [15]

Spetch, M. L., & Grant, D. S. (1993). Pigeons' memory for event duration in choice and successive matching-to-sample tasks. *Learning and Motivation, 24,* 156–174. [14]

Spetch, M. L., & Wilkie, D. M. (1983). Subjective shortening: A model of pigeons' memory for event duration. *Journal of Experimental Psychology: Animal Behavior Processes, 9,* 14–30. [15]

Spetch, M. L., Wilkie, D. M., & Pinel, J. P. J. (1981). Backward conditioning: A reevaluation of the empirical evidence. *Psychological Bulletin, 89,* 163–175. [4]

Spiker, C. C. (1970). An extension of Hull–Spence discrimination learning theory. *Psychological Review, 77,* 496–515. [13]

Springer, A. D., & Miller, R. R. (1972). Retrieval failure induced by electroconvulsive shock: Reversal with dissimilar training and recovery agents. *Science, 177,* 628–630. [14]

Staddon, J. E. R. (1979). Operant behavior as adaptation to constraint. *Journal of Experimental Psychology: General, 108,* 48–67. [11]

Staddon, J. E. R., & Motheral, S. (1978). On matching and maximizing in operant choice experiments. *Psychological Review, 85,* 436–444. [10]

Staddon, J. E. R., & Simmelhag, V. L. (1971). The "superstition" experiment: A re-examination of its implications for the principles of adaptive behavior. *Psychological Review, 78,* 3–43. [8]

Standing, L. (1973). Learning 10,000 pictures. *The Quarterly Journal of Experimental Psychology, 25,* 207–222. [14]

Stavely, H. E. (1966). Effect of escape duration and shock intensity on the acquisition and extinction of an escape response. *Journal of Experimental Psychology, 72,* 698–703. [9]

Steinert, P. A., Infurna, R. N., & Spear, N. E. (1980). Long-term retention of a conditioned taste aversion in preweanling and adult rats. *Animal Learning and Behavior, 8,* 375–381. [14]

Steinman, F. (1967). Retention of alley brightness in the rat. *Journal of Comparative and Physiological Psychology, 64,* 104–109. [13]

Steirn, J. N., Weaver, J. E., & Zentall, T. R. (1995). Transitive inference in pigeons: Simplified procedures and a test of value transfer theory. *Animal Learning and Behavior, 23,* 76–82. [15]

Stephens, D. W., & Krebs, J. R. (1986). *Foraging theory.* Princeton, NJ: Princeton University Press. [11]

Stickney, K. J., & Donahoe, J. W. (1983). Attenuation of blocking by a change in US locus. *Animal Learning and Behavior, 11,* 60–66. [5]

Stimmel, D. T., & Adams, P. C. (1969). The magnitude of the frustration effect as a function of the number of previously reinforced trials. *Psychonomic Science, 16,* 31–32. [10]

Stoffer, G. R., & Zimmerman, R. R. (1973). Airblast avoidance learning sets in rhesus monkeys. *Animal Learning and Behavior, 1,* 211–214. [13]

Stonebraker, T. B., & Rilling, M. (1981). Control of delayed matching-to-sample performance using directed forgetting techniques. *Animal Learning and Behavior, 9,* 196–201. [14]

Straub, R. O., Seidenberg, M. S., Bever, T. G., & Terrace, H. S. (1979). Serial learning in the pigeon. *Journal of the Experimental Analysis of Behavior, 32,* 137–148. [15]

Suarez, S. D., & Gallup, G. G. (1982). Open-field behavior in chickens: The experimenter is a predator. *Journal of Comparative and Physiological Psychology, 96,* 432–439. [7]

Suiter, R. D., & LoLordo, V. M. (1971). Blocking of inhibitory Pavlovian conditioning in the conditioned emotional response procedure. *Journal of Comparative and Physiological Psychology, 76,* 137–144. [5]

Sullivan, L. G. (1984). Long-delay and selective association in food aversion learning: The role of cue location. *The Quarterly Journal of Experimental Psychology, 36B,* 65–87. [7]

Sutherland, N. S., & Mackintosh, N. J. (1971). *Mechanisms of animal discrimination learning.* NY: Academic Press. [13]

Swartz, K. B., & Rosenblum, L. A. (1980). Operant responding by bonnet macaques for color videotape recordings of social stimuli. *Animal Learning and Behavior, 8,* 311–321. [9]

Sytsma, D., & Dyal, J. A. (1973). Effects of varied reward schedules on generalized persistence of rats. *Journal of Comparative and Physiological Psychology, 85,* 179–185. [10]

Szakmary, G. A. (1979). Second-order conditioning of the conditioned emotional response: Some methodological considerations. *Animal Learning and Behavior, 7,* 181–184. [5]

Tait, R. W., Kehoe, E. J., & Gormezano, I. (1983). Effects of US duration on classical conditioning of the rabbit's nictitating membrane response. *Journal of Experimental Psychology: Animal Behavior Processes, 9,* 91–101. [4]

Tait, R. W., & Saladin, M. E. (1986). Concurrent development of excitatory and inhibitory associations during backward conditioning. *Animal Learning and Behavior, 14,* 133–137. [4]

Tarpy, R. M. (1969). Reinforcement difference limen (RDL) for delay in shock escape. *Journal of Experimental Psychology, 79,* 116–121. [15]

Tarpy, R. M., & Koster, E. D. (1970). Stimulus facilitation of delayed-reward learning in the rat. *Journal of Comparative and Physiological Psychology, 71,* 147–151. [9]

Tarpy, R. M., & Mayer, R. E. (1978). *Foundations of learning and memory.* Glenview, IL: Scott Foresman. [1]

Tarpy, R. M., & Sawabini, F. L. (1974). Reinforcement delay: A selective review of the last decade. *Psychological Bulletin, 81,* 984–997. [8, 9]

Taukulis, H., & Revusky, S. H. (1975). Odor as a conditioned inhibitor: Applicability of the Rescorla–Wagner model to feeding behavior. *Learning and Motivation, 6,* 11–27. [7]

Terrace, H. S. (1979). *Nim.* New York: Knopf. [15]

Terrace, H. S., Gibbon, J., Farrell, L., & Baldock, M. D. (1975). Temporal factors influencing the acquisition and maintenance of an autoshaped key peck. *Animal Learning and Behavior, 3,* 53–62. [4]

Terrace, H. S., Petitto, L. A., Sanders, R. J., & Bever, T. G. (1979). Can an ape create a sentence? *Science, 206,* 891–902. [15]

Teyler, T. J. (1991). Memory: Electrophysiological analogs. In J. L. Martinez & R. P. Kesner (Eds.), *Learning and memory: A biological view* (pp. 299–327). San Diego, CA: Academic Press. [11]

Theios, J., & Blosser, D. (1965). Overlearning reversal effect and magnitude of reward. *Journal of Comparative and Physiological Psychology, 59,* 252–257. [13]

Theios, J., Lynch, A. D., & Lowe, W. F. (1966). Differential effects of shock intensity on one-way and shuttle avoidance conditioning. *Journal of Experimental Psychology, 72,* 294–299. [9]

Thistlethwaite, D. (1951). A critical review of latent learning and related experiments. *Psychological Bulletin, 48,* 97–129. [2]

Thomas, D. R. (1962). The effects of drive and discrimination training on stimulus generalization. *Journal of Experimental Psychology, 64,* 24–28. [13]

Thomas, D. R. (1993). A model for adaptation-level effects on stimulus generalization. *Psychological Review, 100,* 658–673. [13]

Thomas, D. R., Curran, P. J., & Russell, R. J. (1988). Factors affecting conditional discrimination learning by pigeons: II. Physical and temporal characteristics of stimuli. *Animal Learning and Behavior, 16,* 468–476. [13]

Thomas, D. R., & Jones, C. G. (1962). Stimulus generalization as a function of the frame of reference. *Journal of Experimental Psychology, 64,* 77–80. [13]

Thomas, D. R., & Lopez, L. J. (1962). The effects of delayed testing on generalization slope. *Journal of Comparative and Physiological Psychology, 55,* 541–544. [13]

Thomas, D. R., Mood, K., Morrison, S., & Wiertelak, E. (1991). Peak shift revisited: A test of alternative interpretations. *Journal of Experimental Psychology: Animal Behavior Processes, 17,* 130–140. [13]

Thomas, D. R., Strub, H., & Dickson, J. F. (1974). Adaptation-level and the central tendency effect on stimulus generalization. *Journal of Experimental Psychology, 103,* 466–474. [13]

Thomas, D. R., & Thomas, D. H. (1974). Stimulus labeling, adaptation-level, and the central tendency shift. *Journal of Experimental Psychology, 103,* 896–899. [13]

Thomas, D. R., Windell, B. T., Bakke, I., Kreye, J., Kimose, E., & Aposhyan, H. (1985). Long-term memory in pigeons: I. The role of discrimination problem difficulty assessed by reacquisition measures II. The role of stimulus modality assessed by generalization slope. *Learning and Motivation, 16,* 464–477. [13]

Thomas, G. (1981). Contiguity, reinforcement rate and the law of effect. *The Quarterly Journal of Experimental Psychology, 33B,* 33–43. [8]

Thomas, G. V., Lieberman, D. A., McIntosh, D. C., & Ronaldson, P. (1983). The role of marking when reward is delayed. *Journal of Experimental Psychology: Animal Behavior Processes, 9,* 401–411. [9]

Thomas, G. V., Robertson, D., Cunniffe, G., & Lieberman, D. A. (1989). Facilitation of responding in a filled-delay trace autoshaping procedure: An occasion-setting hypothesis. *Learning and Motivation, 20,* 225–241. [4]

Thomas, G. V., Robertson, D., & Lieberman, D. A. (1987). Marking effects in Pavlovian trace conditioning. *Journal of Experimental Psychology: Animal Behavior Processes, 13,* 126–135. [9]

Thomas, R. K., & Noble, L. M. (1988). Visual and olfactory oddity learning in rats: What evidence is necessary to show conceptual behavior? *Animal Learning and Behavior, 16,* 157–163. [15]

Thompson, R. F. (1972). Sensory preconditioning. In R. F. Thompson & J. S. Voss (Eds.), *Topics in learning and performance* (pp. 105–129). New York: Academic Press. [5]

Thompson, R. F., Groves, P. M., Teyler, T. J., & Roemer, R. A. (1973). A dual-process theory of habituation: Theory and behavior. In H. V. S. Peeke & M. J. Herz (Eds.), *Habituation: Vol. 1. Behavioral studies* (pp. 239–271). New York: Academic Press. [5]

Thorndike, E. L. (1898). Animal intelligence: An experimental study of the associative process in animals. *Psychological Monographs Supplement 2* (No. 4, Whole No. 8). [1, 8]

Thorpe, G. L., & Olson, S. L. (1990). *Behavior therapy: Concepts, procedures, and applications.* Boston, MA: Allyn and Bacon. [8]

Timberlake, W. (1983a). Appetitive structure and straight alley running. In R. L. Mellgren (Ed.), *Animal cognition and behavior* (pp. 165–222). Amsterdam: North-Holland Press. [12]

Timberlake, W. (1983b). Rats' responses to a moving object related to food or water: A behavior-systems analysis. *Animal Learning and Behavior, 11,* 309–320. [12]

Timberlake, W. (1983c). The functional organization of appetitive behavior: Behavior systems and learning. In M. D. Zeiler & P. Harzem (Eds.), *Advances in analysis of behavior: Vol. 3. Biological factors in learning* (pp. 177–221). New York: Wiley. [4]

Timberlake, W. (1986). Unpredicted food produces a mode of behavior that affects rats' subsequent reactions to a conditioned stimulus: A behavior-systems approach to "context blocking." *Animal Learning and Behavior, 14,* 276–286. [6]

Timberlake, W. (1993). Behavior systems and reinforcement: An integrative approach. *Journal of the Experimental Analysis of Behavior, 60,* 105–128. [4, 12]

Timberlake, W. (1994). Behavior systems, associationism, and Pavlovian conditioning. *Psychonomic Bulletin and Review, 1,* 405–420. [12]

Timberlake, W., & Allison, J. (1974). Response deprivation: An empirical approach to instrumental performance. *Psychological Review, 81,* 146–164. [11]

Timberlake, W., Gawley, D. J., & Lucas, G. A. (1987). Time horizons in rats foraging for food in temporally separated patches. *Journal of Experimental Psychology: Animal Behavior Processes, 13,* 302–309. [11]

Timberlake, W., & Grant, D. L. (1975). Autoshaping in rats to the presentation of another rat predicting food. *Science, 190,* 690–692. [4, 6]

Timberlake, W., & Lucas, G. A. (1989). Behavior systems and learning: From misbehavior to general principles. In S. B. Klein & R. R. Mowrer (Eds.), *Contemporary learning theories: Instrumental conditioning theory and the impact of biological constraints on learning* (pp. 237–275). Hillsdale, NJ: Erlbaum. [4, 12]

Timberlake, W., Wahl, G., & King, D. (1982). Stimulus and response contingencies in the misbehavior of rats. *Journal of Experimental Psychology: Animal Behavior Processes, 8,* 62–85. [9, 12]

Todorov, J. C. (1973). Interaction of frequency and magnitude of reinforcement on concurrent performances. *Journal of the Experimental Analysis of Behavior, 19,* 451–458. [10]

Tolman, E. C. (1932). *Purposive behavior in animals and men.* New York: Appleton-Century-Crofts. [2, 11]

Tolman, E. C. (1948). Cognitive maps in rats and men. *Psychological Review, 55,* 189–208. [11]

Tolman, E. C., & Honzik, C. H. (1930). Introduction and removal of reward, and maze performance in rats. *University of California, Berkeley, Publications of Psychology, 4,* 257–275. [11]

Tolman, E. C., Ritchie, B. F., & Kalish, D. (1946). Studies in spatial learning: I. Orientation and the short-cut. *Journal of Experimental Psychology, 36,* 13–24. [11]

Tomie, A., & Kruse, J. (1980). Retardation tests of inhibition following discriminative autoshaping. *Animal Learning and Behavior, 8,* 401–408. [3]

Tomie, A., Murphy, A. L., Fath, S., & Jackson, R. L. (1980). Retardation of autoshaping following pretraining with unpredictable food: Effects of changing the context between pretraining and testing. *Learning and Motivation, 11,* 117–134. [3, 10]

Trapold, M. A. (1970). Are expectancies based upon different positive reinforcing events discriminably different? *Learning and Motivation, 1,* 129–140. [13]

Trapold, M. A., & Fowler, H. (1960). Instrumental escape performance as a function of the intensity of noxious stimulation. *Journal of Experimental Psychology, 60,* 323–326. [9]

Traupmann, K. L. (1972). Drive, reward, and training parameters and the overlearning–extinction effect (OEE). *Learning and Motivation, 3,* 359–368. [13]

Triana, E., & Pasnak, R. (1981). Object permanence in cats and dogs. *Animal Learning and Behavior, 9,* 135–139. [15]

Trivers, R. L. (1971). The evolution of reciprocal altruism. *Quarterly Review of Biology, 46,* 35–57. [12]

Troisi, J. R., Bersh, P. J., Stromberg, M. F., Mauro, B. C., & Whitehouse, W. G. (1991). Stimulus control of immunization against chronic learned helplessness. *Animal Learning and Behavior, 19,* 88–94. [10]

Tsuda, A., Ida, Y., & Tanaka, M. (1988). Behavioral field analysis in two strains of rats in a conditioned defensive burying paradigm. *Animal Learning and Behavior, 16,* 354–358. [12]

Turner, C., & Mackintosh, N. J. (1970). Continuity theory revisited: Comments on Wolford and Bower. *Psychological Review, 77,* 577–580. [13]

Turney, T. H. (1976). The easy-to-hard effect: Transfer along the dimension of orientation in the rat. *Animal Learning and Behavior, 4,* 363–366. [13]

Uhl, C. N. (1973). Eliminating behavior with omission and extinction after varying amounts of training. *Animal Learning and Behavior, 1,* 237–240. [8]

Uhl, C. N., & Garcia, E. E. (1969). Comparison of omission with extinction in response elimination in rats. *Journal of Comparative and Physiological Psychology, 69,* 554–562. [8]

Umiker-Sebeok, J., & Sebeok, T. A. (1981). Clever Hans and smart simians: The self-fulfilling prophecy and kindred methodological pitfalls. *Anthropos, 76,* 89–165. [15]

Urcuioli, P. J., & Zentall, T. R. (1986). Retrospective coding in pigeons' delayed matching-to-sample. *Journal of Experimental Psychology: Animal Behavior Processes, 12,* 69–77. [14]

Uzgiris, I. C., & Hunt, J. McV. (1975). *Assessment in infancy.* Chicago: University of Illinois Press. [15]

Vaccarino, F. J., Schiff, B. B., & Glickman, S. E. (1989). Biological view of reinforcement. In S. B. Klein & R. R. Mowrer (Eds.), *Contemporary learning theories: Instrumental conditioning theory and the impact of biological constraints on learning* (pp. 111–142). Hillsdale, NJ: Erlbaum. [11]

van Haaren, F., & van Hest, A. (1989). Spatial matching and nonmatching in male and female Wistar rats: Effects of delay-interval duration. *Animal Learning and Behavior, 17,* 355–360. [14]

van Kampen, H. S., & Bolhuis, J. J. (1993). Interaction between auditory and visual learning during imprinting. *Animal Behaviour, 45,* 623–625. [12]

van Raaij, W. F., van Veldhoven, G. M., & Wärneryd, K.-E. (Eds.). (1988). *Handbook of economic psychology.* Dordrecht, The Netherlands: Kluwer Academic. [11]

van Willigen, F., Emmett, J., Cote, D., & Ayres, J. J. B. (1987). CS modality effects in one-trial backward and forward excitatory conditioning as assessed by conditioned suppression of licking in rats. *Animal Learning and Behavior, 15,* 201–211. [4]

Vaughan, W. (1981). Melioration, matching, and maximization. *Journal of the Experimental Analysis of Behavior, 36,* 141–149. [10]

Vaughan, W. (1988). Formation of equivalence sets in pigeons. *Journal of Experimental Psychology: Animal Behavior Processes, 14,* 36–42. [15]

Vaughan, W., & Greene, S. L. (1984). Pigeon visual memory capacity. *Journal of Experimental Psychology: Animal Behavior Processes, 10,* 256–271. [14, 15]

Verplanck, W. S. (1962). Unaware of where's awareness. Some verbal operants—notates, moments, and notants. *Journal of Personality, 30,* 130–158. [8]

Viney, W. (1993). *A history of psychology: Ideas and context.* Boston, MA: Allyn & Bacon. [1]

Vogel, J. R., & Nathan, B. A. (1975). Learned taste aversions induced by hypnotic drugs. *Pharmacology Biochemistry & Behavior, 3,* 189–194. [7]

Volpicelli, J. R., Ulm, R. R., & Altenor, A. (1984). Feedback during exposure to inescapable shocks and subsequent shock–escape performance. *Learning and Motivation, 15,* 279–286. [10]

Volpicelli, J. R., Ulm, R. R., Altenor, A., & Seligman, M. E. P. (1983). Learned mastery in the rat. *Learning and Motivation, 14,* 204–222. [10]

von Fersen, L., & Lea, S. E. G. (1990). Category discrimination by pigeons using five polymorphous features. *Journal of the Experimental Analysis of Behavior, 54,* 69–84. [15]

von Fersen, L., Wynne, C. D. L., Deluis, J. D., & Staddon, J. E. R. (1991). Transitive inference formation in pigeons. *Journal of Experimental Psychology: Animal Behavior Processes, 17,* 334–341. [15]

Wagner, A. (1959). The role of reinforcement and nonreinforcement in an "apparent frustration effect." *Journal of Experimental Psychology, 57,* 130–136. [2]

Wagner, A. R. (1969a). Frustrative nonreward: A variety of punishment? In B. A. Campbell & R. A. Church (Eds.), *Punishment and aversive behavior* (pp. 157–181). New York: Appleton-Century-Crofts. [10]

Wagner, A. R. (1969b). Stimulus selection and a "modified continuity theory." In G. H. Bower & J. T. Spence (Eds.), *The psychology of learning and motivation* (Vol. 3, pp. 1–41). New York: Academic Press. [5]

Wagner, A. R. (1976). Priming in STM: An information processing mechanism for self-generated or retrieval-generated depression in performance. In T. J. Tighe & R. N. Leaton (Eds.), *Habituation: Perspectives from child development, animal behavior, and neurophysiology* (pp. 95–128). Hillsdale, NJ: Erlbaum. [5]

Wagner, A. R. (1978). Expectancies and the priming of STM. In S. H. Hulse, H. Fowler, & W. K. Honig (Eds.), *Cognitive processes in animal behavior* (pp. 177–209). Hillsdale, NJ: Erlbaum. [5, 6]

Wagner, A. R. (1981). SOP: A model of automatic memory processing in animal behavior. In N. E. Spear & R. R. Miller (Eds.), *Information processing in animals: Memory mechanisms* (pp. 5–47). Hillsdale, NJ: Erlbaum. [6]

Wagner, A. R., & Brandon, S. E. (1989). Evolution of a structured connectionist model of Pavlovian conditioning (AESOP). In S. B. Klein & R. R. Mowrer (Eds.), *Contemporary learning theories: Pavlovian conditioning and the status of traditional learning theory* (pp. 149–189). Hillsdale, NJ: Erlbaum. [6]

Wagner, A. R., & Larew, M. B. (1985). Opponent processes and Pavlovian inhibition. In R. R. Miller & N. E. Spear (Eds.), *Information processing in animals: Conditioned inhibition* (pp. 233–265). Hillsdale, NJ: Erlbaum. [6]

Wagner, A. R., Logan, F. A., Haberlandt, K., & Price, T. (1968). Stimulus selection in animal discrimination learning. *Journal of Experimental Psychology, 76,* 171–180. [13]

Wagner, A. R., Siegel, S., Thomas, E., & Ellison, G. D. (1964). Reinforcement history and the extinction of a conditioned salivary response. *Journal of Comparative and Physiological Psychology, 58,* 354–358. [4]

Waller, T. G. (1971). Effects of irrelevant cues on discrimination acquisition and transfer in rats. *Journal of Comparative and Physiological Psychology, 73,* 477–480. [13]

Waller, T. G. (1973a). Effect of consistency of reward during runway training on subsequent discrimination performance in rats. *Journal of Comparative and Physiological Psychology, 83,* 120–123. [13]

Waller, T. G. (1973b). The effect of overtraining on a visual discrimination on transfer to a spatial discrimination. *Animal Learning and Behavior, 1,* 65–67. [13]

Walters, G. C., & Glazer, R. D. (1971). Punishment of instinctive behavior in the Mongolian gerbil. *Journal of Comparative and Physiological Psychology, 75,* 331–340. [9, 12]

Wanchisen, B. A., Tatham, T. A., & Mooney, S. E. (1989). Variable-ratio conditioning history produces high- and low-rate fixed-interval performance in rats. *Journal of the Experimental Analysis of Behavior, 52,* 167–179. [9]

Warren, J. M. (1965). Primate learning in comparative perspective. In A. M. Schrier, H. F. Harlow, & F. Stollnitz (Eds.), *Behavior of nonhuman primates: Modern research trends* (pp. 249–281). New York: Academic Press. [13]

Wasserman, E. A. (1974). Stimulus–reinforcer predictiveness and selective discrimination learning in pigeons. *Journal of Experimental Psychology, 103,* 284–297. [13]

Wasserman, E. A. (1993). Comparative cognition: Beginning the second century of study of animal intelligence. *Psychological Bulletin, 113,* 211–228. [15]

Wasserman, E. A., & Bhatt, R. S. (1992). Conceptualization of natural and artificial stimuli by pigeons. In W. K. Honig & J. G. Fetterman (Eds.), *Cognitive aspects of stimulus control* (pp. 203–223). Hillsdale, NJ: Erlbaum. [15]

Wasserman, E. A., Chatlosh, D. L., & Neunaber, D. J. (1983). Perception of causal relations in humans: Factors affecting judgments or response–outcome contingencies under free-operant procedures. *Learning and Motivation, 14,* 406–432. [8]

Wasserman, E. A., DeVolder, C. L., & Coppage, D. J. (1992). Non-similarity-based conceptualization in pigeons via secondary or mediated generalization. *Psychological Science, 3,* 374–379. [15]

Wasserman, E. A., Franklin, S. R., & Hearst, E. (1974). Pavlovian appetitive contingencies and approach versus withdrawal to conditioned stimuli in pigeons. *Journal of Comparative and Physiological Psychology, 86,* 616–627. [3]

Wasserman, E. A., Hugart, J. A., & Kirkpatrick-Steger, K. (1995). Pigeons show same–different conceptualization after training with complex visual stimuli. *Journal of Experimental Psychology: Animal Behavior Processes, 21,* 248–252. [15]

Wasserman, E. A., Hunter, N. B., Gutowski, K. A., & Bader, S. A. (1974). Auto-shaping chicks with heat reinforcement: The role of stimulus–reinforcer and response–reinforcer relations. *Journal of Experimental Psychology, 104,* 158–189. [4, 6]

Wasserman, E. A., Kiedinger, R. E., & Bhatt, R. S. (1988). Conceptual behavior in pigeons: Categories, subcategories, and pseudocategories. *Journal of Experimental Psychology: Animal Behavior Processes, 14,* 235–246. [15]

Wasserman, E. A., & Molina, E. J. (1975). Explicitly unpaired key light and food presentations: Interference with subsequent autoshaped key pecking in pigeons. *Journal of Experimental Psychology: Animal Behavior Processes, 1,* 30–38. [10]

Watanabe, S. (1988). Failure of visual prototype learning in the pigeon. *Animal Learning and Behavior, 16,* 147–152. [15]

Watanabe, S., Sakamoto, J., & Wakita, M. (1995). Pigeons' discrimination of paintings by Monet and Picasso. *Journal of the Experimental Analysis of Behavior, 63,* 165–174. [15]

Watson, J. B. (1913). Psychology as a behaviorist views it. *Psychological Review, 20,* 158–177. [1]

Watson, J. B. (1916). The place of the conditioned-reflex in psychology. *Psychological Review, 23,* 89–117. [1]

Watson, J. B., & Raynor, R. (1920). Conditioned emotional reactions. *Journal of Experimental Psychology, 3,* 1–14. [1]

Watson, R. I. (1978). *The great psychologists* (4th ed.). New York: Lippincott. [1]

Wearden, J. H., & Burgess, I. S. (1982). Matching since Baum (1979). *Journal of the Experimental Analysis of Behavior, 38,* 339–348. [10]

Wearden, J. H., & Doherty, M. F. (1995). Exploring and developing a connectionist model of animal timing: Peak procedure and fixed-interval simulations. *Journal of Experimental Psychology: Animal Behavior Processes, 21,* 99–115. [15]

Weisman, R. G., & Palmer, J. A. (1969). Factors influencing inhibitory stimulus control: Discrimination training and prior nondifferential reinforcement. *Journal of the Experimental Analysis of Behavior, 12,* 229–237. [13]

Weiss, J. M., Goodman, P. A., Losito, B. G., Corrigan, S., Charry, J. M., & Bailey, W. H. (1981). Behavioral depression produced by an uncontrollable stressor: Relationship to norepinephrine, dopamine, and serotonin levels in various regions of rat brain. *Brain Research Reviews, 3,* 167–205. [10]

Welker, R. L., & McAuley, K. (1978). Reductions in resistance to extinction and spontaneous recovery as a function of changes in transportational and contextual stimuli. *Animal Learning and Behavior, 6,* 451–457. [10]

Welker, R. L., & Wheatley, K. L. (1977). Differential acquisition of conditioned suppression in rats with increased and decreased luminance levels as CS+s. *Learning and Motivation, 8,* 247–262. [4]

Westbrook, R. F., & Greeley, J. D. (1992). Conditioned tolerance to morphine hypoalgesia: Compensatory hyperalgesia in the experimental group or conditioned hypoalgesia in the control group? *The Quarterly Journal of Experimental Psychology, 45B,* 161–187. [7]

Westbrook, R. F., Harvey, A., & Swinbourne, A. (1988). Potentiation by a novel flavour of conditioned place aversions based on both toxicosis and shock. *The Quarterly Journal of Experimental Psychology, 40B,* 305–319. [6, 7]

Westbrook, R. F., Provost, S. C., & Homewood, J. (1982). Short-term flavour memory in the rat. *The Quarterly Journal of Experimental Psychology, 34B,* 235–256. [5]

Wheatley, K. L., Welker, R. L., & Miles, R. C. (1977). Acquisition of barpressing in rats following experience with response-independent food. *Animal Learning and Behavior, 5,* 236–242. [10]

Whillans, K. V., & Shettleworth, S. J. (1981). Defensive burying in rats and hamsters. *Animal Learning and Behavior, 9,* 357–362. [12]

White, K. G., & Bunnell-McKenzie, J. (1985). Potentiation of delayed matching with variable delays. *Animal Learning and Behavior, 13,* 397–402. [14]

Whitney, L., & White, K. G. (1993). Dimensional shift and the transfer of attention. *The Quarterly Journal of Experimental Psychology, 46B,* 225–252. [13]

Wickens, C., Tuber, D. S., & Wickens, D. D. (1983). Memory for the conditioned response: The proactive effect of preexposure to potential conditioning stimuli and context change. *Journal of Experimental Psychology: General, 112,* 41–57. [14]

Wickens, D. D., Nield, A. F., Tuber, D. S., & Wickens, C. D. (1973). Stimulus selection as a function of CS_1–CS_2 interval in compound classical conditioning of cats. *Journal of Comparative and Physiological Psychology, 85,* 295–303. [4]

Wilcoxon, H. C., Dragoin, W. B., & Kral, P. A. (1971). Illness-induced aversions in rat and quail: Relative salience of visual and gustatory cues. *Science, 171,* 826–828. [7]

Wilkie, D. M. (1974). Stimulus control of responding during a fixed interval reinforcement schedule. *Journal of the Experimental Analysis of Behavior, 21,* 425–432. [13]

Wilkie, D. M., Summers, R. J., & Spetch, M. L. (1981). Effect of delay-interval stimuli on delayed symbolic matching to sample in the pigeon. *Journal of the Experimental Analysis of Behavior, 35,* 153–160. [14]

Williams, B. A. (1979). Contrast, component duration, and the following schedule of reinforcement. *Journal of Experimental Psychology: Animal Behavior Processes, 5,* 379–396. [9]

Williams, B. A. (1984). Relative stimulus validity in conditional discrimination. *Animal Learning and Behavior, 12,* 117–121. [13]

Williams, B. A. (1985). Choice behavior in a discrete-trial concurrent VI–VR: A test of maximizing theories of matching. *Learning and Motivation, 16,* 423–443. [10]

Williams, B. A. (1991). Behavioral contrast and reinforcement value. *Animal Learning and Behavior, 19,* 337–344. [9]

Williams, B. A., & Dunn, R. (1991). Substitutability between conditioned and primary reinforcers in discrimination acquisition. *Journal of the Experimental Analysis of Behavior, 55,* 21–35. [10]

Williams, B. A., & Royalty, P. (1989). A test of the melioration theory of matching. *Journal of Experimental Psychology: Animal Behavior Processes, 15,* 99–113. [10]

Williams, D. A., & Overmier, J. B. (1988). Some types of conditioned inhibitors carry collateral excitatory associations. *Learning and Motivation, 19,* 345–368. [3]

Williams, D. A., Overmier, J. B., & LoLordo, V. M. (1992). A reevaluation of Rescorla's early dictums about Pavlovian conditioned inhibition. *Psychological Bulletin, 111,* 275–290. [3]

Williams, J. H. (1964). Conditioning of verbalization: A review. *Psychological Bulletin, 62,* 383–393. [8]

Williams, J. L., & Maier, S. F. (1977). Transituational immunization and therapy of learned helplessness in the rat. *Journal of Experimental Psychology: Animal Behavior Processes, 3,* 240–252. [10]

Williams, S. B. (1938). Resistance to extinction as a function of the number of reinforcements. *Journal of Experimental Psychology, 23,* 506–521. [11]

Willner, J. A. (1978). Blocking of a taste aversion by prior pairings of exteroceptive stimuli with illness. *Learning and Motivation, 9,* 125–140. [7]

Wilson, J. J. (1964). Level of training and goal-box movements as parameters of the partial reinforcement effect. *Journal of Comparative and Physiological Psychology, 57,* 211–213. [10]

Wilson, P. N., Boakes, R. A., & Swan, J. (1987). Instrumental learning as a result of omission training on wheel running. *The Quarterly Journal of Experimental Psychology, 39B,* 161–171. [8]

Wilson, R. S. (1969). Cardiac response: Determinants of conditioning. *Journal of Comparative and Physiological Psychology Monograph, 68* (Pt. 2). [4]

Winston, M. L. (1987). *The biology of the honey bee.* Cambridge, MA: Harvard University Press. [1, 15]

Wise, C. D., Berger, B. D., & Stein, L. (1973). Evidence of noradrenergic reward receptors and seritonergic punishment receptors in the rat brain. *Biological Psychiatry, 6,* 3–21. [11]

Wise, R. A. (1978). Catecholamine theories of reward: A critical review. *Brain Research, 152,* 215–247. [11]

Wise, R. A. (1989). Opiate reward: Sites and substrates. *Neuroscience and Biobehavioral Reviews, 13,* 129–133. [11]

Wise, R. A., & Bozarth, M. A. (1987). A psychomotor stimulant theory of addiction. *Psychological Review, 94,* 469–492. [7]

Wise, R. A., Yokel, R. A., & DeWitt, H. (1976). Both positive reinforcement and conditioned aversion from amphetamine and from apomorphine in rats. *Science, 191,* 1273–1275. [7]

Witcher, E. S., & Ayres, J. J. B. (1984). A test of two methods for extinguishing Pavlovian conditioned inhibition. *Animal Learning and Behavior, 12,* 149–156. [3]

Wolford, G., & Bower, G. H. (1969). Continuity theory revisited: Rejected for the wrong reasons? *Psychological Review, 515,* 518. [13]

Wolpe, J. (1958). *Psychotherapy by reciprocal inhibition.* Stanford, CA: Stanford University Press. [1]

Wong, P. T. P., & Peacock, E. J. (1986). When does reinforcement induce stereotypy? A test of the differential reinforcement hypothesis. *Learning and Motivation, 17,* 139–161. [8]

Wood, S., Moriarty, K. M., Gardner, B. T., & Gardner, R. A. (1980). Object permanence in child and chimpanzee. *Animal Learning and Behavior, 8,* 3–9. [15]

Woodruff, G., & Starr, M. D. (1978). Autoshaping of initial feeding and drinking reactions in newly hatched chicks. *Animal Learning and Behavior, 6,* 265–272. [4, 6]

Woods, P. J., Davidson, E. H., & Peters, R. J. (1964). Instrumental escape conditioning in a water tank: Effects of variations in drive stimulus intensity and reinforcement magnitude. *Journal of Comparative and Physiological Psychology, 57,* 466–470. [9]

Woods, S. C. (1976). Conditioned hypoglycemia. *Journal of Comparative and Physiological Psychology, 90,* 1164–1168. [7]

Woods, S. C., & Shogren, R. E. (1972). Glycemia responses following conditioning with different doses of insulin in rats. *Journal of Comparative and Physiological Psychology, 81,* 220–225. [4, 7]

Worsham, R. W. (1975). Temporal discrimination factors in the delayed matching-to-sample task in monkeys. *Animal Learning and Behavior, 3,* 93–97. [14]

Worsham, R. W., & D'Amato, M. R. (1973). Ambient light, white noise, and monkey vocalization as sources of interference in visual short-term memory of monkeys. *Journal of Experimental Psychology, 99,* 99–105. [14]

Wright, A. A. (1972). Psychometric and psychophysical hue discrimination functions for the pigeon. *Vision Research, 12,* 1447–1464. [13]

Wright, A. A. (1974). A psychometric and psychophysical theory within a framework of response bias. *Psychological Review, 81,* 322–347. [13]

Wright, A. A. (1992). Testing the cognitive capacities of animals. In I. Gormezano & E. A. Wasserman (Eds.), *Learning and memory: The behavioral and biological substrates* (pp. 45–60). Hillsdale, NJ: Erlbaum. [15]

Wright, A. A., Cook, R. G., Rivera, J. J., Sands, S. F., & Delius, J. D. (1988). Concept learning by pigeons: Matching-to-sample with trial-unique video picture stimuli. *Animal Learning and Behavior, 16,* 436–444. [15]

Wright, A. A., & Delius, J. D. (1994). Scratch and match: Pigeons learn matching and oddity with gravel stimuli. *Journal of Experimental Psychology: Animal Behavior Processes, 20,* 108–112. [15]

Wright, A. A., Urcuioli, P. J., & Sands, S. F. (1986). Proactive interference in animal memory. In D. F. Kendrick, M. E. Rilling, & M. R. Denny (Eds.), *Theories of animal memory* (pp. 101–125). Hillsdale, NJ: Erlbaum. [14]

Wright, A. A., Urcuioli, P. J., Sands, S. F., & Santiago, H. C. (1981). Interference of delayed matching to sample in pigeons: Effects of interpolation at different periods within a trial and stimulus similarity. *Animal Learning and Behavior, 9,* 595–603. [14]

Wynne, C. D. L. (1995). Reinforcement accounts for transitive inference performance. *Animal Learning and Behavior, 23,* 207–217. [15]

Wynne, J. D., & Brogden, W. J. (1962). Supplementary report: Effect upon sensory preconditioning of backward, forward, and trace preconditioning training. *Journal of Experimental Psychology, 64,* 422–423. [5]

Yelen, D. (1969). Magnitude of the frustration effect and number of training trials. *Psychonomic Science, 15,* 137–138. [10]

Yeo, A. G. (1974). The acquisition of conditioned suppression as a function of interstimulus interval duration. *The Quarterly Journal of Experimental Psychology, 26,* 405–416. [4]

Yin, H., Barnet, R. C., & Miller, R. R. (1994). Second-order conditioning and Pavlovian conditioned inhibition: Operational similarities and differences. *Journal of Experimental Psychology: Animal Behavior Processes, 20,* 419–428. [5]

Young, S. L., & Fanselow, M. S. (1992). Associative regulation of Pavlovian fear conditioning: Unconditional stimulus intensity, incentive shifts, and latent inhibition. *Journal of Experimental Psychology: Animal Behavior Processes, 18,* 400–413. [7]

Zach, R. (1978). Selection and dropping of whelks by northwestern crows. *Behaviour, 67,* 134–148. [11]

Zach, R. (1979). Shell dropping: Decision making and optimal foraging in northwestern crows. *Behaviour, 68,* 106–117. [11]

Zach, R., & Smith, J. N. M. (1981). Optimal foraging in wild birds? In A. C. Kamil & T. D. Sargent (Eds.), *Foraging behavior: Ecological, ethological, and psychological approaches* (pp. 95–109). New York: Garland. [11]

Zahorik, D. M., & Maier, S. F. (1969). Appetitive conditioning with recovery from thiamine deficiency as the unconditioned stimulus. *Psychonomic Science, 17,* 309–310. [7]

Zahorik, D. M., Maier, S. F., & Pies, R. W. (1974). Preferences for tastes paired with recovery from thiamine deficiency in rats: Appetitive conditioning or learned safety? *Journal of Comparative and Physiological Psychology, 87,* 1083–1091. [7]

Zajonc, R. B., Marcus, H., & Wilson, W. R. (1974). Exposure, object preference, and distress in the domestic chick. *Journal of Comparative and Physiological Psychology, 86,* 581–585. [12]

Zaslav, M. R., & Porter, J. J. (1974). The effects of reinforcement frequency on performance in a multiple fixed-ratio schedule. *Animal Learning and Behavior, 2,* 54–58. [2, 10]

Zeiler, M. D. (1984). The sleeping giant: Reinforcement schedules. *Journal of the Experimental Analysis of Behavior, 42,* 485–493. [9]

Zeiler, M. D. (1987). On optimal choice strategies. *Journal of Experimental Psychology: Animal Behavior Processes, 13,* 31–39. [11]

Zeldin, R. K., & Olton, D. S. (1986). Rats acquire spatial learning sets. *Journal of Experimental Psychology: Animal Behavior Processes, 12,* 412–419. [13]

Zentall, T. R. (1993). Animal cognition: An approach to the study of animal behavior. In T. R. Zentall (Ed.), *Animal cognition: A tribute to Donald A. Riley* (pp. 3–15). Hillsdale, NJ: Erlbaum. [15]

Zentall, T. R., Edwards, C. A., Moore, B. S., & Hogan, D. E. (1981). Identity: The basis for both matching and oddity learning in pigeons. *Journal of Experimental Psychology: Animal Behavior Processes, 7,* 70–86. [15]

Zentall, T. R., & Galef, B. G. (1988). *Social learning: Psychological and biological perspectives.* Hillsdale, NJ: Erlbaum. [1]

Zentall, T. R., & Hogan, D. E. (1977). Short-term proactive inhibition in the pigeon. *Learning and Motivation, 8,* 367–386. [14]

Zentall, T. R., & Hogan, D. E., & Edwards, C. A. (1980). Oddity learning in the pigeon: Effect of negative instances, correction, and number of incorrect alternatives. *Animal Learning and Behavior, 8,* 621–629. [15]

Zentall, T. R., Jagielo, J. A., Jackson-Smith, P., & Urcuioli, P. J. (1987). Memory codes in pigeon short-term memory: Effects of varying the number of sample and comparison stimuli. *Learning and Motivation, 18,* 21–33. [14]

Zentall, T. R., & Sherburne, L. M. (1994). Role of differential sample responding in the differential outcomes effect involving delayed matching by pigeons. *Journal of Experimental Psychology: Animal Behavior Processes, 20,* 390–401. [14]

Zimmer-Hart, C. L., & Rescorla, R. A. (1974). Extinction of Pavlovian conditioned inhibition. *Journal of Comparative and Physiological Psychology, 86,* 837–845. [3]

Zola-Morgan, S., Squire, L. R., Amaral, D. G., & Suzuki, W. A. (1989). Lesions of the perirhinal and parahippocampal cortex that spare the amygdala and hippocampal formation produce severe memory impairment. *Journal of Neuroscience, 9,* 4355–4370. [11]

Name Index

631

Subject Index

delayed gratification, 300
discrimination, 446–447, 450–451, 452–455, 462, 470
drug self-administration, 193–194
drug tolerance, 207, 208, 210–211, 213–214
electrical self-stimulation, 339–340, 377
environmental cues, 186
feeding system, 410
fleeing behavior, 399–400
foraging, 375
frustration theory, 308–311
generalization, 441
habituation, 131–132
heart rate, 94
incentive contrast, 274–276
interstimulus intervals (ITI), 96–98
interval conditioning, 95
joint processing, 485–486
latent inhibition, 125–126, 127, 128
latent learning, 350–352
learned helplessness, 315, 316–321, 322–326
learning sets, 459–460, 470
maturation rates, 517
memory, 493–494, 496, 499–504, 514
misbehavior, 413–414, 415–416
negative transfer in, 333
neurochemistry, 343
nocturnal nature, 85–86, 105
odors and, 216, 276–277
omission training, 226–229
overlearning-reversal effect, 456, 458
passive avoidance, 402
persistence and, 306–308
poison and, 176
punishment, 229–230
radial arm maze, 506–508
reaction potential, 347–348
reasoning, 564
reinforcement, 235–236, 245, 264–270, 297, 331
Rescorla-Wagner model and, 161–162
response-outcome (R-O) associations, 355–357
retroactive interference, 498–499
rewards, 279–280
second-order conditioning, 108–109, 111–113, 144–145
self-control, 298
sensory preconditioning, 117–119
simultaneous conditioning, 91
social reinforcement, 278–279
stimuli-outcome (S-O) associations, 357–358
stimulus-response (S-R) associations, 150
stimulus-stimulus (S-S) conditioning, 114, 153–154
summation test, 58–59
taste aversion, 182–185, 187–189, 190–195, 197–198
thigmotaxis, 402
time horizons, 372–373
Reaction, autonomic, 94, 251–252
Reaction potential, 346–348
Reactive inhibition, 348
Reasoning
analogies, 548–550
cognitive development, 551–556
transitivity, 550–551
Reflex arc, 10
Rehearsal, 274, 476–477, 515
Reinforcement, 240–241
consummatory response theory, 342–343
contingency, 248, 361–362
definition of, 233–234
learning vs. performance issue, 274–276

neurological mechanisms of, 339–343
Premack principle, 234–236
schedules of, 253–263, 285, 294–304
Reinforcers, characteristics of, 244–245, 250
learning vs. performance, 274–276
magnitude, 264–269, 279–280
odor of, 276–277
reward immediacy, 269–274
sensory, 276
social, 277–279
Relational techniques, 561
Relative response rate, 296
Reminder treatment, 498
Reproduction
copulation, 204–206
courtship, 203–204
Rescorla-Wagner model, 158–165
Research, strategies for, 376
Resemblance, laws of, 13
Response, 237–240
maintenance, 290
in Pavlovian conditioning, 47
shaping, 242–243
specificity of, 233–244
Response-deprivation hypothesis, 362–363
Response-outcome (R-O) associations, 355–357
Response-reinforcer contingency, 246–249
Retardation-of-learning
Rescorla-Wagner model and, 161
technique, 59–60
test, 74
Retrieval theories, 133–135, 142–143, 473, 496–505, 517
Retroactive interference, 473, 479
Reward, 331
brain physiology for, 341–342
conditioning, 251
frustration theory, 310
immediacy of, 269–274
law of effect and, 379
magnitude, 279–280
neurochemistry for, 343
positive system of, 377
size, 32, 42
Reward training, 226, 270–274
avoidance learning and, 232
naturalistic behaviors, 282–283
reinforcer magnitude and, 264–267
Rhetoric, 10
Rote, learning by, 531, 563
Running speed, analysis of, 41

Safety, learned, 192
Scalar-expectancy theory, 562
Science, goal of, 24
Scientific method, 24–41
Sea lions, studies using
imprinting and, 420
language, 565
Search images, 196–197
Second-order conditioning, 215
defined, 107
interstimulus interval (ITI) and, 110–111
spatial contiguity, 112
stimulus consistency, 111–112, 112–113
studies of, 108–109
theories of, 113–117
training levels, 113
unconditioned stimulus (US), magnitude of, 112